India

V.S. Naipaul was born in Trinidad in 1932.
Since he started writing in 1954 he has won
many prizes including the Booker Prize for
the novel IN A FREE STATE (1971). Among
his works of non-fiction are AMONG THE
BELIEVERS: AN ISLAMIC JOURNEY (1981);
FINDING THE CENTRE (1984); and A TURN
IN THE SOUTH (1989). His novels include
GUERRILLAS, A BEND IN THE RIVER and THE
ENIGMA OF ARRIVAL. He lives in Wiltshire,
England.

INDIA

A Million Mutinies Now

V.S. NAIPAUL

Minerva

A Minerva Paperback
INDIA

First published in Great Britain 1990
by William Heinemann Limited
This Minerva edition published 1990
by Mandarin Paperbacks
Michelin House, 81 Fulham Road, London SW3 6RB

Minerva is an imprint of the Octopus Publishing Group

Copyright © 1990 by V.S. Naipaul

A CIP catalogue record for this title
is available from the British Library
ISBN 0 7493 9128 6

Printed and bound in Great Britain
by Cox & Wyman Ltd, Reading

Contents

Bombay Theatre

Bombay is a crowd. But I began to feel, when I was some way into the city from the airport that morning, that the crowd on the pavement and the road was very great, and that something unusual might be happening.

Traffic into the city moved slowly because of the crowd. When at certain intersections the traffic was halted, by lights or by policemen or by the two together, the pavements seethed the more, and such a torrent of people swept across the road, in such a bouncing froth of light-coloured lightweight clothes, it seemed that some kind of invisible sluice-gate had been opened, and that if it wasn't closed again the flow of road-crossers would spread everywhere, and the beaten-up red buses and yellow-and-black taxis would be quite becalmed, each at the centre of a human eddy.

With me, in the taxi, were fumes and heat and din. The sun burned; there was little air; the grit from the bus exhausts began to stick to my skin. It would have been worse for the people on the road and the pavements. But many of them seemed freshly bathed, with fresh puja marks on their foreheads; many of them seemed to be in their best clothes: Bombay people celebrating an important new day, perhaps.

I asked the driver whether it was a public holiday. He didn't understand my question, and I let it be.

Bombay continued to define itself: Bombay flats on either side of the road now, concrete buildings mildewed at their upper levels by the Bombay weather, excessive sun, excessive rain, excessive heat; grimy at the lower levels, as if from the crowds at pavement level, and as if that human grime was working its way up, tide-mark by tide-mark, to meet the mildew.

The shops, even when small, even when dingy, had big, bright signboards, many-coloured, inventive, accomplished, the work of men with a feeling for both Roman and Sanskrit (or Devanagari) letters. Often, in front of these shops, and below those signboards, was just dirt; from time to time depressed-looking, dark people could be seen sitting down on this dirt and eating, indifferent to everything but their food.

There were big film posters on billboards, and smaller ones repeating on lamp-posts. It was hard, just at this moment of arrival, to relate the romance the posters promised to the people on the ground. And harder to place the English-language advertisements for banks and airlines and the *Times of India* Sesquicentennial ('Good Times, Sad Times, Changing Times'): to the stranger just arrived after a night flight, the city suggested by those advertisements was like an almost unimaginable distillation – a special, rich liquor – of the humanity that was on view.

The crowd continued. And then I saw that a good part of this crowd was a long queue or line of people, three or four or five deep, on the other pavement. The line was being added to all the time; and though for stretches it appeared to be standing still, it was moving very slowly. I realised I had been driving past the line for some time; perhaps, then, the line was already a mile long. The line was broken at road intersections: policemen in khaki uniforms were keeping the side roads clear.

What were these people waiting for? What was their chance of getting what they wanted? They seemed peaceable and content, even in the sun and the brown smoke of exhausts. They were in good clothes, simple, Indian-style clothes. People joining the line came almost at a trot; then they became patient; they seemed prepared to wait a long time. I had missed the beginning of the line. I didn't know what lay there. A circus? I believe there had been posters for a circus earlier on the road. An appearance by film stars? But the people in the line didn't show that kind of eagerness. They were small, dark, patient people, serious, and in their best clothes; and it came back to me that somewhere along the line earlier there had been flags and emblems of some sort.

I was told, when I got to the hotel in downtown Bombay, that there was no public holiday that day. And though the crowd had seemed to me great, and the line quite remarkable, something the newspapers might have mentioned, the hotel people I spoke to couldn't tell me what the line might have been for. What had been a big event for so many thousands somewhere in mid-town Bombay had sent no ripple here.

I telephoned an acquaintance, a writer. He knew as little as the hotel people. He said he hadn't been out that morning; he had been at home, writing an article for *Debonair*. Later, when he had finished his article, he telephoned me. He said he had two theories. The first theory was that the people I had seen might have been lining up for telephone directories. There had been trouble about the delivery of new directories – Bombay was Bombay. The second theory was something he had had from his servant woman. She had come in after I had telephoned, and she had told him that that day was the birthday of Dr Ambedkar, and that there was a big celebration in the suburb I had passed on my way from the airport.

Dr Ambedkar had been the great leader of the people once known in India as the untouchables. He had been more important to them than Mahatma Gandhi. In his time he had known honour and power; he had been law minister in the first government of independent India, and he had drafted the Indian constitution; but he had remained embittered to the end. It was Dr Ambedkar who had encouraged the untouchables – the *harijans*, the children of God, as Gandhi called them, and now the Dalits, as they called themselves – to abandon Hinduism, which had enslaved them, and to turn to Buddhism. Before his thought could change or develop, he died, in 1956.

No leader of comparable authority or esteem had risen among the castes for whom Dr Ambedkar spoke. He had remained their leader, the man they honoured above all others; he was almost their deity. In every Dalit house, I had been told, there was a photograph of Dr Ambedkar. It was a photograph I had seen many times, and it was strange that a better photograph hadn't been used. The Ambedkar icon was like a grey passport photograph reproduced in an old-fashioned newspaper process: the leader reduced to a composition of black and white dots, frozen in an image of the 1940s or 1950s, a plumpish man of unmemorable features, with the glasses of a student, and in the semi-colonial respectability of jacket and tie. Jacket and tie made for an unlikely holy image in India. But it was fitting, because it went against the homespun and loincloth of the mahatma.

The Dr Ambedkar idea semed better than the idea about the telephone directories. There had, indeed, been a religious stillness about the people in the line. They had been like people gaining merit through doing the right thing. The Dr Ambedkar idea made sense of the flags and the emblems of which I had had a memory. The people I had seen were honouring their leader, their saint, their deity; and by this they were honouring themselves as well.

Later that day I talked to an official of the hotel. He asked for my impressions of Bombay. When I told him about the Ambedkar crowd, he was for a moment like a man taken aback. He was at a loss for words. Then, irritation and unhappiness breaking through his well-bred hotel manner, he said, 'The country's going from bad to worse.'

It was a version of what I had heard many times about India. India had changed; it was not the good and stable country it had once been. In the days of the freedom movement, political workers, honouring Gandhi, had worn homespun as an emblem of sacrifice and service, their oneness with the poor. Now the politician's homespun stood for power. With industrialization and economic growth people had forgotten old reverences. Men honoured only money now. The great investment in development over three or four decades had led only to this: to 'corruption', to the 'criminalization of politics'. In seeking to rise, India had undone itself. No one could be sure of anything now; all was fluid. Policeman, thief, politician: the roles had become interchangeable. And with money – the money of which the crowded, ugly skyscraper towers of Bombay spoke – many long-buried particularities had been released. These disruptive, lesser loyalties – of region, caste, and clan – now played on the surface of Indian life.

The Dalits, for instance. If they had still been only the mahatma's harijans, children of God, people for whom good things might be done, objects of sentiment and a passing piety, an occasion like the morning's Ambedkar anniversary wouldn't have given anyone thoughts of a world about to undo itself. But a certain amount of money had come to the people once known as harijans, a certain amount of education, and with that there had also come the group sense and political consciousness. They had ceased to be abstractions. They had begun to do things for themselves. They had become people stressing their own particularity, just as better-off groups in India stressed their particularities.

And the Dalit particularity was perhaps not the most important one in the city of Bombay. Just outside the hotel was the Gateway of India. This was a British monument: a high, magnificent arch, commemorating the arrival in India in 1911 of the King-Emperor, George V. The imperial associations of the arch were now absorbed into the poetic idea of the gateway; and the paved open area around it was a popular afternoon promenade. On either side of that imperial monument simple and quite small signboards had been put up, with one word in the Devanagari script, black on white – giving the name of the city as *Mumbai* rather than 'Bombay'.

Those *Mumbai* boards spoke of an internal fight. Bombay was a cosmopolitan city. That was how it had been from the start, and that was how it had developed; it had drawn people from all over the sub-continent. But, in independent India, Bombay had found itself in the state of Maharashtra; and in the mid-1960s a Maharashtrian regional movement had started. This movement wanted Maharashtra to be for the Maharashtrians. In the beginning the movement's hostility had been aimed mainly at poor migrants from South India; but other people had felt threatened as well. The movement was known as the Shiv Sena, the Army of Shiva, taking its name from Shivaji, the 17th-century warrior-leader of the Maratha people. The newspapers had been critical; they called the Sena 'fascist'. But the Sena had not ceased to grow. Two years before, it had won control of the Bombay Municipal Corporation.

The corporation building was in the confident Victorian-Gothic style of British Bombay. A wide, solid staircase, with Victorian metalwork below a polished timber banister, led to the council chamber. The walls there were half-panelled in a rich red-brown wood, and the desks and chairs were set in arcs and semi-circles around the mayoral chair. The councillors' chairs were upholstered in green. But the mayoral chair had a saffron cover. Saffron is a Hindu colour, and here it was the colour of the Shiv Sena. Saffron satin filled the Gothic arch below the gallery on one end wall of the chamber. In front of the saffron satin was a bronze-coloured bust of Shivaji; above the bust, on the satin, were a round shield and crossed swords, also in a bronze colour.

High up on the wall at the back of the mayoral chair, and above the Gothic arches (springing from grey marble columns), were portraits of famous old Indian mayors of Bombay from colonial days. The men in the portraits were dignified; they wore wigs or

Parsi caps or Hindu turbans or Muslim turbans. The dignity of those men, and the nationalist pride their dignity would once have encouraged, had now been superseded.

The council chamber was so perfect in its way, so confident, its architectural details so considered, it was hard to imagine that it had all been negated by the simple saffron of the Sena. It made me think of the Christian cathedral in Nicosia in Cyprus, taken over by the Muslims, cleansed of much of its furniture, and hung with Koranic banners. It made me think of the Marathas of the 17th century, in the vacuum between the Moguls and British, raiding as far north as Delhi, as far east as Bengal, and setting Maratha rulers on the throne of Tanjore in the far south.

The visitor, coming into Bombay from the airport, might see only small dark men in an undifferentiated crowd, and dust and fumes; might see, between the concrete blocks, a mess of makeshift huts and the parasitic shelters those huts spawned, one kind of dependence leading down into another; might see what looked like the unending smallness of men. But here in the corporation chamber, in the saffron and crossed swords of the Sena, were the emblems of war and conquest.

It made the independence struggle seem like an interim. Independence had come to India like a kind of revolution; now there were many revolutions within that revolution. What was true of Bombay was true of other parts of India as well: of the state of Andhra, of Tamil Nadu, Assam, the Punjab. All over India scores of particularities that had been frozen by foreign rule, or by poverty or lack of opportunity or abjectness had begun to flow again. And it was easy to see how someone like the man in the hotel, who had grown up with another idea of India and its development, could feel alienated and insecure.

Some such feeling of alienation I had known myself when I had first gone to India, in 1962. That had been a special journey for me: I had gone as the descendant of 19th-century indentured Indian emigrants. Such emigrants had been recruited from the 1860s on, mainly from the eastern Gangetic plain, and then sent out from depots in Calcutta to work on five-year indentures on plantations in various parts of the British Empire and even elsewhere. People like my ancestors had gone to Fiji in the Pacific;

6

Mauritius in the Indian Ocean; South Africa; and to some of the territories in the West Indies, principally the Guianas (British Guiana and Dutch Guiana) and Trinidad. It was to Trinidad that my ancestors went, starting some time in the 1880s, as I work it out.

These overseas Indian groups were mixed. They were miniature Indias, with Hindus and Muslims, and people of different castes. They were disadvantaged, without representation, and without a political tradition. They were isolated by language and culture from the people they found themselves among; they were isolated, too, from India itself (many weeks away by steamboat from Trinidad and the Guianas). In these special circumstances they developed something they would never have known in India: a sense of belonging to an Indian community. This feeling of community could override religion and caste.

It was this idea of an Indian community that, near the end of the last century, the thirty-year-old Gandhi – at that time hardly with a political or historical or literary idea – discovered when he went to South Africa and began to work among the Indian immigrants there. And it was during his 15 years in South Africa that intimations came to Gandhi of an all-India religious-political mission.

I was born in 1932, 15 years before the independence of India. I grew up with two ideas of India. The first idea – not one I wanted to go into too closely – was about the kind of country from which my ancestors had come. We were an agricultural people. Most of us in Trinidad were still working on the colonial sugar estates, and for most of us life was poor; many of us lived in thatched, mud-walled huts. Migration to the New World, shaking us out of the immemorial accepting ways of peasant India, had made us ambitious; but in colonial and agricultural Trinidad, during the Depression, there were few opportunities to rise. With this poverty around us, and with this sense of the world as a kind of prison (the barriers down against us everywhere), the India from which my ancestors had migrated to better themselves became in my imagination a most fearful place. This India was private and personal, beyond the India I read about in newspapers and books. This India, or this anxiety about where we had come from, was like a neurosis.

There was a second India. It balanced the first. This second

India was the India of the independence movement, the India of the great names. It was also the India of the great civilization and the great classical past. It was the India by which, in all the difficulties of our circumstances, we felt supported. It was an aspect of our identity, the community identity we had developed, which, in multi-racial Trinidad, had become more like a racial identity.

This was the identity I took to India on my first visit in 1962. And when I got there I found it had no meaning in India. The idea of an Indian community – in effect, a continental idea of our Indian identity – made sense only when the community was very small, a minority, and isolated. In the torrent of India, with its hundreds of millions, where the threat was of chaos and the void, that continental idea was no comfort at all. People needed to hold on to smaller ideas of who and what they were; they found stability in the smaller groupings of region, clan, caste, family.

They were groupings I could hardly understand. They would have given me no comfort at all in Trinidad, would have provided no balance for the other India I carried as a neurosis, the India of poverty and an abjectness too fearful to imagine. Such an India I did now find, in 1962; and, with my idea of an Indian identity, I couldn't be reconciled to it. The poverty of the Indian streets and the countryside was an affront and a threat, a scratching at my old neurosis. Two generations separated me from that kind of poverty; but I felt closer to it than most of the Indians I met.

In 1962, in spite of five-year plans and universal suffrage, and talk of socialism and the common man, I found that for most Indians Indian poverty was still a poetic concept, a prompting to piety and sweet melancholy, part of the country's uniqueness, its Gandhian non-materialism.

An editor of an economic weekly, a good and dedicated man who became a friend, said to me in Bombay, when we talked of the untouchables, 'Have you seen the beauty of some of our untouchables?' India was the editor's lifelong cause; the uplift of the untouchables was part of his cause; and he was speaking with the utmost generosity.

There was a paradox. My continental idea of an Indian identity, with the nerves it continually exposed, would have made it hard for me to do worthwhile work in India. The caste or group stability that Indians had, the more focussed view, enabled them, while remaining whole themselves, to do work – modest, improving things, rather than revolutionary things – in conditions which to others might have seemed hopeless – as I saw during many weeks in the countryside, when I stayed with young Indian Administrative Service officers.

Many thousands of people had worked like that over the years, without any sense of a personal drama, many millions; it had added up in the 40 years since independence to an immense national effort. The results of that effort were now noticeable. What looked sudden had been long prepared. The increased wealth showed; the new confidence of people once poor showed. One aspect of that confidence was the freeing of new particularities, new identities, which were as unsettling to Indians as the identities of caste and clan and region had been to me in 1962, when I had gone to India only as an 'Indian'.

The people once known as untouchables lined up for more than a mile on a busy road to honour their long-dead saint, Dr Ambedkar, who in his icon wore a European-style jacket and tie. That proclamation of pride was new. It could be said to be something Gandhi and others had worked for; it could be said to be a vindication of the freedom movement. Yet it could also be felt as a threat to the stability many Indians had taken for granted; and a middle-class man might, in a reflex of anxiety, feel that the country was going from bad to worse.

The Bombay stock market had boomed. Papu, a twenty-nine-year-old stockbroker, had made more money in the last five years than his father had made in all his working life. Papu's father had migrated to Burma during the British time, when Burma was part of British India. When Burma had become independent, and had withdrawn from the Commonwealth, Papu's father, like other Indians, had been made to leave. In India, Papu's father had gone into trading in stocks and shares on his own acount. He read the financial pages carefully and he made a modest living. 'On the stock market,' Papu said, 'if you succeed seven times out of 10, you are doing well.' Papu's father, not a formally educated man, had done well according to his own lights.

Papu, better educated, and operating in a far larger economy, had done very well, even by his own standards. The last five years, he had said, had been exceptionally good; and he felt that the next ten years were going to be pretty good as well.

But Papu had become anxious. He didn't know where the new aggressiveness of Indian business was going to lead, and he wasn't certain how far, with the strong religious feelings he had, he would be able to fit into the new scheme of things. He had also grown to fear something his father had never thought about: Papu, at the age of twenty-nine, lived in dread of revolution and anarchy. The fear was partly a fear of personal loss; but it was also an extension of Papu's religious concerns.

Papu came of a Jain family. The Jains are an ancient, pre-Buddhist offshoot of Hinduism, and they aim at what they see as absolute purity. They don't eat meat; they don't eat eggs; they avoid taking life. Every morning a Jain should bathe, put on an unstitched cloth, and walk barefooted to his temple to pray. And yet the Jains are famous in India for their skill as businessmen.

Papu's office was in the stock market area of Bombay. At road level it was not easy for the visitor to distinguish this area from other areas in central Bombay. The lobby of the tall building where Papu's office was had a special Indian quality: you felt that every day, in the name of cleaning, someone had rubbed the place down with a lightly grimed rag, and – in the way that a fresh mark of sandalwood paste is given every day to an image – given a touch of black grease to the folding metal gates of the elevators. Roughly painted little boards gave each elevator a number; and there was a little zigzag line for each elevator, so that in the lobby people created a floral pattern.

On the upper floor where we got off the walls still hinted at the lightly grimed rag. But in this upper lobby, which was much quieter, people clearly didn't have the anxiety they had downstairs about being seen or about giving offence, and they had spat out gritty red mouthfuls of pan-juice, sometimes in a corner, sometimes broadside, in great splashing arcs, on the walls.

After this informality there was an office. Desks, clerks, office equipment. There were framed colour pictures of Hindu deities on the walls, and some of the pictures were garlanded. Papu's chamber was a small inner room. Computer screens blinked green. On one wall were three pictures of deities side by side. The goddess Durga, riding on her tiger, was on the right; a garland of marigolds hung over the glass.

I asked Papu about Durga. He didn't answer directly. He began to talk about his Jain faith and its application to what he did.

He said, 'Basically, we are without the killer instinct, which is what businessmen should have.'

I said, 'But you do so well.'

'We are traders.' The distinction was important to him. 'The killer instinct is required in industry, not in trading. Which is why the Jain community is not involved in industry. If I'm trading on the stock exchange now, and I cannot get some money out of a guy, I wouldn't hire a mafia guy to get it out of him. Which is what happens here in something like the building industry – if I'm a builder, I have to have my own mafia connections.'

'How long has it been so?'

'It's growing in the cities. After 1975' – the time of Mrs Gandhi's Emergency – 'all the mafia dons gave up smuggling and took up building. They will "encourage" people, for instance, to vacate land, so that the land can be used for building.'

It was what many people spoke about. It was part of the 'criminalization' of Indian business and politics.

Papu said, 'It is a problem. I don't know how long this' – he indicated his own room, with the computers, and the outer office – 'is going to continue. We're doing well right now. We're vegetarians, but I don't know how long we can go on without going out there to fight.'

It was strange, this stress on vegetarianism just there. But vegetarianism was fundamental to Papu's faith. In the mess and flux and uncertainty of life, vegetarianism, the refusal to be impure, was something one could anchor oneself to. It was an exercise of will and virtue that saved one from other kinds of excess, including the excess of 'going out there to fight'.

Papu was of middle height. His vegetarianism and his sport – which, unexpectedly, was basketball – had given him a fine, slender physique. He was strong, without pronounced muscular definitions; he was curiously like one of the smooth marble figures of Jain sculpture. His eyes were serene; his face was squarish and well-defined, his skin smooth and unmarked.

He thought that if the nature of trading changed, if the killer instinct entered it, Jains would have to fight or give up. From what he said, it seemed that so far Jains had preferred to give up. They had left the building industry. In Bombay, as in Delhi, they had given up those trades which required them to carry cash or valuables.

He began to speak again of his faith, and when – taking his own time to come back to my early question – he spoke of the goddess Durga, he didn't speak of her as a deity with special attributes. He spoke of her simply as God.

'I have to think of God whenever some things happen. I lost my father in the beginning of this year. My father died of a heart attack. At a time like that the feeling comes that there is some external factor I can't do anything about.

'I am now using computers, the way they are doing in the developed countries. There is a time that there is a feeling in me that if I'm able to beat the market, it's because I'm able to take on these developments. But then – when something like this happens: my father, his death – I get the feeling that my intelligence or my aggression is worth nothing. Here I am, in this business. I forecast stock movements, price movements. There is an obsession about the work, as you know. And then suddenly this feeling – that I can't foresee my life. That is the time I feel there is something like God, and I wish to have faith.

'In the last year that feeling has been coming any time I'm excited or very sad. Earlier, if I had been excited, I would have expressed my excitement. You would have been able to see it. But now I know that at the end of the day, after the excitement, something sad might happen. So why get excited?'

'I can understand older men having these thoughts. But you are not old.'

'We have this saying on the Bombay stock exchange: "How many *Diwalis* have you seen?"' Diwali, the Hindu festival of lights. 'Which is a way of saying, "How old are you?" The friend of mine who owns this firm is only thirty, and he's been very successful these last five years. He's encountered two income-tax raids, and several ups and downs. Things which my father would have taken a lifetime to experience, he's done in five years. So we say it isn't the number of Diwalis you've seen, it's the number of crackers you've burst. For me the same is true, not only in business, but in life. I go to the temple every morning. I basically pray to have control over certain feelings.'

'Grief?' I was thinking of his father.

He misheard me. He thought I had said 'greed', and he said,

'Greed and fear. The two feelings associated with my business. I walk into the temple, hold my hands together, and wait there for five minutes.'

'Who do you address when you do that?'

'Something you think of who's controlling the world.'

'You don't think of a particular deity?'

'If you're doing business, the picture you would have would be of the goddess Lakshmi. On other occasions it would be Saraswati. Lakshmi is the goddess of wealth, Saraswati is the goddess of wisdom. And when I think of the children in the slums, I have to think of God. That is the time I think there is a certain womb I came out of – which is why I'm here today, and not there. Now, why am I here, and not there, in the slums? Nowhere in the organized learning I received at school and college do I get an answer to this question. The answer is: God. A couple of times a day I think these thoughts.'

'Did your father think these thoughts as well?'

'My father was a self-made man. He was only a matriculate. He had to be more involved with his work. Basically, a man thinks of these other things when he's taken care of food and shelter. Although my father must have been having the same thoughts, he had to be doing his duties to his family. I'm a little more comfortable at a younger age. That is one of the reasons why this comes up.'

'Can anyone be successful in business without some aggression?'

'Aggression creates a vicious circle. I'll give you an example. We have a man called Ambani here. He's going to become the largest industrialist in India in a couple of years. This man would really give you the true picture of how business success works in India. He is a good administrator and a good manipulator. Those are different words. An administrator organizes his business, a manipulator manages the world outside. Ambani's got the foresight, and finally he's got the aggression. If you compare him to old industrialists like Tata and Birla, he's one generation ahead. Birla had the licences. He put up industries, he's manufacturing goods. This man Ambani goes one step ahead. He makes and breaks policies for himself. Now he sees a demand for polyester. It's shiny and it lasts and lasts. It's perfect for India, where people can't afford to buy too many clothes. So he gets into polyester, and he makes sure that nobody else is involved in it. After this he takes the next step

– making the raw material for polyester. Then he wants other people to make polyester so they can use his raw material. This backward integration will get him to a situation where he will control the textile industry in India. Polyester will be the largest market.

'If I want to go out into any business in India, that is what I would have to do. Something like that.

'But there is another side. There is a firm here called Bajaj. They are the second largest scooter-manufacturer in the world. Three years ago, when the Japanese entered India, we thought that Bajaj would soon be out. He's not only able to stay, but he's grown much more than all of them. He's a Harvard graduate. But it's a conventional family, with all the culture and conventions of Indians. They've gone through personal taxation at 97 per cent and inheritance tax as high as 80 per cent, and yet today they are still very large. This gives me confidence that it can still work.'

By 'it' he meant the traditional Indian way, the way that fitted in with 'all the culture and conventions of Indians'.

Papu said, 'The important point here is your asking me how to be sucessful without aggression. The problem is discipline. I don't find my non-vegetarian friends have the will-power and discipline and character that the vegetarians have. When we started out being vegetarians we never thought of these things. But now, looking back at life, we find the non-vegetarians have a problem.'

Papu had a plan of sorts for his own future. He wanted to work for the next ten years, to exercise the business faculties with which he had been endowed. He wanted in those ten years to make enough money to live on for the rest of his life. And then he wanted to devote himself to social work. But he had doubts about his plan. He had doubts especially about the wisdom or efficiency of giving up. If he personally went out and did social work, wouldn't that be a waste of his natural talent? Wouldn't he serve his social cause better if he continued in business and devoted his profits – which would grow – to his social work?

These ideas were worrying him. He was uncertain about his promptings, and that worried him even more. He thought that, living the kind of life he did, the concern he felt for the poor was at the moment only 'hypocritical'.

'If I say I should be doing social work, why should I be here in an air-conditioned office? If I have a genuine feeling, I should be out there in the slum, working. But up to the age of forty I may have to continue to live like a hypocrite. And then I would do what I want. Today I am getting so great a return for my input. This makes me feel I should be working harder. This makes me feel I should not be entitled to these luxuries.

'The earlier generation of Jains, when they thought of social work, used to build marble temples. We find that to be not very right, maybe because there are already so many temples. We think of orphanages and hospitals. Our generation thinks more of social work than of religion.'

'Are you really as nervous of the poverty as you say?'

'I am sure there's going to be a revolution. In a generation or two. It cannot last, the inequalities of income. I shudder when I think of that. I am very sure that the Indian mind is religious, fatalistic. Even after all the education I've had, I still think that destiny will take me – I'll get there whatever I do. This is why we haven't had a revolution. Now, with the growing frustrations, even if people are religious there is going to be a revolution. The tolerance is being stretched too far.'

'What form do you think the revolution will take?'

'It won't be *anything*. It will be totally chaos.'

For some, like the Shiv Sena, the revolution had already started. Nikhil, a young magazine journalist I had got to know, took me on a Sunday morning to meet a Sena 'area leader' in the industrial suburb of Thane. The Sena had 40 units in Thane – 40 units in one suburb – and each unit had a leader like Mr Patil, the man we were going to see.

Thane was one hour north of downtown Bombay by train. The coaches were broad and roomy and basic, built for the heavy duty of Bombay suburban travel, no-nonsense affairs of undisguised metal poles and brackets and bolts. A prominent metal label in each coach gave the name of the builders: Jessop and Co., Calcutta, once British, now Indian.

We passed blocks of flats, mildewed and grimed; swamps, drains; browned patches of field; dust, children; and, always, the shacks and the rag-roofed dependent shelters they encouraged, the existing shack or hut or shelter providing one ready-built wall for the newcomer, the tide after tide of human beings that came into

Bombay all the time, sometimes undoing in a night the rehabilitating effort of years. The Shiv Sena, in its early days, had wanted Maharashtra for the Maharashtrians; it had campaigned against immigration into Bombay from other states. What could be seen from the train was explanation enough.

Even in Thane, one hour out, there was a feeling that living space was still immensely valuable. In a working-class lane near the railway station – just past the bright stalls, some with fruit, some with cheap watches, some with Sunday-morning fripperies, shiny fairground goods – a simple apartment could cost two and half lakhs of rupees, 250,000 rupees, about £10,000.

The entrance to Mr Patil's house was off this lane, in a passageway between two two-storey houses. Mr Patil lived upstairs in the house to the right, an old house; the house to the left, which was still being built, and had unexpected architectural style, was going to be substantial. The yard at the end of the passageway was like an old Port of Spain backyard, with a busy outdoor life; though the crumbling brick dependencies against the back wall had the Bombay constriction, and spoke of people making do with very little room.

In the plot or yard on the other side of the back wall, and not far from that wall, was the weathered concrete frame of a projected building of some size that looked as though it had been abandoned. If that building had gone up, it would have blocked out some of the light from Mr Patil's yard; the yard would have felt hemmed in. As it was, with the openness at the back, there was, curiously, no feeling of oppression in Mr Patil's yard, even with the crowd and the general noise – many scattered sounds, many varied events, running together to make something like a sea sound.

The wooden staircase up to Mr Patil's floor was steep (saving space), and called for care. The construction was interesting, with each thick plank mortised into the side boards. In the little verandah or gallery at the top there were taken-off shoes and slippers, but we were not asked to take our shoes off.

There was a visitor before us in the room inside. He was a police inspector in khaki uniform, and he was sitting in an arm chair next to Mr Patil. The inspector hadn't taken off his boots either. They were quite splendid boots, and must have been personal, not part of his police issue. They were ankle-high, of soft leather, with nice indentations and ridges, and they were ox-blood in colour.

The inspector was in his late thirties or early forties. He was serious and respectful, but also self-respecting. Mr Patil was frowning; the frown could be read as an expression of his authority. He was small and had begun to get plump. He was young, in his late twenties, and the way he was sitting gave prominence to his little paunch. The paunch looked new, something he was still learning to live with, like the roundness of his thighs, which was causing his trousers noticeably to tighten. He was barefooted in his sitting room. That was custom; but it was also a mark of his privilege: the local dignitary, receiving at home.

The police inspector had come that Sunday morning to ask for the Sena's help with a local 'Eve-teasing' problem. The sexual harassment of women in public places, often sly, sometimes quite open, was a problem all over India. The particular incident the inspector was worried about had caused two groups in the area to square off against each other. In that crowd and closeness it didn't take much for nerves to tear; trouble came easily.

The sitting room was pink-washed, and it had a terrazzo floor. In its furnishings and decorations it was, making allowance for period details, like rooms I had known in Trinidad in my childhood, the rooms of people who had begun to feel they were doing well and had begun to respect themselves. There was a Sony television set, with a video. A patterned lace cloth covered the Sony, and there was a doll on the cloth. On the pink walls there were plastic hibiscus sprays on sections of plastic trellis-work. A double bed occupied one corner of the room; two bolsters in faded pink were set symmetrically on it at an angle one to the other; and some clothes of Mr Patil's hung on a hook of some sort.

Mr Patil's mother was sitting flat on the terrazzo floor in the open doorway to the left. The room beyond must have been the kitchen. I fancied that a smell of frying fish was coming from that room, but I might have been wrong. Perhaps the Patils didn't eat fish; in India such details were important, and could be serious caste matters. There was at any rate a smell of cooking; and it must have been this which – while the police inspector and Mr Patil talked – drew a little tiger-striped ginger cat across the sitting room to the doorway where Mr Patil's mother was sitting. The cat was a surprise: I thought Indians didn't care too much for cats. This was an Indian cat, lean in neck and limbs, heavy only in belly, more scrawny and desperate than the chubby cats of England.

17

Mr Patil's mother was wearing a red or pink patterned sari, tied in a way which enabled the legs to be wrapped separately. She was very short, with much slack, tired-looking flesh, and she wore thick-lensed glasses. She was sitting in the doorway to enjoy the Sunday-morning company; though it was also plain from her manner that she didn't want to intrude into any of the serious business her son might have to deal with.

The serious, impressive police inspector rose at last. He said he was glad that Mr Patil had been so understanding. Both groups in the Eve-teasing affair had enough supporters to cause real trouble in the locality, he said; and in these matters it was the policy of the police to try to reconcile people. Then he left, and he could be heard picking his way lightly down the steep steps in his boots.

Mr Patil frowned harder, set his mouth, and waited to hear what I had to say. He had no English, only Marathi. Nikhil translated for me. I said I wanted to know first of all about the locality, and about Mr Patil's family.

Mr Patil said his family had spent their entire life right there, in that locality. His father had worked in the tool room of a factory in central Bombay for 40 years. What did the factory make? Neither Mr Patil nor his mother knew. The factory was closed down now, finished. But what was important was that his father had been in regular work. Because of that the family had not known hardship when they were children. They knew hardship as a family only when their father died, in 1975. In India there were no pensions.

Mr Patil had a dark, square face. He wore a moustache. His hair was getting thin.

He went out to work after his father died. He found a job in the packing department of a company that made transistors. A girl cousin told him about the job. She worked in the factory; in fact, she still worked there. He didn't get much in the packing department, 300 rupees a month, working eight hours a day. He didn't like what he had to do, but it was a job. He had made a lot of friends in the factory; many of them had remained friends.

He never thought of himself and his family as poor. He never thought of himself as rich or poor. He always felt he was middle class – using that word in the Indian way. And what he said carried an echo of what Papu, the Jain stockbroker, had said: a man has to take care of food and shelter before he can notice other things. Just as Papu's success had given him the social concerns that his more harassed father had never had, so, though the Shiv Sena spoke of the deprivation of Maharashtrians, that idea could come to people only when they had ceased, in fact, to be absolutely deprived.

How, growing up in that locality, had ambition come to Mr Patil? Had he been ambitious as a child? He had. He wanted to be famous. He didn't want to be famous for any particular thing; he just wanted to be famous. At one time he thought he would like to be a famous cricketer. But now he wasn't ambitious in that way; he had scaled it down. He just wanted to do what the Supreme Leader of the party wanted him to do.

He was ten years old when he had first seen the leader. He had seen him right here, in this locality. That would have been in 1969 or 1970. He saw a poster one day announcing a visit by the leader. At that time he had never heard of the leader: the Sena was only three years old, and the leader wasn't as famous as he became later. But Mr Patil noticed the poster about the leader's visit. This was during the festival of Ganpati. And now, in Mr Patil's talk, religion and Sena politics began to run together.

Ganpati, Ganesh, the Hindu elephant god, with his long, friendly trunk, his bright eyes, and big, contented belly, was adored in Maharashtra. He was very important in the Patil house: the family kept a Ganpati image in the house. Every year there was a festival dedicated to Ganpati. The festival lasted nine days, and there was a big event on each of those days. Mr Patil as a boy would go to the big event on all the nine days of the festival; he did that every year.

He said, in Nikhil's translation of his Marathi, his mother (much paler in complexion than he) nodding while he spoke, 'Everything good that has happened to me has come through the grace of Ganpati. Every month there is one day devoted to the worship of Ganpati. I travel then 110 kilometres to worship at the huge shrine of Ganpati at Pali.'

On the wall at the back of the Sony television there was a colour photograph or picture of this image at Pali: the broad, spreading belly of the deity a violent, arresting red, not altogether benign.

I asked whether this idea of Ganpati as the bestower of good luck had always been in his family. He said yes. What had been the first time in his own life he had associated Ganpati with something good?

He scratched his thin hair. The tiger-striped ginger cat or kitten was now sitting below the chair on which the police inspector had sat, and was looking delicately around. Mr Patil's mother, sitting on the terrazzo floor in the doorway, which appeared to be her own place of sitting, lifted her head, as if thinking herself of the first time her son had been blessed by the god; the thick lenses of her glasses created pools of light over her eyes.

On the wall above the bed with the symmetrically set bolsters was a fluorescent electric tube; fluorescent tubes were used in India because they were cheap. There were two little windows in that wall. In one window the iron bars were set vertically; in the other window – for the variation and the style – the bars were set horizontally. Both windows had similar curtains, each curtain gathered up with a sash in two places.

The little pink-walled room was really quite full of things to look at: much thought here, much pride. There was a wardrobe, and there was also a black-framed glass case or cabinet about three feet high. On top of the cabinet was a very big multi-coloured candle, to balance the doll on the Sony. Among the things on the shelves were a set of stainless-steel tumblers and eight china cups with a flowered pattern. The glass cabinet and the things in it – leaving aside the aluminium tumblers – were like things I had known in my childhood. They were still here in a kind of wholeness: my heart went out to them.

Mr Patil said at last, 'I never used to go to school. I used to just roam around, play cricket. I was finally told that I would be thrown out of the school. So I prayed to Ganpati. I was about fifteen or sixteen at this time. I told Ganpati that if I wasn't thrown out of the school, I would make the pilgrimage to Pali. And I wasn't thrown out. The headmistress had a change of heart. When she called me she said she was only going to warn me that time.'

Having remembered that, he remembered other occasions of Ganpati's grace. 'Three or four years ago my mother fell ill. High blood pressure. She went to hospital. She was on oxygen. She couldn't talk. I went to Pali to the Ganpati shrine and I made an offering of a garland and a coconut. When I came back, my mother was much better.'

And his mother – sitting in the doorway, not flat on the floor, as I had thought, but on a thin piece of wood, perhaps an inch high – put her palms together while her son spoke, and said, in Nikhil's translation, that she folded her hands in gratitude to Ganpati.

Even at his birth there was some element of mercy and blessing. This was in 1959. There were very bad riots in the locality. People were throwing stones. Taxis were not easy to get, but his father managed to find a taxi-driver who said he would try to take Mrs Patil to the hospital. The taxi had to drive five kilometres through the riots to the government hospital. It got there safely, and as soon as his mother went in, she was delivered of him.

Mother and son told the story in relay, and the mother, sitting on the floor, again put her palms together and said that it was Ganpati's mercy.

And then, two years or so ago, there was a serious crisis for him. The crisis was in his political life, and it lasted nine days. That was a very long time to be on the rack. He made a pilgrimage to Pali, and vowed to Ganpati that if he came out of his crisis, he would make an offering of 101 coconuts.

Wasn't that like trying to buy something from the god?

'My faith is rooted in reality. I am not in the habit of offering 101 coconuts and asking to be made prime minister of India.'

Was this faith in Ganpati something deep in himself, always there? Or did he, after he had prayed, look for some sign from the deity?

He said, in Nikhil's translation, 'Even when things look bad I hear a voice inside. I suppose you can call it self-confidence.' Nikhil gave the Marathi word he had used for 'self-confidence': *atma-vishwas*. That was Ganpati's greatest gift.

I said, 'How did you take 101 coconuts up to the shrine?'

'You can buy the nuts at the shrine itself.'

He told me more about the Ganpati festival. Every year you had to get a new image from the image-maker. You kept the image at home for as long as you wanted, but at the end of the festival you had to throw away or immerse the image. It was the tradition in their family to keep the image for one day and a half; then they took it to a lake not far away and immersed it. It had been his mother's ambition all her life to bring the Ganpati image home from the image-maker's with a musical band. Recently, she had been able to do that. Her other son had got a very good job, and the family had hired a band and brought the image to the house, and they had had the band again when they had taken the image out of the house to the lake.

With this talk of Ganpati, of shrines and pilgrimages and vows

21

and offerings, I began to get some idea of the mysteries the earth held for people like the Patils, the glory that sometimes touched their days, the wonders they walked through. There was more to their world than one saw. Thane was an industrial suburb. But the land itself was very old; it had its sanctity; and the same people could live naturally with many different ways of feeling.

It was during this auspicious festival of Ganpati – right here, in this locality, in these lanes I had walked through seeing only the surface of things – that Mr Patil, when he was ten, had seen the poster about the visit of the leader of the Shiv Sena. He had gone to the meeting, to look at the leader. The leader at that time was running his own weekly magazine and was better known as a cartoonist. The young Patil boy didn't find the leader physically impressive when he saw him. He saw a thin man, with glasses, in a buttoned-up long coat. But as soon as the leader began to speak the boy's blood began to 'boil'. The leader's speech lasted 30 to 35 minutes, and at the end people like the young Patil, whose blood had boiled at the thought of all the injustices the true people of Maharashtra had to endure, began to shout their acclamation of the leader.

'Weren't you too young to understand talk about discrimination against Maharashtrians?'

'No. I used to hear a lot about how the Muslims and outsiders were creating problems for Maharashtrians. I used to hear it at home and on the streets. My elder brother used to tell me about it.'

'Your father?'

'He had no interest in it at all.'

The father didn't have the security of his sons. It was as with Papu's father.

And though for a long time after this the ten-year-old boy had heard no more big Shiv Sena speeches, he began to lend a hand when the party wanted people to put up posters and banners. Later, when his father died, and he had gone out to work with the transistor company, he began to do political work for the party in the evenings. He continued to do that party work even when he found a new job. In the new job he was concerned with exporting manpower to Dubai and the Middle East. He got 950 rupees a month, as against 300 with the transistor company. He took people for interviews.

Didn't he want to go the Middle East himself, to make some money?

'I didn't pass my matric at school. So if I'd gone I would have had to do some menial work.'

'You didn't think there was anything wrong in sending people from here to a Muslim country?'

'Not all Muslims are enemies.'

His work for the party at that time was to sit in the Sena office in the evenings and listen to people's complaints. The Sena always believed in the social side of things. There was a lot to be done that way. People needed help. Some people had water for only four hours a day. In many buildings water didn't rise above the first floor. Even after he had been appointed area leader of the Sena – that appointment had come three years before – he still did that kind of social work. When we had arrived, for instance, there was a lady in the kitchen with his mother. She had come to complain about a water-connection. She had paid somebody 1000 rupees for the connection, and so far she had had no connection and no water. The area leader had to interest himself in the problems of the people; it was good for the party politically.

Did his blood still boil? Or had he become calmer, with the success of the Sena, and his own position as area leader?

His blood still boiled. 'There is a place called Bhiwandi, about 25 kilometres from here. When India lost a cricket match to Pakistan, they used to let off crackers in the marketplace, the Muslims there. When I was small I could do nothing about it. But now I can't bear it. There used to be groups of Muslims who used to come over from Bhiwandi to Thane here. The local people were so full of resentment against those Muslims that they had clashes with them in 1982, and they broke open the Muslim shops and sold the goods to the people. They sold towels for two rupees. The Muslim shops have come back now, but they live in fear. The Shiv Sena is very powerful. I will tell you: the Muslims even give donations to the Shiv Sena.'

Nikhil said on his own, 'But isn't this extortion?'

Mr Patil didn't think so.

I wanted to know – thinking of his adoration for Ganpati – what was more important for him: religion or politics? In Nikhil's Marathi translation this came out as: *dharma* or *rajnithi*?

Mr Patil said, 'Dharma.' Religion. But this wasn't the personal faith in Ganpati he had talked about. With the Sena's success and growth, the Sena's ideas had grown bigger: the religion that Mr Patil meant was Hinduism itself. 'There is a plot to wipe Hinduism off the face of the earth.' It was a Muslim plot, and that was why it was vital to keep Hinduism alive.

Two more thin Indian cats or kittens had come into the sitting room – a tabby, and another ginger-coloured cat – and they were walking about inquiringly. Some friends or relations of the Patils had also dropped in, to listen to what Mr Patil had to say to his visitors.

I asked whether Hinduism could be kept alive, if Indian business and industry kept on growing as it had been growing.

He didn't see any contradiction. 'If you want to survive, you have to make money.'

'That isn't the Gandhian attitude.'

'I have contempt for Gandhi. He believed in turning the other cheek. I believe that if someone slaps you, you must have the power to ask him why he slapped you, or you must slap him back. I hate the idea of non-violence.'

This was in keping with his Maratha warrior pride. I wondered how much of Maratha history he knew. What ideas of history were afloat in this locality, in all these narow lanes? Did he know Shivaji's dates?

He did. He said, '1630 to 1680. I know all that. Shivaji saved the Maharashtrians from atrocities. But then the English came, and they committed atrocities on everybody else.'

I could understand the larger communal mood here, the conflict between Hindus and Muslims. But I wondered about the meaning caste would have in an industrial area like this, where people lived so close together. What were the Sena's relations with the Dalits? From the little I had seen, the Dalits had developed the beginnings of that self-confidence, the *atma-vishwas*, which had been part of Ganpati's gift to Mr Patil. Did that touch some chord in him? Did his concern for Hinduism lead him to some fellow feeling for them?

He was rigid. 'We have no differences with them. They don't consider themselves Maharashtrians or Hindus. They are Buddhists.'

Hadn't they been driven out of Hinduism by caste prejudice? Was there no sympathy for them? When he was a boy, his blood had boiled when he had heard his leader speak of the discrimination against Maharashtrians. Didn't he think that Dalits had cause to feel like that too?

He didn't think so. Dalit anger was something the Dalit leaders and the people called the Dalit Panthers – in imitation of the Black Panthers of the United States – were encouraging for political reasons. 'They have no reason to be angry. They've not suffered as much as they say. And the present Dalit organizations are linked to Muslim groups.'

I asked Nikhil whether that was so. He said yes. 'Both those sections, the Dalits and the Muslims, are alienated. And someone thought it would be a good idea to bring them together.'

Alienation: it was the common theme. Mr Patil was triumphant now; but his blood still boiled. Even now he felt that his group might sink, and that others were waiting to trample on them. It was as though in these small, crowded spaces no one really felt at home. Everyone felt that the other man, the other group, was laughing; everyone lived with the feeling of siege.

The time had now come to go with Mr Patil to the Sena office. We said goodbye to his mother; and she, still sitting, lifted her head, her eyes lost below the concentric circles of her thick glasses, and brought her palms together again. Together with some of the people who had come to hear Mr Patil talk, we went out of the pink room to the verandah, past the taken-off slippers and shoes at the door.

We went first to the end of the verandah to look at the view at the back: the brick sheds against the back wall, the abandoned structure next door, with rusty reinforcing iron rods coming out of the concrete. One of the men with us said in English, 'Unauthorized.' So, in spite of the apparent haphazardness all around, there was some kind of municipal regulation.

We went down the steep staircase to the passageway between the two houses, and then out into the sunlight of the paved lane. A little way to the right was the local Sena office, Mr Patil's domain. Structurally, it was a concrete box, a one-roomed shed; but it had been decorated on the outside to look like a fort, with a formal and very simple kind of crenellation at the top, and with the concrete wall painted to suggest blocks of grey stone with white pointing. It was quite startling in the dust and dirt and crumble of the lane. It looked like a stage set or like something from a fairground. But it was a reminder of the warrior past of the Marathas. The past was real; the present power and organization of the Sena was real.

We hadn't been asked to take off our shoes before we went into Mr Patil's sitting room. But we had to take them off now before we stepped from the lane into the Sena office: this, though it was dustier than his sitting room, was Mr Patil's true shrine. The inside walls were painted blue. The floor was paved with stone flags – the people of Maharashtra build naturally and well in stone.

There was a desk against the far wall, with a high-backed chair, like a throne. As soon as we entered, Mr Patil went and sat on the high-backed chair, as though this was part of the formality of the place. In front of the desk were nine folding metal chairs; they were for visitors, and they were painted in the same blue colour as the wall. On the back wall, above Mr Patil's chair, there was a picture of a tiger: the tiger was the Sena's emblem. The only other picture on that wall was of the leader of the Sena. On the desk there was a bronze-coloured bust of Shivaji, and there was another, similar bust on a pedestal set at an angle in the corner away from the desk. The busts were of plaster of Paris, and each carried a fresh mark of sandalwood paste, which was a holy or sacred mark, on the forehead. There was a tall dark-green iron cabinet near the door, and the lighting was by fluorescent tube. A cuckoo clock on a wall – a reminder of Mr Patil's sitting room – was the only decorative thing in the little cell.

The Sena office was a Sena fort, and there were 40 like it in Thane. In one way, it was martial make-believe; in another way, it was perfectly real. There were constant group fights in the locality. Some of the fights were between the Sena and the Dalits, especially those of the Dalits who called themselves Panthers; and there were also fights between the Sena and some Congress groups. The fights were serious, and sometimes deadly, with swords and acid-bulbs as weapons. The Sena also fought to protect its supporters against criminals and thugs. Some of the Sena supporters were stall-holders such as we had seen on the way from the railway station; there were always people trying to extort money from them.

While we were talking in the office, Mr Patil leaning back in his high-backed chair, Nikhil and I leaning forward on our blue metal chairs (the blue scratched down to rust at the edges), there was a sound of tramping in the lane. It sounded almost like a little aproaching disturbance, a little event. And we saw, passing in the sunlight in front of the door, a number of handcuffed young men, roped together with what looked like new rope, roped together upper arm to upper arm. The roped-up men were in two files, and they were being marched or led, without shouts or haste or roughness, by a squad of policemen in khaki uniform.

Nikhil said, 'But that's unconstitutional. People can't be handcuffed just like that. The Supreme Court has handed down a ruling.'

The men being led away seemed to have dressed for Sunday. Their shirts were clean and stylish; the shirt of one man had broad vertical black and silver stripes. They were very young men, all slender, some thin.

The man who had said, of the unfinished concrete structure at the back of the Patil house, 'Unauthorized' – that man now again spoke one word, with the Indian affirmative shake of the head, to explain what we had seen. He said, 'Without.'

Without what?

Railway tickets – everyone around me knew, everyone was ready to explain.

What did Mr Patil think of what we had seen?

He was easy about it. 'It's an everyday occurrence. They are being taken to prison, and they will have to stay there for three or four days. Some are poor people. But some do it for the kicks.'

We went out of the office into the lane. The policemen and their prisoners had almost gone out of sight. The little disturbance had passed; the life of the lane was closing over it.

In a canal (or worse) off the lane I saw an animal of some sort parting the dark green-brown water. A dog? A cow – one of the small Indian variety of cow? A calf? It was hard to see the dark creature against the dark water. But then a round snout rose flat and pink above the surface: a pig. And, vision established now, I also saw, paddling on ahead, their irregular white markings looking from a distance like light on the dark canal, or foam, a number of little black-and-white piglets, paddling and bucking about in the murky water.

The man who had said 'Unauthorized' and 'Without' now said, 'Dalit pigs.'

What did he mean by that? Many Indians, Hindus and Muslims, considered the pig unclean; some could hardly bear the sight of the animal. Was there some Dalit intention to provoke – in these pigs (that few dared touch) being turned loose in a crowded area?

That wasn't so.

The man who had said 'Dalit pigs' said, 'The Dalits eat them on Sundays.' So the pigs were not only part of the Dalit separateness; there was also a formality about Dalit pig-eating. The man added, 'They also sell pigs.'

Just a little way up the lane – where the policemen had passed – many small boys were playing cricket with an old, smooth, grey tennis ball. The Sena fort; the slender young men in their nice shirts handcuffed and roped up; the cricket, the gentlemanly, stylish game from halfway across the world – everything was open for inspection here. And so much more was innocently on view: just below the surface, human emotions and needs, and ideas of mystery and glory, ran riot.

On a white wall somewhere near Mohammed Ali Road in downtown Bombay I had seen this slogan painted in tall black letters: LIBERATE HUMANITY THROUGH ISLAM.

Mohammed Ali Road had a reputation. It was the main thoroughfare of the Muslim area of downtown Bombay. The area was spoken of as a 'ghetto', and it was so often in the news, in such worrying ways, that people tended to use newspaper language to describe it. It was 'volatile', a 'flashpoint'; it was where communal riots could begin and, having begun, could spread like fire.

It was dreadfully crowded, with every kind of smell and noise. The brown-black smoke from cars using kerosene-adulterated fuel was like a hot fog in the sunlight. It burned the skin and felt jagged in the lungs. It was part of the general feeling of oppression; and the slogan about Islam, seen through this smoke, had the effect of a scream. The slogan was in letters as high as the wall on which it was painted, and it was in English. It wasn't for the people of the ghetto; it was for people outside, people like the Shiv Sena, who might think of making trouble.

Nikhil knew a young man who lived in the Mohammed Ali Road area. The young man's name was Anwar. Early one evening, after he had finished his work, Anwar took us to see where he lived. Anwar was very small and frail, with a suggestion of some inherited debility. But he had a compensating passion about his Muslim faith, and he was full of fight.

The early evening traffic on Mohammed Ali Road was very slow. The shops and the pavements were as jammed as the road. The electric lights created the effect of a ceiling or canopy and appeared to press down on everything, adding, with the hot smoke, to the feeling of crowd and abrasion and life lived at an extremity. It was too noisy to talk in the taxi.

At a certain point we got out of the taxi, and then we followed Anwar away from the lights and the smoke to an area of sudden smallness. Narrow lanes opened into narrower, and they were lined with little low houses. Some way off, Mohammed Ali Road glowed and roared; but the lights here were dim, the lanes were full of shadows, and the near noises were domestic and subdued. We were not in unregulated slum. The lanes were straight and paved, and – though the scale was very small – there was a regularity of lay-out and building that suggested an official housing project. Anwar said that this was so; we were in a municipal settlement.

His house was a narrow section of a wire-netting and concrete row. For two or three feet from the ground the walls of the front room were concrete; above that they were wire netting. A white sheet stretched over the wire netting screened the front room of Anwar's house from his neighbour's on one side; the screen was on the neighbour's side of the wire netting. Anwar's house, his section of the row, was perhaps no more than nine feet wide. The wire netting and concrete were painted blue. The front room might have been six feet deep. It had a passageway on one side, with shoes and slippers on shelves built into the concrete wall. This passageway led to the main, middle room. Beyond that, Anwar said, was the kitchen.

Somewhere in the upper space of the middle room was a sleeping loft. The sleeping loft was important. Without it houses like this wouldn't work, wouldn't be able to provide space for whole families. This was the first I had heard of the Bombay sleeping loft. I heard a good deal more about it in the days that followed; and I began to understand how large families – not always slum-dwellers or pavement-sleepers – managed to live in one small room. At night all over Bombay sitting rooms changed their function; the various portions of a house like Anwar's (essentially that main middle room) became simply a place for sleeping in. A sleeping loft utilized to the full the space, the volume, of a room.

We had been talking in the lane outside Anwar's house. We hadn't yet gone inside the house. Our talk encouraged a young man from the adjoining house or section to come out to have a look at us. He was of medium height, with a good physique, and he was freshly dressed, as if for relaxation, in a singlet and khaki shorts. It was momentarily astonishing to me that someone of normal size and so reasonably turned out should have come out of such a restricted space. We fell silent when he came out and stood in the lane in the dim light, in his patch of territory, saying nothing; and, as though we felt we had been indiscreet or discourteous talking in the open about the houses of the settlement, we went then, almost as if for the privacy, into the wire-netted front room of Anwar's house. The young man came back into the front room of his own house and stood about for a while. In the dim light there he or his pale shadow, changing size, could be seen against the white-sheet divider or screen – the sheet fixed to the wire netting on his side – like a figure in a puppet play.

Someone in Anwar's family had made preparations for our visit. A clean sheet had been spread on the string bed in the front room, as a courtesy to Nikhil and me. At Anwar's invitation, we sat there. Anwar's father then came out from somewhere in the middle room. He was our host now; and Anwar was sent to buy cold lemonade.

Anwar's father, a small man, though not as small as Anwar, looked frail and unwell; and I thought that some of the son's apparent debility would have come from the father. He was very dark, with a very thick, silver beard. That beard was like the old man's only physical vanity: it was expertly trimmed and combed, and it rippled and shone. And more than physical vanity was there: in India different groups wear different styles of beard, and Anwar's father's spade-shaped beard was a Muslim beard. That was the beard's forthright message.

He said he was sixty-four. And before Nikhil and I could say anything, he said he knew he looked much older – and that was true: I had thought of him as close to eighty. Europeans didn't look as old as Indians, he said. He knew; he had once worked in an Italian firm, and he had seen Europeans of seventy looking healthy and working hard. Indians aged as they did because of the conditions they lived in. Here, for instance, they didn't just have traffic fumes; they also had mill smoke, from a cloth mill. Still, he was sixty-four. That was something; his father had died at forty.

Anwar came back with some chilled bottles of lemonade. This was formally offered, bottle by bottle. We drank a little – the lemonade was very sweet, and seemed to have some chemical tincture – and we tried to make general conversation, though we were really too many in the space, and voices and sounds came to us from all directions, and that white screen (pinned to the other side of the wire-netting divider) began to seem ambiguous in its intention, not wholly friendly.

I asked the old man whether there were thieves in the settlement. It had occurred to me that the very openness of life there, and the communality of it (as of a commune), might have offered people a kind of protection.

The old man said there were thefts every day. And there were quarrels every day. The quarrels were worse. A lot of the quarrels came about because of the children. People hit other people's children, and the parents became angry.

He had lived under every kind of pressure. So had Anwar. Perhaps – if, in circumstances like these, there could be said to be a scale in such matters – it had been harder for Anwar, who was more sensitive, better educated, and, in the outside world, had a harder fight in the technical field he had chosen.

Playing with the lemonade, considering the old-fashioned courtesies of father and son in that setting, the humanity that remained to them, the old man's calm acknowledgement of the better health and strength of others, the better conditions of life of others, I began to feel an affection for them both. I felt that if I had been in their position, confined to Bombay, to that area, to that row, I too would have been a passionate Muslim. I had grown up in Trinidad as a member of the Indian community, a member of a minority, and I knew that if you felt your community was small, you could never walk away from it; the grimmer things became, the more you insisted on being what you were.

With the old man as our host in the front space of his house, the wire-netted enclosure, and with Anwar being only his father's son there, our talk could only be formal. I didn't feel that difficult questions could be pressed. For the talk to go beyond the part-time job the old man had been lucky enough to find, for Anwar to

31

talk more freely, and without the worry about being overheard, we had to go somewhere else.

So, gently, trying to avoid accident, we laid our lemonade bottles down on the blue concrete wall against the wire netting; and the old man, who had been getting a little restless himself, read the sign well. He stopped talking, created a pause, and we said goodbye.

We went out again to the narrow lanes, where dim lights threw big shadows. Around the corner, a child was defecating in a patch of light. In somebody's front room a big colour television set on a low stand flickered and flashed away, without anyone watching. Anwar said they had no television in their own house. His father said that television was against Islam.

We came to where the low-roofed settlement ended, and Bombay proper began again. Beyond a boundary lane or road was a tall block of flats. The enemy were there. That was a Shiv Sena building, Anwar said. When there was trouble the people who lived in those flats threw bottles at the people who lived below.

Past that building, we came to the roaring main road. We went to a small milk bar Anwar knew: fluorescent tubes, ceramic tiles, grey marble, a sink, tumblers of glass and stainless steel.

I said to Anwar, 'So you live constantly on your nerves?'

Nikhil interpreted the reply. 'It plays havoc with his nerves.'

As worn-away as his father, his dark face thin and tremulous, he sipped at the milk he had ordered.

He said, Nikhil translating directly for him now, 'Those children. You have these clashes between children which turn into blood feuds with adults, and I feel helpless to do anything about it. Fights take place between neighbours all the time. When they are Hindus and Muslims – Hindus are in a minority here – it turns into a communal riot. It gets very bad during cricket matches. When there was the World Cup last year – the one-day cricket matches – people became nervous about the India-Pakistan matches. But then neither India nor Pakistan went into the finals. When Pakistan lost the first semi-final to Australia, the Hindus went wild, and they threw stones and broke the asbestos roofs of the huts.'

How those fights troubled him! Both he and his father had spoken with special dread of fights between neighbours, and I wondered whether they had been talking about themselves. I tried

32

to find out. I asked him about the blood feuds – was his family affected in some way?

His reply was unexpected. 'My brothers have the reputation of being *goondas*, thugs. They're not the right kind of people. Because of this reputation, neighbours think twice before starting anything.'

Tough brothers – they would, for some reason, have been physically quite different from Anwar and his father. Tough brothers, not the right kind of people – yet they enabled Anwar to talk tough himself. Did that little house contain them all?

I asked Anwar, 'That man next door, the man who came out to look at us – how do you get on with him?'

'He's studying at a college outside Bombay. You can just imagine the kind of brothers I have – I have six brothers, and my father still has to work.'

Some family split here. Perhaps the brothers Anwar was talking about, the toughs, might have had a different mother.

He said, 'I don't think of them as my brothers.' But then immediately he softened that. 'The environment has made them what they are. They had to become thugs, to survive. I will tell you this story about the foolhardiness of my brothers. You've been reading in the papers recently about the don who's become the new king of the Bombay underworld. Some time ago, when this don got a contract to kill someone in the locality, he came on a reconnaissance to our area. And – you wouldn't believe – one of my brothers picked a fight with him.'

'What sort of man did the don have to kill?'

'The man the don had to kill was in the business of sending people to the Middle East – manpower export – and he must have cheated someone. But my brothers saw this don as someone intruding on their turf. They exchanged insults and abuse, my brothers and the don, and each side said they would see what the other did. My brother got an Ambassador car and they packed it with weapons. They were planning to attack the don's area, but someone tipped the police off, and my brothers were caught. They were released in a couple of days. Someone here bailed them out.'

'Your brothers have money, then?'

'They make money and then they start gambling.'

'You would say that they, too, are living on their nerves?'

'They don't have the mental make-up I have. If the occasion

33

arises, they will give their lives without a thought. It's the environment.'

In that talk of his thuggish brothers ready to give their lives there was, now, a kind of inverted pride, as when he had spoken of the fear his brothers inspired in the neighbours.

I asked him about the riots of 1984. People spoke of them as a fearful Bombay event, historical, a marker.

He seemed to blow at his milk, as if to cool it. But the milk wasn't warm. That constant parting of his lips, that seeming expulsion of breath, was only a trick of the muscles of his thin face, part of the tremulousness of his face.

He said, 'That was when the will to fight came to me. I was in the final year of the matriculation. There is a Muslim cemetery near Marine Drive, and there is a day near the Ramadan period when it is necessary to visit that cemetery. A group from this area went. At two o'clock in the morning we were walking back home. Some of us were wearing skullcaps, Muslim caps. We passed a Shiv Sena stronghold. We were pelted with stones. We complained to some policemen. They didn't listen. In fact, they followed us for two miles. They thought we were the troublemakers. That was the first sign we had of the riot. Before that night there had been no sign of any trouble. Actually, the real trouble was very far away, about 25 kilometres from here.'

It became hard in the milk bar to hear what Anwar was saying. Above the noise of traffic in the road, there were now querulous voices in the bar itself, Indian voices, specially edged to cut through most sounds of man and machine – above all, the rising and falling cicada sound of motor-car hooters.

Anwar said, 'We returned to this area about three o'clock in the morning. Some of us were bleeding from the stones, and people asked us what had happened. I should tell you that on that night, *shab-e-baraat*, Muslims stay awake right through.

'The next day I had forgotten about the incident. But when I went with a friend to a house near here, I found it full of weapons. That was the doing of one of the big dons. His men had stocked up, to retaliate. Soon after, firing began in the locality. There was curfew throughout the day, and then they banned gatherings of more than five people. In the colony itself' – the area where he lived – 'police infiltrated to check whether people had weapons.'

'Did the presence of the police calm people down?'

'I have no confidence in the police. I will tell you. You can't kill cows in public here – there's an abbattoir you have to take your cows to. But you can pay a policeman, and kill a cow in public. When goats have to be sacrificed at the festival of Id, most Muslims take their goats to the abbattoir to have them slaughtered. But there are some local hoods who insist on killing the goats in public. It's a macho act, to challenge the police. When the police come, the hoods say, "If you interfere, you won't leave here alive."'

He had slid away from the subject of the riots of 1984; he had gone back to the subject of the toughs.

I said, 'These fights with the police excite you?'

He said, with some solemnity, 'It is exciting. I like it. It happens because the police discriminate against the Muslims, and the Muslims have contempt for the police.'

'But what's the point of the game?'

He didn't answer directly. He said, 'There are very few sensible people among the Muslims.' He spelt out the Urdu word he had in mind for 'sensible': *samajdar*. 'There are few educated Muslims here. People who are educated will never get involved in that kind of fighting.' He semed slightly to have changed his attitude to the fighters.

'So it will just go on?'

He said, with his curious mixture of melancholy and acceptance, 'I see no end to it. I don't see how it can end.'

'How did the riots end that time?'

'Mrs Gandhi came and asked people to try to settle things. But things get settled and then – they burst out again.'

I thought of the narrow lanes and the low wire-netting dwellings, with sleeping lofts below the fragile asbestos roofs. 'What was life like during the riots? Did people sleep?'

'When there are riots, you don't know the meaning of sleep. You can't sleep. It's a big sin if someone of your faith is assaulted and you do nothing about it.'

'Don't you think that someone like you should be trying to live somewhere else?'

'I can't take such a step.' It was what I thought he would say. 'There are so many family ties. It is mandatory for a Muslim to honour those ties.' Family, faith, community: they made a whole.

'What advice would you give a younger brother, or someone coming up?'

35

The advice wasn't about going away or breaking out. It was more immediate. It was about surviving, here. 'I would tell him that he should think of retaliating and fighting back only if the person in front of him has made a mistake.'

'Mistake?'

'If someone abuses you, for instance.'

Abuse, quarrels, fights within and without: that was the world he lived in, and, physically, was so little equipped for.

I mentioned the slogan I had seen: LIBERATE HUMANITY THROUGH ISLAM.

He said, 'I agree with it totally.'

'When did you learn about Islam?' How, living where he did, would he have had the time, the privacy, the calm?

'I learned from my parents. And I've also read the Koran.'

'There are so many people in Bombay who feel they know the way to liberate humanity.'

He appeared to change his point of view. 'It's the nature of the world. When people gather in groups, each one will say that his is better than the others.'

I thought again of the family with the big colour television set near his house. I asked about them.

'They have a business, making ready-made clothes. They make a little money.'

People in business, making money, and yet living here: it was proof again of what people said, that all you required in Bombay was accommodation. Once you had a place to sleep, anywhere, on a pavement, in a hut, in a corner of a room, you could get a job and make money. But – did the people with the television set show off a little?

The people with the TV and the tailoring business didn't show off, Anwar said. But my question had touched something. He said, 'They know that TV is forbidden in their religion.' Then, as often, Anwar softened what he said. 'But they don't want their children to go to other houses to watch TV, and to be turned away. That can cause trouble.'

'Why do you think so many of the dons in Bombay are Muslims?'

'I've told you. There are few educated people among the Muslims. They go off the rails when they're young.'

'Are they religious people, these dons?'

'They are all loyal adherents of Islam.'

'Defenders of the faith?'

'It is inevitable that they will fight for Islam. It is a contradictory role. They will continue their criminal activities, but at the same time they will read the Koran and do the *namaaz* five times a day. The community does not admire these people. But the people are enchanted by the way the dons behave with the common Muslims.'

'They are the community's warriors?'

'They organize our underground. *Tanzeen-Allah-ho-akbar* – that's what it's called. It is organized by a don. It was created after the riots. We have meetings and decide strategy. We meet every month, even if there is no trouble.'

'What do you think will happen to the children in your colony?'

'The future is awful for them. All those children see murder, assaults.'

'Have you seen murders?'

'Yeh, yeh.' It was an Indian affirmation, rather than American or English, and it was a spoken with a side-to-side swing of the head in the Indian way.

The bar-owner had begun to talk loudly to the bar in general about the people at the far end – he meant us – who had been occupying a table for too long. I was going to leave a fair sum for him, but he wasn't to know that. I had my back to him, and I thought I shouldn't turn around to look at him; I thought that if our eyes met he might be driven to a deeper rage. Nikhil, who had been facing him all the time, and occasionally reporting on his mood, ordered *gulab jamun* for everybody; and Anwar, who had already worked his way through two tumblers of milk, began – appearing all the while to blow at it – to eat a portion of that rich milk sweet, steeped in syrup.

He said, 'I saw my first murder when I was ten. We were playing badminton in the colony. There was a hut close by, and there were two men who began to quarrel. These two men usually slept on the same hand-cart at night. They were both about thirty. They had begun to quarrel, and then I saw one of the men running away. We went to see what had happened, and we saw that the man on the hand-cart had had his head nearly severed. He wasn't dead. He was in the throes of death.'

'What clothes?'

'Underwear. Shorts and a singlet. And the body in the throes of death caused the hand-cart to capsize.'

'People ran up?'

'Only children. About six or seven of us. And as the body fell to the ground, it spurted blood on us. I was very frightened.' He began to laugh, eating his sweet, sucking at the thick syrup in his aluminium spoon. It was the first time he had laughed that evening. 'We were still children. It didn't occur to us that this was a police matter. Our first reaction was to go and wash the bloodstains off our shirt.'

'How many murders have you seen since then?'

'Ten or 12.'

'Why do you laugh?'

'It's part of everyday life to us here. The reasons for those murders are very small. For instance, one day two men with umbrellas had a little collision. One man went to hit the other man, and the other man ran into a house, and the man chasing him ran in after him. I was talking to friend just there, and I saw it. The man doing the chasing pulled out a knife and killed the other man, just like that. Eighty per cent of people in this locality carry weapons.'

The bar-owner hadn't been pacified by the extra orders for gulab jamun; he had continued to complain. And when Anwar finished his sweet, we prepared to leave. My thoughts went back to the people with the big television set.

'The people with the TV – are they very religious?'

'They are devout people. They are more religious in some ways and less religious in others.'

'In what ways more religious?'

'They offer namaaz five times a day. I offer namaaz only once.'

Formal prayers five times a day – and yet, to Anwar and his father, that faith, obsessive as it was, was flawed.

'Can you see yourself living without Islam?'

'No.'

'What does it give you?'

'Brotherhood. Brotherhood in everything. Islam doesn't teach discrimination. It makes people help people. If a blind man is crossing the road, the Muslim doesn't stop to find out what creed he belongs to. He just helps.'

'What do you think will happen to your colony?'

'I don't see any solution.'

'It will just go on as it is? You really think it will be the same when you reach your father's age?'

'Yes.'

'You don't ever think of going away?'

'At the moment I have no intention to do so.'

'Are you a Sunni?'

He looked surprised. He didn't think that I would know about Sunnis. To him his faith was something secret, something outsiders couldn't really know about.

I wanted to know whether there were other Muslim groups or sects in his colony. I asked whether there were Ismailis or Ahmadis among them. He said he had never heard of those groups. Were there Shias?

'There are no Shias in the community.'

'Isn't that strange?'

'I don't find it strange.'

His orthodox faith was the one pure thing he had to hold on to. He couldn't imagine life without it. It was a stringent faith. It shut out television; it had no room for heretics. All the many rules and celebrations and proscriptions were part of the completeness of Anwar's world. Take away one practice, and everything was threatened; everything might start to unravel. It was correct, for instance, for Muslim men to pee squatting; and I heard later, from someone who worked with Anwar, that Anwar insisted on doing this at the modern urinals in his place of work, though it created problems for him.

Many of the people one saw on the streets and in offices lived in a small space. From small spaces, every morning, they came out fresh and clean and brisk. Whole families, not slum-dwellers or pavement-dwellers, lived in one room; and they might live in the same room for a generation.

Mr Raote had grown up in a family like that. He was one of the earliest members of the Shiv Sena; he had been among the 18 people, no more, at the very first Shiv Sena meeting in 1966. Now, with the victory of the Sena in the municipal elections, he was a man of authority, chairman of the Standing Committee of the Bombay Corporation. He had his own little office in the Victorian-Gothic Corporation building, with a waiting room and a secretary and straight-backed chairs for people with petitions and needs. But he had lived for the first 28 years of his life in the one room where he had been born, in the suburb of Dadar, in mid-town Bombay.

In Dadar Mr Raote now lived in the top flat of a tall block he had built himself, after he had turned developer in his thirties. But the tenement with the one room which had been his home for more than half his life was within walking distance, and he took me to see it one morning.

We took the lift to the ground floor of his building, went out to the sandy front yard, went from the front to the back through a passage in the building, between shops with stylish signboards; and from the back walked to the next main road. Mr Raote was very well known; his walk created a little stir; people were respectful. It couldn't have been open to many people to have the past (and a triumphant return to it) so accessible, just at the end of a short walk.

We turned off, very soon, from the footpath of the main road into a yard with an old two-storey building. We went round to the back and went up the steps at the side of the building to a verandah or gallery at the top. This verandah (like the one on the lower floor) ran the length of the building, and the floor was laid in the Maharashtrian way with slabs of stone. Separate rooms opened into the verandah. The room at the end was where Mr Raote's family had lived.

We looked in from the doorway, and saw new carpentry and paint, in contemporary styling and colours. 'It's been done up,' Mr Raote said. The room next to it was darker and plainer; it was more like the room Mr Raote had known. It was about 15 feet deep by 10 feet wide, with a kitchen at the back and with a loft for storage and sleeping. All the rooms on that upper floor had a common bathroom and toilet.

Before we had come over, Mr Raote had said, 'My father made us study. You will recognize the difficulty when you visit the spot.'

And now, standing in the verandah where he had walked and run thousands of times, looking down at the yard which would have been shared with all the people from all the rooms in the building, I wondered how life had been lived in that small space, how five brothers and two sisters and father and mother had managed. How did children sleep and play and get ready for school?

Mr Raote said his father and mother used to awaken the children at four in the morning. Between four and seven they did their exercises – running, push-ups – and they studied. They had to do it all before seven. What made it difficult after that? The crowd in the building and yard, the noise? Mr Raote said, 'The atmosphere.'

As a top Shiv Sena man, Mr Raote had a reputation for roughness. And he had been a little rough with me when I was taken to his office to be introduced to him. When he understood that I wasn't looking for material for another hostile interview, that I was more interested in his background and development, his manner changed. He was interested in his own story; his idea of himself was of a man who had struggled.

He was now chairman of the Standing Committee of the Corporation, he said; but his first job in the Corporation had been as a clerk, in 1965, when he was twenty-one, and his salary then had been 218 rupees a month, £16. He offered that fact almost as soon as we began to talk seriously. And then he offered another: when he was a boy, he said, he used to help his father make coffins.

I liked that detail. He liked it too. He wanted to tell the rest of the story. He asked me to come to his flat in Dadar, and he sent his Ambassador car for me early one morning. The windows of the car had the dark tinting that had become fashionable in Bombay; there were two small plastic fans that made for fair comfort; and on the dashboard there was a little picture of Hanuman, the deity who stood for strength.

When I was taken up to the flat, Mr Raote was still doing his puja. Waiting, I went out to the terrace and looked at the view north and south, all the great length of Bombay, unexpectedly green from this height. When Mr Raote had finished his puja, I went into the sitting room, and he began to talk.

'When I was born, my father was working as a mechanic in All-India Radio, AIR. This was in 1944. He was getting 300 rupees a month. It was sufficient. I grew up thinking of myself as lower middle class. We had no luxuries, but we had enough to eat. We used to have a kind of soaked-wheat cereal in the morning, *satva*. You become very strong if you eat that. It takes two hours to prepare.

'I studied up to 11th standard in Marathi. Then I joined the college. About this time my father retired from AIR, and he became a jack of all trades. There was a big drop in his earning.

He used to earn 75 to 90 rupees a month as a carpenter in the film studio, working for many hours at a time.

'He also used to go as a carpenter to prepare coffins. I used to go with him sometimes. Making coffins is a very specialized thing. It isn't easy to get that bend at the shoulders. The plank has to be one; it mustn't be cut. And you have to have a very good bottom in a coffin, because the whole pressure of the body falls on that bottom. We would get four annas, a quarter of a rupee, for a coffin for a small child. Twelve annas for a medium-size coffin. For a bigger-size coffin, six feet or six feet five inches, we used to get one rupee and a quarter. That was just for the labour. In a day we would be able to prepare five or six coffins. Normally a person wouldn't go to make coffins. It's a casteless occupation – not for a person of caste. But we did it for the cash.

'My father wanted to see at least one of his children become a doctor. My sister was admitted to the college for science. I completed my own Inter Science studies. My first choice after this was for the military. I wanted to be an officer, but I had no one to advise me. I joined the Indian Navy training course in 1962, and went to the exams and all. But I was a month too old, so I had to come back again. Then I tried to become an engineer. It was hard to get into a school in Bombay. I got admission to the Sholapur Polytechnic – that's far away from here. My father said he couldn't pay the expenses, and he couldn't. The expenses in Sholapur would have been 200 rupees a month. So I had to give that up too. That was in 1964. The next year I put my name down at the state employment exchange. We were still living in that one room. I joined St Xavier's Technical Institute for evening classes.

'So already there were these two or three failures in my life – not getting into the military, being too old for the navy training course, and not getting into an engineering school. It's a frustration at that age. That's the age when boys can develop ambition. If they don't develop ambition, they start to drift.

'My mother and father gave me encouragement, and my intention to do something in life was always there. I had the confidence.'

I remembered what Mr Patil, the Shiv Sena area leader in Thane, had said about confidence, *atma-vishwas*: it had been given him by Ganpati. I asked Mr Raote whether he thought he had got his confidence from Ganpati.

He said he had got his confidence from religion in the larger sense, rather than from Ganpati in particular. 'He is not a special deity. Everything in India begins with Ganpati or Ganesh. No Hindu puja starts without him. The religion we have is from childhood. It is part and parcel of our life. No Hindu family will give up the morning puja. We have a special garment for the puja. Religion definitely gave us confidence. It built our character.

'We are coming now to the most important aspect of my life. I've told you about my failures and frustration, and how I gave up and put my name down at the state employment exchange. In 1965 I took a job as a clerk in the Bombay Corporation. The salary was 218 rupees. Was that a good wage? To the man who has no earnings, whatever he earns is good. And my main ambition at this time was that my sister should become a doctor, as my father wanted. We did secure her admission to a medical college. And she was offered three scholarships – from the British Council, Tata's, and somebody else. We chose Tata. They gave the complete tuition fee. The books we got from other people.'

Mrs Raote had been in and out of the sitting room, but in a self-effacing way. Now, smiling, she came up to us with an open photograph album. She had heard us talking about religion, and the photographs she wanted to show were of a religious occasion: the thread ceremony for one of her sons. This prompted Mr Raote to go and bring out the unstitched length of cotton – mauve, with a band of another colour – which he wore when he did his puja. Mrs Raote was a pale-complexioned, handsome woman; and, as so often in Indian homes, the simple and apparently artless devotion of the wife to her husband was something that made an impression.

Mrs Raote withdrew. The open album rested on the sofa. And Mr Raote went on with his story.

'I should add something else at this point. In 1962, three years before I had taken the job with the Corporation, and at the beginning of the time of my failures and frustration, I had come across a weekly called *Marmik*. This was a cartoon weekly, the first in the Marathi language. It was edited by Bal Thackeray. He and his brother and his father wrote the whole paper. *Marmik* always had a big cartoon on the front cover. It was this that caught my eye. The circulation of the paper was about 35 or 40 thousand at that time.

'And now, in 1965, with my sister in the medical college, and me in the Corporation as a clerk, and my father working as a carpenter in the film studio, *Marmik* really began to work on my mind. Every week the magazine spoke about the injustices done in Bombay and Maharashtra to the sons of the soil. And I found I was terribly attracted to the emotional personality of Bal Thackeray and his father, as expressed in the magazine. I even tried to meet Bal Thackeray. He was living in Shivaji Park.'

Mr Raote waved to the west, to an area of green: Bombay from this height all clear before us, from the Gateway of India and the Fort area in the south, to the hills and suburbs of the north: the great city, from this height all its squalor lost below the green of trees, now truly Mr Raote's own.

'There was an announcement in *Marmik* in May 1966 about a youth organization that was to be founded. It was to be called the Shiv Sena. I started visiting Bal Thackeray's house. Actually, the coconut was broken on the 19th of June 1966 at his house.' The breaking of a coconut at the start of an important venture is with Hindus a kind of puja or religious act. 'Eighteen people were there. At 8.20 in the morning.'

'Was that time chosen by a pundit?'

'No. It just happened. I was one of the 18 people there. Four of the 18 were from Bal Thackeray's own house: Bal Sahib himself, his father, and his two brothers. The first meeting lasted about half an hour. It was in the main room of their small house. Their father occupied that room, being an old man. He wrote everything on a Marathi typewriter. It is still there in the house, as a memorial of him. It was Bal Thackeray's father who gave the name Shiv Sena.' Shiva's Army. 'It just seemed natural and right. And we pledged ourselves at that meeting to fight the injustices done to the sons of the soil.

'That was how the Sena began. Bal Sahib used to hold small meetings here and there. Four months after the founding of the Sena he announced a public meeting on the issue of injustice. That meeting was to be on the 30th of October 1966. It had a tremendous response. Four to five lakhs.' Between 400 and 500 thousand people. 'And a number of gymnasiums in the town began to be attracted.'

What were those gymnasiums? I had never heard of them before.

'The gymnasium is a Maharashtrian institution. My father was too poor to send us to a gymnasium. But, as I told you, he made us run and exercise in the mornings. The gymnasium has been a

Maharashtrian institution since the time of our great saint, Ramdas Swami. He was the guru of Shivaji.' Shivaji, the warrior leader of the Marathas in the 17th century, the founder of Maratha military glory. 'Ramdas was a very practical guru. His message in part was that you should exercise and keep your body fit. One of Ramdas's famous sayings is, "Don't talk. Act."'

And now again Mrs Raote came to us, this time with a big, thick book in Marathi. It was a book of Ramdas's verses, a well printed modern edition, with a dust jacket. This made Mr Raote go and bring out some other big Marathi books: the verses of other classical Maratha teachers, Dineshwari, Tukaram, Eknath. These names were not really known to me. The books all looked new, and were well printed and well produced; but they were too bulky to handle easily, and I felt they were sacred household objects rather than books to be physically read. They were passed to me one by one, and I held them for a little and passed them back. They were then laid out on the sofa, next to the open photograph album with the snaps of Mr Raote in his puja cloth at the thread ceremony for his son.

I wondered how, in the conditions of Bombay, in the conditions Mr Raote had grown up in, people had kept in touch with their sacred books.

He said there had been no problem. 'In a traditional Maharash-trian household the elders would recite, morning and evening, *slokas* or verses from the writings of the famous gurus, so that a child, whether he had actually read the texts or not, would be aware of those verses. Nowadays it's done by tapes.'

There was a small shelf of such tapes in Mr Raote's sitting room, in a corner which seemed, from the objects laid out in it, to be a kind of holy or sacred corner.

He said, 'Maharashtra is a land of saints.' He played a part of a tape with a chanting or singing of Ramdas's verses – and the rhythms took me back 40 years and more to the *Ramayana* singing I had heard in my childhood. Ramdas's verses had endured, Mr Raote said, because of their rhythm. 'Ramdas's slokas have a special, simple, repetitive rhythm.' They were not musical for the sake of being musical. 'They are addressed to the mind. Each and every Maharashtrian, even if he lives in a hutment, has a culture.'

He stopped the tape, and returned to the story of the early days of the Shiv Sena. The Sena, the army of the land of saints, had caught on fast. But even as the Sena grew, Mr Raote's personal life declined. Between the founding of the Sena, in June 1966, and the big public meeting four months later which established it as a power in Bombay, Mr Raote's father died.

'The whole family was now on my head, and I had to continue as a clerk in the Corporation. I've told you that my first choice was always for the military, and I applied at this time for the Air Force pilot aptitude test. I got through the preliminary test in Bombay. Out of 1500 in my centre, only 12 were selected for a further interview at Bangalore. I was one of the 12. I went to Bangalore, and I got through all the aptitude tests of the Air Force. But the most delicate test – the machine test – was the one I failed. As part of that test, 100 questions had to be answered in five minutes. The speed of the questions baffled me. I had had no guidance in these matters. You need to practise to answer 100 questions in five minutes. There are schools today training people for examinations like that. But not then. And this failure was added to my frustration at having to serve in the Corporation, although I was never interested in service.'

I had noticed in other people this Indian use of the word 'service'. In one way it was related to 'civil service'; in another way it was related to the old-fashioned English use of 'service', meaning domestic service. The meaning of the word in India lay somewhere between the two. 'Service' in India stood for employment; but it also meant working for somebody else, working for wages, being dependent. (Mr Patil of Thane, for instance, speaking of his father who had worked for 40 years in the tool room of a factory, had said that his father had been 'in service'.)

'But I had to serve in the Corporation until my sister had got her M.B.S. degree. And I got married in 1968. My father-in-law and mother-in-law made me get married. I was doing the evening classes at St Xavier's Technical Institute, and I would have preferred to get married after I had finished my studies. It was a love-match.'

He used the English words, 'love-match', running them together and making 'love' rhyme with 'how', so that the words seemed to have become Marathi words.

'We belonged to different castes. I used to give lessons at that time. She was one of my students. That was how this affair came

46

up.' This giving of lessons was unexpected, another side of the Corporation clerk. 'She used to live over there, in that house.'

From the top of the block where we were he waved to an area of green and roofs not far away: Bombay, from here, an immense city, but the spaces he had moved in always small, village-like.

'There was opposition to our association from both sides. The castes were different, but they were not all that different. Caste wasn't the reason for the opposition. In our family we didn't want love-match. Our tradition is the proposed marriage.' The arranged marriage. 'It was the same on her side. So my in-laws, or the people who became my in-laws, compelled me to get married. And this marriage became another burden.

'To reduce this burden, I asked my wife to give up her studies and go into service. She gave up her studies and became a telephone operator. This was a government job, in the state secretariat. She got between 171 and 180 rupees a month, about £9, after the rupee devaluation. This was in 1969. We had a child in 1970. But, with my wife in service, I was not much worried by this.

'Then at last, in 1972, my sister got her M.D. She informed me on the phone at 12 o'clock one day that she had got through. And that same day I resigned from the Corporation. Eight years I had been in service – while my sister was becoming a doctor, as my father wanted. The day she became a doctor, I resigned. I had no job to go to, but I resigned. All that we had was my wife's job. Her job in the state secretariat had been a temporary one, but then fortunately she got a job as a telephone operator in the Corporation. It was an accident that she joined the Corporation when I left it.'

During the later years of service there had been Mr Raote's parallel life with the Sena. The Sena had risen, had begun to march, had become feared. In 1968 it had won more than a third of the seats in the Corporation. It had launched an agitation about the borders of Maharashtra; it had called a strike that had brought Bombay to a standstill for four days. Immigrants from South India had grown especially to fear the Sena. And Dadar, the suburb where we were – with a view of Shivaji Park, near where Bal Thackeray's house was, and with a view of the two-storeyed tenement where Mr Raote and his family were still living at that time in their one room – Dadar, as Mr Raote said, was 'the epicentre' of the Shiv Sena earthquake.

I had a memory myself of that early Sena time, from the other

47

side. This was in 1967, a year after the Sena had been founded. I had been visiting a Parsi acquaintance. He was a 'boxwallah', as the word was in those days. A boxwallah was an executive in a big firm, usually a firm with foreign affiliations; and in those days, before the Indian industrial boom, to be a boxwallah was to be secure, even exalted. The man I knew had married a Hindu woman of a well known family; and it was surprising to hear now, from people who should have been far above the day-to-day stresses of Indian life, that this 'mixed' marriage had made them both liable to physical attack from the Sena in their area.

It was evening; we were high up; there were lights below, some pale and yellow in the shanties. My vision of Bombay began to change: the 'poor', the people down there, were acquiring individuality and had begun to stake their own claim to the city; piety (or rage at their condition, or disgust) was no longer a sufficient response. The man I knew – speaking in 1967 with something of the passion I was to find this time in Papu, the young Jain stockbroker – said, of the dangers of mob attack, 'I try not to worry about it. I tell myself that, if I find something starting to happen, I must think it's like being in a nasty road accident.'

Yet at that time, 1967, and for years afterwards, Mr Raote, one of the original 18 of the Sena, had been working as a clerk in the Corporation, his salary rising over eight years from 218 rupees a month to 272 rupees and 50 paise (100 paise make a rupee), travelling back and forth on those crowded suburban trains between the Victorian-Gothic building where he worked and the tenement in Dadar where he had been born and where he had continued to live, in the same one room: carrying the grief for his father, the high ambition for his sister, his own frustrations at not being an officer, then an engineer, then something in the Indian Navy, daily feeling his clerkship in the Corporation, his 'service', as a humiliation.

Outside, he was unknown. But as the Sena had grown, he had risen in the Sena. All the time he had left over from work he gave to the Sena. He thought that in those days, between the Corporation and the Sena, he was working for 20 hours a day. He found himself running 22 Sena areas in central Bombay; he became close to the top leaders; he was put in charge of the Sena's election organization. He began to be known; his name began to get into the papers.

Yet, when he resigned in 1972 from the Corporation, all they had was his wife's telephone-operator salary. Then he appeared to have some luck. Just two days after he left the Corporation, he found a job as a shop supervisor in the tube-well section of one of the most highly regarded engineering firms in India. His salary was to be 750 rupees a month, nearly three times what he had been getting in the Corporation. This was a great piece of good fortune, but it hardly lasted. His Sena reputation undid him.

The Maharashtrian workers began to treat him as a Sena organizer rather than a shop supervisor. They wanted him to start a union. This kind of excitement couldn't be kept secret from the management. The works manager called him in one day – the works manager was an old army officer: the kind of man Mr Raote had longed to be – and began to question him. Had he come to work, or had he come as an activist?

Mr Raote couldn't endure the questioning. 'I am a hot-tempered man. I resigned that very day. I had been with the firm for one month and 22 days.'

Mr Raote paused here. He was coming now to the part of his story he especially wanted to tell; this was the period of his life he had wanted me to know about almost as soon as he had decided to talk seriously to me, in his office in the Corporation.

So, sitting at home now, after his morning puja, with the open photograph album and the sacred Marathi books laid out on the sofa, he paused. Then he said, 'That was when my starving started. That was my most difficult time.'

Though it was the time of his glory in the Sena.

'I began to work the whole day for the Sena. My wife used to feed my family with what she got from her job. And now – since it was a love-match – there began to be trouble in our family. My mother and my wife couldn't get on.'

Whether arising out of a love marriage or an arranged marriage, it was the eternal conflict of Hindu family life, a ritualized aspect of the fate of women, like marriage itself or childbirth or widowhood. To be tormented by a mother-in-law was part of a young woman's testing, part, almost, of growing up. Somehow the young woman survived; and then one day she became a mother-in-law herself, and had her own daughter-in-law to torment, to round off a life, to balance pain and joy.

'I decided at last to leave my place.' To leave, at last, the one room at the end of the upper verandah. 'I left with my wife and children. We went to stay at my mother-in-law's place.'

That wasn't far away. Like the tenement he had left, the building he moved to could be seen from the flat where we were. He would show both places to me later from the roof terrace: the drama of small spaces and short distances, the settings themselves always accessible afterwards, never really out of sight, and perhaps for this reason cleansed (like stage sets) of the emotions they had once held.

'If my mother-in-law gave me food, I had food. If they didn't give me food there, I would starve for the day. In those days I didn't have a penny in my pocket, not even for a cigarette. But, being a proud person, I have never gone down in front of anybody for anything. I prefer starving. And those were my starving days. Since that time, you know, I have only one meal a day. That meal is at night. I never eat in the mornings. I have only coffee.

'One of my maternal uncles used to visit me at that time. Twice or thrice a week. He was absolutely poor, but he used to take me to a hotel.' The word 'hotel', as used by Mr Raote, and pronounced *ho-tal*, was more of a Marathi or Hindi word than an English word, and meant a restaurant, usually of a simple sort. 'He would give me a meal. Poor food. And a cup of tea, and a cigarette.

'One day my father-in-law didn't come home. He didn't come home the next day either. We began a long search for him. After four days he came back on his own. We found him in the road. He had had a road accident, and he had been discharged from the hospital. After this he became "psychiatric". He used to harass everybody. So I had to stay away from my mother-in-law's place during the day. I was quite homeless. I used only to sleep at my mother-in-law's place.

'Then one of my father-in-law's friends offered me a place in East Dadar. We went there, and it was there that my second son was born. During all this tormented time my wife was pregnant. In East Dadar I got settled nicely. I had a peaceful life. I used to get there at 11 in the evening, after my work for the Sena. This was in 1973–1974.

'This period of my life lasted four years. I used to walk kilometres to take the Sena meetings. I never grumbled then. When, later, I was elected to the Corporation, and began to talk there, all that I poured into the speeches came from these years I've been telling you about.'

What had supported him? Had he felt 'guided'?

He had felt guided. He had a guru. In what I had thought of as the holy corner of the sitting room there was – not far from the small shelf of devotional cassettes – a large, perhaps more than life-size picture of a handsome, bearded man, just the face. I had seen the picture as I had come in; but with the feeling I had had that the corner was holy, and private, I hadn't looked at the picture more closely. That man – with features of almost unnatural regularity and beauty, in the picture – had been Mr Raote's guru.

It was of religion that now, near the end of the morning, Mr Raote wished to talk. He took me to his puja room. It was next to the sitting room. The shrine was a deep, chest-high recess in a wall. The images were freshly garlanded; there was a husked coconut with a tuft of fibre or coir at the top. Right at the back of the recess, and fitting the back, was another picture of the guru, perhaps trimmed to fit the space, but similar to the picture in the sitting room: the devotee, and the shrine, would be held in the gaze of the guru. Fresh flowers were placed on the shrine every day; the coconut was changed every month. Mr Raote spent an hour and a half every morning on his puja. He sat on a deer skin. The skin was then rolled up and placed on a high shelf.

Some days later, when I went to see Mr Raote again in his flat, I got the rest of his story.

At the end of that four-year period of starvation, good fortune came to him quite suddenly. In the garage of a friend, right here in Dadar, he began to make furniture. It was a new turn for him; but he wasn't absolutely a novice. At school he had done woodwork and furniture-making as a special technical subject. Now, in the friend's garage, he began to make sofas, tables and chairs; and he sold the pieces he made. He discovered he had talent.

He had made much of the furniture in his flat. Against one wall was a special table he had designed. It was like a Pembroke table, with two fold-down flaps on either side of a central plank. But in this design the central plank was very narrow, about eight inches, making it ideal for the small, multi-purpose spaces of Bombay dwellings. The design found favour; it was adopted by all the leading furniture-manufacturers of Bombay. Mr Raote also special-ized in study units that doubled as room-dividers. The pieces he made were all his own designs: the ideas just came to him. 'The moment I started working in the furniture business I thought of these things.' He also made doors. He had made all the doors in his flat, and designed and made all the decorated teak architraves. The flat was a special kind of triumph for him, a proof of his success and a demonstration of his talent. There was much in it I had taken for granted and only now, with his help, began to see.

His success grew. He began to do woodwork for big buildings on subcontract; and then he thought he would go into the building business itself. Two years after he had started making furniture, he put up his first big building in partnership. Though his journey had seemed long to him, he was at that time only thirty-three. Since then he had done 15 or 16 big projects.

'But in all my business I have tried, as a member of the Shiv Sena, to accommodate the middle-class Maharashtrian. So, instead of becoming a multi-millionaire as a builder, I prefer to follow the path of the leader, to follow the principles he has laid down.'

This devotion to the Shiv Sena and its leader was like an aspect of Mr Raote's religion. He had always had courage, and confidence, the gift of religion, the *atma-vishwas* of which Mr Patil of Thane had spoken.

'In my rise, my falls, whatever the problems, I faced them boldly, whether as a businesman or social worker or head of a family. Up to the time of my college days I had my father pushing me on. Then in 1964 I came across the great saint who had set up his ashram at Alibagh.'

This was the guru whose picture was in the corner of the sitting room and at the back of the shrine in the puja room. Mr Raote, from what he said now, had come in contact with him in the year he had had the great disappointment of not being able to go to the engineering college at Sholapur.

'I used to go to see him for his blessing. I never asked anything of him. I went to him only for his blessing, to serve him because he was a saint, and I feel he changed my entire life. He died in 1968. But I feel he is still blessing me whenever I need his blessing. Though he is not here physically, in the actual body, he always gives me and my family his presence. Look,' Mr Raote said, taking me to the teak front door of his flat. 'My door has no latch. It is always open.'

I had caught Mr Raote just in time to get the end of his story.

Though, when we were making our arrangements, he had told me nothing about it, it turned out now that I had caught him, that second morning, on the very day he was going off to his ashram for nine days. He was going alone, without his wife.

'I go every year, without fail. These nine days of my year I cannot give to anybody else.'

He had done other pilgrimages. He and his wife had been six times to the cave of Amarnath in Kashmir, 13,000 feet up in the Himalayas, where – an ancient miracle of India – every year in the summer an ice phallus formed, symbol of Shiva, waxing and waning with the moon.

He said, 'I love that Himalayan place.'

The worldly man who wanted to be an officer and an engineer, the Sena worker, the devout Hindu: there were three layers to him, making for a chain of belief and action.

Papu, the young Jain stoockbroker, speaking of the Shiv Sena, one of the many components of the threat around him, said, 'All our problems are economic. We wouldn't have a problem if we didn't have an economic problem.'

He was taking me that afternoon – after trading on the stock exchange had ceased – to see where he lived, and especially to see the slum by which he was surrounded. Dharavi, as its name was, was a famous slum. There were people in Bombay who claimed, with a certain amount of pride, that it was the largest slum in Asia.

We were in a yellow-and-black taxi, and moving slowly: sunlight and crowd and hooter-din, the hot exhausts of buses billowing black, grit resting on the skin. And then, in the middle of this, a glimpse of purity: a group of thin young boys in white loincloths, walking fast on the other side of the road.

The boys were Jains, Papu said, *munis*, aspirants to the religious life, and they would have been the disciples of a guru. Munis didn't have a fixed abode; they were required to move about from place to place and to live off charity. There were places attached to temples where they might spend a night; they asked at Jain houses for their food.

How would they know that a house was a Jain house?

'Normally there is a board at the entrance, or an emblem of some sort, or some kind of tile. Nowadays you can even get stickers. But usually there is an attendant with the young munis. He takes them round and shows them the houses. It is said that the purpose of this discipline is to control the ego. In Jainism knowledge is very important. A brahmin is supposed to be the most intellectual person; he is the person to whom everyone listens. It is to become someone like that that the munis go around asking for their food. To gain knowledge, they have first to keep the ego under control.'

But the rituals and traditions came from a more pastoral time. Did they serve their purpose when they were acted out now in the streets of Bombay?

Papu's attitude was that rituals had to be constantly adapted. Jains, for instance, were supposed to bathe every morning and walk barefooted in an unstitched garment to the temple. In Bombay many Jains could still do that; Papu's mother did it in the suburb where she and Papu lived. But Papu himself couldn't do it. He might walk to the temple after his bath, but he couldn't walk barefooted and he couldn't go in an unstitched cloth, because nowadays he went to the temple on his way to work.

I told him about my visit to the Muslim area and my talk with Anwar.

He said, 'The aggression can be made creative. We used to play basketball with a Muslim team from that area. The aggression of the young Muslim boys made them good basketball players. It gave them the killer instinct.' The killer instinct which Papu saw in the Indian industrialist, but which traders like himself didn't yet have. 'If I hit them, they hit back. And they play to win. Whereas I come back home satisfied with a good game. If they hit me, I wouldn't hit back. I suppose I might complain, that's all.'

He talked again about his wish to retire at forty to do social work. I knew, from what he had said before, that he had doubts about the idea, doubts especially about the possible waste of his God-given talent, which, if properly used, might produce more funds for his welfare work. Now – sitting in the taxi, in the dust and afternoon glare, at the end of his working day – doubts seemed to have taken him over and enervated him. He wasn't even sure about the social work he was doing on Sundays among people of the slum in his area.

'Every Sunday a group of us, mainly Jains, feed the slum people. We feed perhaps 500 of them. We start at about 10.30 in the morning. For many of the people we are feeding it may be the only big meal in the week. It may keep them going. I am doing it to help them – there can be no doubt about that. But there is also in me a feeling of relief from the guilt which I always have. Whatever I do for them, I know there are limitations. Perhaps I should try to help them to help themselves. My father's idea about this was: "I would like to teach them fishing, and not give them fish." If I'm giving them a square meal, it ends there. What I think I would like – even if it means helping only five kids rather than 500 – is that the five I help should be able to make a living.'

He was obsessed by the idea of charity, of what he, with his blessings, might do for others. Charity was like an an expression of the religious life, the prudent life, the pure life.

We came at last to Sion. This was the name of the suburb where he lived. He asked the driver to drive round the area of 'quarters'. His spirits, low during the drive out, went lower. He spoke of prostitution and despair in the back streets; but he didn't look at what we were driving through. The 'quarters', though, were only government quarters, apartment blocks for government employees. As a piece of urban development, it was depressing – Indian architecture at its most ignorant and inhumane, concrete block after concrete block set down in scarred, bare land looking in places like a rubbish dump – but it wasn't the slum I had been preparing myself for.

That slum, the famous one, was, in fact, on the other side of Sion. Papu had, however, stopped talking about it. And I began to feel that, though the idea of showing me the slum had been Papu's, his mood had changed during the drive out, and he couldn't face it now.

We went to the street where he lived. It was in the middle-class area of Sion, some way from the quarters, and on the other side of a thoroughfare. It looked a well-to-do and established street; there were big trees; and well dressed men and women, office workers, were waiting for buses. The flat Papu had bought on that street had cost the equivalent of £100,000 – and we were an hour away from central Bombay, and close to a very big slum. That gave an idea of what had happened to property prices here. It explained why the big problem for most people in Bombay was the problem of finding room, a place to stay, a place to sleep; and why the huts and shanties and rag-structures filled so many of the city's nooks and crannies.

The sandy yard of Papu's block was swept and clean and bare. In another city it might have seemed a drab yard. But here it was noticeably clean, noticeably bare; and it was as though the emptiness of the yard was an aspect of its cleanliness.

Papu said, 'This is a co-operative block. That means that the people here are vegetarians. The people in the other building' – the neighbouring block, architecturally similar – 'are mixed vegetarian and non-vegetarian. Property values are higher here because this building is vegetarian. If you cook fish, there is a smell that it generates. If there is a non-vegetarian in a building, you may sometimes see a goat tied up in the yard for a couple of days, and then one day you won't see the goat, and you'll know it's been killed and eaten. But it's changing for young people in our community. When they go out they feel that the rest of the world eats meat, and they can get the feeling that they might be feeble, without manhood. Everybody tries to change things to suit himself.' That was also what Papu thought about rituals: they were being adapted all the time.

We took the old-fashioned lift to his flat. He showed the distinguishing Jain sticker above his front door, and the Hindu marks on the front doors of other flats. His sitting room, looking out on to the street and the school across the street, was big and uncluttered. It was of a piece with the yard: the emptiness of the space was like luxury. The walls were clean, the terrazzo floor gleamed.

I asked about my shoes. He said it wasn't necessary to take them off. But later he said something which made me feel I should have taken them off without asking. We were talking about ritual acts; and he said that a Punjabi friend had said that the floor of the sitting room where we were was truly a floor one could walk barefoot on. What the friend meant was that normally the ritual of taking off shoes – before entering a temple, for instance – meant walking on filth, getting your clean feet dirty in the name of a ritual cleanliness.

Papu said, 'I like the concept of purity. I like it as a way of life.'

His mother came out and was introduced: a grave, silent lady, part of whose life had been spent in Burma, until, with the independence of the country, the Indians had been expelled. She brought her palms together in the Hindu gesture of greeting – and I remembered that she walked barefooted every morning to her temple.

'In India religion enters every sphere of activity,' Papu said. He opened a drawer. 'These are company reports.' He took one out. 'This is the annual report of a South Indian company.' He showed the photographs at the front of the report. They recorded the visit of a holy man to the company's headquarters, and showed him standing in the middle of the board of directors, all the directors standing stripped to the waist and in puja garb.

'They are one of the most efficient cement plants in the country,' Papu said. 'At the back of our minds we always have this idea that following religion or rituals is not going to harm us at all. So why not do it? There was the father-in-law of one of my friends. He told me one time that to succeed in a certain thing you've got to feed a cow every day with certain things. Say, wheat. Feed a cow every day with wheat. Well, at that stage in my life, if I'm working towards a goal, I don't want to leave a single stone unturned. And I know that by doing this thing I'm not going to harm myself. So why not do it?

'There are certain places of worship in Bombay – temples, mosques, even churches – where people go on certain days. On Tuesdays they go to Siddhi Vinayak Temple, devoted to Ganesh. Why Tuesday? No one really knows, but all the people there are probably doing it for the same reason, and on the same principle: Why not do it?'

'A materialist attitude?'

'Certainly. Ninety per cent of us call to God when we need something. There is a church here that Hindus go to. It's something they believe in, but it isn't their religion. If you're a Hindu, how can you go to a church?'

On the sloping middle shelf of the wall unit there was a copy of *Fortune* magazine and a book, *Elements of Investment*. Papu was aware of the oddity: those practical books and magazines, his own Jain faith, his need for a comprehensive purity, the setting, the other faiths around him.

Tea was brought out, on small stainless-steel trays. It was a Jain tea, vegetarian, nothing prepared with eggs. There was a puri, and various fried things made from flour and ground lentils.

I thought that Papu had given up the idea of the visit to the great

57

slum of Dharavi. But his spirits had revived in the sitting room of his flat, and after our tea he took me to a back room, to show me the view. The slum was closer than I thought. It lay just beyond the railway tracks that ran at the back of the street on which Papu's block stood. Papu's middle-class area, so established-looking when one came to the street, was contained in a narrow strip between the area of the quarters and the area of the great slum.

He said, of the slum, 'You wouldn't be able to stand the stink.'

A little later, with the determination and suddenness with which people go out into bad weather, he said we should be going.

We set out on foot. The slum was only a short walk away. We began to cross the busy, dusty bridge over the railway lines. The afternoon traffic was hectic. We had barely got down the hump of the railway bridge, when Papu, losing a little of his resolution, said we should take a taxi.

To stress the extent of the slum, he said, 'Look. No tall buildings from here to there.' It was a good way of taking it in. Otherwise, moving at road level, one might have missed the extent of the flat ragged plain, bounded by far-off towers.

And then, in no time, we were moving on the margin of the slum, so sudden, so obvious, so overwhelming, it was as though it was something staged, something on a film set, with people acting out their roles as slum dwellers: back-to-back and side-to-side shacks and shelters, a general impression of blackness and greyness and mud, narrow ragged lanes curving out of view; then a side of the main road dug up; then black mud, with men and women and children defecating on the edge of a black lake, swamp and sewage, with a hellish oily iridescence.

The stench was barely supportable; but it had to be endured. The taxi came to a halt in a traffic jam. The jam was caused by a line of loaded trucks on the other side of the road. The slum of Dharavi was also an industrial area of sorts, with many unauthorized businesses, leather works and chemical works among them, which wouldn't have been permitted in a better regulated city area.

Petrol and kerosene fumes added to the stench. In this stench, many bare-armed people were at work, doing what I had never seen people doing before: gathering or unpacking cloth waste and cardboard waste, working in a grey-white dust that banked up on the ground like snow and stifled the sounds of hands and feet, working beside the road itself or in small shanties: large-scale rag-picking.

Papu said he hardly passed this way. In the taxi he sat turned away from the slum itself. He faced the other side of the road, where the loaded trucks were idling, and where, in the distance, were the apartment blocks of the middle-class area of Bandra, on the sea.

The traffic moved again. At a certain point Papu said, 'This is the Muslim section. People will tell you that the Muslims here are fundamentalists. But don't you think you could make these people fight for anything you tell them to fight for?'

The stench of animal skins and excrement and swamp and chemicals and petrol fumes, the dust of cloth waste, the amber mist of truck exhausts, with the afternoon sun slanting through – what a relief it was to leave that behind, and to get out into the other Bombay, the Bombay one knew and had spent so much time getting used to, the Bombay of paved roads and buses and people in lightweight clothes.

It had been hard enough to drive past the area. It was harder to imagine what it was like living there. Yet people lived with the stench and the terrible air, and had careers there. Even lawyers lived there, I was told. Was the smell of excrement only on the periphery, from the iridescent black lake? No; that stench went right through Dharavi. Even more astonishing was to read in a Bombay magazine an article about Papu's suburb of Sion, in which the slum of Dharavi was written about almost as a bohemian feature of the place, something that added spice to humdrum middle-class life. Bombay clearly inoculated its residents in some way.

I had another glimpse of Dharavi some time later, when I was going in a taxi to the domestic airport at Santa Cruz. The taxi-driver – a Muslim from Hyderabad, full of self-respect, nervous about living in Bombay, fearful of sinking, planning to go back home soon, and in the meantime nervously particular about his car and his clothes – the taxi-driver showed the apartment blocks on one side of the airport road where hutment dwellers had been rehoused. In the other direction he showed the marsh on which Dharavi had grown and, away in the distance, the low black line of the famous slum.

Seen from here, Dharavi looked artificial, unnecessary even in

Bombay: allowed to exist because, as people said, it was a vote-bank, a hate-bank, something to be drawn upon by many people. All the conflicting currents of Bombay flowed there as well; all the new particularities were heightened there. And yet people lived there, subject to this extra exploitation, because in Bombay, once you had a place to stay, you could make money.

And people could be made by the conditions in which they lived. As animals could be made by the conditions in which they were reared: as chickens (to call up a Trinidad memory of 40 years before), reared in a small cage, found it impossible to walk when they were released, and half hopped, half flew, as they had done in their cage. So people who lived in the little spaces of Bombay dwellings got used to those spaces; got used to the communal life of those spaces, and could find the other life, the life of privacy, emotionally disturbing.

Mr Ghate was a high Sena official. He had grown up in the mill area, in one room in a chawl or millworkers' tenement; and he still lived in a chawl, though it was open to him, as a man of position, to live in better accommodation in a better area. He had tried to do that some years before, but it had ended badly. His wife had suffered in the comparative seclusion and spaciousness of the self-contained apartment they had moved to. This was more than moodiness; she had become seriously disturbed. Mr Ghate had moved back to a chawl, to the two rooms he had now, back to the sense of a surrounding crowd and the sounds of life all around him; and he was happy again.

I went to Mr Ghate's chawl in the company of Charu, a young Maharashtrian brahmin. Without Charu, I might not have been received by Mr Ghate. Mr Ghate, Charu said, was one of the 'brash' men of the Sena; and 'brash' was Charu's brahminical word for someone rough and aggressive.

Mr Ghate lived at the top of his chawl block. Without Charu, I don't think I would have made it even to the internal staircase of the place – I was so demoralized, so choked, driven so near to a stomach-heave, by the smell at the entrance, with wet mangled garbage and scavenging cats and kittens in a little patio, and then, in the suddenly dark passage, by the thick warm smell, catching at my throat, of blocked drains. It was Charu, with his brahmin's sense of duty, with his feeling that an appointment should be kept, who (constantly looking back at me, and sometimes even stretching out a hand, like a father leading his child from sand to sea for the first time) led me on and on, up the chawl steps, past open doors giving glimpses of family living spaces.

Hot air should have risen; but at the upper level the air was fresher. A tiger emblem outside a door, the Shiv Sena emblem, identified Mr Ghate's room or apartment. It overlooked the main road. The little windows, frosted glass in green-painted frames, were open behind their wire-netting burglar-proofing; the traffic fumes they let in were even refreshing.

Mr Ghate had two small rooms. One, beyond a curtained doorway, was the kitchen. The room we were received in, where people would have slept at night, doubled in the day as a kind of Sena office. It was full of papers. They were in a fitted cupboard against the side wall – an unexpected modern touch. Among other decorations on one wall was a poster, perhaps originally from an oil company, with a colour photograph of a tiger and the English words, *You observe a lot – by watching.*

Mr Ghate's father had been a millworker. He earned 400 rupees a month, a little over £30. The family had been large, five brothers and two sisters. There had been four sisters, but two had died. The one room they had all lived in was the standard chawl room, 10 feet by 10 feet; and it had worked out quite nicely when they were children. In the mornings they just had tea for breakfast, no cooked food. From seven in the morning till one in the afternoon the children went to school. This meant that in the mornings, for a month or so at a time, Mr Ghate's father would have had a certain amount of room for himself. Mr Ghate's father did shift work at the mill; every month the shift changed.

I remembered what Mr Raote had said about the culture every Maharashtrian had, and I asked Mr Ghate whether he had gone to the gymnasium as a child. He said no; but the question had some meaning for him, because he added immediately that he had taken part in sports. I asked about religion. How, growing up in his chawl, had he learned about religion and the teaching of the saints? He said he wasn't himself a religious man – so there had been a kind of break with the past. But, he said, his father had done the puja at home; though neither his father nor his mother was educated, and until he went to college his family had never owned a book.

It sounded a basic life, a hard life. But everyone had rubbed along. Things changed when he got married. His wife left her family chawl for Mr Ghate's chawl; and then there was a child. The time came when 10 people were living in the 10 feet by 10 feet room. There were 'differences', and constant quarrelling. So Mr Ghate had taken his wife and child to 'staff quarters' – a self-contained apartment in an apartment block – in a suburb 30 or 40 minutes away by train.

It should have meant a new life – the distance from the family, the end of the quarrelling, and the space: after 100 square feet for 10 people in the chawl, they had 300 square feet for three people in the new apartment. But it had led to calamity. Mr Ghate's wife had lived all her life in a chawl. Now, left alone for much of the day in her self-contained 300 square feet, not seeing anyone, not having anyone to talk to, she had become frightened. She had begun to suffer seriously from claustrophobia, and she had been taken close to breakdown.

So they had come back to the mill area, where they had grown up, and Mr Ghate had had the good fortune to find a place in a chawl. The two-roomed suite or apartment such as he had was called in Bombay a 'one-roomed kitchen'. The main room was actually a little bigger than the standard 10 feet by 10 feet chawl room. Five of them lived there now, and there was no space problem.

He had bought the rooms in 1985, and the mechanics of the purchase were like this. The chawls, many of them decades old, from the very beginnings of the Indian industrial revolution, were originally attached to mills, and were meant to accommodate millworkers. Technically, the millowners still owned the chawls; but (because of rent-control laws) the millowners no longer looked after the chawls, had virtually abandoned them; and tenants were nowadays free to sell the lease of the rooms they held. A buyer paid a premium to the sitting tenant, and then the buyer paid rent to the millowner. In 1985 Mr Ghate had paid a premium of 35,000 rupees for his two rooms, about £1400. But now all he paid to the millowner in rent was 12 rupees a month, 50 pence – which no doubt explained why the millowners had stopped looking after the chawls.

Mr Ghate was now a protected tenant; he said he could stay in his two rooms forever. And from the way he talked, that was what he intended to do now, after having tried to break away. Not everyone was like him, he said. Many people who didn't have the means dreamed of moving to an apartment. He had the means; he could get a loan from the bank; but he was perfectly happy where he was.

Reviving in the fresher air of his room, I began to see it a little with his eyes. I noticed the amenities. There was a ceiling fan; there was a sturdy step-ladder for climbing up to the loft. Below the loft was a utility area, with various conveniences: a clothes cupboard, a wooden stool, a clothes-horse (now hung with towels), a length of hose pipe, and a rubbish bin in blue plastic with a pedal-worked cover. The utility area was at Mr Ghate's back, near the open window. The area at the front of the room was more the office part of the room, and it had that big fitted cupboard. Mr Ghate, as though apologizing for the extravagance, said he had bought the cupboard last year, because with his Sena work he had many papers to deal with.

There were more than papers behind the glass doors of the cupboard. On a top shelf were tumblers and plates in plastic and stainless steel. On other shelves were photographs, and a gold-coloured plaque with the new Marathi slogan of the Sena I had heard about: *Say it with pride: 'I'm a Hindu'*. The Sena, as it had become more powerful, was trying to be less regional. It was appealing now to a more general Hindu sentiment, and some people found this as worrying as its earlier call of Maharashtra for the Maharashtrians.

I wanted to hear a little more about chawl life. Charu and Mr Ghate talked for a while in Marathi, and then Charu summed up.

'He likes the life here. He grew up in this atmosphere. He doesn't feel a bigger room or apartment would make any difference to him. He doesn't envy or hate other people's wealth. He values people for their mind alone.'

'What is it about the life here that he likes?'

Talking in Marathi to Charu, Mr Ghate seemed to get carried away as he described the advantages of chawl life.

Charu said for him, 'In a chawl you always know what's happening everywhere. You know what's going on in all the other families. You hear everything, you see everything. In this way people live life together, sharing one another's problems. There is no *life* in an apartment.'

There was a lot of life in this chawl. On the upper floor alone, where we were, there were 40 rooms. Five toilets served those 40 rooms. You saw people all the time.

'Doesn't he want privacy?'

Charu's reply was emphatic. '*He doesn't want privacy*. He says that those who want privacy can always move out to a block.' There was a touch of sharpness in that, after what he had said earlier about people who didn't have the means but wanted to move to apartment blocks. 'If you need some privacy for reading and writing, it's always available here after one o'clock in the morning.'

'Does he often stay up?'

'Yes. He often reads until 2.30, 3 o'clock in the morning. Otherwise there is no chance of reading and writing here.'

'Doesn't he believe that a little more privacy would lead to better education?'

'Your intelligence, or the reading you do, doesn't depend on whether you live in a block or a chawl. It is more your tendency – your aptitude, your character.' And he referred to a famous recent case where a local boy from a slum came first in a Maharashtra state examination.

'Shouldn't he be offering a better life to his followers?'

The reply, in Charu's direct translation, was severe. 'I don't want to help anybody to a luxurious life. This is a millworkers' area.'

'He wants people to remain millworkers?'

The question was slightly altered in translation. Charu seemed to have put it as a personal question, and he got a personal reply.

'He himself has a job in a bank. One brother works in a state corporation. Another, younger brother works in a mill. But that brother is not too educated; he didn't have the intellectual capacity. That brother now gets 1000 rupees a month. That isn't a good wage. To live in Bombay satisfactorily, you need a minimum of 2000 rupees.'

I tried to go back to the question, in a different way. 'What ambition does he have for people in this chawl?'

I missed again. The question seemed to have been put as a question about the future of the chawl, and Mr Ghate gave a literal reply.

'This chawl is ninety years old. It's of sound construction, and it will last for another 50 years. But I have my doubts about its future. The families here are poor. If this chawl is damaged they will not be able to rebuild or to buy their own places somewhere else. They will have to leave Bombay, if anything happens to this chawl.'

On the wall at his back, just below the loft, were Sena pictures and emblems. In addition to the poster with the tiger, there was a big bronze-coloured plaque of Ganesh against a saffron-coloured backing, and there was a framed picture of the coronation of Shivaji: an idea, like something from the Indian cinema, of power and glory and glitter.

That idea would have been full of meaning for Mr Ghate. I wondered how it squared with the work he actually did for the Sena, and the conditions of the chawl. When he considered the chawl, what did he actually see? Who looked after the chawl now, and cleaned the common parts?

Mr Ghate said the tenants themselves cleaned the chawl. I asked why they hadn't done anything about the blocked drains and the rotting garbage at the entrance.

He said, 'Bombay will never be beautiful. There are certain inherent defects. The drains were cleaned some time back, but they got choked up again. There are also problems with people. *Absence of civic sense.*' The last words were in English.

Shouldn't the Sena, with its special social philosophy, do something about that?

'It's a perennial problem. You have to start with the children. It's not an economic problem. These people throw rubbish out of the window.'

I asked about his own background. His family came from a village near Goa, he said. He still had relatives there, and they came to stay every year for 10 or 15 days. They felt attracted to Bombay and would have liked to live there. But they knew that a decent life in the city would be hard to come by, and so they went back.

There were women's voices in the kitchen, beyond the curtained doorway. Mrs Ghate, who had been in the kitchen all along, pulled the curtain back, and said that there had been an accident somewhere in the chawl. An old woman had just come with the news and wanted to know whether Mr Ghate would see her.

He said he would. The old woman was a little frantic. She stood in the doorway and said with tears that two of the children in her room had got burnt. Their father was at the mill, and there was no one who could help.

Mr Ghate said immediately that he would send the children to the hospital in his car. He hurried out to attend to that, and Charu and I were left alone in the room.

Charu told me some more about the communal life of people in Bombay. He said that the love of the communal life stemmed from the life in the joint or extended family: that was a full life, of a constant crowd, and shifting, passionate relationships between the various groups or sections of an extended family. Charu said his own wife, who was doing an M.Sc. degree in child development, couldn't read if she was alone; she preferred to read when there was someone talking near by. Even now, his wife liked staying with her family in their old flat, for the company, the warmth, the constant reassurance of human voices.

Since Mrs Ghate had pulled it, the curtain in the kitchen doorway had remained pulled back. I could see that there was a puja box in the kitchen, something quite basic, nothing like Mr Raote's recessed wall-shrine. Mr Ghate had said that he was not a religious man; the puja box in the kitchen must have been for his wife's sake.

When he came back to us, Mr Ghate looked troubled. He had got the children to the hospital. But he was now worried about his wife. She fell easily into depressions. She knew the affected family, and the accident to the two children was already having a bad effect on her.

Still, the incident showed how important it was for the Sena to have a representative in a place like the chawl. The Sena was known for its social work, and people felt they could approach him.

I asked whether the communal life of the chawl and of other packed areas made political organization easier.

'The chawl is like a bigger family. The area is an even bigger family.'

And other groups could be organized easily as well?

He didn't answer.

He was a stern, dark man. His concern for his wife, which he talked about so openly, was like the one soft thing in him. He had got married in 1970. He was twenty-one then, and his wife was eighteen. The love story he had to tell was in some ways like Mr Raote's in far-off Dadar. The girl who became his wife lived in another chawl. He began to go to that chawl to give lessons to a friend who was weak in mathematics. He had got to know the girl's family; he had begun to give lessons to the girl as well; an attachment had developed.

The girl's father was a teacher. (Mr Ghate's millworker father had never owned a book.) He didn't like it when Mr Ghate dropped out of his engineering college. At that time, too, the Shiv Sena had a bad and violent reputation. The girl's family thought Mr Ghate was an idler. It was this family opposition to Mr Ghate that first threw his wife into a depression.

Mr Ghate said, 'She's extremely sensitive.'

One day they were sitting together, Mr Ghate and the girl, in a hotel. A *ho-tal*, a simple restaurant. The girl's sisters and her brother saw them. Mr Ghate felt that it would be difficult after this for the girl to go back to her family room. So he took her to an uncle's place in an apartment block. The next day they got married. That hadn't been his intention at all when he took the girl to his uncle's. But he saw that it was the only thing he could do; the decision to get married was entirely his own. The marriage was done with Vedic rites, simpler than the traditional Hindu marriage rites.

So his marriage had been a love marriage. Had other members of his family followed his example?

He said a sister had made a love marriage a year or so before.

'It's happening more and more, you think?'

'Yes.' But then, in spite of the romantic story of his own marriage, he became stern. He was clearly unhappy about his sister's marriage. 'Love marriages don't last, unless there is an understanding of minds. A marriage doesn't survive if it's based on physical attraction.'

'Was there opposition to your sister's love marriage?'

His reply was ambiguous. 'There was no opposition. She got married purely out of physical attraction.'

'What was the man's job?'

'Ayurvedic doctor.' *Ayurveda*, traditional Hindu medicine.

'Well off?'

'Fairly well off, but not independent. That's why I wanted my

67

sister to get a job. They're staying at Sion. Just recently I got her a job.'

Sion was Papu's suburb. Was Sion a euphemism for Dharavi?

I asked, 'Staying in quarters in Sion?'

'They're staying in a proper block. But I don't really know. I have nothing to do with my sister now. I've got her a job, and that's all I want to know about her.'

'But why?'

'The boy is not on his feet.'

'How much is she getting in her job? The job you got her.'

'About 900 rupees.'

'You don't want to go and see how she's getting on?'

'No, no. I've given her a job. They have a child. But no. My sister is not on the same wavelength, and I don't like that. Her way of life is very cheap. She has cheap expectations. To her, I am not too educated. But I believe that my way of thinking is superior to my sister's. Her thinking is: "You must have your own block. You must have a lot of money." But she doesn't have the capacity.'

The translation was Charu's, and I wasn't sure what Mr Ghate meant. He had said earlier that he valued people only for their mind, and perhaps he was saying now that his sister's material ambitions outran her education and made her absurd.

'And she doesn't adjust to people,' Mr Ghate said. 'My wife is adjustable. But my sister can't adjust with my wife.' Perhaps the trouble lay there.

'Is your sister a good-looking girl? Handsome?'

'*Not totally.*' He spoke the words in English. With the affirmative Indian side-to-side swing of the head, he added, in English again, '*Fair.*' Then he restated his position. 'I don't value much the blood relation. My relatives never helped me. Only my friends helped me. Now that I've got a name and position, a lot of my relatives come to me. But I don't give them too much attention.'

'Why do you say that your sister's ambition is cheap?'

He didn't reply.

I put it directly to Charu: 'Shouldn't he, as a Sena man, be encouraging people like himself to have ambition?'

They talked, Charu and Mr Ghate, and Charu gave Mr Ghate's reply. 'What is important is for a person to know whether he is really suited to have that ambition. People come to me all the time to ask for help. But I don't think they deserve help by rights. They should be worthy.'

I asked him about the tiger poster on his wall. He said a friend had given it. He spoke the English words, '*You observe a lot – by watching.*' He spoke the words in an awkward, fractured way, but he seemed to load them with a special, even mysterious, meaning. I asked about the Shivaji coronation or durbar in the other picture. What year was that? He didn't know the year.

His sister had tried to break away. He hadn't forgiven her, for that and for the love marriage which, in his own life, he considered part of his strength and character. He was a hard man, made by the chawl life from which he could now never separate himself. Perhaps, with the Sena pride that was his anchor, he felt – with everything else – that old ideas of honour and correctness had been violated by his sister.

Perhaps the sister was going to be all right; perhaps she would be able to stand alone, without the supports of family and clan and caste. But this was also no doubt how, in Bombay, people fell through the cracks into the abyss, and some – the lucky ones – were cast up again in places like Dharavi, not far from where, with the ambition that in her brother's eye was so absurd, inviting trouble, the girl now had an apartment 'in a proper block', almost certainly something in one of those characterless 'quarters' that had thrown Papu into a gloom a few days before.

It was said by people one met, and by columnists in the newspapers, that Indian society was being 'criminalized'. What was meant was that, with all the frustrations of India, political parties and business people were using gangsters to get their work done or to speed things up: to deter political defections, to encourage political donations; to enforce payment of a debt, to compel adherence to an unwritten 'black-money' contract.

Crime now paid very well. The gangs fought like politicians for territory, and the gang wars of Bombay were in the news. The newspapers and magazines were running articles about the wars that were like accounts of the opaque political disputes in many of the states of the Indian Union. They were opaque for the reason that the politics were opaque: there were no principles or party line, there were only personalities. People only had enemies or allies, and the relationships of both gangsters and politicians were constantly shifting. The killings in the crowded Bombay streets were, like the politics, about power and leadership. And, as the dust cleared, the newspapers and magazines began, competitively, to feature profiles of the don emerging as the king of the Bombay underworld.

This don was like a politician in another way: he was so written about, so interviewed (though he was based outside India, in the Gulf, in Dubai), that all the articles about him were like one another. Like many people in the public eye, the don had become his newspaper profiles; he had nothing new to say.

I thought it would be better for me to meet someone lower down, not of don status, someone not so interviewed, someone who had not formalized his experience to such a degree, and might still have something to say. I didn't really believe that such a meeting could be arranged – I was a visitor, passing through, with nothing to offer – but the gangsters of Bombay loved their publicity, and were especially interested in people who wrote in English. They wanted to be known abroad as well.

My contact was Ajit. Late one afternoon we took a taxi out to Dadar; it was a drive I was getting to know well. After we left the taxi, we walked a little way, through the relaxed late-afternoon crowd, to a pan-shop next to a cinema. We waited there for a while, among the cinema dawdlers, until someone greeted us; and then someone else came. We followed this second man. We turned into various rich-looking residential streets, and finally entered a tree-shaded house by a side door, losing what remained of the daylight when we went in.

It was a new apartment house. The ground-floor apartment we went into was well furnished in an Indian bourgeois, furniture-shop way. And it was strange, there, among those feminine furnishings, and in a very dim electric ceiling light, in an atmosphere still of Indian decorousness (shoes taken off at the entrance and left inside the front door), to be looking at Indian faces expressing Indian welcome and civility, and to hear in Indian-English voices, relishing the moment of theatre, that I was among gangsters.

There were about six or seven men in the small sitting room. They were young men, in their late twenties, and all of them, except for the leader, the man who now began to do the talking, had faces one would have expected to see on university teachers or men working in banks. Many of the men were standing when we came in, and they remained standing.

The leader was sitting alone on a fat, over-stuffed sofa. Like a prince showing favour, he asked me to sit beside him. He was dark, with a well-formed mouth with a full and curved lower lip, and with prominent eyes with well-defined eyelids – the kind of features that were stressed by the artists of some Rajput courts.

And I didn't know what to talk to him about. I had expected to meet one man alone; I hadn't expected a roomful. I was further put out by the sudden loss of daylight and its replacement by a dim ceiling bulb that made me stare hard and was like a physical irritant.

I had been hoping, in whatever talk I had had, to take things slowly, to approach the subject of crime and the gangs with some circumspection, and to light on my material on the way. But it became clear, from what the leader said, that he wanted to start *in medias res*. He wanted to talk right away about the gang wars that were going on, and to stake a claim for his gang and his group. But I knew very little about the Bombay gangs. I didn't know about the personalities and rivalries and famous battles; and I couldn't take advantage of the openings the leader was giving me.

He seemed at last to understand my difficulty. He must have been disappointed, but he didn't show it. He began, instead, to help me with the beginner's story he must have thought I was writing. He said he knew he was going to die sooner or later from a policeman's bullet. I felt he wanted that to be quoted. And then, as though letting a novice reporter into the sensational material he thought such a reporter needed, he told me what his group did by way of crime.

They did a certain amount of protection; in that line they 'worked with' stall-keepers. They did the numbers game. They had recently broken new ground: they had done a kidnapping for a political party, snatching and holding a student leader of another party at the time of the students' union election. A profitable and growing business for them was encouraging people to give up controlled tenancies, releasing land or a building for redevelopment. They also did a certain amount of 'biscuit' work – stealing melted-down gold 'biscuits', which was one way in which people liked to keep their black money. What was nice about that was that when someone lost his biscuits he couldn't complain to the authorities. The biscuit business was a nice business; all you needed was information, and you could get good information from the police. At one time, when they were younger, and money wasn't as plentiful as it now was in Bombay, they used to do black-market theatre tickets. A neat little business, really: you bought up all the seats for a popular film, and had touts sell them at a premium. But that was in the old days; it wasn't worth their while now. The one thing they didn't do was contract killing; they couldn't kill a man they had nothing against.

His manner was confidential. He leaned close to me on the over-stuffed sofa and talked without raising his voice. He was like a businessman outlining his services, giving a prospectus. He didn't move or gesture a great deal; his tone was even; the energy and unreliability were all in his eyes.

The other men in the room were not still. They were moving about all the time, looking through the iron-barred window: the light of the street lamp now falling on the trees just outside. Somone gave a whistle, two or three times. And then – Indian courtesy – a man came in, with cold cola drinks for the visitors.

The leader – with the dark, perfect face – disturbed me more and more. He was acting, of course: the physical stillness, his quiet, confidential manner, the absence of gesture, were studied. But even when his words had the effect of humour, he didn't intend humour; he meant what he said; he believed in power and physical authority.

And there was another man in the room who was beginning to disturb me. He had remained standing, alert, sometimes looking out of the window. He had a bandaged hand. At first I had seen breeding and Indian civility in his face; but then his face had begun to seem empty, and I had found it harder to read. He was a brahmin, or a man of a caste not much lower, gone wrong.

That hand of his was bandaged, I now heard, because it had been slashed by someone from another gang: part of the current gang war. As the leader spoke of that attack, the man began to undo the bandage, to display the fearful wound, the twisted fingers: however strong the will, flesh was only flesh.

'He's all right,' the leader said, in his even way. 'Vithal's all right. That hand can still hold a knife.'

And I wasn't to go away and worry about the wound: the blow

72

had been avenged already. The leader himself had avenged it. He had been sitting in a restaurant in the neighbourhood – not a *hotal*, but a proper restaurant, a famous one frequented by gangsters – when he had seen the slasher in a car outside. He had run out of the restaurant and – just like that, without any thought for the consequences – he had fired at the slasher in the car. The slasher had fallen to his knees then, and he had cried and embraced the leader's feet and begged to be spared. (That was the way the story was told: at one moment the slasher was in the car, then he was out of it.) The leader, exchanging the gun for a knife (to give logic to the story as it was told), began to work the knife over the slasher's shoulders as he knelt, giving the man repeated shallow stabs, and he had said to him, 'You are crying. I don't have to kill you now. You cry and you hold my knees. Why should I kill you?'

The leader, telling the story, repeated those words two or three times. He hadn't made many gestures so far; but now he acted out the small, back-and-forth stabs over the kneeling man's shoulders.

It was a big moment for the gang, that moment of revenge, with the slasher embracing the leader's feet. Vithal and another man seconded what the leader said, and they and others stressed the sequel. The slasher, after that incident, had ceased to be a man. He became ridiculous; no one was afraid of him; he had to be dropped from his gang, and was now a nobody in Bombay, with no one ready to take him in.

'Vithal is all right,' the leader said. 'That hand is all right. It can use a knife.' And then, as though we were colleagues and he was talking to me in an allusive way of things we both knew (and also to explain a gap in his story), he said, 'I like a knife. It's surer. You can't be sure with a gun. You fire, you think the man is dead, but the bullet hits the ribs.'

He told a story of an attack they had made on a rival gang one Christmas at a funeral. They had gone among them with their knives. They had taken the other people by surprise, and they had done a lot of damage before the other mourners even knew what was happening.

One of the things that had thrown me at the beginning – apart from the light and the number of people in the room – was the idea I had had, perhaps from a misunderstanding of something Ajit had said, that the people I was among were Muslims. I had begun to talk to them as though they were Muslims, and had then found out that they were Hindus, with their own ways of communal feeling.

So far, the leader had done most of the talking. But when I asked about the Muslims in the gangs, Vithal said he didn't trust the Muslims in his own gang and preferred not to work with them. The Muslim gangsters came from poor areas. They, the people in the room, were 'middle-class people'. They came from this middle-class suburb of Dadar, like the great Indian cricketers, Gavaskar, Patil, Shastri. Vithal, slowly bandaging up his mangled hand again, looking down at it without apparent emotion, said, as though making an old joke, 'It's something to do with the water.'

The Muslims turned to crime, Vithal and the others said, because their values were lower. The Muslims had more than one wife and they had very large families. And, in a curious inversion of pride, the men in the room said that while Muslim gangsters were heroes to the Muslim community, Hindu gangsters like themselves were outcasts.

Though outcasts, they were religious. They felt protected by the deity of a temple, Santoshi Mata. She was a version of Durga or Kali, the goddess of power.

The leader said with perfect seriousness, 'She's the goddess of the victory of good over bad.'

They were religious people: they wanted that known. It was their policy, for instance, never to harass the poor.

The leader said, 'If you do that, the poor will curse you. And the curse of the poor is a very damaging thing.'

They slept in different places every night; they had their safe houses, like the one we were in now. No one knew where the other slept. They met in different places every day. They had ways of communicating. Every day when they got up they waited for news, of the gang war, of the way certain jobs had gone. And the leader said he had recently got married. The girl had been dazzled by the glamour of the life.

Before we left, the leader asked Ajit for 15 copies of a newspaper of a certain date. There was an article about him, or an article in which he was mentioned, in the issue he wanted.

Publicity like that, recognition like that, was precious to him; it was his link to the world outside. As a Hindu outlaw, still deep in his faith, with his Hindu community still a focus for some of his pride, he was really a lost man. Things were desperate for him and

74

Vithal and many of the others. They couldn't withdraw from the life; they couldn't hide. To do so, they would have to go far away, to the other side of India, beyond the reach of the gangs. Everyone among them now had something to answer for. What the leader had prophesied for himself held for them all: they would all die from police bullets.

It was early evening when Ajit and I went out into the streets again. The street lamps in the residential area fell yellow on trees and cast multiple shadows. The well-stocked shops and stalls in the main roads were brightly lit. From what we had heard, some of the stalls were receiving protection; it gave a new character to the scene.

The men we had been among had an almost cinematic idea of their roles, and had perhaps modelled themselves on certain film stars. It was hard, while they talked, and while one was in their presence, absolutely to believe in what they said, it was so much like something out of a film or a book about gangs and crime and murder. They had been boasting. But, according to Ajit, much of what they said was true. The men in that room had been responsible for eight killings. Vithal, with the chopped hand, was especially deadly.

And they were all doomed. The gangsters at the top, the men the newspapers and magazines called the dons, could be famous public figures, could be courted by political parties and film people, could put their money into the making of films, could be absorbed into the glamour of Bombay. But the men below, the men in the middle, like the men we had been among, were doomed.

They had fallen as children for the life of crime. As children, Ajit said, they would have been attracted by the glamour of the famous criminals in their area, who might have a meal in a restaurant and not pay, who might stop at a fruit stall and choose a fruit and walk away without paying: gestures of style. It was a Bombay-given idea of style for which those men had thrown away their lives: an idea of style with elements of pathos to the outsider, style that was like an expression of the stress and nerves of the city of small spaces: style, a human need, which Anwar felt in his colony, and Mr Ghate's sister had felt in her chawl.

*

75

The gangsters made offerings to the temple of Santoshi Mata. Mr Ghate's sister – though expelled from her family for having gone against custom and contracted a love match – had married an ayurvedic doctor, someone, that is, who was full of traditional lore. However much they had to be modified in the city, the rituals of the past adhered to many people, and there was a need in Bombay for men who knew about rituals.

That was why the pujari, the professional performer of pujas, had come to Bombay. He came from the state to the south of Maharashtra. He belonged to the priestly group of the Chitrapur Saraswat brahmins. More particularly, he belonged to one of the seven priestly families attached to a famous temple where there was a deity that had been revered for more than 300 years.

It could be said that the pujari had grown up in an ashram. The pujari's father had been a pujari, and his father before him – that was as far as the pujari could trace his ancestry. The pujari had lost his father at the age of ten, but it had been a joint family, and the ten-year-old boy had been instructed in pujas and rituals and texts by his father's brothers.

To belong to a priestly family was to have distinction in the community, but it didn't mean having money. Very little hard cash came the way of the pujaris attached to the temple, and the boy had never gone away for a holiday. His boyhood had been spent almost completely in the temple, and his studies there had been only of religious matters. Towards the end of his time of study, a secular modern college had been started in the town, but the pujari had gone there for only one year. So he really hadn't had much modern education; and when the time came for him to start earning a living, there was no modern job he could do.

Like his father and grandfather, he could only be a pujari. It was hard. The seven priestly families – joint families – had produced a lot of pujaris, and there simply wasn't the work for all of them locally. Matters were made worse because very many people of the local Saraswat brahmin community had migrated to Bombay.

The young pujari decided to follow them, to see what might come his way in Bombay. Bombay was an unwelcoming city, but the pujari had some luck. He had an aunt in the city, and he was able to stay with her for a year. That couldn't be regarded as a fixed arrangement, though, because the aunt had a son who was close to the age of marriage; this son would be bringing home his bride when he got married, and the pujari would have to go somewhere else. Still, for the time being, there was a place to stay.

And there was also work. Since the temple from which the pujari had come was famous in the community, and since, in fact, the pujari's family was known to people who had made pilgrimages to the temple, and there were people in Bombay who had known the pujari as a child, there was no question – as with a new lawyer, say, waiting for a brief – of the pujari having to hang around and wait for people to come and ask him to do the rites to bless a new flat or cleanse it of its former spirits. He began to do little pujas almost as soon as he arrived in the big city.

He was a shy young man of twenty-four, still with country ways and temple ways. When he did pujas for people in those early days, and they asked what the fees were, he would brush aside the subject of money and say he left it to them. People took advantage of this, but in the beginning he didn't know. When he realized what was happening he decided to standardize the fees. When he left it to people to pay what they thought fit, they would give him as little as 350 rupees for a wedding – which meant chanting verses solidly for six hours, and doing complicated things all the while. Nowadays his fixed charge for a wedding was 1000 rupees, and there were no complaints.

So he settled into Bombay, built up his practice, and when after a year or so his aunt's son did get married, the pujari was able to move out without suffering hardship. He became a 'paying guest'. This was a special Bombay condition: it meant he rented sleeping room or space in somebody's apartment, in a room or loft. It was enough for him.

He discovered that, as a professional pujari in Bombay, he had certain advantages. There were five pujaris from the community in Bombay. Two were older men; a third had learned the business in Bombay from his father. The young pujari, still fresh from the temple source, as it were, had a certain appeal for the old-fashioned or conservative folk. Only one pujari was younger.

There was a sixth pujari in Bombay, but he was so famous and established, so grand, his methods so modern, that he could be considered to be in quite another category. This pujari had so adjusted old ritual to the pace of Bombay life that he could recite the complete wedding verses – which normally took six hours – in three and a half hours. This pujari was sixty-three years old, and because of his speed with the verses he was known as 'The Electric Pujari'. This man had also taped certain pujas – taped the verses connected with the pujas – and marketed them to the community abroad, in various oil states in the Persian Gulf, mainly. He was said to charge 1000 rupees for a wedding tape, and proportionate sums for shorter pujas. He had done so very well that – according to the story – he and his wife (an officer in a bank) had gone on a long holiday trip to London and the United States; and even on this trip – success attracting success – the Electric Pujari had performed three marriages and three thread ceremonies. He was so important in Bombay now, he had become a Shiv Sena leader, and had put money into a Marathi-language film.

Of the Electric Pujari the young pujari said, 'He's an enterprising fellow.' But the young pujari didn't want to compete with this old lion. He didn't want to do puja tapes. He was content doing things in the old-fashioned way he did them. He thought there were people who appreciated this way. Because of the Bombay traffic – he could spend hours every day just getting from place to place – he could do no more than three pujas a day, and that was enough for him.

He made on an average 1000 rupees a month (on an average: weddings didn't come every month), and he was content. There were also the food gifts: the rice and coconuts and fruit and pulses, things needed in pujas as consecrated offerings: a portion of the too-abundant store laid out by the devotee used up in the ritual itself, the rest given to the pujari to take away. So, going from house to house every day (living the kind of life the Jain *munis* lived in traffic-ridden Bombay, finding food at the homes of the faithful), it must have seemed to the pujari that in Bombay the world had been made whole again for him, after the scarcities of the far-away temple.

He was a small, even dainty man of thirty, not much above five feet. He was sweet-faced, with a little moustache and the pale skin of his community, and he was dressed in white. His dhoti had a light-brown edging. He wore a necklace of sandalwood beads, and he had a white nylon shopping bag for his belongings. His voice was as soft as his smile and his eyes. He was the picture of the serene and gentle brahmin: he looked as content and unfussed as he said he was.

His talk of pujas and gifts of food – and that nylon bag or sack to take away offerings, no doubt – brought back memories. There had been so many pujas in my grandmother's family in Trinidad when I was a child, so many ritual readings from the scriptures and the epics. They had given us less the idea of what we were than the idea that in Trinidad we were apart. These readings – sometimes going on for days – had been in a language I didn't understand. I remembered them as holiday occasions, punctuated – at certain stages of the ritual, when clarified butter and raw brown sugar fed and sweetened the sacrificial fire – by the ringing of bells, the blowing of conches, the play of cymbals.

These occasions had fixed in me the idea of the privilege of pundits. They were the star performers on these occasions, and everything was done to pamper them. The best blankets or sheets were spread for them to sit on; the best food was kept for them, and served to them in state at the end. Afterwards, when the religious moment had ceased, had turned to ashes, as it were, and the pundits were no longer strictly on show, it remained their privilege discreetly to go and gather up the coins that had been thrown on the sacred fire on the decorated shrine, as well as the coins that had been thrown on the brass plate with burning camphor – emblem of the sacred fire – that had been taken around the people watching the ceremony: you threw your coin on the plate, passed your fingers through the camphor flame and took your fingers to your forehead.

To me, they were memories from far back, almost from another life. And here they were whole, in an unlikely setting. I met the pujari in Nandini's apartment. Nandini was a journalist who worked for an advertising magazine. She was of the community of the pujari. She herself had no belief in rituals and no need of them, but the pujari seemed still to be called upon on certain occasions by her family. The apartment was in the neighbourhood of Dadar. It was an apartment in a block – four floors, 10 apartments on each floor – and we were on an upper floor: a respectable middle-class Bombay apartment:verandah, front room, back room.

With a memory of the excitement I had felt as a child at the idea of money being raked out from the warm ashes of the shrine, and coins being picked up warm from the plate with the burning camphor, I asked the pujari whether people in his community put money on the plate with the burning camphor. He said the custom didn't exist in his community. But sometimes people from outside the community put money on the plate when the sacred fire was taken round, and then even people in the community, not wishing to be outfaced, followed suit – and all that money was his.

He told me about the deity of the temple-and-ashram, the *math*, where he had grown up. The deity there was the Lord Bhavani Shankar. Who was he? The friend of Lord Shiva. What were his attributes? The pujari behaved as though I was testing him. Bhavani Shankar, he said, was a reincarnation of Yama, the Lord of Death.

He said, 'You pray to him so that the soul may rest in peace.'

'Isn't that a Christian idea?'

It wasn't the Christian idea; he didn't seem to know the Christian idea. He talked on in his soft way, with his smile and his bright eyes, and Nandini interpreted.

'Our community believes in the soul, the *atma*, that merges with the Lord.' And almost at once – he was a pujari, a performer of ritual, rather than a guru or philosopher or theologian – he outlined, again as though he felt he was being tested, the ritual that had to be performed after a death. 'On the 14th day after a person dies you have a ceremony where you have to prepare all kinds of food – certain dishes in addition to the dishes the dead person liked – and there is an elaborate puja. After the puja you put all the dishes on a plantain leaf and you leave it out in the open. The expectation is that a crow will come and peck at what is laid out on the plantain leaf' – Indian crows are rapacious and swift and watchful – 'and we take that as a symbol of the soul merging with the infinite.'

That was the kind of thing he had studied at the temple. It was an immense course of study. There were rituals at death; there were rituals at birth.

'There is a cradling ceremony. You have then to refer to the *Panchang*. That's an ancient text; it's printed now in various Indian languages. You refer to that text to cast a horoscope and find a name. That's common Hindu practice. It isn't restricted to our community. I had to learn that, and I had to learn the details of all the other ceremonies. Let's suppose you move into a new apartment. You have to exorcize the spirits that are there. The new apartment should be pure. To achieve that, again you have to go through quite an elaborate puja. When a child is eight there is a thread ceremony. And there is the wedding ceremony, of course – six hours, with the pujari chanting all the time.'

I wanted to know whether the details of the rituals were absolutely fixed, or whether there were disputes between pujaris – as, long ago in Trinidad, there were disputes between pundits, sometimes about small things: the correct form of Hindu salutation, for example.

The pujari said, 'In recent times the pujaris have been taking shortcuts, especially with the marriage ceremony. They think a six-hour ceremony is too long.' He didn't like the shortcuts. 'There is no meaning to it. I feel that once you start taking shortcuts it all goes down the drain.'

That was another point. How much of that complicated Hindu theology – evolved layer upon layer over millennia – had already gone down the drain in Bombay? For me, in Trinidad, only two generations away from India – though the Hindu epics still had a charge – whole segments of Hindu theology had been lost; later, parts of it were to be recovered, but only as art-history. Without its setting and its earth, Hindu theology seemed to blow away, as it had blown away after centuries from the cultures of Java and Cambodia and Siam: irrecoverable now, the emotions and the elaboration of belief that had supported the building of Angkor.

The pujari said he always took care to explain the verses he chanted. He had also bought some books published by the Arya Samaj – the reforming Hindu movement, more active earlier in the century than now. The Arya Samaj books explained the significance of some of the ceremonies he performed, and helped him to explain them to devotees.

Did he himself sometimes have trouble with the theology?

'I've grown up with it. It's part of me.'

'Bhavani Shankar. The friend of Shiva, the reincarnation of Yama. These are difficult ideas by themselves. When you run them together, they become harder.'

He said again, 'You pray to Bhavani Shankar so that the soul merges with the Lord.' Speaking then of the various deities, he said, 'To understand God, each one has his own way. In our *math* we have given him that persona, Bhavani Shankar. The math has been there for 300 years, and the deity has been there for centuries.'

'Is the deity there very different from Ganpati at Pali?' This was Mr Patil's deity, the bringer of good fortune, the bestower of confidence.

The pujari said, 'In my eyes all deities are the same. Ganpati is

81

actually the deity I like most, because Ganpati is the Lord of Learning.'

'Isn't that Saraswati?'

'Ganpati's other name is Vidia-Dhiraj. The Lord of Wisdom. When it comes to God, there is no end to learning. You probe deeper, and you always get more. Once you are in the profession, you don't feel like giving it up. It is my livelihood, but at the same time through it my search for knowledge goes on. My faith has been so built up over the years, is so strong, that it wouldn't be the same if I did something else, if I was working in a bank, for instance.'

The pujari's younger brother worked in a bank. This brother had been trained as a pujari, too, but he had also gone to the local college. This was what was happening now to young men of the pujari class, the pujari said. They were turning away from their traditional work. One man, for instance, a fully trained pujari from the temple, was writing the accounts in a hotel in Bombay, near the airport. The younger generation didn't want to go into the profession. The pujari didn't blame his brother for working in a bank. Everybody didn't have the same kind of faith; and even if the brother had decided to come to Bombay and be a pujari, he would have had a lot of trouble finding accommodation.

'How much does your brother get in the bank?'

'Twelve hundred rupees a month.'

'That's about what you get.' And perhaps a good deal less, if the pujari's daily gifts of food, and other things like cloth, were taken into account.

In the beginning, the pujari said, it had depressed and worried him that he hadn't had a chance to study properly at the modern college in his temple town. He used to feel he was going to have a hard time making a living. But he no longer worried about the education he had missed, especially now that he was earning almost as much as his younger brother, who had gone right through the college and had ended up in a bank. Sometimes kindly people told him he should be thinking of some additional, modern occupation, just in case. Even if he was earning almost as much as his brother, that still wasn't a great deal in Bombay.

'But,' the pujari said, 'the first thing people ask you if you go for a job is, "Are you a graduate? Have you done this course or that course? Do you have any job experience?" So the best thing for me is to continue in this profession.'

'You talk as though you've looked for other jobs.'

'I haven't. But I've seen a lot of graduates sitting at home because they have no employment.'

Even if he didn't want to think of a back-up profession, it must have occurred to him that travelling in Bombay was going to get worse, and that it would take him longer and longer to get from puja to puja. Shouldn't he, then, be thinking of doing something on the lines of the Electric Pujari, to safeguard his future?

He talked as though he had considered it. 'I don't believe in that.' He meant preparing his own puja cassettes. 'You are too busy *fast-forwarding* and *rewinding*.' He used the English words. 'Your concentration is disturbed. The whole purpose of doing the puja is lost.'

I said that in a temple ashram a pujari could be poor, and not lose dignity. Even now, it was probably all right in Bombay, being a poor pujari. Was it always going to be like that? Bombay was changing all the time; there was a lot more money around now. Wasn't there the risk that, as a poor pujari, he might start to fall in people's esteem?

'Let others have material wealth. I have peace of mind.' In fact, he said, smiling, he wasn't doing badly. He wasn't a paying guest nowadays. He had just bought an apartment of his own, a 'one-roomed kitchen', as they called it in Bombay, an apartment like the one where we were talking. Three hundred and ninety-three square feet, 75,000 rupees.

I made a simple calculation. He had been in Bombay six years, and he said he made 1000 rupees a month. So the apartment cost more than his entire earnings for the six years. Did he have a mortgage?

He said, with his sweet smile, 'No. Savings.'

Savings! So he had been living more or less on the gifts he got as a pujari, and had hardly been spending what he picked up in puja fees.

He said, 'I paid by instalments. Because I am a pujari, the contractor gave me special consideration. He is a man of my community.'

'Not many people have that kind of luck in Bombay.'

He said simply, 'I accept it as a divine favour.'

It turned out that he had even begun to think of getting married. It wasn't going to be easy for the woman he married, since he would be out all day travelling to do his pujas. So he was thinking that it would be nice if he could have a *working wife* – he used the English words – and that, of course, would help with the expenses and all that side of life which I appeared to be so concerned about.

Did he have pleasures?

It wasn't a good question. There was no division in his mind between work and pleasure. He was a pujari; he served God; that wasn't a matter of work and hours. Still, he set himself to thinking. And his gentle black eyes were bright and smiling as he thought. Pleasure, pleasure – what might pass as pleasure?

He said, 'I like decorating the shrine.'

He looked inwards always. But – we were in Bombay, a city of many faiths and races and conflicts. How did he see the city? What did he feel when, for instance, he saw the tourists around the Gateway of India and the Taj Mahal Hotel? What did he feel about the crowds, the people among whom he – in his pujari's garb – would almost certainly stand out?

'I'm indifferent to it. I have my work. It keeps me busy. I don't have the time to go visiting. I don't have the time to look around me.'

He had been in Bombay six years, and was going to be there as far ahead as he could see. But the only person he still looked up to and revered was the head of the Chitrapur Saraswat brahmin community.

He looked inwards and was serene; he shut out the rest of the world. Or, as might be said, he allowed other people to keep the world going. It wasn't a way of looking which his fellows in the community had (some of them in the Gulf, among Muslims). But it made him a good pujari.

Subroto – who came from Bengal, and worked in Bombay in the art department of an advertising agency, but was reconciled to living in the city as a paying guest, the buying or renting of an apartment of his own being too far beyond him – Subroto took me one afternoon to meet a friend of his, a film writer who had fallen on hard times. Hard times in Bombay meant hard times. For the film writer it meant a fall almost to the level of his potential audience, the people who (as the writer himself was to say) filled the sweaty, broken-down cinemas, and looked to the screen for release.

The writer lived in an apartment block in Mahim in mid-town Bombay, near a vegetable market that gave off warm rotting smells. In this apartment block there were 10 apartments to a floor, as in Nandini's block; but the block wasn't as well kept as Nandini's. As Subroto and I went up the concrete steps we had glimpses, through open doors, of clutter in small rooms, and sometimes of figures stretched out in afternoon rest on beds or on the floor; and my fancy was ready – in the general atmosphere of the place – to work up these figures and postures into more sinister tableaux.

We came to the floor we wanted, and followed a verandah or gallery, very bright in the afternoon sun, to where it opened into a room freshly painted and almost bare. This room, of slanted sunlight and shadow, had two beds against opposite walls, two folding chairs, and three pieces of basketwork on one wall as the chastest kind of decoration, a touch of home, perhaps a touch of Bengal. In that setting, with its clear and sharp details, the details almost of improvised stage properties, there was my host the writer, a tall man in white Bengali costume, a man in his forties, handsome, ironic, with the hint of a suppressed rage, a man to whom my heart at once went out.

I realized a little while later that the room, so plain and without disorder, would have been specially prepared for our visit. It was the only room in the apartment. Two people lived and slept in that room. There was an adjoining kitchen area, beyond a doorway with a curtain.

The writer said: 'Calcutta is where I studied. I keep on drifting back. It's my home town, mentally. It's where I feel comfortable. That's where I feel things are happening all the time, and that's where I acquired the ambition of being a film writer. It is difficult for a film writer to survive – I knew that, and for 11 years I was a cost accountant. That was the time efforts were being made to make India a very big industrial country. A lot of building was going on in many parts of the country, and I was a cost accountant in the construction industry. I got shifted from one place to another and went all over the country, and often stayed in wild and empty places. I became a nomad, and have remained that way since.

'One fine day I just got up and went away from my job. It

85

happened here, in Bombay. I had come to Bombay with my firm. Bombay was becoming a very industrial city at that time, in the late 60s. And I went away from my job here and I got involved in a lot of theatre activity. I used to read a lot in my time off when I was with the building industry; in some of the places where we were you had nothing else to do. And when I came to Bombay I found that a lot of the friends I had here, people I had met elsewhere, were theatre people.

'In the 70s a lot of theatre people became film people. There was a government Film Finance Corporation. Money was up for grabs. So a lot of my friends grabbed this money and joined the movement, and a lot of good films were made. But then these good films didn't get released. They made the seminars, they made the festivals, and a lot of very long articles were written about them. But unfortunately the films themselves were never seen because they were never released.

'I will tell you how I managed when I left the building firm. I was living on the roof of a high-rise building with two friends, under the water-tank. We bribed the watchman. That's how we lived for one year. The best view in town, and free. This was in 1969. I was twenty-seven. The only thing we could afford was country liquor. The deal with the watchman was like this: we would bring a bottle one night, and he would bring a bottle the next night. The result was that we became drunkards up there. We had no option. The watchman wouldn't allow us a free evening to ourselves – that was part of the deal.

'The watchman was from Nepal, and he told us frightening stories about Nepal. He told us he walked for 27 days to get from his village to the Indian border, and he was starving for those 27 days. He came here to get a job, and when he got his first pay packet he went to a restaurant and ate so much food he came down with dysentery. When he got drunk he used to say, "Everybody should be shot!" And we would agree with him.

'We were making up stories, trying to write screenplays. Then one of our friends got some money. And he made a film. Three of us had collaborated on the screenplay, and when the film came out my name was not on the credits. This was my first lesson in art cinema. We were very emotional and foolish. Instead of beating the hell out of the director, we said, "I'm not going to work with you again." Which suited him.

'Let me tell you how I got into the commercial side.

'At that time whole villages in the Punjab were migrating. Many of them were being smuggled into England. Very few of them had valid passports and what not. There was a very famous actor in the commercial cinema who said he wanted to make a film about these Indian emigrants. The actor was very famous. In fact, he was at his peak.

'By that time I had left the top of the high-rise and the Nepalese watchman, and I was staying in a boarding house. Two of us were sharing a room. We never had a room to ourselves in those days. My friend was working for this famous actor, and this actor was looking for a bright young man. And that's something else you'll learn: they're *always* looking for bright young men. I apparently fitted the slot. I was young enough, and the famous man thought I was bright enough.

'The only other option I had at that time was to go back to construction work. The Gulf was opening up at that time, and my old firm were threatening to send me to the Gulf. I was actually still under contract to that company, and had been under contract when I walked out on them – for this great freedom to be a writer.

'So word got to the actor, and the great man sent for me. His office was in Santa Cruz, near the airport. Santa Cruz was part rich, part very slummy. The actor's office had become part of the slums. In the 30 years since he'd built his offices there, the green had gone and the slums had come. Slum all around, and in the middle there was this ramshackle office building. And I found that the interior of the building had nothing to do with what was outside – it was plush, carpeted, centrally air-conditioned. Nothing to do with the outside. I had walked into the dream factory.

'The office was big – colossal. I had to walk through two rooms to get to the actor's private chamber. And that was huge. What struck me were the books on the walls. Those editions of the Nobel prizewinners in 30 volumes. The *Encyclopaedia Britannica* was on the other side, and there were marvellous globes and expensive coffee-table books about animals and flowers. The screenplays of all the so-called film classics of the West were on the other side. Right above his head, in fact.

'He started talking about this film about Indian emigrants. He gave me the outline of the plot. I said – '

I broke in to ask the writer, 'What was the outline?'

87

'Two lines. Just two lines. I said, "It's a very brilliant idea." He looked at me with sparkling eyes and he said, "That's a very intelligent remark to make."

'Let me tell you a little about this famous actor. He was perennially young. He *is* perennially young. He was about fifty then, perhaps fifty-one, fifty-two.

'"So," he said. "Let's try to do the line-up."'

I asked, 'He wanted that straight away?'

'He wanted it right off. That was my first lesson in this new course. How to write a film script for commercial films.

'I was very excited. I thought it was the biggest thing to happen to me, as I picked my way back through the slums outside. I went back to my boarding house. That was in the middle of one of the ugliest slums in Bombay, one of the ugliest of those so-called fishing villages. I burned the proverbial midnight oil that night. Luckily, my roommate was a Punjabi. He knew what the emigrants were like, and he gave me some ideas of their characteristics. I wrote a couple of scenes.

'I took them in to the office the next day. The actor read the scenes in front of me – four scenes in seven pages – and he clapped his hands and said, "This is wonderful! Let me just look at these pages. I will work out some 'lines' and we will talk about it tomorrow."

'The next day came, and he said, "I've thought out everything." And for three hours he told me a story – the story of the film we were supposed to be working on. It was a horrifying experience. It had nothing to do with the village or the humiliations of the emigrants. It was like every other commercial story – it was about spies and shootouts and gangs. It was pretty awful.

'So I looked at him. And at that moment it flashed through my head: "If I tell him it's a very good story, I've got a job." So I told him, "It's a very good story." And he paid me on the spot. Advance money. A contract was made. It was quite favourable to me. He gave me 5001 rupees that morning. It's an Indian custom, that extra one rupee. Even if it's a million rupees, they will pay you that extra one rupee. It's for good luck. Though actually I think the one rupee was my payment for saying it was a good story, and the other 5000 rupees was for my good luck in thinking I should say it. So I thought, "Keep on saying it's a good story."

'It took two years to make that film. And I wrote nothing. Not one single line. I will swear by anything you want that I didn't write a single line. I just kept listening to his rubbish every second day, and I kept saying, "Wonderful!"

'I was making 10,000 rupees a month for saying yes to him. That was what everybody else was saying to him. This great man used to live in a very strange world. If you are a star you live in a very strange world. You manufacture a world where everyone keeps on saying yes to everything you say. If you say no, you are out of that world. And permanently. The rejection is like Jehovah's revenge or something. They live in this world, and they lose touch with reality, with the audience, with the audience's taste. That's why so many films fail. And when they don't run, there's always a fall guy.

'He would call me into his office apparently for a story session, and I would listen to him talking about the wonderful films he was going to make. These people, their heads are like a bubbling kettle. I would listen to him for anything from two hours to seven hours, eight hours. And this went on for two years.

'The film came out. My name was on the credits. But I hadn't written anything, I swear to you. Because there was no *written* script. This was what I learned: that films can be made from scraps that come out, scraps of conversation. In fact, a writer was looked down on. A film writer was supposed to *talk* – to be a talker of scenes, rather than a writer. So that they could get a *feel* of the scenes without having to read. Because reading is something *nobody* in the film world does. The writer is the odd man out.

'They *talk* about stories. They talk about scenes. Even if you write a scene, they shoot it differently. They change while editing, while shooting. And all actors here fancy themselves to be writers. An actor may come and, if he's got clout, he may change a line.

'This was in 1972. I was thirty, and everybody thought I was a brilliant young man. Until the film came out. And it flopped. It didn't run at all. And I learned another lesson: that when a film doesn't run, invariably the writer has to take the blame.'

'How much had been spent on the film?'

'Close to nine million rupees. It was extraordinary. Huge houses would be erected for the village scenes. Places where even maharajas wouldn't stay, and those houses were supposed to be village huts. The hero was an unemployed village youth. The clothes he wore in the film had been stitched at a cost of a lakh of rupees.

And he would stand in those lovely clothes, and employers would tell him, "This job is not for you." The man saying that – playing the employer, the owner of the factory – he would be an extra, earning 30 rupees a day in those days. And he would be wearing shabby clothes of his own – because you don't have to find clothes for an extra.

'I hated every moment of it. I hated myself for doing it.'

I said to the writer, 'But you knew what Hindi films were like.'

'Yes and no. I saw Hindi films, but I didn't know how they were actually made. And they're still being made the same way. How can it be otherwise? Nobody who made a film went to see a cinema show with the audience. In those days they would have this private viewing theatre. They never saw the film with the sweaty audience. The halls are terrible. They are advertised as air-conditioned, but the air-conditioning often doesn't work, and it's hot and humid and sweating and it's packed.

'So I took the blame, and I went away from Bombay. And I drifted around for a while, mostly in Calcutta and Bengal. I didn't want to return to the film industry at all.

'But it's hard to leave the film industry. A friend wanted to make a film in Bombay. So I came back, and started up again. At that time I had the reputation of being a very good script-writer, without having written a script. Many of the things I had worked on had remained at the ideas stage, and ideas can be brilliant. Then this friend, with four disasters behind him, wanted to make a quick, cheap film. He wanted to make it just to survive – a film which we could make quickly.

'There was a well-known actress who was a friend of the group. We thought we could cash in on her name. So we started shooting without knowing where the next day's money was going to come from. After eight days the money ended, and the shooting stopped. We didn't know what to do. And then – you wouldn't believe – a man came and said he wanted to back the film. He was acting for somebody, and I actually believe we got the backing because the person for whom the man was acting liked the story of the film.

'It was the story of a husband's adulterous affair. In Hindi films the standard treatment of this kind of story is that at the end, after the affair, the husband cries and goes back to his wife, and she cries and takes him back. In our film, when the adulterous man came back crying to his wife, she sent him away. This was the story, and for some reason it appealed to someone and they wanted to back it.

'The film was made. It ran – to our surprise, and the surprise of everybody else. At the end of the film, when the wife kicked the husband out, women would stand up and clap. This wasn't only in Bombay; it was in some smaller cities as well.

'We made two other films. Both were very great successes. We became quite famous, in fact. And at that point my friend wanted to cash in on the fame – he wanted to make big-budget films. Offers were coming.

'So it was back to square one. The commercial cinema – saying yes to distributors and stars. And yet at that time we had the clout to keep on making good films.

'So I gave up, and I left Bombay again. But there is something you should know. A film writer gets used to working with a particular director. He knows the director's style, and the director knows the writer's ways. It isn't easy, after this kind of relationship, for a writer to team up with another director.

'So after four years I came back – to team up with the same man, after he'd had another four disasters. Much bigger disasters than the four he'd had when we met and did the quickie. I've been here for a year now.

'How did I manage during those four years? I starved. I did odd jobs. Ghost-writing. I became involved in projects that didn't take shape. And here I am back. And while I was starving I got married – I thought it was just the right time.'

His silent Bengali wife, in a fresh green sari, brought out tea from the kitchen area behind the curtain – where she had been for much of the time – and she laid the tea on a little side table. Subroto was lounging on one of the beds – there was no other place for him in the room.

I asked the writer to describe the apartment where we were.

He said, 'We are in an apartment in Mahim. It's a rented apartment, in a standard four-storeyed Bombay block. We have one room. It's 10 feet by 10 feet. It's a one-roomed kitchen apartment, as they call it.'

He stood up and raised both arms – in his loose cotton tunic – and looked at the ceiling. The gesture filled the little room.

He said, 'This is my room. This is my only room under the sun.'

The room faced west. It was full of light. The verandah was so dazzling that Subroto at one stage thought of closing the door to it.

The writer said, 'I'm working on three films now. It's very difficult in India to survive on one film. This time I've discovered that although they don't follow a screenplay, they have more respect for it. I hope it will last.'

'You think you're a better writer now than you were at the beginning?'

'When I first came I had great notions of what a film writer should be. I was wrong then. I thought that a screenplay was close to a novel or a play. I really thought it was a novel that got shaped up into a play. What I've realized is that a film writer has to know a lot about film technique – the limitations, for instance, and where you can do away with words totally. We write *visuals* – that's what a screen writer is supposed to do. The screen writer is actually a link between all the crafts of film-making, and I'm talking of the actors as craftsmen also. Much of it is in technical shorthand – it's much better if you write it like that. The technicians understand the technical shorthand. They understand it emotionally. The cameraman understands not only the visual of a close-up, but also the emotion. To the layman that kind of writing might be boring – it's like reading the blueprint of a bridge, but that blueprint is full of meaning for an engineer. A script-writer had better learn that part of the technique. Or he's wasting his time, and other people's time. The writer's contribution is really to give a conceptual vision of the whole film – because the technicians can only work one shot at a time. Actually, it's a director-writer team that makes a film.

'So now I've been back for a year. The first six months were hard. People were indifferent, because I'd left the club.'

'Looking back now at your first experience, with the actor, don't you think that something might be said for talking a film – as he used to do?'

The writer was unforgiving. 'That is the enemy. That complacent attitude – that is the enemy.' He jumped a thought or two and said, 'I think I will make money this time. I've got enough for the next month, from the film work I've been doing. At the moment I'm clearing debts.'

'Who are the nice people in the film business?'

'Everybody and nobody. It's totally success-oriented. They worship success. And the success is very concrete, you see. A film opens on a Friday, and by Monday you know the fate of the film. You know the box-office figures. There's nothing abstract about that. It's all there in cold figures. And if the film runs, people are very nice to you.'

At the beginning he had seemed full of rage, with an irony that sometimes threatened to turn to bitterness and self-pity. But he had grown softer as he had talked. When he had talked about the nature of film writing, he had become contemplative, working through to the right words, and he had seemed then to be even at ease with himself.

I felt his attitude to the film industry might have changed.

He said, 'I'm losing my cynicism about it.'

I said, 'It may be because you have a new feeling for the art.'

'People make bad films or good films. But one can't say there is no such thing as screen-writing. There is. And one thing you do learn is that life goes on. There is no such thing as failing in life. You fail at a particular point. The joy of an artist is not to think of success or failure, but to just go on.'

I asked about his way of working.

'We rent a hotel room for five days or seven days. And we talk out the film. Then I'm left alone, and I'm given four weeks or six weeks to write the treatment – basically, scenes without dialogue, in sequence. And then we get together for another three days. And then I'm left alone again. This time it comes out with dialogue, and it takes about two weeks.'

He then said something which made me wonder whether, in spite of what he had said about making money this time, he hadn't with one part of himself given up ideas of succeeding again in the cinema. He said his thoughts had been turning to real writing, the writing of prose, for the printed page. And he wanted to know whether he could send me things he had written or might write.

I said my judgement would be worthless. I had given all my adult life to writing; I had thought about it every day. I wrote, and experienced, in my own way; the two things were linked. My judgements were good only for myself.

He smiled. 'My judgements on other people's screenplays are worthless too.'

Subroto and I left soon after. We went down the narrow, twisting concrete staircase, half-walled on one side and rubbed to shininess. We saw again through open doors the life of single rooms: the people, and the great amount of clothes that in those small spaces couldn't be put away or stored. The smells from the rooms became stronger lower down, the grime more perceptible.

When we stepped out into the bright, dusty yard, there was a call from above, and we looked up at the writer and his wife in her green sari looking down at us from their balcony, one of the 40 balconies of the apartment block: like theatre boxes, from where we were. The sun fell on their heads and faces. Like people suddenly playful, they both smiled and gave small waves.

At the end of the dusty yard there was a tree with a circular, concrete-walled, earth platform at its foot. On this platform, against the trunk of the tree, was a small black image garlanded with marigolds, and there appeared to be a man watching over it. The image was a living deity, and it had fresh holy marks, of sandalwood paste, on its forehead. Past that, we were in the dusty street.

We began to walk to Dadar railway station. It was only a short walk, and Subroto apologized more than once for not taking a taxi. Outside the vegetable market, where the smells were high, boys were lifting wet vegetable rubbish with their bare hands into Ashok Leyland garbage-compacting trucks. Dadar station – with its high, gloomy platforms, its crowd, the echoing sound of the crowd, the stalls, the shoeshine boys and men, the twist of slow-burning rope tied to a metal pillar for people to light their cigarettes from – gave a feel of the big city: as though trains and the constant movement of people had the power, by themselves, to generate excitement.

I asked Subroto, 'Do you think he is going to make it this time?'

'He isn't going to make it.'

We went over the footbridge to the platform on the other side of the rails. Everything in that footbridge was worn, without identifiable colour, years and years of dust seeming to have eroded and dulled metal and to have got into the heart of every piece of timber.

Subroto said, 'He's not positive.'

By that Subroto meant that the writer, in spite of what he had said about making money now, was as he had always been: he didn't really want money or possessions. Even if, with marriage, the writer had changed, Subroto said, the writer's old reputation was now working against him. He had been too scornful of people in the business; he had made too many enemies. There was an influential man, influential in films and in politics, the kind of two- or three-sided figure who was now appearing in Indian public life, who had wanted the writer to do a treatment of a particular story. The writer, Subroto said, had read the outline in the great man's office and then, in a rage at having been asked to work on such rubbish, quite literally thrown the sheets of paper with the story outline in the great man's face.

All the way back to downtown Bombay, against the metallic clatter of the big, open coaches, Subroto talked of art and design and the work he hoped to do. He lived in Bombay only as a paying guest; he didn't think that would ever change. But his talk of his vocation and what he might do was selfless; what he had said about the unworldliness of the writer seemed to be true about him as well.

The shacks and shanties beside the railway lines went by; the dusty light turned golden. I thought of Subroto, and I thought of the writer in his apartment: such a setting for a man who talked of his craft with so full a heart and mind, such refining of his artistic experience: such a mismatch between dreams and setting. It was what had struck me on that first morning in Bombay when, on one side of the road, I had seen the long, patient line of people waiting to honour Dr Ambedkar, and, on the lamp standards on the other side of the road, the small, repeating posters for a new film, a product of the Bombay commercial cinema.

I had heard, vaguely, some years before, of the Dalit Panthers. I had got to know little of them beyond the name, which had been borrowed from the Black Panthers of the United States. It was a romantic borrowing; it encouraged the – too simple – belief that the Dalits (or scheduled castes or harijans or untouchables, to take the wounding nomenclature back through its earlier stages) were in India what black people were in the United States.

I heard now, from Charu, in our many taxi-rides up and down Bombay, of the man who had founded the Dalit Panthers. He was Namdeo Dhasal; he had a parallel reputation in Bombay as a Dalit poet. He was now about forty-seven, though he wasn't sure of the exact year of his birth. He had been born in a village 100 miles or so inland, and he had migrated to Bombay 30 years before. He had lived for a long time in the brothel area, among criminals and prostitutes. Golpitha was the name of that area, and it was the name of Namdeo's first book of poems, written in Marathi, and published in 1974, when he might have been twenty-seven. In that same year Namdeo had founded the Dalit Panthers, and he had immediately become a man of some political standing in Bombay.

The poetry side was a surprise to me. It was surprising that, in the small spaces of Bombay, and with the crowd and frenzy, there was a living Marathi literature, with all the high social organization that such a literature implied: the existence of publishers, printers, distributors, critics, buyers. It was as surprising to me as the idea of the Maharashtrian gymnasium had been, when I had heard about it from Mr Raote.

Namdeo had not been the first Dalit to write. There had been earlier Marathi voices from the depths. But they had written in received, literary Marathi. Namdeo's great originality was that he had written naturally, using words and expressions that Dalits and no one else used. In his first book of poems he had written, specifically, in the language of the Bombay brothel area. That had caused the sensation; he had been praised and condemned.

Charu, who was a Maharashtrian brahmin, and quite learned in Marathi writing, said there were a number of words in Namdeo's poems that he couldn't understand. He gave me this translation of a poem called 'The Road to the Shrine', from Namdeo's first collection.

> *I was born when the sun became weak*
> *And slowly became extinct*
> *In the embrace of night.*
> *I was born on a footpath*
> *In a rag.*

[And the 'crude', Dalit word used for 'rag' was *chilbut*.]

> *On the day I was born I was an orphan.*
> *The one who gave me birth went to God.*
> *I was tired of this ghost*
> *Haunting me on the footpath.*
> *I spent most of my life*
> *Washing away the darkness in that sari.*

[But the word used for 'sari' was not an elegant one: it was *luggude*, and it referred to the way village women tied their saris, wrapping

96

the garment around each leg separately, creating a kind of sari-breeches.]

> *I grew like a person who has lost his fuse.*
> *I ate excrement and grew.*
> *Give me five paise, give me five paise,*

[There are 100 paise in a rupee]

> *And take five curses in return.*
> *I am on my way to the shrine.*

Even in that rough translation, improvised by Charu in a busy hotel lobby, the poem was moving. It was much more moving to Charu. He said that the voice was absolutely new in Marathi; and he told me that Vijay Tendulkar, the contemporary Marathi playwright, had compared Namdeo to Tukaram, the 16th-century Maharashtrian poet-saint, whom I had heard about for the first time from Mr Raote.

In the poem Charu had translated, the mingled suggestions of sex and degradation were harsh and undermining, and the ideas of untouchability and brothel-area sex, childbirth and rags, all coming together, were like an assault. This was the passion that Namdeo had put into his politics and the Dalit Panthers.

But that name, which he had borrowed from the Black Panthers, was like a foreshadowing of what was to come. Like the Black Panthers, the Dalit movement, with its success, began to fragment. That pitch of passion couldn't be sustained; there was the temptation to many to make their peace with the wider society. And though Namdeo became famous and courted, he began to lose his followers. Soon even his literary reputation began to recede. He had done a fair amount of work; he had written two novels, in addition to his poetry; but his most recent book had been published in 1981, seven years before. He wasn't writing so much now; and he had contracted a debilitating illness.

He had no telephone. But Charu knew where his house was, and we went there one afternoon to leave a message for him. The house was not far from the Golpitha area he had written about. It was a house, though, not an apartment; and it was in a reasonably wide and clean lane. Just across the lane from the front door of the house an old open jeep had been parked or abandoned and was now, mysteriously, bleaching away, its tires squashed and perished, its metal body almost bare, yet still looking whole.

Charu called from the lane. After a little while a dark young woman, bright-eyed, fine-featured, opened a leaf of the front door. She and Charu spoke in Marathi, and we went up the concrete steps that were set against the front wall of the house and led directly from the lane to the front door.

The room we entered ran the width of the house. It was the main room of the house. The walls were a lilac colour, and recently painted, in an eggshell finish. There were white-painted rattan chairs with dark-green cushions; and from one of the sturdy beams of the ceiling a basket chair hung by a chain. A feature, this hanging chair, a touch of luxury; and a plump young woman in a blue georgette sari, a visitor, was sitting in it, with her feet on the floor and moving with deliberation back and forth.

The dark woman who had welcomed us was Mallika, Namdeo's wife. She was stylishly dressed, in a kind of long peasant skirt in lightweight material. The skirt swung as she walked about the terrazzo floor on her small bare feet, and her tinkling Marathi voice filled the room as she welcomed Charu and me.

There was a very large colour photograph of a white baby on one wall. On another wall were small colour snapshots of Namdeo: full-cheeked, paunchy, but with a face that was still strong. On the opposite wall was a photograph of Mallika's own father. He had been famous, a folk singer, a member of the Communist Party, and a Muslim. A small red flag hung on the wall behind the television set at the far end of the room, not far from a framed copy of the famous grey-toned photograph of Dr Ambedkar in a jacket and tie.

The woman in the blue sari in the basket chair had not been introduced to us. We had addressed no word to her; and she, as private as always, and seemingly quite content, had continued with small movements of her feet to move the basket chair back and forth. Now, without social disturbance, she got up and went inside.

Mallika herself then went inside, skirt swinging, and after some time brought out tea for us on a kind of woven tray, very pretty. I was beginning to understand that very little Mallika did was casual, that in everything she did, or had some control over, she aimed at prettiness or elegance: in her dress, her walk, the colours of the room, the big colour photograph of the white baby, and even in her dogs, a pair of white, fluffy, combed Pomeranians, slightly listless in the Bombay heat, that she had bought four years before, for their beauty.

We left our telephone numbers with her. She said she would ask Namdeo to get in touch with us. Abruptly, then, with no intermediate atmosphere, we were out of the front room or hall into the lane where the abandoned jeep squashed its rotted tires. And at the end of that short lane we were back in a more familiar Bombay.

Charu told me later that the story of that marriage – Mallika's and Namdeo's – was famous. Mallika had written an autobiography in Marathi, *I Want to Destroy Myself*, and the book had been a bestseller. In Marathi that meant a sale of 10,000 copies.

Mallika's book was a story not only of love, but also of disillusion and pain. Almost as soon as she and Namdeo had married, things had begun to go badly for the Dalit Panthers, and Namdeo's behaviour had changed. She had suffered. She had been introduced to shocking things. Namdeo had a venereal disease; he continued to go with women from the brothel area. But she was tied to Namdeo, by the child they had had, and by her love for him. She was passionate about the freedom of women; but in her own life, because of her love for Namdeo, she found that she had lost some of her autonomy. After 10 years of love and torment she had written her book.

The book was sexually frank; and though that kind of writing was not unknown in Marathi women writers, Mallika's created a sensation, because it offended many people's caste sensibilities. Though Mallika's father had been a Muslim, her mother was a Hindu, of a caste just below the brahmin caste; and people had been upset and wounded by Mallika's story of her love for Namdeo and her later turbulent life with him.

No message came from Namdeo, and late one morning Charu and I went back to the house. Mallika wasn't there, but someone let us in. Before we could leave a note, Mallika came. She had been out shopping, and was wearing a light chiffon sari that billowed about her, a small, rust-red motif on white; and she was carrying in her hands, almost as part of her dress, just a few turnips or carrots with their green: the vegetables looking in her hands like emblems in a kind of Italian renaissance painting.

And then Namdeo himself appeared, with a friend. Namdeo was sturdy, paunchy, dark, unexpectedly avuncular. He would not have stood out in a crowd. I saw suggestions of forcefulness only in his eyes and forehead; but that might have been because I knew who he was. It was hard to see in him the poet or the Panther. There was a curious placid quality to him; it was as though his inner fire had burned out. And then I remembered what Charu had said about his illness. It was his illness, that other external enemy, that had finally weakened him, and given him the easy, affable, and yet somehow distant manner he now showed us.

He spoke no English. Yes, he said to Charu in Marathi, he would like to meet us. Tomorrow. Yes, come for lunch. No? Well, come after lunch. From two to five. Come then.

He went inside then with the man who had come with him, and Charu and I said goodbye to Mallika and left. It seemed easy enough, arranging that meeting, now that we had met Namdeo. But Charu thought it had been too easy. He had his doubts about the appointment. And I learned later – from other people – that in the matter of time-keeping and appointments Dalits had a poor reputation.

And it was as Charu feared. When we went to the house the next day, Namdeo wasn't there. This was Mallika's news when we went up the concrete steps from the lane to the front room or hall. And just as, the first time we had gone to the house, there had been a young woman in the basket chair, to whom we had not been introduced, so now there was someone in the front room who was not mentioned: a thin dark woman sleeping on a mat on the floor, just like that.

We followed Mallika to the kitchen at the back, and then through a side door to a small room at the side of the house, with a high, deep-embrasured, iron-barred window. This was the room Mallika had prepared for our meeting with Namdeo. It had two of the painted rattan chairs, a table with a table-cloth, and, in one corner, an old-fashioned, pretty electric table lamp with a draped woman in bronze-coloured metal, holding a torch.

Waiting there for Namdeo, I talked to Mallika. I asked her about the house. I could see that it was unusual, but I felt I wasn't in a position to see it correctly. I brought too many outside ideas to it. I asked her to describe the house for me, so that I could begin to see it as people in the area might have seen it.

Something of what I intended got lost in the interpreting, and Mallika said, 'This is my parents' house.' The house, therefore, of one of the most famous folk singers of Maharashtra, the house of a successful man. 'It is the house where I grew up. It's nice to stay in a house where you've been since your childhood.'

She and Namdeo had done a certain amount of renovation. They painted the house every two years. As for the area, it was an area of working people; but middle-class people also lived on the street. She knew everyone there. When her father was alive their family had been looked up to.

But her parents had had a mixed marriage. Her father was a Muslim, her mother a Hindu. Had that made for problems?

'I didn't know my father was a Muslim. My mother was a Pathari Prabhu. A little lower than brahmins. These Patharis eat fish. Pathari Prabhus are the original Bombay people, and that is how they have been eating fish.' Eating fish, that is, though they were very nearly brahmins, because they were a coastal people.

She had learned about the Pathari Prabhus from her mother's mother, when she used to go and stay there. She hadn't been particularly interested in her mother's relatives; she hadn't gone out of her way to make inquiries about them because they were the kind of people they were. What she knew about that side of her origins was more a kind of 'idle knowledge' that had come to her as she had grown up.

I asked her about her book. Had she intended it to be as daring as it had turned out?

'I didn't think like that. It was necessary for me to write that book. I had no choice. It wasn't open to me to separate one side of my life from the other side.'

She was wearing a lightweight sari, a simple pattern on a pink ground. She was sitting on one of the white-painted rattan chairs. In the room was a steel wardrobe, olive-green, with a long mirror on one door – it was a kind of wardrobe I had been seeing in Bombay. On top of the wardrobe was a tarnished little globe. The masonry or plaster of the window-sill was nicely bevelled; the eggshell finish of the paint, added to that bevelling, made me want to run my hand over it.

In her book – sections of which Charu had translated for me at great speed, before we had come out – she had said, talking of her love for Namdeo, that she felt 'a blank' at the thought of leaving him. I told her I had been taken by that.

She said, 'Even now I love Namdeo, and am willing to give him everything. Even though he has some negative points. There is a kind of thread running through our relationship. Even when I don't want him, I want him. Even now, whatever is good in me, whatever is creative in me, I would suppress for his sake. I know that if I do certain things he will go out of my life. I don't want that. Then there is my child. We are in a kind of vicious triangle. I love Namdeo. The child loves me. Namdeo loves the child.' The child was thirteen.

The book hadn't been flattering of Namdeo. Some people thought it had even damaged him politically. Had Namdeo read the book while she was writing it?

'If I hadn't written the book, I would have gone mad. Namdeo didn't read it. He used to read my poems. But he wouldn't read my prose. I showed him the manuscript of the book, but he didn't read it. It was only when the book was published that he read it. But then for a year before he had been suffering from his nervous illness.'

She was smaller than her erect posture and her hips suggested. Her dark arms were slender, even thin. She had a big red spot between her pencilled eyebrows. She had a watch and bangle on her right wrist, and eight or nine thin silver bracelets on her left arm.

'He didn't say anything about the book, but there was a change in his behaviour. He has never mentioned the book to me to this day. But I know that when other people have said to him that he should write a rejoinder, he has defended my book. His argument then is that this woman who has lived with him all these years, and has seen it all with her middle-class eyes' – there it was, the social comment, the comment on her family house perhaps, the comment on the way Mallika saw herself in relation to Namdeo, and the way he saw her – 'his argument is that this woman has every right to express what she feels about the marriage.'

Now, Mallika said, a little of the earlier relationship, when she had first loved him, had revived. He was still under treatment for his illness, and he had stopped drinking. His drinking had caused many clashes between them, and he used to beat her. But she felt that much of that had been due to his political frustration, witnessing the quick decay of the Dalit movement he had started.

Her understanding didn't make it less hard for her. 'I would get angry. I would cry. I would shout. I would find it extremely humiliating. I loved the man, but I never thought my life would be so degraded – after I had gone against everybody and married him. Because I had gone against everyone, I felt I couldn't give up on the marriage just then and tell people what a failure the marriage had been. I also felt that if I kept quiet I would have to bear it forever, and that was not my nature. Everybody reacts to a situation in a way which comes most naturally to them, and I turned to writing.

'I wrote the book straight off, within a month. I wrote it sometimes in the front room, and sometimes here, at this table. Sometimes I wrote in the kitchen also.' The kitchen, seen through the doorway, with a door to the right leading to the front room or hall. 'There was no fixed time for writing. I wrote whenever I could.'

'Was Namdeo in the house when you were writing?'

'He was very much in the house.'

'Did he have any idea what you were writing? You weren't nervous?'

'I didn't know what he would do. I thought he would beat me up or throw me out, and go to the court.' To get custody of their child. 'I think a mother should have a right to her child. But according to Indian law the father can have custody of the child after the child's seventh birthday. So, even if I left, I had no guarantee that one day Namdeo wouldn't come and take away the child.'

A good half of the book she wrote in those tormenting circumstances was a reliving of her early love for Namdeo.

It had begun 14 years before. She was sixteen, and she had gone to the resort town of Lonavala, between Bombay and Poona, to do some studying. She had gone with her brother-in-law Anil, who had leftist leanings, and with a famous Marathi film-actor and director. Anil was writing a film-script.

On the fourth or fifth day of this Lonavala interlude Namdeo appeared. He came late one night with another man from the Dalit movement. Mallika had already met Namdeo. She had met him in her family house – the house where we now were. Namdeo used to come to the house to hide. This was in 1974, when the Dalit movement was at its peak, and there were riots in the Bombay district of Worli.

'He had never paid much attention to me. This surprised me, because the boys here found me attractive. But he never paid me much attention. I read his poems, and I realized he had leftist leanings. I gave him my poems to read.

'He came now to Lonavala. At that time Lonavala had a very poetic atmosphere, a pre-monsoon atmosphere. It looked as though it was about to rain, but it never rained. There were quite a few similarities between us. He liked rain and I liked rain. He liked poetry and I liked poetry. Our literary opinions more or less matched, and even now, in literature, we have very many things in common. I was at the age when you really fall in love with somebody.'

She laughed. And when I said I thought that that time in Lonavala was still romantic to her, she laughed again and lifted her thin arms with the thin bracelets, and clapped her hands.

'Then he would talk about politics, and how the police were harassing him and beating him, and I would find it very thrilling. I felt I wanted to be close to him. This wasn't a sexual feeling. I felt compassion. I felt I wanted to put my hand on his head.'

'You had no caste feeling about the man?'

'I had no caste prejudices. I didn't know about his caste, and I didn't think it was essential to know that.'

Perhaps her communist father, the folk singer, had trained her that way. Yet caste would have been in everything Namdeo did. He was a caste leader, and caste still attached to him. In the house that afternoon, in the front room or hall, which Mallika had decorated with such care, there was a thin dark woman in dark clothes sleeping on a mat. That woman, I now learned from Mallika, was Namdeo's mother.

'She is seventy. Because of Namdeo's politics and the ups and downs of his career, she's had a nervous breakdown. Namdeo was her only son. She always had the fear in those days, in the 70s, at the height of the movement, that somebody would beat him up and kill him. Whenever she put on the TV she felt that somebody was going to read out that news. That pressure was always on her, and led to her breakdown.'

But – going back to the earlier point – the fact was that, at sixteen, Mallika had no caste feeling about Namdeo.

'Practically everybody at Lonavala knew we were getting close to one another. We had been together for about 15 days. Anil, my brother-in-law, would joke about it. It was he who asked one day whether I liked Namdeo, and he said we were quite suited to each other. So that same night, after we had had dinner, all of us who were staying in the bungalow – it hadn't begun to rain, but it was cool: Lonavala is cool – I called him into an inner room, away from the people sitting outside, and I said to him, "What do you think of me?" And he said, "Do you want me to put it in words?"'

She raised her hands and the eight or nine thin silver bracelets slipped down her thin arm.

'After this my brother-in-law talked to him. He asked him some questions about his background and his feelings. Namdeo didn't like this. My brother-in law said to him that I had come to Lonavala to do some studying. "Since you've come she hasn't read a single word. She is still at page 153."'

'What book was that?'

'A history book. So my brother-in-law said to Namdeo, "You better leave." The next day Namdeo left.'

But hadn't her brother-in-law encouraged Namdeo? Yes, Mallika said; but when her brother-in-law had spoken to Namdeo about his intentions, he wasn't speaking in anger or in rebuke; he was only speaking formally. Namdeo, though, hadn't like being questioned at all; so he had been asked to leave.

'Just before Namdeo left Lonavala, he took my hand. He called me "comrade" and he gave the "red salaam", the communist salute. This excited me. Before he went he taped something by me – it was a song I used to sing night and day. I heard later that he would play that tape to his friends in Bombay.'

They were married four months later. After the schoolgirl romance, the sexual side of marriage had been disagreeable for her. That was one of the things she had written about openly in her book. 'The pleasure came when the routine started. It was then that I started getting the pleasure. The psychological pressure lessened with the experience.' She hadn't had any idea of the sexual give-and-take in a relationship. And it amazed her, it enchanted her, to be able to give her body and herself to someone she loved. She wrote of this in her book, and people reacted in different ways to her frankness. Some people 'threw themselves at her feet' in admiration; some people abused her.

The marriage itself came under another strain almost at once. 'Within two months of our marriage the Panther movement started breaking up. Dalits stay in small settlements and pockets, little groups. Each pocket and settlement began to have its own leader, and poisonous things began to be said about Namdeo in those settlements. His marriage to me added to his troubles. I was the daughter of a well-known communist, and the Dalits don't like communists. The reason for that is simple. Dr Ambedkar, the hero of the Dalits, didn't like communism. Every Dalit has Dr Ambedkar's picture in his house. So the Dalits hate communists.

'The next year, 1975, there was the Emergency. There were something like 350 court cases against the Dalit Panthers – speeches, fighting, etc. The government withdrew all those cases when the Panthers supported the Emergency. That wasn't really what Namdeo wanted to do. And though he never said anything about it, I feel that was when he began to feel compromised. But that was when I, too, needed him most – in July of that year I had had my child. I needed Namdeo, and I felt he was neglecting me.'

'Because of political pressure?'

'His setbacks and frustration. That helped to send him away from me. So his political life had an effect on his personal life.'

'Do you still find him an attractive man?'

'Much water has flowed down the Ganges, but if he were to come in this room now, I would feel like a young girl. I would feel I had just fallen in love with him. Nothing has really changed in that. There are many other men who may be physically more attractive or intellectually superior. But I don't want them.'

I asked her about the 'five-star life' that – according to his critics – had come to Namdeo as a Dalit Panther, a man in the news.

Mallika said, 'This downward journey began right at the Emergency.'

Namdeo's mother had got up from her mat in the front room. Through the doorway I saw her in the kitchen, a thin dark figure in dark clothes, moving silently, like a shadow.

Mallika said, 'Namdeo is a born politician. If he decides tomorrow to write his autobiography, there would be just a page for me. That is why his political ups and downs had its repercussions on his private life. This is one of the questions I asked in my book. Why should this affect me? Why isn't he helping me with my life?

'After the Emergency he became unpredictable. His friends in the underworld began giving him money. One day he would have 10,000 rupees. The next day he wouldn't have a rupee. And we both had a common trait – money never stuck to us. Namdeo used to say it was middle class to keep money in the bank. So whatever money he had he spent – and on high living.'

Ever since 1975, just a year or so after its time of glory (and a year or so after Mallika's Lonavala romance), the Dalit movement had been in decay. She used an English word: *numb*. The movement fragmented and fragmented again, and there were allegations and counter-allegations about money being taken by various people from various sources. The Dalits, as a result, had lost faith in the people who had been their leaders.

It was now five o'clock. We had been with Mallika for three hours. And at this moment – when our meeting would have been ending, if he had been there for it – Namdeo appeared. His mother was still in the kitchen.

And it was as Mallika had said: Namdeo was in the house; she was aware of his presence; her thoughts were of him. She began to speak to us with only half a mind – speaking simple pieties about the Dalit movement – but then she calmed down again.

I asked about the violent sexual imagery in some of Namdeo's poems, the conflation of sex and excrement and degradation. When she had married Namdeo, her thoughts had been all of romance; even the sexual side of marriage had shocked her. Had she, after that first shock, become wholly accepting? Wasn't she still unsettled, just a little, by certain things in Namdeo's poetry?

No; she wasn't unsettled in any way. What she felt, more than shock at some of the words and images, was Namdeo's great power as a poet. 'It's quite true and pure poetry. It's not just an imitation. I look upon him as one of the greatest poets in Marathi. We've had people who've changed the course of poetry. He's one of them. *He's a milestone.*' She spoke the last words in English.

Namdeo came in from the kitchen to the little room where we were. His glasses were on his forehead. He smiled and was polite. He made no reference to the meeting he hadn't come for. He said only that there were people waiting for him, and he couldn't stay to talk.

He was busy that day with his political work. He was organizing a demonstration by prostitutes in the Golpitha district, he said. He showed the black-and-white posters he had just picked up from the printers. He asked whether I would like to come to that demonstration. I said yes. He gave me a copy of the poster, and we arranged to meet at the house the day after the demonstration, when he would have more time. And then he was out of the room.

I asked Mallika, 'Does he show you his poems?'

'If he writes something here, he will show it to me. If he writes it somewhere else, he will show it to the person nearest him, whether that person understands poetry or not.'

All the shocks of her relationship with Namdeo appeared now to lie in the past – the discovery, for instance, in the first year of their marriage, that he had a venereal disease. She had written about that, and about other discoveries she had made. She lived more easily now with the things she had written about; and she thought her life with Namdeo could go on forever as it was going on now: 'a middle-class family state'. She was not, besides, in a position to do anything extreme: she always had to think of her child.

'I want the child to become my friend. I don't want the child to grow up like his father – the negative aspects.'

'What negative aspects?'

'Raging, cursing. The movement is the first thing Namdeo thinks about. So, whatever our relationship, he will never break his ties to the movement.'

The movement was now stalled. People might come together on certain issues; they might shout slogans and march. But people no longer had a direction or a purpose.

I told her about the long line of people I had seen on the way in from the airport. What would their mood have been, waiting to pay tribute to the long-dead Ambedkar?

'Emotional. Dalits will sacrifice anything and everything for Ambedkar. He is not an extra god for them. He is God. They would slaughter their wife. Anything for Ambedkar.'

Charu added on his own, 'Like Christ to the Christians.'

Mallika agreed.

I asked whether she had been supported by any religious faith during these years.

'Whenever things were bad I turned to myself.'

'No faith?'

'I have faith in myself. I have faith only in my own existence.'

The first part of Mallika's book had ended (in Charu's spoken translation): 'Male ego is the most hideous thing in our present society. Women find quite a pleasure in boosting it. It reminds me of a story in which the tree itself gave its branch to a woodcutter who had only an axe-blade and no handle . . . I do not believe that for anybody called Namdeo I should surrender my entire life.' But the book was also an account of her obsession with the man and his poetry and his cause, and her consequent loss of freedom. The second part of the book ended: 'This has been the journey of a defeated mind.' And though what she had done had been done for the sake of a man, she had always been alone. 'There was nobody with me.'

Charu and I got ready to leave. And now many of the details of the house had a fuller meaning: the photographs of Mallika's father and mother, the colour snaps of Namdeo, the red flag (made by Mallika's son) in the front room, the dark, shadow-like, silent figure of Namdeo's mother who had had a breakdown many years before (and was about to die now), the framed certificate to Namdeo from the Bombay Russian House of Culture, the icon-picture of Dr Ambedkar, the poster for the prostitutes' meeting Namdeo was planning. On one wall, above the very big colour photograph of a white baby (Mallika said she simply liked the picture) there was a framed drawing by her son: brown rocks, black boulder, red sun, black birds. In the up-and-down scratching of the brown crayon, which had given volume and solidity to the rocks, I had seen a great subtlety, and had thought that the picture was a contemporary Chinese print.

The prostitutes' meeting that Namdeo was organizing in Golpitha was to be on Tuesday. On Sunday there was an item in a newspaper that I was to be the 'chief guest' at the meeting. Other newspapers picked up the item the next day; and though people I knew in Bombay began to telephone me, some with worry, some with amusement, I didn't think the newspaper story was of any consequence. I thought that misconceptions or exaggerations of that nature would blow away.

From the impression of busyness Namdeo had given, and from the serious-looking black-and-white Dalit Panther poster, I expected the meeting to be quite an event. But when Charu and I went we found hardly anything. There were Dalit Panther banners across some lanes; there were many policemen and police vehicles about; but there seemed to be no extraordinary stir.

We had gone early, to get something of the atmosphere of the brothel area. We went walking in the narrow lanes: the lights, the signboards, the booths, the people sitting out, some on string beds, in the shadows at the side of the lanes; the piles of wet rubbish, the smell of drains; prostitutes and their 'mistresses' and money-lenders and prostitutes' clients all part of the same display, the mixture of sex and innocence and degradation as undermining as in the poems of Namdeo's that the area had inspired.

The evening life of the area was going on. The prospect of Namdeo's Dalit Panther meeting – to protest against what was seen – was hardly causing a tremor. The meeting was to take place at the end of one of the lanes, dark and without motor traffic, but full of activity, with a walking space only in the middle, between the booths and stalls and the string beds. In bright light at the end of the lane, on a platform spread with white sheets, seated musicians were playing country melodies.

No one seemed to be attending. But as Charu and I got nearer, men with cameras, and men and women whom Charu recognized as newspaper reporters, came out from the shadows. And Charu and I understood that, for that evening, so far as the newspapers were concerned, we were the story.

I thought we should go away. Charu and I turned and walked back to the other end of the lane. The newspaper people followed us. When we were at the end of the lane, and near a brighter main road, Charu said it would be wrong to leave just like that. We would anatagonize the newspaper people, who had given up their evening for this event; and they might go away and write hostile stories. He thought it would be better for him to go and talk to the newspaper people – he knew them: some were his friends – and explain matters to them.

He led me to a cigarette stall, and asked me to stand there and wait for him. He went back down the lane, and was soon lost in the darkness and the crowd. But the photographers didn't go away. They stayed a few feet from me, keeping their eyes on me (in case I tried to run off), while the musicians, their white platform bright and distant at the end of the dark lane, played their rocking country rhythms. All at once a photographer took a picture; and at that flash all the photographers began to click and flash away, creating the effect of dud fireworks around me.

At last Charu came back. He had news. Namdeo had arrived, and – unusually – Mallika had come with him. It was essential now for me to go back and be with them for a little, Charu said. If I didn't do that, they might feel that I was letting them down. Already, Charu said, even if I wasn't aware of it, and couldn't understand the reason for it, a certain amount of caste hostility was building up in the people of the lane, who had witnessed our coming and going. It would take just one little spark for there to be trouble. There was another reason, Charu said, why I should go and be with Namdeo and Mallika. Mallika, after all the time she had given me, had gone to the further trouble of writing me a long letter in Marathi; she had given him the letter to pass to me.

A length of matting covered by some kind of cloth, a version of a red carpet, had been laid down the middle of the wet, dirty lane. Down that we walked, back towards the musicians, who were playing on. We turned into a little room: Mallika was there, welcoming, smiling, in a fresh sari, and Namdeo. I was glad to see them, glad that Charu had made me come back. Women of the area garlanded me. It was what the photographers wanted; and it was those happy pictures – rather than the furtive ones in the dark lane – that made the newspapers the next day.

In the taxi back, Charu translated Mallika's letter: many sheets of foolscap in a beautiful, stylish script. She was concerned that I might not have understood the two sides of her way of feeling: her love of freedom, her love for Namdeo. But she had, in fact, said it all when we had met.

We went to see Namdeo the next day at the house. That was the arrangement we had made some days before. But Charu was nervous, and even worried. We hadn't stayed for Namdeo's meeting; he might have felt that we had walked out on him. He might have felt that we had damaged him politically, and there was no knowing what he might do. He was an unpredictable man.

When we got to the house Mallika told us that Namdeo was there. He was inside, eating. He came out and greeted us and right away went back in. We saw all the day's newspapers in the front room: they had been unfolded and looked at. I hadn't read the stories that had accompanied the photographs. Charu had; and out of a wish to make peace for both of us (and rebuking me for not having accepted Namdeo's offer of lunch when it had been made some days before), he settled down, at Mallika's invitation, and with Mallika serving him, to eat an enormous meal in the front room. He ate all she gave him, and then he asked for more.

But Charu had been too nervous. Mallika was happy with the way the evening had gone. She even wanted me to know that the musicians at the meeting had been part of her father's folk-song troupe. Namdeo was very happy. He was eating at the back, but that didn't mean anything. When the eating was over, Charu's in the front room, and Namdeo's in the back room, we all met in perfect amity in the back room, with the olive-green metal wardrobe with the tall mirror, and the bronze-coloured lamp-stand; and Namdeo made it clear that he was ready, as he had promised, to give me the whole afternoon.

Still, bearing in mind what Charu had said, I didn't think I should talk right away about the prostitutes' meeting. I thought I would begin with his poetry. I told him about the early poem Charu had translated for me, 'The Way to the Shrine'. I asked about the sexual violence of that poem and other, later poems of his I had got to know.

He replied at great length. Charu, perhaps out of a continuing nervousness, and perhaps also out of his interest in literary matters, allowed Namdeo to talk for a long time before he translated or summed up; and Namdeo talked slowly, reflectively.

In the middle of Namdeo's Marathi I caught the English words *not sexual*. He said 'The Way to the Shrine' was not one of his best poems. He gave this interpretation of the poem. The poet was like an orphan in the land of his birth. The shrine that the poet was going towards was a real place, a famous sea-side mosque in Bombay; but Bombay was a cosmopolitan city, and the shrine of the poet's pilgrimage could be any of the city's sacred places. The 'darkness in the sari' and 'the ghost in the footpath' was the social system into which the poet had been born. The darkness in the sari was not a sexual image – even the lowest woman would have her own code. The darkness in the sari meant ignorance: the poet had spent much of his life washing away this darkness, this ignorance.

But he had written better poems. He wished I had got to know some of those. He had written a poem about water. It was quite a well-known poem.

Water is taught caste prejudices . . .

That idea about water was important to him. He referred to it more than once. It came from his memories of the strict untouchability that prevailed in the village near Poona where he had grown up. The upper castes used the river upstream; the scheduled castes used the river downstream; and the upper castes used the river first.

He had a memory of something that had happened when he was in the second standard. The village children didn't have caste prejudices; they would play together. One day he went bathing in a pond with some upper-caste boys. The guard spotted him and threw stones at him. He had defiled the pond. He was chased and stoned. He ran bleeding back to his own settlement and hid there. His mother was abused, and afterwards his mother beat him for defiling the pond and causing trouble.

He thought he was born in 1940, but he couldn't be sure. Even at school – this would have been in 1951 or 1952 – the scheduled-caste boys would have to sit outside the school-room. They weren't allowed to touch any source of water; water had to be poured into their cupped hands. A teacher couldn't touch a scheduled-caste child. When a teacher wanted to punish a child from one of those castes, he threw things at the child.

His family was of the Mahar caste. They lived in a joint family: the wives and children of three brothers, about 25 people in all, lived in one house. Namdeo's father didn't live in the house; he had migrated to Bombay, leaving his family behind. The family had land. They lived by farming, and also by the traditional duties of their caste.

As Namdeo was talking of the traditional duties of the Mahars in his native village, we were joined in the small inner room by a man I had seen in the house before, one of those silent, unintroduced, unexplained people who appeared to have the freedom of the house. This small, dark man, with a thick moustache and an orange-coloured tunic, stood beside Namdeo's chair, and listened with especial attention now, shaking his head in solemn affirmation as Namdeo spoke of the duties of Mahars.

Mahars had to summon people to the revenue department. That was an official duty, for the government, and in the old days it could mean travelling long distances in all kinds of weather. Other duties were more traditional. When someone in the village died, it was the Mahars who were entrusted with the task of informing all the relatives of the dead person. Mahars also disposed of dead bodies. In return, the Mahars were given an allowance of grain three times a year by the upper-caste villagers.

The friend of the house solemnly swung his head from side to side, staring down at a point half-way to the floor, so that it was as if, while Namdeo spoke, the friend of the house was nostalgically remembering the old ways.

He repeated now, 'Three times a year.'

Mahars had another privilege. This was like a daily ritual, and Namdeo spoke long about it, and the friend of the house listened and looked down at the floor and shook his head.

Mahars, Namdeo said, had the right to call on the upper-caste houses every day and ask for bread. If there were 10 Mahar households in a village they would divide the upper-caste households among themselves, and each Mahar household would be allotted certain caste households to call on. The Mahar who had that task would leave his house early in the morning with a woven basket or a metal basket on his head. When he got to the upper-caste house he would make his obeisance and ask for bread. He would ask for bread twice. If the bread wasn't given then, it was the right of the Mahar absolutely to demand it. The Mahars did this every morning. And the upper-caste people would give bread, letting the bread fall into the basket, without themselves touching the basket.

'Without touching,' the friend said.

This was the way the caste system worked when it was still strong, before 1955. After that it began to break down. Instead of grain and certain rights, Mahars could be offered money for what they did; but sometimes they weren't offered anything. So while their duties in the village remained the same, such rights as they had had began to diminish. Ambedkar was powerful at that time; and Mahars and other scheduled-caste people began then to make political demands.

Among the scheduled castes in that area, Mahars were the only ones with the right to own land. That was why Namdeo's family had land and made a certain amount of money from farming. That right of the Mahars, to own land, had come about for an interesting reason.

Once upon a time, there was a raja of Bidar. He wanted to send his daughter to a certain place. The Mahars were the people who traditionally carried the palanquins, and the raja ordered the local Mahars to carry his daughter to where she had to go. The Mahars understood the seriousness of what they had been asked to do; as a precaution, to avoid accident or misunderstanding, they castrated themselves before setting out. The raja's enemies started to spread a story that the raja's daughter had been carnally used by the Mahars. The raja summoned the Mahars and questioned them. They displayed themselves to him, and said they had castrated themselves before taking the princess. The raja was so pleased he gave the Mahars land. That was how the Mahars became the only scheduled caste in the area to own land.

Namdeo had seemed to take much pleasure in the romantic tale; just as, earlier, encouraged by his friend, he had seemed, with something like nostalgia, to call up the caste practices of his village. I asked Charu to ask him about this nostalgia: I thought I might have missed something.

Namdeo spoke for a long time, and his friend in the orange-coloured tunic was as encouraging as always.

Finally Charu reported: 'He's fully aware of the pain he's undergone. But there is also a poet and writer in him, and as a poet and writer he wishes to search out his own roots. Pain has always been part of his psychology. There was no question in the old days of complaining. You were a Mahar and you did your duties, and that was that.'

It wasn't all pain for him in the village. The village teacher had the prejudices of his caste, and he neglected Namdeo. But this neglect gave Namdeo some freedom as a child. He enjoyed taking the cattle out to graze; he went swimming in the river.

In 1958, when he was seventeen or eighteen, and in the fourth standard, he left his village and came to Bombay. He remembered that *Mother India*, with the actress Nargis, was showing in the cinemas. He stayed in a slum area with one of his uncles, who had two rooms in a chawl. The chawl was called 'Dhor Chawl', after the Dhor caste, a caste who disposed of dead cattle and ran the tanneries. Only people of that caste were living in the chawl. So

Namdeo didn't leave caste behind in his village; caste followed him to Bombay.

He didn't go out to work. He went to school. In the school in the village he had been a failure in the fourth standard; in Bombay, in the same standard, he stood first. It was then, too, that he began writing poetry.

All his poems came straight out, 'in a flow'. He had read about Bob Dylan and Eldridge Cleaver. And he had read some Negro poets; and Leroi Jones. He had read them in English. He understood English, though he couldn't speak it. There was no direct influence, but he was aware of those poets. He also knew Allen Ginsberg, Rimbaud, Rilke, Baudelaire, Lorca, the last four in English translations. He'd read all the major mid-20th-century poets.

And though, from a distance, his career seemed to be like the careers of a number of Black Power people in the United States – he had become someone the newspapers and magazines wrote about, and in the end he had become more famous than his cause – yet, talking to him in this little room of the Bombay house, I felt that he was the prisoner of an Indian past no one outside could truly understand. It had been harder for him to break out, to reject the past, than it had been for black people in the United States. And now Namdeo was again, if in a different way, a prisoner of India, with its multiplicity of movements and desperate needs; he could easily sink again. It wasn't really possible for him, as it might have been possible for a black activist in the United States, to withdraw, to settle for ease.

I asked whether he was now more a poet than a politician.

'The roles are not separate. I am against this caste system. I express it in my politics and in my poems. Poetry is a political act. Politics is part of my poetry.'

Only now I thought I could refer to the adventure of the previous night.

'You will keep on working with the prostitutes?'

'I will keep on working on various problems. Prostitutes are a major problem.'

'Are there Dalits who are jealous of you?'

'There is a jealousy of me. There are allegations that I am a communist.'

When he had first come out to greet us, before going in again to continue eating, he had seemed casually dressed, a man at home, with a brownish shirt and a many-coloured dhoti. In fact, he had dressed carefully. The shirt was elegant, fawn-coloured, thick and textured; and his dhoti had a plaid pattern. He fitted into the room, with its walls in an eggshell finish, and the plastic flowers in a vase on the window-sill in front of the vertical iron bars: a lot of Mallika's taste here.

I said, 'Mallika says your poetry is a milestone.'

'I feel surprised when people say things like that. Marathi literature is so poor. There were nice poems like Tukaram's, and then there was nothing for hundreds of years.'

His life was very public now. Was it possible for him to write poetry while living such a public life?

He misunderstood the question. 'I'm not really troubled. I don't expect to be praised.'

'Mallika said you defended her right to publish her book.'

He didn't make a direct comment. 'It's a conflict between two cultures, two backgrounds. Mallika's mother was a traditional Hindu. Though her father was Muslim, her culture was traditional Hindu middle-class culture.'

'You defended her book.'

'Her book was damaging to me, it is true. My image outside was that of a progressive, and Mallika's picture was damaging. But Mallika was right. I've always been an Ambedkarite. That's been part of my being, and I feel that Mallika has a right to say what she feels about her husband.'

Then, explaining himself, not waiting for me to ask questions, he began to speak of some of the things I might have heard about him or wanted to know about him.

'My political rise started in 1971–1972. Before that I was living in that Kanthipura area in the underworld. Money was easy to come by. It was a red-light area, full of ignorance and the mafia and cruelty. It's a cruel area, and that had an effect on me. It had a tremendous impact on my character. When you are young, you are tough and militant. Your energy can take you on to a good path or a wrong path. If I didn't have my special past, and if I wasn't aware of Ambedkar's movement, I might have been one of the big men of the underworld, and I mightn't have gone into politics. Because of the way I had been brought up, I was full of anger and ready to fight at the slightest provocation. Some of the fights I got into came close to murder. Everybody in the Bombay underworld knew me.'

The afternoon had gone; dusk was almost upon us. Our talk had taken a long time, because Namdeo had always spoken at length, and I had had to wait for Charu's translation or summaries. I was tired. Charu was tired, and he had missed the visiting Russian circus to which he had been hoping to take his wife that evening. I got up, ready to leave. But Namdeo didn't want it.

He said, 'You haven't asked me about my personal life.'

And then, like a man doing what was expected of him, giving full value, he spoke the things people said about him and sometimes used against him.

'I used to be a taxi-driver. From 1967 to 1971. I used to go with prostitutes. I have tried all kinds of vices. *Now I'm too much normal and gentleman.*' The last sentence was in English. 'Even after I got married, I used sometimes to go to prostitutes. When the Dalit Panthers split, I used to drink very heavily. I started the Panthers, and then they put me in a minority. It was a great blow. It saddens me still.'

'Why do you think you lost your power?'

'I was ahead of my time. I tried to expand the definition of Dalits – to take in all the oppressed, not just the scheduled castes. If you really want to break untouchability, you have to get into the mainstream. I wanted to be in the mainstream. That was why I wanted to expand the definition of Dalits. But the reactionaries among the Dalits didn't want to be in the mainstream. Their feeling was that, to break communal feelings, you have to be communal yourself. And those were the people who put me in the minority.'

Then there was his illness. That came in 1981; that was also the year he had published his last book. He had spoken in a cool, open way of his life and failings, while the friend of the house with the thick moustache and the orange or saffron tunic (looking more and more like a religious garment of some kind) had listened and looked down at a point half-way to the floor and shaken his head affirmatively from time to time. And Namdeo spoke now of his illness in the same way. It was as though he was detached from his life, and observing it from a distance. He was no longer looking for praise or approval: he spoke of Mallika's right to publish her critical book as though the other possibility, of anger and suppression, had never entered his head.

He had spoken of his own past violence. But he was calm now: it might, after all, have been something he had inherited from the Hindu culture around him.

'What does Ambedkar mean to the Dalits?'

'There was a time when we were treated like animals. Now we live like human beings. It's all because of Ambedkar.'

So, just as greater meaning could be read into the house with the eggshell lilac walls and the white-painted rattan chairs, so a greater understanding became possible of the long, patient line of dark men and women on one side of the road on the morning I had arrived: not just the poor of India, but an expression of the old internal cruelty of that poverty: people at the bottom, full of emotion, with no politics at that moment, just rejecting rejection.

2

The Secretary's Tale

Glimpses of the Indian Century

Nikhil said one day, 'I know a man here called Rajan. He is the private secretary of an influential politician and businessman. He says he met you in Calcutta in 1962.'

I couldn't remember, and I still didn't remember even when Nikhil took me one afternoon to Rajan's office. Rajan was a small, sturdy man of the South with a square, dark face. His office – or the suite of which it formed part – was one of the most spacious and stylish offices I had seen in Bombay. It was in the international style, in cool, neutral colours, and it was beautifully air-conditioned. Rajan was clearly a man of authority in that office. He wore a fawn-coloured, short-sleeved Mao outfit, which might also have passed as a version of Indian formal clothes, or might simply have been a 'safari' suit.

He said, 'You came to Calcutta in 1962, during or just after the China war. You were with some film people. In those days I myself took a great interest in films and the arts – it was the most hopeful period of my life. Someone from the Film Society at the end of one evening introduced me to you. My duty was to take you back to the drug-company guest house where you were staying.'

The painful war in the background, the mingled smoke and autumnal mist of Calcutta, the small, ceiling-lit rooms of the Film Society, full of old office furniture: one or two moments of the vanished evening began to come back, but they were the merest pictures, hard to hold on to. And nothing remained of the end of the evening.

'I was twenty-two,' Rajan said. 'I was working in an advertising agency. I was a kind of clerk. My salary was 315 rupees a month. I was tipped to be an assistant account executive, but that wasn't to be.' Three hundred and fifteen rupees, £24, a month.

'When did you leave Calcutta?'

'It's a long story,' Rajan said.

And later that afternoon – while we sat outside the club house in Brabourne Stadium, the old international cricket ground of Bombay, and had tea, and watched the young cricketers practising at the nets (at the other end of the ground: the high, scaffolded back of the big stage built for the Russian ice show, part of the visiting Festival of Russia) – and on another day, in a hotel room not far from his office, beginning after his office work, and talking on until late in the evening, Rajan told me his story.

'I was born in Calcutta in 1940. Our family came from the South, from what in British times was known as the province of Madras and today is the state of Tamil Nadu. My grandfather used to be some kind of petty official in one of the law courts near the town of Tanjore. He was respected by people for his honesty and courage. Courage in the sense that if something wrong happened, or if someone asked him to do something his heart wouldn't let him do, he would turn violent or resist it in any form he thought fit.

'A Britisher was above him. He wanted my grandfather to be a witness in a lawsuit and say what was not true. I know only that it ended up in a kind of fracas, and my grandfather took off his footwear and hit the Britisher. He realized that after that life would be difficult for him in Tanjore. He decided to migrate to the North with his only son, who was a student at that time. This would have been early in the century, between 1900 and 1905. He chose to move to Calcutta, which was the British headquarters. He could make a living there and have some kind of life.

'In Calcutta he stayed with some friend or distant relation till he found his feet. He got his son to learn stenography. South Indians, brahmins especially, had a better grasp of English because they were more exposed to it, and they would get jobs as secretary, stenographer, or even typist. These were probably the most widely followed professions for the South Indian or Tamil brahmins in British times – and this is something that has changed only very recent years. Otherwise, as a class, South Indian brahmins served as teachers or as priests or as petty clerks. Or, if they enough, they would take up a job in one of the departments. These were the days when government job was a most prized thing aspiration of the bulk of the Tamil brahmins who had done some schooling. And quite a few of them migrated to the North, to the big cities, Bombay, Calcutta, Delhi.

'After he settled, my grandfather lived in Howrah, on the other side of the river from Calcutta city. It was one of those typical Calcutta residential houses – a *pucca* house, a proper house, not *kaccha*, something unfinished or improvised, and it was in a respectable middle-class locality. These places could be rented. It was a locality where there were other people from the South who had similarly migrated, and it gave them some security to live among their own kind. There was no ill-feeling at that time towards South Indians in Calcutta – those times were different. In fact, South Indians were widely respected by the Bengalis. It's quite different today. Since the 1960s South Indians in Calcutta feel they don't belong, in spite of their having been there for many decades. Which is perhaps one reason why I left Calcutta and moved to Bombay – but that was many years later.

'My father became a stenographer when he was seventeen or eighteen. This would have been about 1909, and he would probably have worked in one of the British companies. He was a capable stenographer, and he told me he had twice won the 50-rupee government prize for speed in English shorthand and typing. He continued to live in Howrah, in my grandfather's dwelling, which was a portion of a residential house. In Calcutta there were no such things as flats or apartments or tenements. There were just parts of houses – with the landlord occupying a part of the house, and renting out the rest with little adjustments here and there.

'In a few years both my grandfather and grandmother passed away, not leaving much by way of money or property. But my father moved to better jobs over the years. A stage came, in the decade between 1915 and 1925, when he was quite well paid. He had enough money not only to look after his family more than comfortably, but also to acquire some status symbols, like horses and phaetons. He had a few Arab horses driven by Muslim coachmen. Why Muslim? In those days they were the most widely available for those jobs. In those days, for certain trusted jobs, Hindus wouldn't mind having Muslims around them.

'I myself don't have any memory of this period of my father's life. These are all versions narrated to me by my eldest sister, without me asking for it. And narrated also by people who used to know my father very closely. Some of them would come out with remarks like: "Rarely have South Indians lived in Calcutta in such status or style as your father did." When I was a kid, when I was thirteen, fourteen, fifteen, when I was at school, I heard this when I ran into them at some social gathering. There would be talk then of someone doing well in life, or of someone having failed, and there would be talk of my father's past glory. When I heard these stories I felt a mixture of both pride and sadness.

'My father, during this time of well-being, took to the typical British style of dressing – complete with top hat, the suit, the waistcoat, double-toned shoes, the tie. And he also spent his leisure hours playing tennis. He started a tennis club close to his house. As a South Indian, his living expenses were meagre. All South Indian or Tamil brahmins were vegetarians without exception in those days, of course. So 200 rupees a month was quite a sizeable salary. An average family could make do with 30 or 40 rupees.

'He was a deeply religious man, as most of the South Indian brahmins were. Apart from tennis, the only thing on which he would spend his time were his pujas and *bhajans*, devotional songs. He was quite recognized for his singing of bhajans. He became a leader of the community in the locality. With this result: he kept new migrants from the South, young men coming in search of a livelihood, in his house. He fed them and clothed them and trained them in shorthand and typing. There was almost a regular stenography class in our house. And he helped them into jobs with British firms.

'My father used to respect the British. His ability to get along with the British people, and his love for the English language itself, probably did not make him look at them only as some kind of people to be hated. He never had a bent for politics of any kind.

'My father got married three times. He lost his first wife, and then he married a second time, so that his second wife could look after his first two children. When his second wife died, leaving in turn two or three children, he was forced by his relations to marry a third time. In those days such marriages were not difficult. Despite their impecunious situation, the Tamil brahmins were invariably good breeders. They would be happy to give away their daughters to anyone who wanted to marry them, so long as they were sure of the basics – that the man belonged to the same

123

community, and the man was capable of supporting his wife and family.

'In 1935, when my father married for the third time, he was forty-three. His third wife, my mother, was eighteen. There was a child in 1937, a boy, but he barely lived six months, largely because of my mother's poor health. I was born in 1940.

'By this time my father had married off his first two daughters, and he had one more daughter to marry off. He also had a son from his second marriage still going to school. These were the uncertain war years. My father at that time was a godown or warehouse keeper. It was a responsible job – most of the items in the godown were imported. The godown was owned by the Japanese firm of Mitsui. My father had taken this job with the Japanese in 1936, after he had married my mother. And he continued with it until, with the war, these Japanese operations in India were closed down. When this happened, my father moved to the newly created government department of the DGMP, the Directorate-General of Munitions and Production.

'When the war ended, my father gave up this job. About this time Mahatma Gandhi's independence movement was taking on more serious proportions, and the Muslims too were becoming agitated. In 1946 there were very bad Hindu–Muslim riots in Calcutta.

'But before this, my mother had fallen seriously ill. When my mother was close to death, she asked my elder stepsister – who had married a former army man – to bring me up. So when my stepsister and her husband left Calcutta, I went with them. I was six. My mother died a month later.

'Almost at the same time the big Hindu–Muslim riots took place in Calcutta. In the riots, the house in which we had been living was burned down. We had left Howrah long before and had moved to the city proper. When my father lost his job with the DGMP at the end of the war, we had moved to a single-room tenement in a large building. This was the building that was set on fire during the riots and burned down – with the room where my mother had died, and where we had stored almost everything that had belonged to us.

'My father was forced during the riot to get into a jeep and leave everything behind, paying all that he had, several thousand rupees, to save himself, paying that to the people who transported him. They dumped him and others like him in Howrah railway station, leaving them to take trains to their chosen destinations away from the city.

'I was with my sister and her husband far away, where my sister's husband was working as a food supply inspector for the state government. He had been discharged from the army, Auchinleck's army, in 1945. He had been one of the Viceroy's Commissoned Officers, as they were called, and when he left the army he had the rank of *jemadar*. These people, the VCOs, had been drafted into the army before the war, at a time when the British felt they would soon be facing a war situation. As a kid I used to admire him. I used to look forward to seeing him. In my eyes he was some kind of a hero. He was always well turned out. He had a lot of gifts for us – chocolates, canteen supplies. The only thing I didn't like about him was the smoking.

'I realized what was happening to my father in Calcutta. I used to see the photographs in the papers, and people talked about the horrors. This sequence – of my having seen my mother dying slowly over many months in one room, with my aged father nursing her; and then my being handed over to my sister's charge, and moving with her and husband to an altogether new place, on the other side of India, where people spoke another language, Marathi, which I couldn't understand – this sequence put me into a spell of utter gloom and depression.

'I look at it as depression now. At the time what I did was just sit outside the house, on the steps, just crouching, leaning my head on my arms, sitting all by myself on the steps outside my stepsister's house. I spent hours like that, confused, not knowing what to think.

'Suddenly one morning my father landed, and I suppose he restored me to a certain amount of life. Then he left again, promising to take me away, back with him, after things settled down. This was just before independence.

'My brother-in-law started playing truant from his job. He would leave us, and go away for weeks on end, and not tell us where he was going. My sister wrote to my father for help. But my father was yet to settle down himself. He was almost fifty-five at this time. After various moves with my sister and her husband – who kept on changing jobs, and in every job kept going off, as he had been used to doing – my father came and took me and my sister away to Calcutta, where he had at last found a place to stay.

He had also found a job, in an import company. This was in January 1948, the month when Mahatma Gandhi died.

'I spent some time with my father. Then my grandmother came and took me back to her village in the South, and put me in a school there. But this village life didn't suit me, and in 1950 I returned to Calcutta, to my father. He began to educate me at home. It was only in 1952, when I was eleven, that I actually entered a school. My father couldn't come with me. So I went to the school myself and got myself admitted after a test, in Class 8.

'My father was teaching me mainly English. He didn't attach much importance to the other subjects. Because of his love for the English language, and because he was now aged, he would get me to read out the editorials and leading articles from the *Statesman*, although often I didn't follow what I was reading. He would ask me to underline the difficult words and phrases, and leave me to write down the meanings as my home work for the afternoon.

'My father's income had gone down, and the place where we were living was in a locality where the rents were low. The locality had a sprinkling of leftover Britishers in the mansions around us, a sizable number of Muslims, and an equally large number of Anglo-Indians and Christians. The whole family – there were six of us now: my father, my stepbrother, my stepsister and her two children, and myself – had one very large room. About 20 feet by 16 feet or 18 feet. We had to share the common tap and toilet.

'There were few South Indians in that locality. The family didn't quite fit in. So my father decided to shift over to a place where mixing would be more easy, and my school would be closer. I had joined a South Indian school.

'I studied there for three years. I had problems every year at exam times with various minor ailments, and it was really only my general good performance that saw me through from one class to the other.

'We had moved to a three-room flat. My brother had started earning by then.

'I completed school in March 1955. My father passed away two months later, in a street accident very close to our house. My father was an early riser. He had gone to the market to buy flowers for the morning puja; and, as he was returning, a motorcycle on the wrong side of the road, with three people on it, dashed against him, and he fell unconscious. We found him in a pool of blood, with the vegetables and the flowers he had purchased strewn all over.

'We took him to the hospital by taxi, together with one of the men from the motorbike, the other two having vanished. This man wasn't injured. He was only pretending; and when he saw it was only my brother and me holding our father, he opened the taxi door at a street corner, and ran away. My father stayed in the hospital for three days. Three painful days. He never regained consciousness. He passed away.

'The whole family now had to live on my brother's 150-rupees income, £14 a month. He was working as a secretary to a British factory-manager, the factory being located in one of the suburbs. So we had to leave the three-roomed flat. We moved to a smaller place near to my brother's factory.

'I couldn't think in terms of going on to a college. I didn't want to be a burden on my brother. And I wanted to be on my own in any case. So I decided to learn the most obvious thing – typing, to begin with. There was a typing school not far off from our new place. The fees were four rupees a month. My brother paid in the beginning, but then I was able to earn some money to pay the fees myself. I did odd typing jobs at the institute. I was on the lookout then for any kind of employment, but things were not easy. Often I used to walk 10 or 12 miles to look up a friend, in the hope of finding a job through his help. I was about sixteen at this time.'

Rajan, though sturdy, was a short man. I wondered what his physical condition was like at the time he was talking about.

I asked him, 'Did you feel strong or weak?'

'I didn't feel physically energetic enough all the time. But what kept me going was the determination to be on my own. I'll tell you something I did one day. I even approached a Britisher in my brother's factory. He said, "You're too young. You should be at school." Another person I approached said, "But you haven't even grown a moush." A moustache.

'I suffered spells of gloom and melancholia. It was almost what I felt when I used to sit on the steps of my sister's house. I often even thought of ending my life. There were the suburban trains. And there was always the Hooghly River. But the counsel of a close friend of mine changed my mind.

'I had no adolescence. I stepped directly from childhood into adulthood. And I felt undernourished. Our food had gone down after my father's death, because my brother had to feed so many mouths on his meagre income. An added dimension to my none too happy life at this time was my relationship with my stepbrother, who was supporting us all. We could never get along. He was almost nine years senior to me, and he would always beat me up badly. It was on one of those occasions, when he had beaten me up badly, that I was driven to thinking in terms of ending my life.

'Things brightened up the next year, 1957, when I ran into a friend who said he could fix me up in a job in a Marwari concern. The Marwaris were taking over from the British in Calcutta, and were then the principal business people in the city – and they continue to be so. They were taking over the jute mills, the tea gardens, the coal mines, etc.

'I took a job with one of those family concerns as a typist. The salary was to be 90 rupees a month, seven pounds. I was just about able to get myself a second pair of trousers and a shirt. It was a long journey to the office and a long journey back. In that month I spent no more than 10 rupees on myself, and I handed over the rest of what I earned to my brother as my contribution to the family expenses. I travelled on the second-class train. I didn't go to a movie. I didn't spend more than two annas, one-eighth of a rupee, a penny, on my lunch.

'A month after I joined, I was summoned by one of the directors. I had put the carbon in the wrong way when I was typing out a statement. I was sacked. Luckily, within seven days, I ran into another friend – we were on the same tram – and he took me to another employer. This was also a Marwari. He interviewed me in his house. His company was a newspaper company, which is today India's largest.

'I was to work in their newly opened advertising department. I typed out advertising reports. I got 125 rupees. So I was doing slightly better. I contributed a full 100 rupees to the family, and spent 25 rupees on myself, including the tuition fees at an evening college I had just joined, doing Intermediate Commerce.

'We could now afford to shift back to the old locality in South Calcutta. We lived in a flat shared between two families. My relations with my brother continued as before. But he had stopped beating me, after I had one day returned a slap he had given me.

'I stayed for a year with the newspaper group. Then I left and went to Lipton's for a salary of 10 rupees a day. The manager there recommended me to his own advertising agency, and for six years, from 1958 to 1964, I worked with that advertising agency. That was when I met you. It was a good time for me. I was a member of the British Council. My love for the English language drew me to people proficient in the English language – journalists, film-makers, copywriters, and advertising people generally.

'I liked the advertising profession. It was different. It made me think. It was not drudgery. My other jobs had been drudgery. And I particularly liked the people in the profession – the artists, the account executives, the printers, the copywriters. I joined the advertising agency on 270 rupees. The senior director liked my English, and I worked for him. He liked the interest I showed in the work. He promoted me to assist him in various campaigns. Soon I was tipped to be an assistant account executive. I got on with other people in the firm as well, because I was the youngest of the lot, and could converse fluently in their language, Bengali. Bengalis appreciate that. I got an annual increment of 15 rupees. In 1964 I was getting 330 rupees. I was promised promotion, to be an assistant account executive. And finally, when it didn't come, I resigned in a huff.

'I became an assistant to an advertising and short-film producer who had taken a liking to me. I picked up the basics of film-making. He paid me 350 rupees. I even shot certain sequences on my own. But the Pakistani war of 1965 put an end to that kind of film-making company, and I had to find another job. During this time I met important people in the Calcutta creative world. That made me very happy. I always thought I had a creative urge in me, which hadn't found expression because I hadn't had a settled life and a proper foundation.

'Somebody told me I should go to England. It was because of that I took a job with Air India, for the free flight to England. At the end of my first year I went to England for a visit. But I had to return, because of that recurring problem in the family about my stepsister and her husband. At the end of my second year with Air India I made a trip to the United States.

'The Air India salary was 350 rupees. It was too low – the rupee had been devalued in 1967. I even had to do a part-time job in the evening. At last, I answered an advertisement from a manufacturing company. On the strength of my experience I was given a job in the management cadre, for thrice the Air India salary. The bosses soon promoted me and put me in charge of a purchasing department.

'So, after all these years, I found myself on the other side. But I couldn't identify myself completely with the management, because I knew too well what life was like for others. But then the political situation in Bengal was becoming turbulent. Labour was unruly. The leftists had more or less gained control of the unions and the state. And the physical conditions in the city also started deteriorating. More and more firms were coming under the control of the Marwari capitalists. And then there was the oil crisis of 1973. I was in charge of procurement of oil for the factory. I really faced a rough time. Plus the power shortages, the difficult transport, and the labour militancy I had to put up with as part of the management staff. You might say I had found the right kind of job, but at the wrong time. I hated going to work in the mornings.

'At the end of 1973 I quit – the problems in the job, the conditions of life in Calcutta. These things were compelling me to move out of Calcutta. I could only think of Bombay as the alternative, because my occasional trips to that city earlier – because of my job with Air India – had impressed me with its cosmopolitanism and its opportunities.

'So, without having a job in my hand, I moved to Bombay with my little savings. In Bombay I stayed with a relative almost my own age who was running a photographic studio in a distant suburb. He had no room. But I used to live in the studio, sharing the common toilet with other tenants in the building, and an open space for my bath. We used to store water for our photographic needs, and out of this I used to bathe.

'And I slept in a kind of loft that I specially made for myself. It was almost twice or thrice the size of an average coffin. It was just below the roof, and above the false ceiling of the front portion of the shop. I would climb into it by using the window bars as steps, and then I would slide myself into the small opening. I was comfortable. The air would come through the opening around the roller shutter. Often I would find this little loft to be the most convenient place for doing my reading and occasional writing – of letters, not articles.

'I was earning a meagre sum, having started working in the studio. I would send most of this back to my people in Calcutta, because the four children of my sister were growing, and my stepbrother now had his own family to look after.

'Initially I thought I would be able to build up the photography business with my relative, as I knew a little bit of photography as an amateur. But after a while, my savings having dried up, my relation turned out to be none too helpful. When I needed money he wouldn't give it, and when I asked for the money I had already spent on the studio he wouldn't return it.

'So it was a strained relationship, although, helplessly, I continued to live there, sleeping and reading in my cubby hole, because accommodation of any kind was one real problem in Bombay. As the situation worsened, I decided to give up the idea of any photography business and having to depend on my relation.

'As a first step, I put an ad in the classified pages of the *Times of India*. That must have cost me about 14 or 15 rupees – the paper charged concessional rates for job-seekers. I got 40 replies.

'The advertisement I wrote read something like this: "South Indian secretary with over 10 years' experience, with impeccable English, seeks interesting position in advertising, public relations, travel, etc." I shortlisted the replies by choosing not to respond to companies located in the suburbs on the Central Railway, especially factories. The travelling conditions there were difficult and would involve a change of trains half-way from where I was living with my relation – that was an hour and a half away on the Western Railway line.

'I decided to attend only four interviews, all of which were to take place around the Victoria Terminal in Churchgate, and were in offices rather than factories or workshops. Nothing happened the first day. I didn't come to accept the jobs for varying reasons – salary, office atmosphere, and the interviewer himself. In fact, I told off one of the interviewers when he asked a very absurd question. "Why did you leave Calcutta after all these years? Those beautiful women there – you should have stayed at least for the *rasgolla*-like women there.' I thought that was too degrading to women. Probably he found I was more than he required. It was a trading company, and he was one of those uncouth characters who had suddenly come into money.

'The four interviews I had arranged were to last two days. Two a day. At the end of the first day I was somewhat despondent. I didn't want to return to Calcutta. On the other hand, I didn't want to make my life more miserable by being without much money and continuing to live with my relation. So I decided that if I didn't get a job the next day, I would have to return to Calcutta, from where my sister had been persistently writing to me.

'The following day I came all the way from the photographic studio to Churchgate. On arrival at Churchgate station I went to Satkar Restaurant opposite the station. The board said: "Tea and Snack Bar". I ordered myself an idli and a coffee – idli was about 60 paise and coffee was 40 paise – because I thought that was all I could afford, with my money touching the bottom.

'As I was finishing my coffee, I looked through the papers, the letters from the firms I had shortlisted, to see who were the people I still had to look up. And there I found this call from a man who described himself simply as "Municipal Councillor". His address was on "A" Road. I asked the waiter where "A" Road was. He said, "You are sitting on the very same road." I found that the address the municipal councillor had given was just a stone's throw away.

'I made for it, and discovered it was an office within a residence. After I had waited for a while, a gentleman came in. This was my first sight of the man with whom I was to work for the next 14 years. He was a tall man – no, average, five foot seven, five foot eight. Very fair, not heavily built. He looked well groomed, well dressed.

'He took me inside his office, and after a very brief conversation, 15 minutes, he straight away asked me to join him. Although I was readily impressed by the man, by his speed and quick decision, I did not accept his offer straight away, as I had to ponder over the salary offer he had made, which was 900 rupees. But he made no secret of his keenness to engage me. It looked almost as though he had guessed my situation, decided how much I should get, and made me an offer. To this day I don't know whether he knows much about me, my background, my life away from the office.

'He asked me to ring him back as soon as I had made up my mind, and he hoped he wouldn't have to wait too long, because he had made up *his* mind that I was the kind of man he was looking for. I went back to the restaurant – it was a different waiter – and, after weighing the situation, had very nearly come to the conclusion that a job in hand was better than none. I phoned him up the next day, and joined him the Monday following.

'When I got this job, there was an effort on the part of my relation in the photographic studio to patch up our relationship. But I didn't want it. I stayed for three months after that in the cubby hole in the studio. Then I continued to move from place to place as a paying guest with various families – with problems of their own, of all kinds. I had a suitcase of clothes and another suitcase of books and knick-knacks. Two suitcases of possessions – that was all I had.

'In my work for my employer I began to know people of importance. I enjoyed that. He was a civic leader and I could see that he was an ambitious man. I thought I would have opportunities of rising with him. And, indeed, he has risen in all directions. He is more famous and powerful and wealthy now than when I first went to work for him.

'People who deal with me in my office might say that I have risen with him. But I feel it hasn't been exactly in the manner I had hoped for. For a long time, while I worked here, my nomadic life as a paying guest continued, with my two suitcases, until I met a very kindly family – very hard to think of in a place like Bombay – who were generous enough to offer me a room all to myself, although in an old building. This was in 1980. I was forty years old. At that age, for the first time in my life, I had a room of my own. This was a dream in a place like Bombay, where people have to sleep on the pavement and in drainpipes – and it was perhaps the best thing to have happened to me.

'Until three years ago I lived on this charity, in a single room in that old house, with a common privy shared by 40 people. I couldn't think of marriage then. My salary, though very good by Bombay standards, couldn't have bought me a dwelling of any kind. But I've since been lucky, despite the odds, to acquire a flat or apartment of my own.

'And then a friend of mine felt I should settle down. This friend knew that I had seen my responsibilities to my sister's family through. He put an ad on my behalf in the matrimonial pages of the paper. It's the classified ad which has brought me things, and now again the ad came into my life and changed the course of events for me.

'Among the people who responded to the advertisement my friend had inserted for me was my prospective father-in-law. I had given my background and age in the ad. I had hidden nothing. I said I wanted a lady who would look forward to a simple life. I got about 90 replies, perhaps 100. They were from various parts of India. I think I got so many replies because I had said in the advertisement: "Caste, community, widows, divorcees, no bar." I wanted a lady, though, who was already in Bombay, because that would settle many problems. Bombay life is so hard – there are language problems for people not knowing Hindi – and transport is hard, and generally the style of life is hard here. It isn't an easy thing to get acclimatized to.

'In about half an hour with my prospective father-in-law he was able to understand my basic character. The meeting took place in the coffee shop of the Ritz Hotel. He had come over to my office, but I had to keep him there for a couple of hours, this seventy-year-old man, because I wasn't free when he came. He is a Keralite, but a brahmin. An average-sized man, bald, quiet-spoken, with the real stamp of patience on his face and in his demeanour. He was a retired electrical engineer in charge of purchase for a public-sector undertaking – part of industrializing India. He had been all over the country, and his children were broadminded.

'About a week after this meeting I went to their house at about 10.30 at night, after a full day's work. She was in bed. Her father woke her up. I spoke to her. She had been working for a nationalized bank for 10 years, took interest in yoga, and was not given to speaking much. She was average in her looks. She wasn't fat, but because of her height she didn't look lean. She was about four foot ten. She wore specs.

'And after conversing more or less through her father and her mother, I felt I should meet her again and let her speak her own mind in a private talk, without the parents. After three days I met her once again in her cousin's place. The cousin appreciated this attitude of mine, and made all appropriate arrangements, for privacy, etc. Over a cup of coffee we talked for a little over half an hour – she had just come back from her office in the bank. She wasn't a great dresser. I had the impression she didn't worry much about her attire.

'After three days I telephoned her at her office, and this time we met in a restaurant. And by and large we agreed that we should get married. We got married in about 40 days. I wanted a civil marriage – no dowry, no give, no take; no crowding around with relations and friends; no party, no feasts, no gifts. But they didn't want a civil marriage. So I called my cousin to perform the rites. I was totally without religion myself; I had never made a special effort to understand Hindu theology or principles.

'I am happy at last in having a purpose in life, now that I have a family of my own. I've put an end to my otherwise unsettled life. Marriage came to me when I was forty-five. My wife was thirty-nine. We both had to wait a long time for this mercy. And God has blessed us with this added happiness that – at this late stage – we have had a child.

'I am still left with the feeling that I might have risen much higher, given a litle more understanding and sympathy. Or perhaps in another country. What keeps haunting me all the time is the feeling that I am doomed to rise no more than I have risen. Even in this job I have been like a ship's ladder. The sea rises, the ship rises, and the ladder rises with it. But the ladder cannot rise on its own. I cannot be independent of my employer and rise in life.

'And yet I have, positively, a sense of fulfilment. When my father died, we were almost penniless, despite our earlier well-being. My sister brought me up early. And when my brother-in-law deserted her, it became my turn to take care of her and rear her children. I was able to do it. Today they are all well placed. I look upon them as symbols of my achievement.

'And yet, too, I thought I would be some kind of creative person – like the persons I knew in Calcutta, when I first met you in 1962. But that kind of life and companionship has always eluded me. I started off as a secretary, and am still a secretary, and shall probably end as a secretary. I haven't risen beyond what my father and grandfather could rise to, at the beginning of the century. The only consolation is that, even as a secretary, I am not as badly off as most other secretaries are. And perhaps, even, I no longer believe I am just a secretary.'

3

Breaking Out

As soon as I got to the airport at Santa Cruz, the airport in Bombay for internal Indian flights, I felt like a refugee. There was a crowd at the entrance; and criminally inclined young men of the neighbourhood were trying to extort money from passengers for moving luggage a few feet from taxis to the doorway.

Policemen were guarding the doorway against the young men, but they seemed not to be offering protection to people outside, even when they were almost at the door; and the young men, understanding this, ran two or three at a time to people just arriving, fell shouting on suitcases and bags, and tried to create an unbalancing atmosphere of frenzy. They were small and thin, these young criminals of the neighbourhood, and they were in tight milk-chocolate-coloured trousers of some synthetic fabric that showed up their frailty in hip and thigh. Their faces were small and bony, and their necks looked as though they might easily snap. Their wretchedness of physique didn't make them less threatening: they called up the very thin, fawning-sinister figures of some of the Cruikshank illustrations for Dickens.

Crowd and noise and threat and urgency outside, taxis coming and going in the mid-afternoon sun. Crowd inside as well, and noise, but it was a different kind of noise: it was more stable: it was the noise of people going nowhere. There was only one internal airline in India; it was a state airline, and it was in a mess. It was said by various spokesmen that the flights of this airline had to be late because many of them originated in Delhi, and there was fog in Delhi on many mornings. There were other problems. The airline had never had enough aircraft, and in the last few weeks a number of aircraft had been withdrawn for one reason and another. Services were now in chaos. But air travel remained a necessary badge and privilege for important people, scientists and administrators and business executives; and for weeks a fair portion of the country's most eminent men and women was, at any given moment, becalmed in the country's airports, as if by an act of enchantment. Items in the newspapers regularly told of depleted conferences on important subjects in this town and that town. Yet the demand for seats, especially at this holiday season, was greater than ever, and I had been able to get a ticket for this flight to Goa only through the intercession of an influential friend.

In the airport hall the information screens flashed news of ever more flights delayed or abandoned. It was as though there had been some national emergency or disaster. The many grey-and-white screens gave constant, silent electronic jumps, delivering the bad news above the heads of the crowd, who were going nowhere but were not still, were in constant, very slow movement. My own flight to Goa had been delayed for five hours already. Now the screens, whenever (as in a lottery) the number of the Goa flight came up, promised a further delay of four hours. But some people had been waiting in the hall all that day.

From time to time there were the sounds of aircraft taking off. They were tormenting sounds: the planes taking off were the actual planes people were waiting to board, but at that moment different flight numbers were attached to them, and they were starting on roundabout journeys, with many stops, before coming back to Santa Cruz.

My own flight to Goa would be in a plane that was coming from an unlikely town. This was told me by an athletic-looking man from Delhi, who went five times a year to Goa on business and knew the ways of the airline. This was all the information I had to hold on to; since after a certain time of night there appeared to be no airline officials anywhere, not even the young girls at the quaintly named Facilitation Desk. The advice of the man from Delhi was to watch out for the announced arrival time of the flight from the unlikely town he had told me about. If I added an hour's turn-around time to that, I would have the time of my flight to Goa.

I wasn't to give up hope, the man from Delhi said. He knew for sure that the flight wasn't abandoned. He had a cousin in the catering business – or he might have said that his in-laws did some of the catering for the airline – and he knew that his cousin or his in-laws had distinctly received orders for a plane-load of food-boxes for the Goa flight that day. This meant, he said, that the flight might even leave before midnight. This was the way of privilege in India: to know someone who knew someone who had a connection, even a tangential one, with an important organization.

All this while – the bright light of mid-afternoon giving way to late-afternoon smokiness, to dusk, to undeniable night, to a dim fluorescent evenness in the hall – an elderly American lady had been standing next to the barrow or cart with her luggage. She wasn't relaxed; she didn't lean on the cart; her aged body was rigid as if with the fear of theft and the need to protect her goods. Her eyes were now blank, as though, not through tantric excess or meditation (which she might even have come to dabble in), but only by waiting in an Indian airport hall, she had arrived at the inner calm the famous gurus had the secret of. She had been waiting since morning and would have to wait several hours more. She was now mentally so far away that even when the pretty, plump Indian Muslim woman (herself waiting since the previous evening) got up from her chair and offered it to her, it was some time before the American lady understood she was being spoken to. When she understood that she was being asked to separate herself from her cart, her old lady's face filled with alarm, and, speaking no word, she stood more rigidly in a protective posture beside her goods.

She was standing not far from the check-in counter. The air-conditioning in that corner was very cold. I hadn't felt it at first. But then I was glad I had a thickish jacket. Even with that jacket I began to feel stiff after a few hours. I gave up the chair I hadn't wanted to leave, and I joined the very slow refugee movement in the hall. I discovered a bookshop. I bought two Indian paperbacks, a book of cartoons by the cartoonist Laxman, and *Khushwant Singh's Book of Jokes*, and discovered in five minutes (what I might have guessed) that humorous books require a full life and a contented mind; that where empty time stretches on without limit, the short joke, requiring only a few seconds' attention, can be wearisome to the spirit, and can make a bad situation worse. Better simply to endure.

There was a restaurant. It was on an upper floor. It was comfortingly warm after the frigid conditions near the check-in counter. It took about half an hour, a plateful of cashew nuts I didn't need, and a pot of tea I didn't need, for me to realize that the musty, tainted smell of the restaurant was more than the smell of warmth, was the smell of an enclosed and airless room; that the air-conditioning there had broken down.

Cold downstairs, hot and dusty and choking upstairs. Outside, in the night, was the fresher, un-conditioned air; but to get at that somebody would have had to break the sealed glass.

And just as, according to some people, you can empty your mind in a meditation chamber by focussing on a single flame, so – among the becalmed travellers moving about in slow whorls in the aqueous fluorescent light, people increasingly like people in an allegory, darkly reflected in the glass that sealed them in, conversation now fled from most of them – so, thinking only of my flight number, I found that with every passing quarter of an hour I was taken more and more out of myself. I was taken far away from the man I had been earlier that day, and was becoming more like that American lady I had seen (when I had been more in command of myself), standing rigid beside her goods on a barrow: Indian architecture and air travel giving me, as it had given her, the Hindu idea of the illusion of things.

There was no escape. With every passing hour, the possibility of a return to the hotel in Bombay (would there be room?), and the hiring of a car for the 12 or 14-hour drive to Goa (where a hotel booking had to be taken up, or lost forever), became less and less a practical proposition. So between heat and cold I moved, with-drawn, living feebly on rumour.

But the man from Delhi was right. There was a plane to Goa; and when – time having ceased to matter – we swarmed and bumped aboard, there were the food-boxes of the Delhi man's story, the grey cardboard boxes (with white-bread sandwiches and a pastry of some kind and an apple from the North) that his friends or relations had prepared for the airline for that day's Goa flight. The plane felt over-used. The airline in-flight magazine was dog-eared. A piece of the overhead trim had shaken loose; every time the stewardess tapped it back in, it quivered out again. But there was Goa at the end of the very short flight. And it was interesting, getting out into the clean night air, at last, to see the name of the place spelt out in the Hindi Devanagari characters: *Go-wa*.

It was now well past midnight. We got into a cramped tourist bus. There was very little space between the seats, and the glass was tinted: it was like a continuation of the constraints of Santa Cruz. After some time we came to the Mandovi River. And there, literally, was a break in the journey. There was no bridge over the Mandovi River. There had been a bridge, a new one, until quite recently. But after standing for 10 years or so, the bridge had fallen down one day, and the Mandovi was now crossed by ferries, rough contraptions that looked as old as the century, but had been built only after the bridge had fallen down. Luggage was manhandled down from the roof of the bus on to Indian earth and then into the ferry, and then, at the other bank, out of the ferry and up on to the roof of a second bus: technology giving way (furtively, in the Indian night) to the India of many feeble hands doing simple small tasks.

And when, two days or so later, I saw the collapsed bridge in daylight, only the mighty piers standing, the linking pieces not there, it seemed to sum up the experience of that long day and night, the fracture in reality.

Nikhil, talking to me one day in Bombay of his religious faith, which was profound, had told me of his devotion, especially in times of crisis, to two figures: Sai Baba (not the current figure with the Afro hairstyle, but the original turn of-the-century teacher), and the Image of the Infant Jesus.

Nikhil came of a Hindu family, and his choice of Jesus – which at first was what I thought he meant – seemed unusual. But Nikhil had a particular image in mind, and he told me of the reason for his faith. He had once had some worrying legal problem in connection with his work. In this anxiety he had come across a leaflet about the Image of the Infant Jesus. The leaflet recommended that in times of special need prayers should be offered up to the Infant Jesus every nine hours. This was what Nikhil had begun to do. It meant getting up at a difficult time every two or three days, but it also meant that his days were built around the act of prayer. Nikhil lived with this devotion to the Image of the Infant Jesus over many weeks, and at last the legal problem that had been worrying him disappeared. Nikhil remained grateful. It was irrational, he said; he knew that; but he couldn't help it.

Nikhil must have told me about the whereabouts of this image, but I hadn't taken it in. At the hotel in Goa one morning I saw, at the entrance, a new, well-cared-for minibus with the words INFANT JESUS painted above the windscreen. I asked the driver about it. He pointed to a cream-coloured plastic figure – like a toy from a corn-flakes box – on his dashboard. The driver was a Christian Goan. He told me that the original image was in a church in Old Goa.

It was a famous image, of tested efficacy. The plastic image on the minibus dashboard was the merest symbol of the real thing. The church the minibus driver spoke of was, in fact, the famous cathedral of Old Goa, where Saint Francis Xavier was buried.

This cathedral, and the other Portuguese buildings of Old Goa, some way inland on the Mandovi River, were quite staggering in the setting. So far from Europe (six months' sailing even in the 18th century); so bright the light; the white beaches speaking more of the empty islands of the New World (but empty only after they had been 'dispeopled': they would have been populated and busy at the time of the discovery) rather than the crowded villages and towns of old India, with its tangled past. Part of that Indian past was right there, in Old Goa: in the Arch of the Viceroys, which had been created out of an arch of the – barely established – Muslim ruler the Portuguese had dispossessed. Through that arch, it was said, every new viceroy of Goa ceremonially passed when he arrived.

In another old building, now the museum, there was a gallery with portraits of all the viceroys of Goa. The portraits had been done in batches. One portrait was of Vasco da Gama. A fabulous name, but the portrait of him, as of the other viceroys, was clumsy, a kind of poor shop-sign art. The art of the colonisers didn't match their venturesomeness. This deficiency fitted in with what one knew of the brief period of Portuguese vigour; and it perhaps explained why, outside Old Goa, so little remained of Portugal, adding to the unreality of the damp-stained rococo ecclesiastical buildings of Old Goa.

Still, it was the early date of the Portuguese empire in India that continued to astonish. Every day I was reminded of it when – far from Old Goa on the Mandovi, and just with a sight of the remains of great red-stone military fortifications, all circles and straight lines, on a tropical beach – I sat down to eat in the hotel, and saw an old European print of Goa reproduced on the paper place-setting. The engraved legend gave the year of the arrival in India of the fierce and victorious Portuguese viceroy, Albuquerque: 1509. He conquered Goa the next year. Just 18 years after Columbus had discovered the islands of the New World, and before that discovery had proved its worth; nine years before Cortés started on his march to Mexico. In India itself, before the great Mogul emperor Akbar was born.

Haters of idolatry, haters of all that was not the true faith, establishers in Goa of the Inquisition and the burning of heretics, levellers of Hindu temples, the Portuguese had created in Goa something of a New-World emptiness, like the Spaniards in Mexico. They had created in India something not of India, a simplicity, something where the Indian past had been abolished. And after 450 years all they had left behind in this emptiness and simplicity was their religion, their language (without a literature), their names, a Latin-like colonial population, and this cult, from their cathedral, of the Image of the Infant Jesus.

Nearly everything else of Portugal had been swallowed up in the colonial emptiness. There had been a statue of the poet Camoens in the main square of Old Goa – Camoens, the author of the *Lusiads* (1572), the epic of the expansion of Portugal, and the true faith, overseas. But the statue was taken down (and placed in the museum) after Goa had been absorbed into independent India; and a statue of Mahatma Gandhi was put up in that 16th-century Portuguese square.

Camoens knew Goa and East Africa and Malaya and China; he was like Cervantes in Spain, an old adventurer in imperial wars. He was the first great poet of modern Europe to write of India and Indians; and he wrote out of the hard-won knowledge of a decade and a half of 16th-century wandering. There is a wonderful living sense of south-western India in his poem, not only in its account of kings and castes and religion and temples (the great Hindu kingdom of Vijayanagar, destroyed by the Muslims seven years before Camoens published his poem, is felt to be in the background), but also in dozens of smaller things: the Indian ruler, for instance, who receives the just-arrived Vasco da Gama, chews pan to the 16th-century Portuguese rhythms of Camoens's verse.

It might have been thought that Goa would have been as proud to claim Camoens as it was proud to claim Saint Francis Xavier. But the statue had been taken down; and though the hotel place-setting repetitively proclaimed the antiquity of Portuguese Goa, there was no copy of his poem in the hotel bookshop, and no one there even knew his name. India had its own priorities and values. The tourists who came in coaches to the square of Old Goa came less for the architecture (and the statue of Mahatma Gandhi) than for the Image of the Infant Jesus in the cathedral. They bought bundles of wax tapers and lit them in a cloister.

Old Goa was very old. Almost as many years separated it from the present as separated the final Roman defeat of Carthage from the fall of Rome itself. And Portugal (though it lived on in 20th-century Europe) had become the museum here. A new middle-class India had become the tourists. That was an astonishing twist in history. Portugal had arrived in 1498 and triumphed in 1509-10. Just over half a century later the great Hindu empire in the South, the empire of Vijayanagar, was defeated and physically laid waste by a combination of Muslim rulers; almost at the same time, in the North, the Mogul power was entering its time of glory. It might have seemed then that Hindu India, without the new learning and the new tools of Europe, its rulers without the idea of country or nation, without the political ideas that might have helped them to preserve their people from foreign rule – it might have seemed then that Hindu India was on the verge of extinction, something to be divided between Christian Europe and the Muslim world, and all its religious symbols and difficult theology rendered as meaningless as the Aztec gods in Mexico, or the symbolism of Hindu Angkor.

But it hadn't been like that. Through all the twists and turns of history, through all the imperial venturings in this part of the world, which that Portuguese arrival in India portended, and finally through the unlikely British presence in India, a Hindu India had grown again, more complete and unified than any India in the past.

History in Goa was simple. In the long colonial emptiness the pre-Portuguese past had ceased to matter; it was something to be picked up from books; and then the 450 years of Portuguese rule was like a single idea that anyone could carry about with him. To leave Goa, to go south and west along the narrow, winding mountain road into the state of Karnataka, was to enter India and its complicated history again.

Just as Portuguese rule had given a great simplicity to the history of Goa, so British rule gave a direction to later Indian history and made it easier to grasp. Events, at a certain stage, could be seen to be leading up to British rule; and, thereafter, events could be seen leading to the end of that rule. To read of events in India before the coming of the British is like reading of many pieces of unfinished business; it is to read of a condition of flux, of things partly done and then partly undone, matters more properly the subject of annals rather than narrative history, which works best when it deals with great things being built up or pulled down.

Historical names were on that road down through Karnataka. Bijapur was one such name. It was the name of a Muslim kingdom, established almost at the same time as the Portuguese in Goa (Goa had, in fact, been taken away from Bijapur). The name was associated in my mind not with Goa or Old Goa, but with a fine, Persian-influenced 17th-century school of miniature painting: the very name brought the faces and the postures and the special colours and costumes to my mind. But how did Bijapur fit into the history of the region? What were its dates, its boundaries? Who were its rulers and enemies? It was hard to carry all of that in the mind: I would have to look it up in the books, and even then (though I would learn that it had lasted two centuries) I would get no more than the bare bones of dates and rulers. Its achievements, after all, hadn't been that great; there was nothing in its history to catch the mind, as there was in the art (and the architecture, from my reading: a certain kind of dome). And so that name of Bijapur, and the other historical names on the road south, were like random memories in an old man's mind.

There had been too many kingdoms, too many rulers, too many changes of boundaries. The state of Karnataka itself was a new creation, post-British, post-independence, a linguistic state, answering the new pride, the new sense of self, that the nationalist movement had fostered.

The land was sacred, but it wasn't political history that made it so. Religious myths touched every part of the land outside colonial Goa. Story within story, fable within fable: that was what people saw and felt in their bones. Those were the myths, about gods and the heroes of the epics, that gave antiquity and wonder to the earth people lived on.

All the way south through Karnataka there were buses full of young men strangely dressed, in black tunics and black lower cloths. They looked like young men on a holiday excursion, but the black they wore was unsettling. When I got to Bangalore I learned that the men in black were on a pilgrimage. They were going to a shrine in the southernmost state of Kerala. The shrine honoured Ayappa, a Hindu ruler and saint of days gone by. The pilgrimage was essentially a Hindu affair; but the pilgrims to Ayappa were also required, in an unlikely way, to do honour to Vavar, an Arab and a Muslim, who had been a friend and ally of Ayappa's.

Only men could go on that pilgrimage, and for 40 days they had to live penitentially. No meat, no liquor, no activity conducive purely to pleasure; and they had to stay away from women. The last stage of the pilgrimage was a 25-mile walk up a hill to the shrine of Ayappa. There, on a particular day in January, a divine light appeared. Not everyone who went on the pilgrimage went for the light; most people walked up to the shrine on days when there was no light.

I learned all this from a young man who befriended me in Bangalore. His name was Deviah; he wrote about science for a daily newspaper. He came from a farming family; produce from the family land was still sometimes sent to him in Bangalore by the night bus. Deviah had been on the pilgrimage for the first time eight years before. He had gone when he was feeling low, and was oppressed by thoughts that he had done very little in the five years since he had left college. He thought he had been changed by the pilgrimage – the discipline of the 40 penitential days, the long walk up to the shrine, the companionship on that walk, and seeing the way people had begun to help one another. He also felt he had had professional luck afterwards; and he had gone almost every year since then. Deviah didn't believe in the divine light. He thought it might be only burning camphor, and the work of a human agency; but it didn't lessen his faith. It didn't lessen his wonder at the story of Ayappa.

This was the story Deviah told.

'Ayappa was a real figure, about 800 years ago. He was born in interesting circumstances. Raja Rajashekhar didn't have children. He and his queen did penance to Shiva and asked for the gift of a son. One day when Raja Rajashekhar was out hunting on the banks of the River Pampa – which in Kerala is as holy as the Ganges in the north: it can wash away your sins – he found a boy child with a

bell attached to its neck. The raja began to look for the parents of
the child. A *rishi*, a sage, appeared – in fact, the rishi was Lord
Shiva himself – and told the raja that the child was meant for him.
The raja, the rishi said, was to take the child to the palace and
bring him up as his son. "But whose child is he?" Raja Rajashekhar
asked. The rishi said, "You will find out on the boy's twelfth
birthday."

'So Raja Rajshekhar took the foundling to the palace and looked
after him. That palace is still there, by the way. It is not like the
maharajas' palaces you see today. It is quite a small house. The raja
looked after the child as his own, and it began to be understood
that the boy would succeeed Raja Rajashekhar when the time came.

'The raja's chief minister didn't like that. During all the years of
the raja's childlessness the chief minister had grown to believe that
his own son would one day inherit the kingdom. So, from the very
start, the chief minister hated Ayappa.

'When Ayappa was ten years old, something unexpected happened. The queen gave birth to a son. But Raja Rajashekhar had
grown so attached to Ayappa, the foundling, the gift of the gods,
that he made it clear that Ayappa was still to succeeed him on the
throne.

'The queen and chief minister now began to conspire. Their plan
was this. The queen was to pretend to fall ill. She would say she
had a headache. The palace doctor – who was also in the conspiracy
– would make a show of doing everything he knew. The queen's
headache wouldn't go away, and at last the doctor would say,
"There is only one thing that can save the queen's life. She must
be given the milk of a tigress."

'That was what the queen, the chief minister, and the doctor
plotted to do, and that was what they did. Raja Rajashekhar was
driven to despair. How could the milk of a tigress be obtained?
How could anyone milk a tigress? The queen and the chief
minister, however, knew very well what would happen. They knew
that Ayappa was valorous, and they knew that, though he was only
ten, as soon as Ayappa heard of the queen's need, he would
undertake to go out and bring back the milk of a tigress. And that
was what Ayappa said he intended to do. Raja Rajashekhar knew
it would be suicide for Ayappa to try to milk a tigress, and he
forbade the boy to leave the palace. But Ayappa used a trick and
got out, deceiving the raja in order to save the queen.'

That was how the first part of the story ended. When Deviah began the second part, he said, 'So far we've been dealing with history. Now we enter the realms of mythology. In order to understand why Ayappa was born, we have to go back 3000 years.'

And, slipping easily down the aeons, we began to travel back to the time of the gods.

Deviah said, 'Ayappa was really the son of Shiva and Vishnu.' They were both male deities, but for the purposes of the story Vishnu had to be considered to be in a female incarnation: Deviah had no trouble with these transformations. So the Ayappa who went out into the forest to get the milk of a tigress was not the mere boy the queen and the chief minister thought. He was the son of two of the gods of the Hindu trinity.

Deviah said, 'When he was wandering in the forest he came across a demon, and he killed the demon.' There was a story attached to this demon. Deviah was quite ready to break off the main narrative and give the inset story. I asked him not to.

He said, 'All right. To cut a long story short, the monster or demon Ayappa killed in the forest was a female monster, and she had been terrorizing the *devas*.' They were the gods – residing and having their councils in the place where gods reside. (Ayappa must have killed the monster by some means not available to the gods. There would have been another story here, and Deviah almost certainly knew it.) When the monster was killed, there was rejoicing among the gods. They, of course, knew what Ayappa's predicament was. 'So,' Deviah said, 'out of gratitude, the gods turned themselves into tigers and tigresses, and Ayappa came back to Raja Rajshekhar's palace riding a tiger. The tiger was believed to be Brahma.' The son of Shiva and Vishnu, riding Brahma: completing the Hindu trinity.

Deviah said, 'This forest expedition of Ayappa's had lasted two years. The queen's headache had long been cured. In fact, she had lost her headache as soon as Ayappa had left the palace to go and milk a tigress. And the day Ayappa returned to Raja Rajashkehar's palace, he was twelve years old.'

The identity of Ayappa – coming back riding a tiger – was now clear to everyone. It was what the rishi, who was Lord Shiva himself, had prophesied: that on the foundling's twelfth birthday his parentage would be known. And now all enemies, all the conspiring of queen and chief minister, vanished like morning mist, and Ayappa in due course entered into his inheritance.

The wicked chief minister, who had wanted his own son to rule, fell ill with an incurable disease – a real disease. One night Ayappa appeared to him in a dream and told him to go and wash away his sins in the River Pampa. So he did, and was cured; and then, calling Ayappa's name, the chief minister ran all the way to the temple which Ayappa had been divinely guided to build at the top of a hill. He, the chief minister or former chief minister, thus became the first of Ayappa's pilgrims.

What about the Arab in the story? He belonged to the historical Ayappa figure, Deviah said. He would have been a raider or a pirate. He had been defeated by Ayappa, and then he had been an ally. No attempt had been made to get him to give up his religion; when he died, a mosque had been built over his grave. This mosque stood at the start of the 25-mile walk up the hill to the temple of Ayappa, where the divine light flared every year on the 14th of January. All pilgrims had to pay their respects to the mosque. That was why there were many Muslims among Ayappa's pilgrims. This was something else that attracted Deviah. He liked the mixture of the two religions.

I had never, before this journey, heard of the Ayappa pilgrimage. And perhaps if I hadn't got to know Deviah I might have taken the black-clad figures for granted, part of the crowded Indian scene, and might not have thought to ask about them. The appearance of the divine light at the shrine coincided with a harvest festival in the South, and with a great religious fair in the North; the pilgrimage, the walk up the sacred hill, had perhaps been grafted on to something quite ancient, something to do with the change of the seasons. As the pilgrimage to Ayappa and Vavar, it had been going on for centuries, Deviah said; but in recent years, for some reason, and in spite of the 40 days' penance and the long walk up to the shrine, it had become very popular. A million and a quarter men were expected to be at the shrine at the time of the appearance of the divine light; and some newspapers said that during the year 25 million men might have made the pilgrimage – though, even for India, that figure seemed rather high.

Perhaps the popularity of the Ayappa cult had to do with the fact that people now had a little more money; that roads were better, travel easier, and more buses were available; that more men, young and old, could now, for the best of reasons, get away from their families for a little and become tourists. The Ayappa buses could be like tourist buses; they sometimes took the pilgrims to some of the sights on the way – though this was wrong, Deviah said, since sightseeing was a pleasure; and an Ayappa pilgrim should do nothing that could be construed as a pleasure.

People had a little more money now. It showed in the Karnataka countryside on the road south from Goa. Indian poverty was still visible, the middens, the broken-down aspect of houses and lanes. But the fields, of sugar-cane and cotton and other crops, looked rich and well-tended; the village houses were often neat, with plastered walls and red-tile roofs. There was nothing like the destitution I had seen 26 years before, when I had travelled through on a slow, stopping bus. There were none of the walking skeletons, with their deranged eyes. The agricultural revolution was a reality here; the increased supply of food showed. Hundreds of thousands of people all over India, perhaps millions of people, had worked for this for four decades, in the best way: very few of them with an idea of drama or sacrifice or mission, nearly all of them simply doing jobs.

No corner of this land was without its connection with the gods: mocking when it was a land of scarcity and famine, but more fitting now. Tractors pulled trailers loaded with cotton in big, fat, hessian-wrapped bundles, the cotton forcing its way, like a kind of strained liquid, through the brown sacking. At the same time people in village yards were engaged in biblical-looking tasks, threshing, winnowing. The land was almost beautiful, almost without pain for the beholder.

It was a kind of regeneration that could have come only slowly. There would have been false moves, failures, wasted labour. As there seemed to be even now: a forest department had been at work, planting eucalyptus trees in blocks beside the road. The planting had been successful; for mile upon mile there had been something like shade on both sides of the road, refreshing to look on. But all of that, the work of years, might have to be levelled now, the land stripped again, a fresh start made: the latest word about the eucalyptus was that it was a killer tree, greedy of moisture, desiccating rather than protecting the field it stood beside.

The road was very busy, reflecting the agricultural activity. But the trucks, though decorated with love, were overloaded in the Indian way, and were driven fast and close to one another, as though metal was unbreakable and made a man a god, and anything could be asked of an engine and a steering wheel and brakes. Between Goa and Bangalore that day 10 or 12 trucks had been wrecked, and some people had almost certainly been killed, in seven bad truck accidents. Trucks had driven off the road into ponds; trucks had driven into one another. Driver's cabs had crumpled, glass had shattered. Axles had broken, wheels had splayed at odd angles; and sometimes trucks, like vulnerable, soft-bellied animals, had turned upside down below their cruel loads, showing the wretchedness and rustiness of their metal underbellies and the smoothness of their recapped tires.

Through this old, new land we came to the town of Bangalore. It was 5000 feet above sea level, and was known in the old days for its rain and mild climate, its race course, its Simla-like civilities. Bangalore – though it had a British cantonment or garrison area – had been part of the princely state of Mysore, one of the largest princely states in British India. It had a palace. The royal family of Mysore had been known not only for their great wealth, second only to the fabulous but idle wealth of the Nizam of Hyderabad, but also for their responsibility as rulers, their pride in their state and their people. They had been known as builders of colleges and hospitals and irrigation systems, planters of roadside trees and big public gardens. Bangalore had been a place to which people retired or withdrew from the steamier India of business and work.

Since independence Bangalore had changed. The climate that had attracted retired people began to attract industry, and Bangalore had grown. It was the centre of the Indian space research programme; it was one of the more important centres of the Indian aircraft industry. Every kind of scientific institution was in Bangalore. The tree-lined roads of the garden city of the maharajas was now full of the noise and smell and fumes of three-wheelers and cars. It was no longer a city for walking in.

*

The development of Indian science and technology interested me. What sort of people had made the move, and given India an industrial revolution in 50 years?

In Bombay I had fleetingly talked to Dr Srinivasan, chairman of the Indian Atomic Energy Commission, at a social gathering at his apartment. He had told me then that his grandfather had been a *purohit*, a priest, a kind of pujari. His father, now eighty-six, and living in Bangalore, had been a schoolteacher.

Late one afternoon, a day or so after I arrived, I went to call on Dr Srinivasan's father. The old man was in a dhoti; he had a thin red caste-mark down the centre of his forehead. He was an extraordinarily handsome man, small, slender, fine in every way. He had the face of a man with a deep internal life. He showed an old passport-sized photograph of his father, Shadagopachar, the purohit. Shadagopachar was in his purohit garb, one shoulder bare. His eyes were bright, focussed on the camera, but his appearance was masked by his caste-marks: the thin red line down the middle of the forehead, and two much thicker marks going up from the eyebrows. Those thick white marks were of mud, a refined mud that was still sold in little cakes in the shops. The white mud on the forehead was the symbol of the feet of the Lord.

The family had migrated to Bangalore in the 1890s from a town 40 miles or so away. In Bangalore Shadagopachar had been taught Sanskrit and instructed in all the Vedas by his uncle. But purohits earned very little – four annas, a quarter of a rupee, for a puja – and Shadagopachar also had a job in the maharaja's government as a lower division clerk. He collected files, filed them, and bound them, and in this job he earned between 11 and 15 rupees a month. Graduates at that time earned from 25 to 30 rupees, around two pounds; but Shadagopachar was only a matriculate.

Shadagopachar wanted his son to pass the university examination because graduates could get good jobs with the government, and make much more than they could make as purohits.

'But we were all taught Sanskrit. We were all taught to do the morning and evening prayers. There was a midday prayer as well, but because we had to go to school we would do that prayer in the morning before we went to school. When I graduated, I applied for a job in the education department. This was in 1925.'

That was how the schoolteaching career had begun. But the knowledge of Sanskrit and the general religious training he had received from his father had also stayed with him. Out of that confluence – the new education, the purohit or brahmin's difficult, abstract learning, the concern with the right performance of complicated rituals, the stillness that went with the performance of some of those rituals – there had come a generation of scientists. The old Hindu Sanskrit learning – which a late 18th-century scholar-administrator like Sir William Jones had seen as archaic and profound as the Greek, and had sought, in a kind of romantic, living archaeology, to dig up from secretive, caste-bound brahmins in the North – that old learning had, 200 years later, in the most roundabout way, seeded the new.

It might have been coincidence, but the two scientists I met later in Bangalore – men of different disciplines and from different parts of the country – also had purohit or priestly grandfathers.

Subramaniam's family came from a small village which, with the post-independence reorganization of Indian states, was now in the neighbouring state of Andhra.

'My ancestors lived for a long time in that area. There is a small spot not far from the village – this spot's out in the middle of the jungle – and there is a small shrine in that spot. Our family say that the deity there is our deity.

'The first ancestor I know about is my great-great-great-grand-father. There is a strange legend about him. The legend is that there was this tiger who was making a nuisance of himself in the area. This ancestor decided to tackle it. He wrapped himself in blankets, took a machete, went to the place where the tiger attacked people, and stood there, inviting the tiger, so to speak, to attack him. The tiger did, and my ancestor hacked it to death. I heard the story as a child. It was just this story of physical valour. Perhaps exaggerated. And that's about as far back as I can go.

'My family considered themselves to be part of Mysore State, the maharaja's state. My grandmother – she survived until the 1960s – divided the world into three parts. The first part was the Raja's Land, *Raja Seemay*. That was Mysore State, where things were nice and good and pleasant, and where people who were fortunate like ourselves lived. The second part of the world was what she called *Kumpani Seemay*, the Company's Land. At the time I didn't connect the words – the Company was the East India

Company, and the word was still used by her in the 1950s. The Company's Land was part of India, but it wasn't as nice as the Raja's Land. It was true that some of our relatives lived in the Company's Land, but you had to have sympathy for people who lived there. Beyond these two areas was the rest of the world. This way of thinking was something that was just natural to my grandmother.

'We are a family of brahmins. In a way we are priestly, but my grandfather was not a priest. He was a small landowner, and he was also a minor government official. As a village official he would have been paid 10 rupees, perhaps five rupees. The village would have considered him comfortable, but not rich. He was comfortable socially rather than economically. There were many in the village richer than him.

'My grandfather realized that education in English was essential, and he made sure his son got that education. And so my father, who was born in the 1900s, was the first man in our family who went to schools where English was the medium. My father just applied to a school and got in. Nowadays it's a rat-race to get your child into schools; the demand is great. But then my father just applied. He probably walked to school. Our village didn't have a high school. Many people walked long distances to school. I myself – and this was in the 1940s – walked several miles to school.

'I don't know what led my father to science. I personally feel that the scientific tradition is not alien to India. I think that science comes naturally to Indians. Many Indians like to think of themselves as having a tradition of pursuing knowledge, and science is knowledge as it was understood by Bhaskara, one of our old or ancient scientists. Today in India you can buy Bhaskara's treatise on astronomy of 600 or 700 AD, and there is extant a famous medical treatise of about the same time. I must make it clear that I don't for a moment believe all these other people who run around saying that everything – atom bombs, rockets, aeroplanes – was invented by ancient Indians.

'But Indian knowledge became out of date. The measure of that is that what Newton wrote in 1660 was not understood or appreciated in India until the middle of the 19th century. On the other hand, in 1000 AD, and for a century or two after that, there was a knowledge that India had which would have surprised Europe. Especially in mathematics. In 1000 AD Indians were confident in their knowledge. We have evidence for that. But by 1800 that confidence had vanished. Raja Ram Mohun Roy was the first man who publicly acknowledged that the fact of the matter was that there were many things we knew nothing about.'

Ram Mohun Roy came from Bengal. He campaigned against the burning of widows on their husbands' funeral pyres. He sought, more generally, to purify Hinduism, and to bring the new learning of Europe to India. He was India's first modern reformer, and his dates are astonishing: he was born about 1772, and died, during a mission to England, in 1833.

I told Subramaniam what I had read somewhere about the Mogul emperor Jehangir (who succeeded the great Akbar, ruled from 1605 to 1625, and loved the arts): Jehangir had scoffed at the notion of a New World on the other side of the Atlantic.

Subramaniam said, 'And Aurangzeb' – ruling from 1650 to 1700, a period of rapid Mogul decay – 'referred to England with contempt. He said it was a tiny island, its king like a minor raja in India. This was late in the 17th century.

'In my own family that realization – that our knowledge was out of date – came to my grandfather. But it was too late for him to do anything about it. He was born in the 1880s and died when he was fifty-five. But, as I said, he was determined that his son should have the new education.

'After high school, my father came to Bangalore, to the university. And then he wanted to do research. At that time in India one of the biggest names in research was Meghnad Saha, a Bengali. He was professor of physics at Allahabad. He had made a name for himself a few years earlier with a paper that showed how ionization was related to temperature. This paper of Saha's was in 1922, and his formula, Saha's formula, is still the basis for understanding the composition of the stars. Saha, incidentally, was a great nationalist.

'My father decided he would like to go and work with Saha. And he actually did. For a man who was a first-generation college student it would have been a bit of an adventure for him. I think my father would have been financially supported in Allahabad by his father and father-in-law. My father kept a journal in Allahabad, and one of my projects is to look at that journal.'

The science, the venturesomeness, and then the journal: the longing for new experience, and then the wish to put order into that experience – that was impressive, in a man not long out of a village.

Subramaniam, with his own wish to categorize and define, said, 'I think it's a demonstration of the two points I've made. The first is that the tradition of science is not new. And the second is that I don't think that in my father's mind there was any feeling that he was doing something entirely alien when he was doing science. I think a feeling for that – science and mathematics – was central to many Indian minds.

'My father came back and taught physics in high schools in Bangalore and in other places in Mysore State. Mysore State was in many ways advanced. In a quiet way. The maharajas, and the ministers they had, were quite often in a peculiar way liberal and forward-looking. One side of them was conservative, but there was another side which looked to the future. Have you heard of Visweswaraiah? He was an engineer who was appointed *diwan* or chief minister in 1910 or thereabouts. He was responsible for many projects in the state which made it the model state in the country. Mr Gandhi, in the 1930s, when he came to Mysore, said it was *Rama rajya*.'

It was something many people in Bangalore had mentioned to me. *Rama rajya*, Rama's rule or kingdom – it was the highest Hindu praise: Rama the hero of one of the two great Hindu epics, the embodiment of goodness, universally loved, the man who in any situation could be relied upon to do the right thing, the religious thing, the wise thing, a figure at once human and divine: to be ruled by Rama's law was to know bliss.

Subramaniam said, 'There was a tradition in the state of benevolent rule. And Visweswaraiah was ahead of his time. He made a five-year plan in the 1920s or 30s. The same man set up the University of Mysore. And Mysore was the first state where electric power was available. The rulers had a lot of local pride.

'My father settled in Bangalore, and then my grandfather also came here. We grew up in an Indian joint family, a large family. My grandfather was a man who took his religious life seriously. He headed his family, and he did his pujas. I don't think he was doing anything else at that time. He died in the latter part of the 1930s.

'The feeling grew in my father that there might be conflicts between the science he knew and practised, and the way he lived. It did produce conflicts in the house, especially in a house which was very religious, as my grandfather's house was. My father had the feeling that many things we were doing didn't make sense. Rituals, for example. Caste barriers.

'He tried to reconcile the two. He developed a certain outlook of his own – Hindu or brahminical, as he saw it, rooted in a certain respect for ancient Indian scholarship and philosophy. But it tried to be free of all the things he associated with prejudice. There was one thing he did – at that time it was an improper thing to do, and not so minor. All brahmin children go through an initiation ceremony – it's a serious affair, and usually it's done when the boy is young, six, seven, eight. My father had a very good friend, not a brahmin, and he insisted that his friend join in this function that was being performed for his own child – me, as a matter of fact. That raised eyebrows. This was in the 1940s. But my father was very clear in his mind about this matter.

'About rituals, I think my father went through a stage when he rejected them, and then finally he accepted them in a certain modified form. So, in his later years, he used to perform puja, but in a very unobtrusive way. I remember arguing with him about the puja he performed, and he said it was sufficient that it gave him a certain mental peace and privacy for a part of the day. He can be described without paradox as a man who was conservative in one way and liberal in another. In matters of caste, etc., he was liberal. But he was not westernized at all.'

I asked Subramaniam, 'Do you perform pujas?'

'I don't perform pujas. But I still have a feeling for the small shrine in the jungle, with the family deity.'

'How does a family get a deity like that?'

'A family deity is something given to you. It might have been adopted at some stage. Some event fixed it. Some teacher perhaps. It may be that a person asks a favour of some temple and is granted the favour, and becomes a follower of a deity of that temple.

'My father remained a teacher almost all his life. After he retired as a teacher he worked in a mental-health institute, mainly helping with the electronics on an electro-encephalogram, to measure "brain waves". And, by the way, one of the bits of research they did was on a sadhu. They put electrodes all over his head and tried to find out how these brain waves were behaving when he went into a trance. They did find that he was in fact very calm.

'My father spent the last 20 years of his life writing books on science in the local language. He saw that that was the way things were going to be changed – that you speak of science in the language of the people, and not in English. Those books were pretty good. Some very good. He wrote on energy long before energy-conservation became a topic. He wrote on astro-physics. He wrote a little book about sound. This talked about the physics of sound, and then it tried to tell the reader how this physics was related to the music he heard, the local music. This book was written in the 1940s. It's a small book. It used to be sold for two annas.' One-eighth of a rupee, less than a penny.

'How did you think of yourself when you were growing up? Poor? All right?'

'I felt we were middle class.' Middle class in the Indian way, meaning not poor, but with a suggestion of simplicity and making do, not middle class in the European or American way. 'Not rich. A strained middle-class house. There was never money to spare. Never. I would say that this was something which was taken as part of life, not something we went around thinking about all the time. There are certain advantages in the big joint families: things are taken care of. It's like a little state: you have friends, you carry on.

'The fact that my father had done science influenced me. And my father had literary friends, because he had written books in the local language. Quite often there would be arguments in the house about science, religion, literature. It was a very educated atmosphere, very cultured, very stimulating. The background was simple only in an economical sense. Not at all in a cultural sense. And this is quite important in an old country like India.'

I understood what he meant. It was what I felt – in a lesser or different way – about my own Indian family background in far-off Trinidad. I felt that the physical conditions of our life, often poor conditions, told only half the story: that the remnants of the old civilization we possessed gave the in-between colonial generations a second scheme of reverences and ambitions, and that this equipped us for the outside world better than might have seemed likely. But I also recalled something else: the shoddiness of the Indian books we bought, sometimes out of piety towards the ancestral land. I remembered the poor paper, the broken type, the oily ink, the sloping lines, the uneven margins, the rusting metal staples. The idea of India was part of our strength, and it received part of our piety; yet there was this other idea of the Indian reality, of poor goods, of poor machines poorly used.

Subramaniam said, 'If I go back to the time the British were here – and my recollections are vague: I was born in the 40s – we saw then that things made in England or Europe – there was little of U.S. goods – we saw them as good things. We saw Indian things as not so good quality. I think that people of my father's generation must have had a remarkable mental or intellectual strength to preserve their souls in the middle of all this Indian shoddiness. People knew that things were not very good. But they had some inspiration they drew from a real or imagined greatness. They had some innate feelings of old cultural strength, which preserved them. So you would see people admiring things from Britain, but at the same time we were going to say, "That's great, but we're not going to capitulate to that."'

'Didn't it give you some doubts about the possibility of an Indian industrial revolution, and the capacity of Indians to manufacture things that would feel finished and real?'

'I never had any doubt about that. Never. We saw that as a matter not of whether, but when. We complained that it was too slow.'

'You don't think the shoddiness had a psychological effect on people?'

'I felt a little ashamed. There was certainly a feeling that a lot of businessmen were making money without making quality goods, and that gave a feeling of ill-gotten wealth. One looked forward to a pretty distant future when things wouldn't be so. We saw that the answer was to have a strong science in the country. My own feeling was compounded of shame, ignorance and hope. I think these attitudes would not have been widely shared. On the hope there would have been widely different views.

'Quite a few Indians at that time felt that the British Raj would last forever – not a large number, but quite a few. One of my most vivid recollections was of an argument between my father and my mother's father. He was a doctor.'

'A doctor!'

'As I told you, the background was simple only in an economic sense. The argument – during the war – was about what the future might be. My grandfather, the doctor, thought that Europe, the West, was very powerful, and that it was almost impossible for

India to get rid of the British. And even if the British lost the war, the Germans would be there. So he saw the future as still dominated by the West for a considerable time. And he also thought that Indians were incapable of taking care of the country – running it, ruling it.'

That sent me back to another set of early feelings about my ancestral culture. In Trinidad, in the late 30s and early 40s, I used to see poor Indian people sleeping in the squares of Port of Spain. These people were peasant emigrants from India; they had served out their indentures 20 years or so before, had not been given their passages back to India, and had then become destitute, abandoned by everybody. In the colonial city they were further isolated by their language; and they were to live on the streets until they died out. The idea came to me, when I was quite young, seeing those destitutes, that we were people with no one to appeal to. We had been transported out of the abjectness of India, and were without representation. The idea of the external enemy wasn't enough to explain what had happened to us. I found myself at an early age looking inwards, and wondering whether the culture – the difficult but personal religion, the taboos, the social ideas – which in one way supported and enriched some of us, and gave us solidity, wasn't perhaps the very thing that had exposed us to defeat.

Subramaniam said, 'I felt that, but in a different way from you. The foreigner was here. The country had become slaves and had been plundered. But that wasn't just because of the culture. It was because over the centuries we had become weak and stagnant.'

He began to talk of the pattern of Indian history.

'I go back to Alberuni's comments about the Hindus.' Alberuni, the Arab historian of about 1000 AD at the court of Ghazni, in what is today Afghanistan. Subramaniam had mentioned Alberuni at the beginning of our talk. Alberuni's book was one of the sources for what was known about ancient Hindu science and learning; but Alberuni had also written some famous words about Hindu arrogance in that learning.

'We became complacent. A system had been evolved here whereby the preservation of the country's culture and its social organization was independent of the military masters who ruled the country. The country was run on principles that assumed that kings would change, that wars would be fought, but that society would go on, pretty much undisturbed by those events.

'Up to a point that is why Hindus are a-historical. If you look at what Indian culture remembers – we preserve our books on mathematics, astronomy, grammar. We preserve Bhaskara and Charaka.' Seventh-century scientists. 'Among the things which are preserved are not the names of kings or their battles – that is not part of our tradition. We know Bhaskara and Shankaracharya.' Shankaracharya, a ninth-century philosopher who travelled all over India, revitalized Hindu philosophy, set up religious foundations (which still exist) in certain places, and is thought to have died at the age of thirty-two. 'But if you ask, "Who ruled this part of the country in 1700?" people wouldn't know, and basically they wouldn't care.

'That, however, has been the weakness of the country, and it has brought on us military defeat. But it changed with the British. When the British came here, it slowly became clear to Indians that these political and military defeats were things they couldn't ignore. What in other places would have been a natural reaction, a natural assumption, in India had to be an intellectual conclusion. It took a long time. The realization came very late, in the 19th century.

'It was a widely shared feeling. That is why people went to English schools. I went to an English-medium school. But it was a very Indian school. It was run by people who were orthodox Hindus, but convinced that we had to learn English, science, technology. It was very stimulating. I remember lots of disagreement among my teachers about the future. Even Gandhi was a subject of controversy. Looking back on it, I am astonished that there were some people there, teachers, maybe half a dozen – and their wages would have been very low – who were actually driven by the desire to get people to learn. You got a feeling of mission. I remember one of my teachers who, for no reason I can imagine now, took a great deal of interest in me, gave me a book on the lives of great scientists, and did so out of his own pocket.'

'Was he a brahmin?'

'He was a brahmin. It was a brahmin-inspired school.'

I thought of the brahmin contribution to the independence movement, and the regenerative social ideas that had come with that movement. I thought of the brahmin contribution afterwards to science.

I said, 'So the brahmins have in a way paid their debt back?'

'I'm not sure they've paid it back yet. They're responsible still for many things on our social landscape.' Subramaniam broke off here, to continue on a related theme. 'A great social revolution took place in this state after independence, and it was as a consequence of independence. The social revolution was that the identity of the politically powerful classes changed in a few years. It was a bloodless revolution, but it was a revolution, though people outside India don't know about it. Before independence, the administration in the state was in the hands of brahmins. A few years after independence, power changed hands – and I mean the way power changed hands in other parts of the world. The people who now sit in the offices are of a different social class.

'The prime minister's science adviser was saying the other day that the trouble with Indian science is that it is too much a brahmin science, and that we needed a more lower-caste kind of science. But the fact that so many brahmins are in science is only a development of history.'

'Do you feel threatened?'

'No doubt about it. Entrance to universities is not based strictly on merit. There are quotas for different classes. Many brahmins feel now that even education has become difficult. There are the quotas, and private colleges are expensive. It may partly be responsible for the large number of Indian professionals abroad.'

My thoughts, as I had driven down from Goa, through the untidy but energetic towns, full of the signs of growth, and then through the well-tilled fields at harvest time, had been of the Indian and, more specifically, Hindu awakening. If Subramaniam was right, there was a hidden irony in that awakening: that the group or caste who had contributed so much to that awakening should now find itself under threat.

Education and ambition by themselves would have taken people nowhere without an expanding economy. Perhaps, even, the expanding economy explained the shift in Indian education. For Pravas, an engineer, the expansion had started some time before independence, when the old British emphasis on law and order (especially after the Indian Mutiny of 1857) had been modified by the idea of development.

'Many people were sucked into that process. There was an explosive growth in India around 1930. It built momentum around 1947, had a big growth thereafter, and is now slowing down. In

1962, when I was thinking of universities and a career, I had a choice of professions and institutions. People today have to struggle hard. But these things have a positive side.

'The average aspiration of the Indian is to grow under a shadow – and this is all right as long as someone else throws the shadow. In concrete terms, this means you look for employment, you try to get into structures created by other people. That's how we got governed in the first place. The attitude is: "As long as the local environment is the same, I don't care who is running things at the top." I read something in a paper some time ago. It was to the effect that, before the British came to India, the Indians were like bees in a garden. And that's fine, as long as someone else looked after the garden. And then of course the Britishers became both the owners of the garden and the gardeners, the *malis* – with those other guys, the bees, going happily from flower to flower.'

'What about the positive side of the struggle today?'

'That shadow area I talked about is becoming congested now. It is forcing people to go out on their own. It is forcing them to be entrepreneurial.'

Pravas came from far away, from the east of the country. His grandfather had been a priest, and his father entered government service as a clerk.

'It is almost the standard Indian success story. My father would have got into the service in the mid-40s, the time at which the administration was just beginning to pick up. There was still not a lot of science and industry, or anything like that. But the structure was expanding. This was a precursor of development. When the real development came, there was non-traditional administration. Traditional administration would need police, soldiers, clerks and lawyers. Non-traditional administration needed industrialists, artisans, engineers, doctors, scientists, entrepreneurs. Because my father entered the service at the precursor stage, he wasn't a scientist.'

'What sort of things did your father read?'

'He retained quite a lot of tradition. He chanted *mantras*. My grandfather was a good old classical ritualistic purohit, according to what I've heard. Performing the rituals was his profession. Whereas with my father, if you want to trace the transition, the mantras were chanted out of familiarity, reverence, a way of expressing your gratitude to God – you had these mantras reverberating in your head since childhood. I make no difference between that and the young man today in a video or audio surrounding who chants, formally and informally, Hindi film songs.

'My father is taller than I, and he makes a good sight sitting there cross-legged, chanting, with his back straight. I think the posture is beautiful. My father is seventy-six, and his back is still straight. But with my father the chanting of the mantras has been, in quotes, "degraded" from a livelihood to pleasure. Oral pleasure, if you like; nostalgia; a protection against fears. A gamut of feeling – all this I call pleasure, since it's done out of volition.

'We lived in a small princely state in the east. My grandfather was one of the priests of the royal family. Not really a big king: it was a feudal kingdom of maybe 100 or 200 square miles.'

A small princely state in the east, a priest serving the ruling family. I said, 'That is really old India.'

Pravas said, 'The degree of cultural change that I have personally gone through and digested would break a person elsewhere. When I was a child, and we went to visit my ancestral place, we would go in bullock carts – it was the only mode. Or walk. That was as recently as 1960. You wouldn't have what we think of as a bathroom. You would go down to the river.'

'Were you aware of hardship?'

'At the time it seemed normal. Everybody did that in the village. And for years, going back to the village after I had left it, going back for a day or so, it was more like a picnic. Before you recognized you were deprived, you were out.

'Most of the kings in those days had a policy of encouraging a certain amount of intellectualism. It was a cause for pride. In direct terms that meant they made sure that their people, the priestly caste, the intellectuals, didn't have to depend on other people for their security. So they gave a piece of land to the purohits. A gift of land to a purohit or anybody else couldn't be taken back. It was a gift in perpetuity. It would have been considered a sin of the lowest order to recover a gift. In that kingdom there were between five to 10 priestly families. The religious rituals were very specialized. Some purohits did certain things, and other purohits other things.'

'They were privileged people?'

'Yes and no. The piece of land wasn't much. It was a subsistence piece. It was only to see that the person didn't die. It was something to fall back on, but nothing more than that. The purohits didn't have a lot of clothes. They had two dhotis or something like that. Compared to the tradesmen, people selling grain or timber or oilseeds or oil, they would be poor. Compared to the beggars, they were well off.'

'So the brahmins were kept by the kings in an ambiguous position?'

'If you look at it from the economical point of view, then of course it looks incongruous. But it had a logic of its own. The brahmins had status and royal protection. The king would deal severely with any act of aggression against the priests. And the kings would encourage intellectual exchanges. Debates, chanting, *yagnas* or big pujas, with brahmins from other kingdoms as well, perhaps – everybody competing, or co-operating in a competitive sense, to show their own excellence. Sometimes you would have a thousand brahmins sitting and chanting, but with each man keeping an ear for who was singing well or badly. It's precisely what happens at scientific or intellectual conferences today.

'The internal factor is that the priestly community was born and brought up with the psychology that they didn't expect more. It's so much part of the internal system that it's gone down to the folk level. The Lord Vishnu has two wives – Lakshmi, the goddess of wealth, and Saraswati, the goddess of wisdom. The two wives would naturally be at loggerheads – a depiction of the fact that the intellectual life seldom goes with wealth: you have to choose one of them. So, by a combination of circumstances, this priestly class didn't look for riches, and they wouldn't be given riches. A perfect matching of interests.

'In my father's life the balance was of a different kind. He didn't have an assured security, like my grandfather. He had to work to provide for his family. His life was half ritual, half the struggle for survival. The balance was between the two.

'In certain communities you are supported by the scaffolding of the society. If you are in a merchant caste, dealing in oilseeds or cotton straw, and you wish to graduate to dealing in radios, the scaffolding is the same. You only change the commodity. There is a group movement there. Whereas, in a case like my father's, he wasn't moving with the society – the society wasn't moving in a coordinated way. Quite a lot of young men were doing the same thing at that time, but all of them were doing it individually. Not only did my father have the difficulty of clearing the way, but every time he moved back, to my grandfather's house, there would have been conflict. It would have been like moving between a hot and a cold room.'

'What sort of conflict?'

'In the older society, you would keep your purity both genetically and externally. You would only marry certain people, and you wouldn't have contacts beyond a certain point with people of a lower caste. You wouldn't be able to eat food cooked by someone of a lower caste. Eating was considered a sacred activity. Food was looked upon as a sacrifice to the gastric juices. There were rigid prescriptions about the time you could eat, in what direction you faced while eating, who served, and how much you ate. Food was dissected to the last detail. Different classes of people ate different amounts. For instance, in the scriptures it is prescribed that for intellectuals doing very little physical work the right amount of food would be the rice cooked from a handful of rice grains held in the fist.

'Hinduism is a trinity-based religion – there are three options for everything. So food was of three kinds – *sattvik*, *rajasik*, *tamasik*. Sattvik foods encouraged intellectual pursuits, clarity of mind, purer thoughts. Sattvik foods were very light – most grains, a certain amount of clarified butter, the lighter vegetables. Rajasik food is work-oriented.'

(From Deviah I later had a more comprehensive list of sattvik foods: leafy greens, milk, curds, butter, rice, wheat, most sprouts, most pulses (except a kind of dal), sweet potatoes (but not potatoes), fruit. From Deviah I also learned that rajasik food was more than work-oriented. Rajasik food encouraged both valour and passion, and Deviah gave this list: *urad* dal, meat, wine, spices (true brahmins don't get on with spices). As for tamasik food – which Pravas with apparently brahminical scruple didn't go into (and about which, fearing the worst, I didn't press him, not wanting him to go off on this detour) – Deviah said it encouraged sloth. Strangely, though, the tamasik list that Deviah gave seemed quite subtle, with some elements of the rajasik; and some of its vegetables seemed to be light enough for the sattvik diet. This was Deviah's tamasik list: onion, garlic, cabbage, carrot, aubergine, potatoes, urad dal, meat. Urad dal and meat were both on the rajasik list.)

Pravas said, 'The sattvik is mind-oriented. Such people were expected to do what they did because it should be done, and not because you get a reward. Such people did what they did out of an internal motivation. Brahmins were identified with the sattvik tendency. Therefore they couldn't eat certain foods.

'The whole thing was ritualized in every way. For example, if your father was alive, you shouldn't face south when you ate. This wasn't an all-India prohibition, but it was more than local. So it was a serious matter if the shadow of a lower-caste person fell on your food. If it happened while you were eating, that was that. You stopped eating. The food became impure. And I forgot: nobody should touch you while you were eating, and you had to eat in a certain posture. Some people were so "orthodox", in inverted commas, they couldn't even hear the voice of a lower-caste person while they ate. These people ate deep within their houses.'

'Would they get angry if they had to stop eating because of the shadow or the voice?'

Pravas said with a smile, 'Brahmins are not supposed to get enraged. They would just stop eating. Rage is not considered a brahminical quality. Though a large number of the brahmins I know, 80 per cent, say, are very short-tempered.

'So my father moved between these hot and cold rooms, as I've called them. It was a perpetual struggle for him. He had to face a lot of questioning when he went back to my grandfather's. Had he been eating food cooked by non-brahmins? Or wearing the right kind of dress? That was important in those days. My grandfather never wore long trousers; he wore the dhoti. My father wore half and half – dhoti and trousers. But the food business wasn't a joke for them. In that value system it was sacrilege to break any of the rules.

'Because of his background my father was philosophically oriented. Even within that his reading was different from my grandfather's. My grandfather would practise the hard-core Sanskrit, the original mantras as written in the Vedas or Puranas. It is the hallmark of ritualism that you don't necessarily understand the deeper meanings of everything you do, and my grandfather didn't necessarily understand what he chanted. Ritualism is perhaps, though not very crudely, a show-act.

'My father wasn't a performer; he didn't have that pressure. So he tried to understand what he read. He read a lot of interpretations by newer philosophers. This led him to read in many languages. He read modern philosophical works in Bengali, and he read in English. I grew up with volumes and volumes of his books in Devanagari and English. He made relatively small forays into other topics. The core was philosophical.

'And there was something else. In addition to the old Puranic values, my father had the diffusion from nationalistic values, essentially Gandhian. Gandhianism was almost a mass hysteria in India, but of a healthy kind. It was the good old values, but packaged in a modern-looking way, very mass-based. The old values looked intellectual and were intellectual, and therefore maintained a distance from the masses. Gandhi found a way of making old truths appear simple. And I grew up with quite a few of those Gandhian slogans. "Work more, talk less."

'In my house the continuity of the brahminic value system remained, and then I also made my own change from an old world to a new world, from a hot room to a cold room. But this time the change was different. Nobody asked me, "Why are you wearing long pants?" Or, "Did you eat food cooked by a brahmin?" But, like my father in his government job, I didn't have a scaffolding. I had, so to speak, to break down the door myself.'

'Why did you go in for science?'

'There's the milieu and the current value system. The third factor is a sense of mystery.'

'Mystery?'

'It's one of the strongest motivating forces. All religions are replete with miracles. Mystery attracts, and science has that mystery. I felt that mystery, subconsciously. Put two chemicals and the colour changes – that's the simplest mystery. Or make a machine like an electric fan which runs apparently without any motive force.

'I have made one more level of transformation than my father did from his father's time. I am more liberal in outlook than my father. I've probably become more questioning, because of what we may call "science". I'm less knowledgeable about rituals. My

167

father got a part of what his father had, and I have only a part of the rituals my father had.

'I grew up in my intimate family surroundings up to the age of fifteen or sixteen. That's the time you pick up the rituals, because you are not allowed to perform certain rituals before a certain time. For example, there are some rituals that only married men can do. But at that age I went away from home, going back only for a few days a year. So I missed a lot of the ritual side. And now I have only half the faith in it.

'I don't do it, but I have a nostalgia for it. My roots are in it. It is not alien to me. If someone says to me that I shouldn't eat rajasik food – eggs or something – I don't find it strange. I understand, unlike a modern nutritionist. And, in the philosophy line, I have done more of what my father did. I diversified, even more than him, into other schools of Indian philosophy and schools of other philosophies. My father had gone from the basic Vedic to the broader Indian philosophy. I have gone from that to a more global approach.'

I said, 'With your scholarly approach, you probably actually know more about Hinduism than your grandfather.'

Pravas said, 'Probably I can articulate it better in a Western sense, but I cannot say I know more than my grandfather.

'Change is a continuous process. You can discern a change only once in a generation. Because once you discern it, you are already there. So in these last 50 years I can discern only two changes, but they are large because a continuing process is being focussed at two or three points. The next big change will come with my son. There are spans of transition. There are much bigger spans with the succeeding generations.

'My son will go through a very large change in circumstances in many ways. In the family, in the school surroundings, in the job market, everywhere. I grew up in a half ritualistic background. My son will have no ritualistic background. But if my son loses the rituals even further, he could still be rooted locally, within his peer group. There will be many like him. Society is moving that way.

'The food restrictions and so on that I talked about are known to some, but not known to most in my generation. They don't know that such things existed and exist. And yet they are perfectly at balance in the local surroundings. If you get too attached to your roots in the old sense, you might actually become unrooted, fossilized. At least in form, at least in style, you must get into the new stream, get the new roots. More of India is doing that. Style becomes substance in one generation. Things that one starts to do because other people are doing it – like wearing long pants, in my father's case – become natural for the next generation.'

I thought that the changes he was talking about might have been in some way like the changes that had come a generation or two earlier to the Indian community in Trinidad, the peasant India that my grandfathers had taken with them, an apparently complete world, with language and rituals and social organization: an India that had, in its New-World setting, even during my childhood, begun to disintegrate: first the language going, then the reverence for the rituals and the need for them (the rituals going on long after they had ceased to be understood), leaving only a group sense, a knowledge of family and clan, and an idea of India in the background, an idea of India quite different (more historical, more political) from the India that had appeared to come with one's ancestors.

Pravas said, 'For you the change was not subversive.'

The word was arresting.

He said, 'The change wasn't from within. It was external. Here change is gradual. It's happening all around me – in my father, my brother, everybody. I cannot distinguish any longer what is alien.'

And (extending what Pravas said) there was a further, and fundamental, difference between the new generations in India and our immigrant community far away. For people of that community, separated from the Indian earth, Hindu theology had become difficult (as it had become difficult for people of formerly Hinduized areas of south-east Asia); the faith had then been half possessed by many, abandoned by many. It had been part of a more general cultural loss, which had left many with no strong idea of who they were. That wouldn't happen in India, however much ritualism was left behind, and however much the externals changed.

Pravas said, 'There will remain a few primordial principles. People will lose all the details about individual behaviour – eating and sleeping and so on. All these things will go away. But in the group memory some streams will remain perennial. Faith and its expression is one of those primordial streams, though the details may get blurred.

'Recently there has been on TV the serials of the epics, the *Ramayana* and the *Mahabharata*. Most of the people on the streets of Bangalore haven't actually read those epics. They haven't read them in the original or in an English version or in any version. They take them for granted; they're there. They would have known the main characters and the broad theme. They wouldn't have known the details; they wouldn't know the inside characters. But the TV serials were an instant success.'

And now, for Pravas, there were all the frustrations of modern Indian life. As he described them, they were like the frustrations of the visitor: the difficulty of travel by air or train or road; the crowded, dangerous city streets; the poisonous fumes; the difficulty of doing simple things, the difficulty of arranging the physical details of day-to-day living, which the industrial revolution was meant, after all, to simplify.

Pravas said, 'Sometimes even I despair. And it is perhaps only something in my make-up that stops me going to the mafia.' To straighten people out, to get things done. 'There are no rules in the Indian streets.' That wasn't a simple or frivolous matter. Pravas rode a motor-scooter; he arrived always, when he came to see me, like a kind of spaceman, with his big helmet. 'You feel a little bit like being in a jungle, and this can transfer to a larger view of things. It can, and does. It actually translates into a loss of productivity. I am a far less productive person than I ought to be. A lot of energy goes into these things, those traffic jams, that chaos. Friction in society is like friction in the machine.'

I thought of his grandfather, one of the five or 10 priests of the king of a small state in the east. He lived on very little; he had only his subsistence piece of land to keep him from absolute want, if the king withdrew his favour. He had no other skill – the little state at that time didn't require many skills. That was an arbitrary world, where change could come suddenly and overwhelmingly to a man. It was like the India which had been overrun again and again by this army and that; it was the India of unfinished monuments, of energy going to waste, creating an impression of randomness. That was a jungle, too. Did Pravas's grandfather live with something like that idea?

'I never knew my grandfather. He died when my father was twelve or thirteen. I have no memory of his world, but I can reconstruct it. He was part of a static society. He was not different from his father or grandfather. So, even if there was friction, he wouldn't discover it, because he didn't have the bike.'

The bike – Pravas had been talking of the Bangalore traffic and his own motor-scooter. I liked the metaphor: it made the static past understandable.

I began to wonder whether many of the frustrations Pravas spoke about were not rooted in the past, whether they hadn't been created by the smallness of Indian expectations, the almost pious idea – like the idea behind Gandhian homespun – that a country so poor needed very little. I wondered whether there wasn't deep in India even now a psychology of shoddiness, an extension of the idea of holy poverty, the old religious-political feeling that it was wrong, wasteful, and provoking to the gods (and the ruler) to get above oneself. And I asked Pravas, as I had asked Subramaniam, about the psychological effects on him, as he was growing up, of the shoddiness of Indian manufactured goods.

He said, 'I didn't have much to compare with when I was growing up. I might have seen my grandfather's watch, but I never saw an Indian watch and had nothing to compare. So I didn't feel bad. I didn't grow up with too many imported goods. The things we used were made locally, or we simply didn't have them. We used a lot of the products of Indian artisanship – metal plates, not china, and metal plates have been made for thousands of years. Textiles had been made long before I was born. So the basic needs were met by local goods. When you are small, besides, your needs are very small.'

About the shoddiness of Indian goods he saw now he was philosophical. 'Compared with contemporary goods elsewhere, they are bad. Compared with the nothing we had 50 years ago, it is something. It only means we have started late. Japanese goods 50 years ago were shoddy.'

The new world was so new: it had begun for some people with their grandfathers, and for most with their fathers. And people had travelled so far so fast that many active people had a success story to tell, their own sometimes, or that of someone in their family.

I had got to know Kala. She was of Tamil brahmin origins. She did the publicity for a big organization. She was in her twenties, and unmarried. She was diligent and methodical; she had a reputation as a worker. She was grave, self-possessed, educated. But I didn't know enough of India, and especially of that brahmin South from which she came, to guess at her background.

And then, at lunch one day, speaking of it as of a fairy story, she said that her grandfather had started from nothing, had been so poor as a child that he had studied by the light of street lamps.

(Hadn't that been said of many other people? Hadn't there been another very poor boy somewhere – without paper or pencil or slate – who had had to work out sums on the back of a shovel with a piece of charcoal? I thought of Kala's story as a piece of romance. And then, some weeks later, in a small brahmin 'colony' in Madras, I saw a small boy one evening actually sitting with a book below a street lamp. The lamp was too dim to read by, but the brahmin boy was there cross-legged with his book, acting out ambition and struggle and self-denial, doing the virtuous thing he and his parents had heard about.)

I asked Kala the name of this ancestor. It was the name of a princely-state administrator; it was a name famous in pre-independence India. The boy who had studied by the street lamps had risen to power and wealth.

From Kala's manner, I might have expected someone like that grandfather in her background. What was unexpected – and yet a little thought would have shown that it was in keeping with that brahminical background – was that, on Kala's mother's side, there was a *sanyasi* ancestor, an ascetic, someone who had renounced the world to go and meditate on the river-steps or ghats of Banaras, among the pyres and temples beside the Ganges.

Such strands of old India did Kala carry in her make-up. She knew she was part of the movement out of old India that Pravas had spoken about; but she didn't know it in the same analytical way. When Kala meditated on her family past, as she did with something like obsession, her thoughts were of her mother, who had been caught by that movement forward, had been trapped between the generations, and had had her life distorted.

Kala took the story about her grandfather reading under the street lights seriously. She had heard the story when she was nine or ten from her mother, and then later on in more detail from her grandfather himself. She said, in her grave way, 'When there is a power failure, and the lights go off, and one becomes irritated, then I think of this man, this boy, who didn't have lights at all in his house.' It was probably so. 'This was in Madras in the early 1900s. His parents had sent him to his grandmother's house in Madras to live.' And though Kala didn't say, I thought that this would have been part of the brahmin migration to the cities that occurred in so many people's stories. In Madras, Kala's grandfather lived in a brahmin area near an important temple.

'My grandfather has told me about having to wait at the temple every evening to collect *parsad*, the consecrated food offerings. That food was his evening meal, and his grandmother's meal as well. We visited that temple recently, the temple of Kapaleshwar, one of the two famous old temples of Madras. My grandfather showed me a stone lion on which he used to lean or sit while he waited for the evening puja to be over, to collect his food and go home. The pundits used to scold him: "Can't you even stand and wait respectfully while the puja is going on?" This time, when he went back as a very old man, the priests were standing outside to receive him.

'When he finished the school in Madras, he came to Bangalore, to go to the college here. He stayed with a relative, and he went on his own and got himself admitted to the college.' It was interesting, how that recurred in stories of the past: the child going on his own, without a parent or adult, to get enrolled in a school. 'While he was in college, he married my grandmother. He was a teenager, and she was eleven, if I remember right. In those days, when children were married, they stayed in their parents' house until they grew up. I should tell you that, as I knew them, my grandmother and grandfather were a romantic and devoted couple. I asked him about those early days of his marriage, and he told me that sometimes after his classes at the college he would go down to the market and pick up things for the home, including sometimes beads and coloured threads for my grandmother, his wife.

'The father of that eleven-year-old bride was the sanyasi I told you about. He was a boy sanyasi, and he was in Banaras. The man who became his father-in-law is supposed to have heard in some way of this sanyasi far away in Banaras – Banaras is many hundreds of miles from here – and he had heard that this sanyasi was destined to marry his daughter.' Sanyasis are renouncers of the world; they have no households; they don't marry. So this idea of the destiny of the sanyasi was a strange one.

Kala said, 'They, the people who became the in-laws of the

sanyasi, would have been religious people. They must have been in touch with astrologers; they must have had their daughter's horoscope read. So the man of the family went to Banaras, or he sent someone, to look for this boy sanyasi who had appeared in his daughter's horoscope. They went to Banaras, and they looked among all the holy men there, and they found the boy sanyasi. They put this proposal of marriage to him. But he was firm; he didn't want to re-enter the world. So they came back. But then various things happened, and then they went again to Banaras, and somehow they said certain things, and they persuaded the sanyasi to give up his ascetic life and to leave Banaras and to come here and get married. Not long after this marriage, the sanyasi's wife had an accident, and she began to lose her sight. She was sixteen when she got married.'

'Didn't the astrologer see that?'

Kala said, 'I don't know.' The story that had been handed down to her was like myth: it was full of wonders, but it had its gaps.

'Do you have any story of what the sanyasi said after his wife lost her sight?'

'There are no reports of the sanyasi's reaction.'

'How did he make a living?'

'The sanyasi became a priest at Palani, and in time a high official there. Palani is a famous temple town. The deity of Palani is a manifestation of Shiva. I go there almost every year with my mother. She believes in the temple.'

'What does that mean?'

'She believes in the power of that temple.'

'Do you believe in it?'

'I love my mother, and I believe in her. My mother was very close to her grandmother, the wife of the former sanyasi, and I believe there would have been some family feeling for the Palani temple. Though I go every year with my mother, it doesn't mean much to me. I'm not a particularly religious person myself.

'Palani is a rich temple. There are temples that are richer, but Palani is pretty rich, and many pilgrims go there. Temples are rich from the lands they have, and from the offerings the devotees make. One of the richest temples in the South is the temple at Tirupati. There is a story about it. The deity of that temple, Srinivasa, took a large debt from Kubera, the Lord of Wealth. The goddess Lakshmi gives wealth; Kubera owns it or hoards it, or lends it out. And the story at Tirupati is that the money that people give to the temple is being saved by Srinivasa, the temple deity, to repay the debt to Kubera. Many people believe in that story and that deity. There is a huge *hundi*, a huge cloth bin, and you throw the money in that. You throw anything – gold, silver, diamonds. I believe there have been people who have thrown in revolvers and bloodstained knives, hoping to be forgiven for the crimes they have committed with those weapons. And it is said that the very big offerings of money come from people who have made it illegally. Palani doesn't get anything like the offerings at Tirupati, but it gets.'

'So the sanyasi became a man of power?'

'The impression I get is that he was a very saintly man, and that he wasn't interested in things like power. He died when his daughter, my grandmother, was quite young. She was about fourteen. She had already been married, but she was living in her own parents' house – that was the custom. Before his death, the sanyasi had said to his wife, "If ever you have to depend on anybody, go and stay in the house of the husband of our eldest daughter." So my grandmother went to live in her husband's house, the house of my grandfather, and the whole family went with her.'

'How had that marriage been arranged – between your grand-father and grandmother?'

'We are a fairly small sub-sect of Tamil brahmins, and I guess that people were more sub-sect-minded in those days. Possibly everybody was distantly related. People kept records, or remembered, or kept track of everybody else – somebody's cousin's mother-in-law or something. This clannishness exists today in vestiges. People still keep track of distant kinspeople – which doesn't make sense to me.'

But Kala was in a position to make her own life. She had been educated; she had her job; she was free to come and go. Fifty years before, there would have been no job for her; the publicity job she did wouldn't have existed; even the kind of company she worked for mightn't have existed. People 50 years before would have thought and felt differently; the idea of the clan would have been comforting.

Kala said, 'Perhaps two generations ago the world didn't seem so small a place as it seems now.

'After his time in the college, my grandfather passed an examination, and he joined the government service. He rose. He was very dynamic. He had the reputation of being bold and honest. He went abroad many times.'

This was how Kala told the story, lingering over the boyhood and the street-lamp studying, and then racing away to the great success. It was almost like a proof of what Pravas had said, that with the development of the Indian economy, people had been sucked in and taken upwards.

'In the course of his life he had nine children. He also had his mother living with him, and his mother-in-law, and his sister-in-law. My grandfather was the only earning person in that house. There wasn't much money going around, but all his children were taught horse-riding, swimming and music, and they went in for trekking. I am sure this was a consequence of his career in administration.

'It's all like a story to me. As I knew my grandfather's place, there were no horses, no stables, no swimming. I've also heard of a palace the family lived in, when he served a princely state. There were peacocks in the garden. The stories are true. But those were different times. I feel no nostalgia; I just think it would have been a nice place to visit.

'By the time my grandfather was having this palace life, my mother had been married. So she didn't live in the palace. She just visited it. She had a baby daughter whom she took for a speedboat ride, when the baby was a month old or something. She said she knew the baby wouldn't remember the ride, but she wanted to share everything she knew with her daughter.'

And though Kala didn't say, I thought that the month-old baby girl might have been Kala herself.

'This part of the story, the story of my mother's marriage, is the most painful part. It is not pleasant and not easy for me to talk about it. My mother went to British schools, convents. She was very good in everything she did – music, sports, academic work. She was very bold and confident.' It was noticeable, Kala's approving emphasis on boldness. 'She wanted to do a lot of things. She thought she would like to be a doctor. She enjoyed going to school and wanted to study further. She was still very much a child at heart. She used to read a lot, English novels. Marriage was not on her mind at all. She was a child, a schoolgirl, almost like a

British schoolgirl.' Kala, always grave, was now close to tears. 'She says she wasn't a very beautiful child, but I know that she was a very beautiful woman.

'She got married when she was fourteen, and there was nothing she could do about it. She said she would have just liked to be left alone. She was very distressed, and her elder brother and her boy cousins were also distressed. They, the boys, told her that she could run away – and they would take care of her.'

'Whose idea was this marriage?'

'It was her father's idea. My grandfather's idea.'

'Have you talked to him about it?'

'No.'

'Why not? You know him.'

'I know him pretty well. But he is no longer the man he was then, and I am sure that if he had been the man he is now, he would not have done what he did.

'My mother was in the 10th standard. I don't ask her too many questions about that. I find it too painful, and there is nothing I can do about it, sitting here now. Maybe it's a cowardly attitude on my part, not wanting to know more. She completed school – after her marriage she stayed on for a few more months. It was all quite embarrassing for her, the last few months. People kept asking her whether she was married – many of her friends were British girls or Anglo-Indians. All of them were a good deal older than her. Many of them had boy friends. There were a lot of Tommies around in Bangalore. This was in 1946.'

It was unsettling, this glimpse of 1946 and the real world, in what had up to then been like a far-off story: 1946, the British still in India, still in that cantonment area of Bangalore, but with independence coming, and with the deadly Hindu–Muslim riots about to happen in Calcutta.

I said, 'That year sounds very recent to me. It was just a year or so after Somerset Maugham had published *The Razor's Edge* – about sanyasis and people looking for self-realization.'

Kala said, 'That was a book she liked. She continued to read a lot. It was all wrong, that marriage,' Kala said, carefully using restrained language. 'They should have let her be. She would have become a far greater woman if they had left her alone.'

'Didn't your mother tell her father that the whole thing had become very embarrassing for her at school, after the marriage?'

177

'I don't think my mother would have told her father that.

'The next bit I don't find easy to talk about. She couldn't study any further. For a few years after her marriage she was virtually a chattel, working for the large joint family of her husband. Hard physical work – washing clothes and scrubbing vessels. She had no time to herself, no freedom. She wasn't allowed to go and visit her people when she wanted to. She could make no decisions as to what she would like to do with her own life. Somebody always decided for her.'

'What did your father think about all this?'

'My father was a quiet, easygoing, peaceable sort of person. His family was ruled by the older women in it.'

'Your grandfather was a distinguished man. How could he have married his daughter into that kind of family?'

'They were well thought of. They were an aristocratic family. They were considered to be philanthropists. They probably didn't practise what they preached. Many of the women of the family were in social welfare organizations. They were far better formally educated than they permitted my mother to be. It all comes down to double standards, a lack of sensitivity, a touch of cruelty.'

Cruelty, yes: it was in the nature of Indian family life. The clan that gave protection and identity, and saved people from the void, was itself a little state, and it could be a hard place, full of politics, full of hatreds and changing alliances and moral denunciations. It was the kind of family life I had known for much of my childhood: an early introduction to the ways of the world, and to the nature of cruelty. It had given me, as I suspected it had given Kala, a taste for the other kind of life, the solitary or less crowded life, where one had space around oneself.

But I didn't think that what Kala said about double standards was appropriate. Hindu family life was ritualized. Just as there were rituals for every new stage in a person's life, so there were roles that people were required to fill as they progressed through their allotted years. Mothers-in-law were required to discipline the child brides of their sons, to train the unbroken and childish girls in their new duties as child-bearers and household workers, to teach them new habits of respect, to introduce them to the almost philosophical idea of the toil and tears of the real world: to introduce them, in this chain of tradition, to the kind of life and ideas they had been introduced to by their own mothers-in-law.

Such a disciplining of a child bride would have been considered virtuous; the cruelty, however willed, however voluptuous, would have been seen as no more than the cruelty of life itself. The social work the women of the family did would have been directed to people several layers below, many times more abject. The very wish to do social work would have issued out of an idea of virtue and correctness at home. The concept of double standards came from another world, came from Kala's world today.

Kala said, 'It was a total shock for my mother. She was the only daughter-in-law. She would be the last person considered for any kind of treat or outing. There wouldn't be room in the car for her. And she was still so much a child herself. Everyone was so much older. She was hit sometimes.' This was too painful for Kala to talk about. 'Both her mother-in-law and her husband hit her. Somehow, suddenly, as soon as she was married she was expected to turn into an adult.'

'Have you talked to your father's family about this?'

She hadn't. 'By the time I knew about it, everyone was so much older. There was no point in picking a quarrel. This life went on for five years.'

'Your grandfather was a man of such dignity and honour. Didn't he do anything for his daughter?'

'Hindu parents were not supposed to question what was being done to their daughters after they had been married. It wasn't that they didn't know; they were not supposed to question. They would, nowadays.

'In these five years my mother talked a lot to my father. She talked to him, and eventually they decided that they shouldn't live in that house any longer. My father applied for a job in a tea plantation in the Nilgiris. He got the job, and they moved there.

'That was where I grew up until I went to my boarding school. It was a nice colonial town. As I knew it, there were just the vestiges of colonialism – a Christian culture, parties. It didn't matter what religion you practised. There were no visible British people living there; there were lots of Anglo-Indians. The houses were colonial in design – high ceilings, wooden floors, big gardens, porticoes, servants' quarters some distance away from the house. It felt normal to live there.'

To Kala's mother it might also have been a version of, it might have echoed, the convent life from which she had been snatched five or six years before.

'The happiness began for you in the Nilgiris?'

'I think so. But the marks are still there. What might have been. It's all been a tremendous waste, the waste of potential in a woman nobody considered important. I value freedom a great deal now. My mother has always taught me how important education and financial independence are.'

'You aren't married?'

'I have nothing against the institution, but I don't see it as a goal.'

'Does your mother worry about that?'

'She would like me to get married. But not with any specific time limit. She wants me to be happy. And I feel that, compared to what she went through, anything I go through would appear trifling.'

She was still part of the story she had told me, over two or three meetings. She was full of the emotions of it, and unable to see in it the historical progression that I thought I saw.

She said, on another day, 'I do think about the individuals involved, all of them, and I sometimes wonder what they really felt at certain moments. I think all of them were very courageous people. Each of them displayed some kind of courage in making the changes that they did make. I wonder whether I would be able to display the same sort of courage, if I were put in a difficult or trying situation.'

'I don't think any of us can really know how our grandfathers and grandmothers thought or felt.'

Kala said, 'The world they lived in was very different.'

Prakash, a minister in the non-Congress state government of Karnataka, invited me to breakfast one Sunday morning. The minister's house was near the hotel, and Deviah came and walked there with me.

We had to walk carefully, picking our way over broken or unmade footpaths. Level or fully made footpaths are not a general Indian need, and the Indian city road is often like a wavering, bumpy, much mended asphalt path between drifts of dust and dirt and the things that get dumped on Indian city roads and then stay there, things like sand, gravel, wet rubbish, dry rubbish: nothing ever looking finished, no kerbstone, no wall, everything in a half-and-half way, half-way to being or ceasing to be.

Deviah and I would have liked to talk while we walked, but it was hard. We were being kippered all the time by the gritty smoke from cars and scooters. The dust these vehicles kicked up took a long time to settle down, so we walked in dust as well. By the time we reached the minister's house we had become part of the Bangalore road scene, with dust and fumy grit on skin and clothes and shoes and hair and glasses.

This invitation to breakfast gave a touch of the specialist industrial fair, of drama and American rush, to the politician's life. And, in fact, this early-morning time was when ministers and politicians of importance were very busy. Suppliants (with their own idea of the drama of the occasion), rising and getting ready in darkness, went at dawn to wait outside a great man's house – just as, in ancient Rome, a client's first duty in the morning was to run to the house of his patron, to add to the crowd there, for the sake of the great man's dignity. As in old Rome, so in modern Bangalore: the more important the man, the greater the crowd at his door.

Prakash wasn't among the top crowd-pullers. He had a more sedate reputation as an educated and competent minister, a shrewd and serious politician, yet capable of detachment: someone a little out of the ordinary in state politics.

He lived in one of the houses built by the Karnataka government for state ministers. These houses stood together in an area or park of their own. They were two-storey concrete houses, light-ochre in colour, and they were on biggish plots. There wasn't a crowd outside Prakash's house, such as I had seen at other people's houses, but there was a fair enough press of suppliants – patient, almost idle – to establish the man's importance. There were parked cars and security people in the yard. The parked cars suggested privilege: they looked as though they belonged to people with easy access to the minister.

Deviah and I were in that category that Sunday morning. Nothing was said, but the fact seemed to be known; and, road-stained though we were, the suppliants yielded as we approached, and a path to Prakash's front door opened between them. From the outside, the house had looked only like a house. It wasn't so.

We walked through a number of grimy, official-looking rooms that might have been the much used offices of some government department, and appeared to be staffed by government clerks. We came then to a more personal sitting room, more personal but still with an official feel, with many low armchairs around a low centre table. The day's newspapers, flat and new and undisturbed, were neatly laid out on the table in two staggered rows, each paper showing only its masthead. Some of the mastheads were in English or Hindi; others were in regional scripts.

Prakash, true to his character, didn't keep us waiting. Almost as soon as he had been told we had arrived, and before I could pick up one of the papers, he came in from an inner room to greet us, a small, brisk, confident, humorous-looking man in his forties; and he immediately led us to the room adjoining, a dining-room – this part of the house now quite private and personal, quite different in its atmosphere even from the sitting room – where a big table was laid for a most serious kind of Indian breakfast. And almost as soon as we had sat down at the table, Mrs Prakash appeared, in a fresh blue sari, and began serving us: the ritualized duty of the conservative Hindu wife, personally to serve food to her husband: a duty, but also now, considering what her husband was, a high privilege. How many of the people waiting outside would have envied her that familiarity with the minister, that attending on him; to how many would she have appeared blessed.

I asked about the men he had been seeing that morning, the men who had been waiting outside the front door, and had made way for us as people infinitely more privileged. The most important one among them, Prakash said, was a village accountant in government service. He had been charged with misappropriating 5000 rupees, about £200, from the land revenue which it was his duty to collect. This man had been suspended from his job, and he had travelled all night on a bus, making a journey of 200 miles, to see the minister that morning. Prakash had seen him for seven or eight minutes. The man said he had paid back the 5000 rupees, and he wanted Prakash to help him to be reinstated in his job. Prakash had told him that he could do nothing; the departmental inquiry would have to take its course. And that was it: after the 200-mile night journey, and the morning wait at the minister's house, and the seven or eight-minute audience, the village accountant would just have to take the bus back to his village.

Prakash's wife kept on bringing little side dishes, and serving us from dishes that had already been placed on the table. She brought from time to time fresh hot puris, crisp and swollen.

Prakash, eating away elegantly with his fingers, said, 'Now that fellow will take the matter to the High Court – after the departmental inquiry.'

I said, 'So it will become like a career to him?'

Prakash said, 'If the High Court finds there has been a technical flaw in the departmental inquiry – '

'And most often there is,' Deviah said, also eating, picking at this and that.

Prakash said, 'If there's been that technical flaw, he will get his reinstatement, and his back wages. During his suspension – he has been suspended – he will be getting a subsistence allowance of 75 per cent of his salary.'

I said, 'What sort of background for that kind of man?'

Prakash said, 'Such a man will be the son of a farmer or a local artisan. In government service he will be getting about 1200 rupees a month.' About £48. 'That's why everybody in a village tries for a government job – unless they have good land. If he loses his case, he will go back to nothing. He will have to depend on agriculture.'

The man we were talking about was thirty-six. He had three children. He had come to see Prakash because he belonged to Prakash's constituency. This was in the Bellary district, and agriculture there would have been very hard. Bellary was known in the state as a 'hot area', with summer temperatures of 105 degrees.

Prakash said, 'He might have misappropriated this sum of 5000 rupees over one or two years. People come to pay their land revenue, and he takes their money. Small sums, 25 rupees or so at a time. He gives bogus receipts. And then one day a superior officer asks why farmers here and there are not paying their land revenue. He makes some simple inquiries; he sees the bogus receipts; and the foolish fellow is caught.'

Deviah said, 'He might even think it's unfair, when so many bigger people all around him are taking and getting away.'

I asked Prakash, 'Did the man cry? Did he drop to the ground and hold your legs?'

Prakash, with his witty way of talking, said, 'He might have cried the first night, after he'd been caught. But after a year he's become hardened.'

I liked that 'hardened'. Prakash, in real life or civilian life, the life before politics, had been a country lawyer, and he knew his people.

'But now he's grown fatalistic. He talks of *karma*, fate. It is the Hindu way.'

'Would people in his village look down on him or ostracize him now?'

'At his level people wouldn't bother with that kind of theft. I don't think they would even know about it. The upper class in India take theft for granted. It's only the middle class who are still maintaining these values, and worrying about theft and corruption. It's in the social fibre. It's everywhere. At an appointments board someone will jump up and say, "I'm sorry, I can't interview the next candidate. He's my brother-in-law. You must excuse me." Perfectly nice and correct, but it is also an indication to the panel that the candidate in question is the man's brother-in-law.'

He broke off and, lifting a side dish, said, 'Everything in this house has been provided by the government. Every cup, every plate. How can a man give up this life?' He was referring not to himself, but to others. 'It's in the social fibre, as I say. In the old days the maharajas used to get their land revenue. But in addition to that people would go and offer them gifts – gold, ornaments, fruits, coconuts. They would offer it on a plate, and the plate would be of brass or silver, according to your status. The present-day maharajas are the ministers. Indira Gandhi was a maharani.

'Buying religious favours is another equivalent. There again you have different levels of gifts. Some people might give only a coconut. Do you know the story about the temple at Tirupati?'

It was the story I had heard from Kala.

Prakash said, 'You give money there to help Lord Venkateshwara to repay his loan from Kubera. He borrowed the money to get married.'

Kala had left out the last detail. Perhaps it was so, detail added to detail, that difficult mythological stories grew in the minds of people here.

We got up from the breakfast table then, to go to the State Guest House. Prakash had thought we would have more privacy there, and not be troubled by suppliants.

A fresh batch was waiting outside the front door. One small, smiling fellow, in sandals, was neatly dressed in tight brown trousers and a clean beige-and-yellow Polyester shirt in a check pattern. He was a driver. He was pining for a job with the government. He wasn't unemployed, but he was working for a private firm, and the pay there wasn't as good as it would have been with the government. Prakash had given the man a recommendation some months before, but the man hadn't got a government job; so he had made this morning trip to Prakash again, to complain and plead.

And as royalty, moving among a welcoming crowd, finds a word or two for a selected few, so Prakash, moving among his breakfast suppliants – but not strictly like royalty, more like a medical professor in the ward of a teaching hospital – found words to say to a few, but the words apparently spoken to the suppliant were really words spoken to Deviah and me about the suppliant, and were spoken as though the suppliant wasn't absolutely with us, as though Deviah and I were medical students making the round of a hospital ward, and Prakash, our professor, was talking about people prostrate on their beds or with bandaged limbs in slings and pulleys.

One man did look like a hospital case, and he was showing a very dirty, very creased official form in the local Kannada script which seemed to say – Prakash knew about this man, had met him earlier that morning – that his wife was a cancer patient in a Bangalore hospital. The man's story was that he had come to Bangalore to put his wife in the hospital; he wanted now to go back to his village, but he didn't have any money; he wanted 42 rupees for the bus fare.

The fellow looked quite spectacularly broken down. He was thin and half-starved, with a worn tunic made from some kind of commercial hessian sack, with the commercial lettering on the sacking only half washed out. The top of his nose was skinned, down to the red flesh, and he was carrying a baby and a feeding bottle.

As soon as we came within prostrating distance, this fellow, holding the baby in one arm, made a dive with his other hand for Prakash's feet, in an exaggerated gesture of respect – taking care, during his downward sweep, first to set the feeding bottle upright on the concrete surround of Prakash's house. Prakash made a gesture to the wretched man to get up. The man got up, bent down again to pick up the feeding bottle, dandled the shaken-up baby a little, put the bottle in the baby's mouth, and fixed wild eyes on Prakash. Prakash looked at the man, not really returning the gaze, looking more with something like social or academic distance, and – seeming to assess the man while he spoke – gave Deviah and me a little lecture about the man's condition.

People who were taken into the hospital could have their spouses stay with them, Prakash said. It was a legal provision. If this fellow said he wanted the fare to go back to his village, it was because he chose not to take advantage of that facility. The fellow was probably making the rounds of ministers and other people that morning. Prakash himself had already that morning issued instructions to someone on his staff to give the fellow a couple of rupees, though he wasn't sure that the fellow was genuine.

'And if he does get the 42 rupees for the ticket back,' Deviah said, 'he will probably travel without a ticket.'

The presentation of need was extraordinary. Perhaps it was too much of a production, with the baby and the bottle and the sacking tunic. But the wild-eyed man looked a genuine wreck, genuinely ill and wasted.

Prakash was cool. Leading us now to his car, as though the lecture was almost over, he said that people like that didn't come from the traditional begging groups or castes. They fell into the way of life by accident, or example, or encouragement; they were surprised by the rewards. And then, Prakash added, with an alliterative flourish, 'They become addicted and adjusted.'

(And Prakash was right. More than a week later, when Deviah and I were talking to a state legislator in his room at the legislators' hostel, this wretched man appeared, with the baby and the milk bottle, but without the sacking tunic, and without the official-looking form that said his wife was in the cancer hospital. The legislator's assistants drove the man away immediately, and he went off without a word. He wasn't as wild-eyed as he had been at Prakash's; his skinned nose had begun to heal, and he looked curiously rested. He was as careful with the baby as he had been at Prakash's; perhaps he had borrowed it against a deposit of some kind.)

We went on in Prakash's car through the dusty roads to the State Guest House. Minister at home, minister here too: people jumped about at his appearance. I began to feel the range of his power, began a little to see Karnataka through Prakash's eyes; though the room we were shown into, for our private talk, was a rough little hostel bedroom with a high urine smell, and with the one table in it too low for me to write on.

We went to the main guest house. It was a big stone building in the centre of the tawny grounds. When we were settled in the wide verandah on the upper floor, I asked Prakash about political power in India. How did people come by it? What were a man's qualifications for power?

Caste, he said, was the first thing of importance. A man looking for office or a political career would have to be of a suitable caste. That meant belonging to the dominant caste of the area. He would also, of course, have to be someone who could get the support of his caste; that meant he would have to be of some standing in the community, well connected and well known. And since it seldom happened that the votes of a single caste could win a man an election, a candidate needed a political party; he needed that to get the votes of the other castes. So the whole parliamentary business of political parties and elections made sense in India. It encouraged co-operation and compromise; the very multiplicity of Indian castes and communities made for some kind of balance.

Power achieved here, Prakash said, was very great, in the surroundings of Indian life, the surroundings of struggle and making do. And the fall, the loss of power, was equally great, and could be very hard to bear.

The chairs in the stone verandah were heavy and ugly, government chairs, bleached and dulled by sunlight; and there were very many of them. The verandah, not yet in direct light, was nevertheless full of glare. The trees in the brown-grass grounds were few; the shadows emphasized the light and the dryness. The big rolled-up green blinds were the only decorative touch in the verandah, and they added to the bare, dull, official feeling of the State Guest House.

Prakash said, 'When the average politician falls he will have nowhere to go, and no cushion. He may be an advocate in a country area, or a son of a peasant or landlord, or son or brother of a petty merchant; but not a man with a lot of money. And many may not come from a movement.'

'Movement?'

'Movement would be the independence movement, or the movement against Indira Gandhi's Emergency, or the peasant movement here in this state, or the labour movement, or any people's movement. When you don't come from such a movement, and you have nothing to fall back upon when you lose power, you are in a hurry to make money.

'The power gives so much of comfort, perks, and status – a bungalow, all fully furnished, all personal attendants and secretarial staff. A chauffeur-driven car, and facilities to stay in government bungalows and guest houses when you travel out, and air tickets – you can fly around at the expense of the government. But when you come out of power, if you have no means, you may have to go back to the semi-urban area from where you came. There you can hardly afford to have a secretary or servants. You may have one servant, but not the bunch of servants you had as a minister. Or the free telephone calls.'

Prakash appeared to be speaking against these things, but I thought I could detect a certain lingering over the details of privilege. He had been a minister for six years, and now his government, from what I could decipher in the newspapers, was in some trouble.

I said, 'Servants. You talk a lot about servants. Are servants very important to these men from the country areas?'

Prakash was a lawyer, ironic, bright: he detected my drift. He said, 'In the good old days too many servants, for the big landlords, the zamindars, and the feudals, gave a status. Today it is the power. Servants are there to make your life comfortable. If you are a minister, and you travel on an aeroplane, there will be somebody to buy you a ticket. There will always be a block of seats for the government, and these will be kept till the last minute; so there is always a chance that you will get a ticket. And your P.A., your personal assistant, will come right up to the airport to see you off' – Prakash again lingering over the details, savouring the things he still enjoyed – 'and at the destination somebody will come and receive you. There will be a vehicle at your disposal, and your reservation of accommodation has already been made.

'But as a man without power' – and now, as a preacher painting a picture of purgatory, to balance the heaven of success, Prakash began to darken the details of Indian air travel – 'many a time you will not know where to buy a ticket, where to stand in a queue, how to get your baggage checked. In a western society, which is so very orderly, between a man with privileges and a common man there won't be a big gap in the physical arrangement of life, arrangement of travel and comforts and stay.

'Even in western countries it is an innate thing in a man to look to be in power. And it is all the more so in India, because the power means everything here. When an American president leaves the White House, it makes no difference as far as his lifestyle is concerned, and his physical comforts. Many a time in India it wouldn't be like that, unless you have a will to live in austerity, like the old gods of the Gandhian era.

'Our new-generation politicians don't have that spiritual power, and they feel the difference. They try for a while, after they have fallen, to capitalize on their so-called contacts with the authorities. They undertake certain commissions for people who want things done. But those contacts very soon go away. And the industrialist who courted you drives by in his big car to his rich house in his nice area, and he doesn't even look at you.

'Because of industrialization, and the green revolution in the rural areas, a new class of nouveau-riche persons are emerging, and these people are being exposed for the first time to university education, comfortable urban life, stylish living, and western influences – materialistic comforts. During this transition period, we are slowly cutting from the moral ethos of our grandfathers, and at the same time we don't have the westerner's idea of discipline and social justice. At the moment things are chaotic here.'

I would have liked him to talk more personally. But it wasn't easy. The political crisis in his government, the glimpse of the possibility of the end of things, was encouraging him to put a distance between himself and the delights of power. It was at the same time bringing out his political combativeness. It was making him moralize in an old-fashioned way (almost as though he had already left office) about Gandhianism, materialism, and the dangers to India of the super computer the people in Delhi were talking about.

At last he said, 'I wasn't rich, but I wasn't poor. My family could live in comfort and with security. This was in Bellary. I have land there, and much of what I needed was produced on my land – millet, rice, tamarind, chili, vegetables, and fuel. I can go back any time. But after six years in office here I can notice a change in my children. Their formative years have been spent in this opulence and status, and people giving so much concern and attention to them. Now they don't wish to go back to the village. For me it's nothing.

'Bellary is very hot. And many of these relatives and friends of mine feel a little awestruck when they come here. The friends may have a little jealousy, friends from the village, or people who worked along with me in the old days and have seen me walking the streets of a small place. Now they feel I've become all-important, and there is a jealousy – and this is apart from the ruthlessness of the system, where my own colleagues are pulling down my legs when I am climbing up fast. This is innate in the system, but the jealousy is different.

'Even my voter, he will be more comfortable to talk to me when I am there, in my abode. But when he comes here and sits on a sofa' – it was interesting, getting this idea of the world as it appeared to Prakash's voter, seeing even the drabness of the State Guest House transformed – 'when he sits here, with this big garden, lawn, police people, attendants, it makes him ill at ease, and immediately he feels I am too far away, and that personal equation goes away or changes.'

Car doors banged outside the Guest House. Someone, or some party, had arrived. Very quickly after the banging of the doors a briskly moving group of men in coloured robes came up the steps and walked through the inner room: big men in big shoes, taking firm strides. I saw this only at an angle; I was sitting slightly turned away from the inner room. And then Prakash, lowering his voice, told me it was the Dalai Lama who had arrived.

It was a little unlikely, but I was half prepared. I knew that the Dalai Lama was on tour in India. In Bombay I had read in the newspaper one day that the Dalai Lama was coming to the city to visit Buddhists there. I wasn't sure what was meant by that. When people in Bombay spoke of Buddhists they didn't mean Tibetans; they were more likely to mean Dalit neo-Buddhists. But I hadn't asked further about the Dalai Lama's visit to Bombay. And now, without any announcement I had heard of, with only a few cars, and few state policemen, he had come even further south, and was really far from home.

The Dalai Lama moved so fast that, almost as soon as Prakash had told me who it was, the figure had gone through the inner room, half hidden by an assistant walking close to him, swinging a briefcase. The end of a stride, the swing of the assistant's briefcase – that was all I had really caught.

Afterwards, monks came out to the wide verandah where we were sitting. After the rush of their arrival, they were calmer. From the bareness of the verandah they looked down at the scorched lawn and gardens. Their heads were shaved, and they wore sweaters below their dark-red robes. It seemed at first that they were only staring at the strange aspect of the Indian South. But they were looking for their followers.

Prakash told me there was a Tibetan 'camp' near Mysore City, about 100 miles to the south. There, on land that had been given them by the Indian government, the Tibetans grew maize, did dairy farming, and knitted their distinctive sweaters. There had been no Tibetans in the grounds of the State Guest House when we had arrived. But gradually, in small informal groups, the Tibetans from the Mysore City camp – who had been waiting in the streets outside – began to appear on the burnt lawn, the women in traditional Tibetan dress, the men in jeans, bright-faced, handsome people, who perhaps now, after more than a generation away, were beginning to lose touch with home: another Asian dispossession, part of the historical flux.

My thoughts for some time were with those people. The monks remained on the verandah, looking out, as though they wanted to fix their gaze for a while on each person in the small, scattered, waiting groups. And even when Prakash began to speak again, I felt we were continuing to be part of that wordless Tibetan scene.

Prakash said, 'Our people, because of the long tradition of the rajas and maharajas and feudal lords, they always look with awe and fear on the seat of power, and at the same time they nourish a dislike and hatred towards the seat of power. But there is a dichotomy. They like an accessible, simple, compassionate, benevolent man in the seat of power. But at the same time they have a mental picture of power – of pomp, pageantry, authority and aristocracy. These things don't go together many times.

'In a case like me, they would like to see me as their good old humble country lawyer – as before 1983, when I came to power and became a minister. But they will respect my authority only if I'm surrounded by a group of officers, and if I myself assume postures.

'On the 16th of February 1983 I took the oath of secrecy and office as a minister at Bangalore. On the same day there was a communal disturbance at Bellary – with a police firing, seven deaths, arson and looting. I immediately that night left for Bellary by car, 200 miles down. And I immediately assumed the authority there, and started directing the District Inspector of Police, the Deputy Commissioner of Bellary, and other officers. And I was able to control the disturbance in a day.

'As a lawyer, I had appeared before the Deputy Commissioner of Bellary in several cases, where I used to address him as "Your Honour". But, as a minister, there was a transformation. I started giving him commands. Within a day there was a change in me. And people wouldn't have liked it, and the situation wouldn't have been controlled, if I had just been a *mofussil* lawyer. It's a very strange society we've created. Democracy has made it possible for people like us to have a different role.'

And his government had cut down on ministerial pomp. There had been a lot more in the Congress days: police escorts, red lights flashing to warn off cars, sirens. In those days people couldn't just turn up at the ministers' houses; they had to have an appointment.

Power came from the people. The people were poor; but the power they gave was intoxicating. As high as a man could be taken up, so low, when he lost power, he could be cast down. So the legislators were in a frenzy from the start, and in constant movement, like a group of penguins in an Antarctic blizzard, the ones at the outer rim seeking to work their way through the seething mass to the warm centre. The politics of the state, the comings and goings which filled the local newspapers, were the politics of alignment and realignment. When a majority became shaky, a politician's vote in the chamber became an asset: it could be sold any number of times. Recently (I heard this from another politician), there had been 10 very difficult men who required a lakh of rupees, 100,000 rupees, £4000, for every vote they cast in the chamber. The government and opposition parties had to raise funds to meet these expenses; the ways they chose to raise those funds could be controversial.

The politics of the state, as reported in the newspapers, were opaque to the visitor. In the politics of alignment and realignment there were no principles or programmes. There were only enemies or allies: penguin politics. What was true of this state, Karnataka, was true of other states as well. There were very many columns of the newspapers that one could ignore, or take as read. Political knowledge didn't come from learning the names, just as computer skill didn't come from trying to learn a computer programme by heart. The programmes could be changed or abandoned; the politicians could disappear, or move about very fast.

It seemed miraculous that there was government at all. But, with the growth of the Indian economy, active governments generated the greatest profit for all. And out of the political frenzy there had come a kind of balance: for the first time in the history of India, perhaps, most people felt that they or their representatives, someone of their group, had a chance of getting to the warm centre of power and money.

Prakash was that day in the midst of yet another crisis of some sort, which was taking up a lot of space in the newspapers. We walked down to the asphalted area around the Guest House, where four or five middle-aged men, chewing pan, in fresh cream-coloured homespun tunics and dhotis, with an air about them of sweet conspiracy, were waiting for him in the bright light – a little distance away from the cars and khaki-clad policemen of the Dalai Lama's party. Legislators were being asked that day to sign a loyalty statement, and there was much of the eternal counting of Gandhi-capped heads. Homespun clothes, once the clothes of the poor, now no longer worn by the poor, worn only by the men to whom the poor had given power.

People of all conditions spoke with respect of the days of the old maharajas, and there was a reminder of old Mysore glory in the three-mile-long wall of the palace park in the centre of Bangalore. The palace there had been only the summer palace of the maharajas. It stood deep within the park and couldn't be seen from the road. The park itself, immensely valuable as land alone, was now the subject of litigation, and was closed to the public.

The main palace was in Mysore City, 100 miles to the south. I heard from Deviah that there was still a barber in Mysore City who had been in the service of the 25th and last maharaja. There was also a brahmin who had acted as a pundit of some sort to the maharaja. The barber was said to be full of stories; but Deviah and I went to Mysore one day to see the brahmin.

The road was good, one of the roads of the old Mysore State. It was shaded for long stretches by the big rain trees that had been planted in the time of the maharajas, and were now looked upon almost as part of the continuing bounty of the maharajas. And there were rich green fields that had come into being because of the irrigation works undertaken by the famous chief minister of the 24th maharaja.

Mysore City was built around the palace. We had a glimpse of part of the grounds as we entered the city. Tempting; but that spaciousness and splendour were for later. Our business that morning lay in the city itself, in a small concrete marriage hall, which the former pundit of the maharaja was now supervising. The marriage hall was new and quite ordinary-looking, but it belonged to a foundation that had been set up by the ninth-century philosopher Shankaracharya. So the pundit, though he might appear to be doing commercial work, was still close to religion.

He was a small man of seventy-two. Three broad bands of white ran horizontally across his forehead, and there was a red-and-sandalwood dot between his eyebrows. He had a gold-set ruby earring in each ear. His white tunic was buttoned over a small belly, and this belly was curiously narrow and long; so that, buttoned in the tunic, the pundit appeared to have the shape of a cucumber. The white holy marks on his forehead came from the ash of burnt cowdung. The cowdung was burnt for that purpose on a special day, Shiva-ratri, Shiva's Night. Deviah told this story about Shiva-ratri: every day Shiva watches over the world, but there is one day when he falls asleep, and Hindus on that day (or night) have to stay awake, to watch.

We met the pundit in the office room of the marriage hall. It was a small plain room, with cream-coloured walls, and with an iron chest in one corner and some bedding on the red concrete floor. A red telephone stood on a shelf in another corner, next to a board with four keys. One wall had inset shelves, painted green. Old fluorescent light tubes with attached electric wires (no doubt meant for use in the marriage hall, and stored here as a precaution against theft) were on one shelf; loose electric bulbs were on another shelf; a stack of thin booklets of some sort, together with a number of old-looking paper-wrapped parcels, were on a third shelf. From a nail or a hook at the side of the green inset shelves a woven bag hung flat against the wall. The wall was like a piece of furniture: it was a place for putting things or hanging things.

The pundit was born in 1916. His father was not from Mysore, but from Tamil Nadu; he acted as agent for an absentee landlord, and he was also a dealer in grain. The pundit's mother came from Mysore. Since women return to their parents' house for the birth of their children, the pundit was born in Mysore. He was then taken to Tamil Nadu by his parents; but when he was ten his father died, and his mother's father brought him back to Mysore and put him in the Sanskrit College in Mysore City.

He had a Mysore government scholarship to the Sanskrit College. Anybody who wanted to study Sanskrit was given a scholarship. He started with a scholarship of two rupees a month, about 16 pence. Two rupees were quite enough for a boy of ten in 1926; the salary of a first-division clerk at that time was 30 rupees.

The pundit was not a fluent talker. He waited for questions, and Deviah translated his replies.

Deviah translated: 'It was my grandfather who put me in the college. He was a cook in the palace, and I don't know whether he knew about the scholarship when he put me in the college. We weren't living in the palace; we were living in a rented house outside the palace. My grandfather used to cook for the palace pujas. He cooked the food that was consecrated. He earned 18 rupees a month. Though he was a cook at the palace, he never ate there. He ate at home – this was his custom as a brahmin. He lived for 92 years.'

The pundit studied at the Sanskrit College for 20 years, from 1926, when he was ten, to 1946. Over those years the two-rupee scholarship he had started with was increased, bit by bit.

One of the important things he studied was astrology. He studied that for five years. He had a teacher who was a very famous astrologer.

'There is no end to learning as an astrologer. Just as science keeps on developing, with new discoveries, so I've not stopped learning about astrology.'

On the desk at which the pundit sat was a little dark-blue or grey plastic bag – plastic, not leather, which was the skin of an animal and unclean. On the wall above his head was a framed colour picture of Shiva and his consort. Light had bleached the colours. Both figures had been given as much beauty as the artist could give: a feminine beauty, of an almost erotic nature.

The pundit said, 'We can tell a person's blood group by the day he was born. We have three blood groups, and we can say whether people are compatible or not. They don't have to take a blood test. There is no difference between astrology, medicine, and *dharma-shastra*.' Deviah translated this as 'traditional learning'. 'To learn astrology, you first have to learn all the other sciences. Before you prescribe certain medicines, you have to look for certain planetary conditions, because certain medicines work only under certain circumstances. Certain medicines work only under the rays of the sun, or the moon, or Mars or Mercury.'

He could predict the future. 'If you give the correct time of birth – but it has to be down to the minute – I will tell you everything correctly. If there's a minute's error, it makes a world of difference. The place is also important.'

In 1946, after 20 years, he came to the end of his studies at the Sanskrit College. He had lived for all this time on his scholarship from the state government. In his last year at the college this scholarship was 15 rupees a month. He was now thirty, and he was at last free to get married. He married the daughter of a man who worked as a clerk in the palace. He also found a job; he became librarian at the same Sanskrit College, at a salary of 45 rupees a month. He stayed in that job for 16 years.

One of the projects he worked on as librarian of the Sanskrit College was the translation of all the Puranas, the sacred old texts of Hinduism, into Kannada, the local Mysore language. This project was sponsored by the maharaja, and the pundit's work on it came to the maharaja's notice. The maharajas in India had lost their titles in 1956, but they still had their privy purses; and in Mysore the maharaja still had considerable ceremonial standing as state governor, *raja pramukh*.

One afternoon in 1962, on a day of the full moon, the pundit had finished his puja and was sitting at home, when a servant came from the palace. The servant had been sent by the maharaja's secretary, and the message was that the pundit was wanted at the palace by the maharaja. The maharaja would have told his A.D.C., and the A.D.C. would have told the secretary, and the secretary would have told his servant.

The pundit must already have had some idea of what the maharaja wanted, or he must have been given some idea by the servant. Because, when this call from the palace came, the pundit straight away sent word to the palace, to both his father-in-law and his grandfather, the one a palace clerk, the other a cook.

The grandfather hurried home. He was happy for his grandson's sake, but he was also nervous. He said to the pundit, 'You have been trained as a scholar, a *vaidhika*. But the work you are going to do now is that of a *loukika* – worldly work. You may not fit in. Think of that.' He also gave his grandson detailed instructions about how he was to behave when he came into the maharaja's presence.

At about three in the afternoon, when it would have been very hot, the pundit left his house to walk to the palace. He was dressed as a brahmin, in his dhoti, and with a shawl over his shoulders. Otherwise he was bare above the waist. He was barefooted. It was his way; he had never worn footwear of any kind; to this day he never wore anything on his feet – and, indeed, when I looked below the desk or table at which the pundit sat, I saw his bare feet flat on the red concrete floor, the skin dark and thickened at the soles, padded and cracked. It was no trouble either to walk barebacked in the afternoon sun; the pundit was used to that.

It was about half a kilometre to the palace. He met the secretary in one of the inner rooms, and the secretary sent him in directly to the maharaja, who was in the palace library. The library consisted of three rooms, each about 40 feet long by 25 feet wide. They were all full of books, with hardly a place to sit down. The books were in all languages.

In one of those rooms the maharaja was sitting. The pundit went up to him and did the obeisance his grandfather had trained him in, bringing the palms together and bowing low. The maharaja was wearing a djibba and a dhoti, and he was in a 'social' mood.

'What did he look like?'

'He was a tall man, built like a king. Hefty.' He wasn't thinking only of the seated figure he had seen that day in the library; he was thinking of the man he had later got to know. 'In the morning, after his puja, when he came out with his holy marks on his forehead, he looked like God.'

The maharaja – but that wasn't the word the pundit used: he used the English word 'Highness', pronouncing it in a way that made it sound part of the local language – the maharaja, Highness, told the pundit that he had been chosen to work in the palace.

'I hadn't applied for the job or anything. So bravely I told

Highness what my grandfather had told me, that I had lived all my life as a vaidhika, and couldn't now live as a loukika. And Highness said, "I am using you here only for vaidhika work. I want you to be *mukhthesar*."

'I knew what the duties of a mukhthesar were. They were to organize all the pujas of the palace, to choose the purohits or priests, and to supervise what they did, to make sure that the pujas and rituals were correctly carried out.'

The maharaja spoke to the pundit for half an hour. He told him what he would have to do. There were 10 permanent purohits in the palace; the pundit would have to supervise them, and all the additional purohits who might be called in on special occasions. The pundit would also have to look after the jewels of the palace temple. People who worked in the palace were given a special allowance of 20 rupees a month, and the maharaja told the pundit that he would be getting this allowance. The allowance was given because palace staff were on call all the time and had no leave. The salary itself would be 150 rupees; as librarian at the Sanskrit College the pundit was getting 45 rupees a month.

'It was my duty to do it. Whatever Highness said, I had to do. I was already an employee of Highness, because the Sanskrit College belonged to Highness.'

After his audience in the library the pundit walked back to his family house. He told his father-in-law and grandfather the news, and his grandfather was pleased. He said, 'We've all got good names in the palace. You should do your work well and keep our good name there.'

As someone working in the palace the pundit had to have a uniform. He immediately went to the palace tailor to be measured. He ordered two suits, and the charge was 200 rupees, more than a month's salary. But for some reason the maharaja wanted the pundit to start working in the palace right away. So the pundit was in a quandary about what to wear – the uniforms he had ordered from the tailor weren't going to be ready for some days.

The pundit said, 'I did a mad thing. I borrowed my father-in-law's uniform. We were the same build.' And that was a mad thing to do, because a brahmin shouldn't wear other people's clothes: it was as unclean as drinking from a vessel used by someone else. 'For three days I wore my father-in-law's uniform. Then I had my own from the palace tailor, the two suits. I got them on credit. I didn't have 200 rupees. I paid with my salary, and paid it off in three or four instalments.'

He wore white trousers and a long coat. The coat was white for the mornings, black at night. He wore the Mysore turban, white with a gold band; and he got a white sash. No shoes: inside the palace no one wore shoes, not even the maharaja. The maharaja wore shoes only outside the palace.

On the cream-coloured wall of the marriage-hall office where we were talking there were finger-prints of grime, the eternal grime of India. The floor was dark red, and some inches up the wall were skirting areas in the same colour. Pale-green doors led to other rooms; over a padlocked door – leading perhaps to the marriage hall itself – was a gay *No Admission* sign in a wavy scroll. And, as in an Indian city street, where nothing was absolutely clean or finished, there was in this room, in the corner with the iron chest, a lot of half-swept-up dust and old fluffy dirt, together with the rags and the broom that might have done the sweeping and the wiping. The desk at which the pundit sat was of steel, and painted grey.

The pundit's working hours, as palace mukhthesar, were long. They were from six in the morning to two in the afternoon. He would go home then for an hour, and go back to the palace and stay till seven. That was on ordinary days. On certain days, like the days of the Dussehra festival, the pundit could stay at the palace until midnight. This was because at Dussehra the temple jewels were on display, and the pundit would have to stay and see that the jewels were put back in the palace vault.

When the maharaja was away, 'on camp', the pundit was free and could rest. The maharaja went away on camp four or five times a year, for 15 days or so at a time. Sometimes he went abroad; then he was away for a month.

'Highness used to go on pilgrimages. Highness had this habit, that if he read in an old text, a Purana, about a certain temple – in any part of the country – he would say, "Let's go there." The next day he would be ready, and about 25 people would go with him. He had one or two special railway coaches, which would be attached to the scheduled trains. He used to take cooks, body-guards, a purohit, an astrologer. Sometimes he used to take his family. Highness had a "craze" for visiting temples. There is no temple that he didn't see – he was such a devotee.'

In 1965 the pundit, as mukhthesar, was allowed quarters: a small house with two rooms and a 'hall'. The rent was 10 per cent of his salary. Three years later, in 1968, he was given a special ceremonial uniform. He didn't have to pay for this uniform; it was a gift of the maharaja. The long coat was red, with gold facings and gold buttons. The buttons had a phoenix symbol and the letters *JCRW*, which were the initials of the maharaja: Jaya Chama Rajendra Wodeyar. The trousers were of silk, and biscuit-coloured.

I wondered whether it wasn't too gaudy for him, as a brahmin.

'I was proud of it. When I wore that dress, nobody could stop me anywhere, in the street or in the palace.' He even had himself photographed in that uniform.

He rose in the service. The maharaja called him *Shastri Narayan*, 'Lord of the Shastras', 'Great Scholar'. But then there began to be signs of things going bad outside. In 1971 the maharajas of India were 'de-recognized' by Mrs Gandhi's government, and the maharaja lost his tax-exempt privy purse of 2,600,000 rupees, worth at that time (after the devaluation of 1967) £130,000. Still, the maharaja continued to promote his mukhthesar. In 1972 the mukhthesar was appointed assistant secretary; there were two assistant secretaries in the palace. The pundit had entered the palace at a salary of 150 rupees; over the years this had doubled to 300; now, as assistant secretary, he was getting 500.

'Highness received the catalogues of various booksellers. He ordered 300 to 400 books a month. The palace secretary bought them for him. Highness bought Penguins and books of the Oxford University Press. I had to read or look over or taste the new books, and give a summary to him of books I thought might interest him. He was interested in philosophy and history. He talked about philosophy with me and with others. Highness liked to have a scrapbook. I knew the sort of thing that interested him, and would point certain passages out to him. Certain passages he would want typed out, for his own speeches and writings.

'Highness had two crazes, two madnesses. Temples. Second, books – buying them and reading them. He used to read throughout the night. I was associated with both his madnesses. In his reading room he allowed no one. He had his own system of arranging or storing books. He kept them on the floor. No one was to touch them while they were there. When he had finished with a book, he brought it to me and asked me to catalogue it and put it on the library shelves.'

I wanted to know what English books the maharaja read and discussed with his mukhthesar, his Shastri Narayan. I was expecting to hear the names of Aldous Huxley, Bertrand Russell, Christopher Isherwood. But the pundit couldn't help me; he couldn't remember the name of any English writer.

In 1973, two years after the maharajas had been de-recognized, there was a strike by the palace staff for better pay. At one time there had been 500 workers in the palace. At the time of the strike there were 300. The maharaja gave the strikers the increases they asked for. It was too much for him. The next year everybody on the palace staff was given a gratuity and sent away. The pundit himself was given 19,000 rupees, nearly £1000. But not long afterwards the maharaja sent for him, and five or six others, and took them back. He continued to be mukhthesar and assistant secretary, and the work was just as hard as it had been.

'For some people,' the pundit said, 'Highness never changed.'

But there had been a price for the maharaja's favour. Because of his irregular eating habits, the pundit said, he had developed an ulcer. As a brahmin it wasn't possible for him to eat outside his own house. He couldn't eat at the palace; even his grandfather, who had been a cook at the palace, had never eaten there. And because of the long hours the pundit had had to work in the palace, his digestion had become disorganized.

One day in 1974, when he was fifty-eight, he began vomiting blood. He was taken to the hospital. He stayed there for eight days. He was about to be discharged when the news came that the maharaja had died. That was how it had happened – as suddenly as that. The doctors advised him not to think about the maharaja's death; it would be bad for him. They postponed his discharge from the hospital; they kept him in for two more days. So, after all the years of personal attendance as mukhthesar, superintendent of pujas, he had not been present for the death of the maharaja, and the important rites afterwards.

The pundit said, 'To this day I try not to think about Highness's death.'

I didn't think he was exaggerating. The story we had heard had come out with much trouble; it had taken many hours. For nearly 50 years, as student, librarian, mukhthesar, he had lived on the bounty of the maharajas; and for 12 years he had personally served the maharaja. But the story of his life and his service with the maharaja existed in his mind as a number of separate stories, separate little stories. He had never before, I think, made a connected narrative out of those little stories.

After he left the hospital, he stayed home for a year. And then he saw this job as manager of the marriage hall advertised, and he took it.

'It's a job.'

Had he really succeeded in putting such an important part of his life out of his mind? Did no feelings now remain in him for the palace?

'No feelings. The times are not suitable for that kind of living any more. Times have changed.' He said the words simply, without any stress. There was still a royal family, but there was no maharaja now. The son of the former maharaja was a member of parliament on the Congress side.

Four times a year now he went to the palace, to make offerings to the head of the royal family. He went as a brahmin, as he had always gone: bare-backed, with a dhoti and shawl, and barefooted. But now he didn't go as an employee or palace servant. He went as a man in his own right. He went as a representative of a great and ancient religious foundation – though he just managed a marriage hall for them – and the gifts he took were not a retainer's gifts, but priestly offerings: a garland, two coconuts, and kumkum for the red holy marks on the forehead.

Nothing in the former mukhthesar's account had prepared me for the extravagance of the maharaja's palace. A fire in the last century had destroyed the old palace; the one that now existed, the palace where the pundit had gone for his first interview with the maharaja, had taken 15 years to build, from 1897 to 1912; just after – to think of comparable extravagance – the Vanderbilt château at Biltmore in Tennessee. A European architect had designed the palace, and it answered every kind of late-19th-century British-Raj idea of what an Indian palace should be. Scalloped Mogul arches; Scottish stained glass made to an Indian peacock design; in the main hall, hollow cast-iron pillars (painted blue), made in England, to a decorated pattern – the guide still knew the name of the manufacturers; marble and tile floors, Mogul-style pietra dura, white marble inset with coloured stones in floral patterns, and Edwardian tiles.

Many of the sightseers in the palace – everyone still required to be barefoot – were young men in black, pilgrims to Ayappa. Busloads of them had come, and there was a touch of vanity and even boisterousness about them, a touch of the visiting football crowd. Deviah didn't like it. The days before the pilgrimage should be days of penance, he said, days of doing without pleasure; Ayappa pilgrims shouldn't be breaking their journey to walk through a palace.

There was a very wide, shadowed, cool gallery where the maharaja in the old days would have shown himself to his subjects. The scalloped arches framed the very bright, brown gardens outside; the vistas here had the scale of the vistas through the arches and gateways of the Taj Mahal. And here especially – feeling the cool marble below my feet, in the deep recess of the pillared gallery, with the heat and the harsh light outside, like a complement of privilege – I thought of the pundit and his employer: privilege and devotion meeting in mutual need.

Among the palace treasures displayed was a gallery of Hindu deities. Some of those deities seemed to have been touched, like the palace itself, by a mixture of styles: the increasing naturalism of Indian art in the 20th century had turned ancient Hindu icons into things that looked like dolls.

Deviah thought so too. He didn't like the 'calendar' ideas of Hindu gods which were now widespread. 'The gods look like girls, women. I can't accept the idea of gods being made to look like women. Rama was a brave man, when you get to know about him.'

The palace design, with its garishness and mixture of styles, its European interpretation of Indian princeliness, expressed – paradoxically – a kind of Indian self-abasement before the idea of Europe. The gallery with the deities, speaking of a Hindu faith that was like something issuing out of the earth itself, expressed the opposite. The doll-like quality of some of the deities – modern-looking and camera-influenced though they were – even added to the mysteriousness.

The royal family of Mysore had taken a special interest in the festival of Dussehra. For the 10 days of the festival the jewels of the palace temple were on display until midnight, watched over by the mukhthesar; and on the last day of the festival the maharaja himself had taken part in the procession in the city. It was a great sadness for the people of Mysore, the guide said, when – after his de-recognition – the maharaja had to stop appearing in the Dussehra procession. His place had thereafter been taken by a large image of the family deity – and the image was there, in the deities' gallery.

In a gallery around the main hall of the palace was the 24th maharaja's celebration of the festival. There were panels all the way around with sections of a continuous, realistic oil painting, based on photographs, of almost the entire Dussehra procession of 1935. The faces of everyone, the guide said, could be identified. The uniforms of all the courtiers and the various grades of attendants were as they had been – the bare feet unexpected, but not immediately noticeable. The painters had taken delight, too, in rendering the details of the street, the buildings and shops and cars, the shop signs and advertisements. The painting hadn't absolutely been finished. Nine painters had worked for three years, from 1937 until the death of the 24th maharaja. The 25th maharaja, whom the pundit served, hadn't been interested in art; and the Dussehra picture sequence – like many old Indian monuments, and for the same reason: the death of a ruler – was left unfinished. There were a few blank panels at the very end of the gallery.

There had been no hint of that dereliction in the pundit's account of his master. Nor had there been any hint of what was to be seen in the trophy room: the 25th maharaja had travelled in many countries, and shot wild animals. The towering neck and head of a startled-looking giraffe was among the trophies. It had been killed in Africa, and stuffed in Mysore; one of the world's most accomplished taxidermists lived in Mysore at that time. Another trophy was the lower, curving half of an elephant's trunk, made rigid and converted into an ash-tray or ash-bin, with an iron grille at the top for stubbing out cigarettes and cigars.

People spoke readily of the days of the maharajas. But no one I met seemed to possess the whole story of the end of the 25th and last maharaja of Mysore. Various people had various pieces, which sometimes didn't match. He had borrowed far too much from local businessmen – that was one story. Another was that he had had unsuitable favourites. A third story was that he had been involved in a lawsuit; and the prospect of having his ancient name – naked, without its titles – shouted three times by a court usher, in a place where his word had once been law, was so tormenting to him that he had taken an overdose of sedatives.

One version of the death was that he had swallowed a crushed diamond. Kala said that the swallowing of a diamond to commit suicide was a recurring piece of business in local Kannada-language films: people in extremity bit at the diamonds on their rings, and then began writhing in agony. So the story of the swallowing of the crushed diamond gave appropriate grandeur to the tragedy of the last maharaja, which remained mysterious.

I was told that he was fifty-five when he died. This made him three years younger than the pundit, though the pundit had said nothing of the maharaja's age, had left all that side of the man vague. Even after his death, misfortune followed the maharaja, someone said. The people around him began to pull off the rings from his fingers, and they had to pull hard, because the maharaja was very fat – that was what was contained in the pundit's respectful description of him as 'hefty', 'like a king', 'like God'. And, in this story, that bad death was followed by an unhappy cremation. The pyre was of sandalwood. Sandalwood is expensive (it was a monopoly of the old Mysore State). People began to pillage the pyre of half-consumed sandalwood pieces; and the next day it was discovered that the body had been incompletely burnt.

Folk tales had been generated by the idea of the tragedy of the last maharaja, de-recognized, impoverished, and finally hopelessly in debt. But nothing of that had entered the pundit's memories. He remained true to the man he had found: his memories were of the pure and devout man he had served indirectly and directly for 18 years.

In Bangalore three miles of wall enclosed the 500 acres of the summer palace grounds. The big and very valuable site was the subject of litigation; the public were not allowed in; special permission was required. The grounds were unkempt; films were sometimes shot in them. The palace was in red-grey Bangalore granite, and it was said (fancifully) to be modelled on Windsor Castle. The grass was burnt brown; the paths were of red laterite; sometimes in the grass were red anthills three or four feet high, like some melting-down spire top from the architectural imagination of Gaudí. The lamp standards were broken, one or two leaning, many of the white globes broken or vanished. And all around was the traffic and the smoke and the cicada sound of the car horns of Bangalore, a city now of business, science and industry.

On the road between Bangalore and Mysore City was the river-island fort of Tippu Sultan, who had in the late 18th century ruled here. He had been defeated by the British, by Wellington. Old history, not known to everyone in England now, its place in the imagination having been taken over by later wars, later villains. The British had installed the Mysore maharajas in place of Tippu. They were not upstarts; in the 14th and 15th centuries the Wodeyars had been satraps of the mighty Hindu kings of Vijayan-agar. By an unlikely twist they had been restored to power. Now they were receding fast into the difficult Indian past, beyond the reach of the imagination – like so many of the historical names on the road down from Goa.

4

Little Wars

Aqui a cidade foi, que se chamava
Meliapor, fermosa, grande e rica;
Os ídolos antigos adorava,
Como inda agora faz a gente inica.
Camoens: *The Lusiads* (1572)

Here was the beautiful, great and rich city
called Mylapore, where the unregenerate heathen
worshipped their ancient idols, as they still do.

Somewhere in the Himalayas, one day in August 1962, when I was
part of the great annual pilgrimage to the ice lingam, symbol of
Shiva, in the cave of Amarnath, 13,000 feet up, I met 'Sugar'. He
was from the South, from Madras, a biggish, soft-featured man.
We had become friends then, and two months or so later, when I
was in Madras, I saw a lot more of him. He was a brahmin, and
lived in the brahmin area called Mylapore, near the famous old
temple. He was a melancholic, withdrawn man: so he had appeared
to me in the Himalayas, and so he appeared to me in Madras, in
his home surroundings. He didn't have much conversation. What
he offered, with a full heart and without any apparent kind of
second judgement, was his friendship, which was of the most
undemanding sort. He was always ready to see one; he was always
pleased to be with one. He was in his late thirties, but he hadn't
married. He lived with his mother and father in their comfortable,
middle-class, Mylapore house.

I was spending a whole year in India that time. Some weeks after
I had arrived I had gone north to Kashmir. I had done some work
there for some months, and then I had begun to move down south.

Sometimes, in country areas, I stayed with young government officers I had got to know. Sometimes I stayed in government bungalows and rest houses, bare shells of places offering the barest facilities – though those facilities, in the Indian countryside before the green revolution, were like luxury.

In the towns I stayed in such hotels as I could afford. Before I had gone to India I had had the idea that, with the many hands available, hotels in India would have been cheap and good, like the hotels in Spain in the early 1950s. It wasn't like that. In India at that time there was hardly a tourist trade, and hotel-keeping wasn't yet a profession. The people who ran modest hotels in small towns could only offer a version of the accommodation they themselves had; the staff they employed would have been like their own ragged house servants.

And then in Madras it was different. The restaurants and hotels that were vegetarian were clean (though the popular non-vegetarian or 'military' places, as they were quaintly called, were as bad as anything in the North). The cleanliness and the vegetarianism were connected; they were both contained in the southern idea of brahminism. At the Woodlands Hotel I stayed in a clean room in an annexe, and ate off banana leaves (for the sake of the purity, and the link with old ways) on marble tables in the air-conditioned dining-room. There were gardens and an open-air theatre or stage in the hotel grounds.

If I had known nothing of the brahmin Hindu culture of the South – if I had known nothing of the arts of music and dance, in both of which brahmins were pre-eminent – I would have begun to get some idea of it there: an idea of caste, like the Elizabethan idea of 'degree', acting as a check on the disorder – cultural, social, physical – which in India could easily come.

But with this idea of a protective culture there also came a feeling of strangeness. It was there, in the dining-room of the Woodlands, in the vegetarian food of the South. This wasn't at all like the vegetarian food, the dal and the roti, I had grown up thinking of as essential Indian food. This vegetarian food of the South – which drew the crowds to the Woodlands – was too subtle, too light; it made no impression on my stomach; it never left me feeling fed.

And the religion was as strange as the food. Sugar wanted me to get to know the Mylapore temple; he worshipped there. But the idea of the temple had played almost no part in the Hinduism I had grown up with in Trinidad. I knew about pujas; they were done at home; my Indian-born grandfather had built a puja room at the very top of the house he had built in Trinidad in the 1920s. What I was most familiar with were the occasional ceremonial readings from the epics and the scriptures. The devotee faced the pundit across a specially made and decorated earthen shrine, laid with a sweet-smelling sacred fire of resinous pitch pine. At intervals during the reading the fire was fed with clarified butter and sugar; and then a bell was rung, a brass gong was struck, and sometimes a conch was blown. Words, with a kind of tolling music – that was the Hinduism I had grown up with, and it had been hard enough for me to understand. The idea of the temple to which Sugar tried to introduce me – the idea of the sanctum, and the special temple deity at its centre – was very far away, even a little unsettling.

With all its welcome and restfulness, in Madras I always had the feeling that I was in a strange place. The sculptured pyramidal temple towers, the palm trees, the bare-backed brahmins among the old stone pillars, the big and beautiful water-tank at Mylapore, with internal stone steps all around – they were like things in old European prints. Because of those temple towers, especially, I again and again had a little visual shock and felt that I was seeing the place afresh; that the culture was still whole and inviolate; that I was seeing what the earliest travellers had seen.

Travellers, the sea: my Madras memories were mixed up with memories of dawn walks to the city beach, which was very long and very wide. At sunrise people washed their cattle in the sea. The sun came up from the sea; the flat wet sand shone red and gold; the ribby, bony-rumped, horned cattle stood on their blurred reflections; and then the heat of the day began.

Less than five years later I was in Madras again for a few days. There had been a state election (but it wasn't for that that I had gone); and the atmosphere in the Woodlands Hotel on the day of my arrival was like the atmosphere in a colonial territory after the election of the party that was going to rule after independence. Motor-cars, music, new clothes, the political heroes of the day recognizable by the extra excitement their arrival caused. And the open-air stage or theatre area of the Woodlands was festooned and decorated, as for a carnival.

Twenty years after the independence of India, this colonial-style celebration. After my introduction to the brahmin culture of the

South, this was my introduction to the revolt of the South: the revolt of South against North, non-brahmin against brahmin, the racial revolt of dark against fair, Dravidian against Aryan. The revolt had begun long before; the brahmin world I had come upon in 1962 was one that had already been undermined.

The party that had won the state election in 1967 was the DMK, the Dravidian Progressive Movement. It had deep roots; it had its own prophet and its own politician-leader, men who were its equivalents of Gandhi and Nehru, men whose careers had run strangely parallel with the careers of the mainstream Indian independence leaders. Until that moment I had hardly heard about them, and had hardly known about the passion of their cause. And what that victory in 1967 meant was that the culture to which I had been introduced by Sugar less than five years before, the culture which had appeared whole and mysterious and ancient to me, had been overthrown.

Sugar appeared, in his brahmin way, not to pay attention to what had happened. He was still living in the house of his parents in Mylapore, still going to the ancient temple, still doing with apparent contentment the modest business job he had always done.

His friendship after five years was as warm as ever. He was still as melancholy as I had remembered him, still with that deep, internal nagging. Perhaps now he was a little more withdrawn. I don't think we talked politics. Instead, in an upstairs room of his parents' house, we talked of certain Tamil books of prophecy he had become interested in. He told me they were ancient books; they had now been published, in many volumes, by the state government.

He couldn't say why he had become interested in the prophetic books, whether he was interested in finding out about his own future, or whether his interest in the books was that of a student. There was an ambiguity: he was clearly fascinated by the books, yet he appeared to be warning me off them, telling me that the priests who read and interpreted those holy books could take a lot of money off people.

He read other books as well. They were in his room. He brought them out: romantic feminine fiction from England, books to pass the time, he said, as though for him the matter of a book was not important, as though in his solitude what mattered was simply the act of reading, keeping the mind going.

Now, more than 20 years later, I was in Madras again; and, again without intending it, I had come at a political time. Another state election was about to take place. The posters of the various parties, and the party emblems, and the pictures of the leaders were everywhere. Some of the posters were enormous, like the cinema posters of Madras; and that was fitting, because the leaders the Dravidian movement had thrown up, after the original Dravidian party had split, had been Tamil film stars. In the posters all the politicians had the round plump faces of Southern film stars, and even people known to be dark were given pink cheeks: it was part of the iconography of leadership.

The film star who had been chief minister for much of the past decade, and whose death had led to the present state election, was shown with dark glasses and a white fur cap. The glasses and the cap had been his trade mark both as a star and a politician. He had been a famous stunt man, a kind of local Errol Flynn figure, and to his admirers he had been almost divine. He had been more interested in being a ruler and a star rather than in the business of governing. It was said that at his death some 18,000 files were waiting for his attention. One of the things he had done was to abolish the Madras Corporation. So Madras was in a mess, with mounds of rubbish everywhere. It was as though this, too, was part of the revolt of the South, this violation of the old ideas of purity.

The politics of colonial revolt in Tamil Nadu had followed a colonial course: theft, waste, stagnation, words, the eternal appeal to old grievances. But those grievances were real. The original Dravidian revolt had not been gone back on, had not been rejected by the people of the state: the election fight now was between factions of the original DMK, and what had remained of the DMK itself.

It was the DMK, the winners of 1967, who won again this time. A few days after my arrival the black-and-red flags of the party were everywhere – black the colour of caste revolt, red the colour of revolution. The flag fluttered in celebration from three-wheeler scooter-taxis; from bicycles. Sometimes in open vans or jitneys raised hands held the flag aloft, the raised hands symbolizing the rays of the rising sun, which was the DMK's election emblem.

I looked up Sugar's name in the telephone directory late one evening. I found a name that was like his, but the address was new. I telephoned. A Tamil voice was at first totally rejecting, totally refusing to understand. But then, as the owner of the voice made the adjustment to my English, his own English began to surface, became quite clerk-like and precise. Sugar was asleep, he said; he couldn't be disturbed now; he had 'retired' for the night; it was his habit to 'retire' at nine. When did he get up? He got up at five. I left my name.

The next day there was a message from Sugar. A woman's voice answered when I telephoned, and after a while Sugar came on the telephone. He sounded ill. I asked him how old he was; I said it was something I had never known.

He said, 'Sixty-four. Not too young.'

'So you were thirty-seven when we met in Kashmir?'

'I was a young man. Like you.'

Now Mr and Mrs Raghavan looked after him. It was Mr Raghavan I had spoken to the previous night, and this morning it was Mrs Raghavan who had taken the call. The telephone was theirs; they kept it upstairs; he lived downstairs; it wasn't easy for him to climb steps now. He had retired from 'service'. His mother had died; his father had died. He had left the family house I had seen him in. He had moved from Mylapore. He lived in a little apartment in the Raghavans' house. He wanted me to come right away. He gave the address and said – curiously, I thought – 'Everybody knows my house.' He spoke with something like urgency. His voice began to break; I thought he was very ill.

He was waiting for me, and when the taxi stopped he ran up to me, calling me by my name – I was about to go through a gate to the wrong house. He was in a yellow singlet and dhoti. He was not as tall as I had remembered. In the Himalayas he had been dark, burnt by the mountain sun; he was paler now. The melancholy of his expression had merged into his invalid's appearance. The flesh on his face and his exposed shoulders had grown softer, suggesting the man who couldn't climb steps.

He led me through the correct gate to the house where his apartment was. The apartment was on the ground floor, and we stepped directly from the garden path to his sitting room. He said, 'Drawing-sleeping,' meaning that the room was his sitting room as well as his bedroom. 'Attached bathroom.' He pointed, but didn't offer to show it. There was also a kitchen, and a room that was his temple. That was his great news for me: his temple. He had set up his own temple in his apartment. There were images there of the three most important deities, the deities of wisdom, strength, and money.

'Come, let me show you. Take off your shoes.'

The last command was friendly but firm, without the diffidence with which the request was usually made, the suggestion that if one didn't want to, one didn't. But friendship was uppermost in his mind: he was offering me this sight of his temple as a gesture of friendship.

I took off my shoes and stood before the black, garlanded, unreadable images.

He watched with me. He had always been tolerant of my lack of faith. Then he took me to the room that was his kitchen. He made a show of hanging his head and letting his drooping shoulders droop a little more. He laughed and said, 'Please don't write about my kitchen.' He knew it wasn't clean, he said. But there was no running water. All the water he used in the kitchen had to be fetched in jars. It wasn't easy for him now to lift a full jar; he gave a demonstration, to show how his body could no longer do some of the simple things he wanted it to do. He became ill if he lifted things that were heavy; so he couldn't keep his kitchen clean. The kitchen was grimy. Dirt and cooking grime had caught on the wire netting over the window, and on the ledges and shelves just below. He was looking after himself now, he said; he was dispensing with things. A girl came in to sweep for him. But (though he didn't say) he couldn't as a brahmin allow that girl into his kitchen.

He was sixty-four now. He was dispensing with things. In the front room, the main room of the apartment, the drawing-sleeping, he had a number of small pieces of furniture pushed together in a jumble at one end. He was going to get rid of that furniture; he didn't need it.

'I want a plain room.'

I asked why he hadn't married.

'Why? Why? How can I answer? I didn't feel like it.'

And that was the kind of reply he gave when I asked him about the temple and how the idea had come to him. The idea had just come to him, he said.

I remembered his interest in 1967 in the prophetic books. I

asked him about that. Had that interest left him now? And, again, I wanted to know how that interest had come to him.

He said, 'Why? Why? These are your sort of questions. How can I answer?' The wish had simply come to him. But I was right about one thing: that wish, to delve into the books of prophecy, was now in the past.

And, considering his new solitude, his stained dhoti and singlet, for the first time since I had known him I asked him directly about his life.

He had worked in the same firm all his life, starting when he had left college. Towards the end he had run the office, been a kind of office manager. He had looked after the files of all the employees. He loved the firm still. At the time of his retirement he was earning 2000 rupees a month, £80. That was enough for a single man. The firm was now giving him a pension of 1000 rupees a month. From some money that the firm had invested for him he was getting a further 1300 rupees. It was enough.

The concrete floor of the drawing-sleeping where we were was decorated with white floral patterns, such as exist on the threshold of many Indian houses. They are usually done with flour, and done afresh every day, but the pattern on Sugar's floor was a plastic stick-on. The walls were blue, tarnished from the rubbing of backs and hands and, above the back of the chairs, from oiled heads. All the pictures on the walls were religious pictures. There was a hanging two-shelf wall cupboard with sliding glass doors; inside, medicine bottles and candles and tablets in foil-covered cards were mixed up with papers and household bric-a-brac. I had never felt this kind of desolation in his parents' house in Mylapore.

I asked whether he had had a happy life.

'A plain life. A plain life.'

Then he began to receive people. They came in through the open front door. The first man to come in was a dark man with fresh holy marks on his forehead: he had done his morning puja, or had been to the great temple.

'He's a landlord,' Sugar said, when the man went into the temple room. 'A moneyed man.'

The second visitor was younger; his features were finer. He greeted Sugar and then, with no further word, went into the temple room. This man wore a formal, reddish-brown long tunic. Sugar said the man was an executive in a big company.

214

'People come,' Sugar said, as though explaining his visitors.

The first man, the landlord and moneyed man, came out and sat against a wall in the drawing-sleeping. When the man in the reddish tunic came out, he sat on a chair that was part of the furniture jumble at one end of the room.

This second man, the executive, was the production manager in his company. It seemed rather late in the morning for him to be here, but he said he came every morning to Sugar's temple, to meditate, and to be calm. They didn't talk a lot when they were together. On Sunday evenings he came for three hours; he had a lot of time on Sundays. Once, during a power failure, he had sat with Sugar for nearly four hours, and they had hardly talked during that time. To come and sit in the room where we were, with the tarnished blue walls, and with a glimpse of the dark kitchen, was a form of meditation. Meditation, which implied the emptying of the mind, wasn't easy, the production manager said: the beginner's thoughts ran too easily to family, job, and things like that. It took years to learn to meditate. He wasn't like Mr Sugar.

This was news to me: that Sugar had this reputation, as a sage, a holy man.

I asked him, 'Can you empty your mind?'

He said, playing it down, yet pleased that – without his saying anything – I knew, 'I have achieved little.'

The production manager said, 'With most god-men you go to get something.' It wasn't like that with Sugar. He came to Sugar just for the peace; he wanted nothing from him.

The brahmin world of Mylapore had been turned upside down. But in Sugar's little blue sanctuary the politics of the streets outside were far away: the red-and-black flags, the 80-foot painted cut-outs of the new heroes (against rough wooden scaffolding). In the little apartment in the Raghavans' house Sugar kept a kind of court and had his own circle, and was perhaps more protected, more looked-up to, than he had ever been in the family house where he had grown up. He was holy, offering peace. It explained one of the things he had said on the telephone: 'Everybody knows my house.'

He said, when I was getting ready to leave, 'You must come and eat with me. I will cook for you myself. I will cook pumpkin for you.'

'Pumpkin?'

'You ate pumpkin every day at Woodlands in 1962.'

There were other things he had remembered that I had forgotten. He remembered that in his family house in 1962, and again in 1967, I had had long, serious talks with his father about books and India.

It was flattering to be remembered in this way, in these details, after so long. I felt it also spoke of a life plain to the point of tears. Yet this plainness had in the end brought its reward. His gifts had become known. Perhaps the very qualities that had made him memorable in the pilgrim throng in the Himalayas – his solitude, his stillness, his melancholy, the feeling of incompleteness and search that he gave off – had attracted others.

Only 33 or 34 per cent of the voters had voted for the victorious DMK party; but the red-and-black flags of the party so multiplied in the city, it began to seem that nearly everyone had voted for the DMK. On walls where it had been painted before election day, the party's election emblem, of the sun rising above hills, was now lovingly reworked and decorated, a little more and then a little more again, seeming further to mock the open palm and the two doves, emblems of two of the defeated parties, emblems until a few days before of great hope and jauntiness, but now abandoned, neglected, no loyal or happy hand adding a celebratory touch of extra colour.

Within a day or so of the election result very big painted signboards began to appear in some places in the city with very big portraits of the three heroes of the party. There were no names, no words; you had to know who the heroes were. They were shown in profile, in a staggered line, each profile like a royal head on a coin; and each hero was done in a different colour. The current leader of the party was done in a kind of brown; the man who had led the party to its first election victory in 1967 in a slatey-blue or grey; and the profile behind these two was that of the old, pink-cheeked man with a long wavy beard who had been the prophet of the party.

The prophet was known as 'Periyar'. It was a Tamil word, meaning a sage or a wise man. I knew the name Periyar, but only just; I knew nothing about the man. I began to learn now, and I was astounded as much by what I learned as by the fact that, with all my reading about the independence movement in India, I had read or registered so little about this prophet of the South.

He was an atheist and a rationalist, and he made two or three speeches a day over a very long life. He ridiculed the Hindu gods. He cruelly mocked caste Hindus, comparing the poverty of their scientific achievements with the achievements of Europe. And then, having it both ways, he also said that the Hindus had copied their gods ('some selected animals, a few birds, a few trees and creepers, a few mountains and some rivers') from the gods of ancient Egypt and Greece and Persia and Chaldea.

This was the first surprise: that someone who – at least in the English translation of his often disorganized Tamil discourses – came over as a humorist and a satirist should have been received by the people of Tamil Nadu as a prophet, and at a moment of political triumph so long after his death should have been freshly honoured. But Periyar had never intended humour when he spoke against Hinduism and caste Hindus. He had once been a believer; and he was as obsessed with the religion and its propounders as only a man once a believer could be.

There was a place in Madras called Periyar Thidal. It was on the site of a former bus or tram depot. Periyar himself had bought the place in 1953, for a lakh of rupees, 100,000 rupees, worth then about £7,500. It was the place from which his organization still operated.

A garlanded black statue of Periyar stood in the middle of the big sandy plot, with this inscription on the plinth: PERIYAR THE PROPHET OF THE NEW AGE THE SOCRATES OF SOUTH EAST ASIA FATHER OF THE SOCIAL MOVEMENT AND ARCH ENEMY OF IGNOR- ANCE; SUPERSTITIONS; MEANINGLESS CUSTOMS AND BASELESS MANNERS. Periyar's grave was in a corner of the plot. All around the grave were polished grey granite slabs engraved with some of Periyar's sayings. One of those sayings, virtually an incantation, was very famous: *There is no God. There is no God. There is no God at all. He who invented God is a fool. He who propagates God is a scoundrel. He who worships God is a barbarian.* This was how Periyar began all his discourses.

It was hard to imagine anything so blunt and bitter being accepted in any part of India, if something else wasn't being offered with it. And what Periyar offered, with his 'rationalism' and his rejection of God, was his rejection of the brahmins and their language; his rejection of the North; his rejection of caste; his rejection of the disregard the fair people of the North had for the dark people of the South.

There was importance, too, in the fact of that grave in the Periyar Thidal. Hindus are cremated; Periyar insisted on being buried. He was more than the rationalist: to the people who listened to him and liked what he said, he was the anti-Hindu.

He was born in 1879, 10 years after Gandhi was born, and 10 years before Nehru was born. His political life began in 1919, and continued until his death in 1973. And that was the second big surprise of Periyar: that he should have lived so long, that his career should have for many years run parallel with that of Gandhi, and that Gandhi, through many of the later years of his struggle and search, should have had at his back this figure of the anti-Hindu who finally became the anti-Gandhi, a man whose life and career echoed and reversed much of Gandhi's own.

Gandhi was a vegetarian. Periyar made a point of eating beef. Gandhi struggled to control the senses. Periyar ate enormous quanties of food, and was enormously fat. One of Periyar's admirers told me, 'He was a *glutton*.' And, in this reversal of values, the word was intended as praise. 'He always had a *biriyani* – rice and mutton, beef, pork. He was never *fussy* about food.' Gandhi was always fussy about his food.

He was different from Gandhi, opposed to him, and yet in some ways – in his discovery of his cause, his working out of ways to serve it, his lifelong adherence to it, and, above all, in his practical business sense – he was like Gandhi. Like Gandhi, Periyar was born into a Hindu merchant caste. Gandhi came from a family of small-scale administrators. Periyar came from a family of well-to-do merchants. Periyar was not as well educated as Gandhi, and it could be said that he was more devout and traditional. Gandhi went against the principles of his caste and travelled to London to study law. Periyar, in his mid-twenties (while Gandhi was in South Africa, fighting hard battles), went to Banaras, to live the life of a sanyasi, to live naked, on the alms of the devout, in the hope of finding some kind of spiritual illumination.

The illumination never came, and he left Banaras and went back to his family business in his own town. He also went into local municipal politics, and then in 1919, when Gandhi had been back in India for some years, Periyar joined the Indian National

Congress. He supported its handloom campaign and took part in the non-cooperation movement.

Then came the break. It had to do with the caste prejudices of the brahmins in the South. Non-brahmins were not allowed free entry to temples. They were absolutely barred from the inner sanctum where the temple deity was; they had to be content with a view from a distance. Sometimes non-brahmins were not even allowed to walk on the lane in front of a temple.

This last prohibition caused an especial commotion in the neighbouring state of Kerala in 1924. Kerala was at that time a princely state, with its own maharaja, and the brahmins of Kerala were even stricter about caste prohibitions than the Tamil brahmins of Madras. Within the compound of the royal palace there was a temple, and there was also a law court. One day, when a sacred temple fair of some kind was going on, the temple lane was closed to non-brahmins. The temple lane was also the lane to the law court. A lawyer called Madhavan, a non-brahmin, had to appear in a court case that day; but (fame comes to people in unlikely ways) Madhavan was not allowed to walk past the temple. Some non-brahmins in Kerala protested and started an agitation; they were jailed by the maharaja. They appealed to Periyar. He came to Kerala and campaigned for a whole year, until the temple lane was opened to non-brahmins.

There was another crisis soon after. It was discovered that, at a Congress school for propagating Gandhian thought, brahmin children were fed separately from non-brahmin children. And then it turned out that the school, though run by a brahmin, was being financed by non-brahmins. The matter was reported to Gandhi; but his response was ambiguous and light-hearted.

Periyar at that moment broke with Gandhi and the Congress. (There is a – brahmin – story in Madras that the break really came because Periyar had been asked to account for money connected with the handloom campaign.) In 1925 Periyar founded the Self-Respect Movement, and it was his brilliant idea then to symbolize his cause by wearing a black shirt. Black-shirted, he campaigned for the rest of his life, for nearly 50 years, against brahminism, caste, Congress, the Hindu religion, the disabilities of women. He established the idea of Self-Respect marriages for non-brahmins, marriages conducted without priests or religious vows. And he preached a crude kind of socialism.

'In the world of the future, there will be no men without character and culture . . . The depravity of modern character is founded on culture, justice and discipline being used for maintaining caste and class differences among men . . . When these capitalist and individualist conditions are absent, the need for depraved character will not arise.'

He offered a vision of a future bright with the fruits of science, and without the need for the idea of God.

'Communications will mostly be by air and of great speed . . . Radios may be fixed in men's hats . . . Food enriched with vitamins will be encased in pills or capsules sufficient for a day's or week's sustenance. The average life may stand at 100 years or more . . . Motorcars may weigh about one hundredweight and will run without petrol . . . Electricity will be everywhere and in every house, serving the people for all purposes . . . No industry or factory will run for the private profits of individuals. They will all be owned by the community at large, and all inventions will cater for the needs and pleasures of all people . . . When the world itself has been converted into a paradise, the need to picture a paradise in the clouds will not arise. Where there is no want, there is no god. Where there is scientific knowledge, there is no need for speculation and imagination . . . The struggle for existence needs to be changed into a life of happiness.'

With this preaching, reiterated day after day, this vision of the pain of caste disappearing together with the idea of God, there went his inherited feeling for the practical side of things. He had been born into a business family, and he remained concerned with money all his life, never denying its value, seeking always to keep himself and his movement independent and free of pressure. His movement was never short of money; the trust he left behind to look after his cause was rich.

His relics were in a big room in the main building at the Periyar Thidal. On a four-poster bed in the front part of the room there was a life-size photographic cut-out (the cinema-advertisement style and election-campaign style transferred to this private museum) of Periyar, very old, with a big beard, sitting cross-legged, in a writing posture. There was a patterned pink blanket on the bed, and the cut-out leaned against a bolster. The poles of the four-poster were white; there was no canopy. A tall revolving bookshelf stood at one side of the bed, with small busts of Buddha and Lenin, souvenir-shop objects, and a statue of a horse, a gift. The horse had no significance; it had been kept by Periyar for its beauty, and as a memento of the giver.

More symbolical gifts were in a glass case: silver implements of iconoclasm: two silver mallets, and two silver sticks, in shape like the stick the aged Periyar used.

The leadership of the Periyar movement had passed to Mr Veeramani. He was the keeper of Periyar's memory, and the guardian of his relics. When he showed me the mallets and the sticks, he reminded me with a laugh of what he said was an old Sanskrit saying: 'The poison of the cobra is in his tongue alone. The poison of the brahmin is from head to foot.' That saying led to another, which Mr Veeramani said was a well known Hindi saying: 'If you see a brahmin and a snake, kill the brahmin first.' (I had heard that years before in a different version, and I had been told then that it was a household saying of the people of south-east Asia: 'If you are in the forest and you see a snake and an Indian, kill the Indian first.')

After the emblems of iconoclasm, the emblems of kingship. Periyar had often been called the white-bearded king of Tamil Nadu. A town in the South had given the old man a decorated silver throne, and that throne was in a glass case, with a silver crown, the gift of followers in another town. Another gift was a silver sceptre, with small heads of Periyar and Buddha at the top; and in yet another glass case were curving silver swords.

Right around this big museum room, at the top of the walls, just below the ceiling, was a set of 33 oil paintings depicting the stations of Periyar's long life. It was as with Bible pictures: you had to know the story. And once you knew, it was all there: Periyar as a naked sanyasi in Banaras in 1904, eating such food as he could find; Periyar 10 years later in municipal politics in his home town; Periyar with the Congress in 1919; Periyar campaigning in Kerala in 1924 for the rights of non-brahmins to enter temples; Periyar campaigning not long after for the abolition of caste distinctions in the Congress school; Periyar founding his Self-Respect Movement in 1925, and wearing his black shirt for the first time; Periyar in Germany in 1932, in the company of 'German atheists'; Periyar in Russia the same year with Russian sanatorium employees; Periyar in 1943, discussing the break-up of India after independence with Mr Jinnah (campaigning for a Muslim Pakistan), Dr Ambedkar (wanting a scheduled-caste state called Dalitstan), Periyar himself hoping for a southern, Dravidian, non-brahmin state called Dravidstan. Later paintings showed Periyar, after independence, painting out the Hindi names of railway stations in the South, in 1952; breaking idols of Ganesh, Ganpati, the elephant god, in 1953, to show that they were only of clay, and quite harmless; in 1957 painting out 'Brahmin' from a signboard saying 'Brahmin Hotel', 'brahmin' meaning vegetarian, as opposed to 'military', non-vegetarian; and in the same year burning the Indian Constitution.

He had been single-minded and unwearying through a long life. In the centre of the room a collection of his personal relics had been laid out by Mr Veeramani in another glass case: his flashlight, his magnifying glasses, his unusually stout stick, his watch, his spectacles, his stainless-steel food tray, his bedpan and syringe and other medical paraphernalia. Almost like Gandhi's relics; and they would have been Gandhian, if Periyar had left nothing else behind. But the property he had left in his trust, including the large city site of the Periyar Thidal, was worth many millions; and this worth had multiplied many times over in the 15 years since his death.

In spite of his love of food and his meat-eating, there was, in his single-mindedness and obsession, something like purity, and it was this quality that made him the anti-Gandhi. But that figure, of the anti-Gandhi, had meaning only because the real Gandhi existed. Gandhi developed and grew; for the first 40 years of the century, from his thirtieth year to his seventieth, he was constantly searching for new political and religious ways. His search made him a universal figure; people to whom the politics were far away could yet refer their own search to his. Periyar was a local figure; he never outgrew his cause. Without Gandhi and the Congress and the independence movement his cause wouldn't have had the power it had; he was riding on the back of something very big. That might have been why I hadn't heard of him.

It was Sadanand Menon, a writer living in Madras, who had taken me to the Periyar Thidal and had given me the background necessary to an understanding of Periyar's life and movement.

Towards the end of the 19th century, with British rule, Sadanand said, the brahmins became dominant in a way they hadn't been for some time. They were dominant in Indian social life, the professions, and in the beginnings of the nationalist movement. But Madras Province (taking in Tamil Nadu and other areas) was very large; Madras was a port; and, as the economy of the province grew, other middle castes began to produce their own prominent personalities. Many of these middle-caste people were well-to-do – like Periyar's own family; many were landlords; some could send their sons to Oxford and Cambridge. As soon as such people had emerged from the middle castes, the antique brahmin caste restrictions would not have been easy to maintain. What Periyar did was to take this mood of rejection to the non-brahmin masses.

Sadanand said, 'His mode of communication was cultural. The Self-Respect Movement began three or four newspapers simultaneously. They laid great emphasis on education. In the 1930s one of the methods of the movement was the method of social discourse – not lecturing down. An educated volunteer would go to a slum area in a city, or to the village square, and he would start reading aloud from a paper. In no time he would have a crowd around him. And he would interpret what he was reading according to the Self-Respect Movement's ideology. This has remained a form till today. It has remained the backbone of the DMK, this direct contact between the party cadre and the people. The other parties don't have this. They haven't even attempted it. I remember in the 1960s going to a place near where I was living, and observing a DMK party worker. He would come on the dot at 6.30 in the evening, carrying the party newspaper, together with an English paper and any other Tamil paper. He would have a hurricane lantern. He sat in a shed, just four poles and a roof, and he read aloud, and he would have an audience of 150 people.'

How deep, or important, was the rationalist side of the movement? How far had people been able to reject God or the gods?

Sadanand said that the rationalist movement as such had become a parody of itself over the years. But political power had come to the DMK, which was the political offshoot of that movement, and there had been an upheaval.

Sadanand said, 'The DMK came to power in 1967' – the year I had come to Madras for the second time, and I had gone to see Sugar and his father in their two-storey house in Mylapore, and Sugar had told me about the books of prophecy – 'and they created a ministry, the Hindu Religious and Charitable Endowments, the

223

HR&CE. The HR&CE minister controlled the enormous resources of the Hindu temples and trusts. Land, fixed assets, jewelry – every temple has enormous amounts of jewelry: the idols themselves, and the daily donations. The donations to a temple are anonymous; there is no means of accounting for them. The temple wealth was unassessable. How could you put a value on a 10th-century Shiva? After this – and this was quite separate from what the government was doing – the idols began to be stolen and were replaced by replicas. Archaeologists have recently pointed out large-scale replacement of temple icons by fakes. The originals have ended in private collections around the world.'

'Didn't the DMK mind about that? Isn't it their art too?'

'The DMK didn't think twice about that. They were dealing with the enemy. At the same time the new government started on a policy of distributing temple lands to the landless. But this was a notional thing. The names of 200 people could be produced who had been given one acre of temple land each, but actually that land might all belong to one man or the party. The people didn't get anything out of it.'

Sadanand spoke of this as the 'looting' of the temples, using that word – originally a Hindi word, and this fact reflecting something of the history of India – in the Indian sense. Had the brahmins been impoverished as result?

'In most of the temples the brahmins became simply the conductors of rituals, the purohits, and certainly there was impoverishment.' But more important, in Sadanand's account, was the downgrading of the temples. 'The temples as originally conceived were largely social institutions. Each temple had schools, granaries, facilities for large-scale water-storage – the origin of the temple tank – hospitals, stalls for cows. They were also patrons of the arts. But the DMK made crude equations. The temple became equated with oppression of a certain sort, and then the whole thing was vandalized, without discrimination.'

The movement claimed to have a link with the non-brahmin past of Tamil Nadu, and especially with the Chola emperors of the eighth to the 10th centuries. But this again, according to Sadanand, was glib and unhistorical.

'The Cholas were democrats, if you can imagine democracy within a feudal structure. But they were also the imperialists of the area, and the Chola symbol of the movement is the symbol of

Tamil imperialism, nothing else. The Cholas were known to be learned people, to have written books on astronomy, and to have been patrons of the arts. The DMK Chola symbol stands for none of this. The Chola kings developed fascinating systems of irrigation in the Tanjore area. The DMK never bothered to look at irrigation.'

Out of their narrowness, their regionalism, their caste obsessions, other things suffered. The English language suffered. The number of people from the state holding positions in the central government declined; many of the central government officers in Tamil Nadu now came from outside. The Tamil language itself deteriorated.

'The movement is not creative any more. Tamil has become a language which is incapable of expressing one modern idea. It's a fosssilized language, and this is reflected in the quality of Tamil journalism. Much of it is frivolous, inane.

'The movement still has a place. But what it keeps reproducing nowadays is this parody. Out of it there has come an impoverished iconography. You saw that flat cut-out of Periyar on the bed. That idea was extended later to the politicians of the movement, the leaders of the DMK and its successor parties. They were projected as giants in 80-foot cut-outs – a substitute for what they have lost. And religious or neo-religious movements have become stronger in Tamil Nadu.

'The current neo-religious movement here is the Adi Parashakti cult. You'll find it at a place half-way between Madras and Pondicherry. It's a cult of the primal mother – the Dravidian religion, as opposed to the Aryan religion, was mother-centred. From that has emerged this new cult. Just this one man, a schoolteacher, claimed one fine day that he had had a dream of this Mother or Shakti coming to him and ordering him to propagate her name. He claims that when he woke up there was an idol of Adi Parashakti growing out of the earth in front of him. The followers of this cult have a uniform, red and red. This is one of the paradoxical fall-outs of the rationalist movement.'

There was a deeper irony. The anti-brahmin movement was not a movement of all the non-brahmin castes. It was a movement mainly of the middle castes. There was, as ever in India, a further lower level, a further level of disadvantage. For these people at the very bottom the DMK offered no protection.

Sadanand said, 'The DMK came to power in 1967, talking of the oppression of the lower castes. In fact, the most brutal attacks on the scheduled castes have happened post-1967. In 1969 40 harijans were burnt alive in a hut. The caste known as the Thevars was responsible. They are a middle caste, a backward caste who have in the last 100 years come up socially and are now powerful, with their own caste association. They are one of the most militant castes. They call themselves the *kshatriyas*, the warriors, of the Tamil hierarchical order. The Dravidian Movement had been founded by the middle castes. When their government came to power, they became the oppressors.'

Sadanand's analysis of the cultural impoverishment brought about by the movement was almost certainly true. It was there in the iconography; it was there in the exaggerations and simplicities and contradictions of Periyar's speeches, where words seemed to have been loved for their own sake, and where speeches, in order to be relished, had to be spun out, conceit upon conceit. But, equally, there was the passion of the followers of Periyar. Periyar had touched something in these people, something deeper than logic and a regard for historical correctness; that also had to be taken into account.

Mr Gopalakrishnan was the proprietor of Emerald Publishers, publishers of school textbooks and books about the rationalist movement. He told me this story.

'My father was a very small businessman. He was of the Mudaliar caste. We were lower middle-caste people. He kept a stall. He sold cigarettes, aerated water, little things like that.

'I became a rationalist in the early 1940s, when I was ten or thereabouts. I was a student at the Sri Ramakrishna High School in Madras. It was a brahmin-dominated school. Even the peons and the watermen, four or five of them, were brahmins. We were only a few non-brahmins in each class. Every day we got sermons from some of our teachers that we were only fit for grazing cattle. We heard that from three teachers in particular. They thought that non-brahmins shouldn't study, and the words they oft repeated were: "Go and graze the cattle."

'We had to go to the prayer meeting in the prayer hall every morning. The prayers were in Sanskrit. They were the same prayers every day; they were boring. I had a non-brahmin classmate who didn't go to the prayer meetings; he would get beatings very often for that. All the boys would come with their caste mark. I used to use a piece of chalk, instead of the so-called sacred ash, to make the horizontal marks on my forehead. My friend never did it, and he was beaten for that, too. He was a creative boy. Ten years later he wrote a play and acted in it – a play with rationalist views.

'One day, when I was at the school, I had a chance of attending one of Periyar's meetings. The meeting was in Saidapet, where we were living, and many people, non-brahmins, were going. At that meeting for the first time I was able to understand why the brahmin teachers were so prejudiced against us. Till then I couldn't understand why they were so prejudiced. I started reading literature published by Periyar's movement, and the magazines they published. It took me four years to become a complete rationalist.

'First of all, in 1947 I stopped going to the temple. Until then I used to go with devotion. It was something I had got in babyhood from my mother and my sisters – the environment was like that. In those days the brahmin priests treated their non-brahmin devotees with contempt. The devotees took it for granted: it was the tradition. I used to take it for granted too, in my early days. The priest used to throw the sacred ash with contempt at the non-brahmin devotees, from a distance, whereas the brahmins were allowed to go to the sanctum sanctorum, where the idol actually stands. The non-brahmin devotees could see the idol only at a distance.

'My stopping temple-going was a gradual process. In my college days I used to read Shaw, Wells, and Russell. Their writings made a big impact, and I had the courage to face the believers in my family and in my society.

'My mother continued to be ritual-minded. She became worried, many years after, that when she died I might do no ritual for her. But then, three months before she died, she called me to her and told me that I wasn't to do any ritual for her.

'Now I ignore the Hindu religion. I don't waste my time discussing it. I never did any ritual for my mother when she died. That was two years ago. What I do every year on that day is to give new dresses to every granddaughter. That's all. There's no community lecture. No flowers. I just have my mother's portrait, that's all.'

More obsessed, with a passion that nothing could assuage, was Mr Palani. He was a small, dark man of sixty-three. He was born in Coimbatore district, and he had fresh memories of the discovery of caste prejudice at his school more than 50 years before.

'I on my own did not have anything like this anti-brahmin feeling. My brother got admitted to the school where I was. I was doing my fifth standard. My brother was in the fourth standard. One recess, being a fresher, he just followed the other boys to a hotel to drink water. He did what the other boys did. He took a brass tumbler and dipped it in the bowl of water and started drinking it. It was a brahmin hotel – a hotel where people don't stay, but take their meals. It was a middle-class hotel. The proprietor was terribly angry when he saw my brother putting his hand in the brass bowl and taking water. He emptied the whole bowl outside, and started shouting at my brother.

'My brother came back weeping to me at the school, and I told him that as we are non-brahmins we are not supposed to take water directly ourselves from the bowl. He should have asked some brahmin boy to take a glass of water and give it to him. Brahmins are lighter in complexion comparatively than we are. My brother said, "Why?" He refused to reconcile with this thing. I started thinking myself. I had just been following the custom that was there. I was eleven; my brother was ten. I had been at the school for a year.

'We went home and talked to our father. He was a government clerk. He was earning 35 rupees a month. In those days this was supposed to meet the requirements of a small family. My father's father had been a weaver. We were of the weaver caste, the *sengunthar* caste. But my father had been educated up to the school-leaving certificate, up to the age of sixteen. He was now thirty.

'When he heard our story, my father said, "This is a custom in these places. So even though it is unfair, you must reconcile." He followed the rules himself – not wholeheartedly, but he followed. In brahmin hotels he wouldn't go into the space reserved for brahmins. In those days there were two compartments in any brahmin hotel, one for brahmins, one for the others. So my father wouldn't trespass into the brahmin compartment.

'We were living in a small tiled house, a house with brick walls and a tiled roof. It was a rented house. We were paying about five rupees a month for it. It was not electrified. We had a servant girl whom we fed and paid about three rupees a month.'

'Did she eat with the family?'

'She wouldn't eat with us. She would eat after us. It wasn't a social discrimination; she was just serving us. She slept in the house. She slept in the adjacent room. We slept – all the children – in the big room. There were three rooms in the house, our parents' room, the children's room, and the servant's room. She came from the village. We knew her family. We had requested them to spare a girl for our house. We were middle-class people.'

'Was that why your brother reacted as he did?'

'I'm not sure. It might have been just a human reaction.' He returned to the story of his political development. 'Then there was the anti-Hindi agitation in 1938. There had been state legislative assembly elections in 1937 on a limited franchise, and a Congress government had come in. This government proposed to introduce Hindi compulsorily in the schools. There was an agitation started by Tamil scholars and educationists, and by Periyar and his group.

'Periyar came to talk one evening. It was still daylight when he began, and when the darkness came the Petromax pressure lamps were lighted. He was a stout man, medium height, with a beard. He was wearing a Tamil dhoti and a black shirt, with a shawl over one shoulder. He was fair-complexioned man. He was a Naicker by caste – merchant community.

'He explained how Hindi was going to eliminate English, and how this elimination of English was going to be a disadvantage for Tamil Nadu. Tamil would become secondary to Hindi in the course of time. Once the language got downgraded, everything related to the culture and the society would also be downgraded. Everybody in the audience agreed with this.

'This speech was followed by others made by Periyar's lieutenants. They were young men and middle-class men. One of them was Mr Annadurai. He later founded the DMK, and led it to victory in the state elections in 1967. He was very eloquent. He swayed the people when he started talking. Schools were picketed on this issue of Hindi, and these leaders undertook a march from the southernmost tip of Tamil Nadu to Madras.'

Seven years before, Gandhi had arrived at the idea of the non-violent political march. After a long period of thought in his ashram at Ahmedabad, Gandhi had hit on the idea of walking from there to the sea, to make salt: wonderful theatre, with a definite physical goal, and an uncertain outcome; and a wonderful symbolic act of civil disobedience as well, since salt – so cheap, so necessary, and used by even the poorest – was a monopoly of the foreign government. Gandhi's 1931 salt march lasted many days; it revived and gave new vigour to the national cause. And in 1938 the anti-Hindi march through Tamil Nadu served the Dravidian cause: the Congress state administration dropped the idea of making Hindi compulsory in schools. But Mr Palani didn't make the Gandhian reference.

He said, 'Five years after that agitation, in 1943, I joined engineering college. That again was a very big thing for me. In my old school I had been an outstanding student. I had won scholarships and all that, and my teachers recommended to my father that I should be put in a college. So I did a two-year arts course in an arts college. A professor in that college, when I finished the arts course, insisted I should do engineering. So I applied to the engineering college. I would not have got admission in the open competition, because the brahmin boys scored much higher marks. But fortunately for me – and for people like me, who came from backward, non-brahmin communities – thanks to another agitation of Periyar, some additional seats were reserved for such backward communities. Had this reservation for the backward communities not been there, I wouldn't have been an engineer. That is what I mean when I say that my joining the college was a big thing.

'Now let me tell you this. When I joined the engineering college, I found that in the mess in the hostel the brahmin boys were fed in the nearest enclosure to the kitchen, and their enclosure was separated from the rest of the mess by a wooden partition. All the cooks in the mess happened to be brahmins. So brahmins had a lion's share of the advantages of the mess. This upset us. We started going earlier and sitting in that enclosure. Because there were more of us than brahmins, they finally agreed to remove the partition, and there was a common mess afterwards. You see, they will try to do something so long as we are dumb. Once we start asserting our rights, they wouldn't have the temerity to oppose that.'

'What about the national cause? 1943 was an important time. Did you take part in the national movement?'

'The national movement was going on. But at the same time, within that, we wanted our self-respect to be recognized.'

'Was your brother as active as you?'

'He was in another college. He was a sympathizer with the cause, but he didn't come out in the open as much as I did. He left everything to me.'

'What did your father and mother think of the rationalist side of Periyar's message?'

'They didn't bestow much thought on that side of things. They sympathized more with the linguistic issue and the reservation of places for non-brahmins. In 1943, while we were not at one with the atheistic aspect of Periyar's philosophy, we were very much with him in his fight for the eradication of superstition and rituals.

'This Tamil civilization of ours is a very old one. Say, about 5000 years old. The cities of Mohenjo-Daro and Harappa – Mohenjo-Daro now in Sind in Pakistan – are Dravidian cities. They go back to 5000 BC. That's what historians say. Till about 2000 years back, the society was a casteless society. What happened at that time was that this foreign civilization came from the north, and they started differentiating among classes. Every century since then there has been a protest by some Tamil intellectuals against the caste system. These intellectuals have always in different degrees been resisting rituals and superstition. But they didn't decry the entire system. They said that religion was necessary and God was necessary. But the Aryans were introducing superstitions.'

'You were religious when you were young?'

'I was a regular visitor to temples when I was very young, with and without my parents. We would go and see, and walk around, and go to the deity, and we would pray for prosperity and education and wealth. I was a believer. Up to my twelfth year. After hearing Periyar, I slowly withdrew myself. After twelve, I was a believer, but not a temple-goer. I started disbelieving the ritual part of the religion. In my younger days I read a lot of mythology, but when I started understanding it was all exploitation, I stopped being interested.'

He went back to his personal story. 'I left engineering college in

231

1948. I was twenty-three. This other thing happened then. I joined the government service, and I was posted as a junior engineer to a small town. My parents were very happy about my becoming an engineer and joining the government service.

'In the small town where I was posted I had to take over from a brahmin officer. On the day of my taking over he gave me a dinner at his house. He was living in a rented house. After the dinner the servant maid took back the vessels inside. I could hear the wife of that brahmin officer telling the servant maid not to take the vessels I had used inside the kitchen, but to put them in the back yard for further washing and cleaning, because those vessels had been touched by me. This upset me.'

'What did you do?'

'I didn't say anything at the time.'

'Had you and the officer eaten together?'

'We had eaten together, sitting on the ground, eating with our hands. That experience left a dent. I pocketed the insult. I didn't do anything. They were giving me the dinner, and it wasn't courteous to shout or rebel or say anything.'

'Your grandfather was a weaver. Your father was a clerk. You became an engineer when you were twenty-three. Isn't your story also the story of a rise and of opportunity?'

'I became an engineer because of reservation. And I resolved to fight for similar privileges for others in similar fields. I wanted to devote myself full-time to that cause. I did whatever I could in my official capacity – allocating funds to backward areas, setting up facilities in remote places. The DMK was founded by Mr Annadurai in 1949. But, being an official, I couldn't join.'

'India became independent in 1947. You've left that out of your story.'

'Periyar hadn't bothered too much about the national movement and independence. He was solely concentrating on caste and religion.' And Mr Palani, treating my question as an interruption, went on, 'The DMK emerged as a political wing out of his social movement and began to involve itself in the political life of the state and the country. The Congress was dominant at that time. In 18 years the DMK took power from the Congress. From being a secessionist movement, the DMK had become a party looking for regional autonomy. Many of my friends, people of my own age group, happened to occupy positions of responsibility in the administration. So I could use their goodwill to see that many social-justice programmes could be introduced.'

In this small dark man were locked up generations of grief and rage. He was the first in his line to have felt the affront; and, from what he had said, he was still the only one in his family to have taken up the cause. His passion was very great; it had to be respected. But I also began to wonder whether so great a rage left any room for a private life, the play of simpler emotions.

'When did you get married?'

'In 1951.' This was three years after that dinner with the brahmin officer.

'What caste was she?'

'Same weaver caste. From a neighbouring town.'

'Why the same caste?'

'It was more to please the parents. And also the girl chosen by my parents appeared acceptable to me.'

'Educated?'

'Moderately educated. Up to school-leaving standard. It was an arranged step.'

'In some ways a backward step?'

'Yes.'

'Dark girl?'

He showed the back of his hand. 'My colour.'

'A religious wedding?'

'Yes. But we didn't have a pundit. We had a senior man from our community who conducted the rites. He just prayed to God to bless the couple. It was a *via media*. Not a brahmin marriage, nor a marriage of Periyar's Self-Respect type.'

'You're still a Hindu? You haven't thought of becoming Buddhist?'

'It's not necessary. So long as you're allowed to propagate your own views, there's no need to go to another religion.'

'How do you arrange the various ceremonies?'

'When my children were born I had no ceremonies. In our forefathers' time there was a religious ceremony connected to each individual event in a man's or woman's life – birth, ear-piercing, puberty for a girl, marriage, pregnancy. All these things we don't have now.'

'What happened to your younger brother?'

'He also became an engineer. He married an educated girl in Coimbatore. Same weaver caste. Again out of deference to parents.'

'How did you marry your own daughters?'

'My first daughter's marriage was conducted in the presence of a very small number of most intimate relatives and friends. My second daughter's marriage was a Self-Respect marriage. It was a Periyar marriage, and it was conducted by a well known academic, a man from our movement.'

He was unrelenting in his cause, though his own need for religious faith involved him in contradictions and compromises; though the caste structures in his own family remained in place; and though, in the garbage of Madras, the broken roads, the absence of municipal regulation, the factionalism and plunder of the DMK administration and its successor administrations, something close to chaos could be seen.

Sadanand Menon had spoken of the 'looting' of the ancient temples of the city. And the great tank of Mylapore temple was indeed sad to see, empty, seemingly about to fall into ruin, with its beautiful internal steps buckled in parts.

I asked Mr Palani about the temple.

He said, 'I would like Mylapore temple and tank to continue and uphold their architectural and cultural part of our heritage. But still at the same time I am against these institutions being used to create differences among people. They say that brahmins alone can take water from the tank and use it in the sanctum sanctorum. Only brahmins can go there. People have tried to go into the sanctum in other places, but they have been prevented by law. About 10 years back, Mr Karunanidhi, the DMK chief minister then – he's chief minister again now, after the election – introduced a law that non-brahmins should be entitled to become priests. The brahmins took the matter up, and the law was struck down by the Supreme Court of India on the grounds that Hindu law as it is today required priests to be brahmins.'

That was where we always came back: brahmin prejudice. It was the fount of his passion. To that passion he was always loyal, however much the way of protest might lead to the undoing of his world. And, really, that brahmin cause, part of the apparent wholeness of the world of the South in 1962, was indefensible.

I asked, 'The servant girl who worked in your parents' house – what happened to her?'

'She got married.'

'Weaver-caste man?'

'Same weaver caste, and they've started a little weaving business. They're just making a living.'

I asked what his feelings were about the various Dravidian governments since 1967.

'The DMK government was very good at the beginning. But power corrupts, and the brahmins are intelligent people. They have their own means of diluting the devotion of these people to social reforms. They promise things from the centre in Delhi – in return for which they want concessions locally. They are pre-eminent in the cultural field. There again they tone down the efforts and intensity put forward by the state government.'

His cause made his world complete, left no room for doubt, supplied explanations for everything. And I wondered again whether there was really no part of him that was private, no part not touched by his cause.

I said, 'You can't withdraw into yourself a little, like the rest of us? You can't shut out the world sometimes and be with yourself alone?'

'My wife complains very frequently that I don't care for the family and the children, that I'm always interested in others and their welfare. I'm afraid she's almost right. I've defaulted in some respects. I've not lived a balanced life or a full personal life. I feel obsessed by my cause. It's the state of affairs that made me live this life.'

I went to see Sugar again one morning. He was always in his little ground-floor apartment in the Raghavans' house when he wasn't asleep. He was always available. He received people all the time, except for a period in the middle of the day. He was a local seer; he counselled; and sometimes he just listened.

The furniture pushed together at one end of the drawing-sleeping had disappeared; the room was almost as plain as he had said he wanted it.

His visitors that morning were a middle-aged brahmin group. And perhaps – it must have been something I had always known, but hadn't really thought about – all his visitors were brahmin. The group that morning looked grave but content. The reason for their content was that they had arranged the marriage of a girl in the family; and they were talking, with excited joyful sadness, about the wedding expenses.

The topic of wedding expenses was in the news: for some time the newspapers had been carrying reports from different parts of the country about Hindu brides being done to death by their husbands' families – often by fire – for not bringing a sufficient dowry or valuable enough gifts. These days a boy's family often required modern gifts, motor-scooters, or expensive electronic goods.

However, thoughts of bride-burning were far away from the group in Sugar's drawing-sleeping. They were just ticking off the expenses of the great day, one by one, and it was as though the ceremony was being savoured, in all its details, in advance.

Sugar said to me, with an air of finality, and with the authority of his position, 'They will have to spend a lakh and a half. I've told them. A lakh and a half.'

That was 150,000 rupees, £6,000. But a fairer measure of the cost was to be had if it was set against the salary of the girl's father, on whom all the expenses were going to fall. He was a middle-rank excutive, and he earned between 7000 and 8000 rupees a month. The marriage of his daughter was going to cost him 20 months' of his salary.

I had arrived almost at the end of the calculations, and the man and the women of the party, and Sugar, were quite happy to go through it again, for my benefit.

The first expense was the *choultry*, the wedding hall. The cost of that, for the two days you needed to hire it, was going to be 6000 rupees. And that was a modest choultry; there were choultries in Madras that cost 10 and 20 times as much. You had to add to that the cost of the electricity, and the cleaning-up afterwards.

'And the sundries,' Sugar said, using a word from his old, office life.

With the sundries, the maintenance of the choultry wasn't going to come to less than 2000 rupees. Then the cook was going to charge 4000 rupees.

'At the very least,' Sugar said. 'Preparing food for 500 people four times a day for two days – that's not cheap. The cook will have to have 10 assistants.'

'Vegetables,' one of the women said.

'Three thousand,' the man said.

Sugar said, 'Provisions. Provisions will be 10,000 rupees.'

I asked about the word. 'Provisions', as Sugar used it, seemed to be quite distinct from vegetables.

Sugar said, 'Rice, condiments, Bengal gram, green gram, rice flour, tamarind, chili, pepper, salt – that's provisions.'

'Saris for the bride,' one of the women said. 'And clothing gifts for relations on both sides. Ten thousand.'

Sugar said, 'I don't see how you could do it for less. And clothes for the groom.'

The man of the party said, 'Five thousand.'

'Jewelry,' Sugar said. 'Fifteen 24-carat sovereigns at 3000 apiece.'

One of the women said, 'Plus 12,000 for diamond ear-rings.'

'Two k.g. of silver vessels,' the man said. 'Fifteen thousand. Stainless steel and brass vessels for the household. That will be another 5000.'

'Honeymoon expenses,' one of the women said.

Sugar said firmly, 'Ten thousand there.' He explained to me: 'Furniture for the first night – cot, mattress, sheets, pillows, two or three vessels full of sweets. Dresses for the occasion for bride and groom.'

The man said, 'And you have to give gifts during the first year of the marriage. You have to give dresses, and clothes for the groom. You also have to give the groom a ring or a watch. The request will be made after the marriage. If you give a diamond finger-ring, the Diwali gifts will come to 5000.' Diwali, the festival of lights towards the end of the year. 'There are four or five other festivals. You have to give 2000 each time during the first year. Add it up.'

Sugar, shaking his dhoti-covered legs very slightly, said, 'One and a half lakhs.' A hundred and fifty thousand rupees.

I said, 'I get a figure of 129,000.'

Sugar said, 'It will be one and a half, by the time you actually start spending.'

I said to the man in the party, 'Yet you look so happy.'

He said, 'It's a happy occasion. We know the boy. He's a nice boy.'

'How do people manage if they have two or three daughters?'

The man said, 'That is why middle-class brahmin ladies are not marrying. They go for jobs instead. In our brahmin community, all our savings go to our daughters' marriage. It gets balanced out if you have a son and a daughter. If you've got only sons, you're lucky.'

'How can people make these high demands nowadays?'

'The parents of the boy – who's getting all these things – his parents say, "We've educated him, and now he's earning lucratively." So, as a compensation for what they've spent on him, they want to make capital.'

Things were not easy for brahmin boys nowadays. Places in educational institutions and jobs with the government were reserved for backward communities, and scheduled castes, and scheduled tribes, and physically handicapped ex-servicemen. Fifty per cent of places were now reserved for backward communities, and there was talk of raising that figure to 70 per cent. That would mean that only five per cent of places would be filled in open competition: that meant that only five per cent of places would be open to brahmins.

The man said, 'That's why we are migrating to other places, greener pastures.'

Mylapore was once famous as one of the two or three brahmin areas of Madras. Now only 40 per cent of the people in Mylapore were brahmins. The others were non-brahmins, including even some scheduled castes. Houses had come up for sale in the normal way, and the people with the money – not necessarily brahmins – had bought the houses. In the villages at one time there used to be brahmin *agraharams*, separate streets for brahmins, where no one else was allowed to walk. Now all of that was gone. Brahmins had moved out of the villages, to better themselves. They had left those village agraharams, and other people had bought the houses. There had been an upheaval, but brahmins were not people who fought back or demonstrated or complained, and people outside didn't know about the upheaval that had taken place.

I said, 'So Tamil Nadu is going to be a *shudra* place.'

I had spoken in innocence. But the man looked startled, and Sugar made a show of covering his face with his hands.

Sugar said, 'Don't write that. If you write that, they will come and burn your house. Don't say "shudra" here. Say "Dravidian". You know how they call us? In Tamil the correct word for a brahmin is *parpannan*. When they want to mock us they say *pa-paan*. To say "shudra" is like them saying "pa-paan".'

The people with the wedding on their minds got up to go. The joy of the wedding in prospect made them talk of the position of brahmins (middle class though they were, and vulnerable) with something like light-heartedness.

When they went away, Sugar looked tired.

He said, 'You see. They come all the time. I heal people. Did you know that? I heal people by faith. I have seen about 1000 or 2000 people. Every day I see two or three or four or five people. Every day.'

His dhoti didn't look fresh; nor did his yellow singlet. There was a slight dampness to the skin on his soft shoulders. He looked unexercised, unwell.

'How do you heal them?'

'You give them burnt cowdung, and chant mantras, and solace them by kind words.'

I was puzzled: he seemed to be setting himself at a distance from what he did for people. He sounded tired.

He said, 'They come for marriages.' He meant they came for advice about the marriage of their children or other relations. 'I have to predict them.'

'How do you do that?'

'Something occurs in my mind, and I tell them.'

He crossed from the low seat where he had been sitting, facing me, and he sat down in the chair just beside mine, against the wall. We both had our backs to the door. We looked at the blue wall of the drawing-sleeping, with the religious pictures, and the centrally placed hanging shelves, cluttered behind the sliding glass panels.

He said, 'Cent per cent correct.' He was referring to the predictions he made for people, and again it seemed that he had changed his attitude to what he did for other people. 'If I say 15th of the month, it may occur on the 10th or 20th – a few days this way or that way.'

'When did this gift come? You didn't have it in 1967.'

'It suddenly came. In 1970. I don't know how it came. One Mr R. told me I'd got this gift. And he said to me, "Use it in a proper way, so that you can be useful to many people." From that day onwards I'm doing these things. I used to go to Mr R.'s house often. It was in Madras. A small house, a poor man. I cannot say he is my guru. He likes me, and I like him, that's all. Birds of the same feather flock together, and he has these gifts as well. I can't do miracles like Sai Baba – I don't want you to think that.

'What happened was this. A friend of mine, a businessman, a middle-class man, a good friend, a man about fifty at the time, he came to tell me that his brother is very sick, is running a 104-degrees temperature. "Sugar, give me something for my brother, to reduce his fever." And other symptoms he's got as well, like fits and other things. And this friend came to my house, and I received him, and asked him to sit for a while, and I took some cow-dung ashes and chanted *Sudarsan* mantra, and I gave it to him.'

'What made you do that?'

'Something. Some forces asked me to do it. At that moment, when I'm doing it, I'm not Sugar. I'm not myself. After a few seconds, I gave that ashes to my friend. He went home and gave it to his brother, and smeared it on his forehead. The brother was all right the next morning. He went to office. I was working myself at that time in an office.

'After that, I cannot sleep for two days. I went to Mr R.'s place and asked him about this. "There is something wrong with me. I cannot sleep. I'm seeing some black figures in front of me. Human figures. Black figures." He asked me, "What did you do yesterday?" I narrated the whole story. He scolded me. "Who asked you to give ashes and other things to your friend? In future don't do it." And he asked me to do the same Sudarsan mantra again. I'm all right in a day or two.

'From that day onwards, I'm not doing anything like that, without getting permission from elsewhere. I see those black figures now, even as I am talking to you. Two figures. Horns on their head. *Madan* – cow-headed man. It is a malevolent figure. He may do so many things. At the moment he is very friendly with me. I have to get permission from him whenever anybody comes to ask for this or that. I will hear it in my head, his permission.

'I want to get rid of this gift. I want to get rid of all these things. Temple, everything. I want to get rid of all these things. I want peace. People are coming and worrying me about their horoscope, and about not getting jobs for their sons, and not getting marriages for their daughters, and lost property. And: "I'm sick, Sugar. Do something for me." I don't know how to get rid of these things. I don't like these things. You come and tell me your daughter is not well. "Do something for me." What am I gaining?

'You've not seen these people. It is for those people I've put up a sign on my door asking them not to come at a certain time – that's when I have my rest.

'It is only on account of these things I'm not well. I get a poor blood flow to the brain. I get giddiness often. I can't climb stairs. Slowly I'm stopping these things, but I'm not telling them.'

I said, 'What will you do when you stop?'

His life in the little apartment seemed built around receiving visitors, waiting for them. It was hard to see how he would occupy himself if he stopped seeing people.

He said he thought he would read. 'Even today I'm reading books. Jack Higgins, Wilbur Smith. Haley, the *Airport* man. So many others. To while away my time I'm reading these things. Any book – whether it is *Gita* or trash.'

Twenty years before, I had noted that about him: his ability to read popular romantic fiction from England – so far away, in every sense, from his life and experience in Mylapore.

He said, 'I want some books to while away my time. It keeps my mind occupied. Sometimes I chant mantras. Some mantras I chant 2000 times, 3000 times, the same mantra throughout the day.'

We were sitting side by side.

I said, 'You will have to get rid of this gift.'

'I will. I have confidence. I know myself. I will do it. I have no peace here. I want to go away from the city to some far-off place, but the doctors won't permit. I must be within kilometres of my doctor.'

He pointed to a chair against the opposite wall, below the hanging glass-fronted shelves.

'I can sit there and read your face, give full details, if you sit before me. But after that I will get a headache. I will suffer for two days.'

But the talk I had heard, the previous time I had come to the little apartment, was of the peace people found with him. One man had talked of emptying his mind, of spending four hours in the darkness with Sugar, during a power cut, and hardly saying a word.

Sugar said, with something like irritation, 'They come here not for peace, but to hear what I may blab about them. It's very good for them to hear about their difficulties and how to get rid of those things. They say they want peace. But they want advice.'

I remembered the landlord, the 'moneyed man', as Sugar had said, sitting patiently in his chair; and I remembered the young business executive, with his fine brahmin face, and the fresh holy marks on his forehead, sitting forward, his feet below his chair, the palms of his hands on the edge of his chair.

Sugar said, 'But I'll keep my mouth shut. And they'll sit here, and talk about politics and other things, and then they'll go away.

'Mr R. knows what I'm going through. He himself is suffering. He is an old man of eighty-six. He will predict accurately. He will tell you about your house in London, how you keep your home. He will tell you all these things with you sitting here in front of him.'

I asked, 'Why did you like me in 1962?'

We had met late one afternoon, at the end of the day's march, after the tents had been pitched, not far from a mountain river. The temperature, even in August, was dropping fast; the colours of the mountain were grey and brown. And he had been there in the twilight, muffled up in his coarse woollen pullover. We had begun to talk just like that.

Sugar said, 'In my last birth we both had met. You might have been my brother, friend, and father. I felt something up there in the Himalayas. I won't forget your name. I will always remember your name.'

'I thought you were a sad man. Were you sad?'

'No sadness then. Nothing. My father was alive. My mother was alive. I liked seeing places in the Himalayas. I was the first in my family to go to the Himalayas.'

'Is there anything I can do for you?'

'God will look after me. I have faith in him. Raghavan charges me little for the apartment. I spend all day here, so you might say I look after the house for them, in a way. We have a mutual understanding.'

'Tell me about this burnt cowdung you give people. Where do you burn it?'

'I buy it.'

So it was a common item, on sale in shops dealing in puja goods. It wasn't something special, something he had made himself.

'It's called *vibudhi*. You can buy it in bags, one kilo, two kilos a time. Mine is not scented. I give three rupees a kilo. Scented, they are selling for one rupee, or one rupee 50 paisa, for a packet of 100 grams. How to make it I don't know.'

A slender young girl in dark clothes came in through the front door. No words passed between her and Sugar. She began to clear up and sweep in the middle space, the space between the temple and the kitchen, both of which places would have been barred to her, since she would not have been a brahmin.

There had been a revolution. The temples had been 'looted'. The streets and walls were ragged and scrawled with election slogans and emblems. Mylapore was said to be only 40 per cent brahmin. But in the little space that was still Sugar's the old world seemed to continue.

In Bangalore Kala had told me of her brahmin ancestor who had left his village and had come to the city of Madras, and had been so poor there that he and his mother had lived on the consecrated food of the great temple of Mylapore. That story – old gods, old temples, poor brahmins – had seemed to me to come from a far-off, fairy-tale time. But the story was of the new world, of a countryside becoming overpopulated, and of the dispersal of the brahmins. The story I had heard in Sugar's apartment of the break-up of the brahmin agraharams or village settlements told of the same dispersal, the scattering of people from their ancestral homes.

But on this kind of journey knowledge can sometimes come slowly; the traveller can sometimes listen selectively; and certain things – because they appear to fit the country or the culture – can be taken too much for granted. When at the beginning of my stay in Madras I met Kakusthan, and heard that he was a brahmin who was trying to live as a full brahmin, I didn't understand how unusual and even heroic this resolve of his was.

He lived in a brahmin colony or agraharam near one of the old temples of Madras. His father had been the one to move there; before that, for many generations, the men of Kakusthan's family had been priests of a temple in a village, now two hours or so away from the city by bus. Kakusthan belonged now, by his profession, to the modern world. He worked for a big business company, and he wrote economic reports and project-assessments of various kinds for them. But the guardianship of the family temple had fallen to him. His acceptance of the responsibility was part of his resolve to live as a full brahmin; and so, while sitting at his office desk and while travelling about on his office work, Kakusthan was dressed as a brahmin priest. He wore the caste-marks on his forehead; his head was shaved; he wasn't bare-backed, but he wore the long cream-coloured brahmin's tunic.

To me, India was a land of caste costume. (Though it was a good deal less so than a country like England, where a whole ritual of costume and colour, marking different jobs, groups, social ranks, sports, leisure activities, gradations of meals, different times of day and year, kept many people in a constant pacific frenzy: in India everyone just had his one costume.) And Kakusthan's antique appearance, when I first met him, made less of an impression than it ought to have done. As for living as a full brahmin, I thought this meant that Kakusthan was the purest kind of vegetarian, not eating fish or eggs or garlic or onions; that he followed the basic laws of ritual cleanliness, not eating or drinking from vessels someone else used; that he used the right hand for clean activities, the left for unclean; and that generally he strove to avoid pollution.

But Kakusthan's brahminism went far beyond that. The purity he aimed at forbade him to eat food he hadn't first offered to his god at home, forbade him even to drink water he hadn't conse-crated in this way. In the great heat of Madras this meant that for him every working day was full of hardship. And, in fact, the brahminical restrictions he had imposed on himself were also a kind of private penance, an act of piety and expiation towards his father and his ancestors.

Kakusthan had been a poor brahmin. As a child in Madras he had been made to suffer because of the brahmin observances his father had forced on him. Periyar's anti-brahmin ideas had gone right down to the children of Madras, and Kakusthan had been so tormented at school and in the streets that he had broken faith with his past. He had wanted to turn his back on his brahmin duties; and he had quarrelled with his father. He had succeeded in breaking away; he had made a life for himself elsewhere. But then in early middle age he had been eaten up by remorse; and he had come back to Madras, to live in the very agraharam or brahmin colony, and the very house, where he had grown up. He lived there now with the determination to be as pure a brahmin as was possible.

The colony Kakusthan lived in was in the Triplicane district of Madras. As a brahmin area, it was second only to Mylapore; and the Parthasarathy temple, which was about 1000 years old and was at the heart of the Triplicane district, was in the eyes of its devotees the equal of the Mylapore temple.

The colony was in a lane at the side of the temple. From the lane the temple wall was unexpectedly high. The stonework was beautiful and precise, and the lower section of the wall was painted in broad vertical bands of rust and white, sacred temple colours. Facing this temple wall, and almost in the middle of the lane, was the entrance to the colony: a gateway like a screen, not very high, with wooden doors, and with the symbol of Garuda, the bird 'vehicle' of Lord Vishnu, painted above the doors.

To the left of the gateway, as you entered, was the stone-walled temple garden, separated from the temple by the lane. The garden was old, possibly as old as the temple itself – and that enclosed formal space, with its own symbolical *gopuram* or temple-tower, seemed to take one back to old, superseded ways of feeling. The colony (though clearly on a sacred site) was not itself old. It had been established as a colony towards the end of the last century or at the beginning of this; and the land had been given by a charitable resident of Triplicane to provide for brahmins who had come from the villages, and were either serving in the temple or simply serving as pundits in the city.

The doors of the colony were closed at night, from 10 to five in the morning; only residents could enter then. The colony was closed at all times to people deemed unclean: smokers, drunkards, cobblers, scheduled-caste people generally, and Muslims. Such people were not allowed to pass through the doorway. Some people had to be let in to service the colony, but they were not allowed to enter the houses.

Past the doorway, a paved path led between low small houses to the central yard. There were wells in the yard, with winches and ropes. Women and girls were drawing water when I went; and the pastoral scene was surprising in the middle of a crowded town. Kakusthan, who was my host and guide, said that brahmins could use only well water for drinking, because well water had a direct connection with the earth. (I didn't know about this brahmin rule. It cleared up an old mystery for me. In 1971 I had gone to India to follow the election in a drought-stricken desert constituency in

Rajasthan, in the north-west. One of the candidates, a God-fearing old Gandhian, much admired, had repeatedly spoken, on the grounds of morality, against the taking of piped water to the desert villages. 'Good old water from the well', he kept on saying, was good enough; piped water would 'tell on the health and morals' of women in the villages. He hadn't explained why he had said that; but – going by what Kakusthan now said – his audience would have understood his caste shorthand.)

Over the years, with the increase in the population of the colony, the level of water in the well had gone down 30 feet, Kakusthan said. Years ago you could just dip your 'vessel' by hand and get your water. Now there was rationing, six pots per family in the morning, six pots in the evening. 'Pots', 'vessels' – these were the correct words, because brahmins didn't use buckets. I didn't know about that either, but the explanation was simple. Modern buckets were made of galvanized iron, and brahmins had to use pots made of brass or earthenware, since these materials had a direct connection with the earth. And there, at the colony well, were the women and girls with their awkward, handle-less pots – and one might have seen only the city pastoral, and missed the caste regulation.

Near the well was a hand-pump. The water got from this was strictly for use in the latrine – though, clearly, its source was the same as the drinking water in the well. The rule about the hand-pump and the latrine seemed fierce and brahminical; in fact, it showed how difficult it was nowadays absolutely to live as a brahmin. The very idea of the latrine was a non-brahmin idea: to enter such a polluted place was itself pollution. No old-time brahmin would have even contemplated the idea. Good brahmins, traditional brahmins, used open-air sites, a fresh one each time. So there was a compromise there, as well as in a number of small things the visitor mightn't have noticed or thought about: the wearing of stitched garments like shirts, the wearing of leather sandals, and even the buying of bundles of food-leaves from the market.

Leaves, to eat your food off, were brahminically more correct than plates. Leaves were used once and thrown away; plates were used more than once and were technically always polluted, however much you washed them. There was a special quality of ritual, and romance, to eating off a leaf. It was something that had survived with us even in far-off Trinidad. After special religious occasions in my grandmother's house, when I was a child, people were fed on banana leaves (as they were in the Woodlands Hotel in Madras as late as 1962). A fresh banana leaf was a beautiful thing to eat off: dark green, with a hollow spine of a paler colour, the leaf itself smooth yet with grip, ribbed, with a slight sheen, impermeable, with no intrusive smell or taste. To eat off a leaf like that not only marked a special occasion; it became associated, in the most romantic way, with religion, making one think of one's remote origins, and of the forests through which the Hindu epic heroes, divinities, wandered during the years of their exile. Even in small Trinidad, though, the forests were far away, and banana leaves were not things you just went out and picked. They had to be brought from miles away; they had to be brought fresh; and they weren't always to be had. It was a wasteful and expensive way of serving food. In Madras, now, the Woodlands Hotel no longer used banana leaves. People like Kakusthan who needed to eat off leaves bought bundles of a smaller, rounder kind of dried leaf in the market. They were not fresh, not particularly clean, and they had no aesthetic quality. The idea of cleanliness had been overlaid by ritual; what was really being honoured was the idea of the leaf, the natural thing used once and thrown away.

In the colony there was a restriction about women I hadn't known about. Menstruating women and girls were segregated during their periods. There was a special room for them in a corner of the colony. This room had two doors, and both were kept closed, so that people walking outside wouldn't be polluted. Kakusthan told me that a menstruating woman was polluting at a distance of 10 to 15 feet: if for some reason you had to talk to a menstruating woman, that was the distance you should keep her at. The women in this separate room had their own latrine and bathroom. They did absolutely nothing for the three days of their period. For them, Kakusthan said, it was a time of 'a full and complete rest'. They read books or listened to music. The room could accommodate 10 women, and in the old days the room was always full; but nowadays, modern life being what it was, with girls going out to work (and with other girls slipping out to the cinema and so on: there was a wicket gate at the back of the colony that menstruating women used), at any given time there would be only five or six women in the room. This segregation made women hate the idea of menstruation, Kakusthan said; yet at the same time they welcomed the segregation, because it gave them the kind of regular little holiday they might never otherwise have.

Only five of the houses in the colony had an upper sleeping room; and these houses were in a row down one side, against a boundary wall. All the other houses were single-storeyed and low, built flat to the ground. So the central yard, all the life around the well, was overlooked by the higher buildings at the back. I wondered whether that didn't raise problems of pollution for the brahmins of the agraharam, being gazed down at by people of other castes, or having the shadows of those taller houses fall on their colony. Kakusthan said the high buildings at the back were no problem. The people who lived in them were of the cowherd caste, *yadavas*, Lord Krishna's caste; between yadavas and brahmins there was mutual regard.

The other immediate neighbours of the colony were Muslims. It might have seemed that the 53 families of the colony were vulnerable, and could easily be overrun in a riot; but for some reason there had never been any communal trouble at all between the Muslims and the brahmins. The Muslims might even – though Kakusthan didn't say this – have acted as a buffer against unfriendly non-brahmins. So, between the temple and the yadavas and the Muslims, the colony enjoyed a kind of security: the houses, Kakusthan said, had no locks on their doors.

The colony – with its wooden doors closed every night, and standing next to the enclosed temple – made one think of some old foundation in Europe, alms-houses, say, in a cathedral close; and there was something of that in the way the colony was run. There was a trust; it collected the rents, did building repairs and general maintenance, and paid the man who watched the gateway. Tenancy of the houses passed down from one generation to the other; most of the families in the colony had been there for decades. Kakusthan's father had got into the colony in the early 1940s.

Kakusthan said that penniless brahmins migrating – in the old days – from the villages to the towns were attracted to the areas around the temples not only because it was easier for them to make a little money by being pundits or mendicants, but also because the temple had tanks and wells, and offered water direct from the earth. The temples were also near the sea. This nearness to the sea was important, because during the lunar and solar eclipses, and on some other occasions as well, traditional brahmins liked to have a dip in the sea.

It wasn't easy, being a good brahmin! The more Kakusthan went into it, the more he came up with needs and observances; and the more awkward the whole business appeared. Perhaps an absolute brahmin way wasn't possible. Perhaps it had always been like that; perhaps at all times brahmins would have had to compromise in one thing or another.

Kakusthan's father had come to make his way in Madras in 1932 or 1933. He was twenty-two then, and married, but he didn't bring his wife with him. Not only did he not have the money; it was also not quite right, at that time, for a husband and wife to break away, as a couple, from the joint-family house.

Kakusthan's father was the first in his family to have gone to an English-medium school. He got only as far as the 10th standard; but he later became a teacher. He was especially good in mathematics, and he gave private lessons in the subject. As with other brahmins of his generation, he was hard to categorize. It could be said that he was a half-educated village man; at the same time, so far as mathematics went, he was gifted and unusual. And there was, in addition, his Hindu and brahmin learning. This was considerable.

In the family village there was an old temple. For 700 or 800 years, since the time of the Chola emperors, Kakusthan's father's family had had special rights and privileges in that temple. They did the pujas for the temple deity, and everything offered to the deity in that temple went first to the deity and then to Kakusthan's father's family. In that temple the privilege of Kakusthan's father's family exceeded that of emperors.

His breeding and ancestry made Kakusthan's father the equal of anyone; yet when he left his village, all that he and his family could raise was the train fare to Madras. He left six people behind in the village: his wife, his parents, the family of his elder brother. None of them had an income; all of them depended on the young man who had gone to Madras on the train.

Having no money at all, Kakusthan's father stayed with relatives in Madras. For some time he lived on charity as a young brahmin, eating at different brahmin houses on different days. But then he began to make a little money from his learning. He knew by heart all the 4000 verses of the Vedas in Tamil. The fact got around, and at pujas the young man would be called upon to recite the 4000 verses. He would get a rupee or two for that, and his food as well. With the money for the verses, and then his fees for the private lessons he gave in mathematics, and his salary as a teacher, he was able in the end to have a decent income. He would have made about 40 to 45 rupees a month, enough to keep himself and the six people he had left behind in the village.

Some time in the early 1940s, after 10 years of this life, Kakusthan's father finally brought his wife to Madras. They found a room for 10 rupees a month, about 75 pence. Children were born. And then, with the help of friends, Kakusthan's father got a place in the brahmin colony, paying more or less what he had been paying outside. He would have been in his early thirties; security of a kind had at last come to him. He moved twice within the colony; some people did that. In 1943 Kakusthan was born.

It was like the beginning of a success story. There had been a good deal of movement – but had there been success? Forty-five years later Kakusthan was showing me round the place where he had spent all his childhood and adolescence, and where he had come back to live for good; and Kakusthan was dressed as a brahmin. He was almost certainly the richest man in his little community. But the community was poor; historical though the setting was, with all its promptings to religious pastoral, with the enclosed temple garden at the front, the well and the winch in the central yard (and with the people of Lord Krishna's cowherd caste in the high buildings at the back), many of the women and girls at the well, filling up their pots of rationed water, looked pallid and undernourished.

The brahmin colony was a little urban slum, lower in energy than the Muslim community on the outer limit of the temple area. And the colony was under pressure. Its already compromised brahminical ways were being steadily more compromised. The most dreadful compromise had been made when the sweepers, the cleaners of latrines, had begun to ask for sums the community couldn't afford. Then, to show the sweepers, and to deter further blackmail, the brahmins had cleaned their own latrines. Kakusthan himself had rallied the young men of the community. He told them that every day every person touched excrement, even if it was his

250

own; and that it was therefore all right for them to clean their own latrines and sewers. At any other time what Kakusthan proposed would have been regarded as a form of caste suicide; but Kakusthan spoke of it as a moral, caste triumph.

He was a small man, an inch or two above five feet, warm-complexioned, well made. His eyes were bright and steady. It was his eyes that gave away his passion – at one time the passion of the renegade, the man who wished to break out at whatever cost, now the passion of the man wishing to honour what he felt to be the true way.

He lived in one of the five houses which had an upper floor, with a sleeping room off an open terrace. The room to which he led me when I first went to his house was at the far end downstairs. It was perhaps against the boundary wall; it was dark and airless, with a slight smell of drains, a little cell, where everything, paint and walls and cupboards and fittings, showed age and use in the fluorescent light, but where no doubt everything was ritually clean. Cleanliness – like pollution – could come easily to a brahmin: a finger flick of water could be deemed to purify a room.

Since I was a visitor, and this was India, Kakusthan wanted me to eat something in his house – though having a stranger in his house wasn't strictly what he should be doing as a man trying hard to live as a good brahmin. Of course, he wasn't going to eat with me; but he wanted me to eat something from his kitchen. That was why we were downstairs. We had passed by the kitchen when we had gone through to the little room at the back; and I had seen, on a table or a stand or a half-wall next to the kitchen doorway, a black image, with a flame burning before it in a tall, sooty oil lamp of bronze or silver. The lamp was of a style that took one back to the ancient world: the wick burned in the mouth of a shallow oil container shaped like a curling leaf, and this oil container was attached to a vertical pole. The black image was of Kakusthan's deity; everything that Kakusthan ate had first to be offered to this deity.

I had my own scruples, too, about eating far from home – far, at any rate, from the Taj Coromandel Hotel. But I felt ashamed of those scruples, and I accepted a little food from Kakusthan's kitchen, and put my lips to the glass of coffee, though the breaking of bread (or a puri) in Kakusthan's back room did make my writing fingers oily. This became hard to ignore; it called for a more than ritual washing outside – Kakusthan pouring for me, not complaining, wasting precious water from the well, one of the six evening pots he was allowed. (And there had been no need for me to feel ashamed, or to feel that I had to eat. Kakusthan was a man of the world. When I next visited him at the colony, some days later, I told him straight out that I was like him, too, and didn't eat away from home. He accepted that immediately. He laughed and said, 'All right, I'll be the untouchable this time.')

That first afternoon, in the dark, fluorescent-lit room at the back of his house, he talked in a matter-of-fact way of his neighbours.

He said, 'It is a poor community. Almost the entire community is poor. The first generation largely consisted of purohits, pujaris, cooks, and a few office-goers. The second generation is somewhat better. There are more boys and girls in the family earning money, with jobs.'

'What kind of jobs?'

'Jobs which were not dreamt of by traditional brahmins. Like operating machines, working as mechanics, and all other industrial manual labour. My neighbour on this side is a cook.'

Fifteen people lived in the cook's room. This wasn't as bad as it sounded: the 15 didn't sleep in the room at the same time. In fact, they had their own reserved sleeping places in the central yard: in the summer, which lasted the better part of the Madras year, everyone slept in the yard or in the open. The cook made the greater part of his money at weddings; but he had to employ so many assistants that the profit on a 1000-rupee wedding job was really very small.

The neighbour on Kakusthan's other side was a 'peon' or office boy. He worked in a government office. There was another boy in the colony who drove a mechanized rickshaw. His father had been a Sanskrit scholar, an authority on the Vedas and Hindu rituals.

'It's really sad,' Kakusthan said. 'The boy himself says, "What can I do, when there is no other means for me? I'm not educated. Nor did I follow in my father's footsteps."'

I said, 'That sounds unusual.'

'He wasn't educated because of lack of parental care.'

And when Kakusthan and I next met, in the hotel where I was staying, it was of the poverty of the brahmin colony beside the great temple of Parthasarathy that he continued to talk.

Kakusthan said, 'The situation today is many times better than what it was in the 1950s, when I was growing up there. I felt the need for better comforts. The people I knew at school dressed better, looked better, were stronger, and more modern in their appearance. I looked more like a village boy – with my dhoti, my religious marks on my forehead, and my *churki*.'

It was, barring the churki, the way he looked now. The churki, the long, uncut tuft or lock of hair at the back of the head, was an antique brahmin badge. Kakusthan no longer had a long churki; the one he wore was just an inch and a half long, but it served his purpose. (Four or five times a year, on an auspicious day, as part of his revived brahminism, Kakusthan had all his body hair shaved – eyebrows, everything, except for the hair under his arms and the churki. He was between shaves when we met; the hair on his head looked like a crewcut, and the short churki wasn't particularly noticeable.) When he was a child he had been made to wear the churki by his father. It wasn't something that many brahmin boys wore in the 1950s; it had been at the root of his torment at school.

Kakusthan said, 'All these things brought contempt and ridicule by other boys, which even today continues. I used to react violently if the boy who ridiculed me was weak, and used to ignore the boy who was strong. I complained to my father about my social plight at school, and his reply would be, "Go and report to the head-master." He would also say that it was to uphold the family tradition that I had to wear those religious marks and have the churki – without which the entire family in the village would be looked down on by other families, particularly as our family as brahmins were serving the deity there.

'My father himself was suffering from the same kind of ridicule in his own school and elsewhere in the city – on the buses, on the streets. The whole brahmin community was suffering at that time from that kind of ridicule, due to anti-brahminism, let loose by the so-called Dravidian Movement.' The *Dravidar Kazagham*, the Dravidian Movement, started by Periyar. 'This was in the mid-1950s, when there was widespread movement against brahmins and their practices. This took the form of breaking idols, cutting off brahmins' churkis and sacred threads, and rubbing off the religious marks on the forehead. In Madras most of the vegetarian restaurants used to boast themselves as "brahmin hotels" – and the Dravidian people would erase the word "brahmin". Now hotels do not have these words in the city. In those days you would have the "brahmin hotel" and the "military hotel".'

The 'military hotel' still existed when I first travelled in the South. It meant a place where meat was served; and – as though accepting the brahmin prejudice against such places, as though revelling in the difference and absolute freedom such a prejudice gave – the military hotels in the South were really very dirty and unwashed.

Somewhere on the bus route between Bangalore and Madras in 1962, somewhere on the red earth of that region, I had my first sight of the military hotel. It was a shack on bare earth, part of the informal bus-stop area. The English words on the signboard – in that old-looking landscape of simple colours, like an exotic view in an English 18th-century print – seemed to go back to the British East India Company's wars against Tippu Sultan. The quaint words seemed to hold something of Indian history, something of the 18th-century Indian anarchy, when armies, of Indian hired troops, fought over the land, without reference to the people who worked in the villages or in the fields.

From one kind of war to another, one kind of consciousness to another: in the main museum room of the Periyar Thidal, among the 33 paintings of the stages or stations in the life of Periyar, was one showing the great man in 1957, when he was nearly eighty, painting out 'Brahmin' from a hotel or restaurant signboard. Periyar in this painting was white-bearded and very grand. He had a whitewash brush in one hand; he stood on a bench or stool to reach the signboard; and he was calmly going about his business, without interference from anyone, policeman or politician or hotel-owner or hotel customer. The colours of the painting were simple, the details curiously literal (the signboard, the stool or bench on which Periyar stood, the painting brush edged with white), as though they were illustrating a well known text; and the effect was that of the calm world of a children's comic strip.

Kakusthan, talking of the humiliations he had to put up with as a boy because of his traditional brahmin dress, said, 'I resisted whenever I could, and I got beaten, even while I was telling my parents that I had to switch to the new ways of life – particularly removing the churki, and wearing trousers. We suffered from the churkis. That was the thing we suffered from the most. When I used to go to school sports, there used to be a lot of amusement when I took part in running-races and the sport known as *kabbadi*. When I ran, my churki would get loose and fall down, and that got a lot of laughs. In kabbadi my opponents would seize me by the churki, hold me by that long strand of hair, and they would win the game.

'I stayed at school until 1958. I joined a college then on a pre-university course, and the irony is that I got into that college only because of my churki and caste-marks. The man who recommended me was a brahmin, and he cherished the same values we had in our family. But I was in that college for only six months. I was subject to more intense ridicule from my college mates. And they were adults now, not boys.

'All this made me very sad. I started feeling entirely different from my father, and begged him to spare me these agonies. But he was firm. He said that family respect and tradition were more important than these passing experiences. I was not convinced. I dropped out of college. I felt I had to be independent.'

Independent – it was a strange word.

Kakusthan said, 'Independent of these practices. I was sixteen. I felt I must be as modern as anybody else.'

'Weren't you frightened when you left the college?'

'I wasn't frightened. I was full of hope that I would be able to do what I wanted once I was away from home. I told my mother these things in confidence. She partly agreed with me, and partly didn't. She understood my feelings.'

I tried to set that family drama of 30 years before in the colony I had seen. In the yard around the well the people would have been more obviously brahminical in their dress and restrictions: people once of authority, now safe only in this little area of theirs. I tried to think of the passions of father and son exploding in the small private space the family had in the colony: the dark small room at the back of the kitchen on the lower level, the sleeping room off the common terrace above, with a view – as you climbed the narrow stone-and-concrete steps at the side of the house-row to that terrace – of the overgrown temple garden, memorial of a calmer time.

'For a few days I stayed at home. My father was very angry. He didn't talk to me. He didn't want me in the house. I had betrayed the family and let down his prestige. He wanted me to be a graduate and a bank employee or a central government employee, even while adhering to my religious pursuits at the temple in our village – where we had much honour as brahmins. He would cite several examples of people who did the two things – wear the long tuft, the churki, and at the same time did good, secure, modern jobs.

'Through friends in the colony, friends of my own age or a little older, I got a job with an electric-bulb dealer as an office boy on a salary of one rupee a day. This was in 1959. But since the father-and-son relationship was extremely strained, there was no peace at home. There was also a mother-father tussle, with mother and father quarrelling, and with occasional beatings for me from both father and mother. So I left home.

'I decided to go to my married sister. She lived in the town of Vellore, 100 kilometres west of Madras. Her husband had become a schoolteacher after retiring from the army. I went to Vellore by bus. I got the fare out of the old college books. My father had bought them new. I sold them to a hawker for a throw-away price.

'It was a Saturday when I left home. Every Saturday and Wednesday I had my traditional oil bath, and my mother used to soap my long hair. She did so that Saturday. I had my morning meal around 10.30, and immediately afterwards I slipped away to the bus stop, not telling any soul I was leaving for Vellore. I had very little money, just enough for the bus fare to Vellore, and I walked from Triplicane to Parry's Corner. Five miles, in the scorching heat. It took about an hour.

'There was a lurking fear in me. Was I doing the right thing? What would be my mother's reaction? This agitated me all through my travel to Vellore. Mid-way I even thought of returning home. But then the other half of my mind compelled me to go on – and I told myself I was only going to my sister's place, after all.

'For a few days I was a welcome guest there in Vellore, at my sister's. But then their sympathies were more with our parents than with me, after I had explained why I had come to them. My sister wrote to my parents that I was with her. My father had been quietly looking for me, but he had been pretending not to be concerned about my disappearance.

'My brother-in-law tried to get me a job in Vellore. But Vellore

256

is a predominantly Muslim town, and I was handicapped by my Hindu-brahmin appearance. Whenever I went with my brother-in-law to get a job, the first question would be: "Why don't you wear pants and become more modern, if you want a job?" But even though I'd left home, I wasn't courageous enough to remove the churki or put on trousers. I was in a dilemma. I had no job, and I couldn't go home. I spent some sleepless nights, even while putting a brave face on things.

'I must have stayed a month at my sister's. And then, reluctantly, I went back to Madras. I didn't go back to my own home. I went to the house of a friend of my mother's. This house was outside our brahmin colony.

'The son of this friend of my mother's also wore the churki and the caste-marks and was obedient to what his parents told him. He was an extraordinarily brilliant boy, in mathematics and statistics. He is today a professor in a big American university. And even then, when I went to his house – he was two years older than me – he was an admirer of the genius Ramanujan, whose mathematical work he and his equally brilliant colleagues would discuss and debate for hours together. They especially discussed the unsolved mathematical problems of Ramanujan's. These boys were college students. I couldn't follow the discussions, but I could admire the deep commitment to the studies they were pursuing – commitment which I didn't have.

'What impressed me most was the way in which the father of the boy took interest in these discussions, and encouraged them by supplying coffee. You must imagine these discussions going on in a house as poor as my father's in the agraharam, the colony. There was an irony. My mother's friend's husband was a Sanskrit teacher, and yet his son was a mathematical genius. My father was a mathematics teacher, and I was a mathematical zero.

'The mathematical debate went on past midnight. I felt sorry I couldn't participate, and I literally wept that night that I had had to disappoint my father.'

Tears came to Kakusthan's eyes. He tried to ignore the tears, to go on talking. But then he began to cry at those memories of 30 years before. He stood up and said, 'Let me take five minutes off.'

He walked to the rear of the hotel lobby and began to walk up and down, a small figure in his brahmin clothes, noticeable, five feet one or two, walking up and down, wrestling with his grief, looking down, in his abstraction like a monk or holy man in his cloister, indifferent to the hotel setting.

Were the tears for himself, for what he might have made of himself if he hadn't been pushed into rebellion? Or were the tears for the unhappiness he had caused his father 30 years before? The tears were for both things: he said when he came back and sat down and collected himself that it was the difference between the two families that had upset him all over again.

'I spent 10 to 15 days in that atmosphere, and was full of guilt that I had left home and studies. This boy I have mentioned would teach me mathematics, and console me that nothing was lost, that even now I could pick up the threads. That gave me encouragement to go back to being a student.

'I went home to the agraharam. I settled there. But I couldn't get back into college. It was the middle of the year. I took a job. I needed the money, to satisfy my social cravings – taking friends to hotels, going to movies, etc. None of these things would have been available to me, if I had to depend on my father. In fact, they were forbidden. At home we never even drank coffee – it was a foreign item, an item invented by the British. And even today in strict brahmin homes coffee is not drunk, because of its intoxicating effects – the caffeine.

'I went back to my job with the bulb-dealer. I got 26 rupees a month. I gave my family 20 rupees, and I kept six – to fulfil all my cravings, without the knowledge of my father. I stayed in that job for a year. And having tasted money power, I was reluctant again to take up studies. So I went back to my old ways again.

'The work was hard. I literally had to hawk the bulbs around the city, sometimes on a bicycle, sometimes walking, when the cycle was punctured. It used to be so hot that sometimes the tires used to burst. Even my father was moved by the arduous nature of my job, which was telling upon my health. I became very lean, with the irregular food. So he got me a job with an engineering consulting firm, making blueprint copies, at 65 rupees a month – a big jump.' Sixty-five rupees, £5 a month, in 1960.

'One day I burnt a blueprint. The engineer slapped me, and went away without saying a word. I was at fault. I didn't blame him. I told my father when I went home. He advised me to take it in my stride as part of life. I was surprised – I thought my father might also want to beat me for the mistake with the blueprint.

258

'I did the blueprints for the company for nine months. Then I was posted to one of the company's construction sites. Work was going on at that site on behalf of one of the big industrial concerns of the South. It was here again, for the second time in my life, my traditional brahmin appearance and approach came to my aid or advantage.

'The managing director of the company we were working for was very pleased with my strict adherence to the brahmin way of life. He was so pleased to see a brahmin boy in churki in charge of a building site, being a *maistry* – especially at this time, when anti-brahmin feeling was at its height. This was in 1961.

'I did not know how important this managing director was, how many businesses he controlled. He asked me about my father, and he sent a message through me asking my father to meet him. I was a little nervous. So also was my father. We didn't know what the managing director wanted or who he was. They met, and the managing director got on well with my father immediately. After hearing about my father's background, and especially his versatility in the 4000 hymns of the Tamil Vedas, he asked my father to be his teacher in the Tamil Vedas. Which my father did. This happy meeting with one of the very great industrialists of the South made my father so happy he wondered how I could have pleased an outsider, when I couldn't please people at home.

'On completion of the job which our construction firm was doing for him, the great man offered me a job in his own organization. He wanted me to begin as an "attender", on a salary of 97 rupees, 52 rupees basic and 45 rupees allowance. "Attender" is another word for office boy. But to get into that organization in any capacity would be today like getting into IBM. I did more typing than office-boy work. So at last I began to rise, and I never stopped – with God's grace. I was seventeen.

'The company opened a branch in Vellore. I got transferred there – to be with my married sister, and to be independent. When the Chinese war came in 1962, I became politically active – which I'd never been before. I gave my rings and ear-rings – things given me by my uncle on the occasion of my thread ceremony – to the war effort. This outraged my parents, and it also outraged my sister, because the things I had given had belonged for some generations to the family.

'A visitor came one day from Delhi. He was a first cousin. He worked in the Delhi office of an American concern. He was shocked to see me in my traditional appearance – and also shocked by the paltry salary I was getting. He asked me to leave the job I was doing and to come to Delhi. He said that, for the same effort I was putting into the firm in Vellore, he would get me twice the salary in Delhi. It was a fascinating offer for me. I immediately decided to accept his offer. But I wasn't sure how my father would react.

'As I expected, my father was reluctant to let me go to Delhi, lest I should deviate further. For four months there was a lot of debate, and many heated exchanges, between me and my father. But in the end it was my father who bought the ticket for me. It cost about 42 rupees, and he gave me some pocket money as well. For the journey itself my family gave me *idli* and *dosas* and fried eatables. They gave me too much. I had to throw away the surplus. Their thinking was that the train might get stranded, and they didn't want me to suffer if that happened. It is even today the normal South Indian family way with travellers.

'Finally, on the third of May, 1963, I charted an entirely new course in my life. I left by Grand Trunk Express from Madras Central railway station at 7.30 p.m. I arrived 40 hours later in Delhi, at 11.30 in the morning on the fifth of May – according to the Gregorian calendar, my birthday.

'The very first thing I did in Delhi – as instructed by my cousin – was to drive straight from the railway station to the barber saloon and remove the churki. That was a moment of great anguish and pain. For 18 full years both my mother and my sister used to rear it – as they would do their own child. They were proud of it. They were jealous of it. I had unusually long hair, longer than my sister's. It used to hit my calf when I undid it. They would wash it and oil it and comb it and knit it together.

'My agony was deeper as the barber, a young man, a real thin-looking man with a moustache, started making probing questions – whether I was sure I wanted what I said. He gave me three chances. He said in Hindi, "Are you sure? Are you sure? Are you sure?" I repeatedly said, "Yes," though in my heart of hearts I was trembling and worried about what my father would say. The barber was so kind and considerate he started cutting it slowly, from below, instead of killing it at one blow – to give me another chance to think again. That was the day I lost all my religious fervour – as Samson lost his physical power.'

That was where the story should have ended, with the flight to Delhi, the cutting off of the tresses at the back of the head, and the start of a new life. But Kakusthan had returned for good to the colony from which he had fled. His story was of a double transformation; and it was of the second transformation that he told me on another day.

Kakusthan said, 'In New Delhi I found myself, and for the next 16 years I lived there. I did a small job for the American firm for which my cousin worked. I also worked as a stenographer for a trade union journal.'

Stenography: the old South Indian brahmin vocation, the vocation that followed on from the doing of rituals, and was the other side of the talent for mathematics and physics.

'I got 50 rupees a month from my cousin's American firm. I got 200 rupees from the trade union paper. And it was during my time on the trade union paper that the second transformation began to take place.

'The trade union movement in India based itself on the principles of Gandhian philosophy: truth and non-violence, duty before right: you produce before you make demands. That is precisely what the Gita tells us, and those were the principles of the Indian National Trade Union Congress. Our day's work at the paper was started with a prayer meeting. That had an effect on me. So did the daily religious column on the back page of the *Hindu* newspaper of Madras. And I also read the writings of Mahatma Gandhi, especially his autobiography.

'In the office there was this religious and spiritual atmosphere. Outside, there was the allurement of Delhi life, the life of money, beauty, everything. For some time it attracted me, that Delhi life. And it worried me – because I didn't have the money. But then the religious books I was reading began to have more pull. So over a period of time I changed again, and I embraced the religious life.

'In this period I took a degree from Delhi University; and I married. I had been attracted by my sister's daughter in Vellore, and I had determined to marry her as soon as I could. The family agreed, but I told them that she should graduate first. I met her educational expenses, and on the last day of her final examination the marriage process started.

'Other editorial jobs with papers and magazines followed after I left the union paper. One such job took me to the town of Ahmedabad in 1980. I was thirty-seven. My father came to see me there, for the birthday of my second son. He was extremely pleased that I was in a good position at last – even though I was minus my churki. He would have been doubly delighted if I had still had the churki.

'The first morning he was there he saw me doing the morning puja. It was something I routinely did, but he was taken aback. We talked for a while about the puja I had done that morning, and the texts connected with the puja. He mentioned some error I had committed in doing the puja, and he hinted that if I had studied better when I was young, the mistake would not have happened.

'I apologized for that mistake. And I apologized for everything that had happened earlier.

'I asked him to induct me into our traditional rituals. I asked him also to teach me the 4000 verses of the Tamil Vedas, and all the other mantras that I would need to know for the rituals in the temple in our ancestral village.

'He said he would teach me. He started that day itself, since it was a Friday and an auspicious day. After 15 days he left Ahmedabad for Madras. Before he left, he promised he would teach me every day for two or three years. But he never came back. He died six months after he left Ahmedabad.

'For 11 days after his death there were elaborate rituals. All those who came, relatives, Vedic pundits, recalled the greatness of my father, my grandfather, my uncle, and the religious way of life of our family, especially in the service of the village deity. I heard that my grandfather had died after a religious argument with the temple pujari about a particular ritual that had not been carried out properly. My cousin had also died in similar circumstances. He had objected to certain rituals that had been introduced at the temple, and then he had lain down in the temple doorway; and people had walked over him. He died a few days afterwards of grief and shock.

'I thought, when I heard these stories, that if my grandfather and other relatives could lay down their lives for the sake of the family deity, shouldn't I at least follow their example?

'I decided to move back to Madras.

'I got a job here. It was easy now, with my experience. And my condition with the firm I approached was that they should have no objection to my external form – no objection to my wearing religious marks on the forehead, having the churki, and wearing the traditional brahmin attire: all the things I hadn't understood when I was younger. It was important for me to get this condition agreed to, since I was coming back to Madras primarily to continue my family's temple obligations.'

I asked him, 'Why this stress on external form? Isn't devotion something you carry in your heart?'

Kakusthan said, 'Perhaps if there had been no temple obligation and honour in our family life and tradition, our life would have been a little more flexible, as in many other normal brahmin families. In all the temple rituals external forms come first, because without the external form I will not be entitled to serve the deity. The external form is as important as the internal. The purer the external form, the purer the internal.'

He had suffered because of the external form. He was entitled to speak as he did.

'I had left the agraharam in 1963. I returned in 1981. I returned to my family house in the colony, and I returned a quite different man, a brahmin fully committed, fully realized. On the first anniversary of my father's death, at the end of the rituals conducted at that time, there was a total break from the past for me: from *loukika* to *vaidhika*, from being in the world to being of the spirit.'

They were words I had heard for the first time in Mysore City, from the brahmin who had been master of religious ceremonies for the last maharaja of Mysore. In the palace where the brahmin had served there had been splendour and extravagance beyond human need, almost as though in the Hindu scheme one of the functions of great wealth was to remind men of the vanity of the senses. But the ruler's great wealth had formed no part of the brahmin's story. The physical needs of men were limited: that was the message of the small plain room where the brahmin told his story.

That was the message, too, of the agraharam or colony where Kakusthan lived, in the set of small rooms he had known as a child. In Christian thinking the eternal opposites are the forces of good and evil. In Hindu or brahmin thought the opposites are worldliness and the life of the spirit. One can retreat from one to the other. When the world fails one, one can sink into the spirit, the idea of the world as the play of illusion.

Kakusthan said, 'I became then, one year after my father's death, what I now am, the man you see. I decided then to live the vaidhika life as far as as possible, to live with all the rigours and discipline that go with it.'

'What are the rigours?'

'I shall not eat outside. I shall eat only what I offer the god at home.' So the oil lamp burned always in front of the image of the god, just next to the kitchen area. 'I shall not even drink water outside. Nor mix with people unchaste. Because, if I don't observe these things, I will be polluting the god of our temple.

'I now live in the colony as a full brahmin. People respect me for the sudden change in my life, and the strict observances now. My family was poor, and this colony is also poor – lower-middle-class people with limited income. Though I am well off, due to the grace of God and the blessings of my forefathers, I want to live nowhere else. Living among these people I know gives me a tremendous happiness and peace.'

We had met over many days, in my hotel and in the colony. Sometimes Kakusthan had met me at the hotel and taken me back to the colony; sometimes he had sent his teenaged son to fetch me. The son was many inches taller than his father, but he was without his father's sturdiness; his eyes were softer.

Kakusthan, whatever he had chosen for himself, was ambitious for his son and wanted the boy to do well at school. And just as, many years before, Kakusthan's father might have asked someone to talk to Kakusthan, so now Kakusthan asked me, the last time we met, to talk to his son and to put to the boy the need for doing well, for geting on with the school books.

The boy, Kakusthan said, was too fond of play. He had gone out that morning, for instance, to play cricket. But that was good, I said. All right, Kakusthan said. But then the boy had gone out again in the afternoon to play cricket.

We were going back to the colony, and Kakusthan had a simple plan for getting me to have a private talk with his son. We – Kakusthan and I – would go up to the terrace overlooking the colony yard directly in front and the walled temple garden to one side. The boy would bring up tea for me, and then Kakusthan would excuse himself and go down to the bathroom.

So, in the colony, the boy brought up a tumbler of tea to me on the terrace; and we began to talk, while down below – in this area where he was king – Kakusthan in his brahmin clothes walked confidently, without hurrying, across the crowded afternoon yard, past the well, to the bathroom in the corner.

The boy loved cricket. He said he loved both batting and bowling. I liked his seriousness about the game. And I couldn't find it in my heart to give him the lecture Kakusthan wanted me to give, about sticking to the books: I couldn't see how, in the conditions of the colony, anyone could do any serious reading or study there. One evening, on the dimly lit paved path leading in from the gateway, I had seen a young boy sitting cross-legged outside his little house, in the dark, before an open book: acting out virtue for his parents' sake, the brahminical love of learning reduced to this ritual form.

I asked the boy, Kakusthan's son, what sort of job he hoped to do. His soft eyes became startled. He knew the question; he was dismayed to hear it from me. He might become a stenographer, he said; he might get a job in an office; it depended on 'fate'.

I was surprised by his talk of fate. Kakusthan had never done so. But Kakusthan had been a rebel all his youth. His son was now very much a young man of the colony, with ideas and ambitions not above those of other young men there. Kakusthan, I believe, would have liked his son to be more forceful. But I didn't want to press the boy. He was years away from getting his degree and taking a job; his world, his way of looking, was going to change before then.

And I told Kakusthan, when he came back up to the terrace, that the boy was going to be all right; that his seriousness about cricket spoke of something spirited and reassuring in him; and the books side and the career side would fall into place when the time came. It was half what Kakusthan wanted to hear; he looked pleased. We began to talk of other things.

It was a late Sunday afternoon, still the Madras winter. The sun was mild; the atmosphere in the agraharam without tension; everyone in the yard seemed to be at play.

The terrace was shaded by an old tree, and Kakusthan and I were sitting in this shade, on the concrete half-wall in front of his sleeping room. I asked him to talk to me about what we were seeing in the yard.

Had I noticed the TV aerials? There were 20 of them, he said. In the colony there were even some colour television sets. People were not as cut off from the rest of the world as they had once been.

'And look at those girls over there,' he said. 'Skipping.'

It would have been easy to miss the significance of that. But 20 years or so ago, he said, those girls wouldn't have been allowed to play like that, in an open yard. Those girls were close to puberty, and 20 years ago the shades of the prison house would have already begun to fall on them.

And, Kakusthan said, I had spoken of the pallor and debility of some of the people in the colony. But some of the brahmin boys now did exercises. That boy, for instance, across the yard, two houses or so away from where the long-skirted girls were skipping – that boy did exercises. The boy was a young man, bare-backed, elegant of posture, not tall. He had the physique found in many kinds of Indian sculpture: broad-shouldered, slender-waisted, smooth-bodied, strength and tension lying within, not expressed in the ripple or indentation of muscle.

Kakusthan approved; he was concerned with physical fitness. He was a small man; his father had been a small man; they had both been subjected to ridicule and physical torment in the town.

From our perch on the terrace we considered both the young man who did exercises, and his father. Where did the young man do his exercises? Right there, in the busy yard; no one minded. He came from a family of 10. Those 10 people lived in that one room whose door we could see. The father was a peon or office-attender. The son who spent so much time perfecting his body was only a clerk.

I said to Kakusthan, 'He's got a good brahmin face.'

'And the colour,' Kakusthan said, with a nod.

He looked abashed then, and lowered his voice: a woman had come up to the terrace, he said, and I was in her way. I was sitting on the half-wall in front of Kakusthan's upper room, and my legs were sticking out into the passage that ran along the edge of the terrace. If the woman had tried to pass she might have touched me, and that would have been wrong; it would also have been wrong for her to talk to me directly. I stood up. Without a word, the woman passed; three or four paces down she turned off into her own little space.

The evening light became softer and yellower. Women and girls went to the well to fill their pots.

When I had first gone to the colony, I had thought, from the way Kakusthan spoke, that the community was fading away, making too many accommodations with the world outside. I realized now that he meant the opposite. The community was learning to adapt: that was its strength.

He said, 'As long as the world exists, brahmins will always survive. Brahmins are indispensable to the society.'

Mr K. Veeramani, a short, brisk man in a long-tailed black shirt, worn in the Indian way, hanging out, not tucked in, looked after the Periyar Thidal and kept the Periyar flame alive in Tamil Nadu.

Periyar had died in the last week of 1973, at the age of ninety-four; and Periyar's second wife had suceeded to the leadership of the movement. She had died five years later; and then Mr Veeramani had become the leader. The movement at that time appeared to have lost its way, to have ceased to matter politically or socially. But now, with the election victory of the original Dravidian political party, the movement appeared once again to be at the heart of things.

Mr Veeramani, as Periyar's philosophical heir, travelled about the state, making speeches, and conducting Periyar-style Self-Respect marriages. In Tamil Nadu, where many people couldn't read and write, speeches were important. People enjoyed speeches, the sound of words; and Mr Veeramani said he could speak for up to two hours at a time, if there was the need. As for the Self-Respect marriages, he did only about eight or 10 a month, about 120 to 150 a year. Not many; but the rationalists, Mr Veeramani said, were only a 'microscopic' element in the state. He didn't think it lessened the importance of his work. This was to preserve as much of Periyar's message as possible. So he looked after the relics – the bed, all the various gifts to Periyar; he explained the iconography of the 33 paintings in the room, showing the stations of Periyar's long life; he published pamphlets; and he led visitors round the grave, reading out the more famous sayings of Periyar's that were carved in grey granite around the grave. Without this work of his over the years, Mr Veeramani said, Periyar's message would have been distorted.

Mr Veeramani was born in 1933, in the town of Cuddalore. His father was a tailor. Tailoring was an 'imported' profession (the way coffee was 'an imported item'), and so it wasn't associated with a particular caste, like weaving. Cuddalore was a port, and Mr Veeramani's father, in addition to his local trade, did a certain amount of tailoring for foreign sailors. Mr Veeramani's father was as a result quite well off; but much of his money went first on a court case (he was an expert in stick-fighting and wrestling, trained people in these arts, and in a roundabout way he found himself dragged into a serious local feud); and then the rest of his money went on medical expenses when he fell ill with filarial fever, caused by infected water.

One of Mr Veeramani's school-teachers was an admirer of Periyar, and important in the Self-Respect movement. This teacher, a man of about twenty-eight or thirty when Mr Veeramani got to know him, had changed his name from Subramaniam (the name of a Hindu deity) to Dravidarmani, which meant 'an important Dravidian person'. He got Mr Veeramani to change his name as well: from Sarangapani, the name of a god, to Veeramani, 'brave man', 'hero'.

When he was about ten or so, Mr Veeramani acted in a school play, and Mr Dravidarmani was so impressed by the boy's talents that he began writing speeches on the Self-Respect theme for the boy to deliver at public meetings. In 1944 in Cuddalore there was a Dravidian Conference. Periyar came to that. There also came a famous atheist Tamil poet who was a disciple of Periyar's. The poet's name was Bharathidasam. He was forty-seven, originally of the weaver caste, and he lived in great poverty in the town of Pondicherry (then a French colonial enclave in British India). He was thought of as the Shelley and the Whitman of the movement. There was a poem of Bharathidasam's that was regularly quoted in Self-Respect speeches. Mr Veeramani gave me this translation of the poem:

The world is still in darkness.
Even people who believe in caste are allowed to live.
The persons who frighten people by religion are still thriving.
When will all this trickery come to an end?

Unless and until this kind of trickery comes to an end,
Freedom and liberty are to be equated with evil only.

Unlike Periyar, who was short and very fat, an avuncular-looking old man, Bharathidasam was forbidding. He was tall and very big. He wore a dhoti, a shirt, and a red shawl – red for the revolution. He lost his temper easily and had the reputation of always speaking his mind.

It was in the presence of this man, and Periyar, that the ten-year old Mr Veeramani acted out the speech his teacher had written for him to deliver at the Dravidian Conference. The speech was in Periyar's broadest anti-brahmin, anti-Hindu style. It was about the absurdity of the Hindu myth that brahmins had sprung from the head of Brahma, kshatriyas or warriors from his arms, banias or merchants from his thighs, and shudras from his feet. How – the ten-year-old asked the conference – could someone not a woman give birth to people from so many parts of the body from which birth couldn't take place?

Periyar was impressed by the speech, and after that Mr Veeramani became one of the recognized speakers for the Self-Respect movement. He used to be billed as the ten-year-old rationalist, and soon he began to write (or at any rate to make up) his own speeches.

In 1949, five years after the Cuddalore conference, there was a split in the movement. It was caused by Periyar's decision, at the age of seventy, to marry for the second time.

The woman he wanted to marry was the daughter of a timber merchant in Vellore. The family were supporters of the movement, and Periyar used to stay in their house when he went to Vellore. The daughter was training to be a teacher; but her mother, though she was a follower of Periyar, was yet sufficiently influenced by traditional ways to want her daughter to give up the idea of teaching and to get married. The daughter was twenty-five; that was thought to be very old. When the daughter got to know what her mother's plans for her were, she left the family house in Vellore and went to stay in a far-off place in a school-teacher's house.

Periyar knew the daughter. When he heard what had happened, he called the daughter away from the school-teacher's house and he put her up in his own house in the town of Erode. He refused to let her go back to her mother's house. He made the young woman his secretary; she also became his nurse; and six years later they were married. She was thirty-one then; Periyar was seventy.

This was the story Mr Veeramani told me, and he was anxious for me to understand why Periyar had married at this late age. Periyar had accumulated a lot of property. He didn't want this property to pass to his relatives. He wanted it to be used for the movement, and he thought that this could be best done by leaving it to his secretary-nurse. Under Hindu law, however, he could make her his legal heir only by marrying her.

Not everyone understood the motives, and an important section of the movement broke away to form their own group. Mr Veeramani, however, at this stage a fifteen-year-old rationalist, remained loyal to Periyar. He remained loyal when he went to the university; he remained loyal when he began to study law. And then, while he was still doing his law studies, something important happened.

In 1957 Periyar was sentenced to six months' imprisonment for burning the Indian Constitution. (There was an illustration of this episode, literal, clear, and cool, in the relic-room of the Periyar Thidal.) Up to this time Mr Veeramani had just been a propagandist for the movement, energetic and with a reputation, but still at a distance from Periyar. Now, with the great man in jail, Mr Veeramani found himself touring the state with Periyar's wife, Mrs Manyammai – as Mr Veeramani called her.

When Periyar came out of jail, he sent for Mr Veeramani. Periyar was in the town of Tiruchy. Mr Veeramani went there immediately.

Periyar said to him, 'What about your future? Are you going to get married?'

It was a surprising question, because Periyar was against early marriages; he thought they worked against the uplift of non-brahmins. Mr Veeramani at this time was twenty-five, and he still had more than a year to do at Madras Law College.

Mr Veeramani said, 'Sir, I don't think marriage is a necessity at this stage. I don't have my own economic independence, and I would like to give my most to the party.'

Periyar said, 'But it's only in the interests of the party that I'm suggesting marriage to you.'

The girl or young woman whom Periyar wanted Mr Veeramani to marry was the eldest daughter of a couple for whom, in 1933,

Periyar had performed a Self-Respect marriage. That Self-Respect marriage had become politically famous, because in 1952 its validity had been challenged in the courts. But – sentiment apart – Periyar's real reason for wanting Mr Veeramani to marry the daughter of that couple was that the family was well-to-do, the father belonging to a merchant community, the mother coming from a landowning family; and marriage to the daughter would enable Mr Veeramani to work full time for the movement.

When Mr Veeramani understood this, he said to Periyar, 'If it is in the largest interests of the party, I will obey your command.'

Mrs Manyammai then went to Mr Veeramani's parents to give them the news that their son was going to get married, and after this she took Mr Veeramani to the girl's house in Tiruannamalai. They went by train and bus and finally arrived at the farm-house where the girl and her mother were staying. There was a lot of fertile land attached to the farm-house – rice fields and groundnut fields. After the usual preliminaries the girl came came out and served some food (a curious remnant of old ritual), and then went back inside. But, in fact, she knew Mr Veeramani well, from his appearances in public meetings.

Six months later the marriage took place. Periyar and Mrs Manyammai sent out the invitations in their own names, so the wedding gathering was like another Dravidian conference. The wedding itself took place on a Sunday afternoon at five. The time was chosen quite deliberately, because orthodox Hindus considered it an especially inauspicious time. The atheist poet Bharathidasam, the Whitman-like figure of the movement, read out a poem he had composed for the occasion.

There was a curious sequel: in his final law examination, Mr Veeramani found himself having to answer a question about the 1933 Self-Respect marriage of his in-laws.

The marriage had worked out as Periyar had hoped. Mr Veeramani had been free to do his work for the Dravidar Kazagham, the Dravidian Movement, and had kept Periyar's name and message alive. And now, after all the ups and downs of the last 30 years, Periyar's more-than-life-size portrait was to be seen in many places in Madras, and Mr Veeramani, keeper of the flame, moved through Madras like a hero.

The house in which Mr Veeramani lived belonged to his wife. It was in the Adiyar area of Madras, near the Theosophical Society.

It was a big concrete house, fifteen years old. It was on three floors, and the Veeramanis occupied one floor.

High up on a wall in the drawing-room was a big black-and-white photograph of Periyar and Mrs Manyammai. Periyar was seated, holding his stout stick with the curved handle. The other components of his appearance were now well known to me: the big, wavy beard, the dhoti, the shawl, the black shirt. Mrs Manyammai, steady-eyed, stood plump and firm in a black sari at the side of his chair, and her right hand rested on the back of the chair.

It seemed fitting for that photograph to have a place of honour in Mr Veeramani's drawing-room: that marriage of Periyar's was like a forerunner of Mr Veeramani's.

Mrs Veeramani served tea and withdrew: dutiful and correct, saying little, and still like someone serving a cause. Though, if one didn't know what that cause was, one might never have guessed, so traditional and demure and self-effacing was her manner.

In that family atmosphere, below Periyar's photograph, Mr Veeramani told me about the practical side of Periyar. He had come from a rich merchant family, and he had made himself richer.

'He was very careful. He was a custodian not only of human rights, but of the party property rights. He multiplied those rights by investing in mills and banks. In 1973 his worth, or his party's worth, was more than two crores.' Twenty million rupees, a million pounds. 'Now the property is worth about 10 crores.' Four million pounds.

'People would give him money. And when, say, he had got 99 rupees, he would take a rupee from Mrs Manyammai, and he would convert those 100 rupees into a 100-rupee note, so that he wouldn't easily spend it. Mrs Manyammai would laugh.' Mr Veeramani laughed too. '"Frugality, thy name is Periyar!" The whole of Tamil Nadu knows it. Even for his signature he used to charge. Instead of garlands, he asked people to give him two rupees.'

He charged for his speeches, and he made two or three a day, travelling an average of 200 miles a day in the van his supporters had given him. His last speech was made five days before he died, at the age of ninety-four. He had married Mrs Manyammai when he was seventy, so that she would inherit his property; but their marriage lasted 24 years, and she outlived him by only five years. Then the mantle had passed to Mr Veeramani.

Mr Veeramani's eldest son was an engineer, studying in Boston. His second son had a degree in commerce, and was now in plastics. And the first daughter was also in the United States, doing a master's degree in information systems. Mr Veeramani's father had been a tailor in the town of Cuddalore. The world had opened out for his grandchildren in a way he could not have imagined.

On the wall opposite the one with the photograph of Periyar and his wife there was a 1989 Tamil Tigers calendar, hanging above a bookcase. The calendar had a big colour photograph of the two Tamil Tiger leaders, Pirabhakaran and Mathaiya. They were shown in sun-struck, hot-looking woodland, and they were in camouflage guerrilla garb. They were both fat and big-bellied, and smiling, as though at the absurdity of the uniform they had put on for the calendar photograph. But they were not clownish at all. They had brought chaos to Sri Lanka. And their calendar for 1989 was here, in Mr Veeramani's drawing-room. The rationalist movement of Tamil Nadu, the anti-brahmin movement, also contained this idea of Tamil glory, past and present.

Until this trip to Madras, Periyar had been barely a name to me; and I had never heard of Mr Veeramani. But for 40 years Mr Veeramani had been at the centre of an immense local revolution, which, with all the economic and intellectual growth that had come to independent India, had taken on the characteristics of a little war; and so far Mr Veeramani had been on the winning side.

The same could not be said of Kakusthan. A good half of his story had been of retreat and flight – until family feeling and filial piety had made him turn back and consciously embrace an archaic way. But perhaps the comparison of Mr Veeramani with Kakusthan wasn't just. Perhaps a better comparison would have been with those brahmins who had moved from old learning to new, from temple rituals to science, the brahmins who (almost in the manner of Mr Veeramani) had broken out of old ways more radically.

Madras, with the sculptured towers of its temples, its special foods, the idlis and dosas, its music and its dance, the museum with the great bronzes, could appear to the visitor to be still a whole culture. It took time to understand that a usurpation had

273

taken place, that brahmins were on the defensive, though they were still the musicians and dancers, still the cooks, still the priests in the temples.

It was hard not to feel sad at the undoing of a culture. But the brahmin cause – if such a cause existed – could not be isolated from all the other Indian causes. It was better to see the undoing of a culture – the rise of Mr Veeramani, the flight and transformation of the brahmins – as part of a more general movement forward.

Bharathidasam, the atheist poet of the Dravidian Movement, wore a red shawl – red for the revolution. The flag of the DMK, the political party that had grown out of the Dravidian Movement, was red and black – red for the revolution, black for the Dravidian cause. The two colours, taken together, might have been thought to stand for all the insulted and injured of Tamil Nadu, all the people whom the especial brahmin rigidity of the South had put outside the pale. But the Dravidian Movement represented only the middle castes – Periyar himself was a man of a merchant caste – who, in other parts of India, had a fairly honourable place in the caste system. Below those middle castes, now triumphant, there were, as always in India, others. They, too, had been shaken up; they too had begun to stake their claim.

Seven or eight years before, in the north of Tamil Nadu, there had been a peasant rebellion – or a Maoist rebellion. It had been destroyed. In the 40 years or so since independence the Indian state had had to deal with many kinds of insurgency, in many parts of the country. The state had learned how to manage, when to stamp hard, when to lay off.

There were survivors of that peasant rebellion. They had been restored to civilian life, and were probably doing better now than they had ever done. The police were still in touch with these men; and it was through the police that a meeting was arranged for me with two of them.

They had been summoned from a district far away, and the meeting took place in my hotel room. A plain-clothes police officer came with them. On my side were two newspapermen, one a crime reporter, to interpret, the other a sports writer, to observe. So there were six of us in the hotel room. The number made for formality. The hotel's tea and biscuits, and the solicitous room-service waiter, made everyone a little stiffer.

I didn't know what to make of the former rebels. They were

very dark, solidly built, and in something like a uniform: long dhotis and loose-hanging cream-coloured shirts. Their hair was thick and long and well oiled, combed back from the forehead and from the sides, and cut at the back in a straight line just above the shirt collar.

The older of the two was the spokesman. He had a heavier build, a chunkier nose, and a shinier skin. He said his brother had been a communist, and it was this brother – later killed by a landlord – who had indoctrinated him. He, the speaker, had indoctrinated the second man, who was younger, and was his brother-in-law. It had been easy to indoctrinate the brother-in-law. His father worked in the Railways, in the canteen. One day the father's toes were cut off in an accident in the railway yard. The son then applied for a job in the Railways. He should have got a job: there was a tradition in the Railways that when a man was injured and had to retire, a member of his family was given a job, for compassionate reasons. But the son didn't get a job, because other people had bribed the assistant station-master or some official of that standing.

The police officer nodded: that was the way it was, at that level – and the officer's compassion was interesting. The newspapermen agreed. It was like that with those jobs.

There were very few brahmins in their village. It was an area of backward castes and *Adi-dravids*, the first Dravidians, aborigines, tribal people. These people were exploited by the big landlords or zamindars. A big landlord here was anyone who owned more than 50 acres. Many of the zamindars were people of the Reddiar community who had come from the neighbouring state of Andhra Pradesh. But there were also Adi-dravid zamindars.

The zamindars employed women for three rupees a day and men for five rupees a day. The minimum wage at that time was five rupees for women and nine for men. The aim of the Maoists was to create enmity between the workers and the landlords. They did this by telling the workers about the minimum wage, and encouraging them to ask for it. The landlords often refused, and brought in workers from other villages. Sometimes the landlords became rougher. The older man's brother had been killed by a zamindar. After that, it was war: that zamindar had to be killed.

Three attempts were made to kill the zamindar. He was shadowed, and one day, when he was on a bus, six of the Maoists got on the bus. But nothing happened. The rebels became indecisive, thinking of the other passengers; and in the confusion the zamindar got away. The second time they waited for the zamindar early one morning in a field. He came; they shot at him; they missed. The third time they got their man. A party of eight assaulted the zamindar's house and threw pin-grenades. They killed three people: the zamindar, his mistress, and a baby. They didn't know about the baby; the death of the baby upset them.

After that they did only two more killings. They were just following orders at this stage. The orders were more like decisions: these decisions were made at group meetings. Their wish was to overthrow the government, and their aim, when they were dealing with people whom they had decided were 'enemies', was simply to kill them.

Then the police began to move in. They threw a vice, a 'wrench', around the area where the Maoists were operating, and the wrench was gradually closed. Thirty Maoists were killed. The two men in the hotel room were lucky. They had surrendered to the police some time before, and were in prison, charged with the murder of the zamindar and his mistress and the baby. (This was how the story was told: it was blurred and unsatisfactory at this point. But because of the formality of the occasion, because of the time gap between what the speaker said and what came out in translation, because of the compression of the translation, it didn't occur to me to ask further questions at the time. It was only later that the blurring became apparent.)

The police could make no case against the two men. They couldn't find witnesses, and the reason was that a warning had been sent out by the two men, 10 days before the hearing, that if anyone came forward to give evidence, he wouldn't be alive the next day. This was said quite coolly in the hotel room; and the plain-clothes police officer, nodding, sucking in his breath, took it coolly too, as though it was all part of the game.

Eventually the two men were released. Since their group had been wiped out, they had nothing to go back to – and here, though the question hadn't been asked, they both said they had betrayed no one in their group. The younger man, the brother-in-law, said that the police had cut the 'nerves' on one of his feet. He showed a dark scar, like a burn mark, on the top of his sandalled foot. But even after that, the younger man said, he hadn't given anyone away. The police officer didn't look put out and didn't try to interfere in what was being said; it was as though that, too, that wretchedness about the nerves and the foot, was part of the game, and everyone knew it.

With the help of the police – and no doubt as part of the state policy of rehabilitation – the two men went into business. Neither did well. The older man went into the tomato business, deciding for some reason to ship his tomatoes all the way to Calcutta. He lost 25,000 rupees, about £1000. The brother-in-law started making *beedis*, cheap leaf cigarettes; he said his employees ran away with the money. Neither man looked cast down by his business failure; they both seemed quite content.

I didn't know what to make of what I had heard. There were so few word-pictures in what they had said, so few details. That might have been because of the translation, or because of the formality of our meeting, or because they had spoken their stories too often. There was an obviousness about them. I was reminded of the obviousness of the gangsters I had met in Bombay; they, the gangsters, were obvious because their lives were, after all, very simple. And perhaps the foot soldiers of a revolution, such as these men might have been, had to be simple people too, receiving messages simple enough for their capacities and needs.

I asked them what they knew about Periyar. And at once, even in the crime reporter's translation, they seemed to say more than they had done up till then – and it might have been because it wasn't a question they were expecting.

They honoured Periyar, the older man said. His father had been a follower of Periyar. But Periyar had struggled against caste alone; he hadn't thought of class. 'He shook us up, but he wasn't relevant to our kind of struggle.' That was the crime reporter's first translation. Later he amended it. What had been said was, in a more literal translation, 'We had no connection.' And that hinted better at the caste gap between the Dravidian Movement and the Maoists.

I asked them about the anti-religious side of Periyar's message. The older man said they weren't religious, but their women were. Though even the women had begun to do without brahmins in their ceremonies.

This sounded genuine. So, right at the end, I began to feel that the two men, whatever their relationship with the police, might have been what they said they had been.

Before they left, the brother-in-law asked to use the bathroom. I had my misgivings, but the police officer waved the man into the bathroom. We waited. There was no sound of a flush. Then the man came out; and carefully closed the door behind him.

Later, opening that carefully closed bathroom door, I found the toilet bowl unflushed, and the seat and floor pissed over. Was it social inexperience alone? Or was there also – in this man who had fought the class war – some very deep caste feeling about the uncleanliness of latrines: places so unclean they were beneath one's notice, places for other people to notice, other people to clean?

I talked this over with Suresh, the sports writer, a day or so later. He said the two men were among the lowest of the low. However little I might have been aware of it, they would have stood out in the hotel lobby. They were far below the shudras, and quite outside the reach of the Dravidian Movement. Would they have had any idea of what was religiously clean and unclean? At that level, Suresh said, though caste and community distinctions might not be easily visible to people above, they were nevertheless rigidly followed.

The shirt and long dhoti and oily long hair of both men had probably been modelled on some star of the popular Tamil cinema. This care with their appearance was a sign that they had moved forward, had been shaken out of their village ways. The little paunches were also an aspect of the self-respect that had come to them with their rehabilitation. They had said that they had given up the revolution, and wanted now only to look after their families. And that, Suresh said – whatever other ambiguities there might have been in their stories – felt true.

I went to say goodbye to Sugar. He was always there in his little ground-floor apartment, a prisoner of his reputation.

I found him giving advice to a man who had brought a computer print-out of two horoscopes. A marriage was being considered, and Sugar was giving an opinion about the horoscopes. He was being firm. The girl's horoscope was not suitable; in six months or so the boy would find someone more suitable. The inquirer, a high-up civil servant, didn't seem to mind. He was from the boy's side. In this business of match-making boys had the whip hand; girls and their families were the suppliants.

I said, 'Does the girl have a bad horoscope?'

'Not bad,' Sugar said. 'Not suitable.'

It was strange, finding him, with his own melancholy, so ready to play the tyrant as a seer. I felt that, in spite of what he had said about the selfishness and falsity of the people who came to see him, and what he had said about giving it all up, he took pleasure in his holy man's work and reputation.

Then he must have felt he had to make me some offering. He made it in the way that was now natural to him.

He looked at me across the little room and said, 'When I saw you in the Himalayas in 1962, your face was *bright*. It was one of the things that attracted me to you. Now you look troubled. Has it to do with your life? Your work?'

I said, 'I was more troubled in 1962. But I was younger. Like you.'

'Will you be coming back to Madras again? Come and see me. Come and see me before two years.' He was exercising his gifts of prophecy on himself. 'After two years – '

He shook his head and, slumped in his chair, his illness and solitude now like pure burdens, he let his glance take in the little space that he had made his own – the drawing-sleeping, without the furniture jumble I had first seen there, with the holy pictures on the wall and the hanging shelves with his headache tablets, the adjoining hall between the kitchen, which he couldn't clean himself and which he could allow no one else to clean, and the temple room with its forbidding images – the little space he was soon to vacate.

5

After the Battle

In India in 1962 I took much of the British architecture for granted. After what I had known in Trinidad and England, British building in India seemed familiar, not a cause for wonder. Perhaps, too, in 1962, just 15 years after independence, I didn't allow myself to see British Indian architecture except as background. I was saving my wonder for the creations of the Indian past. Even Lutyens's great achievement in New Delhi I saw in a grudging way, finding the scale too grand, looking in his ceremonial buildings for the motifs he had got from the Mogul builders, and finding in his adaptations further evidence of vainglory.

I looked in this partial way even at the lesser architecture of the British, the bungalows and houses built for officials in the country districts. They were pleasant to stay in; with their porticoes and verandahs, thick walls, high ceilings, and sometimes additional upper windows or wall-openings, they were well suited to the climate. But they seemed too grand for the poverty of the Indian countryside. They seemed also to exaggerate the hardships of the Indian climate. So that, though absolutely of India, these British buildings, by their exaggeration, seemed to keep India at a distance.

But the years race on; new ways of feeling and looking can come to one. Indians have been building in free India for 40 years, and what has been put up in that time makes it easier to look at what went before. In free India Indians have built like people without a tradition; they have for the most part done mechanical, surface imitations of the international style. What is not easy to understand is that, unlike the British, Indians have not really built for the Indian climate. They have been too obsessed with imitating the modern; and much of what has been done in this way – the dull, four-square towers of Bombay, packed far too close together; the concrete nonentity of Lucknow and Madras and the residential colonies of New Delhi – can only make hard tropical lives harder and hotter.

Far from extending people's ideas of beauty and grandeur and human possibility – uplifting ideas which very poor people may need more than rich people – much of the architecture of free India has become part of the ugliness and crowd and increasing physical oppression of India. Bad architecture in a poor tropical city is more than an aesthetic matter. It spoils people's day-to-day lives; it wears down their nerves; it generates rages that can flow into many different channels.

This Indian architecture, more disdainful of the people it serves than British Indian architecture ever was, now makes the most matter-of-fact Public Works Department bungalow of the British time seem like a complete architectural thought. And if one goes on from there, and considers the range of British building in India, the time span, the varied styles of those two centuries, the developing functions (railway stations, the Victoria Memorial in Calcutta, the Gateway of India in Bombay, the legislative buildings of Lucknow and New Delhi), it becomes obvious that British Indian architecture – which can so easily be taken for granted – is the finest secular architecture in the sub-continent.

Calcutta, more than New Delhi, is the British-built city of India. It was one of the early centres of British India; it grew with British power, and was steadily embellished; it was the capital of British India until 1930. In the building of Calcutta, known first as the city of palaces, and later as the second city of the British Empire, the British worked with immense confidence, not adapting the styles of Indian rulers, but setting down in India adaptations of the European classical style as emblems of the conquering civilization. But the imperial city, over the 200 years of its development, also became an Indian city; and – being at once a port, a centre of administration and business, education and culture, British and Indian style – it became a city like no other in India. To me at the end of 1962, after some months of Indian small-town and district life, Calcutta gave an immediate feel of the metropolis, with all the visual excitement of a metropolis, and all its suggestions of adventure and profit and heightened human experience.

Twenty-six years later, the grandeur of the British-built city –

the wide avenues, the squares, the attractive use of the river and open spaces, the disposition of the palaces and the public buildings – could still be seen in a ghostly way at night, when the crowds of the day had retreated to their nooks and crannies, to rest for the restless vacuity and torment of the new Calcutta day: the broken roads and footpaths; the brown gasoline-and-kerosene haze adding an extra sting to the fierce sunlight, mixing with the street dust, and coating the skin with grit and grime; the day-long cicada-like screech, rising and falling, of the horns of the world's shabbiest buses and motor-cars. The British-built city could still be seen, even in this ghostly way, because so little had been added since independence; so little had been added since 1962.

Energy and investment had gone to other parts of India. Calcutta had been bypassed, living off its entrails, and giving an illusion of life. Certain buildings in central Calcutta seemed to have received no touch of paint since 1962. On some walls and pillars – as on the walls and pillars of buildings awaiting demolition – old posters and glue had formed a tattered kind of papier-mâché crust; you felt that if you tried to scrape off that crust, you might pull away plaster or stucco. The famous colonial clubs – the Bengal Club, the Calcutta Club – were in decay, and Indians now moved in rooms once closed to them. Decay within, decay without: Calcutta in some places had a little of the feel of an abandoned Belgian settlement in central Africa in the 1960s, after Africans had moved in and camped. Camped: it was the word. At independence, with the partition of Bengal into Indian West Bengal and Pakistan East Bengal, there had been a very big movement of refugees from the east. They had camped where they could; they had clogged up large areas in and around the city. And since then the population of the city had doubled.

There was no room by day on the streets or in the large sunburnt parks. There was no place to go walking. You could drive very slowly along a dug-up road and through the crowds to the Tollygunge Club, and there you could go walking on the golf course. But the drive was exhausting; and the drive back, in the kerosene-and-gasoline fumes, undid the little good you might have done yourself. People told you that up to 15 years ago the streets of central Calcutta were washed every day. But I had heard that in 1962 as well. Even then, just 15 years after independence, 16 years after the great Hindu-Muslim riots which had marked so many memories, people were looking back to a golden age of Calcutta.

The British had built Calcutta and given it their mark. And – though the circumstances were fortuitous – when the British ceased to rule, the city began to die.

One of the people I met in Calcutta in 1962 was Chidananda Das Gupta. He worked at the time for the Imperial Tobacco Company, later known less provocatively as the ITC. Because he worked for such a grand British company, Chidananda was one of the select and envied group of Indians known as 'boxwallahs'.

These boxwallahs represented in their own eyes a synthesis of Indian and European culture. They were admired and envied by Indians outside the group because their boxwallah jobs were secure, in addition to being, with the British connection, a badge of breeding. The salaries were very good, among the best in India; and – to add to the boxwallah superfluity – there were company cars and furnished company apartments. And the work was not hard. Any firm a boxwallah worked for more or less monopolized its particular field in India. All that was required of a boxwallah was that he should be a man of culture, and well connected, an elegant member of the team.

Chidananda had another interest. He loved the cinema, and was one of the founders of the Calcutta Film Society. It was at the Calcutta Film Society that I met him one evening. And 26 years later I was to be reminded – by Rajan, the secretary, who had told me his story in Bombay – that at the end of that evening Chidananda had entrusted me to him, asking him to see me safely back to the guest house of the drug company where I was staying. No memory had stayed with me of Rajan, to whom this easy intercourse with film people and Bengali men of culture at the Film Society had come as a joy, a glimpse of a Calcutta far sweeter than the one he knew. Of the society office I had the merest impression: a dim ceiling light in a small room full of old office furniture. Of Chidananda I carried away a boxwallah picture: a slender moustached man of forty in a grey suit.

Chidananda didn't last at ITC. He became a film-maker and writer; that became his career, and it took him away from Calcutta. Twenty years or so later, as a semi-retired man, he had come back to Calcutta. He worked for half the week as editor of the arts pages of *The Telegraph* newspaper. The rest of the week he lived at Shantiniketan, the university founded by Rabindranath Tagore, the poet and patron saint of Bengal.

Shantiniketan was two and a half hours away by train from Calcutta. Chidananda was building a house there, living in the house while it was being built around him. I went to see him there one Sunday.

What did I know of Shantiniketan? I thought of it as a poet-educationist's version of Gandhi's Phoenix Farm in South Africa: something connected with the independence movement, and at the same time a protest against too much mechanization: some idea of music, of open-air classes, of huts as lecture halls: something Arcadian and very fragile, depending on a suspension of disbelief and criticism, and something which – since I hadn't heard about Shantiniketan for a long time – I thought had faded away.

I travelled up in the air-conditioned lounge car of the Shantiniketan Express. It was arranged like a drawing-room with sofas and arm-chairs. Its decorative motifs were Buddhist, and one railed-off part of the car might even have contained a shrine area: a reminder of the Buddhist faith in the regions to the north. I was the only passenger in the lounge car; this explained the fearful price the bell captain of the Calcutta hotel had paid on my behalf. But the effect of luxury was absent: the lounge car was used as a sleeping room by lower railway staff, and three of them were snoring away on sofas.

The land was rice land, the level, treeless land of a delta, with green and brown fields. The green fields were full of water, with rice plants in different stages of growth in different fields. In some fields seedlings stood in the water in bundles, like little stooks, before being planted out in rows. The fields that had been reaped were brown and dry; sometimes stubbled, sometimes cleared and ploughed; sometimes with spaced-out mounds of darker, new earth, to revive the soil, waiting to be ploughed in. Water was being lifted in many different places from field to field, sometimes by electric pumps, sometimes by means of a long, flexible sleeve, lowered by hand into a field with water, then lifted and poured into the other field. Every kind of activity connected with the growing of rice was to be seen on this wide, flat delta: this went on for mile after mile, and it was hard to understand how there could ever have been famine here. But then, near Shantiniketan, the land began to dry out, began to look like flat desert, and unfriendly.

Chidananda was at the station to meet me. Twenty-six years on, we were like actors coming on in the third act of a play, exiting young at the end of act two, and reappearing with powder or flour on hair and eyebrows. He was in casual Indian clothes (and not in the grey boxwallah suit my memory had fixed him in), and he had an old Ambassador car. It was far cheaper to run here than in Delhi, he said; that was one consideration when he had decided to move to Shantiniketan.

The short lane leading out of the station was a tangle of cycle-rickshaws. The car was the intruder here, Chidananda said. There actually was a special railway stop for Shantiniketan, but the people of Bolpur, the stop before, insisted that everyone going to Shantiniketan should get off at Bolpur, to give their trade to the local bazaar.

We got out into the open after a little. There were trees. Many had been planted by the university, Chidananda said, and they had helped to increase the rainfall. The shade, too, was nice; but still it was dusty, very dusty. There were no university mud huts now, just ochre-washed concrete houses. We passed the Shantiniketan temple. It was a hall of pleasing proportions, self-consciously un-ecclesiastical. But it was of its period. It had pierced walls and panes of coloured glass, and from the road it looked Edwardian, and a little gaudy.

Chidananda showed some of the houses Tagore lived in when he was at Shantiniketan. Tagore, Chidananda said, became bored very quickly with a house, and liked to move from house to house: the poet's privilege, the founder's privilege, and perhaps also the self-indulgence of the Bengali aristocrat. I had some feeling as well of the great man licensed or at play in Shantiniketan: there were some university buildings that Tagore had designed himself, attempting a blend of Asian motifs, Hindu, Indian, Chinese. Strange to consider now, the romanticism and self-deception behind that pictorial idea; yet at the time there would have been passion mixed up with the play, the need – against the old and apparently enduring glory of the British Empire and Europe – to assert Asia.

Chidananda's unfinished house was at the edge of the university area. The house, of brick, was to be on two floors. The ground floor was almost complete; about three months' work remained to be done on the upper floor. The land around the house was open on three sides. Chidananda had chosen the spot for the privacy and the silence and the fresh air, none of which could now be had in Indian cities. But the main reason why Chidananda had come to Shantiniketan was that – with all its changes: it was now a university like any other in India – it was connected with the special Bengali culture he had grown up in. The soil was sacred to him, as it was sacred, though in a different way, to the simple Indian tourists who came. These tourists came, not because they knew the poetry or the work of Rabindranath Tagore, but because they had heard of him as a holy man, and it was good to visit the shrines of such people.

Chidananda's father had been a preacher for the Brahmo Samaj all his life. The Brahmo Samaj was a kind of purified or reformed Hinduism which the father of Rabindranath had elaborated in the 19th century. It was an attempt to synthesize the New Learning of Britain and Europe with the old speculative Hindu faith of the Vedas and the Upanishads. It was a direct development of the ideas of Raja Ram Mohun Roy of Bengal (1772–1833), the first modern Indian reformer and educationist. The quality of men like Roy and the elder Tagore cannot be easily appreciated today, when the goods and inventions of Europe and America have changed the world, and simple people everywhere have to make some accommodation to the civilization that encircles and attracts them. In the late 18th and early 19th century Europe, in India, was less a source of goods. In the static conditions of Indian civilization at the time – with all its pressures towards old ways, old virtues – it required exceptional intellectual power to recognize the new gifts of Europe.

Chidananda said, 'The Brahmo faith brings together the essence of the Upanishadic teaching and some Christian forms. Such as a form of service – a service on Sunday morning and Sunday evening. You would sit in pews in the larger churches, and there would be a pulpit. The service would alternate between spoken rituals and prayers, and hymns, many of which were written by Rabindranath Tagore, some by his father. It was Rabindranath's father who devised the mode of the service. The Brahmo separated Upanishadic monotheism and the thought of a universal spirit, which was formless, from Puranic Hinduism – idolatry, many deities, mixed with animism, casteism. It believed in the education of women and the ideals of democracy, and the abolition of the caste system.'

This was the faith that Chidananda's father served all his life. The decision to do so came to him at an early age.

'My grandfather used to take my father to the Sunday service of the Brahmo Samaj from the time he was ten years old. This was in the town of Chittagong, now in Bangladesh.' Chittagong: now associated with the poverty and natural disasters of Bangladesh, but to the Portuguese poet Camoens 400 years ago one of the fairest cities of rich and fertile Bengal: *Chatigão, cidade das milhores de Bengala*.

'At fourteen my father decided he wanted to become a Brahmo. My grandfather had never foreseen such an outcome, and he was outraged. My father left home one night. He literally walked and – to use a modern term – hitchhiked, on bullock carts and boats, to reach Shillong up in the hills, 500 miles away. In those days there was still quite a living tradition of wayside hospitality. My father told me he would walk or go by bullock cart all day, and at evening he would go to the nearest house and ask for shelter for the night, and it would be given.

'He went to Shillong because he knew some Brahmos there. They then helped him with his education, and he went to college with a lot of well-known people, among them Satyajit Ray's father, Sukumar Ray, a great humorist and publisher.

'My father never graduated. He did what in those days was called "First Arts", the first two years of college, and he became a missionary of the Brahmo and was paid a small allowance. Quite soon thereafter he met my mother and fell in love with her – in Ganga, in Bihar, where my mother's father was a well-established doctor. When my father asked for his daughter's hand, the doctor agreed. And my father remained a poor preacher all his life.'

For someone of this background – and perhaps for all devoted Brahmos – Shantiniketan was holy ground, for a special reason.

'Rabindranath's father was travelling through this area in the 1840s. It was like a desert, and he liked the place very much. There was one tree, and he sat under it, and that day he decided to found an ashram on the spot. It was to be modelled on the ancient *brahmacharya* ashram – where you practise celibacy during your student days and learn at the feet of your guru. He did found the ashram, and a long time afterwards Rabindranath founded the university, *Vishwa-Bharati*, India's World University. There is a raised platform under the tree where Rabindranath's father sat. That is considered the most sacred spot at Shantiniketan.

'What Raja Ram Mohun Roy began as a reform movment early in the 19th century Devendranath Tagore made into a religion. It transformed the Bengali middle class. Rabindranath Tagore expanded that religion into a culture. And that culture became Nehru's politics. Because Rabindranath channelled it into a culture, and didn't restrict it to religion, it was soon absorbed by the wider middle class. Today the Brahmo Samaj is still technically there. But the life has gone out of the institution – and into the wider society.'

Chidananda first saw Shantiniketan in 1940, when he was nineteen. He was living with his family in the neighbouring province of Bihar, and his father suggested that he should go and spend a holiday there. He stayed in the guest house. He shared a room with an Indonesian teaching batik at the university. It excited Chidananda to be with someone from abroad, and he was also excited by the Indonesian's name, which was Prahasto. This was a name straight out of the Hindu epic, the Mahabharata. Chidananda immediately had a greater idea of India and Asia; and he felt – what Tagore intended students at his university to feel – that in going to Shantiniketan he had gone to a place that was part of the world, not just of India.

A few days later Rabindranath made a speech at the temple.

'It was very early in the morning, December, quite cold – there were few houses in Shantiniketan then, much more open ground – and we sat on the cold marble floor in the glass temple, with pieces of glass of various colours. When the sun came up it threw all kinds of colours on the faces and clothes of the people. We all sat there and waited for Rabindranath.

'He was wheeled in. Then he got up from the wheelchair. He was very tall, but bent with age. He walked in on his own. He was in a white dhoti and koortah and shawl. I was impressed by that sight. It was like an evocation of ancient India, a romantic feeling of encountering a sage from olden times. He sat on a very low stool. Everyone else was seated on the marble, without any spread.

'Then the singing began. No modern instruments, all traditional instruments. No harmonium, though – Rabindranath disliked it because it has a fixed scale, a western scale, and it is impossible with it to sound the semi-tones or micro-tones which are important to the Indian system of classical music. Then they sang a hymn, one of Rabindranath's hymns.

'He read from a prepared text, in Bengali, with Sanskrit quotations. He was a very big man, six foot two, and he looked very *strong*, and I was struck by the contrast between his voice, which was thin and high, and the largeness of the man. I had expected a deep, rich voice. It took a few minutes to overcome that feeling. But very soon the spell of what he was saying took over. This was December 1940, and the war was very much with us. The subject of his address was the crisis in civilization – he was concerned about the movement towards self-destruction.'

So Chidananda was introduced by Tagore to a way of thinking about the world. It was one of the blessings of the Indian independence movement, that many of its leaders should have been men of large vision, capable of looking beyond their Indian cause.

That first visit of Chidananda's to Shantiniketan lasted two weeks. Less than a year later Rabindranath died. Chidananda, like many Bengalis, felt that Shantiniketan without Rabindranath was nothing; and it was 46 years before he went back again. He went back, in fact, only after he had decided to go and live there. To make that return journey, he did what I had just done: he took the train from Howrah station in Calcutta, and got off at Bolpur two and a half hours later.

'That station lets you into the very worst of the Bengali small-town atmosphere – ugly, noisy, crowded, full of the kind of deprivation I see in the style of urbanization in our country, the deprivation of mind, of basic needs. The station had changed much more than Shantiniketan had changed.

'I went through the chaos of Bolpur. I knew I was going to Shantiniketan, where there would be open spaces and quiet surroundings and trees. It didn't trouble me too much – because you can't wish away the reality of your country. It was good to know it had a hidden heart beyond all this chaos. I've been practising yoga for about 15 years now, and it's helped me tremendously to arrive at this mental state – in which I could take an enormous amount of chaos and confusion around me, for a while, without losing my own peace of mind.

'So even on that first visit I found I liked the place. Some months later I bought some land, as much of it as I could afford, and I began to build right away. An old architect friend, a retired man, a Bengali, drew the plans. He knew the area, the climate, the wind direction.

'It's a changed place. I don't expect it to be what it was. You can't go back to the old days when people here lived in mud houses and went about barefooted by choice. But I feel that, coming back here, I have come back to more free ways of thinking, living, acting. It doesn't make me feel shut in. I've been reading the Upanishads again – a renewed inclination. Formally, I'm an atheist, but I've reached a state where I separate spirituality from theism and religion. To me the Upanishads represent man's effort to understand the universe and himself at the very highest level of spirituality.

'Here it's only two and a half hours away from Calcutta, but I feel I've come a very long way from my previous incarnation. The boxwallah incarnation which you saw in 1962 was quite far away from the roots of my culture and upbringing.'

Chidananda had wanted, when he was a young man, to be a teacher. At one stage he had even wanted to be a Brahmo missionary, like his father. But then his wish to prove himself in the world had led him to advertising and then to the tobacco company.

When the news came that he had got the job, everyone congratulated him. But his wife said, 'Why do you want to take this job? Don't you realize we will become a different kind of people?'

Chidananda said, 'In 1962, when you met me, I was looking after the company's advertising, which was one of the biggest advertising operations in the country. The company itself was a kind of tobacco monopoly dating from the British times. Anything that was made was sold, almost regardless of its quality. I will give you this idea of the complacency of that boxwallah world. There was a highly paid staff manager who spent a large part of his time measuring the carpet that a particular category of officer should get, and discussing the colours of curtains with the wives.

'The boxwallah was manufactured into a highly peculiar animal. The system was created to answer the needs of the British, their life-style, their ways of eating, sitting, sleeping, shitting. The Britishers who came out here for the company looked upon their time in India as a stay in a hotel, where everything was provided – down to the last towel and last spoon – in preparation for the time when they would go back home and buy themselves a house and wash their own clothes. Even servants were provided.

'Within six weeks of joining, I wrote a report saying that the name of the company should be changed from the Imperial Tobacco Company to the ITC. All it caused at the time was laughter.

'Like the administration of the British Empire itself, the commercial empire, which was an extension of the first, separated a handful of Indians from the rest and made them into an integral part of the system of governance. The object was to make them identify more with British interests than with Indian interests. This was done in a very subtle way. The British would unhesitatingly serve Indian officers whether in political administration or commercial administration. I don't think this happened with other empires, and it still doesn't happen with foreign companies operating in India. French or American or Japanese companies almost never have one of their nationals serving under an Indian.

'The company was highly hierarchical. There were two distinct classes, officers and men. We, the officers, would have chauffeur-driven cars, and our wives would be provided with separate cars to go out shopping – choosing carpets and curtains. There were colleagues of mine who would straighten their tie if the chairman telephoned, or send the car home to get a fresh jacket if they were going out to lunch. And, of course, at work the officers had separate lavatories.

'My wife got quickly used to the comforts and loved them. I enjoyed the luxury of the life – it would be hypocrisy to say otherwise. And I must say that way of living left a mark on the nature of our needs in later years.

'My problem was that because of my interest in literature and the cinema I was constantly associating in my private life with people who were utterly different. At the end of the day's work I would go to the office of the Calcutta Film Society. I had founded that along with Satyajit Ray in 1947, the year of independence. Our main work was sticking envelopes and writing addresses. We were lucky to have a fan over our heads – in a dingy office of a film distributor. Here we discussed the greatness of world cinema.

'Ray was closely associated with our work. With his enormous height and his wide shoulders, he came to remind me a great deal of Tagore, and I now see him as the last great representative of the Tagore era. But, unlike Tagore, he has a big, booming voice. He is swarthy; Tagore had fair, delicate skin. In his culture, his Indianness, his universality (not to be compared with fashionable cosmopolitanism), his honesty, Ray has some very Brahmo virtues.

'So I was living a Jekyll and Hyde existence. Western clothes, quite formal, during the day, and the Film Society in the evening. Occasionally a colleague would become curious about my leisure pursuits. He would come to the Film Society to see a French or German film, but he would be repelled by the smell of sweat on the bodies of my close associates, who'd travelled long distances on buses, trams, or walking, and worked all day in offices that were not air-conditioned, and didn't have the means to go back home to change their clothes.

'A very acute illustration of the kind of spiritual disquiet that the Jekyll and Hyde existence caused me came in the shape of something very material. I remember going with my colleagues to the wedding of a British executive of our company with an Indian girl, something that had caused a great deal of consternation in the higher echelons of our management.

'Perforce I was in a western lounge suit, along with my colleagues. Or perhaps it was a lack of strength of will on my part. I found, on that extremely hot and sultry evening, the place full of Bengalis in their comfortable thin poplin koortahs and dhotis. As I was sweating inside my completely unsuitable clothes I suddenly realized which side I belonged to, and I said to myself in disgust, "What have I done to myself?" This incident crystallized a lot of things inside me. I began to consider leaving the company, giving up the style of existence it imposed on its executives.

'I would say there was a lot of underemployment of intelligence in those jobs. Many of us, in sales, went out to the bazaars in Calcutta and in small towns all over the country, but their main job there, I found, consisted in picking up random packets of cigarettes to check the code numbers at the back, which told you how fresh or how stale the cigarettes were.

'So people drifted from breakfast to office to lunch to an outing at the bazaar and then to the club and a late night every night. There was air-conditioning in the office and at home and in the club, so one wouldn't have to spend more than half an hour or an hour without air-conditioning.

'The main virtue of this style of existence was that it prevented you from thinking. If you started thinking it could cause you discomfort. It damaged some of the Indians, permanently affecting their ability to be themselves, and printing on them a kind of pretence. I've seen a fair number of people who've become incapable of holding their own without this protective umbrella. And I've seen people go through an infernal amount of humiliation within the organization.

'These jobs were more or less sinecures. So they would humiliate you by taking away certain visible symbols of authority and leaving you without any work. I've seen people go day in, day out to the office and just sit there, and then go back home – Oxford and Cambridge graduates who, if they had gone into other jobs, might have used their capacities better. The whole office would know about this humiliation. It was made very visible. But for many people resignation was unthinkable. It would have been like being thrown out of a warm and well-lit room into the middle of a winter in northern Sweden.

'At that time Indian business had not expanded that much, and opportunities were very limited. In any case, Indian businesses wouldn't have given the boxwallahs the kind of life-style they had become used to. Nowadays Indian business will give you certain facilities and very expensive life-styles – provided you deliver the goods. They make certain of that: there are no sinecures left in Indian business.

'By the mid-60s the new movement in business had begun. The realities were closing in on the beleaguered boxwallah regiment. The tobacco company changed. It transformed itself over a short period, 10 years – which is quite short for a change of culture. This transformation was brought about by Indians. The British trained their men, but they didn't try to run the business themselves. Today ITC has diversified and is coping very well with the slowdown in the tobacco business.'

That transformation was proof of the positive side of the boxwallah culture; that positive side had to be remembered.

'The work ethic was very high. There was a lot of drive and discipline, though they didn't always know what they were driving at. They were at heart good Indians, patriotic Indians. In 1962, at the time of the China war, about the time we met, I remember there was a meeting of the finance committee. The finance director said, "Well, gentlemen, do you think the next meeting of the committee will be held in Peking?" I answered, "Sir, not unless our prime minister takes to wearing an umbrella under his arm." And I will say this for the British, they liked this kind of repartee, and respected you for it.'

Ashok was 25 years younger than Chidananda. Ashok worked for an old British boxwallah company. The company itself had now been bought over by one of the new generation of super-rich Indian financiers and industrialists, much of whose business activity lay outside India.

Ashok hadn't wanted to go into business for the privileges and position Chidananda had described. He had been more excited by the idea of 'marketing' – modern-sounding, active, up-to-the-minute. (I thought that marketing was just another word for selling, and didn't ask Ashok to define it for me. Many weeks later, in Delhi, it was defined for me by a former advertising man in this precise way: 'Marketing is the identifying and satisfying of an unmet need.' Not the creating of needs – that would have been considered devil's work in a poor country. Just the identifying of unmet needs.)

Ashok's first story – he told me three stories in all – was of his attempt to get into marketing.

'I made a number of false starts. The first was when I did commerce at the university. That was what my parents wanted me to do. I knew commerce wasn't for me, but I gritted my teeth and went ahead with it. I just scraped through the final exams, and that dented my self-confidence. Then I applied to join a management institute. I did that because everybody else was doing it. Inevitably, I didn't get in.

'At that stage my father fixed me up with a chamber of commerce in Delhi. I was there for a year and a half. I came into contact with a number of the industry barons for whom the chamber had been set up; but you also had a number of rustic individuals. It gave me a fair idea of the half-and-half way things were in India. I was drawing a pittance, 300 rupees a month, £15, but I was living in the house of an uncle, and didn't have many expenses.

'One day, at a middle-class party in Delhi, in Defence Colony, I met a Dr Malhotra. He was a portly man of middle height, in a dark-brown suit. I asked him what he did, and he said in an offhand way that he was the director of Imba. I asked him what Imba was, and he said it was the Institute of Management and Business Administration. It sounded familiar, but that was because many of these places have names that sound like that. Anyway, I was terribly impressed. He was a man in his mid-forties. I was in my early twenties. He looked very prosperous, and talked that way too. He was indifferent to me initially, no doubt seeing me as just another young man working somewhere.

'But then the conversation led to the fact that my father was an influential businessman in Calcutta, and Dr Malhotra's attitude to me changed. He became quite interested in what I did, how much I earned, and then he gave his opinion that I was made for much better things. My own gullibility took me along on the wave of his interest. His approval of me was total.

'It was beyond him why someone of my obvious talent should be wasting his time drawing 300 rupees in a nondescript chamber of commerce, when I could have the world at my feet. I said, "Have you anything better to suggest?" He said, "Boy, do I!" He described his Imba institute. From the way he told it, Imba was set up to propagate the discipline of marketing to as many people as possible in the country. And he now had plans to expand from Delhi to the other metropolitan centres.

'The way he told it, his own marketing acumen was sought by the large corporations of India, and he had had something to do with the success of quite a few well-known brands. Just listening to him excited me, opening my eyes to the wonderful world of marketing, of which I had heard so much.

'I thought I wanted to go into marketing. Partly this was because lots of my friends and colleagues were applying to these institutes of management, in which marketing was an important discipline, or they were joining large corporations as management trainees in the marketing division. I didn't understand what the thing was about, but it seemed to me the thing to do. It had a certain glamour, a certain aura.

'I agreed with Dr Malhotra that I was wasting my time where I was. He invited me over to his office the following day, where, as he implied, I might learn something to my advantage. I trotted off the next morning. Before I knew it, Dr Malhotra was offering me a job, at double the salary I was getting at the chamber, and with the enticing prospect of going back and working in Calcutta.

'When I asked him why an obviously successful marketing man like him was interested in a raw beginner like me, someone who had failed to get into the management institutes, he said the way he saw professional qualifications was like this: B.S., M.S., and Ph.D. – Bullshit, More Shit, and Piled High and Deep. Which again made a deep impression on me. Even in my school reports they used to say: "His marks are not a true indication of his ability." So I was ready to fall in with what Dr Malhotra said.

'"It's work experience that counts," he said. And he said he preferred, having the views he had, to pick up raw people like me and make them blossom.

'He asked me to look after the Calcutta branch or, as he called it, the "Calcutta Bureau" of Imba – I think he liked the modern sound of the word "bureau". The job, as he described it, would mean setting up courses, and enrolling corporate and individual members at fairly high fees.

'I had the presence of mind to ask him how this was going to help me learn about marketing. I saw that the job meant selling Imba rather than learning the marketing skills for which Imba was apparently famous. He said this would be only one aspect of my work. Imba itself would be deeply involved in marketing research and counselling for clients. This impressed me. I saw myself developing into a marketing whizz-kid.

'I overrode my father's doubts, and I accepted Dr Malhotra's offer. The day I joined Imba he gave me a box of visiting cards with my name and my grandiose designation as Bureau Executive. I had never had a visiting card before. I was very pleased.

'I was hoping to spend a week or so in Delhi, learning about the workings of Imba, but it was apparent that Dr Malhotra was in a bit of a hurry to see me off to Calcutta. He wanted me to go there and start enrolling the big corporations as members. He said I was to get the help of my father. This gave me a little pause: I began to feel that he was interested in my father, and that something was amiss.

'He packed me off to Calcutta. He paid the train fare. He had indicated to me that he had an office in Calcutta, and that a friend was looking after the office. Shortly after I arrived, this friend telephoned and invited me over. The office was in a congested part of North Calcutta, and when I went I found a dingy little place in an old, ill-kept multi-storeyed block.

'When I asked this gentleman, Dr Malhotra's friend, where my Imba office would be, he pointed to a broken small table in one corner of the room, and he said I could work from there. He went on to add that while in an absolute emergency he could consider some typing work, he would prefer it if I used a carbon and wrote my own letters and reports by hand. He said I could also use the telephone – the only one in the office that worked. But every time I made a call I should make a note of it, and these costs would be debited to Imba.

'And from that desk I actually attempted to run my first marketing training course. Dr Malhotra told me I should negotiate with a hotel for a conference hall, and lunch and dinner and so on for the participants. I was to try to get a good price – he was particular about that – and I actually did so.

'He told me more than once that he was getting a reputed American professor down to Calcutta for the training course. That was the point I had to push. The American idea was important. The management scene in the country was heavily influenced by the management boom that was taking place in America, and Dr Malhotra was certainly sensitive to that.

'I did as he said, and was quite successful in enrolling the 25 candidates or so he wanted for the course. I did this primarily because I met a number of senior corporation people who were family friends. That gave me an entry point, and I found that the rest was quite easy. I went to see them, and they were happy to nominate someone in their firm to attend the course for 2000 rupees a head. I should say that a lot of these senior people expressed surprise and dismay that I was associated with such an outfit – of which they hadn't heard.

'The course itself passed off without incident – except one. The American professor and his wife did come down. He wasn't really well known. He came from some obscure university, and in fact he was running a somewhat similar outfit somewhere in the vast North American continent. He was a cartoon American tourist, paunchy, late forties.

'This professor and his wife were put up in the hotel Dr Malhotra had made me negotiate with, for the conference hall and so on. It wasn't the best hotel in town. It was a couple of rungs below. The professor and his wife didn't like what they saw, but Dr Malhotra told them that this was India, a very poor country, that standards were lower, and that service in these less pretentious hotels was often better than in the five-star hotels, which could sometimes be all show.

'Just when it seemed that the Americans were getting reconciled to their quarters, a rat appeared and scurried across the room. The lady screamed and said, "I can't stand *slithery* things." And, to the chagrin of Dr Malhotra, the Americans insisted on being taken to the very best hotel in Calcutta. This was the Grand Hotel. It was infinitely more expensive. I myself had to make the arrangements.

'The course was seen as a feather in my cap. But then, as soon as it was over, Dr Malhotra said I should start preparing for another – going through the whole thing again. And I myself wasn't happy about the course I had just arranged, because it seemed to me on reflection that it hadn't done anything for me in the marketing way.

'I also wasn't being successful in enrolling members in Imba. Dr Malhotra was greatly interested in this, since each corporate member would bring in some 7000 or 8000 rupees, and an individual member about 1000 rupees. Most people simply didn't know about Imba. Dr Malhotra thought I should be able to enrol them simply because I belonged to an influential family. But I didn't feel I had anything to offer the big corporations. It's hard enough to sell a good product without being pushy. To sell a dud product was well nigh impossible to me at that time, when I was young and shy. And my father's friends were becoming a little more vocal in their protests about my requests to them for 8000 rupees for corporate membership of Imba.

'My weekly, carbon-copied, ballpoint-penned Imba reports to Dr Malhotra made less and less impressive reading. And Dr Malhotra was becoming more and more impatient. He also began to feel that there was some danger that I might leave Imba.

'He flew down to Calcutta and wanted to know why I wasn't producing results. I put it to him that I had joined Imba to develop knowledge and skills in the discipline of marketing, in the classical sense. And what I had been doing in the last couple of months was selling or marketing Imba itself, which had helped neither my knowledge nor my reputation. I suggested to him that what Imba

298

needed in Calcutta was some indigent retired army officer with organizational ability, and not an idealistic twenty-three-year-old man on the threshold of a career. It came to me to say at that point that I hoped we could part amicably.

'We didn't part amicably. He became angry. He said he had invested a lot of money and time in me. I ignored that: I thought he was going to ask for some kind of money back. He became very angry, and said he was going to remove my name from life membership of Imba. It was news to me that I was a life member of Imba, but apparently branch executives or "bureau executives" became that automatically.'

The burnt-out Maoists I had met in Madras had been on the periphery of a much larger peasant movement. This movement had its centre in Bihar and Bengal, almost 1000 miles to the north-east; and it had been at its most active in the late 60s and early 70s. Communism in Bengal had a long history. It was another colonial import, one of the things that had come after the New Learning of the 19th century, and the mixed culture. Even now, in the dead British-built city, and almost as an aspect of its death, there were frequent, solemn communist marches through the litter and rubble and hopelessness. Even now, while a communist party ruled in the state, people could still be moved by the poetry of red flags and revolution.

Dealing in poetry and passion, never really persecuted, at times even hostile to the idea of Indian independence, fighting its own sometimes remote wars, the communist party had split and split. There had been the Communist Party of India; then there had been the Communist Party of India (Marxist); then there had been the Communist Party of India (Marxist-Leninist). It was this last, Maoist faction that had got the peasant revolt going. The revolt had been crushed. But the movement, while it lasted, had attracted and consumed many thousands of educated people in Bengal and other parts of India.

There were survivors. One of them was Dipanjan. He was now a science professor in a college in central Calcutta. It was a real, working college, but physically it was in a state of decay, Calcutta decay.

The signboard was peeling; the windows of the two-storey

building were broken. But there was a gate-man, guarding the double gate. He sent me upstairs to Dipanjan, up a narrow, half-walled concrete staircase at the far end of the main building, to a broken-down room with tables with pieces of simple equipment. The uneven floor was unswept, or swept up to a certain wavering line, where the swept-up dust and the broom that had done the sweeping had both been abandoned, just like that. Dust adhered to all the mouldings or extrusions of the tall dun-coloured doors; the plaster on the wall was broken in many places. The room gave one no sense of applied colour, no sense of surfaces made even or lines made straight.

Dipanjan was a small, slender man with glasses. He wore a short-sleeved beige-coloured shirt and trousers. We went to a tall, cupboard-like room just off a central doorway. A desk and two chairs and some tall metal cupboards took up most of the space. The little bit of wall that could be seen between the cupboards was stained: something brown and oily had dripped down from the window.

I asked Dipanjan, after we had talked for a while, 'Do you see what I see here?'

He said in his soft, steady, precise voice, 'It's like other colleges. It's India.'

But he didn't see all that I saw. He said he could see the equipment on the lab tables: he could ignore what surrounded it. What he did see in a special way, what upset him and worked on his nerves far more than it did on mine, was the unswept dust on the floor.

The college was for drop-outs, he said, 'defeated soldiers' (though they looked active enough and healthy enough in the small college yard). They were people who couldn't get into other colleges. Their chances of getting a job were small – a B.Sc. degree didn't get you a job anyway – and they were not motivated. The girls at the college were better motivated. They didn't have the great need to achieve that the boys had; they didn't have that pressure; and, paradoxically, they made better students. The college wanted more girls. The fees were 30 rupees a month, £1.20, which even in India wasn't a great deal.

In that cramped space off the lecture room we talked that afternoon of his background. In physique and voice, and features and manner, he was a gentle man, a mild man. He would not have stood out in any Calcutta gathering. It wasn't easy to see in him the revolutionary who, 20 years or so before (he was now forty-five), had gone out into the countryside to live among the peasants, preaching the idea of revolution and then, in accordance with the party directive, calling for the annihilation of certain people, class enemies.

His mother had been from a well-to-do family. Her father had been high up in government service, a member of the IES, the Indian Educational Service. Before that, he had been 'a minor scientist', Dipanjan said. He had devised one of the early instruments for measuring radioactive particles, and had made a name for himself.

I said, 'I don't see how you can call him a minor figure.'

Dipanjan, not losing his evenness of manner, said, 'In Calcutta minor scientists are quite common. This is the city of M. N. Saha, S. N. Bose, J. C. Bose, and P. C. Ray. The first three were Fellows of the Royal Society. It is only recently that Calcutta has become a backwater. Even in the 1960s, Presidency College of Calcutta had a congregation of physics teachers which could hardly have been excelled anywhere else in the world at that time. So you must understand why I cannot look upon my maternal grandfather as anything but a minor scientist.'

In the South, science had grown over two or three generations out of the brahminical tradition of abstract learning. In Bengal, in the British-built city of Calcutta, science had come with the New Learning; scientific achievement had come out of colonial competitiveness and the wish of Indians to prove themselves.

On his father's side, Dipanjan came from the Bengali gentry. It was only on this trip that I had heard this word in India. I had thought of 'gentry' as an English word, suggesting people rooted and attached to ancestral land, and protective towards it. And the word here in Bengal was in fact an English word, from the early 19th century. Dipanjan said, 'The British made the gentry hereditary. From their point of view, they were creating a class of hereditary farmers of revenue.'

Dipanjan's father's family came from the Faridpur district. In 1947 this became part of East Pakistan. The gentry of Faridpur were in the main upper-caste Hindus. They rented out their land; the cultivators were Muslims and Hindus of the scheduled castes. During the Hindu-Muslim massacres in Bengal in 1946–47, the

Hindus of Faridpur had to flee: not only the upper-caste landowners, but also the scheduled-caste cultivators. But long before that flight from Faridpur, Dipanjan's father's family had become impoverished. The ancestral land of the family had been so divided that all that had come to Dipanjan's grandfather (and his dependents) was one room in the big ancestral family house.

This grandfather, when he was twenty, joined the government service, in the Accountant-General's Office of Bengal. He was helped by the joint-family system. His son, Dipanjan's father, went to live in an apartment owned by a relation in Calcutta. It was in this apartment that Dipanjan was born.

In 1940 or thereabouts, while he was studying in college, and when he was seventeen or eighteen, Dipanjan's father became a communist. Dipanjan never thought to ask his father later why he had become a communist: he took it as normal. Membership of the party was a serious affair. When, in 1943, Dipanjan's father wanted to get married, he had to get the permission of the party, because his prospective bride came from a family that was in government service. The party gave its permission on condition that Dipanjan's prospective father-in-law (the minor scientist, the IES officer) made out a cheque – for any sum – payable to the Communist Party of India.

After the war, in 1946, when Dipanjan was two and half years old, the party advised Dipanjan's father and mother to go to Hungary for their higher studies. Dipanjan was left behind with his grandparents. Dipanjan's father and mother returned in 1950 – after all the upheavals of partition and independence. Dipanjan's mother had done a teacher-training course in Hungary; she was able to get a job soon after she came back to Calcutta. But Dipanjan's father, who had become a Ph.D. in biochemistry, couldn't get a proper job. He moved from one unsatisfactory position to another until 1955, when he found something in his own field; and then he left the Communist Party. And just as Dipanjan had never asked his father why he had become a communist, so he never thought later to ask his father why he had left the party: it wasn't in the Hindu or Indian tradition, this questioning of elders by young people. There was an odd relic of that Hungarian interlude of his parents: they had both learned Hungarian, and in Calcutta it became their private language, when they wanted to keep things from Dipanjan.

Dipanjan developed asthma when he was seven, in 1951. His mother became protective; the boy lived a retired life, drawing sustenance from books. There were many books in the apartment. There were his father's communist books. There were also the books of the father's uncle, to whom the apartment belonged. This uncle was a nationalist; he had books that took the nationalist side. But Dipanjan at that time was not too interested in politics.

He was getting, though, some ideas about the world. In 1952 he had gone with his mother to a slum, where she was teaching children the alphabet: this was party work. He had also gone sometimes to see some of his grandfather's relatives who had fled from Faridpur in East Bengal. These relatives were living in one of the refugee colonies around Calcutta. Dipanjan didn't understand at the time; but later, when he began to read about the events of 1947, he remembered the refugee colonies he had gone to as a child, and the events had more meaning for him. But he didn't think that his generation had been influenced politically by partition.

He was good at his studies. 'My mother slowly became ambitious for me. And now, with hindsight, I think that must have taken up a lot of my mental space. In 1960, when I was sixteen and about to leave school, my major precoccupations were shining academically and writing poetry. I had become interested in literature, and was writing in Bengali and English.'

He was romantic, but in that setting there was no opportunity for him to meet girls. What was open to him, though, was the city of Calcutta. 'I was fond of the city even then, and even now I am fond of it. My roots are only in Calcutta. I have no village in Bengal to which I can lay claim. I felt Calcutta as a very living city, because Bengali poetry had become really modern in Calcutta, after Rabindranath and after the revolt against him.'

What about the crowds and dirt of Calcutta? Did he see that, or react to it?

'Calcutta has always been like this. It was even worse in British times. To a Calcuttan it is the perennial challenge – to rise above the all-absorbing task of just keeping yourself clean, which is time-consuming, energy-consuming. The challenge is how to do that and find time for other more significant things. That is the challenge faced by the ivory-tower intellectual and the rickshaw-puller.

303

'In J. C. Bose's time there were not many underground drains in the Indian areas of Calcutta. The drains would have been ditches.

'We are cursed with a corrupt corporate life. Cleaning the streets is a corporate act, and they will never be cleaned. Corruption here is a way of life, and it has existed here from the time of the East India Company.'

It was now the end of the working day. The motor-car horns and hooters were shrieking a little more exuberantly or impatiently in the streets outside. The college attendant who had brought tea and sodas – adding wet rings to the little stained table at which we sat – now came to close up, and to padlock doors.

Dipanjan took me down to the staff room on the lower floor. No one was there. The room had an enclosed, damp, musty smell, which not even the ceiling fan could blow away. In one corner there was a small, rough, chalk-faded blackboard, crookedly hung. No piece of woodwork or joinery was elegant or finished. What would have been the effect on the teachers? And on the students, the defeated soldiers?

High up on the wall, just below the ceiling, was a large framed photograph. It was a photograph of J. C. Bose, the scientist whose name Dipanjan spoke with reverence. There was an intention of honour; but, in that setting, whatever work the great man might have done seemed to have led to nothing.

The next day was Dipanjan's day off from the college, and he thought I should come to where he lived. This was in South Calcutta, in a lane so hard to find he drew a detailed map for me to give to the car-driver. Someone whom I consulted thought the journey might take up to an hour, depending on the traffic. So I started early.

The traffic was easy that morning, but after some time the city thoroughfare appeared to shrink, to collapse in on itself from its increased human density. The roadway narrowed; roadside huts and lean-tos, without pronounced colour, just a mish-mash of brown and black and grey, appearing to encroach on space meant for vehicles, hid the solider concrete buildings behind them, and gave the impression of a very long village road set in dirt, such freshness as had come with the morning already burnt up here by brown traffic fumes and sun-shot traffic dust. What seemed to threaten in many places in central Calcutta appeared to have happened here: it was like witnessing the creation of a ruin: a large inhabited city was reverting to earth.

In spite of all the instructions, we overshot the meeting place that Dipanjan had decided on, and we had to go back through the hectic little road and look for it. Dipanjan's map was so detailed that both the driver and I had exaggerated its scale. Dipanjan had said that at one corner of the lane where we were to meet there was the playing field of a sports club. I had been looking for something the size of a football field: the playing field in question turned out to be the size of a small building plot, about a third of an acre, a square of concrete in a field of dust. He had said that there was a furniture shop on the other side of the lane. I had been looking for an emporium of fair size; but the Nufurnico shop was a small one-storey concrete shed. In this part of Calcutta – where needs and activities had contracted – there was a compensating inflation of nomenclature. In the 'playing field', which had a few basketball boards, there was also a sign for Sunny Green Creche, Green Park. Nufurnico described itself as 'Dealers of Foam Matters, U-Foam Matters and Pillow'. Foam matters: it made sense, in a way.

I had time to think about these things – and also to note the very dusty palm trees, which for some time I had failed to see – because I had arrived about half an hour too early. Out of the crooked lane between the furniture shop and the playing field (Dipanjan had thought I might have lost my way if I had gone into that lane on my own) reasonably well dressed people began to appear, walking briskly, some even with briefcases, Calcutta folk somehow with a day's work to do. And then Dipanjan appeared, with the deliberate tread of the other walkers in the lane, but he was sandalled now and in a dhoti: home clothes, for his day of rest.

Forty years before, he said, all this area was rice land. This was one of the areas outside Calcutta where refugees from East Pakistan had settled after 1947; everything here had been built in the last 40 years by people trying to remake their lives. And, indeed, away from that main road, the atmosphere of the little lane (perhaps by contrast) appeared pleasant. There was drainage, and electricity. But here too the numbers of people had grown and grown; even in the last 10 years many of the open spaces Dipanjan had known had been filled in.

Dipanjan's apartment was the lower floor of a small two-storey house. His landlord lived upstairs. Dipanjan made me take my shoes off in the little verandah, which was just a few feet away from the lane. The front room was a combined bedroom and sitting room. It was 10 feet by 10 feet. 'And, what is worse,' Dipanjan said, 'by 10 feet.' He meant that the room was 10 feet high as well: an absolute little cube.

There was a big bed in one corner. There was also a cane-bottomed settee; bookcases full of books and papers in apparent disorder; and some red box files in another corner. The apartment had another room, for the children; and there was also a space – it was the word Dipanjan used: he didn't say 'room' – with the kitchen at one end and the bathroom and W.C. at the other end.

The two children had been waiting to see their father's guest. The elder was a girl of nineteen, who was studying to be an engineer at the university of Jadavpur, not far away. She was smiling, open, handsome, with glasses; there was an outgoing quality about her which I had not seen so far in her father. She said mischievously of her plump brother, who was thirteen and was clearly going to be physically bigger than his father: 'He wants to go to America.' It must have been partly true, partly teasing; but the brother took it well. And then they were both off, into the little verandah, and then a few steps down into the lane.

Dipanjan had moved into the apartment in 1980. They were quite cramped there now; but they didn't think so in 1980. The children felt cramped, though. The little apartment cost 600 rupees a month, £24. There were some neatly kept houses around. There was a nice small house next door, with a hibiscus shrub against the ochre-coloured wall, really quite close to the windows of the room in which we were. That house belonged to an ayurvedic doctor, someone practising traditional Hindu medicine.

They had nice neighbours in the lane; they couldn't complain about that; but the house was terribly dusty. That was why Dipanjan was so particular about getting me to take off my shoes: to keep out the dust which my shoes might have brought in. Trucks often went down the narrow lane; when they did, dust blew straight into the house. And there were mosquitoes.

Dipanjan said, 'That reminds me. I should put on a coil.'

He went to the inner 'space' – his long dhoti was brown or beige, with a plaid or check pattern – and he came out after a while not with the green mosquito coil I was expecting, but with a plastic blue Japanese 'gadget' – Dipanjan's word – that had to be plugged into a power point. The chemical in the plastic container was released by heat.

A sweeping woman, speaking no word, looking at no one, bending down low from the waist, her legs quite straight, passed through the front room, flicking her little broom at those small areas of the terrazzo floor that were not covered by furniture or the red box files.

Dipanjan's wife came in. Her name was Arati. She was of Dipanjan's age. She wore a dark-coloured sari with a small pattern, and a black bodice. She, too, was a teacher: her classes started very early in the morning, and finished at 10.

She wanted to know about lunch. She said that Dipanjan couldn't eat wheat. 'Rice, rice, rice – that's what he wants, three times a day, as often as I give him. He can't digest wheat.' That was an aspect of Dipanjan's 'post-political' life. It had been brought about by Dipanjan's illnesses during his life underground in the villages, and by the badness of water in the delta.

'Amoebiasis,' Arati said. 'It's a chronic condition. Does it occur in your place? It's in most of the third world.'

It was the first time, since I had been talking to Dipanjan, that reference had been made to his life as a guerrilla. And it was unexpected that it should have come in this direct, unheroic way, with this emphasis on his personal frailty – the tormenting things he had known before the dust and mosquitoes of the lane.

Dipanjan sat on the bed. The three small windows of the room, with iron bars and green shutters, lit him from different angles. There were three old photographs on the blue walls, and one small portrait in colour. The photographs were of Dipanjan's father and mother, his father's father, and his father's maternal uncle, in whose rent-controlled apartment Dipanjan's father and then Dipanjan had lived until 1969. This relative had been a nationalist and a journalist; he had edited a proscribed Gandhian journal and had gone to jail in 1942. He was a man of culture, a Brahmo, a man of the Bengal Renaissance. But Dipanjan's greatest admiration was for his father's father, who was an orthodox Hindu. He had gone into the Accountant-General's Department because there had been no money for his higher education, and he had devoted nearly all his working life to looking after his brothers and sisters – which wasn't easy, especially after the calamities of 1947.

The photograph of this grandfather was big. Dipanjan had had it made from a damaged original. Other prints of lesser intensity had been made, but he liked the one he had on the wall.

'He had penetrating and dazzling eyes. I prefer this print because of the eyes. We have all inherited our preoccupation with ethics from him. He was a man of principle. People say he never did a wrong thing in his life.'

The other photograph, in colour, quite small, was of the young Mao.

Dipanjan said, 'You don't recognize him. It was presented by a Dr Bose, who was sent by Nehru to Chiang Kai-Shek in 1939, and ended up with Mao. The photograph is there because it was a gift. You mustn't read too much into it, though I have a strong and healthy respect for the man.'

Among the newspapers on the bed was a financial paper. Dipanjan liked to follow the economic news. The Indian economy was fragile, and he said there could be another depression like the one in 1965, which had led to food riots and given an impetus to the peasant movement.

Arati brought out tea. Dipanjan poured a cup for the driver of the car that had brought me, and took it out to him; he was parked in the yard next door.

Arati said, 'Are you staying for the summer?' She hardly waited for my reply. 'The heat is unbearable. There are so few trees now.'

I said, 'Why do they cut them down?'

'It's because of the people. There are too many people. You can't have people and trees. They've cut down so many trees, the weather is changing. We have colder winters and hotter summers.'

A woman neighbour called conversationally, across the short distance from the lane, 'Arati?' and almost immediately came in. At the same time a cycle-rickshaw went by in the lane, with many young children sitting on two facing benches below a little roof – young children going home from school in a toy-like contraption, reminding me of the baker's cycle-vans I used to see as a child in Port of Spain.

Arati and her neighbour talked in the kitchen space at the back of the front room. Their words were very clear through the open door.

Dipanjan, when he came back from looking after the car-driver, settled himself on the bed, among the newspapers, and began to talk.

'When I went to Presidency College I was not politically active. I sided with the left because of my upbringing, but the political activity in the college at that time was at a low level. Towards the end of my second year, when I was driving myself very hard academically, and it was becoming quite a strain, I began to wonder why I was doing it. I was also dabbling in poetry. My father never read my poems – I didn't show them to him. My mother wasn't interested. They thought it was perhaps a harmful diversion. They never encouraged me. I began to question why I was writing. Quite a few of us at college were assailed with similar problems and doubts, both boys and girls.

'From this time I suddenly became aware of the poverty and misery around me. Until then I hadn't been aware. I saw things and I accepted it as part of the scenery. I will tell you a little story. One day – I still remember – we were going, a friend and I, to see a showing of a picture made from a play of Bernard Shaw. I was about to go there. I had just left my house. And I saw this person – I wouldn't say he was a beggar: he was in no position to beg.

'He was lying on the curb. He was about to die, and fully conscious and silent. He was lying in front of a pathological laboratory. I asked the lab people to phone for an ambulance. The ambulance came, and I found that nobody was willing to accompany the person to hospital. So I had to accompany him. I wasn't very eager to do it, but I accompanied him. He was indifferent. Absolutely. He didn't talk.

'We drove to a hospital. Doctors examined him and on his ticket they wrote that he should be admitted, and they stamped the ticket with a prepared seal: "There is no accommodation in this hospital. Try somewhere else." The driver had to take him back in the ambulance. The driver asked me whether I knew this person. When I said I didn't, the driver said, "We can take him to another hospital, but the same thing will happen there."'

I asked Dipanjan, 'What did the man look like? You haven't mentioned that.'

'He was in rags, caked with dirt. The most striking thing about him was that he had hydrocel, an inflammation of the scrotum, caused usually by filariasis, a tropical parasitical disease. And when he walked he had to carry his scrotum in his hands, it was so heavy.

'I asked the ambulance-driver how often this kind of thing happened, and the driver said often. He said that when they were asked to pick up people like that, they did, without making a fuss. But no one accompanied the person, so their practice was to deposit him on some other street, because they knew that no hospital would accept them.

'Seeing that I felt in some way responsible for the man, the driver said, "There is one place I know where he might be accepted. I'm not sure, but let's go." He drove to this place near the temple of Kali, and there was this little space – just a long dark corridor, with perhaps just a tiled roof, and on both sides destitute people lying on beds waiting for death. So we left him there, and we placed the medical ticket near his head, and we came out.

'This place was the beginning of the place Mother Teresa was building up for such people, and she was quite unknown at the time. I should make it quite clear that I am not making any comment on the utility or validity of Mother Teresa's outlook or work. But I must say that even today there is no other place in Calcutta where a dying destitute will be accepted.'

At this point the electricity failed, as it often failed in Calcutta. Dipanjan's first thought was for the Japanese mosquito-repellent, which depended on heat. Without that repellent, he said, we simply wouldn't be able to sit and talk. He got up and got an oil lamp, lit it, and placed the blue gadget on top of the glass chimney. Almost at once the power came back, so he turned the oil lamp off. We also changed places. I sat on the bed; he sat on the cane-bottomed settee.

He said, 'It was a Sunday morning. A fine day, but it rained in the afternoon, after we had placed the man at Kalighat. I missed the cinema show. I spent about three to four hours ferrying that man around.

'This is just an example. Don't think this is my road to Damascus. It stands out in my mind, but it didn't mark my conversion. It was one of a host of things which were happening around me to which my eye was being opened for the first time. And I began to wander about the streets of Calcutta, sometimes alone, sometimes with friends.'

Sitting on the cane-bottomed settee, thinking of the past, his eyes unfocussed, he raised his slender bare arms against the blue-washed wall.

'From 1964, 1965, onwards, the way I was leading my life started appearing futile and meaningless. I retained a strong attachment to physics and poetry, but began to devote less time to it.'

In 1964 Dipanjan took his first degree from Presidency College, and began to do post-graduate work at Calcutta University Science College. At the same time there was a development in his personal life. He had met and proposed to Arati, and there was opposition from her family. Arati came from a distinguished brahmin family. Dipanjan was of the *kayastha* caste. Of this caste Dipanjan said, 'The kayastha caste is technically a shudra, but in West Bengal and elsewhere their possession of land had effectively Sanskritized them. They are a clerkly caste, scribes since the Mogul times or even before.'

Parallel with this turbulence, there was the economic crisis he had spoken about at the start of the morning.

'Since 1965 prices of rice and other foodstuffs had soared to unheard-of heights. Kerosene disappeared. Factories closed. Retrenched workers committed suicide. Even qualified engineers and doctors couldn't find jobs. In West Bengal there was a great uprising. This movement of the people between 1965 and 1966 completely changed the outlook of our generation.

'The people started off by confronting retailers in markets and insisting that they take their prices down. In places they looted godowns where grain was being hoarded illegally. When the government used the police against them, there was resistance by the demonstrators. From stone-throwing to setting public places and transport on fire – this has been a hallowed tradition of protest since British times. When someone sets a bus on fire, you know that now he means business.'

'Was your family affected by the rise in prices?'

'We personally – my family – could afford it. People were always talking about it – the prices, the crisis, the food riots, the failure of the government, the police firing. The movement was always called the Food Movement.'

It was organized by the ordinary political workers of a communist faction, and not by any of the big men of the party. Then in 1966 the students of Presidency College, Dipanjan's old college, formed a pro-communist movement for the first time. The leaders of this movement were expelled, and there was a six-month student agitation against their expulsion.

One night Dipanjan was coming back from South Calcutta by bus. He saw a crowd in the grounds of Presidency College. He got off the bus to see what it was about. He didn't find anyone he knew, but the next day, when he went back, he discovered that the leaders of the student movement, and others, were his friends. He began to spend more and more time with those friends, in Presidency College, in the coffee house opposite, and in the college hostel.

He began to do political work among those students who were not committed. 'There was a vocal minority who felt they had come to the college to study and build their careers. And we had to persuade them.' There was a feeling that the activists organizing the students and the Food Movement were Chinese agents. Dipanjan had to do a lot of reading to deal with these accusations. He started reading Marxist literature.

'This was the time of the Cultural Revolution in China, and it had tremendous influence in Calcutta – what the Chinese students were doing, and why they were doing it, and why there had to be a cultural revolution after a revolution proper.

'I was very excited. I thought that now I could start making my life meaningful. I had no consciousness of my father's political past in the party, or his uncle's past as a nationalist and a Gandhian. My father had by that time become an ordinary householder; he kept no contact with the party. My mother had also stopped being a communist. My father's nationalist uncle had become a bitter critic of the whole Indian polity. He never voted in his life, declaring that under no circumstances would he enter a process of choosing the least harmful among scoundrels.

'But I still lacked an ideology or philosophy, though all my time was being taken up by politics. I didn't return home some nights. Arati was getting extremely worried. My parents had almost written me off.'

'What were you doing at nights?'

'We would be talking with boys at the hostel until 11. We would then talk among ourselves until 12 or one. Then we would sleep on the lawn of Presidency College.'

This was how he was living in 1967, when he took his M.Sc. and got a job; and when – after all the turmoil with Arati's family – he and Arati were married, four years after he had proposed to her.

'It was a packed and exciting time, emotionally, intellectually. It was the start of my education in the world. I had been leading a sheltered life. I was academically minded. My mother was over-protective – I had this asthmatic condition. My mother cried a lot. It was her ambition for me that suffered greatly. My father, having been once bitten himself, was worried about the direction our movement would take.

'In Presidency College we slowly developed one central idea. We felt that the Indian communist movement had failed because the leadership, which was composed of middle-class intellectuals, had made itself into a bureaucracy. The initiative of the masses had never been developed. And then in April 1967 the Naxalbari incident occurred.'

This was the incident, in North Bihar, after which the Naxalite movement was named.

'I was reading the paper in the morning. I read this item on the front page. Peasants had surrounded a police party with bows and arrows and had shot down a police inspector, in the course of a struggle to occupy the lands monopolized by landlords, illegally for the most part.

'This was a dramatic incident. I just couldn't believe it – that this thing, which we had been reading about in our books, in Marxist literature, in history books, could really happen: that the toiling people could take up arms, and they could fight for their rights. And my mind was made up, and that of most of our friends at Presidency College: that this was the struggle with which we were going to link our lives. In Calcutta the first posters in support of the Naxalbari uprising were put up by us, on the wall opposite Presidency College.'

'Who were your friends?'

'Some had backgrounds like mine. Many of them were sons of impoverished gentry on this side of the border. We were all middle-class people.

'We immediately decided to go among the toiling people. Some of us went back to their villages. And some of us went to the industrial slums. There was a major involvement with the workers of the Guest Keen Williams factory in southern Howrah. A trade union leader there had sought us out. Soon in the villages and in

313

the factories the news began to spread that students were coming from Calcutta to talk to people about how to change their conditions.'

'How did you fit this in with your work?'

'I was working in a morning college. So the afternoon and evening were free.'

'Weren't you nervous about knocking on people's doors?'

'I wasn't nervous about the industrial workers. I could tune to their wavelength. But later, when I left my job – I changed many jobs – and went to the villages, my experiences were traumatic. But that was much later, in 1969.

'In 1967 we were still building up the student movement. I had to run to many places, taking political classes and having group discussions with students, equipping them with propaganda to fight the official party propaganda *against* the Naxalite movement. The party saw it as a threat to their organization.

'For the year or two after that I spent much time in Guest Keen Williams. Arati went with me at times. My life at that time would be something like this. At two a.m. I would return home walking, because the last bus or tram had passed. Or I would spend the time on Presidency College lawn, or in the building or the hostel if it rained. I would have to go back to work by 6.15, 6.30. Classes began then. At 10 I would be back at Presidency College. We would start discussions with the students of the college and with students who had come from colleges all over Calcutta and West Bengal to learn of the movement.

'The police were keeping an eye on us. They sent spies to the college. We caught one and gave him a beating up. There were frequent street fights with the police.'

'What was that like?'

'Whenever you go into a fight, whether it's a private fight or a fight with the police, you are nervous to start with. Then the tension slowly drains out, and excitement takes its place, and finally you are quite ready even to risk your own life. Traditionally in Calcutta you fight the police with brickbats. That is the ordinary kind of fight. A serious fight would involve home-made bombs and country-made guns. But such fights are rare, and only occur at the height of important political movements.'

I found this strange: his ability to talk of disturbances and fights in this academic, Aristotelian manner.

I said, 'You talk of these fights with the police as though you were protected in some way.'

Dipanjan said, 'The communists were then sharing power. We understood their dilemma. We knew that the police wouldn't be able to cross certain limits. This was the first time the communists were sharing power in West Bengal, and they couldn't throw themselves against the students and the workers. The very fact that the police had fired on the peasants at Naxalbari caused a division within the party, and brought over some senior communists on to the side of the Naxalite movement.

'In the evenings, after being with the students, we would go to the factories and the slums, or take political classes and conduct group discussions. We were slowly learning the classical Marxist political ideas – Marx, Lenin, Mao, all of them.

'And then, in 1969, we went to the villages. The communist party in West Bengal is pretty old, even in many of the rural areas, and grassroots leaders who wanted the struggle started helping the students who had come to their areas.

'We had a rule. You must have with you only a *lungi*, a cloth, a vest or singlet, and a towel. You went to the villages, identified the huts of the agricultural labourers or poor peasants, and you told them directly why you were there. You started talking immediately about the political aims – seizure of power by the toiling people. We called this Red Guard Action.

'The pioneers faced a lot of trouble getting their message across. But by the time I went to the villages, this fact was well known among the peasants. We kept just the fare back to the urban centre from which we had come, and no other money. And we kept a dhoti, a shirt, and pair of slippers for use in transit between the villages and towns.

'The peasants fed us when they could. In some new places sometimes they wouldn't, at the beginning. But on the whole everywhere they gave us a patient hearing. We slept in their huts. Usually, if they had only one room, and the hamlet was safe, composed only of poor people, we would sleep on the verandah. But this was a rare luxury. Usually we had to sleep concealed in a loft. As the state increased its repression, we would have to remain concealed the whole day. One or two of us had the experience of having to relieve themselves in pots.'

'Repression' – this, too, was strange: that after all he had gone through he should use this abstract word, and make it sound like something from a political textbook.

He went on: 'Two problems crept up. Amoebiasis, because drinking water is uniformly bad. And scabies. Because we had to bathe hurriedly, and on many days not at all. We lacked the know-how of keeping oneself clean in an Indian village. All the villagers know how to clean themselves with a little oil, a little alkaline ash, a little water – which we didn't. But this didn't really trouble us. This was the most exciting and the most interesting and fulfilling part of our political work: when we were moving among the villagers.

'The major problem at the beginning was that I felt that there was an invisible partition between us and the villagers, that we were talking two different languages. It took a long time to get accustomed to the silences and obliquities of rural India.'

'Make that a little more concrete.'

'Suppose I've come to a village where they're afraid to keep me. They won't tell me that outright. When I went to one such village in the evening, the people suggested to me that I should go with the boys to a nearby *jatra*, a whole-night theatrical performance, a high spot in the annual life of a village. They were hinting to me that I couldn't stay in any of their houses that night.'

'You haven't told me what it was like in the villages.'

'The quality of life was better than in the urban slums. Apart from a lepers' village, where – before harvest time – they had a little wheat, but so little they couldn't make chapattis. They made paste of the flour and served that in very small quantities. Children couldn't digest that paste. Hunger – getting one full meal a day – that was the major determining factor of the quality of village life for five months of the year at that time.'

And I was struck again – as I had been when he was telling of the dying man he had picked up from the Calcutta street – by the way he spoke of the distress of India: as though it was a personal idea, a personal observation, as though his group observed it better than others and with more understanding, as though this distress was something they were entitled to refer to, to explain their actions.

*

It was now well past midday, well past the normal lunch hour. He was tired. He said he wanted to have a shower. Arati had prepared the lunch, and when Dipanjan went to the back space to have his shower, she brought out the food and set it on a little stool for me: simple food, two pieces of fried fish, peas, puris. The fish was bony, not easy to pick at, but Arati said that if I used my fingers I could feel the bones better and get rid of them.

Standing in the little room while I ate, she talked again of the heat of the summer in Calcutta; and again she asked whether I was staying for that. She talked again of the trees that had been cut down. I asked her whether Indians hated trees, whether there was some idea that trees sheltered or encouraged bad spirits. She said no, Indians loved trees; but now there were simply too many people, and the trees had to be cut down.

Dipanjan had left her during her first pregnancy, she said – when he went to live in the villages. She had gone to stay with his parents. That was the Indian way, the custom here: the wife stayed with her in-laws. In order to write about India, she said, you had to spend a lot of time in India. There were so many things of India that were different.

She said she had been sympathetic to the cause in the beginning. But she didn't like that idea of going to the villages, taking revolution to the people. She thought it was foolish. The poor here in India believed in their fate. That going out to the villages had set the revolution back by 40 years. And she didn't like it when the murders began. She didn't like that at all.

Dipanjan and I hadn't got to that yet: Dipanjan had promised that for another day, perhaps tomorrow.

Perhaps, I said to Arati, the flaw had lain in that very idea of revolution, that idea of a particular moment when everything changes and the world is made good, and men are made anew.

She didn't take the point up.

Turgenev had written a novel about that, I said. He had written a novel about middle-class people in Russia in the late 1860s taking revolution to the workers. Perhaps if people had read that book without prejudice they mightn't have made the misjudgement that the people in the novel had made. But she hadn't read Turgenev; she didn't know *Virgin Soil*. Her Russian reading didn't go back so far; her Russian reading appeared to have gone back only as far as the classical political texts.

Standing sideways in the doorway, looking out at the verandah and the white early-afternoon light in the lane, the light that was still only the light of spring, she said reflectively that people in other countries seemed to be withdrawing from Marxism.

She wasn't a tall woman. But she was sturdy; and she was still shapely.

She said she had spent some time in England, when Dipanjan had gone there to do higher studies in physics, after all that business was over. And what she had seen in England, and especially what she had noted about the position of women in England, had further shaken her up. Perhaps, she said, Marx was wrong. And I found it moving: such passion, in that tiny cluttered room, with the threat of the summer to come.

At dinner that evening, in a large apartment in central Calcutta, I met someone who had known Dipanjan as a fellow student at Presidency College. Dipanjan had been a talented and even brilliant student, I heard. Then this Naxalite business had occurred, and there had been the dreadful time when it seemed that Dipanjan, married to someone from a very distinguished Calcutta family, might have been hanged. Since that Naxalite business they hadn't met, Dipanjan and the man who was talking to me.

The man said, 'He was a better student than I was. Now he teaches physics. I do physics – that's the difference between us. The college he teaches at is awful. He must know that. He is wasting his talent there. He should return to the mainstream.'

But that wasn't a subject he felt he would be able to raise with Dipanjan, if they were to meet. The matter was too embarrassing. All that Naxalite, communist involvement – in which, from his own account, Dipanjan for the first time in his sheltered life appeared to have found community, drama, and purpose – now lay like an embarrassment between Dipanjan and the other world he had known.

Perhaps, the man said, Dipanjan was too ashamed to meet the people he had once known. So he lived where he did, and taught in that poor college. It was the same when he had gone to England: he had lived in the simplest kind of bedsitter.

Someone else at the dinner said that this kind of disappearing, this hiding away, was a very Bengali thing to do.

And I thought of Dipanjan coming out of the lane early that morning to meet me – in his cloth and shirt – coming after all those other people from the poor settlement with their respectable fronts, their briefcases and dispatch-boxes. From what he had said at our first meeting, I had got the impression that he taught at his college out of a fellow feeling with the students, 'defeated soldiers'. And my first idea was that some similar feeling of social responsibility had made him live where he lived. But no; it wasn't like that. He lived where he did because he couldn't do better. In the villages he had suffered; in the town now he suffered almost as much, from the dust and the mosquitoes, and his wife suffered from the heat. He had chosen a hard way; and neither he nor his wife was used to harsh conditions.

I went to see him the next morning at the college, and took in again the details of the two-storey building, with its Calcutta-style classical ornament, its pediment, and the columns in pairs inset in the walls on both storeys. The green shutters were coated with the grainy black grime of fumes and dust – you could write in that grime. The small trees in the small college yard were discoloured with dust; only the fresh shoots of the spring showed green and clear. Slowly burning mounds of old, flattened, garden rubbish sent pungent smoke into the air, not unpleasant, a gentler smell of autumn in the Calcutta spring. It was a Calcutta custom, this burning of garden waste even in the centre of the city, and it added to the brown haze. Many broken brown classroom tables and chairs had been placed that morning in a jumble on the small untended lawn of the college yard, where weeds grew out of litter mounds.

Upstairs, broken window panes and door panes had been replaced by wire netting of various meshes. The tarnished label, *Department of Physics*, done with screw-down metal letters, looked incongruous. The wavering line of dust on the red floor – the dust Dipanjan and I had spoken about two days before – was still there. In the choked room or cell at the side, the rings made by the soda bottles and the saucers of two days before had not been wiped.

Dipanjan made a half wave at the rings on the table, a half nod at the dust in the room with the lab tables, and said, 'It will *never* be cleaned.'

We sat in the cell, he in his old chair, I in the one I had sat in, facing each other across the little table. The table was really quite multifariously stained. A narrow strip of white-tiled wall showed behind the olive or khaki-coloured metal cupboards and between the cupboards. Brown drips, from some unknown source, had coagulated on the tiles.

I told him that there were certain things I hadn't found in what he had told me. He had talked of going to the Guest Keen Williams workers in Calcutta. How had he done that? Who was the first worker he had talked to? I hadn't got many pictures from his narrative. He had gone to the villages – how had he done that? Had he just taken a bus or a train to a particular village? Could he go beyond certain abstractions – 'workers', 'villages', 'peasants', 'repression'?

He accepted what I said. He offered to fill in details. He talked first of the time in 1967 when he had gone among the Guest Keen Williams workers in Calcutta.

'One of my friends had been living in the Guest Keen Williams slum for some time, and he had met this second-rank communist leader. My friend asked me to come over to judge whether this man was a genuinely revolutionary man. I took a bus from Presidency College, crossing Howrah Bridge. I got off at Howrah station and caught another bus, and that went through the crowded streets of Howrah to the Guest Keen Williams gate.'

(A week or so later I made the same journey myself, with someone from the Guest Keen Williams company. A year-long company lockout had just come to an end, and the inactivity of a year showed in the yard, in the tropical weeds and the post-monsoon rust. The company was one of those lumbering former British companies that had grown slack during the times of near-monopoly; it couldn't adapt easily to new conditions. The company's troubles of 1966–67 had been the beginning of its long decline. In 1966, when the Indian economy was in a bad way, Indian Railways, on which Guest Keen Williams was more or less traditionally dependent, cut their orders by more than half. For six or seven months in 1967 the points and crossings department, and the crossing-sleepers department, had no work. The bolt and nut department was also affected. Workers got their wages, but they got only the minimum. This was what I was told by the company: this was the background to Dipanjan's story.)

Dipanjan said, 'My friend and I waited for a long time at the gate. We looked at the union shack. We talked to the people there. Workers were coming out of the gate. I saw the variety of the people – Muslims, Hindus, Biharis, Bengalis. I was exhilarated, but the man my friend wanted me to see unfortunately didn't turn up.

'The next visit I remember was this. The company was bringing in some new machines, and some workers were going to be laid off on half pay. The role envisaged for us by the organizer of the splinter communist union was that we should go to the slums inhabited by non-Bengali workers, whom the unions hadn't succeeded in recruiting. These workers were anti-communist.

'Late one afternoon many of us had entered the slums. I found myself in a room in one of the huts, and here is this Bihari sitting on a string bed in the space outside his hut.'

'How old?'

'Middle-aged. Reticent at first. But he smiles, and then I start talking about the machines that were going to come. I talked in Hindi, which I didn't know well at that time. He was friendly but non-committal.

'And here is another scene I remember – some time later. I began to go to this slum in the evenings. I had been asked to speak to the workers about Marxism. By that time the splinter union had a large following. This was a Muslim hut, and I was waiting with one of the workers. I had still not got used to the conditions of their life, and what I remember most after 20 years is that there was a public drain running through the room. That is the main thing I remember. Then I went to the class, to talk on Marxism. I don't think I got my meaning across. They were tired, and I was speaking at too abstract a level, as I now understand.

'I was in this euphoric world. I was very young, and some of the Muslim workers – I am talking now about workers in the docks, where I went later – were telling us to go back home to our parents, who were crying for us, and to go back to our studies. I remember I asked one of these workers, "Why should I go back? And why aren't you coming forward and helping me with my work?"'

'How old was he?'

'This chap was middle-aged. I still remember what he said in his Hindustani: "We have come here to make money." It occurred to me that I was being too theoretical. But the party had said that workers in the town were "backward" compared to the peasants, and I had that rationalization to fall back on.'

I said, 'Arati didn't like you going to the villages.'

'In mid-68 I told her I would be going. When I actually had to go, she was pregnant. She cried. She didn't think it was a great thing to do, but she didn't think it was a foolish thing to do at that time. She felt I was betraying her. To some extent I felt that myself.'

'How did you go to the villages?'

'It was another anti-climax, at first. We had certain well-developed urban centres outside Calcutta. I took a train and went to one of them. It was a two-and-and-a-half-hour journey. I went to a factory-worker's house. I knew the house. I had gone there before on certain errands. He was a refugee from East Bengal. He had built a small house of his own, in a ramshackle and dirty part of the town.

'That same day I met one of the village comrades. He was expecting me. We leave the next day by bus. I have a canvas bag, but with nothing in it, only a dhoti. We get down in the late afternoon. My clothes don't stick out, but my glasses do, and my Calcutta accent. We walk for half an hour and reach the village centre, where all the people support us. That night there is a meeting to decide upon a course of action. I don't attend the meeting.

'At night we go to eat in someone's hut. The village people have arranged collectively for the food. The rice is wet. It's not been strained at all, because that rice-water itself is food, and there is a lot of that wet rice. And I can't eat it. It's a strain for me, because I can't throw it away either. My city stomach is just too small for it. And there is nothing else to eat, and nobody is going to eat a real meal again until the next night.'

'What are you eating off? Plates? Leaves?'

'Metal plates. It's a thatched hut. We are eating outside, in an open space. No lights except for the sky, and quite a lot of mosquitoes. I am disconcerted.'

'Why?'

He switched tenses. 'I was afraid of what I had to face the next day – communication-wise. We slept on a string bed outside the hut – two of us to a bed, and that was pretty uncomfortable, because a string bed sags in the middle. I had a sense of forlornness

322

and apprehension. In the villages there are no lavatories. There are certain fields – with nearby pools of water – that are set aside for the purpose.

'Next morning a better-off peasant (he had a radio) gave us tea – which is not common in the villages: the villagers at that time didn't have hot drinks. In the afternoon we were given another meal – again of rice – because we were going off on another journey on foot. A journey of three to four hours.

'I found it hard to keep up with the peasant guide. We reached our destination in the evening. I was charged up with my politics, but they were going slowly and calmly about their everyday tasks. I noticed that, and I felt like a fool. In the cities everyone was boiling, and here were these peasants, who were supposed to be the main force of the revolution, quite impassive. I felt let down, and I began to feel homesick for Calcutta.

'The next afternoon I began to walk back to the nearest party centre, which was in a very small town. I don't remember any of the physical stress, and I don't think it made any impact on me. All I remember is that I had to walk about six hours, because I had no money – we were not supposed to take any. While I walked, buses were plying.

'This was how I began my Red Guard Action. And then I felt I was doing my work at last.'

I said, 'You know I don't want any names. But none of the people you are talking about have any faces. I can't see them.'

Dipanjan said, 'There are faces. But when we began with the Guest Keen Williams workers we were following the communist tradition in which people are objects, not living subjects making their own lives – and history in that process. Our interaction at the human level was mainly within our own political set. Which is why when that Muslim dock-worker asked me why I didn't go back to my family, it made such an impression on me. Even today I believe that conversation was on a different level.

'I would like to make a further comment. The faces of my friends are with me. But most of them are still active politically, and I want to make no comment on them.'

An event then occurred, on 1 May 1969, which called Dipanjan back from the villages to Calcutta. On that day, at a public meeting on the Calcutta Maidan, the great central park of Calcutta, the communist faction that had been organizing the Naxalite peasant movement announced its separate identity as the Communist Party of India (Marxist-Leninist).

Dipanjan said, 'My parents rejected the new party. Arati was not pleased at all. At this stage she would have liked me to leave politics. Our daughter was to be born in October. I stayed on in Calcutta, working politically in the docks, until the end of 1969. And then I returned to the villages.

'The earlier comrades had been asking the peasants to form their own organizations, to seize political power and, in the process, to confiscate landlords' lands and, later, guns – to harvest forcibly the produce of their lands, to take the produce of the landlords' lands. And build centres of peasants' power, as opposed to landlords' power, in the villages.

'And, in fact, there had been a big peasant uprising in the region in the harvest season. I was too late for that. It was during this uprising that the party line about individual killing arrived. The killings were to be carried out by conspiratorially constituted squads. And this time, when I began my Red Guard Action, I had to ask the peasants to form annihilation squads, as they were called.

'This time, for me, the first trauma about the villages and non-communication was over. I had learned a little. I began this Red Guard Action with more conviction and less nervousness. This was an extensive journey, lasting many months, six months to a year. I moved from village to village, community to community, tribals and non-tribals, untouchables and farmer castes. I really learned about India.'

'What did you feel about the new directive?'

'Many of the comrades before had succeeded in forming squads and carrying out annihilations, mainly in the area covered by the old uprising of the harvest season, based on land and harvest – occupation of land, and forcible harvesting.'

'Were you shocked by the directive?'

'No, no. Indians are basically a very violent people. I was doing Red Guard Action in new areas, and in spite of my best efforts I could not persuade the peasants to carry out a single annihilation – which was a cause of great remorse to me, and led to a feeling of inadequacy.'

'Do you remember how you did the asking?'

'Oh, yes. I asked a peasant in whose hut I was staying. I remember that hut very well. They had a new-born baby, and she was being fed rice-water instead of milk – in a bottle – something which appeared quite shocking to me. These people were like others we talked to. They had very little land, enough for perhaps three months' sustenance. The party had asked us all to concentrate on these people.

'I asked this man, "Who is the most hated landlord of the area?" He named the landlord. I told him, "Why don't you kill him off?" He brings another peasant that evening, and asks me to broach the subject with him. The two of them agree that that landlord should be killed off, but they refused to do it themselves.'

'Did the idea shock them?'

'The idea didn't shock them. As I keep on telling you, we are a very violent people. I tried to convince them, coming and going, for about two months.

'My life was a concealed life in that hut. If the landlord knew of my presence he would have killed me or handed me over to the police. I knew it was dangerous. I knew I had exceeded the law. But killing a man is nowhere considered contrary to any ethical code. You must understand that the *Ramayana* and the *Mahabharata* rule the everyday religious code of the Hindus, just as the Koran does for the Muslims, and these are books which extol killing for a greater purpose. I should think that, like any other other Indian, I had no sense of ethical outrage in advocating killing for a cause.'

'Gandhi?'

'Of the many ideals of Gandhi which the Indians didn't accept, *ahimsa*, non-violence, stands out most.'

'The Jains?'

'They're a strange sect. But it's the wrong perspective of India you have, when you mention these religions – Buddhism, Jainism, and Gandhi. I point to what happened in Kampuchea, Ceylon, Burma, China – all countries ostensibly under the umbrella of Buddha and Confucius. All these peoples are very violent.'

'Let's go back to the villages.'

'As I said, I began to feel inadequate. In late 1970 and early 1971 the movement as a whole faced a setback, and many of my friends started re-thinking.

'In the last few months, before my arrest, I had become involved with tribal people. I got to like them very much. I felt at home with them. I understood their political aspirations. For the first time I had come across a section of peasants who thought and acted politically. I used to talk a lot to a schoolmaster among them. These months were very satisfying, the most satisfying of my life in the villages, more so because the doubts that my friends in the movement had developed about the line of individual killing – these doubts gave me the latitude to talk freely without the party trammels, which I was beginning to find impractical.'

'How many people were annihilated in your area?'

'More than 100 people were killed in the area because of this line. Most of them were landlords.'

But now the police were closing in.

'Our friends had to break off from the party, and many of us had to keep on the move, in Bihar and Bengal. One night, at about eight or nine, we were at a food shop by a railway station in north Bihar. There were some policemen in plain clothes there, shirts and trousers. They were from the Bengal Police, and they were in search of some other Naxalites. They had come to the railway food shop to buy some cooked meat for themselves. One of my friends was recognized, and we were arrested.

'At that time the police had started killing off Naxalites, and my first reaction was that they would kill us off. This reign of terror was by this time six months old, and I had accustomed myself to such a fate – just to keep myself going.

'The policemen at the food stall were older than us. They were not abusive. They took us to the police station. There we immediately tried to influence the Bihari police officer in charge of us to prevent these policemen from Bengal from killing us.

'The Bihari officer, an educated man, said, "I do respect you. You work for the country. But my duty as a police officer places me against you." We laughed at him. "Why are you mocking us? These Bengali police officers will kill us in a few minutes' time."

'They tied us with some ropes, and on the way the policemen gave us some blows, harping on the fact that we were Bengalis. The Bihari police officer was shocked, and immediately informed the whole police circuit of Bihar by radio of our arrest, so the Bengali policemen couldn't kill us, if that had been their intention.

'Most of us were never tried. Only a few were tried and convicted. The rest of us were kept under detention without trial until the amnesty of 1977 in West Bengal.

'I was in prison until October 1972, in Calcutta. In prison I

326

found two things which disheartened me. The first was the quality of the Naxalite prisoners from Calcutta. We had been hearing that they had been killing individual policemen, even traffic constables, and suspected spies. The prison was full with Naxalites, especially young boys, and they were not politically oriented at all. What had happened was that there had been an upheaval against the school system – boys and girls forced into the school system, who had then dropped out, and had been recruited by the party for urban violence.

'The party had fragmented. My own ideas were not clear. I felt there had been maladies within the movement. I felt that my political search had reached a dead end, and I would have to begin anew. And for some time I could not think of myself as a political worker any longer.

'After I came to the Calcutta prison I could meet my parents and Arati regularly. No case could be proved against me. I remained in preventive detention. Finally, I wrote the government that if they released me, I would go abroad for further studies in physics.'

The petition was granted. He was accepted by London University, and his father paid his fare to England. The police went with him right up to the plane. He completed his Ph.D. in London, and then came back to Calcutta. This was in September 1974.

I asked him, 'What do you think now?'

He fingered his glasses, squinted, and looked out through the window. I was sitting across the narrow table from him, in a chair with arms, between the two tall metal cupboards. Behind him was an empty room, with patches of new, level plaster on the walls.

He said, 'The major mistake, the basic misunderstanding of the Marxist position – I feel the people must liberate themselves. The intellectuals can only hand them the equipment for doing so.'

He now did civil rights work, and taught in the slums. 'I see no discontinuity with my earlier political search. Between going to the urban slums, and this teaching in the slums.' He leaned back against an olive-green metal cupboard, and considered the sky. 'Society is so structured that the toiling people can never find their own voice, their own view of the world, their own identity.'

I asked about Arati, and her time in England.

'It altered her world. Because she found for the first time that a woman was not merely or at all the appendage of a some man. I was very happy to come back here. Arati cried for days, and her friends who were brought up never to show their emotions in public were unhappy for her. Given the choice, she would have continued to live in England – this feeling of freedom, and recognition of her as an individual.

'I had this running fight with her from 67 to 72 – I could not convince her that if we stayed with my parents we would always be dominated by them. She did not recognize the domination as such. And only when we went to England she realized what I was saying. Until then she regarded that as part of my eccentricity – which, for example, had led me into the Naxalite movement. I used to say, "Let's take an apartment." Or: "Why don't you stand up to my mother? Why do you carry out everything my father says, even when it is hurting you?" She never knew there could be a different way of life. Nowadays things have changed, and are changing, but in the 1960s she was in no way an exception in her view of life.'

This gave an added point to what Arati had said at her house the previous day, when Dipanjan was having his shower. When Dipanjan had gone to live in the villages, Arati said, she had gone to live with Dipanjan's parents. In India a wife stayed with her in-laws; you moved from your parents' house to your husband's parents' house. India was different from other places; you had to know many things in order to write about India.

But now they lived by themselves.

I asked Dipanjan, 'Are you happy in the little house?'

'Yes. As far as Arati and I are concerned, the material side of life has never been important. Both of us are capable of hard physical toil.'

'What about the disorder of your bookcase there – things just thrown together? And the dust – can I mention the dust? You were saying that the college is a corporate place, and that is why it will never be cleaned.'

He said, 'I am ashamed of that, in my house. Both of us are overworked and can't find the time. Arati works as a teacher of physics in a morning college. She works there from 6.30 to 10 – and you have to add an hour to go there, and two hours to come back. But I am ashamed of that disorder in my house. And say "dust", if you like. My grandfather would have taken me to task. But *no one* is ashamed of this place. That's the difference.'

'Do you feel that the most active part of your life is over?'

'Not at all. My life so far has been the first part of the search.'

'May I ask this? You have spent so much time thinking of others. Isn't that arrogant? Shouldn't you have also thought of developing your own talent? You don't have to answer. If you don't want to answer, I'll withdraw the question and not refer to it.'

'I'll answer. The most brilliant boy of the year before me at Presidency College is now a renowned professor in the U.S.A. He asked me the same question. Not the arrogance part. In physics the questions which interested me I found were beyond my ability to answer. I worked on them; I thought about them. I still work on them – or, I should say, I still read about them. But less difficult questions cannot hold my interest. In poetry I am never satisfied with what I write, and especially because the type of poetry I write can only appeal to a few people like myself. But I find helping others is something I can tackle, although I make mistakes. I keep on learning from them.'

Ashok's first story had been about his attempt to get into marketing, and his entanglement with Imba, the Institute of Management and Business Administration, run by Dr Malhotra of Delhi. His second story was about his marriage, his break with the past.

He said, 'I eventually went into an advertising agency, and was immediately happy. My career righted itself from here. I grew in my job; I learned a lot about the real world of marketing; it was the most productive five years of my career.

'But this went with an upheaval in another aspect of my life. I came from a traditional South Indian brahmin household. My father had travelled on various postings all over the world and had settled in Calcutta. And I had a public-school upbringing in India. Yet so ingrained was the traditional outlook of the family that I had never thought of dating girls, although I was popular, and sang pop songs and Indian classical songs. In this Indian classical side I had been trained at home by a private tutor; it was part of one's traditional upbringing.

'A number of my friends were leading an active social life, but I myself didn't see this as either necessary or indeed desirable. Other people did it, had girl friends, but I felt that wasn't for me. I suppose it was deeply in my subconscious that I would get married in the traditional arranged way – until I actually went to participate in a ceremony of "viewing" a girl with the object of marriage.

'My family had arranged it in the standard way, through the exchange of horoscopes. The girl lived in Bangalore, and I went all the way down there to see her. There were hordes of my relatives there, and her relatives. We were told to arrive at the appointed place, which was of the girl's parents' choosing, at a certain time.

'It was in the evening. The occasion itself involved everybody sitting round in a circle. I was introduced only to the girl's father, and we sat round in a circle in the hall. Savouries and sweets were passed around. And everyone was dressed for the occasion. So peculiar were the arrangements, I wasn't sure who the girl was. There were other girls from her side, and I hadn't been introduced to the girl herself, and the girl's father kept up a constant chatter, asking me a whole host of questions about what I did, and what I liked, and what I disliked, and so on.

'Alarmingly, he also started talking about possible marriage venues. So I found responding in a normal way difficult. He would say, "I would rather hold the wedding in Sholapur than in Bangalore, because I have better facilities in Sholapur. What do you think?"

'And you couldn't say no and you couldn't say yes. If you said no, it would have been rude. If you said yes, it would have been nonsense. So one indulged in a series of diplomatic half-volleys. One smiled vaguely. I was relieved when the hour was over. When people asked me what I thought, I kept saying I didn't know.

'One was supposed to make up one's mind about a girl whom one did not actually get to meeting, with whom one did not exchange a word, and who was just about surreptitiously pointed out by one of my relatives. One was supposed to make up one's mind at the end of the occasion.

'It also disturbed me that the girl apparently had no say in the matter. Certainly everybody – all the 20, 30 people there – was anxiously waiting to know whether I had given the green signal. On these occasions it's all weighted in favour of the boy, and the girl's family occupies the inferior position.

'Many years later a feeling of shame crystallizes around the memory. But at that point the feeling was one of embarrassment, though even today boys and girls get married in the way I chose not to then. In fairness to them, I should say they have no choice.

It's not fair for me to tell anyone to follow my example. Perhaps if it had been handled differently, I might have been less embarrassed.

'At the end, while we were trooping out, saying goodbye, it occurred to me – in a trice – that I wouldn't like to go through this again.

'We went back to our family house. I was confused. In the car were my brother, his wife, my father, and I. I was quite silent, and remained silent. They knew I was unhappy. I pushed off to a friend's house and stayed there till late. I was scheduled to leave Bangalore the next day. What was worrying me was that my family had given the girl's parents the promise that they would revert to them the next day.

'When I went back home later that night, my father and my brother asked me what I had decided to do – did I want to marry the girl? I said no. My father said, "No problem. We'll find another girl."

'I told my father I wasn't saying no because I didn't like the girl's face – that would have been unfair: I hadn't had a chance to talk to the girl. I was saying no to the process, not to the girl. And I didn't want to talk about it any more.

'My elders thought that time would heal things, that this was my first time, and that the next time round would be different.

'I became less and less communicative. It's in the situation that parents and children don't talk openly about these things. Nobody ever asks you what your views on marriage are. It just happens that one fine day somebody presents you with a proposal.

'And it was at this time that, spurred on by the thought that I would have to go through with that viewing process once more or many times more, my mind gradually turned towards the principle of making up my own mind who I wanted to marry.

'There was someone I had known, a marketing executive. Marketing – it's always been marketing for me. But this girl I knew came from another community. I declared myself to her. We agreed that it could be a workable proposition. We knew each other socially. We spoke the same language. But she was of a different community. And when I finally broached the subject to my parents, they were as opposed as I thought they would be. They went into a shell, withdrew – as I had withdrawn after the viewing ceremony at Bangalore. It was difficult to communicate

331

with them, because in a situation like this they had a certain crude logic on their side: in a matter like this there could be no half-way compromise. For them I was about to break the family link with history, tradition, and they could have no vision of the future. For them everything appeared to become black.

'I was on test, too, because the person I wanted to marry wanted to see how I would react to pressure. So it was important to me to stand up. I told my parents I wasn't going to change my mind, but I wasn't in a hurry. They could take their time. It was very hard for them, but slowly they came round. They were counselled by some people in the family and by friends. Our wedding was held in the traditional grand manner.

'Today we are physically apart, in different cities, my wife and I in Calcutta, my parents elsewhere. This distance has helped us to adjust to each other. We meet once in a while, a couple of times a year, and we have a cordial relationship. My brothers and sisters have married in the traditional way, and they live with my parents in the same city. But there is no great bonhomie among them. It is my view that the South Indian brahmin cannot let himself go; everything is restrained.

'Among the younger generation of the family, I became a hero. Quite a few members of the family have done what I have done. And it's not now quite the shock that it had been. But one also has to accept – what my parents felt but couldn't express, what made them go into their shell – that something indefinable has snapped. We've been brahmins for untold generations.'

Fifteen years or so had passed since the end of the Naxalite rebellion, but Debu – who was now a high executive in a big company – still looked forward to a new, true revolution. Debu had taken part in the rebellion in its early stages. He had then fallen out ideologically with some elements of the leadership, and had had to hide from both police and former associates. He could chart, precisely and convincingly, how the revolution of love and compassion had turned into simple nihilism, with people talking of revolution and peasant power, but never actually taking on the state, or the powerful or the protected, concentrating instead on the weak and the exposed. But there was still in Debu some idea that a fresh and better start might be made.

He said, 'The only change – a big change – between then and now is that at that time, in the late 60s, I thought I would be a part of the revolution, and now I know that I shall be a *witness* to it. A supportive witness. I don't think the need for revolution has changed.' And going on from there to talk of his involvement, he dropped a half-thought: 'Once you've tasted blood – '

Tasting blood – strange metaphor.

Debu said, 'Organizing large masses of people.' And he meant something else as well: experiencing the love the people offered to those who were trying to do something for them. 'Love is a trite word. You cannot describe the thing I mean – it was something welling up and touching you. At that time I thought this was to do with loyalty to the party. Now I feel that the party always is the person. That is what I mean by the taste of blood: the people give you a million times more than what you might ultimately give them.'

He was born in the late 1930s, into the Calcutta middle class. But when Debu was young, his father, a professional man, had a serious illness that lasted for some years; and the family became poor. They were helped by friends, but isolated by their own relatives.

Some of those relatives, when they came to visit, said things like: 'When you want to sell those chairs, you must let us know. We might want to buy them.' The chairs were real, not just a figure of speech. When I met Debu again, and he took me to his large apartment, after a little tour of middle-class central Calcutta, and the once British clubs, I saw the chairs in his drawing-room: low, old-fashioned, ebony or black-lacquer Bengali chairs, a complete set. They would have reminded him every day of those hard years of his father's illness; they would have confirmed him every day in the distrust of the class from which he had come.

He had thought for so long about those years that the story came out easily, like a simple fable, together with the political moral he drew from it. There were four components of the Bengali middle class, he said: caste, education, family history, and money. The first three stayed with his family when they fell, but lack of money took them to the outer limit of the class.

He couldn't forget that. Even when his family cirumstances improved, he remained an 'achiever', passionate to do well at school and college. Even when he was playing cricket – at which he was good – that passion to achieve, to do well at his school, was with him. He punished himself. He said that for six years he worked 16 hours a day. Finally, when he was twenty-two, he had his reward. He became an executive in one of the boxwallah companies, at a time when the Calcutta boxwallah world still had 10 years or so to go.

It was only then that he could look around. He read a book about President Kennedy, and decided, with some young accountants, to do social work in the slums. The group had vague political ideas; they were not connected with any political party. Their primary idea was the old Bengali idea of the Motherland, the idea that Bengal had given to the rest of India, Debu said: the idea that India had to be a country one could be proud of. The idea had decayed in Bengal since independence, Debu said. 'In my class the idea is still there, but it is a remnant of the past – considered an anachronism – and in the class above, the industrialists and businessmen, the idea exists more or less as a negative quantity.'

The slum work became serious. Debu was giving it three evenings a week and two mornings a week. He already had a distrust of his middle class. Now he saw, close to, the injustices of society lower down. He saw how the middle classes were responsible; and he saw also the *chain* of injustice.

'You had Sir So-and-so, the landlord of a slum. He would do whatever he was doing to the widowed housewives of that particular slum through his lower-middle-class agent. The agent would have his own agents among the lower class in the lumpen proletariat. This was the chain. If you disposed of the landlord, he would be replaced by someone else. The chain itself would go on.'

After three or four years with his firm, Debu went to the United States on a one-year business fellowship. As part of the deal, he gave lectures on India. He found the experience unexpectedly humiliating. At the end of every lecture there would always be some questioner asking, 'How come you're starving and begging for food, if you're so great?' And there would always be someone making a shaming comparison between India and China.

He started to study Marxism and Indian history, and he decided that when he went back to Calcutta at the end of the year he would join the more radical of the communist parties. This was the time of the Food Movement, when India was going through its worst food crisis. Sixty people had been shot by the police in West Bengal, and people were eating 'milo'.

'This was a derivative of maize which the Americans fed their pigs, and which they had sent over as charity, and the Government of India were dishing out in their ration shops to feed the village poor. I was very ashamed and angry. To me it wasn't the *poor* who were eating it. It was Indians and Bengalis.'

He joined the Communist Party (Marxist) and began to work in the villages. He lived with the peasants. In the main he did propaganda. He also tried to stop black-marketing in rice. He and his fellow workers did this by stopping the movement of rice out of the villages. They also worked to prevent the eviction of sharecroppers.

Debu began to rise in the party. The Bengali *bhadra-lok*, the middle class, loved what was foreign, and Debu found that being a foreign-returned person and an English speaker was helping him up even in the Communist Party (Marxist). This was unsettling, but it was also the time when Debu began to have the almost mystical experience of receiving the love of the people. He placed no limit on the time he wanted to give to the cause, no limit on the risk he was prepared to take; and the people in return gave him love.

'People I didn't know at all – peasants, labourers – no one among them ever said, "You can't stay here. We can't give shelter to this friend of yours."'

He formed a committee to fight revisionism in the party, but then he himself became disenchanted with the party. He found that at the lower levels of the party leadership there was a lot of minor corruption: people were stealing fish or rice that had been collected for the party. When he complained to a higher-level committee, he was accused by them of being a CIA agent. He began to feel that some people were trying to push him out of the party.

But he had also begun to write articles about the peasant movement, and these articles had got the attention of the people who were later to form the Naxalite faction of the party. Some of these articles were read out on Peking Radio; to the Naxalites, as bhadra-lok as any in their love of the foreign, this was the highest recognition. Debu became important in the councils of the faction.

The leader of the faction, when he came to Calcutta, began to stay in Debu's house.

'I had come into this movement through indignation felt abroad at the position of India. And since most of the people of India were poor and lived in villages, this indignation focussed on the poor. I was convinced you needed an *overturning* brought about by the poor, since my class and the class above stank, and no redemption could even begin to come from them. And this is where the abstract part comes: the entire concept of *overturning* came from Marxism as interpreted by Lenin and particularly by Mao. At this time there were two classes of books about Russia and China. On one side were the cold warriors. And on the other were the starry-eyed – Han Suyin, Felix Greene, Edgar Snow. One rejected the cold wariors. I say this with hindsight.

'When the Naxalite movement started – with its attempts to inform and involve the mass of the people – it was quite different from what the other communist parties had been doing. And I want to tell you that I started believing it could be done, it could happen here now. It was the transformation of desire into belief.

'The Naxalites were not using quotations only from Marx, but from Rabindranath and Vivekananda and Romain Rolland. In their wall posters they gave *facts* about poverty, the amount of food available, the wage scales. And one could see people reading them, and even the illiterates understood them when somebody read them out to them. And above all there was the business of not wanting office, staying away from the electoral process – which had become quite filthy, a matter of money and compromise.

'And now comes the agony, for someone like me. If you have to do something big, you have to be organized in a big way. To be organized in a big way, you needed a command structure. And with a command structure you had battles between indiv:duals for positions in that command structure.

'In communist parties you fight your inner party battles with a thesis and a programme for revolution, and then there are debates, accompanied by expulsions and counter-expulsions, until in the end you have a small group of people or an individual left in supreme command. The style in which this takes place varies from country to country – that grows up from the soil, the culture, the traditions.

'In Bengal we were heavily struck by several things. There was the bhadra-lok tradition I've told you about – not in the sense that it led to any gentlemanliness in the struggle, but in the sense that the bhadra-lok is upper caste and Hindu, and has a fixation with the foreign. The upper-caste Bengali is governed by certain laws of inheritance which make internecine war a way of life. That informed our actions very much. We forgot the other political groups, even the extreme communalists. The fight among ourselves was bitter. In this fight you might say that the people became secondary. The level of our intensity was very great; our quarrels were correspondingly bitter. It wasn't at all an abstract ideological war. It was like a family conflict which had strong overtones of violence.

'A second, later development was parallel: the sanction of individual killing.' This went with other things, which Debu now outlined. 'The seizure of college and school buildings, the destruction of laboratories and libraries – since it was considered that this educational system created enemies of the people. The rewriting of our history. The destruction of the statues of people like Raja Ram Mohun Roy and Vivekananda.' Ram Mohun Roy, out of whose teachings the Brahmo Samaj and the Bengali Renaissance had arisen, which had given so much to India and the nationalist cause, and which still remained dear to people like Chidananda Das Gupta. Vivekananda, the religious teacher – qotations from whose writings had appeared on the first Naxalite wall posters. 'They were considered people who had compromised with imperialism, and served the interests of the landlords and the then ruling classes. Along with this came the slogan: "China's chairman is our chairman."'

Stage by abstract stage, from a raw, humiliated concern with the poor and India, to cultural and economic suicide, new compulsions and violations, and a cause far removed from the peasant's hunger.

The leader of the Naxalite faction was called Charu Mazumdar. Debu knew him well.

Debu said, 'I was present at the small meeting in Calcutta when Charu Mazumdar first unveiled that policy, of individual killing. He had already spoken of this in the villages, and had sent out letters to individual units. This was the first time he was talking about it in Calcutta, and I actually went with him to the meeting.

'It was in North Calcutta, in a lower-middle-class home. I remember a short corridor and a small room. The corridor was full of slippers left by those sitting on the floor in the small room. It was a late-evening meeting, a local meeting.

'I had tremendous admiration for Charu Mazumdar then, and I have admiration now. He was the most intense person I had ever met. And he truly believed in what he spoke about. He put tremendous faith in the young and the new. He truly loved the peasant – *much*, much more than the love I felt for them. My love was different. He *believed* in the Indian peasant. He admired them.

'His sense of Indian history was really startling – the essence and dynamics of Indian history. He had no greed, none at all. No sense of personal comfort. There were many thousands of people, at that point, who were prepared to give their lives and follow his command. And he had developed that power without coercion. The only other organization I have known with the kind of power he possessed is the army, and in the army there is a great deal of coercion.

'He was a thin, short man with glasses. His glasses had very powerful lenses. He generally dressed in shirt and dhoti, or bush shirt and trousers. The clarity of his speech and expression was very great. And this was duplicated in his movements.' Debu meant that Charu Mazumdar's movements were economical and precise, without too many gestures. 'He had enormous energy, his movements were swift. And, by God, he could inspire.

'He never ever raised his voice, but he could speak with great emphasis. And in that small room in North Calcutta he started speaking. There were two windows at the back of the room, and they were both open. I noticed those windows, because I was worried that people outside would be listening. There was very little in that room. I remember an unpainted wooden table with lots of books on it, and a radio. The radio was important. Do you know why? That was the link to Peking Radio. All Naxalites gave enormous importance to the radio – "where-yesterday-we-were-mentioned-on-Peking-Radio" sort of thing. There was something wrong with me. In my whole life I have never listened to Peking Radio more than twice.

'There was also a small bare bench at the back. I noticed that no one was willing to sit on it, in spite of the crowd in the room. But ultimately the room became so packed that people had to sit on the bench. Charu Mazumdar was sitting on the floor – that was why people were reluctant to sit on the bench: they didn't want to be higher than he was.

'People were smoking. That was why the windows were open. I was smoking myself. The atmosphere was still free and easy. I think some tea was brought in, but not for everybody – it couldn't get to everybody in the room.

'Charu Mazumdar started by mentioning certain successes the group had had in Bengal and in certain other parts of the country. "You are doing very good work here, I know. And they are frightened of us. You can expect them to attack. Our experience has proved that killing individual oppressors helps to mobilize the people, because the people then perceive that the oppressor can be *destroyed*. Therefore I have just issued this letter." He read out the letter from a handwritten script. It was the letter calling for individual killing. Then he called for questions.

'I was shocked. But I think my own roots came into play then – as it always does. I was shocked, but simultaneously thrilled. The thrill was: "Have we at last found the way?" It didn't enter my mind to question what had been given as fact: that killing had generated large-scale enthusiasm among the poor.

'My shock was on two counts. One, it was so close to murder. But this I rationalized: it's not murder, it's execution. People weren't going to be killed just like that. The individual killings were going to be discussed and agreed upon by the group. The second shock was that virtually all the gurus of Marxism had warned against terrorism. And this sounded like terrorism.

'The questions that came were essentially like this: "What do we do in the cities?" "What happens if the landlord is supplanted by another oppressor?" There were many tactical questions. I was one of the last to ask a question, and I asked it in a very humble way, I must tell you, because, compared to the fellows there, I was from the wrong class, and the fellows sitting there were more active in the field than I was. The question I asked was about Mao and Lenin having warned against terrorism. So how, theoretically, could we support this?

'Charu Mazumdar answered us all. Very quietly, convincingly. We were all convinced.'

I said to Debu, 'Tell me a little more about him.'

'He was about fifty-eight. Wizened, fair. He was from a land-lord's family in North Bengal, and his father was a famous doctor, well-to-do. He was very bright in his studies and did well. He was pulled into the swadeshi movement' – the nationalist movement – 'and from there he transferred to the peasant movement, and made a name for himself. He became a member of the Communist Party. What he did was to transform a militant reform movement – protecting the sharecropper – into the beginning of a revolutionary movement. He did that by deciding that the battle would be carried on against the *state*.'

'Didn't it occur to you that it was madness?'

'At the time I didn't think it was madness. I don't think it is madness now. If there is to be revolution, it has to take on the state.

'That meeting in North Calcutta lasted for three hours. Charu Mazumdar's initial statement was for about an hour and 15 minutes. The discussion was about another hour. Afterwards, little groups would talk to him about their local problems, and leave.

'Up to that time the Naxalites had been occupying schools, defacing statues, etc. Isolated incidents. These things I objected to rather seriously. Up to about April 1970 Charu Mazumdar and others assured me that they were the result of over-enthusiasm. I remember now with hindsight that it was the lower-middle-class and rural schools that were made targets. There was no attempt at touching the elite schools.

'When the directive came that "China's chairman is our chairman", I became very angry, and went to see him. I said, "If the Chinese start coming I will be one of the first with a gun in my hand to stop them." On that topic he immediately kept quiet. But I think that the personal equation we had built up since 1968 – he had stayed in my house, and we had had long discussions – that equation snapped. Later I wrote him a letter. It was a long letter, full of theoretical backing to things I opposed. He didn't reply. At that time the killings had started. The party had moved underground, and all communication was cut.

'That was how I left the movement. From 1970 to 1972 I was involved with a parallel organization. We were mainly doing propaganda. We were hunted by the police. We had to hide from both sides.

'The first policeman was killed in Calcutta in early May, 1970, in a bomb attack. After mid-1970 the action became more general. Traffic policemen were being killed, because they were easy game.

340

There was a funny side. The traffic police were issued arms. The Naxalites snatched the arms, so the traffic policemen chained the arms to themselves. Simultaneously there began the killing of informers.

'And when you start killing *informers*, then you really open the can of worms. You do not refer to his class – you cannot refer to his class, because he has to be within your own ambit to be an informer. Again, with hindsight, I also see that there were no attacks against big targets, the big industrialists, the big landlords.

'And further divisions appeared in the Marxist-Leninist camp. More groups left. By 1973 the Marxist-Leninist camp was divided into 20 factions. The police and their gangs had killed several thousands. By 1973 the movement – that phase of it – was finished.

'I came out of hiding in 1972. The police knew about my break with Charu Mazumdar. The last time I was questioned in detail was in 1972. My great luck was that my last arrest had been in April 1970 – before the first policeman was killed in Calcutta. Then I had gone underground.

'I am doing nothing now. I think in some ways our country has more respect and honour in the world than at that time. From beggars we have become borrowers. I am exercised by the gap between rich and poor, exercised by the lack of patriotism amongst the power-brokers, exercised by the number of industries going sick. And I am exercised by the fact that borrowers generally end up begging.'

Debu didn't tell me about the end of Charu Mazumdar. That I heard from someone else. He was arrested in Calcutta in 1972, and died soon afterwards. He was an asthmatic, and when he was arrested he had a tube of oxygen with him. He must have suffered continuously in the damp and heat of Bengal.

Ashok's first story had been about his attempt to get into marketing. His second story had been about his marriage, his break with the past. His last story was about his life in advertising, and his sighting of the Calcutta boxwallah world, just when that world was about to disappear, giving way to the cruder, richer business world of post-independence India.

Ashok said, 'My first experience of the Calcutta boxwallah was when as a trainee account executive in an advertising firm I was taken to my first client meeting, and was introduced to this very senior executive in the marketing division of the company. The man was portly and appeared to be quite jovial. He was smoking an imported brand of cigarette, and – this was the middle of May, which is something in Calcutta – he was wearing a suit. His office was air-conditioned. The general atmosphere was of a man in a plush office with a leisurely approach to life.

'He appeared to be in no great hurry to discuss the business in hand. We were going into all kinds of trivia about life in general, the cricket series, a little office politics. All kinds of things were being talked about from 11 or so until 12 or 12.15. And then there was this long pause, and it seemed almost a pity that we had to set aside the general discussion.

'My boss broached the subject of business, and this was gone through with great dispatch. I was just observing; I was only a trainee. The business side of things was finished in a quarter of an hour. It was now about 12.30. Lunch was looming. The client asked my boss if he had a luncheon engagement. My boss said no. The client said, "Perhaps we ought to discuss a little more business over lunch."

'My boss instructed me to run to the office and take out an IOU for 500 rupees, and join them at a five-star hotel. The client wasn't inviting us – it wasn't known for clients to invite advertising agency personnel to lunch. The lunch was to be on us. I suppose I was quite excited at that moment. I had heard a great deal about client entertainment, but I hadn't done any, or been part of it, at that time. The lunch that day started at 12.45 and finished at 3.30. Everybody was happy at the end.

'This way of doing things went on till the early 70s. The big companies had more or less a monopoly in their respective fields. They didn't have to sell. They merely allocated. There was never enough to meet the demand.

'That's changed now. There are a lot more companies making the products, and companies are having to battle it out – to meet production volumes, to place them in the market, to persuade the customer. So all of a sudden companies had no room for people who merely dressed well, could talk to the boss's wife, could play a round of golf, and hold their drink. The country itself had started setting up business schools. To a large extent they tended to be textbook American models, and this created problems for companies. But these institutes enabled companies to get a shortlist of candidates. It became a status symbol to recruit an MBA.

'People who in earlier days would have gone up the ladder now began to flounder, because they didn't have the talent to hold down their job. Whereas, before, office life was a pleasant interval between the company apartment and the club house, now, in my firm, if I want to rise, I have some sacrifices to make. For example, I might have to travel 20 days a month. If you're an all-India organization, you can travel to monitor what's happening in the field. You're also doing it because your colleagues are doing it, and it can be seen as a sign of your commitment to your organization.

'In the old days, if an executive went to the wedding of, say, the niece of a dealer, that would have been seen by the dealer as a most enormous favour, and the executive would have been suitably rewarded by the dealer. Today the executive goes to that wedding to keep in with the dealer. So the whole thing now changes. These dealers most of them speak Hindi, and the older social accomplishments – speaking English, dressing well, playing golf – no longer matter. If you're travelling 20 days a month, and you're the sales manager, you're spending all those days in the company of the dealers and your field staff, and almost every evening is a fairly heavy drinking evening.

'I can't say that when I started I had any idea that marketing would be the way it is now. But in my company I am specifically on the advertising side, and this gives me creative satisfaction. Social graces are still a bonus for an executive; they can add sheen to an executive's profile. But what the executive is really expected to have are qualities of a hard-nosed entrepreneurial businessman – which is the kind of man he is dealing with. In his company he has to be a sophisticated communicator; and when he is sitting in a poky little dealer's shop somewhere he has to speak a different kind of language. He is probably drinking tea out of a dirty tumbler – and yet that dealer probably makes infinitely more than the executive.

'Traditionally in India the dealer network is a very potent force. They're a breed apart. They may even be different from dealers in other countries. To a very large extent people in the dealer community have not been educated. But they are naturally talented at making money. They take pleasure in making money, and more money. It's a family business, handed down from generation to generation. They will sit from 10 to 10 at night in their little shops and think nothing of it – that's their life. They keep rolling the money they make into more and more profitable ventures. And they like to show that they have money. The dealers' houses might have chandeliers and wall-to-wall carpeting, quite unnecessary, imported TV colour sets, and curtains and cushions in the most garish colours.

'But these people are important to companies. So you have these sophisticated organizations with their trained manpower from management institutes, who then have to learn to deal with people who are semi-literate but extremely savvy when it comes to money matters. We need them more than they need us, at this moment in our country's development.

'The strength of a dealer's shop or "counter" – that is how it is referred to: So-and-so is a good counter or a poor counter or a reliable counter – comes from his having been, or his family having been, in business for generations. He knows what his market will take.

'The targets are worked out on a counter basis for each town. We might say of a dealer: "He's a good 500-TV-set counter, and I must get him to sell 200 of mine." That's the kind of thinking that's taking place in an executive's mind. And once he returns to his base city or town, with his head muzzy with too much drink and travel, he's on to his computer, feeding it with all this information. No sales manager worth his salt can be found without his strips of Alka-Seltzer – they all have stomach problems – along with their calculators. They're drinking till 11 or 12 at night, and they're up again at 8.30 or 9, to face the new day.

'The boxwallah of the bygone era was really, typically, a shallow fellow, interested in appearances and the good life. We've swung the other way today. Professionally, the executive today is superior to his counterpart of 15 years ago, but his development as a human being is retarded. He is becoming more of an automaton. He physically has little time to think about anything except the turnover and collection targets for the month.

'If I had known that marketing was going to turn out to be like this, I probably wouldn't have wanted to go into it when I was young. I've turned down requests from the company to move into direct selling jobs. I don't want to pay that kind of price. I prefer to stay on the advertising side. And I don't have to do the extra things the sales executives have to do – going to the airport to meet this boss and that boss and take them home and spend an evening with them. I don't have to do that at all.

'Life is hard now for the executive, and the city of Calcutta adds to this pressure, by offering so little in return to a person who's putting in so much effort. After a hard day's work you can find yourself stranded in a car for hours on end, and when you return home there is no power. There are generators, but they make a dreadful din, and are limited. Apart from visiting one of Calcutta's clubs, if he's fortunate enough to be a member, an executive has little choice of places to go. He cannot go out walking because the pavements and the roads don't allow it. The parks are over-crowded. Most of these parks are infested with rich young men and women who take their cars and turn up their car stereos and eat all evening – junk food from hawkers – and throw the litter around.

'The infrastructure of the city is crumbling. The drainage system is perhaps the worst in the world. In the monsoon, major areas of the city are waterlogged for anything up to 72 hours at a time. One year the water never drained away. Carcases of animals appeared, and we were afraid of an epidemic.

'The only section of people here who seem to be thriving in Calcutta are the Marwaris. They came from parts of Rajasthan a couple of hundred years ago. They thrive by being middlemen, buying and selling. This is what they were good at, and they continue to be. They were never known for cultural or technical skills. And they just grew as a community. They have been the only ones, in the last 15 or 20 years, who are able to buy properties in the posh areas where previously only the rich Bengalis or expatriate executives lived. They have participated in the property boom. Today in these areas you have multi-storey buildings coming up – one more nail in the coffin of the city: more cars, more sanitation problems, etc. – with the Marwaris themselves occupying most of the apartments.

'The other aspect is that some of the very rich Marwaris keep buying up companies after buying just enough shares to gain control. And so a number of old firms are now in the hands of Marwaris. Most of them do not nurture or invest in these companies. They strip the assets. They are quite happy to let the company become more and more sick. It is also true that in the earlier era the British didn't bother very much about growth. Their main concern was repatriation of a certain amount of profits in foreign exchange to the parent company, and most British managing directors came here for a short-term period of three or five years.

'At the other end of the spectrum you have the red-flag-waving unions constantly playing cat-and-mouse with the management. The union leaders themselves don't do any work at all. The unions represent what ultimately the true Bengali is like: he is indolent, doesn't want to work, but he wants something for nothing, and he must protect his dignity at all costs. He will publicly despise the Marwari trader, but he wouldn't be able to do the same job himself.

'We put in a great deal of effort. We draw a monthly pay cheque. And for people like us, who are not businessmen, we feel that the city in which we live must offer us something in return. We must at the end of the working day have more than the prospect of just coming back home. You can't go to any cinema house, because most of them have poor sound systems and virtually non-functioning air-conditioning systems – they don't renovate them. I haven't been to a cinema hall in Calcutta for five or six years.

'I have told you how as a young man I longed to break into the world of marketing. I have done that, and I can say that professionally I have done well. But that profession hasn't turned out to be what I thought, and now I feel that those of us in Calcutta who are in the middle between the Marwaris and the trade-union Marxists – the executive class, who used to be an influential part of the city – are slowly being squeezed out of existence.

'The fact is that the problems of Calcutta are of a magnitude that cannot be endured. My wife and I feel now that we won't see improvements in our lifetime. We feel we should be trying our luck somewhere else, and saying goodbye to Calcutta.'

My own days in Calcutta had been hard. When I had first come to Calcutta, in 1962, I had, after the early days of strain, settled into the big-city life of the place; had had the feeling of being in a true metropolis, with the social and cultural stimulation of such a place. Something of that life was still there. But I was overpowered this time by my own wretchedness, the taste of the water, corrupting both coffee and tea as it corrupted food, by the brown smoke of cars and buses, by the dug-up roads and broken footpaths, by the dirt, by the crowds; and could not accept the consolation offered by some people that in a country as poor as India the aesthetic side of things didn't matter.

My feelings went the other way. In richer countries, where people could create reasonably pleasant home surroundings for themselves, perhaps, after all, public squalor was bearable. In India, where most people lived in such poor conditions, the combination of private squalor and an encompassing squalor outside was quite stupefying. It would have given people not only a low idea of their needs – air, water, space for stretching out – but it must also have given people a low idea of their possibilities, as makers or doers. Some such low idea of human needs and possibilities would surely have been responsible for the general shoddiness of Indian industrial goods, the ugliness and unsuitability of so much of post-independence architecture, the smoking buses and cars, the chemically-tainted streets, the smoking factories.

'Everybody is *suffering* here,' a famous actor said at dinner one evening. And that simple word, corroborating what Ashok had said, was like an illumination.

For years and years, and even during the time of my first visit in 1962, it had been said that Calcutta was dying, that its port was silting up, its antiquated industry declining. But Calcutta hadn't died. It hadn't done much, but it had gone on; and it had begun to appear that the prophecy had been excessive. Now it occurred to me that perhaps this was what happened when cities died. They didn't die with a bang; they didn't die only when they were abandoned. Perhaps they died like this: when everybody was suffering, when transport was so hard that working people gave up jobs they needed because they feared the suffering of the travel; when no one had clean water or air; and no one could go walking. Perhaps cities died when they lost the amenities that cities provided, the visual excitement, the heightened sense of human possibility, and became simply places where there were too many people, and people suffered.

Calcutta had had a left-wing or Marxist government for years, and I was told that the money nowadays was going to the countryside, that the misery of Calcutta was part of a more humane

Marxist plan. But things are often as they appear, and it is possible that this is one of the ways cities die: when governments are dogmatic or foolish, killing where they cannot create, when people and governments conspire to frighten away the money and the life they need, when, in a further inversion, the poetry of revolution becomes its own intoxication, and Marxism becomes the opiate of the idle people.

Perhaps when a city dies the ghost of its old economic life lingers on. So, in Calcutta, old firms with famous names are taken over and their assets are broken up; and people invest in real estate, since people always have to live somewhere; and there is an illusion of an economic life. Every few days, in a further illusion of activity, there is a political demonstration; and idle young men, morose and virtuous-looking, take their red flags and slogans through the self-perpetuating misery of the streets; and money and ambition and creativity go elsewhere in India. Without the rest of India to take the strain, the death of Calcutta might show more clearly, and Bengal might show as another Bangladesh – too many people, too little sanitation, too little power.

At the back of the hotel was a market: I looked down on its low, spreading roof. Buzzards perched on the ledges of the hotel, waiting. The ledges were black with an accumulation of blown dust and the grit of brown traffic smoke. The style of the British-built red-brick building opposite the market – the formality, the symmetry, the elegance, the thought, the confidence, the reference to classical ornament – was now oddly at variance with the life of the street, and seemed to come from a dead age.

The sticky-looking asphalt of the cambered street lay between wide, irregular drifts of dust that had hardened to earth in the gutters at the side; the streets would be washed now only by the monsoon. The once paved footpath outside the market had crumbled and in places merged with the earth in the gutters. People went about minute tasks. Men pulled rickshaws. In 1962 this had been offensive to see, but it was said that the poor needed employment. Twenty-seven years on, the rickshaws were still there. The same thing was said about employment for the poor; but the Calcuttans, with their low ideas of human needs and possibilities, appeared genuinely to enjoy the man-pulled rickshaw as a form of transport; and many of the rickshaws looked nice and new, not like things on the way out. Minute tasks: one man walked by carrying a single, limber, dancing sheet of plywood on his head. Other people went about perfectly seriously carrying tiny loads on their heads, no doubt for very small fees.

On important days big circular baskets of trussed white chickens appeared outside the market, and one or two men seemed idly engaged for some minutes throwing trussed chickens from one basket to another. Then one noticed that the basket from which the chickens were being thrown was full of movement, and the basket into which the chickens were being thrown was still. And then one saw that the gesture of chicken-throwing also contained another, the wringing of the chicken's neck: two jobs combined in a single, fluent, circular gesture.

One man might then be seen taking away his own little load of dead white chickens: the chickens artistically arranged into a big feathery ball hung on the handle of his old bicycle, the feathers of the stiff dead chickens hanging down the other way and showing brown-yellow rather than white, with the stiff brown claws and legs like spokes in the feathery ball, like sticks in candyfloss. The man had trouble arranging the load on his bicycle. When he first tried to get on the bicycle and ride away, the chickens got in the way of his knees.

At the end of the day a little green pick-up truck came, and the wide circular baskets, empty now, were stacked in the truck in two piles. When the truck went away, there remained – in this city where rubbish was seldom cleared – only a few scattered white feathers in the dust of the broken and silted-up street.

The British were in Calcutta for a long time. It might be said that the Anglo-Bengali culture – out of which modern India grew – is as old as the United States. Raja Ram Mohun Roy, the first exponent of that culture, was born in 1772, four years before the Declaration of Independence. From Raja Ram Mohun Roy there is a direct line to Rabindranath Tagore, whom Chidananda Das Gupta saw in 1940 when he first went to Tagore's university at Shantiniketan.

On that visit Chidananda heard Tagore, nearly eighty, deliver a talk in the Shantiniketan temple on 'Crisis in Civilization'. In that talk – a famous talk, published a few months after Chidananda heard it – Tagore said he had always believed that 'the springs of civilization' would come out of 'the heart of Europe'. Now, with the war and the coming cataclysm, he could no longer have that faith. But he couldn't lose faith in man; that would be a sin. He lived now in the hope that the dawn would come from the East, 'where the sun rises', and that the saviour would be born 'in our midst, in this poverty-shamed hovel which is India'.

It was an old man's melancholy farewell to the world. Five years later the war was over. Europe began to heal; in the second half of the century Europe and the West were to be stronger and more creative and more influential than they had ever been. The calamity Tagore hadn't foreseen was the calamity that was to come to Calcutta.

In 1946 there were the Hindu-Muslim massacres. They marked the beginning of the end for the city. The next year India was independent, but partitioned. Bengal was divided. A large Hindu refugee population came and camped in Calcutta; and Calcutta, without a hundredth part of the resilience of Europe, never really recovered. Certain important things were in the future – the cinema of Satyajit Ray, especially – but the great days of the city, all its intellectual life, were over. And it could appear that the British-built city – its grandeur still ghostly at night – began to die when the British went away.

6

The End of the Line

One of Satyajit Ray's few films to be set outside Bengal is *The Chess Players*. It is an historical film about the annexation of the kingdom of Oude by the British in the 1850s. Oude was one of the provinces of the Mogul Empire; in the mid-18th century it became one of the successor states of that empire. The city of Lucknow was the capital of Oude, and it was the setting of the Ray film: a work of subtlety, looking at the events of the 1850s as they might have seemed to people at the time. The film was more than a comment on 19th-century British imperialism. It also considered – with understanding and melancholy and humour – the decadence or blindness or helplessness of a 19th-century Indian Muslim culture at the end of its possibilities: where the rulers play chess and conduct petty affairs, while their territory (and its people) pass into foreign rule.

The British annexation of Oude was one of the things that led to the Indian Mutiny of 1857. In colonial times, and for a period afterwards, this was called by some the First War of Indian Independence. But this was a 20th-century view, 20th-century language, and a kind of mimicry, seeking to give to old India something of the socialist dynamism the Russians found in their own history. The Mutiny was the last flare-up of Muslim energy in India until the agitation, 80 years or so later, for a separate Muslim state of Pakistan.

Lucknow was the end of the line for Muslim India. The city is the capital of the state of Uttar Pradesh, which is the largest state in the Indian Union. In its historical heart it is like a graveyard from the days of the Nawabs of Oude, full of the ruins of war. The city was shelled and fought over during the Mutiny; afterwards the

British preserved the ruins as a memorial, and passed them on to independent India.

The hunting lodge of the Nawabs, *Dilkusha*, 'Heart's Delight', is roofless. Much of its plaster has gone, revealing the layers of thin bricks that make up the mass of the walls. It was a local way of building; but the style of the – palatial – lodge, with what remains of the stables, is of European inspiration: the Nawabs of Oude employed Europeans in many capacities. Even in ruin, the hunting lodge remains wonderfully suited to the climate. To stand in the shade of its thick walls, even on a bright and warm day, is to feel cool and relaxed. The climate – that elsewhere in Lucknow, amid the concrete and glass, seems altogether unfriendly – here, a short distance away, becomes quite benign, almost a perfect climate. So, almost certainly, it would have appeared to the designers of the lodge. Among these shattered old walls, one can even think of the Lucknow climate as part of the luxuriousness of the days of the Nawabs.

A more extensive ruin, in a similar kind of style, is the Residency. The British Resident, originally an ambassador or agent, became in time the effective ruler of Oude; and the Residency was built by the Nawabs, over some decades, for this powerful figure. It was a settlement, a little town, not simply a building on its own. It was where, at the beginning of the Mutiny, the British people of the area were gathered together, with Indian servants and Indian soldiers loyal to their cause (or fearful of the mutineers' cause). There were 3000 people in all in the Residency, and they were besieged for three months by the mutineers. When the siege was lifted, 2000 of the 3000 had died. The British among them had been buried in a corner of the Residency; later, fine tombstones were put up in their memory in that corner.

And just as the ruins of the Nawab's hunting lodge were left as a reminder of the end of the power of the Nawabs of Oude, so the damaged buildings of the besieged Residency were preserved as a monument of British courage. The hunting lodge – blown up after victory by the relieving British forces (mainly Scots and Sikhs) – was the more complete ruin. The buildings of the Residency carried very many little dints caused by rifle bullets, with occasional larger excisions caused by non-explosive cannonballs. Perhaps the siege had failed because the mutineers didn't have the weapons for it. Both the hunting lodge and the buildings of the residency showed, below plaster, the flat thin Lucknow bricks that made up their mass.

The Residency was one of the famous monuments of the British Raj. Now, after the withdrawal from India, and the wars of this century, there is hardly room for it in the British memory. But it remains important in Indian history. Independent India inherited the monument, and has kept it up. The Residency is now a public garden, with trees and flowers and paths between the shot-up, weathered buildings.

Rashid, who came of an old Lucknow Muslim family, walked with me in the Residency on my last day in Lucknow. He had in the beginning been neutral, talking of history, pleased to show the famous sights of the famous city, and pleased, too, to show that in Lucknow (unlike other Indian cities) there were still places to go walking in. But in the museum building, with its trays of pathetic mutineers' cannonballs, and other carefully tended imperial relics, its tarnished photographs and engravings with faded captions, Rashid's mood changed. His Muslim sentiments flared up; he became quite agitated at the events of 130 years before, full of rage about the powers of the British Resident and the humiliations of the Nawab, full of rage and grief at the siege that had failed, the chance of Muslim victory which, though so near, had not come. He said, 'Bastards! Bastards!' And he was referring not to the besiegers but the besieged, whose heroism and general predicament, lucky escapes and cruel deaths, were the subject of the museum display.

Not far away, and visible from the ruins of the Residency, was a white marble pillar with a twist at the top, to symbolize the flame of freedom. Independent India had put that monument up, to counter the British Raj's monument to itself. It was a feeble thing, the equivalent in marble of Rashid's rage. Its symbolism was quite crude beside the real, bullet-marked buildings of the Residency, and it was historically invalid: the Indian independence movement didn't grow out of the Mutiny.

No monument of independent India could have solaced Rashid, because, in Rashid's view, independence – 90 years after the Residency siege – had come as another kind of Muslim defeat. Independence had come with the partition of the subcontinent into India and the two wings of Pakistan, so that the Muslims of undivided India had found themselves, as Rashid said, under three roofs.

Many of the middle-class Muslims of Lucknow had migrated to West Pakistan. The Muslim culture for which Lucknow had been known – the language, the manners, the music, the food – had disappeared. Where once Muslims had ruled, there now remained, after what could be seen as 300 years of a steady Muslim decline, the cramped, shut-in, stultifying life of the Muslim ghetto of the old town. There were other Muslims still, middle-class people like Rashid, and upper-class people as well, people sometimes of princely antecedents. But the predominant feature of Muslim Lucknow was that life of the ghetto, where people were ill-equipped and vulnerable, withdrawn and highly-strung.

Lucknow still had something of its old Muslim legend and aura when I went there for the first time, in 1962. Certain frivolities still seemed to speak of the past. People flew kites; special toys were made; special perfumes (including a clay perfume, meant to give the monsoon scent of rain falling on parched earth) were made with a medium of sandalwood oil, so as not to offend the Muslim religious law. Though there were no longer any singing girls, the intricately worked screens on the upper floors of buildings in the *chowk* or bazaar area seemed to speak (like a 19th-century oil portrait of a Nawab, baring one plump breast) of old Lucknow indulgences.

There was no legend now. The upper-class Muslim community, which had been at the centre of the legend, had shrunk; while the general population of the city had doubled or trebled. Shabby, post-independence concrete had spread everywhere; certain thoroughfares had become hellish. The city of the Nawabs had become an administrative city, Rashid said, a district city: an Indian mofussil town.

The hotel, part of the new concrete city, was like a parody of a five-star hotel. It had its 'logo'. It had various cards in the rooms, offering this and that, listing services and asking for comments. It had its door-knob breakfast menus, very difficult to fill in rationally. It had it all. All the best hotel forms had been borrowed; only the services were missing. The 'Do Not Disturb' light didn't function. The red telephone was more or less a dummy, sometimes releasing a faint, seemingly cavern-lost voice, hardly decipherable. The towels, perhaps because of some violent bleach, had turned a pale fluorescent blue, with a thin but thorny nap. The lampshade was broken; the lights were dim and strained one's eyes. A full half of the wall that faced west was of glass. Even now, and it was still only spring, it became quite oppressive in the afternoons, and it was necessary to use the weak-metalled window catch (weak-metalled: the catch seemed ready to bend between one's thumb and finger) to open the window, to let in a lot more hot air, together with the full roar of the traffic and the horns and the hooters.

But, miraculously, out of that window, there was a view that took one back to the past, gave one the illusion of looking at the original of one of the large views done by Thomas and William Daniell in late 18th-century India, and later published in London as aquatints. The view was of the River Gumti – or its lower channel, full, placid, not wide – between its tawny and dusty-green banks.

The Daniells' views were often taken with the help of the camera oscura, and they can suggest immense distances; close to, an Indian aquatint of the Daniells' is full of literal detail, full of human figures, some very small. There was that kind of distance, that kind of minute busyness, to this view of the River Gumti from the hotel room.

Along the top of the bank to the right there was a path, and figures were walking on it down all its length, small, separate figures, the colours of their clothes not easy to catch at this distance. Trees at the back of this path concealed the residential streets on that side of the river bank. More in the foreground, above the full lower channel of the river, but well below the path on the right bank where people walked, there was a wide, irregular, tree-less shelf. Far to to the left, black water buffaloes, small, moving black specks, gave a touch of the African or American wilderness to this river shelf. To the right, and closer, washermen in the mornings spread out their washed sheets and clothes to dry. In the middle of the shelf, at the edge of the flowing river channel, were widely spaced huts, with distempered walls, pink or white, some with advertising copy in Hindi: single-roomed huts with sloping roofs, reflected in the smooth water. These huts belonged to swimming clubs. At the weekends boys swam in the river, keeping close to the bank and the huts.

On the left bank of the river, directly below the hotel, there were Hindu temples. Far away, on the same bank, were the minarets of old Lucknow, reminders of the mosques and *imambaras* in which in 1962 I had looked for the glory of old Lucknow. Below, hidden by trees, were the lanes of the chowk or bazaar, which in 1962 still had a touch of the *Thousand and One Nights*, but which now, Rashid said, showed the final tragedy of the Muslim city to someone who knew how to look.

I went looking with him one morning. It was so crowded and cramped and repetitive in the lanes, the visitor might have seen the area as the expression of a single culture; and he might have missed the distinctions that Rashid saw.

The shops or stalls, as in the usual Indian bazaar, were narrow little boxes, fully open to the road or lane, and set side by side, with hardly a gap between. The floors were a few feet above the lane. Gutters at the side received water and waste from the drains that ran between or under the stalls. This waste water didn't run off to some larger drain, Rashid said. It just stayed there, in the open gutter, and evaporated.

All the shops and stalls had metal shutters; every shop and attached house was built like a fortress, for the days of riot. From time to time, where there should have been a shop, there was a moraine of rubble, as though – out of age, fragility, or rot – the shop and the house with it had fallen inwards, a small demonstration of how the ground level of cities might rise, layer upon layer.

Had there always been a bazaar here? Was it possible to think of a time when this site was bare, a field? Rashid and I walked through a ceremonial gate, an archway, called after the great Mogul emperor Akbar. He ruled from 1556 to 1605. Perhaps the gate had been built in the late 16th century to mark a visit of the emperor's; so the outlines of the bazaar would have been then (in Shakespeare's time) what it was now. There were glimpses of a more recent past – 18th-century or 19th-century – in the small flat Lucknow bricks that could be seen below the broken plaster on some old buildings. The bricks were set in lines that echoed the lines of the structure – in arches, for instance, they were set in

356

concentric arcs – so that they looked like iron filings demonstrating the lines of magnetic force around a magnet.

The outer bazaar was mixed. The shopkeepers were Hindu; the artisans were Muslim. Both groups had their history and special traditions. The artisans did simple work. They beat thin ribbons of silver into very thin, half-crumbling silver leaf or silver foil. They made cheap shoes; they did a local kind of embroidery called *chikan*; they did bead embroidery. The shopkeepers, Hindus, were either merchant-caste people from Uttar Pradesh, or Punjabi *khatris* who had come to the area 200 or 300 years before and had stayed as moneylenders and traders.

One shop out of five was supplying goods for bigger shopkeepers in the same area: thread for chikan embroidery, gold and silver spangles for brocade work, wooden printing blocks for stamping designs on chikan work, the very wide ledgers used for the single-entry style of Indian book-keeping. Some shops sold kites: Lucknow still had that tradition of kite-flying. Some shops sold goldsmith's equipment; some sold fresh flowers, for Hindus to take to the temple. Generally, Rashid said, the shops in this outer bazaar sold basic, everyday items connected with traditional ways of living, Hindu and Muslim.

Very small boys sat cross-legged on the floor of their narrow stalls, at the front, above the gutters, and filed away at the needles which were used in the bigger establishments for doing brocade work. These needles looked like the plastic ink-refills of ballpoint pens; they were of that size, and they had a similar kind of point. They were sold for a rupee each: a boy had to prepare a lot of needles before he made anything like money.

There were many mosques, and some of them might have been built on the rubble of old stalls and houses: the mosque here was like a kind of folk art, over-ornamented, weak in design, painted with love. While Rashid and I walked there came, above the bazaar noise, the amplified, breaking voice of a mullah. There was such passion in that trained voice: he might have been reciting something from the Koran. In fact, Rashid said, the man with the loudspeaker was only saying: 'Give money for the mosque, and have a palace of gold in heaven.'

The simplest kind of faith: though the outer bazaar was mixed, not purely Muslim, the bazaar life was like an expression of the faith of the book and the mosque, and it was possible to feel that

357

everything here served the faith. The most glittering and spangled stalls were the Koran stalls. They were hung with feathery paper tassels of gold and silver. In the general drabness of bazaar goods, those tassels, which were for braiding girls' or women's hair, caught the eye. These Koran stalls not only sold the book; they also sold boxes to keep the book in; bookstands to place the book on while it was being read; incense sticks to go with the reading; and caps to wear while you read the book, since it was forbidden to read the book with your head uncovered. The reading caps were in bright orange, red, or green; there were also crocheted skullcaps.

The shops didn't open before 11, Rashid said. The reason was that, though they didn't live far from their work, the shopkeepers didn't go home for lunch. Once they went to their shops and sat on the floor, on sheets or sacking or carpets or durries, they were there for the whole working day. They were as much prisoners of the bazaar as the artisans who worked for them. The entrances to the shopkeeper's houses were in the narrow passageways off the main bazaar lane; the living conditions in those hidden spaces were not too different from what could be seen of working conditions in the lane.

There was a point in the bazaar when you crossed over from the mixed Hindu-Muslim area to the area that was purely Muslim. The cross-over point was clear enough to Rashid; it wasn't so clear to me. The crowds beyond that point were denser, Rashid said, and the people were smaller; they were undernourished and stunted. And I did see, when I had got my eye in (or thought I had), that many of the children in this part of the bazaar were thin and wizened, with staring eyes, and often had some kind of skin infection.

There were small private schools here and there, but generally the Muslim children of the bazaar were not educated in the modern way. Their parents didn't see how that kind of education could lead to anything for their children. They also felt, in a profound way, that that kind of education was for other people. Education and learning were, of course, good things; but for them as Muslims that good learning, pure and untainted, was to be had only in the Koranic school or the seminary. Nothing outside the faith was for the people of the faith, the people in these squashed passageways and shops. The smallness of the spaces added to the feeling of comfort and protection within, added to the sense of the corruptions without.

Many children – boys – went to the seminary (a big, new building) or the Koranic schools in the bazaar. But most were apprenticed by their parents to various simple bazaar trades when they were eight or seven or six or even five. And if some of the children serving in the stalls or working in the shops looked frightened, it was because, Rashid said, they knew they were going to be 'bashed up' by the shopkeeper to whom their parents had apprenticed them, or the overseers of their employers.

Rashid said, 'It's an unfed world. And what can be more cruel than an unfed stomach?'

And yet, in the purely Muslim area, where Rashid was teaching me to see only gloom, I thought there was a greater feeling of festival and shopping joy than in the drab, workaday stalls of the mixed outer bazaar. Watches were repaired here; kites were sold (kite-selling common to both Hindu and Muslim shops); photographs were framed; people sold kebabs; there were other cook shops; there were even firework stalls.

And always, licensed and provocative, hanging around the stalls, like a decayed reminder of Lucknow's past, were the transvestites and eunuchs of the ghetto, in women's clothes and with cheap jewelry, making lewd jokes and begging: the darkness of the sexual urge finding this ritual, semi-grotesque, safe public expression – in this lane where few women were to be seen, and those who were seen, thin, tiny figures, were clad in black from head to toe. These eunuchs and transvestites sold their bodies; they had a market.

'They are sexual objects,' Rashid said. 'Can you imagine?'

They sat on their haunches at the side of the lane, near the gutters, below the floors of the shops, these sacrificial women-men of Lucknow. Their faces, half male, half female, were worn and lined and crudely rouged; but they had men's teeth, big and blackened and spaced out.

Hammer sounds, muffled and competitive, came from stalls where boys or young men, four or five or six to a stall, sat or squatted and hammered thin ribbons of silver into very fine sheets of silver foil. This foil was placed on sweets or other delicacies, to suggest luxury; it had no other purpose. The silver ribbon was placed between goatskins and beaten with a mallet. About a dozen pieces of ribbon were beaten at the same time, the silver ribbon interleaved, one piece at a time, between the goatskins – I read later that intestines, being more pliable, were most suitable for this kind of work. It took two to three hours to hammer out a piece of ribbon into foil. A sheet of foil was sold for half a rupee or a rupee, according to its size. A young man's working day, therefore, might produce silver foil that could fetch from 18 to 36 rupees. Take away the cost of the silver, and the cost of the stall, and there wasn't much that a young man could earn in a day, from that incessant banging, companionable or competitive, in a small space. The silver foil hammered out in this way was fragile, shredding at the touch of a finger. Almost without purpose as a commodity, it was stored between the leaves of discarded books.

Rashid said, 'All the jobs here have this soul-destroying quality. They are doing it only because their fathers did it before them. They've probably never stepped out of the area. They listen to cassettes of film songs and religious songs, turned up loud, to distract themselves from the deadening labour, whether it's beating out silver foil or doing embroidery or brocade work. They drink a lot of tea in glasses. There is a reason for the tea-drinking. It kills the appetite. When they want to pee, they just go down and pee in the streets.

'It's so basic. The level of education is so low, and so are the needs and the skills. Apart from the transistor and the occasional electric fan, they could be living in another age. Their leisure life is like this. They hire a television set and three video cassettes for 100 rupees. A number of them club together to pay the 100 rupees. And they sit through the night, 40 or 50 of them, watching those three films. There are about 60 firms hiring out TVs and VCRs in this area, and they're all doing good business. There is a little exploitation here, too. Someone with spare cash books a TV for a certain slab of time in the evening – the man doing that will do it every day – and then he sells that time (and the TV) for a premium of 20 rupees or so.

'At the most the only education the children get is the Koran. The women are not educated. They inbreed a lot. First cousins get married. That explains some of the physical degeneracy. The boys marry young, at fifteen or sixteen or seventeen. At forty a man is a grandfather, and burnt out. They eat badly. Meat and bread and no vegetables. They have poor sanitation. Most of them never meet a Hindu or non-Muslim in their lives. The people who go to the

Gulf and make money stay in the ghetto when they come back. They build big houses there, to enjoy the regard of their fellows.

'Most of them are Shias. The highlight of their year is the Mohurram.' The period of mourning for Hussain, the son of Ali, the Shia hero. 'Elsewhere Mohurram runs for 12 days, or 40 days. Here in Lucknow it runs for two months and eight days. One of the Begums of Oude made a pledge once that if a certain wish of hers was fulfilled, Mohurram in the kingdom of Oude would last for two months and eight days. This Mohurram has given the Shias here a shared identity. For those days you cry, you beat your breast, you knife yourself, you moan. It helps them to bear their misery, and it gets them out of the house. This Mohurram has led to tensions with the Sunni majority. With this result: Lucknow has never had a Hindu-Muslim clash, only a Sunni-Shia clash.

'There are any number of mosques in the area, and the call to prayer on microphones and amplifiers comes regularly from all quarters. The words for the Sunni and the Shia are the same, but there is a slight difference in the timing. So you hear 10 calls a day instead of five.

'And then there is Ramadan for a month, when you fast during the day. In that month restaurants close during the day and stay open at night. That gives a real casbah effect.'

In a purely Muslim country people might have been less tense about the faith, and nerves might have been less raw. But here it was known that what lay outside the lanes and passageways of the chowk was outside the faith, and from this world outside there came threats and provocations.

Near the end of my time in Lucknow Rashid told me what the most worrying recent threats had been. There was the man from Bangalore who had petitioned the court to ban the Koran in all its languages and editions in India, on the ground that the Koran preached sedition. The petition was a form of provocation, and should not have been taken seriously. Instead, Rashid said, the judge, a woman, rather too legalistically agreed to consider the petition. This caused rioting. The petition was thrown out later by another judge, who ruled that the Koran, like the Bible, was 'a basic document', and couldn't be the subject of that kind of legal petition.

Then there was the affair of a mosque in the town of Ayodhya, 300 miles away, which the Hindus had turned into a temple. Ayodhya was important, even sacred, to Hindus. It was the birthplace of Lord Rama, the hero of the Ramayana; and there were Hindus who said that after their invasion the Muslims had built a mosque on the site of Rama's birthplace. With independence, Hindus wished to claim the site again. In 1949, Rashid said, the mosque was closed down, because of the danger of rioting. Then, four years or so ago, there had been a development. A Hindu petitioned the district judge for permission to pray there. The petition was allowed; the locks of the place were opened; Hindus took possession, and were still in possession. There had been riots; people had been killed; the bitter squabble was still going on.

The third threat had to do with Muslim personal law. A wealthy Muslim lawyer divorced his first wife and married again. He gave the first wife the lump sum stipulated in their Muslim marriage contract. The divorced wife then went to the Indian courts and asked for a monthly maintenance allowance as well from her husband (this was how Rashid told the story). After 20 years the case reached the Indian Supreme Court. The judge spoke of the deficiency in Muslim personal law, and granted maintenance to the divorced wife. There was an outcry from Muslims at this interference with their personal law, which was part of their faith; and the Indian government, responding to the protests, passed legislation that overturned the decision of the Supreme Court.

Parveen lived in an old-fashioned, spacious, enclosed Muslim house in the old quarter of Lucknow. The front room was the sitting room; the private rooms were at the back. Two years before, Parveen had decided to go into politics. There had been jealousy from other women, Muslim and non-Muslim; but Parveen had begun to make her mark politically, and a little time before she had led a delegation of Muslim women to the prime minister. There were photographs of this occasion on the ochre-coloured walls of Parveen's sitting room.

Parveen was a handsome woman of upright carriage. There were lawyers and landowners and high government officials in her background, and she had the confidence of her class, which had once been the ruling class here. She was a world away from the Muslims in the chowk or bazaar, and the small black-veiled figures who occasionally flitted about the lanes there. She wore no veil; she spoke forcefully and well; and yet there were in her unexpected moments of feminine reserve which reminded you that she came from a special culture, that this Muslim house with its areas of feminine seclusion represented an important part of her nature.

She wanted to go into 'secular' politics; and she meant that she wanted to go, as a Muslim woman, into the politics of the state. This ambition in no way diluted her religious faith. Certain aspects of the Muslim faith were 'the law', she said: they couldn't be discussed. Such an aspect was the aspect of women's rights.

Women enjoyed many rights under Islam. They didn't need to have their rights – which were in any case 'the law' – amended by the state. They enjoyed the right, for instance, of inheriting property from their parents; Hindu women had no such right. Whatever was given to a Muslim wife during marriage was hers to keep; that wasn't so with western women. When a marriage was arranged a man undertook to pay a woman a certain sum if he divorced her. That was enough; the idea of maintenance was repugnant to a Muslim woman. When a woman became a wife, it didn't mean that she had become a servant. After a divorce a husband became a stranger, and there was no question of a woman taking money from him afterwards. Other countries or communities could think of modifying the rights of people according to the needs of the time. But the Koran had laid down the law for Muslims for all time.

The words were strong, but Parveen spoke them easily, when – with Rashid to help with her English – she came to the hotel to talk of her political work. She was a defender of the faith. But the faith – complete, fully formulated – sat lightly on her. At her social level it was even part of her certainty and strength, and seemed to equip her for the public life she wanted to enter.

She had a talent for organizing. She was off that day to meet – informally – a young woman who had been suggested as a prospective bride for her brother. She would go to this far-off town; she would call on a friend. In the friend's house – and apparently quite by chance – there would be the young woman her brother wanted her to meet.

Life was going on for Parveen. She didn't have Rashid's dark vision. Rashid was a bachelor. He was a reader, a solitary. He brooded; his mood changed easily. He loved his apartment; he loved retreating to it.

As for the Muslims of the chowk or bazaar – of course, Parveen said, they were trapped in their ignorance, and it was hard to get through to them. But though people spoke of this ignorance and constriction as a specifically Muslim problem, many other groups in India were in a similar position – people in the rural areas, the scheduled castes.

Perhaps it was that comparison that depressed Rashid. Muslims had once ruled here, set the tone. Now they had been depleted by the middle-class migration to Pakistan; and, in spite of the esteem in which individuals were held, as a group they ranked low.

Rashid was of an old Shia Muslim family. An ancestor in the mid-18th century had been a trader, with seven ships plying out of Bombay. Perhaps they hadn't really been ships, Rashid said; perhaps they had been only dhows. But that ancestor had done well. He had even built an *imambara*, a replica of one of the Shia mausoleums erected in Iran and Iraq for descendants of the Prophet. It was the practice in those days for a Shia who had done well to put up an imambara, as a place where religious discourses might take place.

In the 19th century an ancestor had served at the court of the last Nawab of Oude. When this ruler was exiled to Calcutta by the British, Rashid's ancestor had gone with him, and this ancestor had lived in Calcutta until his death in the 1880s. Rashid's mother's father was an administrator in one of the bigger princely states. He looked after everyone in his family; he wrote poetry; and he dressed like an Edwardian gentleman. Rashid thought – going only by photographs – that this grandfather looked a little like Bertrand Russell.

Rashid's father's father was the first one in his family to learn English. He worked in the railways, in what was then the new railway station of Lucknow – and it is still one of the more impressive buildings of Lucknow. Rashid's father, when he was of age, thought he would go into the police service. At that time upper-class Muslims, landowners, went into the professions; they did law and medicine. People like Rashid's father went into the police service or the administration. Rashid thought that his father was a handsome man. He was five feet eight, which made him an inch or two taller than Rashid. He was slightly marked by smallpox; but at that time nearly everybody had pock-marks.

In those days, if you were someone like Rashid's father, it was easy to join the police service. Somebody took you to the English officer and offered you for the service. The officer would say, 'Send him from the day after.' This happened to Rashid's father. He joined the force as an assistant superintendent; this was the starting officer-rank. But he lasted only three days. He didn't like the drills, and he couldn't bear the abusive language of the instructors. He couldn't see it as just part of the game, part of the toughening-up process; he wanted to get out right away.

He decided after that to go into business. He and his brother opened a shop in Lucknow that sold cameras and photographic equipment. This was in 1911, the year of the coronation of the King-Emperor George V: the high-water mark of the British Empire, and the British Indian Raj. The camera shop that Rashid's father started in that year did well in imperial India. It suited the place; it developed with photography itself, and became one of the best shops of its kind. Branches were opened in other Indian cities, mainly the hill resorts, where people went for their summer holidays. The Lucknow shop was in the main shopping street called Hazratgunj. In those imperial days Hazratgunj – now crowded and a mess – was sprayed with water every evening by a municipal van.

The other shops in Hazratgunj were owned by Englishmen and Jews and Parsis. Rashid especially remembered the shop of a Jew called Landau. Landau had a very big corner shop, and he sold watches. The walk-way outside his shop was roofed or canopied by the floor above. There were wrought-iron pillars downstairs; the residence part of the building was upstairs, with a verandah with slender pillared arches, echoing the solider pillars below. Anderson Brothers were tailors; they closed after independence in 1947. Another tailor was MacGregor. He didn't leave in 1947; he stayed on in Lucknow and died there. MacGregor had Indian royalty and Englishmen among his customers, and men from the Indian Civil Service. 'You could tell that a coat had been made by "Mac",' Rashid said. 'People wore them 30 years on.'

Rashid, who was born in 1944, remembered his father's shop as having showcases in Burma teak. They had been made in Lucknow by Muslim artisans, working to his father's designs. The shop was like a club; outsiders and idlers were nervous of going in. 'Money wasn't the main thing. People came to meet my father and their other friends there.'

Rashid's family house was in old Lucknow. It had a separate section for the women. Guests couldn't go into the main house. They stayed in the drawing-room, which was right at the front of the house and had a separate entrance. The furniture in that drawing-room was in the English style, made in Lucknow: enormous pieces, very uncomfortable. At the back of the drawing-room were a few other rooms, and then there was the courtyard of the main house. In summer the family slept out in the courtyard. Water was first thrown on the courtyard to cool it. The servants then laid out the string beds in rows, and put up mosquito nets on bamboo poles. There was a stand for pitchers in which drinking water was kept, to cool for the next day. A big square table was in a corner of the courtyard; it was covered by a white cloth and had a coloured tablecloth in the centre. Food was put on that square table. Dinner was at nine, when Rashid's father came back from the shop.

Almost as soon as Rashid had got to know this ordered middle-class family life, the family fortunes began to change. When independence came in 1947, Rashid's father wanted to migrate to Pakistan. He had a nephew who was looking after the branch in the hill town of Mussoorie; he asked this nephew to take the stock from Mussoorie to the shop in Karachi, which was now in Pakistan. The nephew did so; but, in the chaos of those days, the nephew got the Karachi shop transferred to his own name.

'So my father was left high and dry. He gave up the idea of moving to Pakistan.'

'What happened to your cousin?'

'He lost his leg in a motorcycle accident. He mucked up the shop, and was reduced to bringing provisions for the school his wife ran. You might say that he was punished. But that brought no joy to us.'

Hindu and Sikh refugees from Pakistan began to come to Lucknow.

'They were strange to us. The people behind our house, though not very rich, were an educated Muslim family. In 1947 they went

366

to Pakistan. Their house was then assigned to a refugee family. One memory that stays in my mind was how the mother of the new family used to make their children defecate on pieces of paper and throw it over the common wall into our courtyard. We made a fuss, and they understood, and stopped. They probably came from the Punjab, although I don't know.

'Slowly you could see new signboards coming up in the town. The old shops belonged to Muslims. Now on the new boards you saw different names. Instead of the staid, English kind of shops you saw garish shops, brightly lit, with music. In Aminabad, old Lucknow, the Sindhis put up rows and rows of cloth shops. The first thing they started doing was shouting and asking you to come into their shops. "Come in, sister. Come and see." This was unheard-of among us. No glass cases there. Rickety little boxes. But a lot of those people who came then have now put up enormous shops full of chrome and glass.

'They were better businessmen than we were. They were better salesmen. They would sell smuggled goods – we never touched them. They would work on turnover rather than a decent margin. And our stocks began to get old and shop-soiled, and less in demand.'

In 1951 the *zamindari* system of land tenure was abolished. 'Land holdings were reduced. Hereditary rights were taken away from the major portion. The zamindari system had been established by the British in 1828. It replaced the Mogul *mansabdari* system, whereby land rights were given to people and they were required to supply a certain number of horses when required – in the mansabdari system your status depended on the number of horses you were assigned. So, in 1951, a lot of the zamindars or big landlords who had big houses in Lucknow – absentee landlords – had to adjust to changing times. A lot of them left for Pakistan. The abolition of zamindari removed our clientele in one fell swoop. All of a sudden the economy changed. And the English customers left. Our shop was "by appointment" to several governors of the province – it was that respected.

'Hazratgunj stopped being whitewashed. The roads were dirtier. You found a lot of pavement shops. It became impossible to walk on the footpaths. The whole atmosphere changed.'

With this calamity in business, there was a family tragedy. The family had a summer house in Mussoorie, and there one summer

Rashid's elder brother was drowned. Altogether, the years just before and after independence had brought blow after blow for Rashid's father: the very bad Hindu-Muslim riots in Calcutta in 1946, the partition in 1947 and the loss of the Karachi shop, the abolition of zamindari, and now the loss of the elder son.

It was harder for the old than the young. Rashid was at the famous Anglo-Indian school in Lucknow, La Martinière, and he was very happy there. La Martinière had been founded by an 18th-century French adventurer, Claude Martin, who, having come to India, had taken service with the Nawabs of Oude. He had an Indian wife or wives, and at his death he left part of his great fortune to set up schools for Eurasian children. A hundred and fifty years on, La Martinière at Lucknow still had a mixed, cosmopolitan atmosphere; and Rashid, during this time of family stress, was able to grow up with a certain amount of security, and almost in a kind of political innocence.

'We had boys from every community in the school, all from the same middle-class background. The families knew each other. I took my world for granted. It was there, the family was there, the extended family, the cousins. Religion was just part of life. It wasn't a burden. A lot of things helped there – the school, and the friends who came to call at my father's house: they were people of all religions. We were made to read the Koran with a succession of moulvis, but we never got beyond the first chapter.

'Our father never forced us to go to the mosque, and I personally have never been. It was my temperament: there was no death-of-God attitude in that. We would go to the *majlis*, at the imambara or at friends' houses, ostensibly to listen to religious discourses about the battle of Kerbala and the death of Hussain, the son of Ali. But, really, it was a social thing. This was the Shia side, as against the purely Islamic part, of our upbringing. The one thing my father was absolutely firm about was that on the 10th day of Mohurram we would go barefoot to Taalkatora-Karabala, a grave-yard with an imambara where Shias were buried. This was an opportunity to visit the family graves also.'

Inevitably, as he grew up, Rashid became aware of all that independence and partition meant.

'It was a foregone conclusion that my sister would marry a Pakistani boy, because Muslims in India weren't doing so well, and the Pakistanis themselves wanted to marry a girl from the old country. Muslims in India weren't doing well, because after partition there were no jobs for them, and a general lack of opportunity. There was the resentment of the majority community. It was but natural. First you fight to get a country, and then you refuse to go.

'It was also the survival of the fittest working. Every Muslim house split after partition. There wasn't a family that wasn't affected. Parents stayed back, sons went away. The ones who stayed back were not ready to face the jungle. A lot of them were landlords, and they lacked the competitive spirit. My brother did brilliantly in his studies, in India and then in the United States. When he came back to India he couldn't get a job for six months. He went to Pakistan and got a job right away.

'Then the language started changing. Children over here were learning Hindi, and Muslim parents did not teach their children Urdu. We literally murdered Urdu. There was no preservation, such as the Armenians did for their language or the Jews did for Hebrew. Next to the religion, the language was dearest to the Muslim heart, because that was the essence of his identity. Urdu was not far from Hindustani, the lingua franca of the elite of the north-west. But Hindustani started changing, started to be more Sanskritized, became Hindi.'

In 1971 Rashid's parents went to Pakistan for the wedding of the brother who had migrated a few years before. While they were there, the second Indo-Pakistan war, the war over Bangladesh, occurred. Rashid's father, now very old, died in Pakistan at that time; his mother stayed on with the married son.

'Another strand was broken in my relationships. Up to this time I had been apprenticed to my father's shop. But when he passed away in Pakistan – and since the business was collapsing anyway – I closed it down.'

The shop had been started 60 years before, in the year of the coronation of the King-Emperor George V; it was closed down in the year the state of Pakistan broke into two. The whole life of the shop – though Rashid didn't make the point – had been contained between those two historical moments.

Rashid began to drift. He went to England and did odd jobs there. He sold six-month accident insurance for two pounds and five pounds from door to door. He had to knock and say, 'Good morning, are you the proprietor? My name is Rashid, and I believe

369

this will interest you.' He hated the business of knocking on doors. One day – memories of Landau, the watch-seller, in the very big corner shop in Lucknow came to Rashid – a Jewish antique dealer from France opened to him, and told him, with some concern, that he wouldn't make it as an insurance salesman in London and he should go back to India. Rashid went to work in a pancake house. He worked in a Kentucky Fried Chicken shop. He learned to cut a chicken into nine equal pieces with an electric saw and to deep-fry the pieces for 11 minutes. He cut up 120 chickens a day.

He left England after two years. He went to Pakistan. He found they had no 'identity crisis' there; religion was not a man's distinguishing feature. But he didn't like the Pakistan money culture, the business aggressiveness of people who, when they had been in Lucknow, had been more easy-going. He didn't like the boasting about money and possessions; in Lucknow that simply wasn't done. He left, and went back to India, to Bombay, and worked for three years in an export company.

He was waiting for an inheritance. He was hoping to use that to go into the real estate business. But then he ran into a communal-minded official, and he began to find all kinds of obstructions thrown in his way. The litigation he had started then had gone on and on. He was near the end now, and the chances were that he was going to get what was his; but he had wasted many active years.

'I had never faced a communal problem before. Communal riots were something that happened to the lower classes. It's like the ethnic trouble you hear about in Pakistan. When I read or hear about it, I know that my brother won't be involved, that his house will be far away from the trouble. So, here, I mixed with my Hindu friends and never gave the matter a thought – until I had to face the wrath of a communal officer. That did shake me – that a man, just by the flick of his pen, could change my life so much.

'The Indo-Pakistan war of 1971 was a watershed not only in Muslim lives, but also in Hindu-Muslim relationships. The myth of Muslim superiority was all finished. Here was India playing a decisive role in the sub-continent. Every Muslim had a soft corner in his heart for Pakistan, and everyone was sad that the experiment had failed after less than 25 years. The dream had died. Then the Pakistani soldiers were prisoners of war for two years. That was a constant reminder.

'I would feel a change taking place in personal relationships. My Hindu friends started lecturing. "What are Muslims doing with themselves?" They started becoming reformist about the Muslim faith and what they saw as our archaic practices. "How long are you Muslims going to carry on like this? How long are you going to be so dependent on your mullahs, your *mohallas*?" The sad fact was that there was a lot of truth in what they said. I was hurt, but we had to take it.'

The main palace of the last Nawab of Oude, the Kaiserbagh Palace in Lucknow, was nearly all destroyed by the British during the Indian Mutiny of 1857. In 1867, when British power seemed secure again, unchallenged, the surviving wing of the Kaiserbagh was given to the Raja of Mahmudabad as a city residence.

Almost 70 years later, the descendant of the Raja became the treasurer of the Muslim League, and campaigned for the formation of a separate Muslim state of Pakistan. Pakistan came into being 10 years later. And then – as though he hadn't fully worked out the consequences of the creation of Pakistan: Lucknow was in India, and many hundreds of miles away from Pakistan – the Raja found that he had made himself a wanderer. It wasn't until 1957 that he commited himself to the state for which he had campaigned. In that year he became a Pakistani citizen; with the result that, during the Indo-Pakistan war of 1965, all the Raja's property in Lucknow, the palaces and land, were taken over by the Indian government as enemy property.

The family property was still alien (rather than enemy) property. But petitions had been made to the Indian government, and the Raja's son, Amir, now lived in the Kaiserbagh Palace that had been granted by the British to his ancestor 120 years before.

I had met Amir in Parveen's drawing-room. He was in Indian evening dress, the long coat, the tight trousers. He was a small man, delicate in visage, sturdy in body, and he had the manner of a prince. An English public school and some years at Cambridge had given him an English style. But when I next met him, in the library of his palace, he was to tell me that when he spoke another language, Urdu, say, and when he was with people – Muslims, Shias – who might have looked up to him as a prince and a defender of the faith, he was quite different. Recent history had given him many styles, many personalities; had imposed strains on him such as his ancestors hadn't known.

Amir was now in state politics, and for three years or so had been a member of the Legislative Assembly in the Congress interest. His father had belonged to the Muslim League, which in the 1930s and 1940s had been opposed to the Congress. But now in India the Congress was the party that best served the interest of Muslims; and, in a further twist, as a politician Amir used the title, Raja of Mahmudabad, to establish the link with his forebears, and to give 'a focus of identification' to the local Shia and Muslim community.

His father's association with Pakistan could have been politically damaging; but Amir said that the people of Mahmudabad, 80 per cent of whom were Hindu, had never shown him or his family any hostility. And Amir honoured his father's memory. His father was a deeply religious man, with streaks of mysticism. He hated his caste, Amir said.

'My father never wanted to be a ruler. He couldn't bring himself to be a raja. He was most uneasy about benefiting from it. He thought income earned from property was tainted, since it wasn't earned by the sweat of one's brow.'

That idea had come to Amir's father when he was a child. It was an idea he had got from his mother. She, Amir's father's mother, came from a family of poor Muslim scholars who considered learning to be superior to wealth.

'My father's father was a maharaja, a man of personality, but not a socialist. He married for a second time, and relations between him and my father became strained. This was no doubt when my father developed his attitude to his caste. One of the first things I heard from my father – which I later understood to be one of the teachings of Ali – was: "You will not find abundant wealth without finding by its side the rights of people that have been trampled." And: "No rich morsel is eaten without there being in it the hunger of those who have worked for it."'

I said that such statements applied to poor or feudal countries. They couldn't apply to all countries.

Amir said, 'People in England may not be able to understand the kind of destitution and misery that exists in India.'

Though Amir didn't say so directly, it might have been his father's religious nature that made him campaign for a separate

Islamic state of Pakistan – not merely a homeland for Muslims, but a religious state. Amir's father began wearing homespun when he was very young. When, in 1936, at the age of twenty-one, he joined the Muslim League, he gave up music, which he and the rest of the family had loved – Indian classical music, western classical, Iranian classical.

Amir was born in 1943. When he was two years old, his ears were pierced. It was the custom in Muslim countries for slaves' ears to be pierced; and the piercing of Amir's ears meant that he had been sold to the Imam: the child had been pledged to the service of the Shia faith. This service began soon. When India and Pakistan became independent in 1947, Amir, then aged four, started on a wandering life with his father and mother.

'After partition my father left India. He was a very committed man, but he wasn't a politician. Just before independence we were in Baluchistan, in Quetta, in what had become Pakistan. On the day of independence we crossed the border into Iran. We went to Zahedan, and from there we went in two buses to Mashhad, and then to Tehran. We went on to Iraq by air. The convoy followed by road. This was in 1948.'

Although they were now living this wandering life, Amir's father had transferred no money out of India. All he had taken with him were books and carpets.

'My father was invited to return to India on certain conditions – that he took no part in public life, that he condemned the Nizam of Hyderabad, and that he spoke out against cow-slaughter. These conditions were not acceptable to my father. He said he was willing to give an undertaking not to eat beef personally, but he couldn't speak out against cow-slaughter, because beef was the cheapest food for Muslims.'

They went, in Iraq, still with Indian passports, to Kerbala. This was the site of the battle where Hussain, son of Ali, had died; it was sacred ground to Shias. On this sacred ground there arose in Amir's father's mind – perhaps it had been there all along – some idea of having his son become an ayatollah, a Shia divine. In 1950 Amir, aged seven, was sent to a religious school in Kerbala. He stayed at the school for two years. And then his father – who had begun to earn a livelihood by importing tea and jute from India – changed his mind, and decided that Amir should have a secular education, after all. This didn't mean, Amir said, a turning away from the religious side of things. Ali himself had said, 'The best form of worship is reflection and thought, and there is no form of worship that is better than reflection, thought and knowledge.' Before Ali, the Prophet had said, 'Acquire knowledge if you have to go to China.'

I asked Amir, 'What did they mean by knowledge?'

He said, 'Ali was once asked, "What is knowledge?" He said, "Knowledge is of two kinds. One is the knowledge of religions." And that is interesting – the plural, *religions*, rather than religion. "The other is the knowledge of the physical world."'

The first idea was that Amir should be sent to a Jesuit school outside India. But then it was decided to send Amir and his mother back to Lucknow; and in Lucknow Amir, now in his 10th year, was enrolled at the Anglo-Indian school of La Martinière. This was when Amir – who had seemed so English in Parveen's drawing-room – began to speak English; until then his languages had been Urdu and Persian.

Culture upon culture now: because the boy who went to La Martinière felt, after his time in Iraq, that part of him was Arab or Iranian. After his classes at La Martinière there were special religious lessons at home every day, in the very room of the palace where we were now sitting – cool, with the solid brick-work of old Lucknow, with a terrazzo floor, and with bookshelves inset in the damp-marked, whitewashed walls.

The Muslim and Shia festivals were also constant reminders of the faith. Amir took 12 days off for Mohurram – 'The principal of La Martinière was most disapproving' – and a further four days for the 40th day after the martyrdom. At the end of Mohurram there were another eight days off, and there were four days more in Ramadan – the month of purification, and of the martyrdom of Ali, and of the beginning of the revelation of the Koran.

During his time at La Martinière Amir was living in the palace with his mother, his two aunts, and his father's brother and his wife. To protect him from untoward influences, he was not allowed to visit other boys or to become involved with their families. He had his own guardian, a childless man, who stayed in the palace day and night. This man – who also had a knowledge of Urdu and Persian which Amir found remarkable – followed Amir 'like a shadow', even when the boy went to the cinema or a restaurant. At

374

La Martinière he would wait in the car, or just outside it, sitting on a carpet on the ground, while Amir was at his classes.

'As a result of this I became a reticent person, extremely withdrawn. I had difficulty in talking. If there were outsiders, I found it impossible to open my mouth.

'I used to wear philacteries underneath my shirt, and boys at school would feel them and tease me. The other thing I used to wear were ear-rings, in my pierced ears. I used to wear an emerald in my right ear, and a ruby in the left. This looked very strange, and I would twist both my ears and hide the stones behind the ear lobe. I took these off – I was permitted to take them off – when I went to England, after the end of my schooling here.'

All this time the Raja, Amir's father, had been living in Iraq. But then in 1957, 10 years after the creation of Pakistan, he took the step which was to cause his family a good deal of hardship: the Raja went to Pakistan, and changed his Indian passport for a Pakistani one.

Amir said, 'My mother became very ill when she heard the news, right here. My mother is a rani in her own right, a woman of great pride. She never tried to take anything from my father. She was also religious. She lost both her parents when she was nine. She was ill when she heard the news about my father in Pakistan, because she felt that the great crises of 1947 had passed – not one voice had been raised in Mahmudabad against my father. Nehru met my father and asked him to think again, and to keep his Indian passport. Nehru said, "You've always acted impulsively. We all would be happy if you return and take your passport back." My father said, "One cannot change one's nationality like one's clothes."'

And Pakistan didn't work out for the Raja. He had had the idea of going into politics, but then he discovered that it wouldn't do for him. He was a Shia, in a country with a Sunni majority; he didn't have a local language in Pakistan; and he was a *mohajir*, a foreigner. His political ideas had also changed. In the 1930s and 1940s, when he was very young, he had wanted Pakistan to be a religious state. He thought now that it should be a secular state. He didn't believe that the Pakistan army would stand for that kind of politics. So he left Pakistan and began to travel again. He spent much time in the old imperial capital, London.

It might have seemed from this account that, in his young man's agitation for the creation of Pakistan, the Raja had been irresponsible; that he hadn't foreseen the political convulsions or worked out the human consequences; that other people had been asked to pay for his Muslim and Shia piety, while he himself had been keeping his options open for as long as possible. Iraq, Pakistan, England, India – these were all countries to which he might have gone, as a man of standing.

But people have their own ideas of their predicament. Of this wandering stage of his father's life Amir said, 'I think it was almost like a penance, you see. I feel it was necessary for him to undergo the same process of homelessness that other people had gone through when they left India and went to Pakistan.

'I used to visit him every year. One of the books he made me read was Pearey Lal's *Gandhi: the Last Phase*. He was greatly moved by the fact that at the time of independence Gandhi was nowhere to be seen. He wasn't in Delhi. He was in Calcutta, mourning and grieving for the tragedies of that city.' The tragedies of the religious riots of 1946, which marked the beginning of the end for the city of Calcutta. 'In the Shia way of feeling, if there is grief and mourning on one hand, and celebration on the other, the Shia tilts to the grief.'

After Amir had finished his schooling at La Martinière his parents didn't know what to do with him, and he lost some time. At last, in 1961, when he was eighteen, he was taken by his father to England and placed in a public school. That was when he was allowed to take off his ear-rings. On the way to England they stopped off in Lebanon, where the Raja had many friends; and later they did a tour of Europe. In Paris they went to a casino and a night-club: the Raja wanted his son to see what these places were like, and he wanted his son to see them first with his father as his companion.

At eighteen, Amir was somewhat old for a public school. But he spent three years there, until he got into Cambridge, to do mathematics.

'I wasn't treated too badly at school. I was still withdrawn. I was friendly with a few boys. I cherished my faith. For me it was a sort of armour. For me the fact that something is secret and personal and internalized gives it a new dimension and a strength. The fact that you can't perform or express it, what you feel, heightens the experience, the power of that.'

Amir was to enter Pembroke College, Cambridge, in 1965. Before that, he was taken by his father on a tour of Pakistan and the Middle East. They met Shia divines, and in Lebanon they stayed with Sayed Musa Sadr.

'I heard world affairs discussed between my father and him in language and idiom which later became part of the Iranian revolution and the uprising in Lebanon. They talked of the presence of the western powers in Lebanon, the kind of regime that existed in Iraq – oppressive, anti-religious. They talked about the Shah in Iran. They talked about the need for bringing about a revolution on the principles of Ali – which I thought most utopian, and said so to my father.'

After this Shia exaltation, this talk of revolution and the rule of Ali, there was calamity. So far, the Raja's political actions and gestures had been without great personal consequences. Now, overnight, everything changed. In September 1965, a few weeks before Amir went up to Pembroke College, Cambridge, there was war between India and Pakistan, and all the Raja of Mahmudabad's property in India was declared enemy property. Had the Raja foreseen that consequence when he became a Pakistani citizen in 1957 – or when, 30 years before, he had started to to agitate for a separate Muslim state?

Amir said, 'Our palace in Mahmudabad, the Qila, was totally sealed – the place where I had grown up, and my father and his forebears. None of my family was permitted to enter it. All the income was taken by the Government of India through the Custodian of Enemy Property. The Cambridge term was about to begin. I got letters from home, saying how the Armed Constabulary had come and surrounded the Qila and sealed every door. Although there was this terrible blow, my family *never* thought of moving to Pakistan.

'The Qila was sealed for a year and a half, during which time there were two big robberies. An enormous amount of very valuable things was taken away. During this period my uncle and my mother petitioned the government to permit them to observe Mohurram in the Qila – that had been our family tradition. Permission was eventually given, with the condition that they were confined to two rooms and one bathroom. They accepted the condition, and they went and lived in verandahs. The imambaras were open, though – that was where the Mohurram ceremonies actually took place.

'I was in Cambridge all this time. I was very distressed. My work suffered. A lot of people didn't know all the background. I talked to my tutor. I used to read the life of Ali, for consolation. And certain chapters and verses of the Koran.'

I asked what the verses of the Koran were.

Amir said, reconstructing a verse from memory, '"I give good tidings to those who are not weak but have been weakened." Let me get the actual verse. I know it very well. I will have no trouble finding it.'

He got up from the white-covered table at which we were sitting, went to the next room, and came back with a small blue-covered book. But he couldn't find the verse in that book. He went to shelves on the opposite wall, took down a bigger book, came and sat again at the table. While he looked in the book he said, 'This verse occurs again and again in the Irani revolution.' He sometimes said 'Irani' for 'Iranian'. At last he found the verse. He read it to himself first of all. I could see that he was moved. Then he read it aloud to me.

'"And we wished to be gracious to those who were being oppressed in the land, to make them leaders, and to establish a firm place for them in the land, and to show Pharoah and Haman and the hosts at their hands the very things against which they were taking precautions."' He paused, and said, 'This gives an understanding of the Shiites right from the time of Imam Ali onwards. The "oppressed" here doesn't mean someone inherently weak, but those who have been made weak by circumstances, and have latent in them the power of faith and action.

'I used to read this at Cambridge. It's a promise, you see, a promise of God's. This is actually about the children of Israel, but it has been used throughout the history of the Shiites as a promise of deliverance.'

Amir read further in his big book, read the fine print of notes, and said, 'It's one of the Meccan revelations. Before the flight to Medina. The Meccan revelations are noted for their poetry.'

I said, 'While the Prophet was still only a prophet?'

Amir said, 'That might suggest he stopped being a Prophet, and would be blasphemous.'

'Before he became a ruler? While he was still without temporal power?'

'That would be better.' He said again, 'The Meccan revelations are well known for their poetic quality.'

While Amir was trying in this way in Cambridge to reconcile himself to the loss of the family property, his father was in Pakistan again. But the next year the Raja came to England, to work at the Islamic Institute in Regent's Park; and he stayed there while Amir did his studies. It was now open to the Raja, as someone working in England, to become a British subject again. If he had done so, he would have ceased to be an 'enemy' or an 'alien', and the Indian government would have released his property in Lucknow and Mahmudabad. But the Raja preferred to carry the cross of his Pakistani citizenship, though it was still bringing hardship to his family.

Amir's academic work developed. After he had done his Cambridge degree, he went to Imperial College in London; and then he went back to Cambridge, to the Institute of Astronomy.

'Things quietened down. I reconciled myself to the situation at home, and resolved to undo some of the problems. But the problems remain. The Qila at Mahmudabad is open now. I use it and maintain it, but it is still not our property. Were it not for my mother's investments and so forth, it would be impossible to live there.'

In 1971 there was the Indo-Pakistan war over Bangladesh.

'It was a blow from which my father never recovered. He died two years later. He was very unhappy when he died – this unparalleled bloodshed by the Pakistan army in Bangladesh, and the materialistic crassness of Pakistan itself. He was very unhappy about the types of rulers and the classes that had come up.'

Amir took his father's body to the shrine of Mashhad in eastern Iran. The Raja had hoped, when Amir was a child, that Amir might have become a famous ayatollah, in the Iranian tradition. This hadn't happened; but Amir was greatly moved by the journey to Mashhad with his father's body.

'Some of the ulema, the religious teachers who had known my father, made the announcement that the body of an *alim*, a Shia divine, a servant of the faith, had come from London. And my father was buried just outside the shrine, in a cemetery where many eminent theologians had been buried. The burial was intended to be temporary – the final burial was to be in Kerbala in Iraq. In 1976 I heard from the Iranians that the Shah had given orders for the cemetery to be turned into a park, and that there was a danger that my father's grave might have been obliterated. But when I went to Mashhad I found that, owing to the intervention of Mr Bhutto' – the prime minister of Pakistan: the Raja had died a Pakistan citizen – 'my father's body had been reburied within the inner shrine.'

So in death the devout Raja had found a kind of fulfilment. His political and religious passion had bequeathed many languages, many cultures, many modes of thought and emotion to his son. He had had his son's ears pierced, to pledge him to the service of the faith; and Amir had indeed inherited something of his father's passion. But with that – his academic work in Cambridge and London had been in astronomy – Amir had also developed religious doubts.

'These doubts began at school and continued at university, and at periods became intense. But the totality of my experience – which is of an historical or cultural nature – is so deep and ingrained in my being that it's now indelible. It's a sort of dialectical process, in which religion, and the concerns of the real world, unfold for me a path in a dialectical manner. I veer towards religion to seek support in worldly matters. And that brings me back to doubts, and then back again to religion. I move back and forth between both worlds.'

(He had arrived, it seemed, at the Hindu idea of opposites: the worldly life, the life of the spirit: *loukika*, *vaidhika*. But that idea didn't interest him.) At Cambridge he had been attracted by some aspects of Marxism. He was especially attracted by the Marxist attempt to analyse history scientifically. But it was his Shia faith that made him receptive to the larger Marxist idea.

'There are a great number of elements and contradictions in my way of thinking. The aspect of Marxism which drew me was its concern with bringing about a just and more equitable society, especially for the oppressed, the insulted and the injured. My instinct was to go to Trotsky and Che Guevara, neither of whom succeeded, though their message lived. Kerbala, you see.' Kerbala, where Hussain, son of Ali, had perished. 'So the world picture given me by Marxism ran into my own religious picture.'

It was this mixture of historical and religious ideas that reconciled him to the long Muslim decline here in Lucknow.

'I find solace in both ways of thinking. The historical way shows me that human destiny is above this – our sufferings, our little problems. This idea of human destiny shows me that we are really moving towards a better world, in spite of all the trouble and conflagration. The religious way teaches me endurance, reconciliation with the divine plan of which this is a part, but with hope and belief in a better future. The Koranic verse I read out to you has been the sustenance of so many peoples throughout the world.

'I felt in my own case it was a great help I was a Shia, because from childhood I was acquainted with people who had fought for ideals and had been vanquished, ostensibly by earthly power, and yet had left such a profound imprint on history. I feel proud that most of my ancestors didn't care about material success so much as about what they believed in. I am very proud of my father's life.' His father admired Gandhi. 'The fact that his possessions were spectacles, sandals, a staff, a few changes of clothes, and books, brought him nearer to the ideal of the Shia ruler, as Ali was. The link between my father and Gandhi was that he realized that religion could be used to bring about a great change of consciousness – about the world and the place of men in it – and also to bring men to action.'

I asked him what the Kaiserbagh Palace meant to him.

'One has a kind of bond with it – all the changes, all the things that have happened, all the forebears. It's almost as if it, the house, is an organic, living thing.'

The wing in which he lived was 400 feet long by 100 feet wide, and it was on two floors. The whole wing was occupied. I asked about the number of servants.

He said, 'Goodness, I haven't counted. Certainly three figures for the retainers and their families. In my mother's kitchen upstairs meals are cooked *every day* for about 40 people, on an average. A great expense. At times I wonder whether it's worth it. But I know I can't leave it. I have a pied-à-terre in London, in Hampstead. That's a refuge. No servants.'

He had returned from the Astronomy Institute in 1978, and had been living in Lucknow more or less permanently since that time. Then, three years ago, he had gone into state politics. After the 1985 elections, he had written to Rajiv Gandhi, reminding him of the links between their two families, and offering to serve. It was suggested to him that he should contest a seat in the state elections. He didn't think he would get the nomination; he thought that there might have been hostility towards him because of his father's past. But he did get the nomination; the hostility he did attract was that of the man he had displaced.

'He grew up here in the palace. His family served our family for three generations. I knew him very well. It's like a film, like something in a novel. Before the elections, he used to come here every day. He's now doing everything he can to finish me off in every way. He's immensely rich now.'

Amir was smiling.

I said, 'You appear to be managing.'

He laughed. 'After all the things we've ben talking about – to come down to *this*!' *This*: the rage of a political rival.

We had been talking for a long time, sitting at a big table covered with a white tablecloth. Behind him were inset bookshelves, part of his library. From time to time during the day Amir's very young son, Ali, had appeared, and idly gone in and out of various doors. We had had lunch, sandwiches and fried fish, not from the kitchen upstairs, but from the Kwality restaurant in Lucknow. (I heard this later from Rashid. He knew the palace servants, and he had seen them at Kwality's when they had gone to get the take-away lunch.)

It was cool in the library-sitting-room of the palace. Wajid Ali Shah, the last Nawab of Oude, had planned the palace on Versailles lines, it was said; but perhaps what was meant by that was only that he had planned to build a lot. The walls were thick; they were made of the thin Lucknow brick and the special mortar of lime and ground-stone. The temperature was so benign that I had stopped thinking about it. But warmth and dazzle were outside all the time, and they made themselves felt as soon as we were out of the library, and in the dust of the drive.

Outside, too, were some of the palace servants Amir had spoken about, thin men standing up and, whether noticed or not, making constant gestures of obeisance and keeping their eyes fixed on their master: men quite unlike the waiters of restaurants or the staff of hotels, or even the staff of the main Lucknow club: men made by the security and idleness and antique etiquette of palace life.

We were going to the Legislative Assembly. Amir wanted to show it to me. But we were delayed for a while. A car came down the drive. It held a constituent. He jumped out of his car; Amir got out of his. The two men shook hands, and Amir told his constituent that he would be back in half an hour or 40 minutes.

He said he saw about 20 people a day. At any rate, 20 people came to see him. It was the side of political life he didn't care for. The people who came to see him often had impossible requests, about jobs or their dismissal from jobs, or about the fixing of tribunals of inquiry. They sometimes even wanted Amir, as their elected representative, to bribe people on their behalf. Amir wasn't like Prakash, the minister, in Bangalore. Amir wasn't amused, as Prakash was, by this aspect of the human comedy; he didn't enjoy the theatre of the morning crowd of suppliants and downright beggars at his door. Amir didn't like being badgered. He had discovered, he said, that people were never grateful for what you did for them; they always felt you could have done more.

The legislature was not in session. We looked at the chamber through the glass door. The formality and ritual of the chamber appealed to Amir. But he was enervated by the pettiness of much of political life. The vendetta of the man he had displaced, however much he appeared to laugh at it, was emotionally draining, an entanglement and irritation he could have done without.

'Politics costs a lot of money, and I feel guilty squandering – if the word can be used – money on politics. I have doubts about continuing.' But to someone of his ancestry there was a special appeal in public life. 'My political life has renewed and revived the link between my family and the people of Mahmudabad which had atrophied since 1936. That was the year my father became a member of the Working Committee of the Muslim League.' And his election victory from Mahmudabad wasn't something he could easily turn his back on. 'It was a moving experience, because the people of Mahmudabad – 80 per cent Hindu – voted overwhelmingly in my favour, in spite of my father's politics. It was an unprecedented majority in the district of Lucknow. My mother was very touched. She said – on election night in the Qila – that she hadn't seen the Qila filled with so many people since her childhood.'

The Hindu spring festival of Holi, which had emptied the Legislative Assembly, had also emptied the school of La Martinière. The buildings were famous: a late 18th-century French or European extravagance in far-off India. The grounds were immense; and, as so often in such settings, one thought with something like envy of the man who, 200 years or so ago, had had the foresight or the luck to buy so much land. The school was important to people who had grown up in Lucknow. It figured in the memories of Rashid and his friends. It figured in the memories of Amir, and in a printed memoir by his father.

It was still a private school; the money available was not enough to keep it absolutely in repair. To approach the school from dusty scrub at the back, to see the weeds sprouting out of the masonry, taking root on ledges, was like seeing something about to become a ruin. It was in better order at the front, more impressive. There were well-watered green gardens there, full of colour.

On this quiet day, with the great expanse of the sunstruck grounds, and their burnt colour, it was again – as with the view of the Gumti River from the hotel window – like being in the original of one of the late 18th-century prints of the Daniells. The Daniells would have been of the period of the self-styled General Martin, would have been of that period when a European soldier of fortune could have sold some of the skills of Europe to an Asian ruler for vast sums.

Some such thought must have been going through Rashid's head as well. His memories of La Martinière had been entirely happy; and an old boy's school pride had made him bring me here. Yet the sight of the Oude cannon cast by the general, still with the general's name in big raised letters, polished to a shine by the innumerable hands that had caressed them – the sight of that on the wide terrace at the front of the school had stirred up old ideas of Muslim and Indian helplessness and defeat; and, quite unexpectedly, Rashid had begun to be enraged by the thought of European and American experts of today, the successors of General Martin, travelling regally about the poorer countries.

He was overcome by his mood. He stayed in the shade in the pillared front loggia, and sent me out into the sun to look at the names of old boys carved on the wide stone steps at the front of the terrace.

Some other idea of loss was working on him, something to add to all that been lost since the 18th century.

He said later, 'All the masters here used to be Anglo-Indians,

384

except for the Hindi master. They were very respected. Their families have now gone to Australia. Their families had been in Lucknow for generations. The Anglo-Indians had been mostly in the railways, teaching, and the police. The railways were absolutely their show. And their colonies, the areas where they lived, were outside the city – lovely, clean places. After 1947 they packed their bags and left.'

Something of that melancholy attached also to Hazratgunj, the main shopping street of Lucknow in the old days, where Rashid's family had had their camera shop, and where Landau the watchmaker had had his big corner shop. Landau's corner was now Ramlal and Sons, a cloth and sari shop, with the slogan, 'Our Collection is Your Selection'. Not far away was the house where MacGregor, the old Hazratgunj tailor, who had made clothes for princes and IAS men and Raj Englishmen, had lived until his death.

The melancholy of the recent past, there. Elsewhere, the memories of the defeats of 130 years before, in the ruins of the Residency and of the Nawab's palace and hunting lodge. Before that, and just as painful now, the reminder of the glory of the older Nawabs: especially in the monument known as the Great Imambara, built as famine relief work in the late 18th century: over-decorated, weak, but impressive by its sheer scale. No great architecture in the old princely city, but many parks, many places to walk in: not many cities in India had this kind of style. But these walks saddened Rashid, as they were saddening him that afternoon, bringing out the tragic Shia side of his nature, the side that dealt in defeat, grief, and injustice.

He said, 'Lucknow is me. It's not the river or the buildings or anything. You don't like your father because he's six feet two inches, and handsome. He's your father. In this way, Lucknow is me. We've been here for generations, on both sides.'

What did it mean, being a Lucknow Muslim?

'It's like the Buddhist idea of "Not this, not this". I'm an Indian, but the temple is not for me. I'm a Muslim, but in its details my faith cannot be the same faith as the one in Afghanistan or Iran or Pakistan. I speak Urdu. I greet people in the Lucknow Muslim way. I say "My respects to you" instead of "Peace be upon you". I derive my sustenance from Lucknow. It gives me my sense of identity – the buildings, the monuments, the culture, the relationships.'

There was a new white palace that could seen above the greenery from many places in the city. It was called the Butler Palace, and the story was that it had been built by Amir's father as a palace of pleasure for a British official, Sir Harcourt Butler. It was part of the property that Amir had lost. It was still in the possession of the Custodian of Alien Property, and it had been rented out for 38,000 rupees a year to the Indian Council of Philosophical Research. The palace, so far as as some of its motifs went, was in the Lucknow style. It wasn't a distinguished building: all that gave it a palace feel were the four many-sided towers at the corners.

In one of those towers an elevator had been installed. Upstairs was a very large philosophical library; many of the volumes were new, and looked unused. No finer or more respectful use could have been made of the building. But, from what Rashid said, that didn't assuage Amir's grief. Amir, Rashid said, had never set foot in the Butler Palace since it had ceased to be his.

I asked Rashid afterwards – at the end of our tour of old Lucknow, the city of schools and palaces – about his visits to Pakistan. I wanted him to tell me a little more. I wanted more concrete details.

He said, 'In India the beggars asked for small change. In Pakistan they asked for a rupee. The customs officers in Pakistan were taller and better built than on the Indian side, and this was the first time I'd seen a Punjabi Muslim. But then I thought – and I wonder whether you'd understand this – "What's the use of their being Muslims, if they speak this crude Punjabi, and not chaste Urdu?" You see, I had associated Muslims with Urdu and culture.

'When I went to Lahore I thought it was a better version of Lucknow: a whitewashed Lucknow, where all the people had had a bath and changed their clothes. It was pleasing to see. There was a funny thing: you looked at the cinema advertisements, and, because they were making copies of Indian pictures – the Pakis can't make a picture to save their lives – you saw the names of pictures you knew, but with new stars, different faces. In Lahore you feel at first you are in a different city of India which you are visiting for the first time. But slowly the differences become apparent. You meet a person, you get to talking. You think he is a Punjabi, tall, well-built, speaking Urdu in a crude Punjabi accent.

386

You ask him where his father is from, and he says Lucknow – and you are left amazed, because you are now so different from each other after 40 years.

'I stayed for two months, but I knew I couldn't belong there, in spite of the wealth. Even the relatives I met had changed. They were more worldly-wise; they were more aggressive. They had become like the refugees who had come from the Punjab and Sind to Lucknow. I had a cousin who was a trader. He had a finger in every pie; he could bribe every officer; he knew that the main thing was to move and make money. He had been made homeless twice, the first time in 1947, at independence, and then in 1971, in Chittagong in Bangladesh. He knew he could depend on nothing but money. Other values didn't matter. He was quite different from the person I remembered.

'Another thing I found over there was that there was no living in the past, as with us here. They had a healthier attitude to partition than the Indian Muslim. What was done was done. They'd started a new life – they'd forgotten the people they'd left behind, even the people who still remembered them and thought of them and had sent messages through me.

'After my two months I was glad to leave. I felt relief to be back in India, after the claustrophobia of an Islamic society. I liked seeing women again on the streets. The dirt and filth of India didn't seem to matter. The people in Pakistan were relaxed enough about their religion. It was just the wretched laws, hanging like a cloud over one: the call to prayers, the moulvi coming to my friend's house and asking why he hadn't seen us at the mosque recently. The thought police. Islam on wheels.

'I felt relief to be back here. That sense of belonging, which I had in India, I knew I couldn't find anywhere else. Yet I also know that I can never be a complete person now. I can't ignore partition. It's a part of me. I feel rudderless. If there had been no partition I might have been a married man with all the paraphernalia of a middle-class Muslim existence. But I've lived all my life so far as a bachelor, and it's now too late for me to change. The creation and existence of Pakistan has damaged a part of my psyche. I simply cannot pretend it doesn't exist. I cannot pretend that life goes on, and I can have the normal full emotional life, as though what had been here before is still around me.'

7

Woman's Era

Some weeks later, when I had left India, and was among my own things again, I looked at a book I had bought many years before but hadn't read in any connected way. The book was *My Diary in India in the Year 1858–9*. The author was William Howard Russell; he was described on the title page as the special correspondent of *The Times*. It was as correspondent of *The Times* that Russell had made his name in the years immediately before, during the Crimean War: his reports about the hospital conditions of the British expeditionary force had caused Florence Nightingale to be sent out to the Crimea. It was with that reputation, and no doubt with the hope of repeating something of that success, that, nine months after coming back to England, he had gone off again, to the Mutiny in India.

Train and ship and train to Paris; train to Marseilles; steamer to Malta and Alexandria; train to Cairo and Suez; three weeks in a steamer to Ceylon and Calcutta. And then by cart and rail and cart to the front.

Russell was thirty-six. He was the only correspondent who had been sent out by a British newspaper to report on the Mutiny 'and the revolt which followed it'. The 'letters' he sent back to *The Times* were duly published in the paper. Then the diary, which supplied the letters, was prepared for the press, 800 pages in all, with yellow-tinted lithographs and an engraved map. It was published in 1860 in two volumes by the firm of Routledge, Warne, and Routledge: Victorian energy making a great effort – a hard journey, and a sustained literary labour – appear effortless.

The Russell of the Crimea was famous enough to enter the history books. I learned about him at school in Trinidad; he was the first foreign correspondent I ever knew about. The Russell of the Indian Mutiny I didn't know; I had never heard of his Indian book until I saw the two volumes in the antiquarian bookshop. They would have been handsome, authoritative-looking volumes when they were new, with an angular decorative pattern stamped on the hard covers bound in purple cloth. Light had bleached the purple colour to a pale brown on the back of both volumes, had caused a fade at the top edge and the bottom edge of the covers, had cracked the purple cloth down one hinge of the binding, and had nibbled away at the brittle top.

I found the book hard to read. I thought the writer took too long to get to India; and what engaged him on the way didn't seem very interesting. When I looked at the later pages I found the tactical military details hard to follow. At the time of the writing those details would have been the hot news from India; they didn't hold me now. There were other things in India in 1858 and 1859 that I found myself looking for.

But after this trip to India, and especially after my walks in Lucknow with Rashid, the *Diary* became a different book. The long journey to India that Russell described was in fact a journey to the battle for Lucknow. The engraved fold-out map at the beginning of the text was labelled 'Plan of the Operations against Lucknow March 1858'. On that map I saw a number of the places Rashid had shown me.

The British army had encamped in the Dilkusha park, the park of 'Heart's Delight'. The hunting lodge of the Nawabs, not yet in ruin, and to Russell's eye like a French château, was the British commander-in-chief's headquarters. It was annoyed by one of the Nawab's cannon at La Martinière. Among the people firing on the British positions from La Martinière were some of the Nawab's African eunuchs – strange that such people still existed in India in 1858. I wonder what Rashid would have made of that detail in Russell's book. Perhaps the detail would have been obliterated by the rage and grief he would have felt at the defeat, and by the sacking of the Kaiserbagh Palace afterwards – in the surviving wing of which I had met and talked to Amir, whose ancestors had been given the palace by the British nine years after that sacking.

One of the yellow-tinted lithographs was entitled 'The Plunder of the Kaiserbagh'. It had been done later in England, and was an illustration of Russell's text: 'It was one of the strangest and most distressing sights that could be seen; but it was also most exciting

. . . Imagine courts as large as the Temple Gardens, surrounded with ranges of palaces, or at least buildings well stuccoed and gilded, with fresco-paintings on the blind windows . . . From the broken portals issue soldiers laden with loot or plunder. Shawls, rich tapestry, gold and silver brocade, caskets of jewels, arms, splendid dresses. The men are wild with fury and lust of gold – literally drunk with plunder . . . I had often heard the phrase, but never saw the thing itself before. They smashed to pieces the fowling-pieces and pistols to get at the gold mountings and the stones set in the stocks. They burned in a fire, which they made in a centre of the court, brocades and embroidered shawls for the sake of the gold and the silver . . . Oh, the toil of that day! It was horrid enough to have to stumble through endless courts, which were like vapour baths, amid dead bodies, through sights worthy of the Inferno . . . suffocated by deadly smells of rotting corpses, of rotten ghee, or vile native scents; but the seething crowd of camp followers into which we emerged in Huzrutgunj was something worse. As ravenous, and almost as foul, as vultures . . . '

Two days before, Russell had got 'a small bit of loot of very little value': a portrait of the King of Oude, which he had cut out of its frame. He had taken the portrait from a room in the Badshahbagh, 'a large walled garden and enclosure, amid one of the finest of the King of Oude's summer palaces'. A small piece of loot, after horrors: the protective ditch around the Badhshahbagh 'was filled with the bodies of sepoys, which the coolies were dragging from the inside and throwing topsy-turvy, by command of the soldiers; stiffened by death, with outstretched legs and arms, burning slowly in their cotton tunics . . . We crossed literally a ramp of dead bodies loosely covered with earth.' More dead soldiers were being burned in the rooms inside. 'It was before breakfast, and I could not stand the smell.'

A more substantial piece of loot came to Russell from the Kaiserbagh: 'a nose-ring of small rubies and pearls, with a single stone diamond drop.' He had a chance that time of getting an armlet of emeralds and diamonds and pearls as well, but the soldier who had looted it wanted 100 rupees in ready cash, there and then, and – 'Oh, wretched fate!' – all Russell's money was with his Indian Christian servant, Simon, who was in the camp. Russell heard later that a jeweller – whether in England or India is not said

– had bought the armlet from an officer for £7,500, a very large sum in 1860.

The ruins of the Residency still had the power to enrage Rashid; he would have found it hard to bear this account of the looting of his beloved Lucknow. And harder perhaps to bear Russell's accounts of Lucknow before its destruction, 'more extensive than Paris and more brilliant'. From the top of the hunting lodge in the Dilkusha, this was the view: 'A vision of palaces, minars, domes azure and golden, cupolas, colonnades, long façades of fair perspective in pillar and column, terraced roofs – all rising up amid a calm still ocean of the brightest verdure. Look for miles and miles away, and still the ocean spreads . . . Not Rome, not Athens, not Constantinople, not any city I have ever seen appears to me so striking and beautiful as this . . .'

Of the Kaiserbagh, which even in that 'wilderness of fair architecture' Russell saw as 'vast . . . a blaze of gilding, spires, cupolas, domes', there remained only the wing where Amir and his mother lived with their establishments. Rashid had told me more than once that in the old days there were no streets around the palace, only gardens, and it was only from Russell's book that I began to understand to what an extent royal Lucknow had been a city of palaces and gardens.

Across the river from my hotel – beyond the higher dry shelf in the channel with the huts now of the swimming clubs, the black buffaloes on some mornings, the sheets and the many-coloured clothes spread out by the washermen to dry, where I had seen the deep perspective views of an aquatint by the Daniells – on that bank there would have been the Badshahbagh, the Royal Garden.

'Such forests of orange-trees, such trickling fountains, shady walks, beds of flowers, grand alleys, dark retreats and summer-houses . . . in which were now revelling some of the Welch Fusileers.'

There was a similar – perhaps French-inspired – elegance in the many courtyards of the Kaiserbagh, the main palace.

'Statues, lines of lamp-posts, fountains, orange-groves, aqueducts, and kiosks with burnished domes of metal . . . Lying amid the orange-groves are dead and dying sepoys; and the white statues are reddened with blood. Leaning against a smiling Venus is a British soldier shot through the neck, gasping . . . Court after court the scene is still the same. These courts open one to the other by lofty gateways, ornamented with the double fish of the royal family of Oude, or by arched passageways, in which lie the dead sepoys, their clothes smouldering on their flesh.'

It is ironical that – as with Bernal Díaz del Castillo's account of Montezuma's city of Mexico in 1520 – the first account of the splendours of 19th-century Lucknow should also be an account of its destruction. It is ironical, yet not unexpected: the history of old India was written by its conquerors.

What was pain for Rashid was also pain for me. I couldn't read with detachment of the history of this part of India. My emotions ran congruent for a while with those of Rashid; but we grieved for different things. Rashid grieved for the wholeness of the Lucknow world he had been born into, the world before partition. This world would have had elements of old Muslim glory: the glory of the Kings or Nawabs of Oude, and before them the glory of the Moguls. There was no such glory in my past. Russell's journey from Calcutta to Lucknow lay in part through the districts from which, about 20 or 25 years later, my ancestors migrated to Trinidad, to work on the plantations there.

That was the lesser India I was looking for in Russell's book. It was the India only glancingly referred to, always assumed: the India that, in Russell's pages, went on working during this time of war, working in the fields, constructing fortifications, clearing away corpses, looking for positions as servants: an India engaged, without ever knowing it, in subduing itself. On the Grand Trunk Road near Benares long lines of cotton-laden country carts creaked one after the other to Calcutta: trade and business going on in the British-run city. The human groups on the road, indifferent to the terrible war, gave the impression of being at a fair. The people who worked the fields were separate from the war; they took no part in the wars of the rulers.

From Russell's book I learned that the British name for the Indian sepoy, the soldier of the British East India Company who was now the mutineer, was 'Pandy'. 'Why Pandy? Well, because it is a very common name among the sepoys – like Smith of London . . . ' It is in fact a brahmin name from this part of India. Brahmins here formed a substantial part of the Hindu population, and the British army in northern India was to some extent a brahmin army. The Indians who were now being used to put down 'Pandy' were Sikhs, whom the British had defeated less than 10 years before.

With that British army marching to Lucknow to put down the mutineers was a host of Indian camp-followers. Russell said they were mostly Hindu. The Muslims among them were domestic servants; the Afghans sold dried fruit. Among the Hindu camp-followers were merchants and their wives and families, travelling with their store-tents. There were drovers, looking after the sheep and goats and turkeys for the army; and there were any number of porters, 'whole regiments of sinewy, hollow-thighed, lanky coolies' carrying chairs and tables, 'hampers of beer and wine, bazaar stores, or boxes slung from bamboo poles'.

Russell, as special correspondent of *The Times*, was attached to the staff mess of the British headquarters, and the mass of army servants ensured that dinner on the march was as formal as ever.

'It was about 5 o'clock P.M., when a wheeling multitude of kites and vultures soaring above the dust, announced that we were near an encampment, and very soon the joyful sight of a plain full of tents met our eyes . . . Our servants came out to meet us, and I alighted at my tent door . . . On entering everything was in its place just as I left it. Our mess-dinner was precisely the same as at Cawnpore; and it was hard to believe we were in an enemy's country.'

Russell noted the 'high delight' with which these Indian camp-followers – making life so comfortable for the British army – 'were pouring towards Lucknow, to aid the Feringhee' – the foreigner – 'to overcome their brethren'. He saw a parallel with the spread of ancient Roman power. Even the mixed speech of the camp-followers he saw as a symbol of conquest.

None of this was easy for me to read. I had had trouble with *My Diary in India* when I had first tried to read it. I had trouble with it now. I made three or four attempts at it, and found myself rejecting it, for literary reasons. I found it Victorian and wordy. I thought the writer too much of an imperial figure, travelling too easily through a world made safe, and taking that world for granted, almost as much concerned with himself and his dignity and his character as a special correspondent as with the country he had travelled to see, and the people he found himself among.

But these judgements, arrived at from scattered readings, always foundered on the quality of Russell's descriptive writing. The trouble I had with Russell's book was like the trouble I used to have, when I was a reviewer, with good books with which I was nonetheless out of sympathy. Such books were hard to write about; they could make one twist and turn, until one acknowledged their quality. So it took time for me to yield to the Russell book, to take it at its own pace, to accept its purpose; and then I found it very good. His aim, he said, was 'to give an account of the military operations', and also 'to describe the impressions made on my senses by the externals of things, without pretending to say whether I was right or wrong'.

The trouble I had with the book was a trouble with history, a trouble with the externals of things he described so well. There was such a difference between the writer and the people of the country he was writing about, such a difference between the writer's country and the country he had travelled to. The correspondent's job for *The Times*; the British army telegraph, which he used to send his 'letters' to the paper; the talk of railways and steamers – Russell's world is already quite modern.

He had been on *The Times* since 1843, when he was twenty-one; and the first war he had gone to have a look at was the Danish War of 1848. Now – calm, experienced, going out to this Indian war – on the steamer from Marseilles to Malta he finds himself among English people going to many places. 'To trace their destinations from Malta would be to cover the East with a wide-spreading fan. There were men for Australia, for China, the dominions of the Rajah of Sarawak, for Penang, Singapore, Hong Kong, Java, Lahore, Aden, Bombay, Calcutta, Ceylon, Pondicherry . . .' For these people much of the world had already been organized; and many of them were equipped, like Russell himself, to understand and to move into new parts of the world.

That impression of an energetic, spreading civilization is heightened by Russell's careful modesty, the character he gives himself as an observer who is conscious of his special reputation but at the same time knows his limitations. He will not compete with other experts; he will not describe again what he knows others have described. So he refuses to say anything about the wonders of ancient Egypt, or to say one word about the 'much-vexed' Mediterranean. Until he sets out on his march from Calcutta, his tone is allusive; he is writing for his equals; he is an imperial traveller, travelling in a well-charted world.

Yet days out of Calcutta, moving at first in a horse-drawn covered cart, he seems to have gone back a century or two. Just days away from the comforts of Calcutta, he is among people to whom the wider world is unknown; who are without the means of understanding this world; people who after centuries of foreign invasions still cannot protect or defend themselves; people who – Pandy or Sikh, porter or camp-following Hindu merchant – run with high delight to aid the foreigner to overcome their brethren. That idea of 'brethren' – an idea so simple to Russell that the word is used by him with clear irony – is very far from the people to whom he applies it. The Muslims would have some idea of the unity of their faith; but that idea would always be qualified by the despotism of their rulers; and the Muslims would have no obligations to anyone outside their faith. The Hindus would have no loyalty except to their clan; they would have no higher idea of human association, no general idea of the responsibility of man to his fellow. And because of that missing large idea of human association, the country works blindly on, and all the bravery and skills of its people lead to nothing.

It is hard for an Indian not to feel humiliated by Russell's book. Part of the humiliation the Indian feels comes from the ambiguity of his response, his recognition that the Indian system that is being overthrown has come to the end of its possibilities, that its survival can lead only to more of what has gone before, that the India that will come into being at the end of the period of British rule will be better educated, more creative and full of possibility than the India of a century before; that it will have a larger idea of human association, and that out of this larger idea, and out of the encompassing humiliation of British rule, there will come to India the ideas of country and pride and historical self-analysis, things that seem impossibly remote from the India of Russell's march.

Nine years after Russell's book was published, Gandhi was born. Twenty-one years after that, in 1890 (when Russell would have been sixty-eight years old, with three more *My Diary* war-books to his name, one in 1861, *My Diary North and South*, about the American Civil War, another in 1866 about the Austro-Prussian War, and a third in 1870 about the Franco-Prussian War), in 1890 Gandhi was a law student in London, coping as best he could with the bewilderment of a cultural journey the opposite of Russell's Indian journey in 1858. Ten years after that, in 1900 (five years after Russell had received a knighthood), Gandhi was in South Africa, campaigning for the rights of Indians who, 20 or 25 years after the Mutiny, had been sent out as indentured immigrants to many of the former slave colonies of the British Empire, to work on the plantations. And then in 1914 (seven years after Russell's death: the 86 years of the newspaperman's life entirely contained within the period of imperial glory), Gandhi was getting ready to go back to India, wondering how to get started there, how to make use of the political-religious lessons he had learned in South Africa.

From 1857 to 1914, from the Indian Mutiny to the outbreak of the Great War – it isn't long, and great things are seeded in that time. But look back over the 100 years before the Mutiny: right through this period there is an unvarying impression of a helpless, trampled-over country, never itself since the Muslim invasions, wealth eternally squeezed out of it, with a serf population always at work, in the fields, building fortifications, for kings that change and kingdoms with fluid, ever-shifting borders.

'I shall never cease thinking, that rational liberty makes men virtuous; and virtue, happy: wishing therefore ardently for universal happiness, I wish for universal liberty. But your observation on the Hindu is too just: they are incapable of civil liberty; few of them have an idea of it; and those, who have, do not wish it. They must (I deplore the evil, but know the necessity of it) they must be ruled by an absolute power; and I feel my pain much alleviated by knowing the natives themselves . . . are happier under us than they were or could have been under the Sultans of Delhi or petty Rajas.'

The words are by a great 18th-century British scholar, Sir William Jones. They come from a letter he wrote in 1786 from Calcutta to an American friend at the other end of the world, in Virginia. Seventy-five years before William Howard Russell's journey to India, Sir William Jones – at the age of thirty-seven – had gone to Calcutta as a judge of the Bengal Supreme Court. There were no railways or steamers then, no short cut through Egypt; the journey to India was around the Cape of Good Hope, and could take five months; one out of three letters between India and England was lost. Sir William Jones wanted to make his fortune in India. For five years he had angled for an Indian appointment, for the great money it offered. He hoped, once he was in India, to make £30,000 in six years; he was obsessed by that figure. Such were the sums to be made out of the servility and wretchedness of India – trampled over, but always working blindly on.

His talk – to his American correspondent – of liberty and happiness was not disingenuous. William Jones loved the idea of civil liberty, and was a supporter of American independence. He had made three visits to Benjamin Franklin in Paris; and at one time he had even thought of going out to settle in Philadelphia. He was of modest middle-class origins (one grandfather a well-known cabinet-maker). Though he was a lawyer and a fellow of an Oxford college, and famous as an extraordinary scholar of eastern languages, he always in England needed the support of an aristocratic patron. That was why he wanted the £30,000 from India: for his own freedom. And he was unusual: he gave back to India as much as he took. In Bengal, while he did his important and original work on Indian laws, and regularly sent back his money to England to add to his growing hoard, he was also – for no money, for love, learning, glory – going deep into Sanskrit and other languages, talking with brahmins, recovering and translating ancient texts. He brought many of the attitudes of the 18th-century enlightenment to India. In the cultural ruins of much-conquered India he saw himself like a man of the Renaissance in the ruins of the classical world.

This is from a very long journal-letter he sent back to his patron, the second Earl Spencer, in 1787, towards the end of his fourth year in Bengal: 'To what shall I compare my literary pursuits in India? Suppose Greek literature to be known in modern Greece only, and there to be in the hands of priests and philosophers; and suppose them to be conquered successively by Goths, Huns, Vandals, Tartars, and lastly by the English; then suppose a court of judicature to be established by the British parliament, at Athens, and an inquisitive Englishman to be one of the judges; suppose him to learn Greek there, which none of his countrymen knew, and to read Homer, Pindar, Plato, which no other Europeans had even heard of. Such am I in this country; substituting Sanscrit for Greek, the *Brahmans* for the priests of *Jupiter* . . .'

William Jones made more than the £30,000 he had set his heart on; he amassed nearly £50,000. It took him almost 11 years to do so. The thought of the money would have comforted him; but the money itself did him no good. His wife went back a sick woman to England. The year after, when he was getting ready to follow her, he died, and was buried in Calcutta. He was forty-eight.

He, and people like him, gave to Indians the first ideas they had of the antiquity and value of their civilization. Those ideas gave strength to the nationalist movement more than 100 years later. And those ideas travelled very far. In Trinidad, in colonial days, and before India became independent, those ideas about our civilization were almost all that we had to hold on to: as children we were taught, for instance, what Goethe had said about *Shankuntala*, the Sanskrit play that Sir William Jones had translated in 1789.

What luck that bit of knowledge should have come our way! Sanskrit was considered a sacred language; only priests and brahmins could read the texts. William Jones had to get the help of a Hindu medical man to translate the play; and even in our own century pious people could get fierce about the sacredness of the language. Nearly 200 years after William Jones had translated the play, someone in independent India asked Vinoba Bhave, an imitation-Gandhi, seen by some as a kind of spiritual lightning-conductor for the country, what he thought of *Shakuntala*. The idle fellow replied angrily, 'I have never read the *Shakuntala*, and never shall. I do not learn the language of the gods to amuse myself with trifles.'

It is a wonder that, with this internal destructiveness, the play survived; that some knowledge of our cultural past should have come down to us. For every Indian the British period in India is full of ambiguities. For me, with my background – the migration from that overpopulated Gangetic plain 20 or 25 years after William Howard Russell had crossed it in imperial, *Times*-correspondent style, with servants and tents and access to the staff mess of headquarters; and the darkness which for so long blocked my own past as a result of that migration – for me there are special ambiguities.

It fills me with old nerves to contemplate Indian history, to see (perhaps with a depressive's exaggeration, or a far-away colonial's exaggeration) how close we were to cultural destitution, and to wonder at the many accidents which brought us to the concepts – of law and freedom and wide human association – which give men self-awareness and strength, the accidents which have brought us to the point where we can in a way meet William Howard Russell, even in those 'impressions made on my senses by the externals of things', not with equality – time cannot be bent in that way – but with something like lucidity.

So I could go only part of the way with Rashid in this contemplation of the recent past. I had no idea of a state of glory from which there had been a decline or a break; and I had no easy idea of an enemy. Growing up in far-off Trinidad, I had no idea of clan or region, none of the supports and cushions of people in India. Like Gandhi among the immigrant Indians of South Africa, and for much the same reasons, I had developed instead the idea of the kinship of Indians, the idea of the family of India. And in my attempt to come to terms with history, my criticism, my bewilderment and sorrow, was turned inward, focussing on the civilization and the social organization that had given us so little protection.

People in India didn't feel as I did. Perhaps – being in India, and having to order their day-to-day lives there – they couldn't feel or allow themselves to feel like that. But in Delhi this time I met a publisher whose sorrow went beyond mine. His name was Vishwa Nath. He was in his seventies. His family had lived in Delhi for 400 years. There was a story in his family that during the Mutiny, at the time of the British siege, they had had to abandon the family house and take refuge somewhere else. One episode out of many: Vishwa Nath's thoughts, as a Hindu, went back much further than the Mutiny, went back centuries.

He said, 'When I read the history of India, I weep sometimes.'

He was fourteen at the time of Gandhi's salt march in 1931. Ever since then he had worn Indian homespun.

He said, 'Gandhi made us a nation. We were like rats. He made men out of us.'

Rats!

But he was speaking almost technically. 'Man as a species has been trying to kill off rats all through his existence on the earth, but he has never succeeded. Even in New York they haven't succeeded. Similarly, we have been subdued, subjected to torture, conquest – but nobody has been able to kill us off. That has been the strong point of our civilization. But how do you live? Just like rats.'

He hated the idea of caste: 'the main reason why we are slaves'.

399

And he had what I had never had: a clear idea of the enemy. The brahmins were the enemy – yet again, and more than 1000 miles north of the anti-brahmin politics of the South.

'The brahmins let the country down, during all those dreadful invasions by the Mohammedans. All through, they went on chanting their prayers, their *havans*: "God will protect us."'

With his homespun and his nationalism, his sense of history, and his reverence for Gandhi, there was his – seemingly contradictory – rejection of religion. The mixture made for a special passion, and Vishwa Nath's passion came out in the magazines he edited and published in four languages. His women's magazines were especially successful. *Woman's Era* was a fortnightly in English. It had been started 15 years before, and it had damaged the older English-language women's magazines. It sold about 120,000 copies now; it was the best-selling women's magazine in English. Vishwa Nath thought he could take it up to half a million.

I don't believe I had ever looked at an Indian women's magazine. I had taken them for granted. I had been aware of them, knew some of the names. It had never occurred to me that in India they would have had a unique evolution. As soon as the idea came to me, I saw that it couldn't be otherwise, in a society still so ritualized, so full of religious rules and clan rules, where most marriages were arranged, and the opportunity or need for adventure was not great.

I had heard about *Woman's Era* in Bombay. Its success was spoken of as something extraordinary; but people I met didn't care for the magazine itself. It was thought uneducated and backward-looking – in spite of what I was to learn later in Delhi of the editor's iconoclasm and reforming mission. The magazine was extraordinary because it had found a new kind of working-woman reader. A reader of that sort who spent scarce rupees on an English-language magazine might have been thought to have social and cultural ambitions. But that wasn't true of the *Woman's Era* reader; and that was part of her oddity. She was content with her old, shut-in world.

The editor of a rival magazine, one of those damaged by *Woman's Era*, said, '*Woman's Era* is naive right through. It is the first magazine of its kind in India to cater for this new group.'

How did she define this new group?

'It has now acquired a bit of affluence, embraced consumerism. It has a bit of education. But this education has been circumscribed by their traditional thinking and by their family's old beliefs – it's a kind of non-education, a kind of parrot education.'

The bookshop in the Bombay hotel didn't stock *Woman's Era*. The woman assistant made it clear that she didn't like even being asked for it. I bought a copy from a pavement magazine-seller. My first impression was that the magazine was dull. If I hadn't been looking for it, I might have missed it in the pavement seller's display. It was well produced but undistinctive, with an unprovocative young woman's face on the glazed-newsprint cover: carefully made up but unprovocative, a woman's view of a woman. And if, without knowing the magazine's reputation, I had looked through its pages, almost nothing would have stayed with me.

The main article, six pages long, with posed colour photographs, was about 'bride-seeing'. This is the custom whereby, before a marriage is finally arranged, a party from the boy's family visits the girl's family house, and the girl is shown to the visitors and put through her paces. Ashok, the business executive I had got to know in Calcutta, had felt so humiliated by his own experience of bride-seeing that he had decided not to do it again. He had done his own courting and made his own proposal, and kept his family out of it. Ashok could do that; he could look after himself. Not many readers of *Woman's Era* were in that position, and the attitude of *Woman's Era* to bride-seeing was quite different. Most marriages were arranged, the writer of the article said. As long as this was so, bride-seeing was the best way of introducing the girl to the boy; and it was not as demeaning as some people said.

The article was, in fact, an article of advice to girls and their families about the best way of dealing with the occasion. In the first place, a girl shouldn't feel rejected, the writer says, if after a bride-seeing a boy says no. It may be only that the 'demand' – the financial demand – of the boy's family is too much for the girl's family. To prevent that kind of misunderstanding, it is important for the girl's parents to check out the boy and his family thoroughly, before the invitation to view. The girl's parents should visit the boy several times. One tip the article-writer gives to the girl's parents is to see, when they are in the boy's house, whether servants, children, and pets like the boy.

For the bride-seeing occasion itself, the girl shouldn't wear too much make-up or jewelry. She shouldn't boast, and she shouldn't say she can do things which she can't do. Nor should the parents try to appear better-off than they are; some families, the writer says, even borrow furniture to make a show. Then there is the question of dignity. The girl and her family are the suitors on such occasions; the boy and his family have to be won over. But: 'The girl's parents should not behave in an ingratiatingly humble and servile manner.' Easy enough to say; but how, in the circumstances of a bride-seeing, can the girl's family keep their dignity? The writer makes one suggestion. 'Some families insist that the girl touch the feet of every boy and his parents who come to see her. This practice is deplorable, goes against the basic human dignity, and is best avoided.'

Still, the unfairness of the procedure remains. "Why can't the boy sit in *his* drawing-room, nicely groomed and smelling of after-shave, with his head bent and his academic qualifications, job certificates, etc., in his hands?"' To that complaint of a girl, which the writer of the article quotes, there is no reply. Except this: if a girl doesn't want to go out husband-hunting on her own – 'and believe me, in our society it is an extremely difficult game' – then the girl has to put up with the bride-seeing visits. 'If the boy's people put on airs and act uppity, they can be forgiven, for tradition and thousands of years of social behaviour have gone into it.'

Later, after I had met Vishwa Nath in Delhi, I could see a little of his passion and iconoclasm in that last sentence. But without that knowledge, the sentiment appeared simply archaic, an acceptance of old ways because they were the old ways and the best ways. And, with that acceptance stated or implied (sometimes with a take-it-or-leave-it tone), the article got on with its business, which was to give the kind of instruction that might come from some worldly-wise person within the family. Dress modestly for the bride-seeing; mind what you say; watch out for trap questions from the boy's family; be respectful towards older members of the boy's family, and affectionate with the children.

Instruction, instruction of the simplest sort – that appeared to dictate the tone of the magazine. That appeared to be the need the magazine was meeting. The customs, like bride-seeing, might be old; but the world in which they were being practised was new;

and in this world the readers of the magazine appeared to be starting almost from scratch.

'Personal Hygiene' was a long article in the same issue of the magazine. It was illustrated with a photograph of a girl bending over a sink and throwing water at her face, and the advice it offered was of the most elementary kind. There was a little flick of irreligion at the very beginning of the text, but to spot it you had to be in the know. 'Today, of course, whether one believes in godliness or not is not a matter of such grave concern, as is the fact that many of us fail to adopt cleanliness and personal hygiene as our chosen religion.' Cumbersome, even imprecise; but the point of the article was the clear and simple hygiene lesson.

'There is no harm in getting dirty, but the problem arises only when we like to stay dirty . . . The importance of keeping our body and our surroundings clean and orderly cannot be stressed over much. Their direct result is good health, peace of mind and happiness.' To be clean, to be 'tidy', was to avoid infections, and that meant spending less on doctors and medicines: it was, therefore, to avoid a certain amount of financial worry.

Stage by stage, then, taking nothing for granted, the writer took the reader through the problems, in India, of personal hygiene. 'An orderliness of the surroundings is the first and essential step.' 'Orderliness' – a euphemism. 'Surroundings' – a strange word, but clearly 'house' or 'apartment' wouldn't have suited everyone's living space. So we begin to understand that the living conditions of the people for whom this article is meant are not always good. Some of the readers of this article would be at the very margin, would just be making do.

Water is important, the article says; enough of it should be available. India is a warm country, and a bath once or twice a day is necessary, 'accompanied by a thorough and strong but gentle scrubbing, using soap and lukewarm water'. After the washing of the body, the washing of clothes. 'Clothes which have once become wet with perspiration should be washed well before they are worn again . . . Cleanliness of the undergarments is extremely important as these are worn next to the skin. If they are used continuously without changing, they are likely to cause irritation of the skin, or more serious conditions.' A full-page advertisement opposite the last page of text is for an anti-lice treatment. Daughter embraces mother; they both smile at the camera. 'She trusts me with all her

problems . . . and I trust only Mediker with her lice problem.'
(Lice! No wonder the young woman in the hotel bookstore made a
face when I asked for *Woman's Era*.)

Simple instruction – it made for dullness, if you were on the
outside. And the stories – there were five in the issue – were like
fables. A fat woman goes with her husband on a posting to Korea.
She is nervous of the hotel food. She fancies that the mutton is
really dog-meat and the noodles are worms. She eats salad and
yoghurt and a little rice for two months; she loses weight and
becomes another, better person. The rich young Indian businessman, back in India to look for a wife, is frightened away by the
flashy girl he had been expected to marry; instead, he chooses the
humble, orphaned cousin who has been living with the girl's family
as a kind of servant. In another story the rich husband is completely
won over by the simple goodness of the poor-relation aunt whom
his wife is trying to hide. Simple goodness – it is the quality most
people in these *Woman's Era* stories turn out to have. There are
references in the magazine to women reading romances, especially
the English romances published by Mills and Boon. But the love
that matters in these stories is family love rather than romantic
love.

Family love, articles of simple instruction on unglamorous
subjects, advertisements for a Procter and Gamble lice-treatment,
advertisements for antiseptic creams, water-heaters: there was
nothing here to exercise the fantasy, to encourage longing. Who
would ever have thought that this was the formula for a best-selling
women's magazine?

Gulshan Ewing was one of the most famous women's magazine
editors in India. She became the editor of *Eve's Weekly* in 1966,
and took it to its great success in the late 1970s.

At dinner in Bombay one evening, speaking informally of the
Woman's Era phenomenon, before she knew (or I knew) that I was
going to take a greater interest in the subject of women's magazines,
Mrs Ewing described the kind of new reader women's magazines
in India had to reach out to. This reader did a job. She got up
early, looked after her family, got them off to school and work,
and then went out to work herself, in an office, perhaps. At half-
past five she left her office. On the way to the bus stop or railway
station she bought the vegetables for the evening meal, and cut
them up on the way home.

I was attracted by that detail of the cutting up of the vegetables on the train home. But it took only one or two suburban train journeys for me to understand that in Bombay the detail was romantic, a vision of pastoral, that suburban trains were so crowded that, far from cutting vegetables on her train, the woman office worker would have had to fight – hard – to get on the train. Later I read a whole story in *Woman's Era* about a girl becoming separated from her sister during a scrimmage to get on a suburban train.

Mrs Ewing admitted the fantasy when I went to see her some days later in her office. She had simply wanted, she said, to describe the position of the Indian working woman in the cities. I might have thought that she was being merely witty in her description; but the life of the working woman was not funny.

'We've talked to these people, and friends of these people. We've had feedback. And what generally happens is that she – the working woman – she's up at the crack of dawn, about five, to fill the water for the day. We don't have 24-hours' running water in most houses. Water comes on early in the morning, goes off all day, and returns in the late evening for an hour or under a couple of hours. That's in the lower-middle-class areas. So when she gets up – tubs, barrels, whatever she can get hold of, she fills. Then she does the morning chores, filling the tiffin-carriers for husband and children, after giving them tea, breakfast, whatever. It's mainly she who does it. Then she's off to work herself. A very long train journey in a crowded train, usually. She hardly gets a seat.'

'What kind of job would her husband have?'

'A clerk, a bank employee. A middle-level job in a factory, earning about 1000 to 1500 rupees. Her job would be anything from 600 to 1000.'

'That sounds hard.'

'Very hard. It's not funny at all. She's away from the children the whole day. She gets off from her office at 5.30 or six. She might first take a bus to the station. Or – this is more harrowing – she might have to take a bus all the way home. There are mile-long queues for the bus sometimes. When I pass I often wonder when they are ever going to get a bus. Before getting to the bus or station she would buy her vegetables or whatever she needs. Her vegetables are there, in her little *thela*, a carrier bag.

'And then she gets home. And before having her own cup of tea, she has to give one to her own lord and master, who's probably sitting with his feet up, already at the television. Ten to one, in spite of the low earning, they have a television. Then the dinner, then a bit of the children's homework – if she's capable of doing that. Her day would end late. She would have to do the washing up. Then she has to think of the water again.'

'How do they keep going?'

'This is their lot, their destiny. They believe this is how it has to be for them. I'm not necessarily describing the reader of *Eve's Weekly* or *Woman's Era*. I'm just making the point of how sad such women can be with so much drudgery in their lives.'

Women in such circumstances needed special magazines. Simple mimicry of European or American magazines wasn't what was required. The idea of glamour might even be wrong.

Mrs Ewing said, 'The only difference between the middle readership of *Eve's Weekly* – which might be secretaries – and the readership of *Woman's Era* is language. *Woman's Era* uses more simplistic language and talks down to the woman. A fascinating explanation of the success of *Woman's Era* was given to me the other day. The women who read *Woman's Era* are really intimidated by magazines. They'd rather pick up magazines like *Woman's Era* that don't make them feel uncomfortable. But I'm optimistic that that kind of reactionary woman's journalism will be on the way out. When we' – she meant *Eve's Weekly* – 'write about bride-inspecting, we get all het-up. And we tell the woman, the girl, that she doesn't have to go through this. But she can only revolt if she is educated enough to be economically independent at some later stage.'

That was the point: that for a girl or woman from that background, with that education, living in those 'surroundings', the idea of revolt was fantasy. *Woman's Era* was addressed to those women. And so the magazine which had at first appeared so characterless to me, so dull, began to say more, began to create a whole new world of India, a whole new section of urban Indian society which wouldn't have been easy for me to get to know.

There were no Indian women's magazines before independence. Middle-class Indian women read the two popular British magazines, *Woman's Weekly* and *Woman's Own*. When the British went away these magazines ceased to be available. Even a middle-class Indian woman would have found them too expensive to subscribe to from India. I was told this by Nandini Lakshman. She was a journalist specializing in media and advertising matters. From her I got a short history of Indian women's magazines.

'When the *Times of India*, a British paper, was Indianized, they started *Femina*. This was in the early 50s. In the early issues they had a British hangover. The editor was a Parsi lady. In those days modelling wasn't considered a good profession in India. So in *Femina* you had pictures of a lot of these foreigners posing in these Indian outfits. The Indian women who modelled came from affluent Indian families who were not so bound by custom and traditional norms. Then unfortunately within a few years the first editor committed suicide. Nobody knows the reason why. She must have been in her late forties. Then you had an Indian editor for the first time.

'*Femina* wanted then to reach out to more women. So they started this Miss India contest. They had contests all over the country – in the major metros, Bombay, Calcutta, Madras, Delhi – and then all the winners had a Miss India competition. Not really middle-class – it was quite a society affair: the affluent, the moneyed, the influential, people who frequented social parties. The contest had a kind of snob appeal. Initially there weren't too many girls who participated, because again a beauty contest was considered below their dignity, even for many of the snob people – because not everybody wins. I suppose it was the fear of being rejected. And, moreover, the chosen Miss India had to participate in the Miss Universe contest. And there, in one session, she had to wear a swimsuit and parade herself. This would have been shocking to all Indians. So in the early days we had Parsi girls and Christian girls as Miss Indias. But even though the middle-class Indian woman couldn't participate, she began to aim towards that. It was something new to her – the glamour, the image. She was partly shocked, partly fascinated.

'*Eve's Weekly* came along at about this time, and they also started a beauty contest. The circulation of both papers then would have been about 15,000. Much later, they started carrying articles about how to drape your sari, how to look good. It was the editor of *Femina*, a man, who began to do that. I suppose he had a more open view of women's expectations.

'In those days you didn't have too many women working. The magazines carried stories like "The Experiences of a War Widow" – or the experiences of people who had lost their husbands during the partition of India.

'The creation of Indian women's magazines was a gradual process – with a growing readership and a wider market, because of growing education and more awareness. *Femina* touched 90,000 in the late 70s; *Eve's Weekly* also. *Woman's Era*, the star today, was launched in 1973. As *Woman's Era* has risen, *Femina* has dropped – to 65,000 today. And now there's a new magazine, *Savvy*, which is the opposite of *Woman's Era*. *Savvy* is three years old, and it already has a circulation of 50,000. It's a monthly. *Femina* is for the older woman. *Savvy* is for the city-bred woman, from eighteen to thirty.

'*Savvy* is a scandalous magazine. It carries a cover story, a personality story, about a woman. She is known as the "*Savvy* Woman of the Month". She has to be a divorcee, or she can have affairs, or she can have her husband beat her up, or she can leave her husband and kids for somebody, or he can leave her for somebody else, or she can have a husband and a lover. And at the end of it all she can still emerge victorious. She manages to have her cake and eat it too. Every month. *Savvy* women are fairly famous, but not always. If I have a gory life, if I want to dare all and bare all, *Savvy* will make a heroine out of me. They have found a market for this: I think they did some kind of research. An Indian woman may not admit that she reads *Savvy*, but she still reads it. *Savvy* is for the metro areas. *Femina* and *Woman's Era* you will find in the small towns, like Nasik and Nagpur. *Savvy* did something on rape a couple of months ago – with photographs – and the women's organizations said it was too blatant, and there was a court injunction, and they had to withdraw all the issues.'

We talked about *Woman's Era*. I told Nandini what Gulshan Ewing had said about the working woman to whom *Woman's Era* was reaching out.

She said, 'That's glamorizing the *Woman's Era* reader a bit. It's the elite voice talking.' Nandini herself was just a generation or two from traditional and small-town life. 'Every day I change two buses and take a train to come to office. And I get up early. But I don't read *Woman's Era*. I cook at home and I come to work, and

I don't find it a drudgery. That's a skyscraper view. The person who says that probably has a lot of servants at her fingertips.'

Nandini didn't see *Woman's Era* as appealing to the working woman. 'It aims at the traditional middle-class housewife. I don't mean illiterate. It is the only magazine that carries five stories, fiction, in every issue. All about: they lived happily ever after. The husband comes back to the wife. *Woman's Era* is very biased towards women. The woman can do no wrong. She is always a good person. She may be a grandmother, or a wife, or a mother-in-law; she is always a good person. Even when the husband is an alcoholic, in the story the wife with her good nature helps him give up the bottle. To the magazine it may not matter why the husband has hit the bottle. They don't tackle that angle. The situations are from everyday life. The readers can identify with each and every situation. In the 1950s, in *Femina* and *Eve's Weekly* the stories would have been remote.'

I said that the *Woman's Era* stories seemed to me to be fables, to be hardly stories.

Nandini said, 'They are badly written. I fail to understand that in spite of such bad presentation and packaging the magazine has such a wide readership.'

Was there an element of instruction? Did women turn to the magazine for simple basic advice?

'The stories are meant to *entertain*. The reader sees the situation as one that may befall her. Mother-in-law and daughter-in-law problems. Or the boy studying abroad. He is engaged to a girl in India, or he is married to her, and he has affairs abroad, but ultimately he comes back to the wife, and they live happily ever after. *Woman's Era* doesn't tackle social problems. They tackle *personal* situations. The editors know what they are doing.'

We talked about the 'bride-seeing' article. It had caused a certain amount of offence. Many people talked about it, and from the journalistic point of view it had to be considered a success.

Nandini said, 'I would condemn bride-seeing. But they don't. Their article has the sub-title, "A Positive Look at the Custom". And they carry photographs like this.'

A posed colour photograph, occupying the top half of the first page of the article, showed a girl bringing tea on a tray to a viewing party. The room in the photograph was small and cramped (perhaps one of the standard 10 feet by 10 feet Indian rooms), and

409

there was almost no space between the furniture: a matching three-piece 'sofa set', a coffee table, and a side table with a big lamp and with marigolds in an earthen pot. Four people of the visiting party were on the sofa; and two of the visiting women were staring hard at the girl, who was standing with the tea tray, in a new sari, her hair freshly done, looking with something like wretchedness at the camera.

Nandini didn't have my outsider's eye. She saw nothing humorous in the photograph; her feelings were absolutely with the young girl. 'It is horrendous. At the end of the article they say that a get-together between the boy and the girl is advisable – they don't say it's a must – and they have a photograph of a boy and a girl facing each other across a table, but not looking at each other and not talking. "Be respectful and affectionate" is a sub-heading.' She read out from the article: '"The boy's sisters and nieces and nephews should be treated with friendly affection."' She was irritated by what she read. She said, 'If a battalion comes to see you, you are not on parade. You are not being bought. In the article they try to take a liberal step. But the arguments justifying the custom are so strong, the liberal step is nullified. They are not appealing to the new woman. They are appealing to the traditional woman.

'My sister is educated, but she went through an arranged marriage. She hadn't fallen in love with anybody, and there was this proposal from these people. So my parents asked her. There wasn't this kind of exhibition. She just met the boy. He is a merchant-navy captain. Both of them liked each other.'

'Would *Woman's Era* readers suffer when they have to go through something like that bride-seeing?'

'They are conditioned to the fact that they have to go through all this. Some women do find it a torture, but they have to go through with it. However educated or affluent a woman is, you have her saying, "Ultimately I would like to get married and have children." But there are also women who accept *Savvy* magazine. There are the two strands now, and these two papers are leaving *Femina* and *Eve's Weekly* far behind.

'When you come to the advertising, you will find food ingredients and certain cosmetics in *Woman's Era* and *Femina*. But not a winter skin-care lotion costing 50 rupees for 200 ml. That would be advertised in *Savvy*. It's not such an easy market in India. It has to be studied.'

From time to time on my journey I bought an issue of *Woman's Era*, and my regard for its journalistic and social achievement grew. I felt it deserved its success. I thought its merit lay in something Gulshan Ewing had mentioned: it did not intimidate its readers.

A recurring theme of its stories was the discovery by a woman – usually a new bride – that the great shame she feels about her poor relations is misplaced. And *Woman's Era* never shamed its readers. In its stories, its recipes, its photographs of interiors (like the cramped small room which illustrated the bride-seeing article), it acknowledged the conditions in which its readers lived; and it never went beyond those conditions. Perhaps that recognition in itself was a kind of glamour; perhaps in no other form – not cinema or television – did women of that group find that recognition.

With that recognition, there was always reassurance. It could be said that reassurance was the dominant tone of *Woman's Era*. In the stories (the themes usually connected with family love) people always turn out to be better and more human than they appear. And there was reassurance again in the articles of instruction or advice. Nothing was taken for granted there. *Woman's Era* will tell you everything about how to pay a visit: don't go unannounced, don't let your children touch things, don't let them jump in their muddy shoes on your host's sofa and cushions. In another number *Woman's Era* – turning the tables, as it were – will tell you how to deal with an unexpected caller: 'Not immediately after their arrival, but some time during their stay, you can give them a tip by saying tactfully, "Had I known you were coming for a stay, I would have provided you with more comforts and adjusted our own schedule." Unless the guest is extra thick-skinned, this should serve to carry the message across.'

Woman's Era will tell you how to write a letter: don't use a crumpled or grease-marked sheet, don't tear a sheet from your daughter's notebook, don't use big words, don't write only about yourself, don't slap the stamps on all over the envelope. The magazine will even tell you how to go to the cinema: don't take food, don't comment on the plot, don't take your baby and walk it up and down the aisle when it begins to cry.

People who don't need this kind of advice don't need *Woman's Era*. And the people who need the advice are never rebuked or ridiculed. The faults are never written about as the reader's faults. They are other people's faults, faults the reader might have observed; there is always some story or fable to soften the correction. *Woman's Era* invites its readers to a special, shared world. The editorial tone is one of concern, almost love.

And when I got to know the editor, Vishwa Nath, I found that this tone fairly reflected his idea of a mission.

He was seventy-two, and he was still very much in control of his printing and publishing business. He was of middle size, brisk, with no great fat on him, looking cool and ready for business in his white trousers and short-sleeved shirt – Indian homespun, but I wouldn't have known if he hadn't told me.

He gave the impression of not being used to talking about himself. He had no personal anecdotes, and didn't draw moral lessons from his experience. He was still engaged in the world; ideas still held him; he was engrossed by his work and it made him look outwards. He loved the idea of magazines; he loved everything to do with print. He was proud of the new Heidelberg presses on the ground floor. At the same time, out of his love of print, he kept, in a caged room on the upper floor, trays and boxes of movable type, Hindi and English, from older days.

His family had first set up a printing press in Delhi in 1911. So in the printing business he had something like an ancestry. As with Indians in other fields, the talent that had appeared to flower after independence had been maturing over a generation or two. His family had been in Delhi for 400 years, but he could trace it back only as far as his great-grandfather, in whose house he had been born in 1916, and where he had lived until 1934. This great-grandfather had been born just before the Mutiny, perhaps in 1854; he was the man who had passed on the story of the family abandoning the house during the British siege and sacking of Delhi in 1857.

There was a more tangible record of that ancestor. At some time in the 1870s he had been employed by a British lexicographer, Dr

Fallon. Dr Fallon was preparing a Hindi-Urdu-English dictionary; and Vishwa Nath's ancestor had travelled about North India with Dr Fallon, recording the words and phrases they heard.

At Vishwa Nath's back, in his office, there was a glass-doored bookcase that rose from the cupboard to the ceiling. Dr Fallon's *Dictionary* – re-bound – was on a shelf in that bookcase. It was 1200 pages long, the pages almost quarto size, 10 inches by seven: *A New Hindustani-English Dictionary, With Illustrations from Hindustani Literature and Folk-Lore*, by S. W. Fallon Ph.D., published in 1879 by Trubner & Co., London, and E. J. Lazarus & Co., Banaras. Every entry appeared in the three languages, in the three scripts; the pronunciation of the Hindi or Urdu word was given an English approximation.

So, just 20 years after William Howard Russell's journey, there had been this other English journey, through some of the same districts, and there had been this other labour, that couldn't possibly have been adequately rewarded. And there, in Dr Fallon's preface, was the acknowledgement of Vishwa Nath's scholarly ancestor: 'Munshi Thakur Das of Delhi.'

Thakur Das, in fact, 30 years or so later, bought the copyright of the *Dictionary* from Dr Fallon. His intention was to reissue the book. That was one reason why he bought a printing press in 1911 – the coronation year of the King-Emperor George V, as Vishwa Nath said: the year when the capital of British India was shifted from Calcutta, and the foundation was laid for New Delhi. But Thakur Das didn't reissue the *Dictionary*. He died almost as soon as he had bought the press. Vishwa Nath's grandfather had then to see to the setting up and commercial working of the press. The *Dictionary* would have been a very heavy labour; and it wouldn't have paid its way. Vishwa Nath said, 'Every single letter, in Hindi, English, and Urdu, would have had to be set by hand. So the press did other work to keep going.' The *Dictionary* was set aside, surviving in the family only in that copy in the glass case in Vishwa Nath's office.

Vishwa Nath said, 'It's now out of copyright, and there are stories that someone has brought out a photo-offset edition.'

Vishwa Nath's grandfather died in the influenza epidemic of 1917. That was when his father and grand-uncle took over the press. They were an orthodox Hindu family. 'A joint family, living together and working together.' But there was friction. 'There was

413

a division in the family. By 1939 the press was almost finished. I wanted to work in the press, but I saw they were quarrelling. So I came out and qualified as a chartered accountant. I never practised, though. I started a new press, on my own, without the rest of the family. I was twenty-two.'

I asked him what Delhi was like then.

'Easy-going, before the war. For six months the city slept. The Government of India used to go out to Simla from April to September – the summer exodus. New Delhi was almost completely deserted. Everybody took it easy, sleeping in the day, doing things leisurely.'

Politics? Gandhi?

'I became interested in 1930.' He was fourteen. 'I wanted to go to prison, but I was a minor. They wouldn't arrest me. That was during the time of the salt march. Gandhi was noted for his stunts. I call it a stunt. The salt march was a stunt, but it was necessary. We had no arms. He went out to the villages and roused the masses. The salt march actually electrified the whole country. I remember the day Gandhi reached Dandi on the sea, we in our street in Delhi prepared salt from a brackish well, and we said, "We have broken the salt laws." From that day of the salt-making I started wearing the *khadi*, the homespun. And I still do.

'The time of the salt march we had processions every day. It was the first time women came out of their houses, came out of purdah in Delhi and all over North India. Some of our relatives courted arrest. My uncle was imprisoned for six months; he later became a minister in Nehru's government.'

It was at that time, too – 'The whole country was in ferment' – that the idea of publishing began to come to him. He liked reading; he spent all his pocket money on books and magazines.

'I used to go to the press, and set type by hand – for play. My father loved printing, and I also loved printing. When I was in the eighth class, when I was eleven, I had decided that I would publish magazines.'

I felt he was speaking for me. In colonial Trinidad, at about the same age, I had developed – largely through my father, a journalist – a love for print, the shapes of letters, the variety of typefaces, a wonder at the way words were transformed when handwriting turned to type. Out of a love for that process I had decided to be a writer, with perhaps less idea of what I was going to write about

414

than Vishwa Nath – in the ferment of India in the 1930s – had of the magazines he was going to publish.

We talked for a while about printing. I asked about Hindi typefaces. I liked them very much. They seemed strong and elegant and logical, and at the same time true to the written script. I asked Vishwa Nath if he knew who had designed the first Hindi typeface. I felt sure that the designer would have been someone from India. Apparently I was wrong.

'Drawings were sent from India to England. The Devanagari script' – the Hindi script, derived from the Sanskrit – 'was cut over there. All the type we used – for Fallon's *Dictionary*, for everything – was imported from England. We kept on importing Devanagari type from England until the 1920s, when type-foundries were set up in India. The paper we used was imported. The machinery was imported. The ink was imported. It was only when Gandhi started this swadeshi movement – the movement for using India-made goods – that there was a quest for producing things in India.'

There was a side of imperialism that had nonetheless to be acknowledged. 'Actually we owe a great deal to those British officers and men and scholars who went deep into our literature, to translate the texts which the brahmins didn't want known outside their own coterie.' That point about the brahmins was something Vishwa Nath wouldn't let go; it still made him bleed, and still drove him on. But always, too, there was his professional side, and it was with a printer's enthusiasm that he spoke of the Hindi type.

'The Sanskrit script is essentially a script for handwriting. It has ascenders, descenders, the letters move right and left, and there are many contractions. It was really a marvellous job to make it – the typeface – in movable type. In English we have 26 letters and two cases, upper case and lower case. In printeries there were literally two cases, one with the capital letters, one with the small letters. When you are setting Hindi you have to have four cases.' For the contractions, the half letters, the vowel indicators. He drew a plan on a sheet of paper, and said, 'No. You will need five to six cases.'

Two rooms away from his office – empty rooms now, at this time of evening, the tables clear, the many chairs unoccupied – was where he kept the trays of old type. He pulled out a few trays and showed them: formes still set, the movable type worn at the edges, shiny. From a gallery on this top floor you could look down at the

Heidelberg machines on the ground floor, and the stacks of printed sheets. There was a smell of ink and warm paper.

In his white homespun, walking briskly through the empty rooms, he was – even without the deference of employees to underline his status – the owner, the man who knew where it all was, because he had arranged for it to be as it was.

When we were back in his big office – the big desk, the swivel chair upholstered in brown velvet, the glass-doored bookcase rising to the ceiling, the books on the shelves, the file copies of his magazines, the black Shiva statue on the cupboard, an old copy of American *Cosmopolitan*: all the varied attributes of his personality – he talked of history and his anti-brahmin obsession.

'When I was young the freedom movement was at its height. We had been slaves for centuries, and when the independence movement started we had to have some tonic – that we were not as bad as the British had called us. To gain our self-respect, we started thinking we had a very ancient civilization – and of course there's some truth in that. But then it also had its weaknesses, and it was those weaknesses that made us slaves for a long time.

'When I started my own press in 1939 – and soon after that began bringing out my own magazines – I started reading our old scriptures. I wanted to find out for myself how great or grand our civilization was. And when I looked into our ancient literature I found that we were lacking something very vital. The more I went into the scriptures the more my mind was turned – and then this thing started.' The thing: the reformist slant of his magazines.

'The Hindu religion is a conglomeration of faiths, 500 religions or faiths. We've had reformist movements from the very beginning. From the dawn of civilization we've had reformist movements against orthodoxy. What happens is that every reform movement degenerates into a sect – the Lingayats, the Arya Samajists, everybody. Buddha rebelled. Mahavir, the founder of the Jains, rebelled. Guru Nanak, the founder of the Sikhs, rebelled. It's a long list. They rebelled and degenerated into sects, and became as orthodox as the previous orthodox people. So I didn't put on those saffron robes and start going about to those conferences, or preaching in public. I published my magazines.'

His first magazine, *Caravan*, in English, was started in 1941. In 1945 he started *Sarita*, for women, in Hindi. Both magazines had a circulation of about 15,000.

'A substantial circulation for that time. There was a big uproar when I published an article that stray cows should be eliminated. They came out in procession. There were posters all over the city. This was in 1950 or thereabouts.'

But there wasn't much rebellion in *Woman's Era*. People even thought of it as a conservative magazine.

He said, 'Rebellion isn't in *Woman's Era*. It's in *Sarita*, our Hindi magazine, which sells three times what *Woman's Era* sells. *Woman's Era* is more for social affairs. It's educative. Teaching women the simple things nobody bothers to tell them about.'

His idea of social affairs was different from Nandini's. She had said that the magazine dealt in personal situations rather than social problems. Their differing uses of the word came from differing world-views, differing assumptions and levels of education. And Vishwa Nath had his own ideas of rebellion.

'In *Sarita* we go full blast, preaching against gods and goddesses, even God itself. Last month we had an article in *Woman's Era*, "Prayers Breed Selfishness and Sycophancy".'

He took a file copy from the bookcase and showed the article. I thought that only *Woman's Era* could have used so heavy a title. It was, though, a fair description of the article, which railed against the prayer practices of people of all faiths. The article was shot through with Vishwa Nath's rage about Indian history. People who abased themselves before God, the article said, could also abase themselves before a despotic ruler. This touch of historical judgement, this mention of a despotic ruler, seemed to remove the contemporary scene, and gave an antique flavour to the article, which, for all its passion and boldness, and its contemporary photographs, came out as curiously inoffensive, a criticism not so much of religion as of foolish individuals trying to make a contract with God.

Was he a religious man? Only a religious man, I thought, could be so obsessed with religion. Only someone of true Hindu inclination could have spent so much time with difficult, speculative Hindu texts. I remembered Chidananda Das Gupta in Shantiniketan: not a theist, Chidananda had felt a 'renewed inclination' in his semi-retirement to read the Upanishads, and – only a few years younger than Vishwa Nath – had found in them the highest level of spirituality, and rewarding.

Vishwa Nath said, 'I am not a religious man at all.' The

Upanishads? 'Play of words. The Upanishads are just a play of words. *Atman*, Brahma – the whole exercise is to prove that atman is part of Brahma, and Brahma is atman. Some say yes, some say no, some say it's half-and-half. The Hindu philosophers spend all their lives hair-splitting.'

The Dancing Shiva was in his office as a work of art, not as a living icon.

'I think religion is the greatest curse of mankind. It has killed more people, destroyed more property, than any other thing. Even today – Northern Ireland, the Middle East. Hindus, Muslims, Sikhs, all fighting each other in India. The oldest profession is not prostitution. It is the priesthood.'

Yet, with this iconoclasm, there was in Vishwa Nath something that was like its opposite: a concern for the family. In India this concern was like a wish to preserve the old social order; and perhaps, like the iconoclasm, it came out of some personal need. This seeming contradiction was at the heart of *Woman's Era*.

Vishwa Nath said, 'The family is the hinge of civilization. My stress is that the family should be strengthened, not destroyed. Woman's Lib is responsible for quite a good deal of the disintegration of the family.'

He saw himself as a man made not only by Gandhi and the independence movement, but also by his family past. Perhaps, with his family past, the family stories of the siege and sacking of Delhi at the time of the Mutiny, and with his reading of Indian history, the invasions and the cruelties which could make him cry, the pillaging and destruction by the Muslim invaders of the great Hindu temples of North India – perhaps there was with him some dread of chaos which younger people – who saw him only as conservative – didn't have.

One reason why he had started *Woman's Era* – the very name a counter-blast to Woman's Lib – was to fight for the sanctity of the family. It was important to do such a paper in English.

'I had to reach women who don't read Hindi. It is the English-reading, English-speaking people who control things in this country. All this feminist Woman's Lib movement is conducted by English-speaking people. You don't find it so much in Hindi or the Indian languages.'

Nandini had said of *Woman's Era*, 'The editors know what they are doing.' The words had suggested that, in India's professional and competitive magazine business, the people who ran the magazine had done 'research' of some sort, like the research the people at *Savvy* were said to have done. But Vishwa Nath, I felt, moved by instinct; no amount of research could have led to his formula.

The *Woman's Era* formula couldn't be copied, because the personality of the editor couldn't be copied, with its many ambiguities: the tears for the past, the iconoclasm, the fear of chaos coming again, the strong nationalist feeling, the homespun, with the over-riding love of print that had come down from the ancestor who, less than 20 years after the Mutiny, had worked on Dr Fallon's *Dictionary*, applying a new kind of scholarship to the everyday India he knew.

In the beginning, at independence, women's magazines (as Nandini had said) had been a borrowed idea, appealing to a few at the top. *Woman's Era* was an expression now of a purely Indian social order much lower down, offering instruction and reassurance, and a subtle transformation of the hard real world, to women just emerging, women whose lives were a tissue of ritual and given relationships, and didn't want to rebel or dream.

The formula couldn't be copied, or transferred. Vishwa Nath himself had tried to apply the *Woman's Era* formula to a general magazine, *Alive*. *Alive* hadn't found a public. What made sense in the shut-in woman's world came out in the general magazine as quirky and insubstantial.

8

The Shadow of the Guru

To awaken to history was to cease to live instinctively. It was to begin to see oneself and one's group the way the outside world saw one; and it was to know a kind of rage. India was now full of this rage. There had been a general awakening. But everyone awakened first to his own group or community; every group thought itself unique in its awakening; and every group sought to separate its rage from the rage of other groups.

Every day the newspapers carried plain official accounts of events in the Punjab: so many killed by Sikh terrorists; so many people arrested for harbouring terrorists; so many terrorists killed by police; so many 'intruders' from across the Pakistan border killed.

In the wide streets and roundabouts of New Delhi there were reminders of the trouble in the north. At night there were roadblocks. At places below the trees there were sandbags, guns, and policemen. In some areas there was a policeman every 100 yards or so. In the city which Vishwa Nath remembered as being empty and sleepy when he was a child (and where the trees would have been little more than saplings: still only a dream of a new Delhi) terrorism had led to the creation of this new and effective police apparatus.

The British forces the correspondent William Howard Russell had seen at the siege of Lucknow had been made up principally of Scottish Highlanders and Sikhs. Less than 10 years before, the Sikhs had been defeated by the sepoy army of the British. Now, during the Mutiny, the Sikhs – still living as instinctively as other Indians, still fighting the internal wars of India, with almost no idea of the foreign imperial order they were serving – were on the British side.

During the assault on Lucknow an incident took place that

sickened Russell, who was a tough man, and a hardened relisher of war. One of the Lucknow palaces – the 'yellow house' on the racecourse – was being attacked by Sikh soldiers. The defenders fought back with spirit; at one stage they shot and killed one of the Sikhs' British officers. When it was clear that the defenders intended to fight to the end, the attacking soldiers were withdrawn, artillery was brought up, and the yellow house was blasted with shot and shell. The defenders were brave men, Russell said; they should have been sung in ballads. But no mercy was shown them in Lucknow. Those who had survived the shelling were bayoneted by the Sikhs and quickly killed – all but one man. For some reason this man was dragged out by the feet, bayoneted about the face and chest, and then placed on a fire. The tormented man struggled; half burnt, he managed to get up and tried to get away; but the Sikhs held him down in the fire with their bayonets until he was dead. Russell, in a footnote, said – a characteristic touch – that he saw the charred bones on the ground a few days later.

Russell was told that during the Punjab war the Sikhs mutilated all the prisoners they took. So this bayoneting and burning of the man who – possibly – had killed their officer might have been no more than their practice. Perhaps it was part of the barbarity of the country; or simply the barbarity of war. Russell loved war, but he had no illusions about it. 'Conduct warfare on the most chivalrous principles,' he wrote, 'there must ever be a touch of murder about it.'

In the Sikh fierceness at the battle of Lucknow there would have been a wish to get even with the 'Pandies' who had helped to defeat them less than 10 years before. There would have been a more general wish as well to get even with the Muslims. And it was historically fitting that the Sikhs should have helped to bring about the extinction of Muslim power in Lucknow and Delhi, because it was out of the anguish caused by Muslim persecution of Hindus that the Sikh religion had arisen, in 1500 – at about the time of Columbus's last voyage to the New World.

People within the Hindu fold had always been rebelling against brahmin orthodoxy, Vishwa Nath had said; and everyone who had rebelled had started a sect with its own rigidities. Buddha had rebelled; Guru Nanak, the first Guru of the Sikhs, had rebelled. Two thousand years separated the rebellions, and they had different causes. Buddha's rebellion had been prompted by his meditation on the frailty of flesh. Guru Nanak's rebellion or breaking away had been prompted by the horrors of the Muslim invasions – the horrors to which at that time no one could see an end.

Guru Nanak's illumination was the quietist one that there was a middle way: that there was no Hindu and no Muslim, that there could be a blending of the faiths. Islam had its fixed articles of faith, however, its fixed, pervasive rules – no room there for Nanak-like speculation and compromise. The full Islamic 'law' could be asserted at any time; and 100 years later, at the time of the fifth Sikh Guru, the persecutions and the martyrdoms at the hands of the Moguls began. Nearly 100 years after that, at the time of the 10th and last Guru, the religion was given its final form, and Sikhs were given their distinctive appearance: the hair not to be cut, and to be wrapped in a turban, a kind of underpants to be worn, and a steel bracelet, and a knife – so that every day, with these intimate emblems, a man would be reminded of what he was.

As the Mogul power declined in the first half of the 18th century the power and numbers of the Sikhs grew. In the ravaged north of India, in the interim between the collapse of the Moguls and the coming of the British, there was for a short time the Sikh kingdom of Ranjit Singh. This was the kingdom that the British defeated with the help of 'Pandy' in 1849. But there was no great humiliation with that defeat; it might even be said that that defeat propelled the Sikhs forward.

The British, at the height of their empire, had a general disregard for all Indians. Even in 1858, while the Mutiny was going on, Russell noted this slighting British attitude towards the Sikh soldiers who were fighting on the British side. But by being incorporated into British India the Sikhs were immeasurably the gainers. They were granted a century of development. Without the British connection, north-west India – assuming that there had been no more regional or religious wars – might have been no more than Iran until oil, or Afghanistan: poor, despotically ruled, intellectually disadvantaged, 50 or 60 or more years behind the rest of the world.

Independence and the partition of India in 1947 damaged the Sikhs; millions had to leave Pakistan. But again, as after their defeat by the British, they quickly recovered. With the expanding economy of an industrializing independent India, with a vast country where they could exercise their talents, the Sikhs did very well; they did better than they had ever done. They became the country's best-off large group; they were among the leaders in every field. And then in the late 70s their politics, always sectarian and clannish and cantankerous, became confounded with a Sikh fundamentalism preached by a young man of a simple village background, a man born in the year of partition. There began then the train of events which were to lead to the daily budget of terrorist news in the newspapers; and the khaki-clad policemen with guns in the green streets of New Delhi.

For 150 years or more Hindu India – responding to the New Learning that had come to it with the British – had known reforming movements. For 150 years there had been a remarkable series of leaders and teachers and wise men, exceeded by no country in Asia. It had been part of India's slow adjustment to the outside world; and it had led to its intellectual liveliness in the late 20th century: a free press, a constitution, a concern for law and institutions, ideas of morality, good behaviour and intellectual responsibility quite separate from the requirements of religion. With a group as small as the Sikhs, where distinctiveness of dress and appearance was important, there couldn't be this internal intellectual life; even the idea of such a life wasn't possible. The religion had reached its final form with the 10th Guru, and he had declared the line of Gurus over. Such a religion couldn't be reformed; reform would destroy it. A new teacher could only re-state its fixed laws and seek to revive old fervour. So it happened that India's most advanced group could be called back by a village teacher to a simpler past.

The preacher's name was Bhindranwale, after the name of his village. His first name was Jarnail; this was said to be a corruption of the English word 'general'. At his first appearance he was encouraged by the Congress politicians in Delhi, who wished to use him to undo their rivals in the state. This seemed to have given him a taste for political power. The word used most often – by admirer and critic – for Bhindranwale in this incarnation is 'monster'. The holy man became a monster. He moved into – effectively, occupied – the Golden Temple of Amritsar, the Sikhs' holiest shrine, built by the fifth Guru (who was more or less Shakespeare's contemporary). He fortified the Temple, making use of its immunity as a sacred place; and, with a medieval idea of the scale of things, perhaps a villager's idea of a village feud, he declared war on the state. To serve Bhindranwale and the faith, men now went out with the mission of killing Hindus. They stopped buses and killed the people in them. Riding pillion on motor-scooters, they gunned down people in the streets. The resulting shock and grief would have confirmed the terrorists in their idea of power, would have confirmed them in their fantasy that it was open only to them to act, and that – as in some fairy-tale – an enchantment lay over everyone else, rendering them passive.

Eventually the army assaulted the Temple. They found it better fortified than they knew. The action lasted a night and a day, and there were many casualties, among soldiers, defenders, and Temple pilgrims. Hindus as well as Sikhs grieved for the violation of the holy place; Hindus also offered prayers there. Police officials were later to show that there was another, cleaner way of isolating the Temple. But at the time – to deal with a novel situation: a murderous insurrection conducted from the sanctuary of a holy place – the army action, heavy-handed though it was, seemed to be the only way.

The damage was done. Stage by stage, then, the tragedy unfolded. To avenge the desecration, Mrs Gandhi was murdered by some of her Sikh bodyguards. And, again, it is as though the men who planned the murder didn't sufficiently understand that their action would have consequences, that by doing what they did they would be putting their community at risk: Sikhs were settled all over India. There were riots after the murder. The most dreadful were in Delhi, where hundreds died. Out of that great fire in 1984, these terrorist incidents in the Punjab, on the frontier with Pakistan, were the embers.

To most people what had happened in the Punjab was a pure tragedy, and not easy to understand. From the outside, it seemed that the Sikhs had brought this tragedy on themselves, manufacturing grievances out of their great success in independent India. It was as if there was some intellectual or emotional flaw in the community, as if in their fast, unbroken rise over the last century there had developed a lack of balance between their material achievement and their internal life, so that, though in one way so adventurous and forward-looking, in another way they remained close to their tribal and country origins.

*

Something went wrong with a tire of my hired car on the road to Chandigarh. It wasn't only a puncture. The much-used, much-recapped tire had also split in an arc half-way down the wall. Chandigarh was more than three hours away, and the other tires didn't look too good. There was no question of taking a chance; the ravaged tire had to be mended before we went on. Help was at hand, though. There was a Punjabi truck stop just a short way down the road – we could see it from where we were – and after we had changed the wheel we went there.

The truck stop was a dusty yard with brick sheds on three sides. Some of the sheds were walled, some open. Advertisements for Apollo tires nailed to a wall gave a reassuring technical feel to the place. At the back and sides of the yard were fields of ripe wheat; down one side was a ditch of stagnant, blackish water. Drivers turbanned and unturbanned sat above the dust on string beds in the open sheds and drank tea. The tea was prepared in an open kitchen at the back (a lot of blue smoke over black earthen fireplaces), and served by two boy waiters in long trousers and very dirty (and now perhaps uncleanable) long-tailed Indian shirts.

While the driver of my hired car manhandled the wheel with the split tire, traffic roared and rasped by, the brown smoke from unmuffled exhausts mixing with roadside dust. Within the split tire there was, surprisingly, an inner tube. I hadn't seen one for years. Over this tube the driver, an unturbanned Sikh, then squatted with the repair man, and after they had pumped the tube up they passed it through water in a red plastic basin. (There was another red plastic basin in which glass tumblers and heavy china cups were soaking on a stand outside the cooking shed.) The flaw in the tube was found, the spot was dried and rasped, some adhesive solution was applied, and a bandage was stuck on. The procedure sent me back to my childhood; it made me think of the way we used to mend bicycle punctures; I had thought it was something that had passed out of my life forever.

Stepping down from the greasy brick platform, where they had been working on the tube, the driver and the repair man selected, from a small collection, a tire so worn it had been finally abandoned. They cut two sleeves out of this tire, one sleeve out of the thin part of the tire, the other out of the thicker part. Both sleeves were then fitted into the tire where it had split; the mended inner tube, pink and deflated and flabby, was also fitted in; and then somehow the driver and the repair man hammered and malleted the whole thing together, pumped the tire up, and bumped it up and down professionally a few times on the grease-blackened earth. Finally, like a man more fulfilled than irritated by the accident, Bhupinder the driver set the nose of his car towards Chandigarh, and we didn't stop until we got there.

The traffic was of all sorts: buses, trucks with towering loads, packed three-wheeler taxi-buses with about 20 people each (I counted), mule carts, tractors with trailers, some of the trailers carrying very wide loads of straw in sacking, or carrying logs placed crosswise, so that they occupied a good deal more of the width of the road than you thought from a distance. There seemed to be no limit to a load. Metal, being metal, was deemed to be able to carry anything that could be loaded onto it. Many bicycles carried two or three people each: the cyclist proper, someone on the cross bar, someone sitting sideways on the carrier at the back. A motor-scooter could carry a family of five: father on the main saddle, one child between his arms, another behind him holding on to his waist, mother on the carrier at the back, sitting sideways, with the baby.

Always in India this feeling of a crowd, of vehicles and services stretched to their limit: the trains and the aeroplanes never frequent enough, the roads never wide enough, always needing two or three or four more lanes. The overloaded trucks were often as close together as the wagons of a goods train; and sometimes – it seemed to depend on the mood or local need of drivers – cars and carts came in the wrong direction. Hooters and horns, from scooters and cars and trucks, sounded all the time, seldom angrily. The effect was more that of celebration, as with a wedding procession.

Chandigarh, when I first saw it in 1962, was a brand-new city. It had been built as the capital of what was then the state of Punjab. It was an empty, still artificial-feeling city in 1962. It was full of Punjabi tourists, running up and down the modern concrete towers Le Corbusier had built for the state assembly, the high court, and the secretariat. The city was now full, built up. It was squabbled over by the two states into which Punjab had split.

Le Corbusier's unrendered concrete towers, after 27 years of Punjab sun and monsoon and sub-Himalayan winter, looked stained and diseased, and showed now as quite plain structures, with an applied flashiness: megalomaniac architecture: people

426

reduced to units, individuality reserved only to the architect, imposing his ideas of colour in an inflated Miróesque mural on one building, and imposing an iconography of his own with a giant hand set in a vast flat area of concrete paving, which would have been unbearable in winter and summer and the monsoon. India had encouraged yet another outsider to build a monument to himself.

Grass grew now between the blocks of the paving. Armed policemen guarded the buildings in the evenings; visitors were driven off. The people of Chandigarh, following a more natural Indian inclination, promenaded in the afternoons on the lakeside, far from the dreadful public buildings. The city over which people squabbled was without a centre and a heart.

But the air was clean. It was still cool; in the evenings it was cold. The hotel garden was full of flowers, and the big shaved lawns, soaked by a fat hose every day, were bright green.

Gurtej Singh was famous as a Sikh who had resigned from the Indian Administrative Service – the highest branch of the Indian civil service – because of his commitment to the Sikh cause. He was represented to me as someone who would give me some understanding of the Sikh alienation. On a number of mornings he came to the hotel, after he had taken his sixteen-year-old daughter to her school in Chandigarh, and we talked. I didn't know then that he had been acquainted with Bhindranwale; that he had gone underground for four years after the army assault on the Golden Temple in June 1984; that he had been charged with sedition, and was still technically on bail.

He was forty-one, tall, just over six feet, slender, with sombre, intense eyes. He was carefully dressed, in pale colours. There was an elegance about his manner as about his physique – nothing of the big-eating Sikh or Punjabi there. It was hard to imagine that he had come from a farming family and a village background, and that he was the first in his family to have received anything like a formal education.

He wanted, the very first time he came, to talk about the importance of water. Punjab depended on the water of its rivers; it didn't like sharing its water with other states. Since 1947, he said, more people had died quarrelling over water than had died during the upheavals of partition. 'The water problem is the crux of the matter.'

But I could hear about water from many other people. I felt, too, that it was a simplification, something to be put forward at a first meeting. Fundamentalism and alienation would have had other promptings as well; and I was more interested, at this first meeting with Gurtej, in understanding how his ideas of religion had come to him.

The first ideas, he said, had come to him from his grandfather. From his grandfather he had also got the idea of 'gentlemanliness'.

'We don't have many rituals. My grandfather taught me the simplest form of prayers. It's just a simple prayer for the well-being of the entire world. It lasted from half an hour to 45 minutes. Every morning my grandmother would get up for the household chores – and that included churning the morning milk – and she would keep on repeating the prayers while at work. She was not an educated person, and she remembered only those things she had heard, the simplest of couplets from the scriptures.

'She got up at four. After she had got up I couldn't sleep, and then I gradually got interested in those prayers of hers. My grandfather would pray in a more formal manner. He would wash himself in the morning and sit with the holy book in his hand. We have a small version, with the daily prayers, and he would carry that with him all the time. The last thing would be the *ardas*, the conclusion of the prayer, the supplication.

'My parents were living in a different village. There was no school in that village, so they had sent me to my grandparents' village, where we had a school next to the house. I went to that school until I was big enough to go away to Dehra Dun, to a boarding school.'

I wanted to hear more about the 'gentlemanliness' of the grandfather.

Gurtej thought. He began to remember; his intense eyes softened. 'He always dressed properly, in clean clothes, and a white turban. He always had his watch with him. He was conscious of time, which no one else in the village was. He was a progressive man. He was the first man to get a radio, the first man to buy a jeep in the village. And he kept a daily diary. He had a contact with some saint, who had taught him to make anti-snakebite medicine. This he religiously used to make before the onset of the rainy season every year, and he would distribute it to the neighbouring villages. People used to come to ask for that medicine whenever there was a case of snakebite.

'Sometimes I used to go with him on a camel to the neighbouring market town. When we passed through a place where the village elders used to sit he would ask me to greet them loudly. And I never heard him shouting at anybody. When he thought the worst of a person he would say '*Dusht*!' – 'Wicked man!' – and then we knew he was very angry.

'He used to give pocket money to me and to his son – who was my uncle – wanting us to be on our own, not depending on him for anything. He would help anybody who came. He was the only person to have a horse carriage, and when people wanted it – for a wedding or to go to hospital – he let them have it. He was widely respected. He was one of the better-off farmers.'

From this protected life Gurtej was taken away when he was sent to the boarding school in far-off Dehra Dun.

'I was in a different sort of culture, and there must have been a yearning in my heart to be in touch with my land, my culture, my people. I began to read the poems of Sohan Singh Seetal. He's a poet and a writer. He is still living in Ludhiana. The books I read at that time were ballads, concerned with Sikh history in the Mogul period and the British period.

'I still remember several poems – which were full of the suffering of my people. One poem was about the general order of massacre given by two or three Mogul governors – that every Sikh should be hunted down. And the mothers from whom the children were snatched, to be cut up to pieces. Young boys being murdered. Women being incarcerated, tortured. The torture of the companions of the ninth Guru – that was in 1675. They were killed in front of his eyes. One was set on fire. This was in Delhi, in Chandni Chowk. Another was sawn alive – put into a wooden casket and cut into two. You see the helplessness and anguish of people at that time. They were doing no wrong. They were just following God according to their own lights.'

His eyes misted over. He found it hard to bear the details of physical pain, which he was yet stressing. Then he related what he had said – almost mythical suffering, but with real, historical dates – to the problems of the present.

'Consciously or unconsciously, a Sikh is all the time trying to avert a situation like this.' Religious persecution. 'And this is what made me support this agitation for justice in the Punjab. It was more of an emotional identification with my people – in the days of the Punjabi Suba, 1957 to 1960.' The agitation then by Sikhs for a Punjabi-speaking state: Gurtej was ten in 1957. 'The intellectual reason came afterwards. What I recall is that as soon as a Punjabi Suba was formed, Hindus started agitating against it. They burnt a gurdwara' – a Sikh temple – 'in Karnal. They attacked a gurdwara in Delhi. Stoning took place. And all over the Punjab towns there was a bit of a commotion.'

So present suffering linked to past suffering. The heroic past ennobled or gave a different quality to the trials of the present.

Gurtej said, 'The fifth Guru was burnt to death.' In 1606, by the order of the Emperor Jehangir, Akbar's son. The fifth Guru, the organizer of the faith, the founder of the Golden Temple. 'The best human being I can conceive of is the Guru' – the singular or the collective noun is used by Sikhs for all the 10 Gurus – 'and I believe them to be motivated sincerely by the good of all the community. Why should they suffer like that?'

'Did you ask your grandfather? Did you talk to him about this problem of suffering?'

'I don't remember having asked him. I think the first time I talked about these things was with Sardar Kapur Singh in 1965–66.'

This man, Kapur Singh, was important to Gurtej. He was born in 1911 to a farming family. A gifted and unusual man, he completed his education at Cambridge, and he gained entrance to the Indian Civil Service, the ICS, the predecessor in British times of the Indian Administrative Service. But then at independence in 1947 there was some trouble about money meant for refugees and also trouble about buying an expatriate's car, and Kapur Singh was dismissed from the service. Kapur Singh claimed that he had been wrongly dismissed, and it might be said that for the rest of his life Kapur Singh fought and refought his case; mixing this grievance with regional Sikh politics, the writing of poetry, and the writing of difficult books about the Sikh religion. This was the man who became Gurtej's mentor. He opened Gurtej's eyes to the position of Sikhs in India.

I wondered whether, before this meeting with Kapur Singh in

1965 (when Gurtej was eighteen), Gurtej had noticed any discrimination against him as a Sikh. He said yes; he remembered that once, when he was queuing up to buy a railway ticket, the booking clerk had been rough with him.

'When you first talked, what did Kapur Singh tell you about suffering?'

'He told me it was an eternal fight between good and evil, and by their suffering the Gurus have only shown that people should identify themselves with good causes. He used to say that a measure of man is the sense of commitment he has. It's the only thing important in man. Otherwise, it's an animal existence. And he would say it's the only way to salvation, serving mankind. And Sardar Kapur Singh's words carried conviction because he had suffered much, and he had no regrets.'

In this way Gurtej had arrived at some idea of the Sikh religion: a special idea of the Gurus, a special idea of the Sikh God.

Of Guru Nanak, the first Guru, who had had the illumination that there was no Hindu and no Muslim, Gurtej said, 'I see him as a man who's conscious of the sufferings of his people, and having an intense desire to change the situation.' He didn't see Nanak simply as another rebel against Hinduism. 'He's not a reformer, he's not a philosopher, he's not a poet – though he expressed himself in poetry. He's a prophet of God.' This idea of the prophet – a Muslim idea, a Christian idea, a Jewish idea – was not held by every Sikh. But Gurtej was firm. 'There's no doubt in the minds of Sikhs. We look upon all the Gurus as *one*.' In this account, therefore, over the first 200 years of their history the Sikhs had a line of 10 God-sent prophets.

Why the emphasis on suffering? How could a believer live from day to day with this idea of suffering?

Gurtej said, 'The stress on suffering is like this. The world is an unhappy place to live in, and unhappiness has to be eliminated. There are only two ways. Either you make somebody else suffer, or you suffer. And I think a man of God must suffer himself, rather than pass it on to somebody else. I regard myself as a man of God. I always have, and always hope to. The very idea of attaining salvation by serving mankind is unusual in this sub-continent. In the other religions here the stress is on monasticism, renunciation, a personal salvation. At crucial times in my life I have found that I would like to decide a thing as the Guru might have decided it.'

This idea of the Sikh prophet went with a particular idea of God. 'For Sikhs he is the fountainhead of all virtues, a living God manifesting himself through his prophets. Of all the prophets, if you ask me who is the prophet nearest to the Guru, I would say Mohammed. Our idea is different from Islam in only one aspect: the dominant element in our concept of godhead is justice and kindness. The Islamic God appears to me to be a little harsh – if you see the punishment renegades got at the hands of Mohammed himself. And when you see the manifestation of sovereign power in Islamic states, there is an element of cruelty, a bit of oppression. We view God as a liberator. Ranjit Singh ruled the Sikh kingdom for 40 years, and he never sentenced anyone to death. This, I think, is the spirit of Sikhism. This is our concept of God as kindness.'

I said, 'There is no such conception of God in Hinduism.'

'Everything is violent in Hinduism. Do you see the Devi strung with skulls around her neck? If you ask me, Hinduism is the most violent of religions.'

Some years before, in England, listening to the radio one day – when Bhindranwale and Sikh fundamentalism and his fortification of the Golden Temple were still far away, and I knew little about them – I had heard an interview with Bhindranwale in the Golden Temple. Sikhism, Bhindranwale had said, was a revealed religion; the Sikhs were people of the Book. I was struck then by the attempt to equate Sikhism with Christianity; to separate it from its speculative Hindu aspects, even from its guiding idea of salvation as union with God and freedom from transmigration. I had thought of Bhindranwale's statement as an attempt, by a man intellectually very far away, to make his cause more acceptable to his foreign interviewer.

So I pressed Gurtej now about his idea of the prophet.

He said, 'If we get bogged down in Darwinian ideas of evolution, and see everything as evolving from something else, we cannot see a finished product right at the beginning. And this is what the prophets do: they present you with a finished product.'

I felt then, from his language and imagery ('Darwinian', 'product'), that his ideas had been worked out and studied; and I had the feeling that he might have been put on to this way of thinking by his mentor, Kapur Singh.

One of the pamphets Gurtej gave me was entitled 'The Trial of a Sikh Civil Servant in Secular India'. It was an English translation of Kapur Singh's account of his fight for justice after his dismissal from the Indian Civil Service, his '30 years of persecution by the state authorities without an income and without an occupation'.

The story as presented in the pamphlet was fragmented and not easy to follow; the translation, besides, was poor and the roughly printed pamphlet was full of printing errors. But it seemed that he had been dismissed on a charge of embezzling government money meant to be given out to refugees from Pakistan at the time of independence. He had been suspended in 1949, and dismissed after a departmental inquiry by the Chief Justice of the Punjab. Kapur Singh's defence was that he had given out the money in question to refugees, but he had thought it 'neither possible nor wise', in the circumstances of partition, to get receipts from refugees who couldn't be identified and had no addresses. The government itself, he said, had directed that 'cumbersome formalities' like the obtaining of receipts should be ignored in dealing with refugees.

One of the points of his pamphlet was that the charge of embezzlement had been brought against him only because he had been protesting against a directive issued in 1947 to all deputy commissioners in the Punjab that 'the Sikhs in general . . . must be treated as a criminal tribe. Harsh treatment must be meted out to them to the extent of shooting them dead so that they wake up to political realities'. Mr Nehru himself had been behind that directive. (Mr Nehru had also been behind a directive Kapur Singh had heard about in 1954, from a Sikh major in the army, that Sikhs in the army were to be 'constantly threatened, terrorized, insulted and kept in subjugation'.) Mr Nehru's mind had been poisoned against Kapur Singh by 'compulsively malignant Hindus and Sikhs with tainted conscience', who had told exaggerated stories about Kapur Singh's Sikh-oriented politics. As a result, Mr Nehru and his home minister 'were on the lookout of an oppportunity for liquidating me'.

The departmental inquiry into the embezzlement charge against

Kapur Singh was conducted by the Chief Justice of the Punjab. He was an Englishman – this was in 1950, just three years after independence. He ruled that Kapur Singh was guilty. 'The British Government was requested to Knight him in recognition of his valuable service to the people of the Punjab during his tenure as Chief Justice. Accordingly he was Knighted by the Queen. Most of his time as Chief Justice was spent in enquiring against me.'

As for Kapur Singh: 'I was dismissed from service and thrown from pillar to post for 12 long years.' He took his case to the Public Service Commission, and after that to the Supreme Court. 'I was driven from pillar to post for another four years . . . Then in accordance with the Guru's exalted words "The ultimate test of truth is to die fighting for it," I started a serious legal battle. I filed a detailed writ against the high-handedness of the government in the High Court at Chandigarh.'

Some months before, in Bangalore in the south, Prakash, the minister, had told me at breakfast about one of his morning petitioners. This man, a village official charged with embezzling a portion of the land revenue he collected, had been suspended from his job; and he had travelled all night on a bus to wait at dawn outside Prakash's door and to plead for the minister's help. Prakash had seen the man for seven minutes, had said that the departmental inquiry had to take its course; and the man had then to go back all 200 miles to his village. It seemed hard, all that travel for so little. But Prakash, in his witty way, had described how someone like that suspended official, after a day or two of tears and fright at his situation, might find, as it were, a second wind in the idea of *karma*, fate, might become quite calm and lucid, and, supported by that idea of fate, might devote the rest of his life to litigation and action for the cause abruptly granted him.

Kapur Singh's religious support was of another kind. '"Irreligiousness is the root cause of all misery" is our ancient thought,' he wrote in his pamphlet. And in his long legal fight he was both consoled and encouraged by the example of the Sikh Gurus who had been persecuted by the Moguls. He began to see his own persecution as 'the destiny of a Sikh in consequence of the power falling into Hindu hands'. When his case was at the Supreme Court, his lawyer told him one day (the account is full of this kind of hearsay), 'All around me I hear it being said that total demoralization of Kapur Singh is necessary to contain the Sikhs, and he must be liquidated in spite of law and regulations.' When his writ was at the Chandigarh High Court he happened one day to be in a shop and there he heard one of the judges say to the shopkeeper, 'He is a dangerous Sikh – a poisonous snake.'

His sufferings linked him to the persecuted warrior Gurus of the Mogul time, and their sufferings had led to his present political predicament. In the 17th and 18th centuries Mogul governors and generals 'got Guru Arjun imprisoned and executed after unbearable torture, conspired to kill Guru Hargobind, attempted to do away with Guru Harkrishan, got Guru Teg Bahadur beheaded, got the infant sons of Guru Gobind Singh bricked alive in a wall, caused a fatal wound on the person of the Tenth Master, inspired the Imperial edict of the genocide of the Sikhs, were responsible for butchering Banda Singh Bahadur and his companions, became the preceptors of the Great Holocaust, and in the 19th century raised the flag of Jehad against the Sikh political power. Their activities ultimately culminated in the . . . formation of Pakistan.' So the litany of religious pain ran together with history and contemporary politics and Kapur Singh's personal calvary. The identification was complete: 'The Mogul king Bahadur Shah had ordered, "Followers of Nanak [should] be executed on sight." I, being a declared Sikh, fell a victim to this Mogul firman.'

It was as though the faith called up this identification with the torments of the Gurus; and as though this identification created in the believer the feeling of injustice and persecution, and perhaps even the wish to be persecuted.

What I would never have guessed from that pamphlet – what I learned from another book of Kapur Singh's that Gurtej gave me later – was that, with that obsession about his case, Kapur Singh had had a full and fruitful life in independent India. He had done his writing; he had been professor of religion at a Sikh college in Bombay; and he had been active in Punjab politics, being both a member of the state assembly and the central parliament in Delhi.

He and Gurtej met in 1965. Kapur Singh was fifty-four, and quite famous in Chandigarh. Gurtej was eighteen, a student at the university in the town. The two men became close. Kapur Singh would begin his letters to Gurtej, 'My dear son'. He bequeathed his books and papers to Gurtej.

One of the titles that Kapur Singh claimed was 'Decorated National Professor of Sikhism'. Gurtej, on his card, described himself as 'Professor of Sikhism'. There was clearly in Gurtej some wish to honour Kapur Singh; and – after reading the pamphlet of Kapur Singh's that Gurtej had given me – I wondered whether in his own career in the Indian Administrative Service Gurtej didn't have before his eyes Kapur Singh's martyrdom in that role 30 years or so before.

Kapur Singh had been dismissed, but he said he had really fought a point of principle, objecting to an anti-Sikh directive. Gurtej, who had joined the service in 1970, had resigned in 1982, also on a point of principle. He had become worried, he said, about serving the ends of justice. 'You can only serve as long as the state remains just.' In the Punjab in 1977, during Mrs Gandhi's Emergency, his doubts had grown. 'I see my people running from pillar to post. They are humiliated, though they don't feel it. They feel it's the normal way in this country.'

It was about his government service that we began to talk when he came the second time to the hotel, early in the morning again, with the shaved hotel lawn shining in patches from its flooding by the big hose, and with the banks of flowers still in shadow.

In 1969, when he was twenty-two, he had got married. It was an arranged local marriage. The following year he joined the Indian Police Service. It was at school – in Dehra Dun, away from home – that his thoughts had turned to that kind of career: quite a change for someone from a farming background. A friend of his was the son of an Indian Administrative Service officer; that first put the idea in Gurtej's mind. Then he heard someone say that the only worthwhile services were the Indian Administrative Service and the Indian Police Service. So he had written the examination. 'I made no special preparation. I just studied hard. After having done my M.A. in history I sat for the Indian Police Service.' He was successful; only a handful of people got in every year.

He shifted the next year to the sister service, the IAS. And, even after all that had happened, he still thought highly of that service. 'It was a good service, and if I were inclined to serve in adminstration, this would be the service I would like to join.'

The IAS was an all-India service, and Gurtej's first posting was in the South, in the state of Andhra. He became disenchanted almost at once.

'I was able to detect one case of death in police custody due to torture. And instead of the police officer concerned being punished, he was actually rewarded – so that he would avoid the punishment. The man killed was a small peasant; his wife appeared very poor to me. I was an S.D.M., sub-divisional magistrate. It's mandatory for an S.D.M. to conduct a divisional inquiry into any death in police custody. I was told to set the matter aside – it had been pending for three years.'

But he couldn't set the matter aside, and the case still worried him. 'After 18 years I still remember the names of the people. It was a pathetic case. I felt very bad about it. The wife had been hunted out of the district so that she couldn't give any evidence against the police. There had been a quarrel between the man – the dead man – and some landlord in the village. The man had probably become a source of irritation to the landlord. People like that don't feel confident enough to attack a landlord.'

I asked Gurtej why he had stayed on in the service, after that experience.

'I thought the time would come when I could do more. But that time didn't come. I started realizing that the corruption has set into the administrative machinery, and that people are really pawns. Whenever politicians are interested in a case, whenever they have a vested interest, it's impossible to take any action.

'In the same year, 1971, a whole family had died of starvation in Andhra Pradesh. It was in one of the revenue sub-divisions. A question was asked in Parliament. I was asked to inquire into it. The district magistrate contacted me later to ask what I thought of the case. I said it was a starvation death. The D.M., the revenue collector, said, "No, no, we can't write that. It will cause a commotion. It will be a bad advertisement in the foreign press." And again, as often with Gurtej, the thought of suffering brought tears close to his sombre eyes. 'It was a family of poor people. The old man died first. They had no means of subsistence. No one offered them food. And then the wife died; and then the children died. Harijans, scheduled caste. The case was taken out of my hands.'

'But you say the IAS was a good service. Weren't there good things?'

'There were good things. I was in the drought-prone area programme. We tried to provide relief to people in drought-prone areas. We provided wells, sources of irrigation. That was a good thing. Though there again I ran into trouble. With the *zilla parishad*, the district council. That's an elected body, and the chairman wanted all the minor irrigation works to be entrusted to his relative. And that relative was sub-contracting it out to others, and he made money on that. The chairman had a big clout in the administration. But I didn't help him. He wanted to humiliate me. He called me to a meeting of the zilla parishad. But that time the democratic process worked – very unusual. The other elected members supported me, and rebuked the zilla parishad chairman for harassing an honest officer.'

Even that didn't reconcile Gurtej to the administrative service. But wasn't politics the art of the possible? And couldn't that be said with greater force of the civil service? Wasn't there – going only by what he had said – an intention of improvement and service to the people?

Gurtej didn't see it like that. He had gone into the service with the highest expectations; they allowed of no worldliness or compromise. He said, 'I am not somebody's minion. I am serving the law, the country's constitution. Why should I play to the whims of some corrupt man? As an officer, if you can't act impartially, there is no meaning in remaining in service. Even for self-respect it is essential that you should feel you are doing what is right.'

Though he was far away in the South, his association with Kapur Singh continued. In 1974 he formally took his vows as a Sikh, going through the ritual which the 10th Guru had laid down. He took *amrit*, drank the consecrated nectar, a mixture of sugar and water stirred with a double-edged sword. Not every Sikh went through this ceremony and made his formal vows.

Gurtej said, 'I had doubts until then whether this sort of ceremony was necessary. Sikhism is committed to ideas; ritualism has no place. I had been following all the tenets of the religion, but had not formally taken this amrit. Sardar Kapur Singh said that it was a formal ceremony that must be gone through, to declare that you are openly committed.'

The actual ceremony was carried out in the Punjab, where he had gone on two months' leave. And it was carried out at the town of Anandpur, where the 10th Guru, Guru Gobind Singh, had performed the first baptism of Sikhs in 1699.

Gurtej said, 'The amrit was stirred with the sword of Ali.'

This was quite bewildering. Did he mean the Ali of the Muslim Shias, the cousin and son-in-law of the Prophet Mohammed?

He did. He said, 'The caliph.'

How had this sword survived more than 1000 years? How had it come into the possession of Guru Gobind Singh?

'It was presented to him by the Mogul Emperor Bahadur Shah.'

So again, in this version of the Sikh faith that Gurtej propounded, there was an Islamic twist, a non-Hindu, non-Indian aspect, a separateness of the faith from the land of its origins.

'During this period in Andhra Pradesh I continued my studies in Sikhism. I wrote an article in 1975 about the martyrdom of the ninth Guru. He was beheaded in Delhi by the Emperor Aurangzebe, in Chandni Chowk. Then I wrote some articles for the *Encyclopaedia of Sikhism*.'

He was encouraged in his studies and writing by his wife, 'a double graduate'. Together they visited important Sikh temples in the South. 'Every year we went to the gurdwara established in the memory of the 10th Guru near the spot where he had been cremated.' The 10th Guru had died in 1708, killed, it is said, by one of his own Muslim followers. The Guru had travelled down to the South – the episode has its ambiguities – to help the Emperor Aurangzebe's successor in a dynastic war.

In 1977, when he was thirty, and after six years in the South, Gurtej went back to the Punjab. His father was ill, with Parkinson's disease; he was soon to die. It was still the time of Mrs Gandhi's Emergency, and there was an agitation against it by the Sikh political party. The agitation was going on from the Golden Temple.

'It kept on nagging people that they were not free. It's all right to make two ends meet and have an animal existence, but there's more to life. We have in India two absolutely opposed ideas about government and politics. The Hindu idea is that government must have every right to do as it pleases. This is how the violations of the constitution are tolerated by everybody. The Hindu idea is that whatever the government does is the law. It is more susceptible to dictatorship. The Sikh idea is that God is the only true sovereign, and that governments have a mandate to govern on the condition that they do justice. I was very happy that my people were resisting this subversion of the laws and constitution during the Emergency.'

Gurtej didn't go back to Andhra Pradesh. 'In 1979 I joined the

Punjab government – an IAS transfer, on deputation – and worked until 1980. It was a good experience. The chief minister was known to me. He was not a crookish man. We worked on a big process of decentralizing certain powers. It was good for democracy.'

He also began at this time to be politically active. 'Bhindranwale was in the air.' This was the fundamentalist or revivalist preacher who was to become the 'monster' of Sikh politics. 'Since 13 April 1978' – the 13th of April is a date that recurs in Sikh affairs: it is the date of the harvest festival, and is chosen as the date of great events: the first Sikhs were baptized on this date by the 10th Guru – 'since 13 April 1978 he had shot into prominence. He was a young man who had recently become the leader of a seminary.' The immediate cause of Bhindranwale's fame was a dispute with a Sikh sect called the Nirankaris. 'The Nirankaris are as old as independence. They were a reform movement started in Sikhism in the late 19th century. And then one Buta Singh took over that movement, and he was supported by the government to create a schism in the Sikh body.' It wasn't clear from this account whether the government that encouraged the Nirankaris was the British Indian government, or the government of independent India. 'In a demonstration aginst the Nirankaris on the 13th of April 1978, 13 of Bhindranwale's followers were shot.'

In this atmosphere of excitement, Gurtej took up political work. He began to help Sant Longowal in the Punjab water problem. Longowal was another religious leader; he was to be murdered in 1985, the year after Bhindranwale and many others were killed in the army action at the Golden Temple.

Gurtej, explaining his association with Sant Longowal, said, 'The Sikh idea is the service of mankind. And here was a representative of my people asking me to be with him in this agitation. Everybody must serve his people first, and through them serve humanity.'

He resigned from the IAS in 1982. 'My deputation was over, and there was trouble over a paper I read about the Sikh problem. I thought that people didn't want me in the service. I think that the administration was objecting to my religious activities.'

He had told me the day before that at the boarding school in Dehra Dun, far from the atmosphere of home, he had read ballads about the suffering of 'my people'; and that Kapur Singh had later talked to him about the persecution of the Sikhs. It didn't seem to me a sufficient explanation of the way he had developed. It occurred to me now to ask him again about his childhood.

How had his family heard of this boarding school in Dehra Dun? Was he sent off alone, or were there other boys from the village with him?

'Three of us were sent. A brother and a cousin and I. Somebody in my grandfather's village was already studying there. The school was run by the Irish Brothers, the order of St Patrick.'

'How often did you go back home?'

'We just came home for the holidays. It has taught me a lesson. I will never send my children to a boarding school.'

'When did you go?'

'1951. From 1951 to 1961.'

'But in 1951 you were just four.'

'Every day I used to sit up in bed and pray that the term should come to an immediate end. We were allowed to go home once in six months, for a month or so.'

An exile from four to fourteen: so the memories he had spoken of the day before, of the camel rides with his grandfather, so gentlemanly with his clean clothes and white turban and watch and horse carriage, and the making of the snakebite serum at the start of the rainy season – all those memories would have been like memories of a lost paradisal life, something far removed from the India to which he would have been awakening over the 10 years in Dehra Dun.

It also occurred to me – but this was two or three months later – that it might have been at that Irish Catholic school, with the example of the Irish brothers for 10 whole years, a school term running for six solid months, and this was in the 1950s, still close to colonial times, in the decade before the discovery by the hippies and others of a spiritual and romantic India, it occurred to me that in his solitude over those 10 years some idea of the greater seriousness or modernity of revealed religion, and some wish to touch his own faith with this non-Indian magic, might have come to Gurtej.

But that idea, about revealed religion, didn't come to me until much later; I couldn't put it to Gurtej. At the time I was too taken with the idea of the four-year-old child sent away from home.

How had he managed? Did he think he had gained anything from the separation and the loneliness?

He said, 'I think if I hadn't gone to the boarding school I wouldn't have been able to appreciate the basic nature of things, and I would never have tried to analyse why certain things function as they do.'

I asked him to talk about the changes that had come about in the village he knew.

'There has been a revolution. Attitudes have changed – towards the joint family system, to begin with. Agrarian relationships have changed. My paternal grandfather at one time had about 3000 acres of land. Every year he would buy some.'

An idea came to him. He broke off what he was saying and added, as if in parenthesis, 'And yet my father wasn't an educated man. He stayed at school until the fourth standard. My grandfather' – the gentlemanly figure of Gurtej's childhood – 'didn't believe in education. When I was doing my M.A. I heard my grandfather, my paternal grandfather, say to my father one day, "Why don't you take this boy out of school?" He still thought I was going to the secondary school. And my father, not wishing to show disrespect, said, "What can I do? He doesn't listen."' And, for the first time since we had met, Gurtej laughed.

'My grandfather was greatly *disturbed* to see me reading. He said I was reading *all* the time. I was the first in the family not to be a farmer, and perhaps the first in the family to be a graduate. In my village there are now 16 people who have their M.A. When I was born there was only one person – and he had done his B.A. and was a teacher. The people are greatly concerned now about what is happening. There is this craze for education. People are paying through the nose to send their children to better institutions.'

He returned to the subject of his grandfather's 3000 acres. 'There's no one with so much land now. There has been fragmentation of holdings. Intensive cultivation, with high-yielding varieties. It's a revolution. I used to go sometimes to see my grandfather in the field, carry his lunch and sometimes buttermilk – he was very fond of buttermilk. The agricultural practices which I saw then are totally extinct today. The cutting of the crops was in April. In most of the land then we had only one crop a year. April was a very hot month. And my grandfather would take about 40 people as labourers, give them sickles, and they would go out to the fields at about four in the morning, to avoid the heat. They would be cutting until 11 o'clock – a whole big row of people sitting in the field and going at it with gusto, holding the stalks in the left hand and cutting with the right, and then moving on, in a competitive spirit.'

After Gurtej the theoretician, the man with ideas about religion and history, this was like another man.

'It was a sort of celebration, this harvesting. The cutters would rest in the afternoon, and go back again in the evening, from 4.30 to 6.30, seven. Now it is impossible to see this sight in any village. Nobody gets up at four in the morning to go to the fields. I think the adoption of machinery has changed the attitude and life. It has given people the education required to handle such complicated machinery, and to that extent they have become more modern. This again is one of the causes of the Punjab problem, which the Hindus in other areas don't understand.'

I said that what he was saying about machinery was true of other parts of India as well, in villages and cities. It was an aspect of the Indian industrial revolution.

He appeared to agree, but went on, 'Agricultural man comes in touch with several aspects of administration very early in life. Because of water, he understands the hierarchy of officials. Because of seeds, he gets to know the universities. He understands the functioning of government much better than people in towns do.'

He went back to the subject of change. 'We used to have sharecroppers. That's gone. The dependence on labour is no more to the same extent. During the harvest the common scene in the evening used to be the sickles being sharpened. The poor carpenter would be at it the whole night, because the sickles were required again in the morning. Today I have several people in my village who make and repair the new agricultural implements. In small towns in the Punjab you now have a long row of repair shops on both sides of the road.'

He thought of something else that had changed. 'Nobody in the village is paid in kind any more. And there is the position of the harijans, the scheduled castes. That has changed. One day, when I was a child, I had water from a well in the village. I didn't know it was the harijan well. My uncle didn't allow me to enter the house. I had to sit there in the entrance, and the village *granthi* – the reader of the Sikh scriptures – was called, and he gave me some water, to purify my misdeed. Today the same uncle has harijans working in his kitchen. They cook for him.

'This has taken place in the Punjab, but it is going to be extended to the entire country. The attitudes of the people are going to change everywhere, and they are going to expect more and more of their government. The government is deteriorating fast. It will not be able to come up to the expectations of the people, and therefore I see a deep-rooted chasm in the country. Utter chaos. Our government has become a sort of mafia – the politician, the government servant, and the trader, none of them primary producers. They are going to come into conflict with the producers.'

Gurtej gave me copies of some of the papers he had written on the Punjab and Sikh issue. One of the papers, written for a university seminar at the beginning of 1982, might have been the one that had got him into trouble with the administration. It was called 'Genesis of the Sikh Problem in India'. It reminded me of Kapur Singh's writing; it was academic in tone, with long sentences and difficult words, and with quotations from the Sikh scriptures in the footnotes. Its primary theme was the separateness of the Sikh faith and ideology from the Hindu; its further theme was that the Punjab was geographically and culturally more a part of the Middle East than of India. The great enemy of Sikhism and the Sikh empire of Ranjit Singh had been – again – brahminism.

'With nothing more tangible than unflinching faith in the Guru, the Sikhs built up an Empire on the foundations laid by the Guru. They planted the saffron flag' – saffron also the colour of the Shiv Sena in Bombay, with material in that colour draped on the wall panels of the Bombay Municipal Corporation, and decorated with crossed swords – 'in the heartland of the customary invaders, humbled the might of China and reduced the god-king of Tibet. Then they turned to liberating India from the English.' But they were frustrated. 'The Brahminically oriented forces within and without the Punjab cooperated in destroying the Sikhs who alone held out a promise of the early redemption of India.'

So, with his pastoral memories of his grandfather's village, the enchantments of harvest and celebration, there was this other dream of glory, based on Ranjit Singh's short-lived 19th-century kingdom. It was a partial view. But that was to be expected; people all over India, awakening to history and new knowledge of their place in the scheme of things, refashioned history according to their need.

What was unexpected in Gurtej's account of his life and beliefs was how much he took for granted. The constitution, the law, the centres of education, the civil service with its high idea of its role as guardian of the people's rights and improver of their condition, the investment over four decades in industrial and agricultural change – in Gurtej's account, these things, which distinguished India from many of its neighbours, were just there. There was no acknowledgement that generations of reformers and wise men – refusing to yield to desperate conditions – had created those things that had supported Gurtej in his rise from the village.

With his pastoral memories, his dream of Sikh glory, there was also his idea of religious purity. He applied this idea to the affairs of men, and rejected what he found. Like Papu the Jain stock-broker in Bombay, who lived on the edge of the great slum of Dharavi and was tormented by the idea of social upheaval, Gurtej had a vision of chaos about to come. Papu had turned to good works, in the penitential Jain fashion. Gurtej had turned to millenarian politics. It had happened with other religions when they turned fundamentalist; it threatened to bring the chaos Gurtej feared.

To be baptized was to take nectar, amrit. The Golden Temple was at Amritsar, the pool of nectar. It was said that there had been a pool here known to the first Guru. Sacred sites usually have a history: it was also said that the place was mentioned in a version of the Ramayana, and that 2000 years and more before Guru Nanak, the Buddha had recognized the special atmosphere of the Golden Temple site. The Emperor Akbar, the great Mogul, gave the site to the fourth Guru, and the first temple was begun by the fifth Guru in 1589, the year after the Spanish Armada. In the chaos of the 18th century the Temple suffered much from the Muslims. The Sikh king Ranjit Singh rebuilt it in the 19th century. He gave the central temple its gold-leaf dome. This gold leaf, reflected in the artificial lake, has a magical effect. Even after the battle-marks of recent years the Temple feels serene.

Bhindranwale came to the sanctuary of the Golden Temple in

1982, and he turned it into his fortress and domain. He was thirty-five. Four years before, he had been only a preacher and the head of a Sikh seminary; now he was a politician and a warrior. He was also an outlaw: pursuing a vendetta against the Nirankari sect, whom he considered heretics, he had been accused of murder.

He was a proponent of the pure faith; he was persecuted; he offered his followers a fight on behalf of the faith. He incarnated as many of the Sikh virtues as any one man could possess. He and his followers controlled the Temple. The guns were smuggled in from Pakistan. From the Temple, killings were planned, and bombings, and bank robberies. Not all of these things were done with Bhindranwale's knowledge; there would have been a number of free-lance actions: the seeds of chaos were right there. The Temple provided sanctuary; it was the safe house. It was not physically isolated from the town; the old town went right up to its walls. Guns and men could come and go without trouble.

In that atmosphere some of the good and poetic concepts of Sikhism were twisted. One such idea was the idea of *seva* or service. When terror became an expression of the faith, the idea of seva altered.

This is the testimony of one man: 'Inderjit was a close adherent of Bhindranwale. He was involved in the murder of Sandhu. Inderjit used to come to Darbar Sahib [the Golden Temple] and ask for any seva from Bhindranwale. He had once come to me also and had offered his services for any action. Since I hardly knew him, and he had come on his own to see me, I did not place any trust in him. He was, in fact, a very suspicious-looking character. He had developed friendship with [some people] who used to go out of the Golden Temple complex for committing terrorist actions. Two days after the assassination of Sandhu, Inderjit came to Darbar Sahib. By his exuberant behaviour and boastful talks he made it quite clear that he had a hand in the killing of Sandhu, and that he prided about it.' Sandhu, in fact, was Inderjit's next-door neighbour. Inderjit's service or seva was to give information about his neighbour's movements to the seven-man killer team. Neighbourliness had no place in this idea of the faith.

Bhindranwale's military adviser in the Temple was Shabeg Singh. He had been a major-general in the army, and had served with distinction in the Bangladesh war of 1971. Then something had gone wrong: he had been cashiered from the army for embezzlement, but allowed to keep his rank. Revenge had become his religion; Bhindranwale's cause had become his.

From the witness quoted above, there is this story of how preparations were made to take on the state: 'As the events were taking place at a very fast pace, it was appreciated that the police entry into the Golden Temple had become imminent. It was decided that the Sikh youth should be mobilized . . . The decision was taken in March-April 1984. Groups of Sikh youth numbering 30 to 50 came to the Golden Temple for the purpose. In the car-parking space in the Ram Dass Langar' – one of the Temple kitchens – 'wooden partitions were erected to lodge them there. In one of the rooms Shabeg Singh used to impart theoretical training about firearms. Demonstrations were given by him and sometimes by a few of us . . . These groups were treated to inflammatory sermons . . . The groups used to stay for two or three days. In all, about 8000 to 10,000 youth would have been covered.'

In this way Bhindranwale made himself politically powerful, and he might have made himself more powerful if he had had more time. But the free-lance terrorist actions continued, and in June 1984 the army moved in. The army had underestimated the strength of the defenders; about 100 soldiers died. This was not the end of the matter. Bhindranwale's followers, and others, occupied the Temple again and made it again a terrorist base. In 1986 the police went in once more; and again after that the terrorists came. In May 1988 the police did what they should have done at the begining: they cut off water and electricity and laid siege to the terrorists within the Temple. Many of the terrorists occupied the central gold-domed sanctum in the middle of the pool. Police marksmen outside the Temple fired at those who tried to get water from the pool. It was the Punjab summer, and very hot. Nearly 200 terrorists surrendered. During the siege the central temple had been defiled, used as a latrine, by the terrorists. Elsewhere in the Temple bodies were discovered of people who had been killed by the terrorists before the police action.

The men who had defiled the central temple had not fought to the end. A Sikh journalist who witnessed the siege was shocked by their surrender. He had been brought up to have another idea of good Sikh behaviour. This idea had already been confounded by some of the terrorist actions. He hadn't believed that people of his faith would kill women and children; he hadn't believed that they

447

would stop a bus and kill all the passengers. He had thought, at first, that these stories had been made up by the authorities. And there were people who continued to believe that the men who had surrendered during the siege of the Temple were not Sikhs at all. A pamphlet written by a retired army officer said that the men were 'government-sponsored . . . criminals . . . given Sikh form and apparel and taught rudimentary knowledge of the Sikh traditions.'

The establishing of a Sikh identity was a recurring Sikh need. Religion was the basis of this identity; religion provided the emotional charge. But that also meant that the Sikh cause had been entrusted to people who were not representative of the Sikh achievement, were a generation or so behind.

Bhindranwale had spent most of his life in a seminary in the country town of Mehta Chowk, not far from Amritsar.

At the entrance to the town there were small shops set in bare earth yards on both sides of the road. One shop had this sign, as spelt here: UNIVERSIL EMPLOYMENT BEURO *Overseas Employment Consultant*. All around were fields of ripe dwarf wheat, due to be harvested in a few days. There were also fields of mustard, and fields of a bright-green succulent plant, grown as animal fodder. Lines of eucalyptus marked the boundaries between fields, adding green verticals to the very flat land: line standing against eucalyptus line all the way to the horizon suggested woodland in places.

Fields went right up to the seminary. The flat land, spreading to the horizon below a high sky, seemed limitless; but every square foot of agricultural earth was precious. The gurdwara or temple attached to the seminary had white walls, and the Mogul-style dome that Sikh gurdwaras have, speaking of the origin of the organized faith in Mogul times. The dome looked rhetorical; it stressed the ordinariness of the Indian concrete block which it crowned. The window frames of the white block were picked out in blue. The main hall of the gurdwara was quite plain, with big-bladed ceiling fans, and a wide railed upper gallery. Coloured panes of glass in the doorways were the only consciously pretty touch.

The seminary building was just as plain. On the upper floor, in a concrete room bare except for two beds, the man who was the chief preacher talked to the visitors. There were no more guns at the seminary, he said; and they took in only children now. Some of those children, boys, came to the room, to look. They wore the blue seminarian's gown that went down to mid-shin. It was bright outside, warm; the gowned and silent small boys in the bare room, come to look at the visitors, made one think of the boredom of childhood, of very long, empty days. Some idea of sanctuary and refuge also came to one. Many of these children were from other Indian states; some – solitaries, wanderers – seemed to have been converted to Sikhism, and to have found brotherhood and shelter in the seminary. That idea of welcome and security was added to when a big blue-gowned boy brought in a jug of warm milk and served it to the visitors in aluminium bowls.

The chief preacher said he had come to the seminary when he was about the age of the boys in the room. He had left his family home to stay in the seminary: that was more than 20 years ago.

It was in some such fashion that Bhindranwale had come to the seminary. He had come when he was four or five. Twenty-five years later he had become head of the seminary; and five years after that – after he had taken on the heretics among the Sikhs – he had moved to the Golden Temple. There, two years later, he had died.

He was from a farming family, one of nine sons, and he had been sent to the seminary because his family couldn't support all their children. What could he have known of the world? What idea would he have had of towns or buildings or the state? In these village roads, that ran between the rich fields, there were low, dusty, red-brick buildings, with rough extensions attached, sometimes with walls of mud, sometimes with coverings of thatch on crooked tree-branch poles. Straw dried on house roofs. Shops stood in open dirt yards.

After 25 years in the seminary, he began to call people back to the true way, the pure way. He would go out preaching; he became known. One man heard him preach in 1977 – a year before his great fame – in the town of Gayanagar in Rajasthan. Three thousand people, perhaps 5000, had come to hear the young preacher from Mehta Chowk, and Bhindranwale spoke to them for about 45 minutes. 'He held them spellbound, talking the common man's language.' What was said? 'He asked people not to drink. He said, "Drinking does you harm, and you feel guilty. Everybody wants to be be like his father. Every Sikh's father is Guru Gobind Singh. So a Sikh should wear long hair, and have no vices." There were many references to the scriptures.'

In this faith, when the world became too much for men, the religion of the 10th Guru, Guru Gobind Singh, the religion of gesture and symbol, came more easily than the philosphy and poetry of the first Guru. It was easier to go back to the formal baptismal faith of Guru Gobind Singh, to all the things that separated the believer from the rest of the world. Religion became the identification with the sufferings and persecution of the later Gurus: the call to battle.

The faith needed constantly to be revived, and there had been fundamentalist or revivalist preachers before Bhindranwale. One such was Randhir Singh. The movement he had started in the 1920s was still important, still had a following, could still send men to war against heretics and the enemy. The head of the movement now was Ram Singh, a small dark man of seventy-two, who had been a squadron-leader in the air force.

He said of the founder of his movement, 'He saw the light. His skin was dark, but when he saw the light he started glowing. He could see the future and also all the things about the past. His skin glowed more than English people's. He had rosy cheeks – the light emanated from his cheeks. He saw the light when he was twenty-six. He revolted against the British government. This was the Lahore conspiracy case of 1920. He was imprisoned for life.

'In the jail one day a padre asked him, "You look healthy. You must have good food." Sant Randhir Singh said to the padre, "I have the worst food." The padre said, "You look happy. Do you have someone with you, or do you stay alone?" The sant said, "I'm never alone." The jailer said to the padre, "The man is telling lies. We never put two prisoners together." So the padre asked the sant again, "Who stays with you?" And the sant said, "Almighty."

'When the sant came out in the 1930s – after 16 years in prison – he began to devote his life to singing religious verses, and reading, and administering amrit to others.'

I asked Squadron-Leader Ram Singh, 'Why is the amrit necessary?'

He said, 'God is hidden within us. He is a name only – in every human being. When you take amrit, only then you become aware of it – that name comes automatically on your tongue.'

He started on a discourse about amrit. 'It's a mixture of pure water and white sugar. The sugar is created out of white sugar and baking soda. It's heated, so that it swells and foams up, so that, solidified, it forms sugar buns. It is mixed with the water in iron containers, and an iron double-edged sword is moved backward and forward in the mixture. This was initiated by the 10th Guru, Guru Gobind Singh. You give amrit to render the receiver deathless. Iron is a magnetic metal. In that iron vessel in which you mix the amrit you have the greatest concentration of lines of magnetic forces. When a conductor moves across the line of magnetic forces you get an electro-magnetic force. That energizes the sugar buns and water, and to a small extent dissolves the iron in it. So it's a little iron tonic as well.'

We were talking in his sitting room. There was a carpet on the floor, and a cloth on the centre table, and knick-knacks on hanging shelves: a clock, a small statue of a rearing horse, a china jar, a colour snapshot of a child, a small silver salver (a souvenir of London), and some small painted flower-pieces.

Squadron-Leader Ram Singh was born in 1916. His father was a farmer, and he had gone to some trouble to give his son an education. Ram Singh joined the air force in British times, in 1939. In 1957 he had taken amrit.

Why had he felt the need? Had there been some personal crisis? He said no. He had read books by Sant Randhir Singh, and he had discovered that without amrit one just couldn't reach God.

He spoke clearly. I felt he wished to be friendly. He had the tone and manner of a reasonable man, a man at peace. He was in a fawn-coloured costume, with a milk-chocolate-coloured cardigan. He wore what looked to me like a head-tie rather than a full turban; it was of a saffron colour. The knife, one of the five emblems of Sikhism, hung in a sheath from a big black cross-band, and it made him look less like a warrior than a bus conductor. His beard was a yellowish grey.

The movement aimed at creating pure Sikhs, and amrit was necessary. 'After you take amrit, you don't eat food not cooked by *amritdharis*.' People who have taken amrit. 'That helps to control the five evils: lust, anger, covetousness, ego, family attachments.'

It would also have created the idea of brotherhood. Was that why some people in the movement had become suspect to the government?

He said they had had trouble with a reformist Sikh group who believed in living Gurus: they believed, that is, that the line of Gurus didn't end with the death of the 10th Guru in 1708. They were a small group, but they were a great and constant irritant. In 1978 one person from his movement had been killed by people from that group, and some people of the movement had gone underground.

But he spoke as one for whom violence was far away. His life was consumed by his faith. He got up – his day began – at midnight. He had a bath, and said his prayers till four. From four till 5.30 he read from the Sikh scriptures. Then he slept until 8.30. That was his life. That was the life that had come to him with the pure faith he had turned to when he was forty-one. It clearly had given him peace.

Just before we left, his son came in. He was a handsome, light-eyed man. He had overcome polio, and was a doctor. He was sweet-visaged; he radiated gentleness; he had all his father's serenity. He was in government service; he said with a smile that they were currently on strike. The silver salver on the hanging shelf, the souvenir of London, was something he had brought back after a trip to England.

The terrorists lived now only for murder, the idea of the enemy and the traitor, grudge and complaint, like a complete expression of their faith. Violent deaths could be predicted for most of them: the police were not idle or unskilled. But while they were free they lived hectically, going out to kill again and again. Every day there were seven or eight killings, most of them mere items in the official report printed two days later. Only exceptional events were reported in detail.

Such an event was the killing by a gang, in half an hour, of six members of a family in a village about 10 miles away from Mehta Chowk. The two older sons of the family had been killed; the father and the mother; the grandmother, and a cousin. All the people killed were devout, amritdhari Sikhs. The eldest son, the principal target of the gang, had been an associate of Bhindranwale. But a note left by the gang, in the room where four of the killings had taken place – the note bloodstained when it was found – said that the killers belonged to the 'Bhindranwale Tiger Force'.

The North Indian village tends to be a huddle of narrow angular lanes between blank or pierced house walls. Jaspal village, where the killings had taken place, was more open, simpler in plan, built on either side of a straight main street or lane. It was a village of 80 houses, and was a spillover from a neighbouring, larger village. Eight years before, some of the better-off people of that village had begun to build their farmhouses at Jaspal, on big, rectangular plots on either side of the main lane.

When we arrived, in mid-afternoon, the people at work on the edge of the village were cautious. We – strangers arriving in an ordinary-looking hired car – could have been anything, police or terrorists: two different kinds of trouble. They frowned a little harder at their tasks, and pretended almost not to see us. It was strange to find that there was no policeman or official in the village, and that less than 48 hours after the murders the village had been left to itself again.

The central lane was wide and paved with brick, and it was strung across with overhead electric lines. The farmhouse walls on either side were flat and low, some of plain brick, some plastered and painted pink or yellow. In an open space below a big tree there were short poles or stakes for tethering buffaloes, and there was a high mound of gathered-up, dried buffalo manure. At various places down the lane – as though the lane also served as a buffalo pen for some of the villagers – there were flat, empty, propped-up carts with rubber tires, and buffaloes and feeding troughs and heaps or pyramids of dung-cakes for fuel. The village ended where the bricked lane ended. Beyond the lane – half in afternoon shadow now, and dusty where not freshly dunged – there was a narrower dirt path, sunstruck, going through very bright fields of mustard and ripe wheat, with tall eucalyptus trees with their pale-green hanging leaves, and crooked electricity poles.

We didn't have to ask where the house of death was. About 15 women with covered heads were sitting on a spread in the wide gateway. The gateway was painted peppermint green, with diamonds of different colours down the pillars. The two big metal-framed gates had been pulled back: a wrought-iron pattern in the upper part, corrugated-iron sheets fastened to the criss-crossed metal frame on the lower part, the resulting triangles painted yellow and white and blue and picked out in red. At the far end of the farmyard – the vertical leaves of the young eucalyptus trees hardly casting a shadow – the men sat in the open on the ground, white-turbanned most of them, their shoes taken off and scattered about them, a string bed near by. The buffaloes were in their stalls, against the low brick wall, over which the gang had jumped two nights before. Such protection at the front, metal and corrugated-iron; such openness at the back, next to the fields.

We were taken to the farmhouse next door. It seemed a much richer place. The yard was not of beaten earth, but paved with brick, like the lane. It was one of the few houses in Jaspal to have an upper storey. This upper storey was above the entrance. It was decorated with a stepped pattern of black, white, green and yellow tiles, and at the corners there was a regular pattern of half-projecting bricks, for the style. The trailer in the courtyard was to be attached to a tractor: it carried the mysterious, celebratory words that all Indian motor-trucks have at the back: OK TATA. And there was something like a flower garden in one corner of the courtyard: sunflowers, bougainvillaea, nasturtiums, plants that loved the light.

We sat on string beds in the open, bright room at the left of the entrance. The brick ceiling, which was also the floor of the upper room, rested on wooden beams laid on steel joists. The concrete pillars were chamfered, with bands of moulded or carved decoration, and painted in many colours – an echo here of the pillars of Hindu temples before the Muslim invasions. Everything in this courtyard spoke of the owner's delight in his property.

People began to come to us. They sat on the string beds, their backs to the light, or leaned against the painted pillars. The Punjabi costume – elegant in Delhi and elsewhere – was here still only farm-people's clothes, the smeared and dirty clothes of people whose life was bound up with their cattle. A sturdy woman in her thirties, in a grey-green flowered suit, grimy at the ankles, came with a child on her hip and sat on the string bed. The woman's eyes were swollen, almost closed, with crying.

The child who now sat on her lap and held on to her was the seven-year-old son of the eldest brother. The boy had been in the room when his father was killed; he had been saved from the burst of the AK-47 only because another brother had hidden with him under a cot. The boy was still dazed, yet still able from time to

454

time to take an interest in the strangers; occasionally, while people talked, tears appeared in his eyes. He had been put into a clean, pale-brown suit, and his hair had been done up in a topknot.

The uncle who had saved him was a handsome, slender man of twenty-three. He had dressed with some care for this occasion, all the visitors coming: a blue turban, a stylish black-and-grey check shirt. He began to tell of the events; while he did so a girl cousin came and unaffectedly rested her head on his shoulder.

The farming day went on. The buffaloes came home, through the front gateway. The heavy chains they dragged rang dully on the bricked yard, and their hooves made a hollow, drumming sound. And village courtesies were not forgotten: water was brought out for the visitors, and then tea.

Joga was the name of the man in the black-and-grey check shirt. What he said was translated for me then by the journalists with me, and amplified the following day by Avinash Singh, a correspondent of the *Hindustan Times*.

The family had had dinner, Joga said, and a number of them were in the room on the living-quarters side of the courtyard. (The opposite side was for the cattle or buffaloes.) Some of them were 'sipping tea'. A little after nine there was a commotion in the courtyard, and someone called out from there: 'The one who has come from Jodhpur, and poses as a religious man – he should come out.'

Joga thought at first that some villagers were calling, but then the tone of the voices convinced him that they were 'the boys', 'the Singhs'. 'The Singhs': the word here wasn't simply another word for Sikhs. It meant Sikhs who were true to their baptismal vows; and in these villages it had grown to mean men from one or other of the terrorist gangs. 'Singhs' was the word Joga used most often for the men who had come that night. The other word he used was *atwadi*, 'terrorists'. Only once did he say *munde*, 'the boys'.

Joga was holding Buta's son on his lap. As soon as he decided that the men who had come were Singhs, he hid with the child below the cot.

Buta, the eldest brother, went to the door of the room. The men outside had called for the man who had come 'from Jodhpur'. Jodhpur had a meaning: Buta, with 200 or 300 others, had been detained in the fort at Jodhpur as a suspected terrorist for more than four years, from June 1984 to September 1988 – just eight

455

months before. Buta had been detained because he had been in the Golden Temple at the time of the army action, and he was known as a religious follower of Bhindranwale's. Buta admitted being a follower; but he said he wasn't a terrorist. He was in the Golden Temple that day, he said, because he had taken an offering of milk for the anniversary of the martyrdom of the sixth Guru, executed on the orders of the Emperor Jehangir in 1606.

This was the man, only thirty-two, but already with many years of suffering, his life already corrupted, who went and stood at the door and looked out at the many muffled men in the courtyard.

The leader said, 'Who is Buta Singh?'

'I am Buta Singh.'

'Come with us. We want you. We have come to take you.' And the man who spoke said to one of his Singhs, 'Tie his hands.'

Some of the men made as if to seize him by the arms. Buta said, 'I won't, I won't.' There was a scuffle, and two of the Singhs fired. A bullet hit Buta just below his ribs on the right side, and he fell backwards into the room. Buta's mother threw herself on her son, saying to the men, 'Please don't kill.' Buta's brother Jarnail and Buta's wife Balwinder also fell on Buta. The Singhs pulled away Balwinder by her hair from her husband, and they fired again with their AK-47s. Buta hadn't been killed yet; but he was killed now, with his mother and his brother. Buta's grandmother was wounded, and was to die in a few days.

Buta's father ran out from his room at the front of the courtyard, the street side. He ran across the courtyard to where the men with the guns were. He tried to grab one of the guns. He was killed with a shot to the head.

After this, the Singhs – there were eight or nine of them – went out of the gateway to the main village lane. Opposite, a little to the right, was the house of Natha Singh, Buta's uncle, the first cousin of his father. They wanted Natha Singh. When the front gate of Natha's house wasn't opened for them, they went around to the back, climbed over the low wall, and they called for him. Natha had five children; the eldest was a polio-stricken girl of fourteen.

Natha came out when he was called. The gang took him out to the lane, and asked him to take them in his tractor to the house of Baldev. They very much wanted Baldev as well. They had a case against him: Baldev, they said, was an amritdhari Sikh, but Baldev had gone against his vows and had been having dealings with a temple priest in the town of Jalandhar. They didn't find Baldev when they got to his house, which was just at the end of the lane, next to the fields. Baldev had heard the gunfire and had slipped away; he had had threatening letters before because of his religious practices. So they had driven back in the tractor with Natha, and in the lane, just outside his house, they had shot Natha Singh dead.

The Singhs had been in the village for half an hour, not more. Then they were gone. It wasn't until eight hours later, at about 5.30 in the morning, that someone of the family picked up the note the terrorists had left behind – now bloodstained and hard to read. The note said that Buta Singh and Natha Singh had been killed because they had been responsible for the deaths two months before of two terrorists just half a kilometre from the village. There was a price of 30,000 rupees on the head of one of the terrorists killed then.

The police said that the gang in question wanted Buta to join them. Buta, as a man who had been close to Bhindranwale until 1984, would have given the group some 'credibility'.

There was another story as well that the villagers told. Shortly after his release from Jodhpur, Buta – who had taken a B.A. degree while in detention – had applied for a minibus permit. This was part of the government's plan to rehabilitate people like Buta. Buta went one day to the town of Jalandhar to see about his permit. He didn't come home at the time he should have done. People in the village made inquiries, and they found that Buta had been arrested by the Central Reserve Police Force in Jalandhar. He was held for nine days.

Buta never told anyone what he had been arrested for, or what had happened during the nine days of his detention. All they knew was that Buta was very frightened when he came back, and never wanted to be alone when he went out of the village – to the tubewell or the local market. (Some said that Buta was afraid of being caught by the police again. But this didn't seem logical. Buta could have been picked up by the police whether he was with a companion or not. A companion, on the other hand, might have deterred an assassin from the gangs.)

We went at last next door, to the house of death, picking our way past the women sitting in the gateway. They were not keening now; they were sitting as silent as the men in the sunstruck yard – no shade there from the vertical eucalyptus leaves, the afternoon sun seeming in fact to catch the leaves in a kind of glitter. The plastered courtyard wall of the living quarters was painted pink, the pierced ventilation concrete blocks above doorways and windows were peppermint green, like the entrance walls: Mediterranean colours. The doors and windows and the vertical iron bars over the windows were a darker green.

The bedrooms were at the front of the building, on either side of the gateway. The doors opened into the courtyard, and the back wall (with iron-barred windows) was also the wall of the lane. There were two rooms on the left. In addition to being used as bedrooms, Avinash told me, they would have been used as storerooms, with wheat and rice in gunny sacks. Buta Singh's father had been sleeping in the room at the corner of the courtyard; it was from there that he had run out.

The bedroom to the right of the gateway was the principal room of the farmhouse. It was where Buta Singh and his wife slept. It was also the drawing-room. There were no chairs now. The chairs and the centre table, Avinash said, had been removed, because it was known that after the murders visitors were going to come. There were two beds side by side. The bedclothes on them were in disorder. There was an extra bed in the room, together with tin trunks and chests. There was a souvenir of the Golden Temple on a shelf, and Sikh religious calendars on the wall. In Sikh popular art the Gurus are shown with the pupils of their eyes half disappearing below the upper lid, so that more white than usual is seen in the eyeball; this way of rendering the eyes suggests blindness and an inner enlightenment. In this room the pictures made an unusual impression.

There was a photograph of Buta's father-in-law, and there was one other photograph, of Buta himself: a studious-looking young man in glasses. The studiousness and the glasses were a surprise, in this setting of the farmhouse and the village. Buta might have cultivated the scholarly appearance; he would almost certainly have been the first man in his family to have received higher education. Buta's wife, Balwinder, was the only graduate in the village; and no doubt it was her example that had made Buta study for a B.A. degree while he had been in detention in Jodhpur.

Two or three generations – not only of work, but also of political encouragement, political security, development in agriculture, the growth of a national economy – had led Buta's family to where it had got. Two or three generations had led to the beginning of an intellectual inclination in Buta Singh. Awakening to knowledge, he would have seen with a special clarity what he had come from. Ideas of injustice and wrongness would have come more easily to him than ideas of the steady movement of the generations; and the fundamentalism of someone like Bhindranwale would have seemed to answer every emotional need, would have appeared like a programme: ennobling complaint and the idea of persecution, offering history as an idea of glory betrayed, and offering for the present the twin themes of the enemy and redemption. That idea had trapped him and swept him away.

The police said he had been killed because he had refused to join the gang. The note left by the Singhs said he had been responsible for the deaths, by police bullets, of two important terrorists. There might have been truth in both statements. It was part of the wretchedness of the situation, where men had to be blooded into the cause, and, once blooded, couldn't turn away. He must have suffered. Everyone said that he was a very religious man. He had bought religious primers for his two young sons; he went twice a day to the gurdwara to pray. Such devoutness! In the beginning it might have met an emotional and intellectual need; later, perhaps, it had become just a praying for protection.

It had ended for him in the next room. The room was at the side of the courtyard. It faced south. The door was open; but, against the pale glare of the dung-plastered courtyard and the sunlit pink-distempered wall, the doorway looked very dark. Inside, in the shadows, brass pots and steel pots glinted on shelves. There were scuff-marks on the floor where Buta and his family had fallen. Not more than 42 hours had passed since then. But the marks might have been made by the people who had come to look. The note left by the killers, when it was found, was soaked in blood. The ground now was black with flies, barely moving.

Only three days before the killing, Avinash told me later, Buta Singh's wife, the graduate, had opened an English-medium school in the neighbouring village. It was something she had wanted to do for a long time. 'I thought my dream had come true,' she told Avinash. 'I didn't know my husband's return from Jodhpur would spell doom for the family.'

Across the lane was the house of Natha Singh, Buta's uncle. His wife couldn't read. She had five children, the eldest with a disability. She told Avinash, 'I don't know what to do. My world is finished.'

It was for Natha Singh that a new spasm of mourning began when we went outside. To the right of the peppermint-green entrance with the multi-coloured diamond pattern, women were now sitting, now throwing themselves down, on the spot where Natha had been killed, when he had driven the tractor back from Baldev's house. On both sides of the dung-dropped lane farming life went on: buffaloes held their heads down to the troughs at the side of the lane, against the walls of houses. Taking out these animals, bringing them back, milking them or unyoking them, feeding them, bedding them down – these things gave rhythm and correctness to a day and were followed like religion.

Two other men from the village had been detained in Jodhpur. While the women keened, and the buffaloes ate, we heard one man's story. On the very day Ranjit was released from Jodhpur, his brother was killed. Ranjit didn't say who his brother had been killed by; this suggested that his brother had been killed by 'the boys'. His brother's body was found 20 kilometres away from Amritsar – not far from where we were. And so it happened that on the day Ranjit returned home, after four and a half years in Jodhpur, his brother's body also came home. That had happened just a month before.

How could they talk so calmly of grief? They had to some extent been prepared by the faith; but they could talk like that because many hundreds had suffered like them. Avinash said that he and other correspondents had seen more than 50 mass killings such as we had heard about that afternoon. Exactly a year and a week before, 18 members of a Rajasthani clan, half of whom were Sikhs, had been killed. The AK-47 was a weapon of pure murder. It could empty a magazine of 32 bullets in two and a half seconds; the bullets sprayed out at many angles, and could kill everyone in a room in those two and a half seconds. In one night in one sub-division of Amritsar 26 people had been killed, including a thirty-day-old baby girl and the ninety-one-year-old head of a family.

We drove back to Amritsar through by-ways and village-ways, looking at the rich, well-cultivated land. It was still afternoon and bright, still safe. After some time we felt we had lost our way. We were on a dirt road between irrigated fields. We saw two men on a bicycle, one man doing the pedalling, one man on the carrier. The man on the carrier was sitting elegantly, sideways, feet together, but not dangling or hanging down. His shoes were locked together and they were lifted, as though above the dust. When we stopped to ask the way, he slid off, with a practised movement, and offered to come with us, to set us on the road to Amritsar.

He was as handsome as his posture on the bicycle had suggested. He was a Sikh, with a trimmed beard. The trimmed beard had a meaning: it meant he had not taken amrit. He had heard about Buta Singh's death, and the other murders, and he thought it dreadful. He himself didn't belong to any of the purely Sikh political groups. He was in business in a small way and he considered himself successful. He enjoyed his success. He had built a house, he said, with toilets and flush system and everything. He had spent four lakhs on this house, £16,000. But he was thinking now that he might have to give up his house and leave the area. He hadn't taken amrit, and he didn't intend to. He didn't think he would be able to live by the strict amritdhari rules, and he didn't want to get into trouble with the boys, as other people had done.

In the Sikh catalogue of the torments and martyrdoms of its founding Gurus, the bricking up alive of the two sons of the 10th Guru has a special place. The story – with its echoes of *King John* and *Richard III* – has some of the quality of myth.

The man who orders the execution of the children – boys aged nine and ten – is the Mogul governor of the town of Sirhind. Only one person objects to the cruelty: he is a Muslim nobleman of Afghan ancestry, the Nawab of Malerkotla. Then he pleads for the bodies to be honourably cremated: Muslims are buried, Sikhs and Hindus are cremated. The governor says, 'All right. We'll grant you a cremation site. But it will be only as big as what you can cover with gold sovereigns.' The Nawab agrees. He lays out part of his treasure on the ground, and the two bodies are cremated there. So two sacred places come into being: the place where the boys were bricked up, and the place where they were cremated. And the anniversary of the martyrdom is marked by a ritual procession from one place to the other.

Where there isn't a sense of history, myth can begin in that

461

region which is just beyond the memory of our fathers or grandfathers, just beyond living witness. This story of the bricked-up children might have occurred 2000 or 200 or 100 years ago. The events can, in fact, be dated. The 10th Guru gave amrit, baptized the first Sikhs, established the Sikh martial order, in 1699, in the town of Anandpur. Two years later he was besieged in the town by the Mogul forces. The siege lasted for three years. The Guru escaped with two of his sons; but the Guru's mother and his two other sons were captured. They were taken to Sirhind. In 1710 Sirhind fell to the Sikhs.

Events which can be dated and analysed, and placed at a proper distance from the present, can also at some stage begin to appear far away; can fade. Myths are fresh; they never lose their force. Though at Malerkotla in 1762 the Sikhs were massacred by an invading Afghan army, in Malerkotla in 1947, at the time of the partition of India and the population exchange between India and Pakistan – the flight of Muslims to Pakistan, and Sikhs and Hindus from Pakistan – in Malerkotla in 1947, because of that Afghan nobleman who laid down gold sovereigns over the cremation site of the two sons of the 10th Guru, no Muslim was harmed. In the 1960s the Sikh political party, the Akali Dal, nominated the Nawab of Malerkotla as their candidate, and he got the Sikh vote in three elections.

I was told this by Amarinder Singh. Amarinder was the head of the house of Patiala. Informally – because the titles of princes have been abolished, and the princes 'de-recognized' – he was the Maharaja of Patiala. All Sikhs are 'Singhs'; in the common surname differences of caste and rank were intended to be submerged. The ideal remains; but almost from the start Sikh chieftains arose, and Patiala was one of the grandest. After Sirhind – where the two boys were bricked up – was incorporated into Patiala territory, it became the family tradition to mark the martyrdom of the Guru's sons with a ritual procession.

'Sirhind was the seat of the Mogul governor. When the Sikhs eventually captured the fort, there was nothing on the spot. No Sikh emblem had survived. The Moguls had destroyed it all. The sites were located where the bricking was done, and the first gurdwara was built. It was subsequently rebuilt. The rebuilding was done by my father in the early 1950s. The tradition was that, on every anniversary, from the site where they were bricked up to the site of the cremation the Guru Granth Sahib was carried on a bier.' A mimic funeral procession, with the Sikh scriptures – as finally established by the 10th Guru – standing in for the Guru's two sons. 'This went on till the 1960s, when the Akali party acquired control of the gurdwara, and they took over the ceremony.'

The family had a special obligation to the faith. 'We are the only family to have been blessed twice by the Guru.' Amarinder was using the collective form of the word 'Guru', as Sikhs often do. The first blessing was given by the sixth Guru, Hargobind (1606-1644), who comforted the crying son of the family: 'What is he crying for? His horses will drink water out of the River Jamuna.' This was the Guru's way of prophesying that Patiala territory would eventually stretch to that river.

A later ancestor was one of those baptized by the 10th Guru. It was to this ancestor that, at the battle of Chamkaur, not long after the disaster of Anandpur, the 10th Guru wrote for help.

'The Guru was surrounded by the Mogul forces in the fort, but he managed to get a message out. In that letter he says, "My home is your home. And I am in danger. Come." But by the time my ancestor arrived, the battle was over.' In that battle the Guru's two other sons died. 'This was the first generation into the Khalsa.' Later, when the Guru was on his way to the South, where he died in 1708 (two years before the Sikhs managed to capture Sirhind), he made a prophecy about the Patiala family and the eventual size of their state.

That letter of the Guru's from Chamkaur was especially precious to the family. It was from that letter that Amarinder's father or grandfather had derived the current Patiala family motto: 'My House Is Your House'. The earlier motto had been 'Heaven's Light Our Guide'; it could still be seen on old Patiala crockery.

On the roof of the palace there was a gurdwara. The only object of Sikh worship is their holy book, assembled over the years by the various Gurus, and given finally the status of a Guru. But in this gurdwara there were also relics of the 10th Guru. After I had washed my hands and covered my head, I was shown some of these relics: a sword of the Guru, in its velvet-covered scabbard; some spears; a letter, the actual transcription of which must have been done by a secretary or scribe.

On the roof of the palace, old pieties: the historical events of 300 years ago absorbed into religion (the 10th Guru died two years after Benjamin Franklin was born). The palace itself spoke of more recent transformations. It was a new palace, built in the 1950s, sumptuous, but without the oriental motifs such as the European architect of the Maharaja of Mysore had lavished on the Mysore City palace of 1912. This new Patiala palace was like a grand European country house, international or neutral in its feel, built for comfort, using the Indian climate well, converting it into an amenity. In its various reception rooms were signed photographs, such as the visitor sees on open days in grand houses in other countries. But here the photographs – of rulers – marked a changing world, a changing vision, an emerging India: the Kaiser, Victor Emmanuel, the Belgian royal family, Tito, Nehru, Indira Gandhi.

There were many pictures, most of them apparently bought in Europe; but few were notable. There had been a school of Sikh painting, developing just before the British time. The works of this school had been small-scale, on paper, a private court art, records of faces for the most part, the sheets assembled in albums or wrapped up in bundles and stored in palace libraries. The taste or judgement hadn't carried over to the art of Europe, larger, in oils, meant for display on walls and serving a purpose that wouldn't always have been clear. So, though there had been an abundance of money, Amarinder's father and grandfather had bought neither old masters nor any of the great names of the century.

The most striking painting was a larger-than-life full-length portrait of Amarinder's father. The Maharajas of Patiala were famous for their great height. The Raja of Patiala whom William Howard Russell met in Patiala in 1858 was more than six feet tall, and heavily built. The exaggeration, in the painting, of Amarinder's father's size, with his regal stance, was monumental in its effect, and breathtaking. Of a piece with that was a large salon-style painting, hung above the wide staircase, of the Silver Jubilee thanksgiving celebration of the King-Emperor George V in London in 1935, with Amarinder's grandfather and other Indian princes, notably Kashmir and Bikaner, shown with the Prince of Wales, the future George VI and Queen Elizabeth, and their daughters Elizabeth and Margaret.

Amarinder said, 'My grandfather was an autocrat through and through. He came to the throne when he was nine years old. He became a full-fledged ruler when he was eighteen, in 1907. From 1907 to 1938 he was a full-fledged ruler. He put Patiala on the map. He picked an able team to run the state. He was a patron of sports, and music. But he was an autocrat.'

His idea of what he owed himself was shown in the palace where he had lived: the old Patiala palace, on the other side of Patiala city.

'It had 1000 rooms and 400 acres. It is now a sports college. It was three-quarters of a mile from my father's room to mine. We actually measured it one day, taking account of all the steps. It was far too big. So my father built this palace in the 1950s. This is still enormous, but at the time it seemed to the family, after the old palace, that it was a little cramped.'

And, before that old palace – the kind of Indian palace that established the idea of the extravagant wealth of the maharajas at the time of the British Raj – there had been the Patiala fort.

'The old fort was used when people had to fight. There is a tower from which people could fire down.'

The fort began to be built in 1714, on the site of the hermitage of a Muslim fakir or holy man. The fakir's fire was lifted into the fort that was built at the time, and that fire had been kept going ever since.

It was in the fort that in 1858 the then Maharaja (or Raja) of Patiala and his courtiers, all in their best clothes and jewels, had ceremonially received William Howard Russell, showing honour to an important representative of the paramount, and now triumphant, Indian power. It is unlikely that the Raja of Patiala would have understood what Russell's job was, but he would have known that Russell's opinion mattered, and he did all that he could to make a good impression. He went out some way from the fort, on his caparisoned elephant, to meet Russell. He offered Russell an elephant as well, and he ceremonially offered a hand – all this ritual of courtesy and welcome in something like dumb show.

The fort was now half in decay. It was in the middle of the bazaar area in Patiala city, with whole streets, or large sections of them, selling shoes, or certain food dishes, or embroidered garments – Patiala specialities. The first courtyard, where Ruseell had entered on his elephant, was now used as a urinal by some people. A house built at a later date for important visitors, a house with classical columns, was falling down. Squatters lodged there; and someone had chalked, roughly, *UNSAFE*.

Within, the fort quickly became a maze of small courtyards and passages and steps. There was a small Mogul-style garden, restful, even in its semi-ruin, after brick and plaster. In the late 19th and early 20th centuries ideas of elegance came to Patiala from Britain and Europe. In the 18th century elegance was provided by the Mogul. There is an irony, though, in the 18th-century Sikh borrowings from the Mogul enemy: today, long after the disappearance of Mogul power, the decorated 18th-century Mogul dome lives on in the Sikh gurdwara, as much an emblem of the Sikh place of worship as the spire is of the Christian church.

Apart from this garden, the fort was built up, all paved, no earth showing. Passages, courtyards, terraces, roofs: crumbling brick and plaster, more perishable than wood. Here and there were small, oppressive, over-decorated, dark rooms, with dark mirrors on the walls and carved ceilings. Here and there a ceiling had collapsed, and it could be seen that the village way of building a brick roof, as in the farmhouses at Jaspal village – the bricks set on end on timber beams – had also been the way of the men who had built for the rajas and rulers. Impossible to restore or preserve the old fort: it was in the nature of this brick to crumble. A palace like this could last only while it was lived in. Here and there small attempts at restoration – concrete patching, whitewash – added to the feeling the fort gave of having been built over many times, grown room by room and space by space to its limit, and then finally abandoned.

In some rooms at the top, even with all the decay, the religious rites connected with the foundation of the town and the Patiala fort – blending Muslim and Hindu and Sikh piety – were going on. It was necessary here to take off shoes, because the site was still consecrated. The fire of the Muslim fakir that had been lifted up into the original fort of 1714 was kept going: it was one of the wonders of Patiala. Only oak was used for this fire, and the ash was offered to make a holy mark (a Hindu form). Hindu images of Krishna and Kali were tended in an adjoining room. In another room, opening on to a roof patio, a dark-complexioned reader was chanting from the Sikh scriptures, with a barefoot attendant swinging a whisk over the holy books, which were covered with very fine silk cloths. So, at the very top of the abandoned fort, as at the top of the contemporary palace, there was a reminder of the beginning of clan or family things.

It would have been touch-and-go for the clan in the early part of the 18th century. But the Mogul power declined; the Afghan invasions and raids ceased; the Sikhs came into their own. Patiala state at the end had territory of nearly 7000 square miles. A fair amount of this came in the early 19th century.

'In the 1830s the Gurkhas decided to take the entire mountain range. In 1830 they marched and attacked our hills. All the hill rajas got together and asked for help, and we sent our troops. It was a six-months' war. The Gurkhas were defeated. The head of the Nepalese general hung on the Patiala gate until it disintegrated.'

Patiala never got on with the great Sikh ruler, Ranjit Singh. 'When Ranjit Singh threatened, Patiala entered into a treaty with the British. Patiala stayed neutral in the Anglo-Sikh wars.' Even before the Sikhs were defeated in 1849, two battalions of Sikh irregulars were recruited by the British in Patiala. When the Mutiny broke out eight years later Patiala remained loyal to its treaty with the British. That support was crucial; without it the British might have been defeated in North India.

'In our family archives there is a letter from the last Mogul emperor, Bahadur Shah. In our archives we keep rulers' personal documents; the other documents have gone to the state. In the palace we have a librarian looking after our archives. The mutineers pressed Bahadur Shah into being their titular ruler, and he wrote letters to all the Indian states asking for their support. But at that time his domain wasn't even Delhi. His domain was literally only the Red Fort. The letter was in English, very flowery, probably written by a scribe. It was a scroll two feet long. But we had this mutual defence pact with the British, and it was that which we had to honour.'

In June 1858, when the Mutiny had been more or less suppressed, William Howard Russell went 'with a party' to look at the defeated emperor in the Red Fort at Delhi. The Red Fort was occupied by British soldiers and Gurkhas (recruited now, like the Sikhs, to replace the soldiers from other mutinous communities). The emperor was squatting on his haunches in an empty passage off a small roof patio. He was a small, withered man of eighty-two, barefooted, in a dirty muslin tunic and thin cambric skullcap. He was vomiting into a brass basin; Russell didn't ask why. The old man was mentally far away from the people who had come to stare at him. He had a habit of poetry, and Russell said that a day or so before he had composed a poem, writing 'some neat lines on the wall of his prison by the aid of a burnt stick'. This didn't arouse Russell's wonder or compassion, only his mockery. He never thought to find out what the words meant.

British people in India at this time were talking of blowing up the Jama Masjid in Delhi, as earlier someone had talked of destroying the Taj Mahal and selling the marble. Even the Raja of Patiala had become suspect to the British, and Russell heard complaints that he had been in communication with the Emperor Bahadur Shah.

It seemed from what Amarinder said that there was some truth in the story. He said, 'A brother of the maharaja was very fond of Bahadur Shah, because he was a poet. And he went to offer help to the emperor. After the Mutiny he came back to Patiala, and the British then asked for him to be handed over to them. Patiala refused, and the British couldn't push it because there were few loyal rulers left.

'So a compromise was reached. The maharaja's brother left Patiala. And he eventually renounced the world, living first in Rishikesh in the Himalayas, one of the Hindu centres of learning and pilgrimage, and then in the early part of the century he moved south to Bangalore.' Bangalore was in the princely state of Mysore, somewhat removed from British jurisdiction. 'There he died in the 1950s, well over a hundred. He became a teacher and a sadhu kind of figure. His wife continued to live in the old Patiala fort. Theirs had been a child marriage. She had come as a child to the fort, and was left by her husband when she was nine. And she continued living in the fort, refusing to leave, until the 1930s. She had never seen anything outside the fort. There was strict purdah in those days. She had never seen a car, a train, people outside the palace, a forest, a field. My grandfather wanted her to take drives. He insisted and insisted, and – it must have been in the early 1930s or late 1920s – my grandfather forcibly took her out in the car to see the things she hadn't seen before. While she lived in the fort she refused to let anyone draw her water from the well. This was because she wanted to live the difficult life she thought her husband was enduring.'

It was hard to believe in this story. If, say, the brother of the

Raja of Patiala was sixteen when he had gone to offer his help to Bahadur Shah, he would have been born in 1840 or 1841. To have died in the 1950s would have made him over one hundred and ten at the time of his death. And his child bride would have died at the age of ninety or thereabouts. Still, the story as Amarinder told it contained many of the great transformations that had come to India from Mutiny to independence. The lifetime of those people would have contained not only the transformation of the Sikhs from ruffianly frontiersmen to farmers and businessmen; it also contained the transformation of their rulers from warrior chieftains to Raj-style maharajas.

Amarinder said, with a wave of his hand, 'My grandfather wouldn't have been able to *understand* this.' And by 'this', Amarinder meant independence, parliament, universal suffrage. 'Do you know, my grandfather kept my maternal grandfather in prison, and kept them out of Amritsar for nine years, for being a member of the Praja Mandal. That was what the people involved in the freedom struggle called the Congress in the princely states. My maternal grandfather was man of character, too. He didn't climb down. All the family's confiscated property was returned only when my parents got married.'

Two generations lay between the jewelled ruler William Howard Russell saw in the Patiala fort in 1858, and the maharaja who ruled absolutely in the 1000-roomed Motibagh Palace from 1907 to 1938. One role followed on from the other: the British connection enhanced the ruler's glory. It was altogether different for Amarinder's father.

'My father had a difficult life. He took over in 1938 when his father died. He was twenty-five. There was the war in 1939, and then from 1945 there was the independence movement. My father was chancellor of the Chamber of Princes. So he lived with instability. With independence he was the first to sign the instrument of accession, and Patiala merged with all the Punjab states. It was a decline for my father personally. From being a ruler he became a governor of a state. Patiala was being considered as the possible capital of Indian Punjab. But the chief minister at the time got it scotched. He thought that Patiala would always have an influence in state matters, so he cooked up the idea of building a brand-new city at Chandigarh. And then in 1958 the Punjab States Union merged with the Punjab, and my father became a *nobody*.'

He stood for the Punjab assembly, but he didn't like politics. He became an ambassador; it didn't assuage his grief. 'He was an introvert. He kept the problems inside. When he died in 1974 – he was only sixty-one – the doctors said his heart was like that of a man of eighty-five.'

Amarinder himself had no problems of adaptation. He was born in 1942; he was five when independence came. 'I've been brought up in a modern environment.' There was a palace education: an English nanny, a German kindergarten tutor, and training by 'a great master' in Sikh scriptures, legends and folklore. There was also a full education outside the palace, in preparatory schools in Simla and Kasauli, in a famous Indian public school, and then in the Indian Military Academy at Dehra Dun. He joined the army, enlisting in the oldest Sikh regiment, directly descended from the two battalions raised in Patiala in 1846. He loved army life, and would have liked an army career. But he had to leave the army to look after the affairs of the family. He later 'grew into politics' – exercising, perhaps, something of the skills of his 18th-century ancestors during the early days of the Patiala state.

Then the preacher Bhindranwale appeared. There was a terrorist crisis; and the army that Amarinder loved was ordered to move on the Temple he held sacred.

'When the chips were down I couldn't let 300 years of history go. It was the Sikhs who made Patiala. The two Gurus have blessed us. I had to stand with our people.'

When I went back to Chandigarh I saw Gurtej again. It was then that he told me – what I suppose was common knowledge – that after Operation Bluestar, the code-name for the army action at the Golden Temple, he had gone underground for more than four years. For the first time he spoke in some detail about Bhindranwale. Kapur Singh, the dismissed ICS officer, had been Gurtej's first hero and mentor; Bhindranwale was the second.

'He was always a religious man. To the very end. He was the son of a small farmer in Faridkot district. The district was named after Farid, a Muslim Sufi saint of the 13th century; his couplets appear in our scriptures. Bhindranwale was born in 1947. He was one of nine sons. He was the son of a second wife. The father had seven sons from the first wife, two sons from the second wife. The father couldn't support all the sons, and at an early age, four or five, Bhindranwale was sent to the seminary.'

Gurtej was also born in 1947. He, too, had been sent away to a boarding school when he was four or five. And he too came from a farming family, though his grandfather had been rich, with 3000 acres.

'The father had a little land, and there was no intensive agriculture at that time. One son went to the army; he is retired now as a captain. Another son went to Dubai and is now back, well-to-do, still farming. Others are also farming.

'Bhindranwale spent all his years in the seminary, and we never heard anything about him until 1976. By then he was married, with two sons. His wife would have stayed in the village; it was an arranged marriage. Bhindranwale was known as a contemplative man, totally unconcerned about the world around him. Sometimes he would go to work in his family fields, and he was known as a very hard worker. Cutting starts on the 13th of April. It's a very hot period; the sun shines harshly. Bhindranwale would start cutting in the early morning and go at it right until the evening, without food or drink. He was a very determined man. This was told me by one of his brothers.'

And not for the first time Gurtej, talking about the life of the village, the life of the fields, fell – easily – into a lyrical strain.

'In 1977 the head of the seminary died. He had nominated Bhindranwale to succeed him. The head of the seminary died during the Nirankari controversy.' The Nirankaris: reformist Sikhs to some, heretical to others. 'His legacy to Bhindranwale was the continuation of this struggle.'

The following year, on the day of the spring or harvest festival, an important day in the Sikh religious calendar, there was a clash between the two groups in Amritsar, and a number of Bhindranwale's followers were killed. With this event Bhindranwale became a figure.

Gurtej said, 'I got to know him in 1980. The high priest who had given me amrit in 1974 had died, and I went to his village for the last rites. And there I met Bhindranwale. He was a very truthful man, a man of his word. He never went back on what he said. He was a man of God. He had unbounded faith in God. While taking decisions he only consulted his conscience. He lived the life of a mendicant.

471

'In 1980 the head of the Nirankaris was killed in his own place in Delhi – just like Indira Gandhi later – and he was allegedly killed by somebody who had been employed as a carpenter there. The Arya Samaji press blamed Sant Bhindranwale for the killing and demanded his arrest. Shortly after that, the head of the Arya Samaji press was killed near Jalandhar, and it was in this connection that warrants were issued for the arrest of the Sant.

'The Arya Samajis control the Hindu press of Punjab. The history of Punjab in this century is full of controversies between Arya Samajis and Sikhs, the essence of the trouble being that the Arya Samajis were attacking the separate identity of the Sikhs. At the beginning of this century the Arya Samajis publicly converted some *chamar*' – untouchable – 'Sikhs back to Hinduism at Jalandhar. And their hair was cut off, plaited together into a rope, and the rope was sold at a public auction. The idea was to ridicule Sikhism and Sikhs.

'At the time the warrants were issued for the arrest of the Sant he was preaching in a village in Haryana. This information was given to him there, perhaps by the Haryana administration, who didn't want any trouble in their area. The Punjab police party arrived after the Sant had left, and they became so angry they burnt his buses and destroyed his holy books. After this, his arrest was enforced at Mehta Chowk, at the seminary. A big crowd had collected on the day of his arrest. After he had been taken away he appealed to the people to be peaceful. The police resorted to firing – at the town itself – and 34 people were killed. The police claimed they had been attacked with swords.

'These three things upset him: the burning of his buses and holy books, his being accused as a conspirator, and the killing of his people. He was in jail for some months. Then he was released unconditionally. In 1982 he went to the Golden Temple. The circumstances were like these. Two or more of his followers had been arrested. And then the people he sent to supervise the legal protection of these men were themselves arrested. That was when he decided to launch an agitation.

'He was a tall man, six feet one inch, as tall as I am, and a lean man. A very forthright man, outspoken. He had very simple habits. He ate very little. In this he was unlike Sardar Kapur Singh, who liked his food. He had an incisive mind. You could discuss things with him. He knew, for instance, that I ate meat, but he didn't mind. He never asked me to stop eating meat. I had a long argument with him about whether it was according to the tenets of Sikhism to eat or not to eat meat. This was in January 1983 at the Akal Takht in the Golden Temple. The discussion lasted two hours. He kept on telling me in a good-humoured way, "You prove it to me that it is according to the tenets of Sikhism to eat meat, and I will polish off one and a half kilos in no time."

'He used to call us for discussions several times, sometimes just for the interpretation of passages in the scriptures. The seminary supported the traditional interpretation. The seminary interpretation is nearer to the Hindu understanding of the scriptures, and it is all expressed in Hindu terminology. Most of the examples are from Hindu mythology. I used to support the more recent, scientific interpretation, established in 1960 or so.'

I asked about this scientific interpretation.

'It was by Sahib Singh – the interpretation of the scriptures according to the grammar of the language. He was a saintly man, a teacher.'

This statement – I took it down without understanding it fully, and considered it only many weeks later – cast a little light on a difficult sentence on the first page of Kapur Singh's pamphlet, 'The Trial of a Sikh Civil Servant in Secular India': 'The basis of grammar and language are certain metaphysical postulates, cultural patterns and human propensities, the logical demonstration of which may not be possible, but without acceptance of which, neither language nor grammar can be properly studied or understood . . .'

And I wondered whether, in these religious discussions in the Golden Temple, Kapur Singh's ideas might not have filtered through Gurtej to Bhindranwale, and encouraged him to go against his seminary training and to say to the BBC radio correspondent, when the Golden Temple crisis was worsening, that Sikhs were not like Hindus but were more like Jews and Muslims and Christians, people of a prophet and a book.

In that interview Bhindranwale also said – in English, in a voice breaking with passion – that Sikhs were subject to such persecution in India they had to 'give a cup of blood' to get a cup of water. This kind of exaggeration from a religious leader had puzzled me; but at that time I hadn't yet begun to enter the Sikh ideas of the torment and grief of their Gurus.

473

What Gurtej went on to say now gave me some idea of Bhindranwale's state of mind in the airless, imprisoned atmosphere of the Golden Temple during the last days.

Gurtej said, 'He was most enamoured of the personality and sacrifices of Guru Gobind Singh. The last days of Guru Gobind Singh he remembered by heart. He remembered the day-to-day doings of the Guru. He really lived it out. If you met him in December on a certain day he would say, "On this day the Guru was doing such-and-such." In fact, he would remember it by the time of the day. It was very remarkable. He would look at his watch and say, "In another two hours the Guru would have been getting his sons ready for the battle." And so on. In the month of December the Guru's sufferings began, because that was when he left his fort at Anandpur Sahib.' Anandpur: the town where the Guru's mother, and the Guru's two young sons – to be bricked up later – were captured by the Moguls.

Shut up in the Golden Temple, Bhindranwale must have begun to see himself as the 10th Guru besieged in Anandpur.

Gurtej said, 'People didn't go to him to talk about history or scriptures. His family rarely visited him. Whenever they came, they came as devotees. He had no time for his family in this period.

'I used to go to see him at the Temple once a month. Never less than two hours. There was some degree of mutual understanding between us. Once he said, "You should come to see me more often." I said, "I have to look after my family." He said, "How many children do you have?" I said, "Two." He said, "I have two children too. God looks after children." And he quoted a passage from the scriptures about migrating birds who leave their offspring behind. He said, "They fly for thousands of miles, and God sustains them."'

I asked Gurtej about the killings done in Bhindranwale's name, and the killings he was said to have given orders for.

'They were made-up stories. The purpose was to defame him.'

After Operation Bluestar – the army assault on the Temple, in which Bhindranwale and many of his followers died, and many soldiers as well – it was given out officially that Gurtej was among the people killed. This alarmed Gurtej. 'A case of sedition had been registered against me in connection with a booklet about Sikh human rights. The meaning of giving me out as dead was that instructions had been given to the forces to eliminate me.' So

Gurtej went underground, and stayed in hiding for more than four years.

'My obituary also appeared in the *Indian Express*. It was flattering by and large. But it said that I didn't eat with Muslims – which is wrong, totally. I wrote a letter to the *Indian Express* saying, "Let any Muslim prepare a tasty vegetarian meal and invite me."' Vegetarianism wasn't the issue. Gurtej wasn't a vegetarian. 'But I don't eat meat killed in the Muslim or Jewish fashion. It's a commandment of the 10th Guru, when we take amrit. Such taboos in religion often have a deeper meaning.'

The point about the *Express* obituary must have been that Gurtej adhered strictly to his Sikh vows. Kapur Singh had written a big book about the significance of Sikh vows; Gurtej had given me a copy of the book. And now – leaving to one side the question of his life underground after Bluestar – he told a story to explain the 10th Guru's injunction to his followers against having relations with Muslim women.

'One of the stories appearing in one of our Sikh texts, *The Fundamentals of Sikhism* by Sewa Dass, relates to a person who had been forcibly converted to Islam in the 1700s. He went to the Guru, who was presiding over the congregation, and said, "I have been forcibly converted." "How have you been converted?" "I've been made to eat cow's meat." "That doesn't make you a Muslim." "I've been circumcised." "That can't make anybody a Muslim." "I've been made to repeat the Kalma." "That's the name of God. It doesn't make you a Muslim." Somebody in the congregation was surprised. He asked the Guru, "How does one become a Muslim then?" And the Guru said, "By marrying a Muslim woman, or having such relations with her." The implication is that marriage is a voluntary act. "If you *accept* that you are a Muslim, then alone you become a Muslim." This is how the Guru comforted the man.'

As much as any story of martyrdom, this story from the final years of the last Guru speaks of the persecution and anguish and violation out of which the Sikh military brotherhood was born. Though that wasn't the point Gurtej made: Sikhism, in his interpretation, was a religion of prophecy and revelation.

When I asked him what had supported him during his time underground, he said 'I was thinking I was suffering with my people. There was another consolation: this was the period I turned most to my scriptures. The main theme of the scriptures is that one lives in the world in such a fashion that one becomes acceptable to God. And I thought I was doing that. I did a lot of reading and writing. So my time underground was instructive. One could contemplate the nature of things.'

'That was what you said about your Roman Catholic boarding school, your schooldays away from home. So your time underground was like a repeat of your childhood?'

Gurtej said, 'I don't know whether character is destiny or destiny is something in its own right. But things do develop which put you in situations that develop you in a definite direction.'

One cause of grief during this time underground was the death of Kapur Singh, at the age of seventy-five. Gurtej had known and loved Kapur Singh for 20 years. The cantankerousness which had irritated Gurtej at their very first meeting was something he now smiled at, as he smiled at other quirks of the man: his liking for his food, his love of ice cream. He could eat a pound at a time. He used to say to Gurtej, 'You must eat ice cream. It's good for your liver.'

Gurtej said, 'He was a rather stout man, not very tall, with thick-rimmed glasses. Always a pen or two with him, looking every bit a scholar, with a book or magazine tucked under his arm, always.'

Kapur Singh had carried his grievance about his dismissal from the ICS for embezzlement for nearly 40 years; he had kept it fresh. The grievance hadn't fatigued Gurtej or raised any doubts in him. He said, 'The idea of injustice is there in every Sikh.' And he was still ready to fight that particular side of Kapur Singh's case. Gurtej had become like a member of Kapur Singh's family; it distressed him that he couldn't be with the old man at the end.

'Finally I was able to get some sort of protection from the High Court. I had applied to the High Court saying that the sedition case against me was false, and the intention of the government was to harass me and harm me physically. The court granted me seven days' time to appear in the lower court and sign my petition and ask for bail. And I did that. I am still technically on that bail.'

This was why, a few months before, Gurtej had been able to visit Kapur Singh's brother, when that brother was dying. The family, Gurtej said, belonged to a sect of Sikhs who, since the days of the first Guru, traditionally became mendicants and teachers – and this was perhaps one factor in Gurtej's admiration of Kapur Singh.

'His father was a small landowner – about 20 acres or so. The other son was totally uneducated. He remained a farmer all his life – while Kapur Singh was educated at Cambridge University. In lieu of this, the younger son got 10 more acres of land. The younger brother was on his death-bed when I met him last year, and he complained that Kapur Singh's relatives were trying to snatch those extra 10 acres from him.'

Gurtej, Kapur Singh, Bhindranwale: they were all men of farming families. Great events had claimed them; but below all the passions – about faith and purity – there were elemental things that could take men further back: to a deathbed anxiety about 10 acres of land.

Sanjeev Gaur, the Amritsar correspondent for the *Indian Express*, was attacked and stabbed one day in Febuary 1984 just outside the Golden Temple.

'There was an old pickpocket of Amritsar who had become a political activist, first for the Indira Congress, and then as a member of the All-India Sikh Students Federation. I wrote a story about this pickpocket for the *Express*. The day the story was published I went to the Golden Temple, and he gave me a very dirty look. My source told me I should be careful.

'A fortnight later I was stabbed by two young boys, one wearing a saffron turban. They asked my name first, and then they started hitting me. Five times they stabbed me in the thigh. And I heard another voice saying, "Drag him inside." I thought that was the moment of death, because I had been reporting for the last month or so about the discovery of five bodies in gunny sacks in the gutters of the Golden Temple – people killed by the terrorists inside the Temple. The people killed were mostly Sikhs – suspected by the terrorists to be police informers.

'The two men who attacked me left me. I began to walk to a clinic. People were looking at me. Blood was oozing out of my trousers. The people who were looking were helpless. If they had helped me, they would have incurred the wrath of the terrorists. And then I asked a cycle-rickshaw-wallah – a lot of them there, outside the Golden Temple – to take me to a doctor, and then two Sikhs helped me. I later learned that the two men who had helped me were communists.

477

'But I should also mention that Bhindranwale condemned the attack. He told some journalists that he didn't believe in daggers – he believed in guns. And two of his main aides telephoned me at home to express their regrets. They said they were not behind the attack.

'Then I was posted to the East by my paper, but deviously, for my safety.'

Dalip, another reporter, told of what happened after the Golden Temple had been occupied by Bhindranwale.

'People stopped going to the Golden Temple. Both my neighbours stopped going, though they wanted to. People were angry about what was happening in the Temple, but the Sikh political party never condemned the desecration of the Temple by Bhindranwale and his guns. The Sikh political party were fighting a joint agitation with Bhindranwale from the Golden Temple, and they were afraid of him. He was a killer. He didn't worry about Hindu or Sikh – once you opposed him, you would be on his hit list.

'I was witness to one killing he ordered. I was sitting in Room 47 on the third floor of the Guru Nanak Niwas. This was one of the rest houses in the Temple where he used to stay with his followers. There were armed men sitting all around, eight, 10 people. This was in the middle of 1983. Suddenly one guy entered. He was a middle-aged Sikh, in shirt and pyjamas, and he was looking glum. His hair was cut and his beard was cut awkwardly. He started talking to Bhindranwale: "Santji, this is what Bichu Ram, a police inspector, has done to me. He took me to a police station and desecrated me. He cut my hair and my beard."

'Bhindranwale immediately asked one of his aides to take down all the details. Fifteen days or so later this Bichu Ram, in charge of one of the police stations, was shot dead.

'The second way of operating, of ordering killings, was to pronounce the names of people whom he wanted killed from a public platform. He did this from the 19th of July 1982 till June 1984. He would make a speech. Always against Mrs Gandhi, Giani Zail Singh [the Indian President], and Darbara Singh, the chief minister of Punjab. And he would say these people should be taught a lesson for having harmed the Sikhs. Afterwards he would talk against some local police officers. And many of the people whose names he spoke would be later killed. Bachan Singh, a senior police officer of Amritsar, was killed, together with his wife and daughter.

'I used to talk to Sikhs. But by and large Sikhs did not come forward to condemn the happenings in the Golden Temple. They were blaming New Delhi – everything was being done by New Delhi. They were never criticizing Bhindranwale and his men. Whenever terrorists were killed the Sikhs were very upset – they spoke of fake encounters. Whenever the terrorists killed innocent people, I never heard my neighbours expressing regret.'

Dalip had Sikh connections; this explained some of his passion.

I said, 'Someone who knows Sikhs well has told me that there was something wrong with the way Bhindranwale and his followers looked. They had the eyes of disturbed people. Was it a kind of communal madness, you think?'

'It's the minority fear, the persecution complex, the death wish. It's a new religion. It has produced great generals and great sportsmen. But it hasn't produced great religious thinkers to strengthen the religion. Nothing happened after Guru Gobind Singh set up the Khalsa in 1699. Since 1699 it has produced no great thinkers.

'It's madness, it's fanaticism. It can't really be explained. It's the tragedy of the Sikh religion that in the post-independence era a man like Bhindranwale has come to be accepted as the most important Sikh leader since Guru Gobind Singh. He was called in his lifetime by many Sikhs the 11th Guru. And he really was a product of Mrs Gandhi. She built him up to fight the Sikh party, the Akalis.'

'Why did educated people give their support to Bhindranwale?'

'Frustration.'

'When did you first see him yourself?'

'The 24th of July 1982. In the Golden Temple. The famous Room 47. I was checked by his bodyguard. Guns in the Temple were seen for the first time in 1982, and it's a perversion of the religion.

'He arrived in the Golden Temple on the 20th of July 1982. He left it dead on the sixth of June 1984. He harmed the Sikhs the most, the Sikh religion the most. He harmed Punjab, and he harmed India.

'The aides questioned me, and when I told them I was a journalist, they smiled and were very happy, and they immediately escorted me inside.

'I greeted him. He was sitting on a string bed, and he was nicely dressed up, wearing that long white cotton gown going down to his knees, and that blue turban. And his revolver hung from a belt around his waist. He had angry eyes – you asked about the eyes. He looked lean and hungry, the type of people who are dangerous. He said, "Who are you?" Very dictatorial. I said, "I'm a journalist." I gave him the name of the weekly I worked for, and I mentioned that I was also the correspondent for a Canadian paper. "Do you want to interview me?" "No, I've just come for your *darshan*."'

Darshan is what a holy man offers when he shows himself: the devotee gets his blessing merely from the sight, the darshan, of the holy man.

'He was very flattered. He smiled and he laughed. He had been very serious when I entered.

'I found an old lady handing over to him bundles of currency notes, and she also removed one or two of her gold rings and handed them over to him. Standing over the old lady was an old man, who I learnt later was General Shabeg Singh.' Major-General Shabeg Singh: cashiered in his mid-fifties for embezzlement, and now acting as Bhindranwale's military adviser.

'Shabeg was lean and thin, middle height, very fair, wearing spectacles, flowing beard, white beard, white pyjama and kurta. He was smiling. I shook hands with him. He said, "I'm General Shabeg Singh. I led the Mukti Bahini in the Bangladesh war." I said, "Sir, you are a general. How did you get attached to Bhindranwale?" I needed copy for a colour story – my first day in Amritsar. His reply was, "I see spirituality in his eyes. He is like Guru Gobind Singh."

'I came out of the Golden Temple a sad man, wondering about the fate of the community, wondering about the general's reply, comparing Bhindranwale with Guru Gobind Singh. I was very sad when I sat at the typewriter. Because I was not impressed by Bhindranwale. I knew he was not Guru Gobind Singh. I knew he was just being used by the Indira Congress to harm the rival Akali party in Punjab. He was an ordinary man on whom greatness was being imposed. Why should the community accept him? Why should General Shabeg Singh not judge him as a man? Why were people just impressed by his angry looks and the armed men around him? He was not an intellectual, not a thinker, and he was not a pious man.'

Dalip meant, I suppose, that Bhindranwale wasn't really a man of God. But what were the noticeable religious aspects of the man? There must have been many.

'He was a vegetarian, a lover of music. He would go to the Golden Temple water tank every morning at three and listen to the music played by the blind musicians from inside the main shrine. They play on the harmonium and recite the scriptures. That music is soothing, divine – and I give him full marks for wanting to be part of that. You feel the presence of God when that music is played in the silence, and there are no people around. He did that every morning for one hour. And he was not a womanizer.'

The vegetarianism, the love of music, the early rising, the sexual control, were run together in this account to give an idea of the austerity of the man that so impressed people in the early days, when he went out preaching and urged people to be like their father, the Guru.

Dalip said, 'He made himself a monster.' Monster: it was the word people used of the later man. 'He began to think he would rule the country or rule Khalistan. He wanted to rule something. He accepted the compliment when people told him he was like Guru Gobind Singh. Subconsciosly, Bhindranwale began imagining himself to be Guru Gobind Singh – a reincarnation of the 10th Guru.

'I will give you two more pictures of him. The first is from the middle of 1983. A colleague on an Indian daily did a big story saying that Naxalites had entered Bhindranwale's camp. I checked out my colleague's story and found it was all right, and I extended it with inquiries from my own sources. Bhindranwale hated the story in the daily, but I learned about that only later. The day after my own story came out, I went to see Bhindranwale. That was my practice, to go and see him after things about him by me were printed.

'The same room in the Temple. Room 47. Now I can open the door and go in coolly – everybody knows me now. I took along a friend with me, someone from the medical college. The moment I open the door of Room 47, I see the angriest look in his bloodshot eyes. They were red eyes when he was angry, which often he was. And I got the message. There were eight or nine of his armed admirers in the room, and two journalists were interviewing him.

'He started shouting at me, in crude Punjabi, at the top of his voice: "How dare you compare me with thieves and scoundrels and lumpens?" That is what he thought Naxalites were. He continued shouting at me in this way for three minutes, and then he ordered one of his men to bring the copy of the magazine with my story. And I, the magazine's correspondent, stood in front of him like a schoolchild who has offended the teacher. I couldn't utter a word – I was so afraid: I could see the guns around, and I knew he could kill me if he wanted to.

'The magazine arrived. He handed it to me. He had cooled down a bit, but he was still very angry. He asked me to translate what I had written into Punjabi. I pleaded that I wasn't good at translating from English into Punjabi. He cooled down more. And then, to my amazement – I realized how shrewd he was – he signalled to me, while he was sitting on his string bed – I was no more than four feet away – to come closer to him.

'He wanted me to come closer to him, and when I went closer to him on his string bed, he pulled my head down and he whispered into my ears. "You are like a younger brother to me," he said in Punjabi, whispering, "and still you write against me."

'The meeting ended, and I came out of the room with my friend, the man from the medical college. He had wanted to see Bhindranwale, and had asked me to take him, because as a journalist I could go in and out of Room 47. I apologized to my friend for the shock treatment.

'I didn't meet Bhindranwale for a couple of days after that. I felt most uncomfortable. I didn't know how to report him. I knew one had to be critical of him, but it was so difficult to be sitting in Amritsar and to attack him. For a few months I kept quiet.

'But the magazine wanted stories, and in October 1983 I did a story saying that Bhindranwale was losing his popularity, that not many people were coming to see him. The magazine played it up: 'The Sant in Isolation', a full two pages, with a big photograph of that big man in his white cotton gown, half smiling, half frowning. And, as usual, after my story appeared, I went to see him.

'He was having a walk on the terrace of the rest house, the Guru Nanak Niwas. Not many people were there – 40, 50, mostly his followers. He started walking with me. Obviously he didn't know about the story. That was the last time I had a friendly chat with him. The next day I went again to see him, accompanying a Canadian TV team as an interpreter. He had learnt about the story by then, and in full public view, on the same terrace of the Guru Nanak Niwas where he had walked with me alone the day before, he told me that if I didn't stop writing against him, then I wouldn't be alive. He said this in Punjabi, in symbolic language. *Sannu uppar charana anda hai.* "We know how to take you up."

'After this I stopped seeing Bhindranwale. I didn't report on him. I didn't do any critical story. I was afraid. On the 23rd of December 1983 he shifted from the Guru Nanak Niwas to the Akal Takht, from the rest house to a sacred building. I went with some local journalists to see him. He was sitting on the floor – 50, 60 people with him. Some fruits and sweets lying near by. He gave me a piece of sweet and a banana, and he made some sarcastic remark, which I don't recall. Obviously he didn't like me any more. Some weeks later a colleague was stabbed outside the Temple. This didn't have anything to do with Bhindranwale, but in the atmosphere of fear nobody went to the aid of the stabbed man. They just stood and watched him bleed. I asked my paper to move me somewhere else.'

Just as Gurtej, talking of the fields and harvest, fell into a kind of lyricism, so I felt that Dalip, talking of the morning music in the Golden Temple, had spoken with a special reverence for the sacredness of the old site. I asked how shocking Operation Bluestar, the army action at the Temple, had been to him.

'Bluestar itself was not shocking to me. What was shocking was the manner in which it was done. It was a very bad operation. I thought Bhindranwale and his men could have been caught easily without bloodshed. I felt sorry for the 93 soldiers who were killed. They chose such a bad day to catch Bhindranwale. And they didn't even catch him.'

He was killed on 6 June; and General Shabeg was killed. Many other people with him managed to leave the Temple before the army action. They lived.

Kuldip was one of those who had been with Bhindranwale right up to the end, but had somehow lived. He had been in hiding for five years. 'It's a hard life, an ascetic life, moving from place to place. The police always get to find where you are, and then you have to move.' He had been active in the All-India Sikh Students Federation: a strange name, because the group was known for its violent inclinations, and the prominent people in it were not really young, and could be considered students only in the broadest way.

Kuldip was about fifty, but he looked older. His face was creased and lined, with a further network of thin worry-lines, speaking of internal stresses even below those stresses connected with his life on the run. He dressed in the palest colours – his turban was of the palest brown – as though he wished not to draw attention to himself. Those colours, the lined face, and the small, quiet eyes suggested a deeper withdrawal.

He came an hour earlier than we had arranged, and he came straight up to my hotel room. He had to wait while I finished a long telephone call. He didn't seem to mind waiting. He sat quietly in the armchair, and I found it hard to believe that the quietly dressed man sitting in the hotel room was the 'activist' I had been told he was. It even occurred to me that he might have been from the police. When we began to talk, I asked him about his life on the run.

He said, 'So many people who are with me have been tortured to death and killed. Hundreds have been killed in false encounters. They are being killed for the freedom of the human race.'

The freedom of the human race?

He meant that. The current Sikh movement was intended 'to undo the political and social injustice of the world.' The goal was 'political power guided by Sikh religious principles and Sikh religious force'. The ultimate goal was 'a universal religious system, a universal spiritual system, universal humanistic values'.

'This is just the microcosmic experiment in the Punjab. Already we had in the time of the kingdom of Ranjit Singh this experiment in Punjab. We would like to recover the Sikh system of that time, the Sikh system of the 19th century, before the annexation of the Punjab by the English. And we want to apply that system to the whole of the world.'

I wasn't prepared for the language. Perhaps, then, he was or had been a student, exposed to the language and views of someone like Kapur Singh.

How did he define the Sikh 19th-century system?

'A secular system, a socialistic system also, a Sikh socialistic system. The main point is having the Sikh religious and political system along with the socialism. Religion and spirituality are intrinsically inseparable parts of the human personality. Similarly, the urge to dominate, to have political power, is also part of the human personality. This is so in animals, in birds also. And why not in human beings? Animals have got their leaders, the birds have got their leaders. Similarly, Khalsa [the Sikh brotherhood, as established by Guru Gobind Singh in 1699] wants to be the leader of the world, as it has got the inseparable elements of that leadership in its character.'

He thought that the goal would be reached in 10 or 15 years. At the moment the struggle was going badly. 'There is no discipline. There is no central leadership. We have lost control, and this thing is now going in favour of the government. Some of these anti-social elements are semi-religious people attracted by the emotional aspect of the movement. They are not deeply read, and they don't have regard for the deeply read and educated people, because these deeply read people don't believe in killing people aimlessly. No doubt there are some government agents also involved, and the blame is being put on the Sikhs. But our group' – the Sikh Students Federation – 'has not so many bad elements, comparatively.'

He had been born in a part of the Punjab that had gone to Pakistan in 1947, at the time of the partition. 'My great-grand-parents were generals in the army of Ranjit Singh. My ancestors fought in both Anglo-Sikh wars, 1843, 1849. One was commander of 300 men, and so was the other. Around 1900 half the family got converted to Islam. They fell in love with some Muslim girl, and got converted. Our parents felt bad about it.' In 1947 the Sikh part of the family came over to India, to a part of the Indian Punjab that later became part of the state of Haryana. They had about 80 acres there. 'One-tenth of what we had in Pakistan. This was the price of our sacrifice for freedom.'

I asked whether it was irrigated land. Water was such a talking point in the Punjab: there was such resentment (in spite of the Punjab's own green, rich fields) of the water of the rivers of the Punjab going to other states.

'Irrigated land, but not so rich.' One brother farmed the family land; one had become a teacher, another wanted to be a lawyer. It

485

was the Sikh pattern: all the middle-class people I met had their connection with the land still, and many could think themselves back easily into old peasant passions. 'Now we've got used to Haryana,' Kuldip said. 'But we are not so well-to-do. We're just hand-to-mouth.'

I asked him about his career.

'In the early days I wanted to become an engineer, just out of love of the word "engineer". But I failed in mathematics. Then I wanted to become a lecturer in chemistry or physics. The life of a lecturer seemed to me very easy, very peaceful.'

I understood him. His words took me back to my own beginnings, to my own uncertainties, when (just the second person in my family to go a university) the life of the university did seem to me peaceful and protected, and I wanted to prolong my time there.

Kuldip said, 'But I failed there too. I got poor marks. At that time I was twenty-five. I was teaching practical science in a college. Then I wanted to be an advocate, but that line I didn't like. Then I got attracted to English literature. I was now thirty. This study of literature fascinated me. I did an M.A. in English literature at a university. It took two years. I got a job as English lecturer in a college.'

'How did you support yourself when you were doing all that studying?'

'At first my parents were giving me money.' This would have been money from the land. 'Then I supported myself, and then for some time I supported my brother who was younger to me.'

For some years, since his mid-twenties, he had been in touch with a well-known holy man, whom he thought of as his 'revered father'. 'I used to listen to him. Other people were also there around him. This was in the town of Sirsa. Then I got attracted to the study of religion. But I liked the study of literature better than the study of religion. Literature is real. Religion is obscure. The Sikh Gurus made the study of religion like the study of literature.' I thought he meant by that that the Sikh scriptures were like literature: the important Gurus were also poets.

When he was nearly forty, then, he got another job, as a research fellow in a college department. That was when he was claimed first by politics and then by Bhindranwale's movement. 'He promised to bear the whole expenses of the English daily which we were planning to start in Chandigarh.'

When I had asked Dalip what he thought attracted people to Bhindranwale, he had said, 'Frustration.' I hadn't absolutely understood what he meant. But now, from what Kuldip told me about his wandering, stop-and-start, and still unresolved career, I began to understand a little more about these men from farming communities who had been cut loose from one kind of life, and were without conviction or vocation in the new world.

I asked him, 'What attracted you to Bhindranwale?'

'His magnetic personality.'

'Did you think he had angry eyes?'

'No, spiritual eyes. Of course, he had the anger of a lion – when he got angry. The movement was very well under control until Bluestar, and this worried the government.'

'Was he a tyrant? Did he want to be a ruler?'

'He wasn't a tyrant. He followed the principles of the Guru. The Gurus gave orders in battle to kill the enemy. But I shouldn't put it like that. The Gurus had no enemy: enmity was thrust on them. Similarly, enmity was thrust on that man.'

What about storing guns in the Golden Temple? Wasn't that contrary to the religion?

'In Sikhism nothing is wrong with guns in the gurdwaras, provided they are not used unjustly. Guru Gobind Singh sometimes personifies God Almighty with the mystical names of weapons. There are so many verses where he praises the strength of arms as he praises God Almighty.'

'I've heard that Bhindranwale began to think he was Guru Gobind Singh.'

'Sometimes in congregations he used to recall the doings of the Guru. He was close in spirit to the Guru. In the Sikh religion anyone who truly follows the edicts of the Guru is said to become so close to the Guru that he becomes the Guru, and the Guru becomes he.'

He told me about Bhindranwale's last days.

'I was living with him in the Temple from the 29th of March 1984 to the sixth of June 1984. I last saw him on the fifth of June. In the evening. We talked about the situation. He was firm. He inspired me with courage. Everybody there was prepared for anything. General Shabeg was standing outside. He sent me to Santji.

'I remember the last words of Shabeg: "The best place to die is

487

the highest place of your religion, and a place connected with your ancestors." And he further said, "The place where we are standing has got both of the highest qualities. So it is best to die here." We were in the Akal Takht.' The council building, it might be said, of the Golden Temple: the Chapter House. 'To bring food from the langar' – the communal kitchen of the Temple: the communal kitchen in the place of worship is an important Sikh idea – 'was very hard. So food was brought over the Temple wall by the people, over the roofs of the adjoining houses. This went on for only one day. We had parched channa in quantity' – chick-peas – 'and that was distributed to us. Water was stored in buckets.

'Four of us were stationed behind the two flags on the first floor. Nobody was worried. We were all happy. Kirtan was going on.' Hymn-singing, from the central gold-domed temple in the pool. 'And they were singing a couplet: "Nobody can kill one whose God is almighty." *Jisda sahib dada hué usnu marna koi*. This inspired us.'

'Did you know about the bodies stuffed into the drains?'

'I didn't know.'

'Does it upset you now?'

'No. All is fair in love and war.'

He became restless all at once, and said he had to go. He said he would telephone me in Delhi in a few days. I walked down the steps with him. He didn't walk towards the hotel desk. He turned smartly about and walked at the side of the flowerbeds on the front lawn, stepped over a low border into the drive, and walked out of the hotel gate.

A day or so later the police announced that a terrorist bombing campaign might be about to start in Delhi. This gave a new twist to what Kuldip had told me about his movements, though it remained hard for me to associate the man with the lined face and subdued eyes, who had sat so stilly in my room, with violent acts.

Gurtej had said at the beginning of my time in Chandigarh, when I had asked him about the emphasis on suffering in Sikhism: 'This world is an unhappy place for many, and it [unhappiness] has to be eliminated. There are only two ways. Either you make somebody suffer, or you suffer.'

On the day Kuldip had mentioned, the telephone operator in the Delhi hotel rang my room and said, 'There is a man on the telephone who wants to talk to you, but he will not give his name.'

488

Before I could decide what to do, the caller had rung off. No further call like that was made; I never heard from Kuldip again. I was relieved in a way; because the news about the bombing campaign had put me – like the people in Jaspal village, and other villages – in a quandary.

9

The House on the Lake

A Return to India

India was full of visitors; the number rose year by year. In all the big towns I went to – except Amritsar and Lucknow – the hotels were packed: trade fair following trade fair, one kind of public or holiday occasion following another, foreign delegations of various sorts treading on one another's heels.

The India I had gone to in 1962 was like a different country. India was not yet a place to which many people went to do business. It was not yet a place to which tourists wanted to go. Hotels of any standard were few and far between. Away from the main centres travel was hard. In some places you spent the night in a room in the railway station; in some places, if you could get the official permission that was required, you stayed at a 'dak bungalow', a post house. It was a lovely name, suggesting old-fashioned travel, and old-fashioned attentions. But when you got to the sunstruck, mildewed, colonial bungalow, with perhaps a few zinnias or thin-stalked roses or nondescript shrubs in its sandy garden, you had to shout for the watchman; and eventually some barefoot ragged fellow appeared and offered to cook for you in the kitchen of his own quarters the kind of meal he cooked for himself, which, when it came, might smell of woodsmoke or the cowdung cakes over which it had been cooked. In the sparsely furnished bedroom the coarse-napped 'bedding' would smell of the brackish or tainted soapy water in which it had been washed; the floor would feel sandy or gritty underfoot; the mosquito net would have tears and holes; the ventilation gaps at the top of the wall would leave one feeling exposed. The night could feel long.

The India I had gone to in 1962 had been like a place far away, a place worth a long journey. And – almost like William Howard Russell a century before – I had gone by rail and ship from

London: rail to Venice; ship to Athens; ship to Alexandria; ship to Karachi and Bombay. Twelve years before, I had travelled to London from the island of Trinidad. There, as the grandson and great-grandson of agricultural immigrants from India, I had grown up with my own ideas of the distance that separated me from India. I was far enough away from it to cease to be of it. I knew the rituals but couldn't participate in them; I heard the language, but followed only the simpler words. But I was near enough to understand the passions; and near enough to feel that my own fate was bound up with the fate of the people of the country. The India of my fantasy and heart was something lost and irrecoverable.

The physical country existed. I could travel to that; I had always wanted to. But on that first journey I was a fearful traveller.

I had planned to spend a year in India; and – though I had no clear idea for a book – I hoped that for part of that year I would settle down somewhere and do some writing. I arrived in Bombay some time in February. Early in April I went north to Kashmir: train to Delhi; night train to Pathankot; and then by bus for a day and a morning (with a halt for the night: moonlight on the terraced rice-fields of Banihal) up into the mountains and then down into the vale of Kashmir.

I put up in a gloomy, mildewed hotel in the town. In its rooms you had no idea of the setting, no sight of lake or mountains or fresh snow; you just had a cluttered backyard town view. I didn't see myself staying there for three or four months. There were the houseboats on the lake, relics of the Raj. But the well-equipped ones – like white barges on the water, echoing the fresh snow on the dark mountains all around – were too expensive for me. These were the ones with the good china and the hand-carved old furniture and the old-fashioned English menus (and still, here and there, the photographs and sometimes the recommendations of English guests of 30 years before – before independence, before the war). The smaller houseboats were shabby. But even if I could have afforded the better ones, I didn't think I would have been able to write and live in one room on a houseboat. It would have been constricting not to be able to walk out when one wanted; I would have felt it as a kind of imprisonment.

It began to look as though, after the long trip north, Kashmir wasn't going to work out. But then, on the second or third day, looking all the time for a good place to stay, I allowed myself to be led by a small man with a big blue jacket and a black fur cap to what he had said was a hotel on the lake itself, with its own garden.

It was hard to credit, but it was as Ali Mohammed, the man with the black cap, had said. I was to get to know him very well. For many weeks I was to see him leaving his hotel base, morning and afternoon, getting into a lake boat with his big bicycle, being paddled to the lake boulevard, and then cycling to the bus station or the tourist department or any other place where he might win a visitor, as he had won me. Though he wasn't pushy or talkative, was really a shy, subdued fellow, liking nothing better than a little smoke on the hookah with his friends in the hotel kitchen at the end of the garden.

The hotel was like a little house. It was called the Hotel Liward – that was the way the word was spelt, and that was how I thought of it. It had two storeys and a pitched corrugated-iron roof. It stood in its own garden in the lake, not one of the floating gardens, thick mats of lake weeds and earth, which could be towed about, but a fixed plot of earth. I rented an upper-floor bedroom at one end of the house. This section of the house had just been built for the new season – the Liward expanded every few years – and the way the building was designed, this bedroom had no immediate neighbour. It had windows on two sides, with views of the lake and the mountains and the snow. It had its own brand-new bathroom. Bathroom and bedroom smelled agreeably of new wood and new concrete. The small sitting room of the hotel was adjacent to the bedroom; I rented that as well, so that I could almost say that I had my own little wing of the Liward.

It was an extraordinary piece of luck for me. The Liward, my time in Kashmir, became a point of rest in my Indian year, a point of rest in my fearful travelling; and perhaps it enabled me to go through with my Indian venture. I had uprooted myself from London, and invested all the money I had in this Indian journey; it would have been hard if it hadn't worked, and I hadn't been able to last.

I stayed at the Liward for more than four months. I got to know all of them who worked and smoked in the kitchen shack at the end of the garden. Ali Mohammed – so important at the very beginning – soon became a figure in the background. Mr Butt owned the hotel, but English was beyond him; we communicated only by smiles and gestures. Mr Butt's right-hand man was Abdul Aziz. He couldn't read or write. But he had an acute social sense and could read faces and situations; he had a prodigious memory; and he spoke an idiomatic English, picked up purely by ear. It was with Aziz that I dealt during those four months at the Liward. It was with Aziz that I made my excursions to the higher valleys. Aziz and Mr Butt planned my expedition to the cave of Amarnath, at the time of the great pilgrimage there in the month of August; and Aziz came with me on that as well, to exercise some control over the retinue they had hired for me.

And I wrote my book. What had been a mere idea, an impulse, a series of suggestions, what at the start of the writing had felt unreal, began to have its own life and to exercise its own power in that room with the two views. That had also been part of the comfort and reassurance of that season, that feeling of a book growing day by day. Aziz and Mr Butt had knocked up a table for me to write at. They had also given me a table lamp.

The next year, in an oppressive furnished flat in south London, I began to write my book about India. I had intended to write one, but after my early weeks I had begun to give up the idea. Travel writing was new to me, and I didn't see how I could find a narrative for a book about India: I was too overwhelmed by the distress I saw. I had kept no journal, made few connected notes. But money had been spent, and a book had to be written. A full two to three months after my return, I began to write. In the writing, the Kashmir interlude became what it had been the year before in India: a point of rest. Calling up events day after day, I found a narrative where at the time there had appeared to be none.

After the book was written – order given to memories, a narrative found, Indian emotions faced and written out – the details began to fade. The time came when I no longer read the book. Kashmir and the Hotel Liward – and Mr Butt and Aziz – remained a glow, a memory of a season when everything had gone well. It was open to me after that to go back to Kashmir at any time. Air travel had simplified the world, had simplified our ways of dealing with sections of our past. Sometimes people wrote me about the hotel; someone sent me a photograph to show the changes that had come to the building. But I never felt the need to go back.

*

This time I went back. I went by air. So I saw the airport which, 27 years before, I had never seen or been near. There had been stringent security checks at Delhi airport, because of the situation in the Punjab. There was security at Srinagar: the Kashmir valley was restless. It had been restless in 1962 as well. But all over India people lived more on their nerves now, and had a different attitude to authority.

The road to the town was being improved. It led past many big new houses; I hadn't seen that kind of private wealth in 1962. The city centre was as mud-coloured and medieval-looking as I had remembered: as though all the colours of Kashmir, by themselves as vivid as the colours in a paint-box, had run together and created the effect of mess and mud. The brick and timber of old buildings – or buildings that looked old – were both the colour of mud. Mud was also the colour of the streets, the colour-effect of the variegated clothes of the people; and mud – with here and there a green algae patch or crust – was the colour of the turgid, steep-banked river that ran through the town. An arm or canal of this river was choked with small unpainted houseboats side by side: and there the houseboats showed very clearly as a slum row, little floating houses permanently moored to the bank, each with its outhouse on the bank.

Some memory stirred, at the grey-brown colour of the house-boats; but the feeling of crowd and constriction was new. Some memory also came to me of someone telling me in 1962 that in the days of the British (though Kashmir was a princely state, with its own ruler) Indians were not allowed to walk on the Bund, the main avenue in the town. That was now far in the past. The Kashmiri-Indian town had burst its bonds and had spread a long way down the lake boulevard. This new development was not the colour of mud. It was a roaring Indian bazaar of concrete and glass and new paint, hotels and shops and signboards. And facing it, on a section of the lake where in 1962 there had been only water, was a long row of tourist houseboats, each houseboat with its signboard: the Kashmiris and the visitors seemingly lined up and facing one another like two sports teams, the visitors handicapped in their houseboats, denied movement and manoeuvre, the Kashmiris nimble on the shore, ready to deal with any landing party, with their irregulars paddling about on the lake, appearing from nowhere, their shallow low boats capable of nosing into the smallest opening. All down this stretch of the lake boulevard was a roar of human voices, as in a market or bazaar.

At the far end of the lake boulevard, and some way beyond this new development, was the Palace Hotel, in its own spacious grounds. I was staying there this time. The hotel had been the summer palace of the Maharaja of Kashmir. It was a big but plain building of the 1930s, low and wide, set well back from the lake and boulevard. The apple orchards planted by the last maharaja but one were in blossom; so were the almond trees. After the mud colours of the town, the colours here were of the freshest spring-green.

I knew the palace as a palace. In 1962 Karan Singh, the maharaja, had been in residence; his official position in the state had been that of governor, *sadr-i-riyasat*; and I had been invited to the palace more than once for dinner. On one occasion I had gone in a tonga, a horse-drawn cart. The horse had laboured and slipped up the long, hard incline of the drive. I could have walked faster. It felt absurd to be sitting in the tonga, but I didn't know what to do. The whole procedure had seemed undignified to the officials watching: they had finally come up in a jeep to rescue me.

No memory remained to me of palace entrance or rooms. The carpet was worn in the corridor downstairs. Upstairs, outside my room, there were warm kitchen smells; and there was a glimpse, through a concrete screen, of the staff quarters. My room was big; the furniture felt inadequate; the coarse-tufted carpet was bright green. No sense of glory or comfort or holiday: just a feeling, in the spring-damp air, of a big building running down, with too many things to put right now, a building too big for those of us who were in it, a building just opened up for the season, needing summer and a holiday life, which, with the religious and political restlessness in the valley, it perhaps wasn't going to get.

The gardens the windows looked out on were in good order, though. The grass had been cut low, the two big trees freshly pollarded, the flower-beds bright with bulbs and seed-packet colours. Two Japanese girls in jeans, having their photographs taken, posed one for the other, squatting in front of the red tulips and giving tinkling little squeals. Beyond and below, seen through spring growth, the new sprays of poplars and the soft lime-green fronds of willows, was the lake. The far-off mountains had fresh snow at the top. It was a privileged, palace view: no sight, from the window, of the new building on the lake shore to the right, the terracing of the lower mountainside; no sight of the houseboat rows to the left.

Somewhere there, to the left, was the Liward Hotel. And it was towards that that very soon, not wanting to delay the moment, I went. I took a hotel taxi. There was a minimum charge. For that charge I could have gone two or three times the distance I did go; I could even have walked. Old Kashmiri irritations began to revive, telescoping the years.

Misled by the crowd I saw ahead on the boulevard, not able with the new clutter on the lake to gauge where the Liward might be, I got off too soon, at the wrong boating steps, and became involved in a haggle with the boatman in charge about the fare to the Liward. The boatman had the height of a child; and, below his brown gown, he had the physique of a child. Pale, marked skin, discoloured in patches; a cadaverous small face on a thin neck; light-coloured hair, bright eyes. His appearance spoke of winter starvation; but his eyes, like his haggling voice, were full of rage. I hadn't seen anyone like that on the boating steps in 1962; but neither had there been the crowd, and the human roar.

We settled for 25 rupees for the crossing to the Liward, a pound: far too much, five times too much.

The water of the lake, streaming through my fingers, was cool. And even with all the traffic, the lake still had its spring-time clarity. It was full of little fish, a delight to see, and the ferns at the lake bottom tossed slowly in the current. (Later, in high summer, the water would cloud.) Where there had been openness in 1962 there was now a long row of houseboats, each with its signboard and steps; and some of the boats seemed to be linked by a railed timber walk, supported on stilts.

We paddled past that; made for a water lane with shop-boats and service boats. And soon – the crossing certainly not worth 25 rupees – there was the Leeward, in that corrected spelling, according to its big signboard. Not the modest cottage and lake garden I had lived in, but an establishment dominant even in the new commercial clutter: solid, concrete-walled, many-winged, many-gabled.

The photograph of the Leeward I had been sent some years before had shown a building two storeys high. I felt that the roof had been raised since then, and a third storey added. The gables were oddly splayed at the bottom ends, thicker, and almost with the curve of hockey sticks. With the steep pitched roof, the effect was Tibetan or Japanese.

I had remembered flat lotus leaves on the lake beside the Leeward garden. A few were still there, but they were not as noticeable as the tall, litter-trapping grass that grew about the landing stage. The hotel had always been at an intersection of water lanes; but now it was as though a residential area had become a business area. Houseboat shops moored to ragged remants of black islets, rough timber and corrugated-iron shops on stilts, and handcrafts emporia faced the Leeward across all the lanes. The Leeward had its own grocery shop in one corner, with a large wall advertisement; and next to that was an emporium of Kashmir leather and wool goods.

From the landing stage a railed path led between two rectangles of garden. It was (apart from the bath-tub jardinière in one corner) a little like the garden I knew. But it was impossible to reconstruct the site, to work out where my sitting room had been, and where the bedroom with the two views. The hotel island, the plot of earth, must itself have been added to.

At one end of the building, opposite the hotel shops, was the office, a small white-walled room with glass windows. A high counter; a brown keyboard; a calendar on the wall; Kashmir tourist folders opened out. There were also posters of Mecca: the kaaba stone, and a dome. There had been no decorations with that religious twist in the old Leeward. Clearly someone had made the pilgrimage to Mecca, or wished to show his allegiance.

There was no one in the office. A little boy hanging around outside seemed to be connected with the hotel. I sent him to look for Aziz or Mr Butt. It was Mr Butt who came. I hardly had to wait. After 27 years, it was as simple as that. He had a white fringe of beard, the beard of a man who had made the pilgrimage. Perhaps in a crowd I might not have spotted him. But here, in his own setting, he was immediately recognizable: the fur cap, the dark colours he liked to wear, the thick-lensed glasses, the slenderness.

He behaved like a man who was unsurprised. We were indeed both like actors in a play, who had rehearsed this moment. In 1962 there had been nine rooms in the hotel, he said; now there were 45. The charge now was 125 rupees per night, five pounds, eight dollars, to include bedding and hot water. He knew precisely how long I had stayed in the hotel in 1962. I didn't have to ask him; he reminded me. I had stayed four months and 15 days. Just as writing, the ordering of events and emotion, made things manageable for me, helped me as it were to clear the decks, so it seemed that putting numbers to things, finding the right numbers, helped Mr Butt to file things away and put a pattern on events.

After the hotel news, which he had given very quickly, the most important thing he had to tell me was that he had made the pilgrimage to Mecca. There was his health. 'But I am good, sir.' And, to prove it, he held my hand and gripped it hard.

I asked how old he was. He had trouble translating the numerals. He said eighty-six first of all, then seventy-six, then sixty-six. Perhaps he was sixty-six; that would have made him thirty-nine in 1962, one year short of forty – that would have seemed to me old then.

He told me about the others. Ali Mohammed, who had brought me that lucky day to him, had gone away. The *khansamah*, the cook, tormented and temperamental, creating all kinds of crises in the cook house and quarters at the end of the garden, had died. But Aziz was still there, very much so. At the moment he was in his own house; he would be back at the hotel in the afternoon.

I said I would come back at about four to see Aziz. Language – or the absence of a common language – lay between Mr Butt and me, as it had always done. Having come to the end of such language as we had in common, we had come to the end of things to say just then. And I took the lake boat back to the boat steps and the small, angry-eyed man.

On the shore there was a hill known as Shankaracharya Hill. There was a Hindu temple at the top; in 1962 Karan Singh used to maintain the brahmin there. Many afternoons I walked up the hill. I got to know the brahmin. He was a jovial hermit, with a woollen cap. When it rained, or was misty or cold, he kept himself warm in the Kashmiri way, hugging a small clay brazier of burning charcoal below a blanket. There had been so many new things to take in: it was only now – going back to the boating steps through this echoing bazaar roar from lake and boulevard – that I saw that on the small hill next to Shankaracharya there was a big television transmission mast; and I wondered about the temple and the brahmin.

I went back to the Leeward at about four. Taxi again from the

Palace Hotel; lake boat again from the 25-rupee steps. A small handsome young man was waiting for me in the office. He had a sleeveless blue padded jacket in some synthetic material, as stylish as his haircut. He said he was 'Aziza's' son – 'Aziza' was what he said: it was, as I remembered, the affectionate form of Aziz.

Aziz's son! He was eighteen. He was a student at a college in Srinagar. He was studying accountancy. Accountancy! But, of course, with all the activity in the lake and the town, there was a need.

And Aziz appeared, coming out of that corridor from which, in the morning, Mr Butt had appeared. Mr Butt had remained slender; Aziz had become broad and paunchy and round-faced. He was wearing many garments: loose trousers, long-tailed shirt, a pullover stretched tight over his paunch, a kind of unbuttonable waistcoat (more back than front), and a lightweight, full-skirted jacket. Strangely, his size made little difference: he remained the man I had known. There was still the energy, the lightness of step, the neutrality of expression, the assessing intelligence, the slight blink, as though he was shortsighted.

What news? Well, he said, the boy – he meant his handsome son – had wanted to become a doctor. But they had talked him out of that. There was no business like the hotel business. And Mr Butt, joining us, chuckled and said, after Aziz, that there was no business like it.

I asked Aziz about Mr Butt's fur cap. I had, in my earlier book, described the effect one day of heavy rain on the fur: having found those words, and having never forgotten them, I had remembered the cap. I wondered now whether the cap, like the white beard Mr Butt wore, had a religious significance; or whether it meant that Mr Butt belonged to a particular clan.

Aziz said, 'You can pay 1000 rupees for that cap.'

That seemed to be all. It was only then I noticed that Aziz was himself wearing a fur cap; and then memory – in a dozen vivid pictures – told me that Aziz had always worn a fur cap, that the cap had been part of his appearance, and that I had seen him bareheaded only once – after some horseplay in the kitchen, which had sent him out laughing and dishevelled into the garden. But I hadn't had to find words for his cap; it hadn't acquired importance for me.

I told Aziz about my trouble at the boating steps, and the charge of 25 rupees. The boatman was waiting with his boat to take me back. Aziz made a gesture and called the boatman over. I felt the boatman didn't like being called: he appeared not to notice.

Aziz himself appeared to forget the boatman. He brought out a box of photographs and he and Mr Butt began to look for old ones. They found one of the hotel in 1962, showing the garden and my sitting room. And they found another, an over-exposed one, of the staff of that time. Mr Butt was there, and Aziz; and Ali Mohammed, blunt-featured and earnest, who had now gone away; and the dead khansamah. The khansamah was tall and really rather fine, with a face more tormented than I remembered. Perhaps his rages hadn't been due just to temperament; perhaps he had been ill sometimes, and in pain.

There had been no more than five or six people in that old group. Now the hotel employed 20 people, and there was even a manager.

What did Aziz do, then?

Aziz's son said: 'He is the commander-in-chief.' And Mr Butt, understanding, smiled.

I asked Aziz about Mr Butt's health. Mr Butt had hinted in the morning that he wasn't absolutely well. Aziz said that Mr Butt shouldn't be smoking, but he smoked his hookah in secret; he couldn't give it up. And Mr Butt, not smiling, made a grave gesture of helplessness.

I reminded Aziz about the boatman, and the 25-rupee crossing charge.

Aziz said, 'You pay *twenty-five* rupees this morning?'

And when I said yes, he looked grave, like a doctor coming upon a bad and unexpected symptom. But then, like a doctor, he was willing to do what he could. He called the boatman over again, and this time the boatman came. Aziz and Mr Butt talked to him. Aziz said later that he had told the boatman that I was an old friend of the hotel's, not 'a three-day tourist'. And more than once during this talk with the boatman Mr Butt said, 'Four months and 15 days.' At the end the boatman smiled and Aziz said that I was to pay the boatman what I wanted. I didn't think this was good enough. Aziz knew that; he suggested that I pay 15 rupees.

Memory had brought back that picture of a skittish, bareheaded Aziz in the garden of the old Leeward – a rare skittishness then, and hard to imagine now in the dignified, successful man in front of me. How old had he been then? To me at the time he had been a mature, ageless kind of man.

'How old are you, Aziz?'

'Forty-eight, fifty.'

That was far too young. But he didn't seem to know; and perhaps, not being able to read and write, having to depend only on his own memory, his ability to relate events in his own life to events outside, he had no means of knowing.

We talked about the Himalayan pilgrimage to the cave of Amarnath that they had arranged for me, with muleteers, tent-pitcher, a cook, and Aziz in general command. Helicopters went to Amarnath now, Aziz said; and there were immense numbers of pilgrims, four lakhs, five lakhs, 400 thousand, 500 thousand.

Aziz said, 'You remember *ghora-wallah*?'

He was talking about one of the muleteers in our party. I would have written about him; the details would have been there in my book; but the man himself, and events connected with him, had slipped my memory. But Aziz remembered, and a memory came back to me of a muleteer who had abandoned us high up in some pass and who, before that, had caused some of our baggage to roll down a hillside – and Aziz had had to do the retrieving.

I would have liked in 1962, after the Amarnath journey, to dawdle for a few more days in the high Himalayas, with the Leeward team and their equipment. But Aziz hadn't wanted that. He had hurried me back to Srinagar, for another – Muslim – religious occasion. In the Hazratbal mosque at the far end of the lake there was a famous relic, a hair of the beard of the Prophet. It was displayed once a year, and Aziz was passionate to get back for that.

He liked big religious occasions, a mingling of faith and fair and holiday; and his news now was that, like Mr Butt, he had gone on the pilgrimage to Mecca. He had gone twice. The pilgrimage took three months. The Indian government made the travel arrange-ments. You went first to Jeddah; and then you took taxis and buses to Mecca. There were toilets everywhere between Jeddah and Mecca. It wasn't like Amarnath. Everything was clean in Mecca. He spoke like a man of the faith; he also spoke like a man who knew a thing or two about hotels and accommodation.

Two pilgrimages to Mecca: that meant money, leisure, success of a substantial kind. It wasn't what I would have prophesied for

Aziz in 1962. And, really, it was extraordinary that Aziz and Mr Butt, with their different talents and natures, should have worked together in the same way for all these years. They had supported one another; Mr Butt had allowed Aziz to grow; and the business had grown beyond their imagining.

I asked Aziz about the fancy gables on the hotel.

He said, 'A style, a style. You should see the new buildings here.'

He had a story to tell about my book. After the book came out the hotel had been called up by the Tourism Department. They said they hadn't liked what they had read about the Leeward. They had read that hotel guests spread their clothes to dry on the Leeward's lawn and hung clothes out of the windows. The Tourism Department didn't like that. Aziz said he had had to tell the government man very firmly: 'You don't *understand* the book.' An old fight, but clearly a fight: Aziz told the story twice.

Success; but the lake was crowded. All India was crowded, Aziz said, as though this was something people now had to live with. Forty years before, you could drink water from the lake (and I remembered people in excursion boats even in 1962 using lake water to make the special Kashmiri tea). Now, Aziz said, and Mr Butt shook his head in agreement, the flush systems of some houseboats emptied directly into the lake.

Then, abruptly – as though explaining the stillness or the flatness of the occasion, and the absence of hospitality – Aziz told me it was Ramadan. They were not supposed to talk much. They were going to break their fast at 7.10 that evening.

Aziz's son, Nazir, went with me in the boat back to the boulevard. He said that Mr Butt had told him and other people about the time I had sat out with them in the garden and smoked the hookah. I remembered the occasion. The smoke of the coarse-chopped Kashmiri tobacco, pleasant to smell, enticing, had turned out to be fierce and gripping in the throat and the lungs, stronger than any tobacco I had tasted, the hot charcoal-and-tobacco smoke barely cooled by the water in the bowl of the hookah.

I didn't think that anyone at the Leeward would have time for that kind of playfulness now. The mood felt different. The lake here was too built up, too busy.

From the lake and the boulevard and the boating steps there was now a late-afternoon roar. An amplified, quavering, nerve-stretching voice was part of the roar. It was the amplified voice of a mullah in the mosque on the boulevard – new to me, that mosque, a plain small building, part of the new development, many houses deep, on the boulevard, below Shankaracharya Hill. The very plainness of the mosque seemed to speak of the urgent need of the new lake crowd.

Aziz had said, after his talk with the boatman, that I was to pay 15 rupees for the crossing. The boatman himself had smiled and had appeared amenable to whatever was decided. But it wasn't the boatman I had to pay. It was the small, angry-eyed, angry-voiced man at the boating steps; and he absolutely insisted on 25 rupees. Nazir, who had come with me partly to protect me against this demand, was abashed. I noticed, though, that he didn't argue with the boating-steps man; he simply offered to pay the extra rupees himself. The lake clearly had its own rules, its various territories and spheres of influence. The Leeward's writ, and Aziz's, didn't run here. I paid what was asked. And then, solicitously, Nazir put me in a taxi and sent me back to the Palace Hotel.

There was more than an hour of daylight left. The view of the lake from the hotel garden beckoned me out again. I walked down to the Palace Hotel steps and took a boat for half an hour. Almost as soon as we had put out, two very small children, in a boat of their own, came alongside and threw mustard flowers into my boat. The gesture took me by surprise. I smiled, the children smiled back and asked for *baksheesh*. They were perfect little beggars: the smile, the whine, the aggression.

And then it was the turn of the salesmen. One by one they came, and besieged my boat. One man said, 'We will do it one after the other.' I thought he was making a joke, commenting on my situation; but he was speaking quite seriously. And they stayed with me, two on one side, three on the other, so that I was at the centre of a little flower-pattern, a daisy-pattern, of lake boats. They showed their goods in detail: saffron, stones, cheap jewelry, and all kinds of pointless things in papier mâché. The salesmen's boats were paddled by little children. The salesmen themselves reclined on pillows and cushions, and gave an impression of following one of the lake's more luxurious occupations. One or two were covered in blankets from the neck down; below those blankets they would have had little charcoal braziers.

*

Nazir and I went on a tour of the lake. We had hardly pushed off from the Leeward landing stage – we were still in front of the hotel – when the little begging children appeared, paddling fast, throwing sprigs of mustard flowers into our boat, and saying, in a sibilant whisper at once demure and penetrating, 'Baksheesh, baksheesh.' Nazir gave them one or two rupees each. He said, 'If you don't give them money, they won't go away.' He was as tender with the salesmen, allowing our boat to be delayed just long enough to give offence neither to the salesmen nor to me.

After we had passed the long row of houseboats we were in open water, and no one came near. We passed what I had remembered as the maharaja's lake pavilion. A memory came to me of a poplar-lined causeway between the lake boulevard and the lake pavilion: there was no causeway now.

In 1962 I had had tea in the lake pavilion one day with Karan Singh and his wife. Karan Singh had a great appetite for Hindu thought, and at that tea he had talked of the ninth-century Hindu philosopher Shankaracharya, who, born in the South, had, in a short life of 32 years, walked to the four corners of India (while India was still itself, before the Mohammedan irruptions), preaching and setting up the religious foundations that still existed. The hill beside the lake where we were was named after the philosopher; Karan Singh took a personal interest in the temple at the top.

The setting for our tea was spectacular: the pavilion, the lake all around, the mountains, the poplar-lined causeway, the long drive rising between orchards and gardens to the palace. I asked who had designed it all. I was expecting to hear the name of an architect. Karan Singh, looking around, simply said, 'Daddy.'

That had fixed the moment for me. But now there was no royal causeway, no tall poplars, only openness, a breeze picking up strength across the water, and blowing our boat against the rough poles and the slack, rusting strands of barbed wire around the pavilion island, where the buildings looked damp and closed, awaiting summer and people.

Nazir and the boat-boy between them poled and pulled the boat around the pavilion island. The lake was still choppy; but it became calm beyond a causeway laid with a big black pipe that took drinking water to the city. In the distance was the Hazratbal mosque. It had a white dome and minaret, and that whiteness stood out against the brown-black cluster of two-storey and three-storey houses.

The dome and minaret were new. Hazratbal had been a plain mosque. There had been riots one year in Srinagar when the famous Hazratbal relic, the hair of the beard of the Prophet, disappeared. I asked Nazir about it.

He said, 'It was found in Srinagar, in a private house.' (I was told later by someone else that a well-connected woman, who had fallen ill, had expressed a wish to see the relic, and it had been brought to her.)

Nazir, talking of this and that, said that he was corresponding with an English girl who had stayed at the Leeward. They wrote once a month.

He said, with unexpected seriousness, and without prompting from me, 'It's in God's hand whether I marry a Kashmiri or a foreign girl. Only God knows the future.' And that mention of God was serious, not idiomatic. Kashmiri girls, Nazir said, were nice, but foreign girls were more 'experienced' – and I didn't ask what he meant by that.

I asked him about religion. He said he went to the mosque every day. He went alone for half an hour or so, to pray for 'everybody'. On Fridays he went for two and a half hours, to pray with everybody else. He had been religious ever since he was ten.

We saw fishermen, scattered, still, almost emblematic against the open bright water, standing or lying on their low boats. We moved slowly towards them, coasting in the calm water after each paddle stroke: it was a wonderful moment of quiet just minutes away from the hubbub around the houseboats and boating steps of the boulevard.

One fisherman cast a small net where he had previously laid bait – a tin can marked the spot. The fisherman, having cast his net, used a long pronged stick, held within the net, to stir up the fish hiding in the reeds and ferns. As the fish rose they were caught within the weighted net; the net was hauled aboard, and the fish caught were kept in a covered, water-filled section of the boat's hull. Two other men were spearing fish: holding a spear, each man crouching a little way beyond the edge of his flat boat, with a dark cloth thrown over his head, the better to see through the water to the fish below. So for minutes they crouched, looking like small unmoving bundles at the edge of a boat, until they attempted to spear a fish, the spear held still until that moment of thrust.

From the openness we moved to the gardens, fixed or floating. The fixed gardens were planted at their edges with willows, whose roots made a cage that kept the soil from being washed away. Just a few hundred yards away from the tourist lake, and as though no middle way was possible, was this old agricultural life of the lake people: weeds and ferns being twirled loose from their lake-bed roots by means of a curved stick, and lifted dripping, mixed with black lake mud, into the flat-bottomed boats, and then taken to fertilize the gardens, where weeds and mud and water were shovelled off all in one with broad wooden shovels.

Women squatted and worked in spinach beds, and children worked with them, as children worked with adults everywhere in the lake, in gardens and on boats. Between the strips of gardens the algae-covered water lanes were lined with low-hanging willows. The houses were of timber and pale-red brick. People washed themselves on one side of a narrow plot; and on the other side young girls used the water to wash pots and pans. Some men, meeting among reeds, stayed in their boats and talked, as they might have done on a street. Some men and boys fished with rod and line. A boat passed with a cottage-cheese seller. Slowly – women and girls paddling their own boats, women and girls more visible here, among the gardens – we came back to the busy highways of the lake, behind the houseboats.

We passed a settlement among willows, rough houses of dusty red brick set in timber frames. A one-roomed shop-stall, with a platform a few feet above the water, had a large picture of the Ayatollah Khomeini of Iran (of whom it was said in Iran, by his enemies, that he was really Indian and Kashmiri).

Nazir said in a whisper, speaking with something like awe and nervousness and distance, as though he was speaking of people who were very strange, 'All this is Shia.'

Aziz had spoken in that way of Shias in 1962. He had spoken of them as people different from himself; once he had even said that Shias were not Muslims. I had barely understood then what he had meant. One afternoon, not really knowing what I was being taken to see, knowing only that it was a Shia occasion, I had gone by boat with some hotel people to see the Mohurram procession in the old town. I had remembered the occasion as a series of medieval pictures: remembering especially the pale, half-covered faces of secluded women, framed in small timber-framed upper windows, looking down at the bloody scene of self-flagellation below.

It had been hard for me, emerging from the soft lake world of willow-hung waterways and lotus and vegetable gardens, to believe what I had so suddenly come upon: bloodied bodies, blood-soaked clothes, chains, whips tipped with knives and razor blades, the exalted, deficient faces of the celebrants, and their almost arrogant demeanour. They pushed people out of their way. I was ready to believe, what I was told then, that much of the blood on display was really animal blood. I hadn't understood the religious-historical charge of the occasion, the undying grief it sought to express. I had only been alarmed by it, and glad to get away from it, glad to return to myself and what I knew.

Nazir said he had been told by his father that I had complained about the Shia drumming during Mohurram. And I felt now that the distance with which Nazir (and his father before him) had spoken of the Shias had contained some wonder that the apparently peaceable lake people we were paddling by had this other, ecstatic side.

It had become cloudy. Clouds came down over the mountains to one side of the lake. A strong breeze began to blow just as we were coming out of a water lane to the open water at the back of the houseboats and the Leeward Hotel. It began to blow us back, and dislodged the awning of our boat. This wind also kicked up the dark-red or russet underside of the flat round lotus leaves, revealing where – among the reeds and the tall grass and the litter around houseboats and service boats – the lotus were. I had been looking for the lotus. The pink flowers came out in June and July; I remembered them as one of the glories of the lake. But the lotus was also a crop here: even in the wind a man in a boat could be seen collecting lotus roots, using a special rod or tool for breaking them off under water and pulling them into his boat – endless, this loading and unloading of boats.

Becalmed, having trouble with our awning, we were 'boarded' by two begging children, throwing mustard flowers, keeping their boat glued to ours, and asking for baksheesh.

Nazir drove them away. It was the first time I had heard him raise his voice; and they respected his voice. He explained, 'They're a bad family.'

Perhaps in some way they had broken the code of the lake. They were thin-faced and very small, starvelings of the lake (like so many others), yet with something predatory and disturbing in the thin-armed frenzy with which, indifferent to wind and rain, having spotted us, they had paddled towards us.

The long row of big tourist houseboats gave us shelter. We moved in their lee, beside the railed timber walk that appeared to link them all. And then, the wind having dropped, we turned into the main river lane, back into the clutter of shops and sheds on stilts or stone walls, service boats with walls of old corrugated iron, timber and corrugated-iron structures on sodden bits of black, nearly bare earth: J & K Unique Stores, Manufacturers of Kashmir Arts and Crafts; a grocery shop; a butcher's stall with cases of bottled soft drinks on the wooden platform in front; the New Pandit Shawl House and the Mir Arts Emporium facing the Leeward's own handicrafts emporium and corner grocery shop; and, side by side on one narrow service boat moored to its own little island, a fur and leather-goods shop, a grocery, and the Sunshine Haircutting Saloon.

And, in this area, what could be heard when the rain stopped, what became noticeable, was the roar of human talk from many directions, as in a covered market, regularly pierced by the cries of children.

It was said that there were now 2000 houseboats in the lake. Every houseboat needed a service boat, or an attached garden. And what people said was that the lake, by which everyone in lake and city lived, the lake which drew the tourists, and was not very large, was shrinking.

The rain returned in the afternoon. Clouds hid the mountains and the lake misted over. The Palace Hotel felt unaired and desolate. There were few visitors; the tourist season was not starting well. The hotel staff, formally dressed, outnumbering the visitors, were subdued; the formality of their dress added to the gloom. The Harlequin Bar was empty; it was serving no liquor. It was a big bar, and there was no crowd now to hide its shabbiness: the carpet, or carpet-like material, that was tacked to the front of the counter was ragged in places.

A secessionist Muslim group had been setting off bombs in

public places in the city. The group had also made a number of demands. It wanted no alcohol in the state; it wanted Friday and not Sunday to be the day of rest; and it wanted non-Kashmiri residents expelled. The hotel people, while they waited for the authorities to take action, had met among themselves and decided to avoid trouble. That was why the Harlequin Bar of the Palace served no alcohol, and why – until some Japanese visitors insisted – not even beer was served at dinner in the dining-room.

In the afternoon, in all the rain, a Muslim holy man, a *pir*, turned up at the hotel, and it woke the place up. The pir was a very small, very thin, dark man, with something like a crew cut. He was in his sixties. He wore a dark-grey gown which came down to a few inches above his frail-looking ankles, and he was barefooted. He came to the hotel in a three-wheel motor-scooter, and when he got out he was carrying a telescopic umbrella. Six cars, full of people, were following his scooter. The pir appeared to be in a rage. He began to shout as he got to the desk. Shouting, waving his umbrella, seizing the arm of a foreign woman tourist, letting her go, he raged down the corridor, knocking down or hitting things in his way.

The staff didn't object. The holy man's curse was to be feared. Equally, his blessing was to be sought. He behaved as he did because he was holy, and because, as someone told me, he was 'in direct line' with God. His movements and his moods couldn't be predicted; but clearly, at this moment, during this extraordinary visit to the Palace Hotel, he was in a state of high inspiration. That was why the six cars were following him. With all the risks, people were anxious to get in his way. A waiter told me that if you had the chance, if you were lucky enough, to sit in front of the pir, you didn't have to tell him of your problems. He knew about your problems right away; and – always if you were lucky – he began to talk about them.

And then he was gone, with his gown and umbrella, and in his scooter, and the cars chased after him, leaving the hotel staff to return to themselves.

At 7.11 – one minute later than the day before – the mullahs' calls from the mosques around the lake announced that the sun had set, and believers could break their day-long Ramadan fast.

Religion, faith: there seemed to be no end to it, no end to its demands. It was like part of the nerves of the over-populated, over-protected valley.

While the maharajas ruled, Hindu sentiment had been protected in the valley. The killing of a cow, for instance, was a criminal offence, punishable by 'rigorous imprisonment'. The portraits of the maharajas, Karan Singh's ancestors, were still there on the main staircase of the building, beyond the main dining-room.

Some of the worn carpets in the hotel now had been in the palace in 1962. They had been specially woven; there had been some talk about them one evening. On a subsequent evening the burning head of a guest's cigarette had fallen on a carpet we had talked about and created a scorch spot. Karan Singh had not flinched, had not expressed, by a hesitation in speech, or a glance, that he was concerned or had even noticed.

His family had ruled for more than a century here; his princely ways were instinctive. It was also interesting for me to see how rulers managed more everyday things. We went to the cinema in Srinagar one evening. We went late and left early, before the lights came up; and then we raced back to the palace. I asked Karan Singh's wife one day whether they stopped at foodstalls, roast sweet-corn stalls, for instance, at sweet-corn time. She said they did; and their practice was to pay more than was asked – leaving me wondering even now whether, with that tradition, the ruler was asked less than his subject, or more.

I wanted to get a shawl, and I asked Aziz and Mr Butt to help me. I went to the Leeward one morning, and for form's sake – with Nazir standing with me – I looked through the stock of the hotel shop. There was nothing there that I wanted, and then – to wait for Mr Butt's real shawl-man – Nazir took me to the Leeward's sitting room. They had all wanted me to see this sitting room; they were proud of it. It was a big room in bright colours on the upper floor; it had tall sliding glass windows; and it overlooked the busy water-lanes in front of the hotel. There was a photograph of the Golden Temple – perhaps this was a political gesture of some sort on somebody's part. There was also a bleached picture of a Kashmiri girl. The girl was famous in legend, Nazir said; she was poor, a peasant girl, but by her singing she had won a king's heart.

Aziz came up to the sitting room. He ordered tea, and had a cup with me when it came. Tea was permissible in Ramadan in certain conditions: Mr Butt, for instance, who was not well, could have tea. Aziz had brought some photographs of himself in Mecca: cheerful, relishing the pious adventure. What a taste he had for life!

I asked him, 'Aziz, do you remember how often I went to the maharaja's in 1962?'

After 27 years, he knew precisely. He said, 'You went to have dinner three times. One time you went for tea.'

Then I thought to ask him what I had never asked in all the months we had been together. Where had he been born? He said here, on the lake. His father had been a Kashmiri, and his grandfather too; he was a pure Kashmiri. His father had been in business. A little shop. Up to 15 years ago, he said, people in Kashmir were poor. Now people were better off; now people were 'good', though – as both he and Nazir agreed – there were so many more of them. But that, Aziz said, speaking now as a man who had travelled, was also the problem of Bombay, Calcutta, Delhi.

I wondered why in 1962 I had asked Aziz so little about himself. Shyness, perhaps; a wish not to intrude; but also perhaps derived from the idea of the writer that I had inherited: the idea of the writer as a man with an internal life, a man drawing it all out of his own entrails, magically reading the externals of things.

Aziz went down, and shortly afterwards I saw the shawl-merchant's boat pull up at the Leeward's landing stage. The merchant came up alone. His loose baggy trousers, of thin brown cotton, were tucked into thick woollen socks pulled up high. He was a man of middle age, slender, sharp-featured and impressive. With his black, kinky-curled fur cap (like Mr Butt's), his black shoes and his black Indian-style jacket, long-skirted, hooked at the top (the top hook was visible), he looked Central Asian rather than Kashmiri. His name was Sharif.

Two lake boys brought up his small tin trunk, carrying it like a palanquin. He took off his shoes, spread a sheet on the carpet of the Leeward's sitting room, below the tall sliding glass windows, kneeled down, took out some embroidered tunics and laid them aside, and then, reverentially, took out the small bundle of his better-quality shawls, wrapped in white cotton. I had absolute faith in Mr Butt's management of this affair; and Mr Sharif's reverence for his goods confirmed what I felt. His stuff was good, thin, light, very warm, suggesting, at certain angles, a kind of ripple in the weaving. He took off his fur cap, showed the needle stuck into the crown, and said – pointing to his somewhat inflamed eyes – that he was more than a seller. He was a maker of shawls.

He wanted 8,600 rupees. I asked for a better price. He said 8,500, and he was firm. I asked Nazir to go and call Mr Butt. Nazir dutifully began going down the steps. On the landing (overlooking the water my bedroom had looked out on: now stagnant, with all the new building and boats, and attracting bottles and wrapping and other litter) Nazir stopped and called me. He wanted to know where I was – how serious I was. He said that Mr Butt knew Mr Sharif very well, and had told Mr Sharif to show me good pieces and give me a good price.

Aziz reappeared. We left Mr Sharif upstairs, and went down to the office. Nazir brought down the shawl I had liked. Aziz felt it and said he would guarantee it for two years: it was what Mr Sharif had said. Mr Butt came, walking in from the front garden. And then Mr Sharif himself came down the steps. So there was a general meeting in the office around the milk-chocolate-brown shawl.

Aziz said 8,500 was too much. Mr Sharif disagreed. Aziz said I wasn't a three-day tourist. Saying nothing, Mr Sharif left the office, and walked down the marble-floored verandah to the hotel shop. I thought he had been offended in some way.

But Nazir said, 'He's going to pray.'

Mr Sharif got a mat from the shop, set it down on the white marble verandah just outside the office, and, while it rained, began to bow and pray. In the office we continued to debate the issue.

Mr Butt said that Mr Sharif was a good man. They had gone to Mecca together. Nazir said that Mr Sharif led the prayers in the mosque. He was not only a man of authority, but also a man of his word.

And Mr Sharif bowed and prayed, the rain pattering on the white marble just inches away from him.

Aziz said, 'Offer 7,500.'

That was how it was settled. The offer was apparently made and accepted without further reference to me. Mr Sharif finished his prayers, rolled up the mat, took the mat back to the shop, came back to the office, picked up an Urdu newspaper that was a couple of weeks old, began to read from it to Mr Butt (whose spectacle lenses were very thick now). Slowly, after he had finished his reading, he folded the finger-ring shawl; and then, with a similar deliberation, he wrapped the folded shawl in a sheet of the Urdu newspaper he had been reading.

While this was going on, Aziz showed me a third photograph of his trip to Mecca, and I asked Mr Butt what I had never asked him in all the months in 1962. What had he done before starting the Leeward? He said he had been a contractor; he had started the hotel in 1959, with five rooms. Thirty years later, the hotel had 45 rooms.

Much money had come to the valley; many people had risen; there was a whole new educated generation. But a good deal of that improvement had been swallowed up by the growth in the population.

The new wealth showed in the new middle-class building on the north shore of the lake, and on the lower slope of the hill with the Hari Parbat fort. At the same time, behind the houseboats, the stultifying old lake life went on (picturesque in sunlight, less so in the wet and the cold after the rain); and the lake was now more populous. More boys than ever shouted and competed for custom at the boating steps. The effect, though the setting was quite different, was like that of the Muslim ghetto of the old bazaar area of Lucknow.

An older style of life, again, seemed to go on in the centre of the old city, where small covered boats choked the canals, where the brick and timber shops were as I had remembered them, and where very quickly after rain the streets became dusty – with the dust from dried mud. At the rim of that old city, though, there were many important-looking new buildings, among them the university and a government building connected with animal husbandry. But then again, in the villages beyond this, as though the two styles of life were quite separate, was the immemorial world of rice-planting.

In small flooded fields people worked with their hands alone or with wooden ploughs. The houses were basic, brown-red brick between timber uprights, on two or more floors. The pitched roofs of corrugated iron were open at the gable ends, and in this space (and sometimes in a dormer window in the roof) were stored firewood, straw or fodder, or grain. Water ran down the hillsides in many channels; willow and poplar cast cold shadows; and boulders and tree-branches made crude and crooked fences in wet yards. And here as elsewhere wood and brick and the clothes of people were the colour of mud.

Even with this wretched-looking village life – people sitting on the platform-floor of open one-room shops, wrapped in grey-brown blankets or gunny sacks – there were the signs of big public works, as though a great effort was needed to support even that style of life, to provide electricity, to build a road, to offer some kind of transport. And always, the children: very small, in smiling groups, outnumbering the adults. The abiding memory was of the children.

Above a certain altitude it semed that people lived in treeless mud. There were little ploughed plots of sodden earth around low houses of stone or timber, with people sitting or squatting at the edge of the mud. Safe above mud and water, straw was hung in bundles on the branches or in the forks of dried or dying trees. Even here there were children, wearing loose grey or brown gowns that made them look like little adults and made it hard, from a distance, to judge their size.

I saw this on a drive to Sonamarg with Nazir. Sonamarg was on the road to Ladakh in the north-east. It was new to me; it might have been that in 1962 the road wasn't good or wasn't open to visitors. The road was closed in winter; it had just been opened for the season. At higher altitudes it ran between walls of snow – melting from below, creating little caverns and snow overhangs; and the just-cleared asphalt surface was being abraded and dug up by runnels of melting snow.

At Sonamarg we were surrounded by thin, shouting boys who wanted us to toboggan down the snow slopes. 'Thirty rupees, 30 rupees.' The boys wore caps and had blotched complexions. From the roadside signs, Sonamarg seemed to mark a kind of boundary between Kashmir and Ladakh. It was no more than a collection of government huts and tourist lodges and shops. There were no fields or houses; the boys must have come from a village some distance away.

Nazir would have liked me to take a slide, to do the holiday thing, and to give the boys some work. Nazir's father was a successful man. He himself, with his nice haircut, his jeans and trainers, his dark-blue anorak (I asked him about it: it was Taiwanese, and cost 500 rupees, £25), was the picture of a young man of the middle class. But here, as on the lake, he had this feeling of solidarity with the Kashmiri children.

Going back down, back to the softer valley, getting an idea of its comparatively restricted size, returning quickly to crowds and small spaces (on the outskirts of Srinagar Nazir pointed out a little orchard that belonged to Mr Butt, but we didn't stop), I felt again, as I had felt at some of the boating steps, that even in this setting of mountains and snow-fed rivers, people had become as hemmed in and constrained as they were in the narrow ghetto lanes of Lucknow.

At the Leeward the next day I said goodbye to them all in the late afternoon, about half an hour or so before they broke their fast at the end of the Ramadan day: goodbye to Mr Butt, Aziz, the man who ran the hotel shop (from whom I had bought nothing), and the slender young man who was the manager of the Leeward. They were all in the little white glass-walled office downstairs, with the key-board and the calendar and the two posters of Mecca showing the kaaba and a golden dome. And just before I left they asked, just for the courtesy, whether I wanted tea.

Mr Butt's last news – the news he wanted me to take away and remember – was that he had made the pilgrimage to Mecca. He didn't speak of it as a penance; he spoke of it as a joy and fulfilment. It made him smile and laugh at the moment of farewell.

With Aziz my last talk was about money. His son Nazir had spent much time with me, and on our excursions had sometimes spent his own money. What would be a good recompense? There was no question of payment, Aziz said. Baksheesh was another matter: that could be one rupee, fourpence, or a lakh, 4000 pounds. That was no help to me at all, but Aziz didn't go beyond that. When I suggested a figure, Aziz's face remained unreadable – and that was how I left him.

In the boat going back to the boulevard, feeling the end of the Ramadan day pressing on us, I made my offering to Nazir. He took what I offered, but it was immediately clear that he had done so only out of courtesy. His face altered; he looked away. I felt I had mishandled the moment: Nazir, though he had done tourist things with me, had perhaps been treating me as a friend. I felt again, but more acutely now, what I had sensed from the beginning: that my relationship with Nazir, an unexpectedly handsome young man with his own new ideas of elegance and self, couldn't but be more complicated than my relationship with his father.

I wanted to save the moment. I said that the gesture I had made had been made out of friendship for him and Aziz and Mr Butt. I said that twice. He softened; some recognition seemed to come to him that he too had to do something to save the moment – so soon to end, at the boating steps, and before the sunset call from the mosques.

The stiffness went out of him. And as we slipped down the busy waterway, past the small houseboat with the leather and fur-goods shop, the grocery, and the Sunshine Haircutting Saloon, we talked about his studies. In a few months he was going to get his school-leaving certificate. For two years after this he would study commerce at a college – preparing for his career in accountancy and, as his father and Mr Butt hoped, his life in the hotel business – and then he would go to the university.

From his grandfather's little shop in the lake, to his father's successful hotel career, to his own prospects as a graduate and acountant – there had been a step-by-step movement upwards. Would it continue?

He had never been out of Kashmir. At the moment the valley (and the mountains around it) was all the world he knew. He was still part of it. Twenty-seven years after I had got to know him, Aziz had remained more or less the same. It wouldn't be like that with Nazir. Already he had intimations of a world outside. Already, through that monthly exchange of letters with a foreign girl, there had come to him the idea of the possibility – always in Allah's hands – of a foreign marriage. In 27 years – hard for me now, in late middle age, to imagine that stretch of time, that boundary in the shades – Nazir wouldn't be the same. New ways of seeing and feeling were going to come to him, and he wasn't going to be part of the valley in the way he was now.

In 27 years I had succeeded in making a kind of return journey, shedding my Indian nerves, abolishing the darkness that separated me from my ancestral past. William Howard Russell, in 1858, had described (and commented on) a vast country physically in ruins, even away from the battles of the Mutiny. Twenty-five years or so later, from a part of the country Russell had travelled through (in

516

such style as was available), my ancestors had left as indentured servants for the sugar estates of Guyana and Trinidad. I had carried in my bones that idea of abjectness and defeat and shame. It was the idea I had taken to India on that slow journey by train and ship in 1962; it was the source of my nerves. (It was the idea that surfaced again, to my surprise, during the writing of this book, when I first tried to read William Howard Russell's *Diary*, and I found myself rejecting the book, the man, and even his great descriptive talent.)

What I hadn't understood in 1962, or had taken too much for granted, was the extent to which the country had been remade; and even the extent to which India had been restored to itself, after its own equivalent of the Dark Ages – after the Muslim invasions and the detailed, repeated vandalising of the North, the shifting empires, the wars, the 18th-century anarchy. The twentieth-century restoration of India to itself had taken time; it could even seem like a kind of luck. It had taken much to create a Bengali reformer like Ram Mohun Roy (born in 1772); it had taken much more to create Gandhi (born in 1869). The British peace after the 1857 Mutiny can be seen as a kind of luck. It was a time of intellectual recruitment. India was set on the way of a new kind of intellectual life; it was given new ideas about its history and civilization. The freedom movement reflected all of this and turned out to be the truest kind of liberation.

In the 130 years or so since the Mutiny – the last 90 years of the British Raj and the first 40 years of independence begin increasingly to appear as part of the same historical period – the idea of freedom has gone everywhere in India. Independence was worked for by people more or less at the top; the freedom it brought has worked its way down. People everywhere have ideas now of who they are and what they owe themselves. The process quickened with the economic development that came after independence; what was hidden in 1962, or not easy to see, what perhaps was only in a state of becoming, has become clearer. The liberation of spirit that has come to India could not come as release alone. In India, with its layer below layer of distress and cruelty, it had to come as disturbance. It had to come as rage and revolt. India was now a country of a million little mutinies.

A million mutinies, supported by twenty kinds of group excess, sectarian excess, religious excess, regional excess: the beginnings

517

of self-awareness, it would seem, the beginnings of an intellectual life, already negated by old anarchy and disorder. But there was in India now what didn't exist 200 years before: a central will, a central intellect, a national idea. The Indian Union was greater than the sum of its parts; and many of these movements of excess strengthened the Indian state, defining it as the source of law and civility and reasonableness. The Indian Union gave people a second chance, calling them back from the excesses with which, in another century, or in other circumstances (as neighbouring countries showed), they might have had to live: the destructive chauvinism of the Shiv Sena, the tyranny of many kinds of religious fundamentalism (people always ready in India to let religion carry the burden of their pain), the film-star corruption and racial politics of the South, the pious Marxist idleness and nullity of Bengal.

Excess was now felt to be excess in India. What the mutinies were also helping to define was the strength of the general intellectual life, and the wholeness and humanism of the values to which all Indians now felt they could appeal. And – strange irony – the mutinies were not to be wished away. They were part of the beginning of a new way for many millions, part of India's growth, part of its restoration.

When I went back to Bombay I got in touch with Paritosh, the film writer. Paritosh worked in the commercial cinema, and he loved the film form: it was his vocation, almost his faith. But he didn't care for the people who made films in India. They made him suffer; they enraged him; and he had had his ups and downs.

When I had met him, five months before, he had just come out of a bad period. During this period he had turned his back on Bombay and films and had gone back to his own city of Calcutta to rest and recover. But then – having married in this period – he had come to the end of his mood of rejection, and he had come back to Bombay to start again. He was living in a mid-town area in a bare one-roomed apartment. 'This is my only room under the sun,' he had said, throwing up his arms, looking at the ceiling, making the room feel very small. But he had prospects: he had come back to Bombay to work on a film with a once successful producer he had known. Every now and then they met in a neighbourhood hotel and discussed the script.

Paritosh was determined to stay the course and to succeed this time. He said he felt he was going to make some money. But his cousin, who had taken me to see him, and had sat in the room with us, was gloomier. Paritosh's temperament would get in the way; he would quarrel with someone, or something would happen; and Paritosh would be back where he had always been. I listened to what the cousin said as we walked back through the crowded streets near a market to the suburban railway station; and I had become depressed, thinking of the fine-looking writer in his bare room. Now, five months on, I wanted to know what had happened.

I didn't have to make a journey to see Paritosh – no overcrowded suburban train, no choking taxi ride through the brown smoke of the Bombay highways. He came to have a coffee with me in the hotel. He was a busy man; he had things to do. His face was suffused now with the pleasure he felt in his busyness; some of the rage had been ironed away.

He had written his film. And the producer had found a backer. They had been able to start shooting, and to show rushes of early scenes to distributors. The distributors had bought the film. The backer had got an almost instant return on his investment, and he had put up money for a second film – Paritosh seethed with ideas. Paritosh had already got his writer's fee for the first film; it was a substantial fee; he had, already, bought a bigger apartment in a better area. In five months his fortunes had changed; this was the kind of thing that was possible in rich, energetic, squalid Bombay; this was why the city drew people all the time.

He had retained a bigger financial share in the second film. This film, Paritosh said, was to be more for himself. The first one, the one that had bought him his apartment, was commercial, popular – but he wasn't using the words to criticise his work: he was only describing a particular kind of film.

What was it about? What kind of story and characters had been filling his head when I had met him in his little room? What was the material he had been banking on? The film was set in a Bombay slum, one of the many shanty towns of the city. The hero was a young slum-dweller; he was a man of possibilities, but he was corrupted by a gangster. A commercial film, but topical, and strong. (And also, as fictions often do, carrying an unconscious echo of the creator's predicament.)

To make the film, Paritosh said, they had had to build their own slum or shanty town. For legal reasons they couldn't use a real place. They had taken photographs of various real places, and they had created a kind of composite Bombay slum. While the film was being shot, they had all lived in the various huts of the set. Just the day before, Paritosh said, they had begun to dismantle the make-believe slum they had lived in for many weeks. It had given him a pang.

December 1988 – February 1990

Acknowledgements

When you travel for a book like this, you often don't know what you are looking for until you have found it. You need a lot of help on the way. On this journey many people helped. They shared their knowledge; they gave names and introductions. Three people, all of them newspaper editors, helped especially, from beginning to end: Nikhil Lakshman, Vinod Mehta, Rahul Singh. Vinod Mehta and Rahul Singh each did a part of the journey with me; but I must stress that I alone am responsible for what I have written. There are a number of other people I would like to remember here. In Bombay: Charu Deshpande; Ajit Pillai. In Bangalore: T. J. S. George. In Madras: K. P. Sunil. In Calcutta: Shekhar Bhatia; Viv Sanghvi; Sunanda Datta Ray; Satyabrata Bose. In Delhi: Rekha Khanna Mehta. In Chandigarh: Kanwar Sandhu. Other people who helped are mentioned in the text; sometimes, for obvious reasons, their names and circumstances are changed.

A Selected List of Titles Available from Minerva

While every effort is made to keep prices low, it is sometimes necessary to increase prices at short notice. Mandarin Paperbacks reserves the right to show new retail prices on covers which may differ from those previously advertised in the text or elsewhere.

The prices shown below were correct at the time of going to press.

Fiction
☐	7493 9026 3	**I Pass Like Night**	Jonathan Ames	£3.99 BX
☐	7493 9006 9	**The Tidewater Tales**	John Bath	£4.99 BX
☐	7493 9004 2	**A Casual Brutality**	Neil Blessondath	£4.50 BX
☐	7493 9028 2	**Interior**	Justin Cartwright	£3.99 BC
☐	7493 9002 6	**No Telephone to Heaven**	Michelle Cliff	£3.99 BX
☐	7493 9028 X	**Not Not While the Giro**	James Kelman	£4.50 BX
☐	7493 9011 5	**Parable of the Blind**	Gert Hofmann	£3.99 BC
☐	7493 9010 7	**The Inventor**	Jakov Lind	£3.99 BC
☐	7493 9003 4	**Fall of the Imam**	Nawal El Saadawi	£3.99 BC

Non-Fiction
☐	7493 9012 3	**Days in the Life**	Jonathon Green	£4.99 BC
☐	7493 9019 0	**In Search of J D Salinger**	Ian Hamilton	£4.99 BX
☐	7493 9023 9	**Stealing from a Deep Place**	Brian Hall	£3.99 BX
☐	7493 9005 0	**The Orton Diaries**	John Lahr	£5.99 BC
☐	7493 9014 X	**Nora**	Brenda Maddox	£6.99 BC

All these books are available at your bookshop or newsagent, or can be ordered direct from the publisher. Just tick the titles you want and fill in the form below. Available in:
BX: British Commonwealth excluding Canada
BC: British Commonwealth including Canada

Mandarin Paperbacks, Cash Sales Department, PO Box 11, Falmouth, Cornwall TR10 9EN.

Please send cheque or postal order, no currency, for purchase price quoted and allow the following for postage and packing:

UK	80p for the first book, 20p for each additional book ordered to a maximum charge of £2.00.
BFPO	80p for the first book, 20p for each additional book.
Overseas including Eire	£1.50 for the first book, £1.00 for the second and 30p for each additional book thereafter.

NAME (Block letters) ....

ADDRESS ....

....

....